D1293311

LOEB CLASSICAL LIBRARY

FOUNDED BY JAMES LOEB 1911

EDITED BY

JEFFREY HENDERSON

SEXTUS EMPIRICUS

I

LCL 273

SEXTUS EMPIRICUS

OUTLINES OF PYRRHONISM

WITH AN ENGLISH TRANSLATION BY

R. G. BURY

HARVARD UNIVERSITY PRESS
CAMBRIDGE, MASSACHUSETTS
LONDON, ENGLAND

First published 1933

LOEB CLASSICAL LIBRARY® is a registered trademark
of the President and Fellows of Harvard College

ISBN 978-0-674-99301-3

*Printed on acid-free paper and bound by
The Maple-Vail Book Manufacturing Group*

CONTENTS

INTRODUCTION

I. The Earlier Dogmatic Philosophies

The writings of Sextus contain not only an exposition of Scepticism but also a critique of the doctrines of "the Dogmatists." The main task of the Sceptic is, in fact, to expose the folly of every form of positive doctrine; and consequently the bulk of these works of Sextus is controversial. Scattered through his pages there are references to almost every known name in the history of ancient Greek thought, and without some previous acquaintance with the main outlines of that history it is hardly possible to appreciate the points or estimate the value of his arguments. Accordingly I give here, for the convenience of the reader, a short summary of the history of Greek philosophy.

1. *The Ionian Physicists.*—Of the School of Miletus the founder was *Thales* (*circa* 600 B.C.). He declared that the fundamental substance of which the world was made is *water*. His successor, *Anaximander* (*circa* 570 B.C.), described that substance as "*the boundless*" (τὸ ἄπειρον), since out of it were formed "countless" (ἄπειροι) worlds. He regarded this primitive stuff as being in itself indeterminate, or of no one definite quality, and evolving into the forms of earth, fire, etc., by a process of "separation" of hot from cold, moist from dry, etc. Also he called his primal substance "divine." *Anaximenes* (*circa* 540 B.C.), like Thales, took one definite element as his primary

vii

matter, but chose *air*, or vapour, instead of water. He explained the passage of this into other forms of matter as due to a process of " condensation and rarefaction."

2. *Heracleiteans and Eleatics.*—In chronological order the first of the Eleatic School, *Xenophanes* of Colophon (*circa* 520 B.C.), comes before Heracleitus. He was less a philosopher than a religious reformer who declaimed against traditional mythology and preached a pantheism which identified the One Universe with God.

As against this Unity of the Eleatic doctrine, which precludes diversity, *Heracleitus* of Ephesus (*circa* 490 B.C.) declared that things are never one and the same but continually changing. Reverting to the view of the Milesians, he looked for one primary world-substance and found it in *fire* ; this, as being also mind-stuff, he called " Reason " (λόγος) and God. By a kind of circular process (" the upward and downward way ") the primal fire passes through the forms of air, water and earth, and returns to its own nature again. The World is " a harmony of opposites," since " War is father of all and king of all," and conflict lies at the heart of things. " All things are in flux " (πάντα ῥεῖ), and since things have no permanent identity the reports of our senses are delusive, and opposite statements about an object may be equally true or false. In fact, to the eyes of God, life and death, good and evil, and all opposites are identical —there is no dividing line, and they are for ever passing into one another. Thus, as a Dogmatist who dissolves all dogma, Heracleitus is acclaimed by the Sceptics as one of the pioneers of their tradition. (*Cf. Pyrr. Hyp.* i. 210 ff.)

INTRODUCTION

Parmenides of Elea (*circa* 470 B.C.) defended the unitary doctrine of Xenophanes as against the flux doctrine of Heracleitus. In his view " only Being is," and change, motion, and Becoming are illusions. The World is a single self-contained Sphere, uncreated and imperishable. In his great poem " On Nature " Parmenides calls this " the Way of Truth " ; but he follows it up by an account of the World and its constituents on the lines of current physical Science (especially that of the Pythagoreans) which he calls " the Way of Opinion," without giving any explanation of how the one " Way " can be related to the other.

Zeno of Elea (*circa* 450 B.C.) supported the doctrine of the Unity of Being by attacking the notions of multiplicity and motion. These notions, he argued, are self-contradictory. As against the possibility of motion he is said to have evolved the arguments known as " The Achilles " (and the tortoise) and " The Flying Arrow." The kernel of his reasoning is that any *quantum* (as of space or time) must be regarded either as consisting of a plurality of indivisible units or as itself divisible *ad infinitum*; but in the latter case, how can the sum of infinite parts make up a finite whole ? and in the former, the unitary parts of the *quantum* must themselves be *quanta* or magnitudes, and as such they cannot be indivisible.

Melissus, the Samian admiral (*circa* 440 B.C.), likewise taught that Being is One, infinite, uncreate and everlasting, motionless and without void.

Thus, in spite of their metaphysical dogmatism, the Eleatics were akin to the Sceptics in so far as they rejected the evidence of the senses and criticized the ordinary belief in the phenomenal world.

INTRODUCTION

3. *Fifth-century Pluralists.*—Hitherto the Cosmologists had attempted to explain the World by assuming either the Unity of its primal substance or its Unity as a static Totality (the Eleatics). And a direct contradiction had arisen between the position of Heracleitus (" All is in motion ") and that of Parmenides (" All is at rest "). We come next to a number of theorists who—though otherwise divergent—agree in adopting a *plurality* of primary substances or principles to explain the world. Also, in relation to the opposing views of Heracleitus and Parmenides, they take up a mediating position.

Empedocles of Agrigentum (*circa* 450 B.C.) assumed as primary indestructible substances " four Roots of all things," viz. the four elements, earth, air, fire and water. He explained all Becoming and change as due to the mixing and unmixing of these elements. As the motive forces effecting these opposite processes he assumed the two rival powers Love and Hate, or Harmony and Discord, which oust each other alternately from control of the World. When Love is in full control, all the " roots " are fused together in a compact mass forming the " Sphere," which he terms " a blessed god." When Hate is in full control, all the " roots " are completely separated, each massed apart by itself. But in the world as we know it both forces are in play, so that its constituents are neither wholly in union nor wholly in disunion. The nature of particular things depends upon the proportion of the " roots " of which they are composed. As regards knowledge, Empedocles declared that " like is known by like," fire and water in the eyes (for example) perceiving the fire and water in the objects of sight by means of effluences. He also regarded the blood

as the seat of intelligence, it being the best mixture of all the elements. And he shared the Pythagorean belief in the transmigration of souls, saying that he himself had in times past been " a bush and a bird and a mute sea-fish."

Anaxagoras of Clazomenae (*circa* 450 B.C.) lived mostly at Athens, where he was intimate with Pericles and Euripides, until he was condemned on a charge of atheism and escaped to Lampsacus. Like Empedocles, he held that becoming and change are due to composition and decomposition of primary indestructible substances : " Nothing becomes and nothing perishes." But the primary substances (" seeds of all things ") are not merely four but numberless, all existing forms of matter (bone, hair, gold, etc.) being equally ultimate. Originally " all things were together," in a chaotic mass of all kinds of matter, then " Reason (*Nous*) came and set them in order." That is Anaxagoras's most important contribution to philosophy—the introduction of Reason or Intelligence as the Moving Cause and the principle of order and harmony in the world. He described *Nous* as alone " unmixed," and ordering the mixed mass of the world by setting up in it a vortex motion which disintegrates the mass and unites like " seeds " of matter with like.

Leucippus of Miletus (?), the first Atomist, was probably a contemporary of Empedocles and Anaxagoras, but we know little that is definite about him. His views were developed by *Democritus* of Abdera (*circa* 420 B.C.). He held that the World is made up of " the Full " and " the Empty," *i.e.* of solid, indivisible molecules of matter, the *atoms*, and empty space or *void*. The atoms differ only in size and shape, and

the forms and qualities of visible objects depend on their atomic structure. The atoms are supposed to rain down through space and collide with one another owing to the differences in the speed of their movement, their speed varying in proportion to their size. As against Anaxagoras's doctrine of *Nous*, the Atomists spoke of " Necessity " as the governing force of the World, allowing only mechanical causation. Sensation was explained as due to the reception through " pores " of " images " projected from the atoms of the object perceived ; but the apparent qualities of objects have only " conventional " reality, the only true reals being the Atoms and the Void. No clear distinction is made between sense and thought, and we can make no assertion about the truth of sense-objects, since these depend on the state of the percipient and the arrangement of the atoms of which he is composed. Belief in gods is due to the " images " projected by certain anthropomorphic beings who dwell in the air. Knowledge is of two kinds, " genuine " and " bastard," the latter being that derived from the senses, the former that of the understanding which discerns the only real existents, the atoms and the void. Democritus appears also to have named " Well-being," or tranquil cheerfulness, as the ethical " end " or " good." The relation of Democriteanism to Scepticism is discussed by Sextus in *Pyrr. Hyp.* i. 213 ff.

The Pythagoreans.—Pythagoras (circa 530 B.C.) was a contemporary of Xenophanes, born at Samos, but mainly resident at Crotona in South Italy. There he founded a religious Order, and a Way of Life akin to that of the Orphics in its asceticism, its belief in re-incarnation, and its precepts for the salvation of the soul from its " body-tomb " ($\sigma\hat{\omega}\mu\alpha$-$\sigma\hat{\eta}\mu\alpha$). But

nothing is known of Pythagoras himself as scientist or philosopher, and as a philosophy Pythagoreanism seems to date from the fifth century, its chief exponent being *Philolaus* (*circa* 440 B.C.). Thus Pythagoreanism is, in the main, contemporary with the other "pluralist" systems mentioned above. The chief subjects cultivated by the Pythagoreans were mathematics, music, medicine and gymnastics. Their main tenet was "Things are numbers," or "The principles of things are the principles of numbers." And, as all numbers are either odd or even, the world is made up of opposites, which can be arranged in ten classes. Even numbers are always divisible by 2 and so are named "Unlimited"; and 1, being the primary odd number, may be called the "Limit." Regarded geometrically, 1 is the point, 2 the line, 3 the plane, 4 the solid. They called 10 (the *Decad*) the perfect number, as being the sum of the first four numbers ("the Tetractys") and thus containing all the elements of number. "Harmony" is the principle which unites opposites and resolves cosmical as well as musical discords. The Universe consists of ten bodies (the heaven of fixed stars, the five planets, moon, sun, earth, "counter-earth") revolving around the "central fire" or cosmic "hearth"; it is surrounded by air which it breathes in and out. Its life lasts for a "Great Year" (10,000 years), at the end of which it starts anew on the same course; and in every such period history repeats itself. Soul was defined as a harmony, and the virtues identified with special numbers.

4. *The Fifth-century Sophists.*—While the thinkers hitherto mentioned dealt mainly with the world of Nature, the group known as "Sophists" were chiefly

concerned with Humanity. It was " the Age of
Enlightenment " in Greece, when old beliefs and
customs were being challenged by a new spirit of
doubt and inquiry. With the rise of democracy every
citizen became a potential politician, and instruction
to fit men for public life was in general demand. This
demand the Sophists laid themselves out to supply.
They were the professional Educators of the public,
and what they taught was " Virtue," as they called it,
i.e. civic excellence, and the arts which enable a man
to succeed in life. And since, for a political career
and to achieve success in the law-courts, debating
power is of supreme importance, the art of Rhetoric
is the most useful aid to " Virtue " ; and we find that
the Sophists cultivated it in particular. The earliest
of the Sophists was *Protagoras* of Abdera (*circa* 440
B.C.) who resided for some time at Athens until he
was convicted of impiety and had to flee.[a] He is chiefly
noted for his dictum—" Man is the measure of all
things ; of what is, that it is ; of what is not, that it
is not " (*cf. Pyrr. Hyp.* i. 216 ff.). This means that
the individual man is the criterion of truth, and denies
that there is any universal standard or any absolute
truth. The subjective impressions of each man are
true for him, but not necessarily for anyone else.
Hence, all opinions are equally true, and falsehood
has no meaning, and contradictory statements are
both equally credible. But to reject objective truth
is also to reject the possibility of knowledge, and this
consequence of Protagoreanism was further developed
by the second great Sophist, *Gorgias* of Leontini

---

[a] So Sextus in *Ph.* i. 56, but the story is doubtful.

INTRODUCTION

(*circa* 440 B.C.). His book " On the Non-ent or Nature" essayed to prove (1) that nothing exists ; (2) that if anything exists it is incognizable ; (3) that even if cognizable it is incommunicable (*cf. Pyrr. Hyp.* ii. 59, 64). In this we see the strongest possible expression of the agnostic tendency and a Scepticism more dogmatic than that of the professed Sceptics of a later age. Another important Sophist was *Hippias* of Elis, the " polymath," who boasted of his ability to give an extempore lecture on any subject, and (like other Sophists) contrasted " law " or convention with "nature" or instinctive impulse. Of *Prodicus* of Ceos we are told that he specialized in linguistics, the precise use of synonyms, and ethical discourses. Other Sophists of the eristic type, who helped to undermine religious belief and to promote intellectual anarchy, were *Euthydemus* and *Dionysodorus*, *Critias* the Athenian (one of " The Thirty "), and *Diagoras* of Melos.

5. *Socrates and the Minor Socratics.*—*Socrates* (469–399 B.C.) was the contemporary of the Sophists and so far akin to them that he held that " the proper study of mankind is man," and was a humanist rather than a physicist. But his aim was exactly the reverse of theirs—to establish morality on a sound basis, instead of proclaiming the futility of the moral law. By means of the *inductive* method and *definition* he sought to build up a system of *conceptual* knowledge which should possess objective truth, as contrasted with the merely subjective opinions derived from sense-perception. As an ethical teacher he preached " well-doing," or right conduct, as the aim of life, and urged self-knowledge and self-control as things more valuable than any external goods, his most

distinctive doctrine being that of the identity of
knowledge and virtue, and of vice and ignorance ;
for " no man," he said, " is voluntarily wicked." But
there is much uncertainty about the details of the
teaching of Socrates, since the " Socrates " of the
Platonic dialogues is by no means always " the
historic Socrates," and the evidence of Xenophon
(our other chief authority) does not appear to be
altogether trustworthy.

Four " Minor Socratic " Schools were formed by
the disciples of Socrates. *Eucleides* of Megara founded
the *Megaric* School in which, it would seem, Socratic
tenets were combined with Eleatic doctrines, and the
indirect method of proof was developed. Its interest
was mainly in logic and dialectic ; and to *Eubulides*
(Eucleides' successor) is ascribed the invention of
many logical puzzles (" the Liar," Sorites, etc.).
Curiously enough, although Sextus often refers to
Diodorus Cronos (*circa* 300 B.C.), he hardly mentions
the earlier Megarics, although many of the Sceptic
arguments must have been borrowed from them.
The *Elean* School was founded by *Phaedo* of Elis,
whose teaching seems to have resembled that of
Eucleides. It, too, is not referred to by Sextus.
Antisthenes founded the *Cynic* School. It subordinated
logic and physics to ethics. Virtue, said Antisthenes,
is the only good, all else is indifferent and of no
account. Virtue is wisdom, self-control and self-
sufficiency : the wise man cuts himself free from all
earthly interests—pleasure, society, religion ; he
stands secure in himself, above all temptation. And,
as in their Ethics, so in their Logic the Cynics stood
for individuality and independence. Only identical
judgements, they said, are possible ; contradiction is

impossible, and therefore knowledge equally so. Thus they reverted to the Sceptical position of Protagoras and Gorgias. Other notable Cynics were *Diogenes* (*circa* 340 B.C.), famed for his blunt coarse speech and his contempt for civilized customs, and *Crates* (*cf. Pyrr. Hyp.* i. 72, 153).

The *Cyrenaic* School was founded by *Aristippus* of Cyrene, who was succeeded by his daughter Arete, and she by his grandson Aristippus. Later members of the School were *Theodorus* " the atheist," *Anniceris*, *Hegesias* (" the *suasor mortis* "). Like the Cynics, the Cyrenaics concentrated on Ethical theory. The *summum bonum*, they said, is *Pleasure*, and pleasure consists in " smooth motion," pain being " rough motion," and the neutral state " immobility." These are the three states of consciousness or psychic " affections " in which sensation consists and to which knowledge is confined. As the causes of these internal states are unknown, knowledge is wholly subjective, and each individual is his own standard of truth—the Protagorean position again. As the end of life is to gain from it the maximum of pleasurable sensations, the " Wise Man " of the Cyrenaics is he who best knows how to secure enjoyment from all possible sources, and to ward off discomfort and pain. Like the Cynics, the Cyrenaics stood for " nature " as against " convention," but they interpreted nature in a very different way (*cf. Pyrr. Hyp.* i. 215, *Adv. Log.* i. 11).

6. *Plato and the Old Academy.*—The philosophy of *Plato* (427–347 B.C.) defies a brief summary. Only a few outstanding points can be mentioned. As against the Sophists, he maintained the possibility of knowledge, and the existence of an objective standard of

truth ; and by identifying the " natural " with the " rational " he suppressed the Sophistic appeal from " law," or convention, to " nature." His theory of knowledge and of Being may be said to be based on a reconciliation of the rival doctrines of Heracleitus and Parmenides. Heracleitus was right in regarding the sense-world as being in a state of continual flux and therefore not a subject of knowledge, but he was wrong in treating it as the only world. Parmenides, too, was right in holding that the world as known must be changeless and self-identical, but he was wrong in trying to force this conception on the phenomenal world. There are, in fact, two distinct worlds and two distinct kinds of apprehension to deal with them. Sensation tells us of the phenomenal and gives rise to " opinion " ; Reason and thought deal with objects supersensible. For the content of his " intelligible " world Plato is indebted to Socrates' theory of concepts. The general (Aristotelian) view is that by " hypostatizing " these concepts he framed his " Ideas." He presents the Ideas as the ultimate Realities, the only objects of knowledge in the strict sense. The logical method which deals with the Ideas is " Dialectic," which combines induction with deduction. The supreme Idea is " the Good." In the physical theory of the *Timaeus*, the " Demiurge " (God, or Mind) frames the Universe with a view to the most Good, by means of harmony and proportion. Ethics is interwoven with psychology ; the soul is a whole with three component parts or faculties (rational, spirited, appetitive), and is defined as " the self-moving "—the source of all motion. Virtue is the " goodness " of the soul both as a whole and in each of its parts—so that virtue is fourfold (wisdom,

INTRODUCTION

courage, temperance, justice). Virtue in the State
corresponds to that in the individual : each class must
be efficient and loyal, and all together must be united
in harmony. Thus Plato's Idealism contemplates the
rule of Reason, acting for " the Best," in all three
spheres—that of the Individual, of the State, and of
the Universe. How far it contains a Sceptical element
is discussed in *Pyrr. Hyp.* i. 221 ff.

Speusippus, the nephew of Plato, succeeded him as
Head of the Academy (347–339 B.C.) and was in turn
succeeded by *Xenocrates* (339–314 B.C.). Both seem
to have amalgamated Idealism with the Pythagorean
doctrine of Numbers. *Polemo* (314–270 B.C.) was the
next Head of the School. Other noted members, or
allies, of the Academy were *Heracleides* of Pontus,
Philip of Opus, *Eudoxus* of Cnidus, the astronomer,
and the Pythagorean mathematician *Archytas* of
Tarentum. The general character of their teaching
was, it seems, in the direction of lowering the standard
of the Idealism of Plato and adapting it to the interests
of inferior minds. The most gifted of Plato's disciples
was undoubtedly Aristotle, the man who deserted the
Academy to found a rival school of his own and to
teach a revised Platonism.

7. *Aristotle and the Peripatetics* (*cf. Pyrr. Hyp.* iv.
31, 136, 218). — *Aristotle* of Stageira (384–322 B.C.)
joined the Academy in 367 B.C., and after Plato's
death, about 335 B.C., founded a School of his own in
the *Lyceum* at Athens, lecturing as he walked about—
whence the name " Peripatetic " (" walking round ").
Aristotle was the great systematizer in all branches
of philosophy and science. In his *Logical* treatises
(" Organon ") he formulates the " Categories," or ten
heads of predicables ; the rules for the conversion of

propositions ; the doctrine of the Syllogism, as based on the Laws of Contradiction and Excluded Middle ; the meaning of Demonstration or Proof as concerned with necessary causes, and how First Principles, or axiomatic truths, are indemonstrable ; problematic or imperfect syllogisms ; the various kinds of eristic argument or fallacy. In his *Metaphysics* he argues, as against Plato, that the Universals, the objects of knowledge, are not separate from the sensibles but *in* them. The first principles of Being are *actuality* and *potency*; and *Cause* is analysed into four kinds —material, formal, efficient and final. *Form* is the essence of things, and the object of cognition, and Form *plus* Matter compose the concrete substance. God is pure actuality, "thought thinking upon thought," the *primum mobile*. In his *Physics* and *Psychology* he postulated *Ether* as a fifth element, and the Earth as stationary in the centre of the Cosmos. Life is the power of self-movement, of which Soul is the principle, it being the "form" or "entelechy"[a] of the body. The faculties of Soul are five—nutritive, sensitive, appetitive, locomotive, rational. In sensation we receive "the form without the matter" of the percept ; and besides the five external senses, each with its proper object, there are three internal senses, memory, imagination, and the central *communis sensus*, with its seat in the heart, by which we note and compare the several reports of the special senses. As the senses deal with the concrete and individual, so the Intellect deals with the abstract and universal ; but though distinct from Sense it is dependent on it for its material,

---

[a] *i.e.* actuality or realization of what is otherwise merely "potential."

being of itself a *tabula rasa*. The intellect is also described as twofold, active and passive. His *Ethics* is chiefly notable for his doctrine of Virtue as consisting in " the Mean " between two extremes, and for his preference of mental to moral virtues. Also, he included bodily goods (health, wealth, pleasure) as well as virtue in his description of the ethical " End " (" Happiness "). In his *Political* Theory he rejects Plato's communism and abolition of private property, and regards the State as a means for the moral advancement of the citizens and as the guardian of justice. He also wrote treatises on biology and aesthetics and rhetoric.

Theophrastus was Head of the Peripatetic School from 322 to 287 B.C., when he was succeeded by *Strato*, and he in turn by *Lyco* (269–225 B.C.). They, and other leading Peripatetics—such as Dicaearchus, the historian, and Aristoxenus, the musician—cultivated the special sciences rather than the metaphysical and logical aspects of Aristotelianism, and empirical interests tended to outweigh theoretical in the later history of the School.

II. The Later Dogmatists

On its theoretical and constructive side the philosophical movement which culminated in the architectonic systems of Plato and Aristotle came to an abrupt end. The philosophic *Epigoni* of the post-Aristotelian age showed less breadth of vision and but little originality of mind: the glory had departed from Israel. This was, no doubt, partly due to the depressing social and political conditions which prevailed in the Greek-speaking world during the third and following cen-

turies. These conditions tended to make men concentrate their thoughts on purely human interests—the welfare, destiny, salvation of the individual—to the neglect of the other departments of philosophy and science. In so far as they were cultivated at all, those other departments came to be treated merely as the handmaids of Ethics, thus reviving the mainly humanistic attitude of the Sophists. Philosophy, in fact, became the substitute for an out-of-date and exploded Religion, and had for its aim, not the attainment of objective truth, but the provision of a subjective spiritual salvation from the manifold ills of life. Its task was no longer theoretical, but the very practical and urgent one of supplying distressed humanity with " arms against a sea of troubles," with shield and buckler against " the slings and arrows of outrageous fortune." Truth was now a matter for the heart rather than the head ; philosophy, like faith, was to be judged by its " works " ; it was bound to be pragmatical. To meet this situation two great Dogmatic systems were evolved, the Epicurean and the Stoic, and, to counter them, the system of the Sceptics. These three were contemporaneous, all dating from the end of the fourth century B.C.

1. *The Epicureans.* — *Epicurus* of Samos (341–270 B.C.) founded his School in his garden (hence " the Garden School ") at Athens in 306 B.C. Epicurus reverted to Democritus for his Physics, and to Aristippus for his Ethics, being both an Atomist and a Hedonist. In his physical theory he followed Democritus closely, except in explaining the collision of atoms as due to slight arbitrary deviations from the straight line in their downward course. The Soul, he said, is material, composed (as are the gods) of a

finer sort of atoms, and mortal. Sensation, with its immediate evidence (ἐνάργεια), is the only criterion of truth; it is effected by effluent images (εἴδωλα, ἀπορροαί) from the external objects impinging on the sense-organs. The aggregation of several sensations forms the notion or concept (πρόληψις), and from notions arise opinion (δόξα) and conviction (ὑπόληψις). This theory of knowledge constitutes " Canonic," the Epicureans' name for Logic. Physics and Logic were regarded as subordinate to Ethics, and in Ethics Epicurus, like Aristippus, held that the Good is Pleasure, but he defined pleasure rather differently—not as a satisfying " smooth motion " but as a state of rest, " painlessness," or absence of all unsatisfied desire, or " unperturbedness " (ἀταραξία). Also he regarded freedom from mental distress, fear and prejudice, as even more important than bodily satisfaction ; and it is the task of the " Wise Man " (φρόνιμος), by means of a kind of hedonistic calculus, to estimate the comparative value of the different kinds of pleasurable affections (πάθη) so as to win for himself the maximum of mental satisfaction and repose throughout his life. Virtue, and the special virtues, are of value only in so far as they contribute to this end. Right and wrong become matters of merely subjective feeling. Religion was abolished as the cause of intolerable mental " perturbation," and the gods were banished to the *intermundia*. Lucretius's great poem *De Rerum Natura* is our most complete exposition of Epicureanism.

2. *The Stoics.*—*Zeno* of Citium, in Cyprus (350–258 B.C.), started his School about 305 B.C. in the " Painted Porch " (στοὰ ποικίλη) at Athens—whence the name " Stoic." He was succeeded by *Cleanthes*, author of

INTRODUCTION

the famous " Hymn to Zeus," who, in turn, was followed by *Chrysippus* of Cilicia (280–206 B.C.), who systematized the doctrines of the School. With *Panaetius* of Rhodes (180–111 B.C.), *Poseidonius* of Apamea (130–46 B.C.), and the later Stoics, the system tended to become more eclectic, with infiltrations of Peripatetic and Academic doctrine. The main tenets of Stoicism were briefly these :—

In *Physics* they reverted to Heracleiteanism, and taught a materialistic monism. All that exists is corporeal : only body can act on body, therefore God is as much corporeal as the world, the soul as the body. The primal world-stuff is *Fire*, which by the " upward and downward way " transforms itself into the other elements and produces the Cosmos, until finally, at the end of the " Great World-Year," it returns to its original form in the World-Conflagration (ἐκπύρωσις) ; and this cyclical process of evolution goes on for ever. This primary matter has two aspects, active and passive : as " artistic fiery vapour " it is the Soul of the World, Reason (λόγος), Thought, Destiny, God. Hence the World, though wholly material, is rational : because governed and permeated by *Logos* (the divine " Word ") it exhibits order, harmony and beauty, as the artistic products of creative design. But the Logos is also the Cosmic Law, which binds all things in the rigid nexus of cause and effect, the bonds of Destiny (εἱμαρμένη). Hence, too, there can be no freedom of the Will for the individual. The Divine Logos contains all the " seminal Logoi," which are the active reproductive principles in all living creatures. Of the four elements, fire and air were contrasted as " active " with earth and water as " passive," and the forms and qualities of things were explained as

due to the action of air or " aeriform tension " (τόνος). The unity of inorganic objects was ascribed to " condition " (ἕξις), of plants to " nature " (φύσις), of animals to " soul " (ψυχή). The souls of living creatures are parts of the Cosmic Soul, and consist of hot vapour or " spirit " (πνεῦμα). Human souls (or at least those of the Wise) persist after death until the Ecpyrosis. The Soul has eight parts or faculties, viz. the five senses, the vocal, the generative, and the *hegemonic* or ruling. To this " Regent Part " all the rest are attached, it being their source of motion, with its seat in the heart, whence the *pneuma* radiates to the various local organs. It is in the " Regent Part," too, that perception (presentations and impulses) takes place.

For their *Logic* the Stoics were mainly indebted to Aristotle. They subdivided Logic into Rhetoric and Dialectic. All knowledge comes through the senses, the mind being a *tabula rasa* upon which sense-impressions are made. The " presentation " (φαντασία) is defined as " an affection (πάθος) arising in the soul " or " an impression (τύπωσις) on the soul " (Zeno) or " an alteration in the soul " (Chrysippus). Of these presentations some come through the senses, others are mental. How are we to distinguish between trustworthy and untrustworthy presentations ? What is the *Criterion* of truth ? Here we come to the most distinctive feature of the Stoic doctrine. The Criterion, they said, is to be found in the subjective reaction of the percipient. If the presentation is true, proceeding from a real object, it wins the " assent " or approbation (συγκατάθεσις) of the percipient : such an " apprehensive presentation " (καταληπτικὴ φαντασία) constitutes the Criterion. In

the development of knowledge they distinguished four stages—sense-perception (αἴσθησις), memory (μνήμη) or retained presentation of an absent object, experience (ἐμπειρία) formed by a plurality of like memories, notions (ἔννοιαι). " Notions " may be either involuntary—termed " common notions " or " concepts " (προλήψεις)—or voluntary, due to the reflex action of the mind. The " concept " is defined as " the natural notion of universals." The reasoning faculty (λόγος) deals with " notions," and all notions, as substances, are corporeal. The concepts were classified under four heads, the Stoic *Categories,* viz. substance (ὑποκείμενον), essential quality (τὸ ποιόν), accidental quality (πὼς ἔχον), relation (πρός τί πως ἔχον). These they called " highest universals " or *summa genera* (τὰ γενικώτατα), and of these the first is also termed Being. In order to include also Non-being, another, still higher, category was postulated— " Something " (τό τι). All qualities, as gaseous currents (πνεύματα), are corporeal ; but essential or intrinsic qualities or " states " (ἕξεις) are distinguished from imported or accidental qualities or " conditions " (σχέσεις). Under " relation " are classed all attributes which imply a connexion between co-existing objects.

In their *Ethics* the Stoics followed the Cynics, declaring Virtue to be the only *Good,* and presenting the Ideal " Sage " as the embodiment of virtue. Like all the post-Aristotelian Schools they regarded Ethics as the crown of their philosophy to which Physics and Logic were merely adjuncts, since Ethics deals with the one thing needful—human happiness and the rules for its attainment. Happiness—the End (τέλος) or Good—they defined as " Living in conformity with Nature " (ὁμολογουμένως τῇ φύσει),

or without contravening the Cosmic " Law " which
is Right Reason (λόγος), which means obeying God or
Necessity. This subjection to the Law of the Logos is
ultimately unavoidable, since " volentem fata ducunt,
nolentem trahunt." Action in accordance with
" Nature " is Virtue, which does not admit of increase
or decrease and is termed a " disposition " (διάθεσις)
rather than a " state " (ἕξις). The four virtues—
wisdom, temperance, justice, courage—are defined
as four forms of knowledge. Between the extremes
of virtue and vice there is no middle state ; but an
important distinction was made between three classes
of conduct—perfect moral actions (κατορθώματα),
" becoming " actions or " duties " (καθήκοντα),
" undutiful " or sinful actions (παρὰ τὸ καθῆκον). The
first kind is peculiar to the Stoic " Sage," the second
proper for those " progressing " towards wisdom
(προκόπτοντες). As the only " goods " are the
virtues and the only " evils " their opposite vices,
there is a large class of things which come under
neither of these heads : these " neutral " things—
such as life, health, wealth, beauty, pleasure, and
their opposites—are, strictly speaking, " indifferent "
(ἀδιάφορα). But, even so, they differ in value and
were divided into two classes, " the desirable and
preferred " (προηγμένα), and " the undesirable and
unpreferred " (ἀποπροηγμένα). Non-rational affections are the " passions " or emotions (πάθη), of
which there are four kinds—one being of the body,
viz. involuntary sensuous feeling, and the other of
the soul, viz. the rational emotion of the Sage, natural
and involuntary states which are harmless, and vicious
or morbid emotions. In all such mental passions there
is an element of intellect and will as well as of feeling.

INTRODUCTION

The primary passions are four—desire, fear, pain and pleasure; and one definition of passion is " an excessive impulse." To give way to such an impulse is to " assent " to it, or approve of it by a perverted act of judgement, and hence " passions " were called " judgements " by Chrysippus. The root of evil passions is " intemperance," " a defection of the whole mind from right Reason," and their fruits are the diseases of the soul we call vices and sins. The Ideal Wise Man or Sage, being moved only by rational emotions, is said to be " passionless " (ἀπαθής). In him virtue and wisdom are personified. He only is happy and at peace with himself, unperturbed by fightings without or fears within, indifferent to externals, self-sufficient and self-controlled, master of his fate and captain of his soul. Their portrait of the Ideal Sage is one of the features of Stoicism which attracted world-wide attention, alike from critics and admirers of the School. Horace alludes to the *sapiens* more than once in his *Satires*, *e.g.* ii. 7. 83 ff. :

> quisnam igitur liber ? sapiens sibi qui imperiosus,
> quem neque pauperies neque mors neque vincula terrent,
> responsare cupidinibus, contemnere honores
> fortis, et in se ipso totus, teres atque rotundus.

Of " the Wise " it was said also that all were friends of all and that they had all things in common and that the whole world was their city and their home (whence the term " cosmopolitan "). They form one of the two classes into which mankind is divided— the " good " (σπουδαῖοι) and the " bad " (φαῦλοι), the sheep and the goats. Here again we note the ingrained ethical dualism of the Stoic system. The " bad," the poor in virtue, we have always with us,

a multitude whom no man can number, but where shall wisdom be found and who exactly are the truly " wise " ? Socrates, they said, and Antisthenes and Diogenes approximated to the Ideal, but the perfect Sage is nowhere discoverable upon the earth ; either, then, he had his being in the far-off Golden Age or he remains for ever a " pattern laid up in the heavens."

I have enlarged thus much upon the details of Stoic doctrine because it is the type of Dogmatism which the Sceptics criticized most frequently and most severely. We pass on now to the Sceptics themselves.

III. Scepticism and the Sceptics

A " Sceptic," in the original sense of the Greek term, is simply an " inquirer " or investigator. But inquiry often leads to an *impasse*, and ends in incredulity or despair of a solution, so that the "inquirer" becomes a " doubter " or a " disbeliever," and Scepticism receives its usual connotation. All down the history of Greek philosophy we have found traces of sceptical thought in the repeated discrediting of sense-perception and the frequent insistence on the folly of vulgar opinion. But, with the exception of Sophists like Protagoras and Gorgias, all the philosophers agreed in assuming that truth existed and that knowledge of it was possible. When Scepticism was revived and reorganized under the name of " Pyrrhonism " its main task was to challenge this assumption and to maintain, if not the impossibility of knowledge, at least the impossibility of positively affirming its possibility. Its watchword was " Suspend judgement."

The history of Scepticism, as a definite tradition or

INTRODUCTION

" School," may conveniently be divided into four periods or stages, viz. :

(1) Practical Scepticism of *Pyrrho* of Elis (*circa* 360–275 B.C.), and his pupil *Timon* of Phlius (*circa* 315–225 B.C.).
(2) Critical Scepticism and probabilism of the New Academy—*Arcesilas* of Pitane (*circa* 315–241 B.C.) and *Carneades* of Cyrene (*circa* 213–129 B.C.). This ended in the Eclecticism of *Philo* and *Antiochus* (*ob.* 69 B.C.).
(3) Pyrrhonism revived, systematized and developed dialectically by *Aenesidemus* (*circa* 100–40 B.C.) and *Agrippa* (? first century A.D.).
(4) Final development of Empiric Scepticism, culminating in *Sextus Empiricus* (*circa* 160–210 A.D.).

A brief account of each of these stages must here suffice.

1. *Pyrrho* of Elis—in spite of some later traditions about him—was probably not at all a full-blown Sceptic, but rather a moralist of an austere and ascetic type—as Cicero represents him (*Acad. Pr.* ii. 130, *De Fin.* iv. 43, 49)—who cultivated insensibility to externals and superiority to environment. Probably he derived from Democritus a deep distrust of the value of sense-perception, but otherwise he seems to have been imbued with dogmatism, though it was the dogmatism of the will rather than of the intellect. We may fairly assume that the causes which led to the Scepticism of Pyrrho and his immediate followers were twofold—firstly, the intellectual confusion which resulted from the number of conflicting doctrines and rival schools, and secondly, the political confusion

and social chaos which spread through the Hellenic world after Alexander's death, together with the new insight into strange habits and customs which was given by the opening up of the East. The natural result of the situation at the close of the fourth century was to shake men's belief in tradition and custom, to dissolve the old creeds and loyalties, and to produce the demand for a new way of salvation in the midst of a crumbling world. Pyrrho, it would seem, shared this attitude, and stood out as the apostle of disillusionment. He would not seek or promise " happiness," in the usual sense of the word, but he sought and taught the negative satisfaction of freedom from care and worry by the cultivation of a neutral, non-committal attitude towards all the problems of life and thought. In self-defence he sought refuge within himself, there to achieve a self-centred " apathy " which his disciples were to acclaim, under the name of " ataraxy," as the Chief End of Man. Probably, then, the main, if not the only, interest of Pyrrho was in the ethical and practical side of Scepticism as the speediest cure for the ills of life.

Timon of Phlius spent the latter part of his long life at Athens. In his earlier days he is said to have sat under Stilpo at Megara, as well as under Pyrrho at Elis. His admiration for the latter was unbounded, although it would seem that he did not copy his ascetic habits too closely. He was a voluminous writer of both prose and poetry—epics, tragedies, satires—but only a few fragments of two of his works have survived, viz. the " Images " or " Illusions " ('Ινδαλμοί), and the " Silli " or " Lampoons " (Σίλλοι). The latter evidently became very popular because of its mordant wit. It consisted of three books, all deriding the

professors of philosophy, and written in hexameters in the Homeric style, beginning thus :

> Come now, listen to me, ye polypragmatical Sophists.

The second and third books were in the form of a dialogue between Timon and Xenophanes, in which the latter expresses his contempt for nearly all the rival schools of thought. It appears, then, that the only philosophers for whom Timon entertained any respect were the Eleatics, Democritus and Protagoras —the most severe critics of knowledge in the form of sense-perception. This exposure of the futility of philosophizing served to support the indifferentist attitude of Pyrrho ; and Timon by his writings (for Pyrrho wrote nothing) popularized the Sceptical view that the way to make the best of life is to eschew dogma and to cultivate mental repose. It is probably a mistake of Sextus (*Adv. Math.* iii. 2, vi. 66) to ascribe to Timon formal argumentation concerning " hypotheses " and the " divisibility of time," considering his ridicule of dialectic and his avoidance of " the strife of tongues " ; and it is very doubtful whether he (or Pyrrho) invented or used any of the technical vocabulary of Scepticism (*e.g.* " Suspension," " No more," " Equipollence ") which is commonly ascribed to him or his master.

2. *Scepticism in the New Academy* (*cf. Pyrr. Hyp.* i. 220 ff.).—With *Arcesilas* Scepticism entered upon a new stage of development. It ceased to be purely practical, and became mainly theoretical. Arcesilas succeeded Crates as Head of the Academy about 270 B.C. He appears to have been influenced by the Megarics as well as by Pyrrho, and was eminent as a dialectician and controversialist. His delight was

to argue *in utramque partem* and balance argument against argument ; and he took up the position that to know we know is an impossibility, and to seek for absolute truth an absurdity. His polemic was chiefly directed against the Stoic epistemology and its doctrine of the " apprehensive presentation " as the " Criterion." He maintained that we can " assent " to no sense-impression as carrying conviction and indubitably true, and that the objective realities are consequently incognizable, and we can only " suspend judgement " about them, unless we content ourselves with fallible " opinion " instead of scientific " knowledge." But the Stoic " Sage " never " opines " ; neither can he " know " ; therefore he must suspend judgement and turn Sceptic. False and true presentations are indistinguishable : no valid criterion exists : we have no guide but opinion, and we can only think, believe, and act in accordance with what seems reasonable (εὔλογον) or probably right. Thus, while Pyrrho had renounced and Timon flouted the Dogmatics, Arcesilas started the practice of refuting them scientifically and systematically, and earned thereby the abuse of Timon for his lapse from pure Pyrrhonism.

Carneades of Cyrene, like Arcesilas and Pyrrho, left no writings, but his views were preserved by his disciple Cleitomachus (Hasdrubal). He was a brilliant teacher, a formidable dialectician, and perhaps the most talented philosopher of the post-Aristotelian period. His energies were mainly devoted to negative criticism of the theories of the Dogmatists, especially the Stoics. He resumed and developed the arguments with which Arcesilas had attacked the Stoic theory of knowledge, and which Chrysippus had, in the meanwhile, attempted to rebut. Neither the senses nor

the reason, he argued, can supply any infallible
" criterion ": there is no specific difference between
false " presentations " and true : beside any true presentation you can set a false one which is in no wise
different. The dreamer, the drunkard, the madman
have illusions of the truth of which they are convinced :
you see two eggs or two hairs and cannot tell the
one from the other : you cannot distinguish the true
impression from the false, or assert that the one rather
than the other is produced by a real object. It is in
vain, then, to look to the senses for certainty ; and it
is equally vain to look to the reason since it (as the
Stoics held) is wholly dependent on the senses and
based on experience. Logic, the product of the
reasoning faculty, is discredited because of the number
of insoluble fallacies for which it is responsible—such
as " The Liar " (" The Cretan says ' I lie ' : is he a
liar ? "), " The *Cornutus* " (" Have you shed your
horns—yes or no ? "), " The *Sorites* " or Chain-
argument (" How many grains make a heap ? Take
10, 20, 30, etc., away, is it still a heap ? "). Chrysippus
when confronted with the *Sorites* in a dialectical discussion is said to have called a halt and refused to
answer, thus giving in to the Sceptic by " suspending
judgement." Reason is thus found to be as fallible
as sensation, and certitude impossible.

Carneades also attacked the Ethical system of the
Stoics, exposing their inconsistency in saying that
Virtue is directed to choosing the prime objects of
natural desire while denying to these objects the
name of " good." He criticized also their Theology,
their doctrines of the Divine Nature, of Providence,
of Divination and Prophecy. The Stoics were fond
of appealing to the *consensus gentium*, or the universal

belief in the existence of the gods : Carneades ridiculed that appeal. For how do we know that the belief is universal ? And why appeal to the multitude who—the Stoics tell us—are all fools ? why call in ignorance as judge ? And as to divination and prognostication, they rest on no principles of science but are mere quackery and tricks of the trade. The God of the Stoics is an incredible Being because he is composed of contradictory attributes. If He is to be infinite, omniscient, all-good, and imperishable, He cannot be either composite or corporeal or animate or rational or virtuous—all such qualities belonging to objects which lie in the sphere of becoming and perishing. In support of their theory of Providence the Stoics brought forward evidences of design in Nature. Carneades retorted by quoting cases of snake-bites and wrecks at sea. Reason, said the Stoics, is a gift of Providence to man : why then, replied Carneades, did not Providence see to it that the majority were endowed with a " right reason " instead of one that only enables them to outdo the brutes in brutishness ? Only a few possess right reason ; so the Stoic God must be miserly in his gifts !

In all this the position of Carneades is purely agnostic. He does not wish to affirm a negative, but merely to show up the untenability of the Stoic dogmas, and to reassert as regards all departments of knowledge the impossibility of attaining absolute certitude. When the pretentious structure of the Stoics had been thus riddled by the arrows of Carneades, their Ideal Sage must have appeared but as a figment to many, and their anthropomorphic Deity as an incredible bundle of contradictions.

But there was a constructive as well as a destructive side to the teaching of Carneades. He took over, modified, and developed the theory of Arcesilas that, despite the impossibility of objective knowledge, a sufficient ground for practical choice and action might be found in the " reasonable " (εὔλογον) or subjectively satisfying. He granted to the Stoics that some sense-impressions or opinions *seem* to the percipient superior to others, and this apparent superiority provided a sufficient reason for preference and consequential action. Impressions being thus subjectively distinguishable, judgements may be graded in value as more or less " persuasive " or " probable " (πιθαναί). Carneades then classified presentations in this way : (1) the apparently false ; (2) the apparently true, which are of three grades—(a) the probable in itself; (b) the probable and " uncontradicted " (*i.e.* by accompanying conditions—ἀπερίσπαστος) ; (c) the probable and uncontradicted and "closely scrutinized" or "tested" (διεξωδευμένη). These apparently true impressions produce varying degrees of " conviction " and deserve proportionate " assent " (συγκατάθεσις) of a relative kind—the only kind of assent possible for the Sceptic who denies that objective certitude is attainable. In connexion with this doctrine of " probabilism " Carneades defended human freedom, in " assent," choice and action, as against the determinism of the Stoics with their rigid theory of Destiny and Necessity ; and he subjected their doctrine on this subject to a searching criticism which exposed its inherent inconsistency.

With Carneades the dialectical Scepticism of the New Academy came to an end. His successors, *Philo* of Larissa (*ob. circa* 80 B.C.) and *Antiochus* of Ascalon

(*ob.* 69 B.C.), surrendered his theory of nescience, and reverted to a more dogmatic position. Both were Eclectics—Antiochus so much so that he asserted the harmony, if not the practical identity, of the doctrines of the Academy with those of the Peripatetics and Stoics, and his teaching was a curious amalgam of them all. This tendency to doctrinal conflation continued to characterize the philosophers of the succeeding generations till the rise of Neoplatonism, excepting only those attached to the Epicurean School and the Later Sceptics.

3. The first of the " Later Sceptics," who revived the original " Pyrrhonism," was *Aenesidemus*, a younger contemporary of Antiochus. Cnossus in Crete may have been his birthplace, Alexandria was where he taught. Though originally an Academic, he denounced Arcesilas and Carneades as dogmatists in disguise rather than true Sceptics, since we cannot know that knowledge is impossible. His treatise *Pyrrhonean Discourses* consisted of eight books in which he explained his dissent from the New Academy, and criticized in detail the logic, ethics, and physics of Stoicism. In another work, *Introductory Outline of Pyrrhonism*, he set forth his famous " Ten Tropes," or " Modes " of procedure, for the refuting of Dogmatism in all its forms. Apparently the order in which they are drawn up was not fixed, since Sextus's order differs from that of Diogenes Laertius ; nor does it seem to be governed by any logical principle. The Tropes themselves merely formulate arguments in favour of the relativity of knowledge, borrowed from earlier Sceptical teachers— Sophists, Megarics, Academics ; and, as Lotze says,[a]

[a] *Logic*, III. i. § 310 (English translation).

" The ten tropes, or logical grounds of doubt, all come to this, that sensations by themselves cannot discover to us what is the nature of the object which excites them."

Besides these ten Tropes, Aenesidemus (in his *Pyrrhonean Discourses*, bk. 5) summarized the arguments against causality and current theories of "cause" in his "Eight (Aetiological) Tropes." These form a list of fallacious methods of reasoning about "cause." His objections rest mainly on the assumption that "cause" is a thing in itself, and causality a real objective quality inherent therein.

Similarly he attacked the Stoic and Epicurean doctrine of "Signs" ($\sigma\eta\mu\epsilon\hat{\iota}\alpha$), or "effects" which point back to "causes," arguing that no phenomenon can safely be regarded as a "sign," because "doctors differ" in interpreting symptoms.

But, to judge by several remarks of Sextus, Aenesidemus was not consistent in his Scepticism. We are told that he regarded "the Sceptic system ($\dot{\alpha}\gamma\omega\gamma\dot{\eta}$) as a road leading to the Heracleitean philosophy, on the ground that the (Sceptic) view that opposites *apparently* belong to the same object is prefatory to the (Heracleitean) view that they *really* so belong." We are told also that he held that the primary world-principle is *air*, which he identified with *time* and number; and that he explained the origin of the world in all its variety from this unitary substance by supposing it to be receptive of opposite qualities, and every whole self-identical in all its parts. He is also said to have reduced the six kinds of *motion* distinguished by Aristotle, and the ten of Plato, to two, viz. locomotion and alteration or transformation;

and a peculiar theory of *Soul*, or reason (διάνοια), is ascribed to him, according to which the reason exists outside the body and is somehow inspired so that it can act from within through the senses. With the theory of reason as external, and therefore not individualized but " common " (κοινή), like the " Logos " of Heracleitus, is connected the further theory, ascribed to Aenesidemus, that some phenomena appear alike to all men " in common," while others appear different to different percipients, and that the former class are " true," the latter "false "— universality of experience thus being the " Criterion " of truth.

How we are to reconcile this hybrid dogmatism with the undoubted Pyrrhonism of Aenesidemus is a puzzling question which has much exercised the historians of philosophy. It has been suggested that Sextus has misunderstood or misrepresented Aenesidemus; or that Aenesidemus did ultimately pass over from the Sceptical to the Dogmatic position; or that his apparent Dogmatism can be explained away as no real surrender of Scepticism but rather an unconscious yielding to the Eclectic influences of his intellectual environment. None of these suggestions seems wholly satisfactory; but perhaps the least difficult supposition is that Sextus is unintentionally misrepresenting Aenesidemus by a loose use of language when he ascribes the dogmas mentioned above to " Aenesidemus and his followers " (οἱ περὶ τὸν Αἰνησίδημον). If so, we may suppose that while Aenesidemus may have given a start to the dogmatizing tendency by enlarging on the points of similarity between Scepticism and Heracleiteanism and claiming Heracleitus as a forerunner, certain of his adherents

INTRODUCTION

pushed that tendency to excess and indulged in an Eclectic dogmatism, after the fashion of Antiochus, which blended Scepticism with Heracleitean and Stoic doctrine.

Of the successors of Aenesidemus we know no more than the names until we come to *Agrippa*, about a century later. To him is attributed the presentation of Sceptical theory in "five Tropes," which are briefly these: (1) Based on the conflict among opinions (ὁ ἀπὸ τῆς διαφωνίας); (2) Every proof requires a fresh proof in endless regress (ὁ εἰς ἄπειρον ἐκβάλλων); (3) Based on the relativity of perceptions (ὁ ἀπὸ τοῦ πρός τι τρόπος); (4) Proof must not presuppose unproved premisses (ὁ ὑποθετικός); (5) Reasoning involves a vicious circle (ὁ διάλληλος τρόπος). Of these (1) and (3) resume and sum up the former "ten Tropes," which exhibited the fallibility of the senses and the relativity of perceptual knowledge; while (2), (4) and (5) are directed against the Aristotelian theory of "immediate" axioms (ἄμεσα) and the possibility of logical demonstration.

Agrippa was followed by Zeuxippus, Zeuxis, and Antiochus, who remain mere names, though we may suppose that they adhered to the tradition of dialectical Scepticism.

4. The last stage in the history of Greek Scepticism is marked by its alliance with medical empiricism (*cf. Pyrr. Hyp.* i. 236 ff.). *Menodotus* of Nicomedia and *Theodas* appear to have been the first of these medical Sceptics, and we may date them about A.D. 150. Galen criticizes the views of both regarding medicine and natural science. *Herodotus* of Tarsus, who succeeded Menodotus, is thought to have belonged to the "pneumatic" rather than to the

" empiric " school of medicine ; but in any case he
was the teacher of Sextus Empiricus.

To one or other of the foregoing Sceptics we may
probably attribute two further developments of
doctrine, viz. a further reduction of the " Tropes "
to two (arguing against the possibility of either
immediate or mediate certitude), and a new distinction between " commemorative " (ὑπομνηστικά) and
" indicative " (ἐνδεικτικά) " signs " (cf. Pyrr. Hyp.
ii. 99).

Sextus Empiricus (circa A.D. 200) is our main authority
for the history and doctrine of the Sceptic School. We
know that he was a Greek physician and that he succeeded Herodotus as Head of the School, but we
know little else about the details of his life. He seems
to have resided for some time in Rome, and to have
been acquainted with Athens and Alexandria. Although named " Empiricus " he seems to imply that
he adhered rather to the " methodic " than to the
" empiric " tradition in medicine. His surviving works
are three—(1) " Outlines (ὑποτυπώσεις) of Pyrrhonism " in three books ; (2) " Against the Dogmatists "
in five books,[a]—1 and 2 " Against the Logicians," 3
and 4 " Against the Physicists," 5 " Against the Ethicists " ; (3) " Against the Professors " in six books—a
book each against Grammarians, Rhetors, Geometers,
Arithmeticians, Astrologers, Musicians, in this order.
Other works ascribed to him are a treatise " On
the Soul " and " Notes on Medicine."

Of the surviving works the Hypotyposes, or " Outlines," is a kind of summary of Scepticism, the first
book stating and defending the Sceptic position, and

[a] These five books are sometimes entitled Adversus Mathematicos, vii-xi. Cf. p. xlii.

the other two books attacking the Dogmatic position. The other two works are usually put together as a whole under the title *Adversus Mathematicos*—which we might construe " Against the Professors of all Arts and Sciences,"—and they resume and expand the critical and polemical arguments of books 2 and 3 of the " Outlines."

Probably there is but little original matter in these works. Sextus was mainly a compiler: he drew freely on the writings of his predecessors, especially Aenesidemus, Cleitomachus (for Carneades), and Menodotus. He was evidently interested in the history of thought, and provides us with much valuable information about the earlier Schools, although he is not wholly reliable. He writes mostly in a plain, dry style, enlivened but rarely by touches of humour. As a controversialist he studies fairness by quoting the opponent's own views, often at great length ; but he wearies the reader by his way of piling argument upon argument for the mere sake of multiplying words —bad argument and good heaped together indiscriminately. Obviously his books are not intended to be works of art, but rather immense arsenals stored with all the weapons of offence and defence of every conceivable pattern, old and new, that ever were forged on the anvil of Scepticism by the hammer blows of Eristic dialecticians. From these storehouses the Sceptic engaged in polemics may choose his weapon to suit his need ; for (as Sextus naïvely observes) the Sceptic is a " philanthropic " person who spares his adversary by using against him only the minimum of force necessary to bowl him over, so that the weakest and most flimsy arguments have their uses as well as the weightiest. Or is Sextus here the veiled humorist?

INTRODUCTION

IV. TEXT AND EDITIONS

The text of Sextus is derived from two main sources
—the Greek Manuscripts and a Latin Translation.
For the *Hypotyposes* the most important MSS.—as
described by the latest editor, Mutschmann—are :

M = Monac. gr. 439, late fourteenth century, containing *Pyrr. Hyp.*

L = Laur. 81. 11, dated A.D. 1465, containing all the
works of Sextus.

E = Parisinus 1964, late fifteenth century, containing all Sextus (plus διαλέξεις).

A = Parisinus 1963, dated 1534, containing all
Sextus (plus διαλέξεις).

B = Berol. Phill. 1518, dated 1542, nearly a dupli-
cate of A.

Of these, the last three seem to be closely akin, so
that we have three main lines of MS. tradition,
derived from the same Archetype, viz. M, L, and
EAB.

T denotes (in Mutschmann's notation, which is
here followed) the Latin Translation, which is preserved in the MS. known as Parisinus lat. 14700
(fol. 83-132). It contains the whole of Sextus except
for two omissions, viz. p. 51, 11-26, and p. 145, 3-160,
20. As it was first brought to light by C. Jourdain
in 1888, earlier editors were ignorant of its existence,
and it is only in the latest Teubner edition that
its readings are reported. The Teubner editor, H.
Mutschmann, dates it in the thirteenth century, and
regards it as equal in importance to any of the Greek
MSS., and derived from an independent Archetype.

There are three early editions of Sextus—by P.

and J. Chouet (Geneva, 1621); by J. A. Fabricius
(Leipzig, 1718), incorporating the Latin version by
H. Stephens (Paris, 1562), as well as additional Notes ;
by I. Bekker (Berlin, 1842), giving the text and index
only. The first volume of the Teubner edition (containing *Pyrr. Hyp.*) was published in 1912, the second
volume in 1914.

A literal German version of the three books of
Pyrr. Hyp., with an Introduction and useful Notes,
by E. Pappenheim, appeared in 1877 (Leipzig) ; and
an English version of *Pyrr. Hyp.*, book i., is included
in M. Patrick's volume *Sextus Empiricus and Greek
Scepticism* (Cambridge, 1899). The latest considerable
contribution to the textual criticism of Sextus is
Werner Heintz's *Studien zu Sextus Empiricus* (Halle,
1932).

The present four volumes include " Outlines of
Pyrrhonism " (in Vol. I) ; " Against the Logicians "
(Vol. II) ; " Against the Physicists " and " Against
the Ethicists " (Vol. III) ; and " Against the Professors " (Vol. IV). " Against the Professors " vii-xi
(*Adversus Mathematicos* vii-xi) is an alternative title
for " Against the Logicians " i-v (*Adversus Dog-
maticos* i-v).

The text in these volumes is based on that of Bekker. Bekker, it may be noted, omitted both the
Tables of Contents prefixed to the several books in
the MSS. and the corresponding Chapter-headings,
although the earlier editors had retained both. In
these volumes the Chapter-headings are restored,
for the convenience of the reader, while the Tables
of Contents are, after Bekker, omitted, as a superfluous duplication.

In addition to the accounts of Greek Scepticism

given in the standard Histories of Ancient Philosophy, attention may be drawn to the special treatment of the subject in *The Greek Sceptics* by N. MacColl (1869) ; *Les Sceptiques grecs* by V. Brochard (1887), copious and clear ; *Die Geschichte des griechischen Skeptizismus* by A. Goedeckemeyer (1905), good for details ; *Stoic and Epicurean* by R. D. Hicks (1910), chapters 8 and 10 ; *Stoics and Sceptics* by E. Bevan (1913), less detailed, but scholarly, suggestive and interesting, and thus probably the best introduction to the subject for the general reader.

The following abbreviations are used in the footnotes on the text :

L = MS. Laur. 85. 11.
M = ,, Monac. 439.
E = ,, Paris. 1964.
A = ,, Paris. 1963.
B = ,, Berol. Phill. 1518.
G = consensus of foregoing MSS.
T = Latin Translation.
Fabr. = Fabricius.
Bekk. = Bekker.
Mutsch. = H. Mutschmann.
Papp. = Pappenheim.

OUTLINES OF
PYRRHONISM

ΠΥΡΡΩΝΕΙΩΝ
ΥΠΟΤΥΠΩΣΕΩΝ

ΤΩΝ ΕΙΣ ΤΡΙΑ ΤΟ ΠΡΩΤΟΝ

Α΄.—ΠΕΡΙ ΤΗΣ ΑΝΩΤΑΤΩ ΔΙΑΦΟΡΑΣ ΤΩΝ ΦΙΛΟΣΟΦΙΩΝ

1 Τοῖς ζητοῦσί τι πρᾶγμα ἢ εὕρεσιν ἐπακολουθεῖν εἰκὸς ἢ ἄρνησιν εὑρέσεως καὶ ἀκαταληψίας ὁμολο-
2 γίαν ἢ ἐπιμονὴν ζητήσεως. διόπερ ἴσως καὶ ἐπὶ τῶν κατὰ φιλοσοφίαν ζητουμένων οἱ μὲν εὑρη-κέναι τὸ ἀληθὲς ἔφασαν, οἱ δ' ἀπεφήναντο μὴ δυνατὸν εἶναι τοῦτο καταληφθῆναι, οἱ δὲ ἔτι
3 ζητοῦσιν. καὶ εὑρηκέναι μὲν δοκοῦσιν οἱ ἰδίως καλούμενοι δογματικοί, οἷον οἱ περὶ Ἀριστοτέλην καὶ Ἐπίκουρον καὶ τοὺς στωικοὺς καὶ ἄλλοι τινές, ὡς δὲ περὶ ἀκαταλήπτων ἀπεφήναντο οἱ περὶ Κλειτόμαχον καὶ Καρνεάδην καὶ ἄλλοι Ἀκαδη-
4 μαϊκοί, ζητοῦσι δὲ οἱ σκεπτικοί. ὅθεν εὐλόγως δοκοῦσιν αἱ ἀνωτάτω φιλοσοφίαι τρεῖς εἶναι, δογ-ματικὴ Ἀκαδημαϊκὴ σκεπτική. περὶ μὲν οὖν τῶν ἄλλων ἑτέροις ἁρμόσει λέγειν, περὶ δὲ τῆς σκεπ-τικῆς ἀγωγῆς ὑποτυπωτικῶς ἐπὶ τοῦ παρόντος ἡμεῖς ἐροῦμεν, ἐκεῖνο προειπόντες ὅτι περὶ οὐδενὸς τῶν

---

[a] See Introd. pp. xxxii ff.

[b] " Doctrine." " School," "system " or " way " are other

OUTLINES OF PYRRHONISM

BOOK I

CHAPTER I.—OF THE MAIN DIFFERENCE BETWEEN PHILOSOPHIC SYSTEMS

THE natural result of any investigation is that the 1
investigators either discover the object of search or
deny that it is discoverable and confess it to be
inapprehensible or persist in their search. So, too, 2
with regard to the objects investigated by philosophy,
this is probably why some have claimed to have discovered the truth, others have asserted that it cannot
be apprehended, while others again go on inquiring.
Those who believe they have discovered it are the 3
"Dogmatists," specially so called—Aristotle, for
example, and Epicurus and the Stoics and certain
others ; Cleitomachus and Carneades and other
Academics [a] treat it as inapprehensible : the Sceptics
keep on searching. Hence it seems reasonable to 4
hold that the main types of philosophy are three—
the Dogmatic, the Academic, and the Sceptic. Of
the other systems it will best become others to speak :
our task at present is to describe in outline the
Sceptic doctrine,[b] first premising that of none of our

possible renderings of ἀγωγή. "Procedure," "way of
thought," "trend," or "line of argument," "leading" (ἄγων)
up to a definite goal, is rather what it connotes.

λεχθησομένων διαβεβαιούμεθα ὡς οὕτως ἔχοντος
πάντως καθάπερ λέγομεν, ἀλλὰ κατὰ τὸ νῦν φαινόμενον ἡμῖν ἱστορικῶς ἀπαγγέλλομεν περὶ ἑκάστου.

Β΄.—ΠΕΡΙ ΤΩΝ ΛΟΓΩΝ ΤΗΣ ΣΚΕΨΕΩΣ

5 Τῆς σκεπτικῆς οὖν φιλοσοφίας ὁ μὲν λέγεται
καθόλου λόγος ὁ δὲ εἰδικός, καὶ καθόλου μὲν
ἐν ᾧ τὸν χαρακτῆρα τῆς σκέψεως ἐκτιθέμεθα,
λέγοντες τίς ἔννοια αὐτῆς καὶ τίνες ἀρχαὶ καὶ
τίνες λόγοι τί τε κριτήριον καὶ τί τέλος, καὶ τίνες
οἱ τρόποι τῆς ἐποχῆς, καὶ πῶς παραλαμβάνομεν
τὰς σκεπτικὰς ἀποφάσεις, καὶ τὴν διάκρισιν τῆς
σκέψεως ἀπὸ τῶν παρακειμένων αὐτῇ φιλοσοφιῶν,
6 εἰδικὸς δὲ ἐν ᾧ πρὸς ἕκαστον μέρος τῆς καλουμένης φιλοσοφίας ἀντιλέγομεν. περὶ τοῦ καθόλου
δὴ πρῶτον διαλάβωμεν λόγου, ἀρξάμενοι τῆς
ὑφηγήσεως ἀπὸ τῶν τῆς σκεπτικῆς ἀγωγῆς ὀνομάτων.

Γ΄.—ΠΕΡΙ ΤΩΝ ΟΝΟΜΑΣΙΩΝ ΤΗΣ ΣΚΕΠΤΙΚΗΣ

7 Ἡ σκεπτικὴ τοίνυν ἀγωγὴ καλεῖται μὲν καὶ
ζητητικὴ ἀπὸ ἐνεργείας τῆς κατὰ τὸ ζητεῖν καὶ
σκέπτεσθαι, καὶ ἐφεκτικὴ ἀπὸ τοῦ μετὰ τὴν ζήτησιν περὶ τὸν σκεπτόμενον γινομένου πάθους,
καὶ ἀπορητικὴ ἤτοι ἀπὸ τοῦ περὶ παντὸς ἀπορεῖν
καὶ ζητεῖν, ὡς ἔνιοί φασιν, ἢ ἀπὸ τοῦ ἀμηχανεῖν
πρὸς συγκατάθεσιν ἢ ἄρνησιν, καὶ Πυρρώνειος ἀπὸ
τοῦ φαίνεσθαι ἡμῖν τὸν Πύρρωνα σωματικώτερον

---

[a] Cf. Introd. p. xxxvii; §§ 36 f. infra.
[b] Bks. II. and III. belong to the " special " part of the
exposition.

future statements do we positively affirm that the fact is exactly as we state it, but we simply record each fact, like a chronicler, as it appears to us at the moment.

Chapter II.—Of the Arguments of Scepticism

Of the Sceptic philosophy one argument (or branch 5 of exposition) is called " general," the other " special." In the general argument we set forth the distinctive features of Scepticism, stating its purport and principles, its logical methods, criterion, and end or aim ; the " Tropes," also, or " Modes," [a] which lead to suspension of judgement, and in what sense we adopt the Sceptic formulae, and the distinction between Scepticism and the philosophies which stand next to it. In the special argument we state our objections 6 regarding the several divisions of so-called philosophy.[b] Let us, then, deal first with the general argument, beginning our description with the names given to the Sceptic School.

Chapter III.—Of the Nomenclature of Scepticism

The Sceptic School, then, is also called " Zetetic " 7 from its activity in investigation and inquiry, and " Ephectic " or Suspensive from the state of mind produced in the inquirer after his search, and " Aporetic " or Dubitative either from its habit of doubting and seeking, as some say, or from its indecision as regards assent and denial, and " Pyrrhonean " from the fact that Pyrrho [c] appears to us to

[c] See Introd. pp. xxx f.

καὶ ἐπιφανέστερον τῶν πρὸ αὐτοῦ προσεληλυθέναι
τῇ σκέψει.

Δ΄.—ΤΙ ΕΣΤΙ ΣΚΕΨΙΣ

8 Ἔστι δὲ ἡ σκεπτικὴ δύναμις ἀντιθετικὴ φαινομένων τε καὶ νοουμένων καθ᾽ οἱονδήποτε τρόπον,
ἀφ᾽ ἧς ἐρχόμεθα διὰ τὴν ἐν τοῖς ἀντικειμένοις
πράγμασι καὶ λόγοις ἰσοσθένειαν τὸ μὲν πρῶτον
εἰς ἐποχήν, τὸ δὲ μετὰ τοῦτο εἰς ἀταραξίαν.
9 δύναμιν μὲν οὖν αὐτὴν καλοῦμεν οὐ κατὰ τὸ περί-
εργον ἀλλ᾽ ἁπλῶς κατὰ τὸ δύνασθαι· φαινόμενα δὲ
λαμβάνομεν νῦν τὰ αἰσθητά, διόπερ ἀντιδιαστέλ-
λομεν αὐτοῖς τὰ νοητά. τὸ δὲ " καθ᾽ οἱονδήποτε
τρόπον " δύναται προσαρμόζεσθαι καὶ τῇ δυνάμει,
ἵνα ἁπλῶς τὸ τῆς δυνάμεως ὄνομα, ὡς εἰρήκαμεν,
παραλαμβάνωμεν, καὶ τῷ " ἀντιθετικὴ φαινομένων
τε καὶ νοουμένων "· ἐπεὶ γὰρ ποικίλως ἀντιτίθεμεν
ταῦτα, ἢ φαινόμενα φαινομένοις ἢ νοούμενα νοουμένοις ἢ ἐναλλὰξ ἀντιτιθέντες, ἵνα πᾶσαι αἱ ἀντιθέσεις ἐμπεριέχωνται, λέγομεν " καθ᾽ οἱονδήποτε
τρόπον." ἢ καθ᾽ οἱονδήποτε τρόπον φαινομένων
τε καὶ νοουμένων, ἵνα μὴ ζητῶμεν πῶς φαίνεται τὰ φαινόμενα ἢ πῶς νοεῖται τὰ νοούμενα,
10 ἀλλ᾽ ἁπλῶς ταῦτα λαμβάνωμεν. ἀντικειμένους δὲ
λόγους παραλαμβάνομεν οὐχὶ πάντως ἀπόφασιν
καὶ κατάφασιν, ἀλλ᾽ ἁπλῶς ἀντὶ τοῦ μαχομένους.
ἰσοσθένειαν δὲ λέγομεν τὴν κατὰ πίστιν καὶ

---

[a] *i.e.* " opposites " includes, for the Sceptics, " contraries "
(*e.g.* " All are wise ")(" None are wise "), as well as " contradictories " (*e.g.* " Some are wise ")(" None are wise "),
whereas the Stoics used it of the latter only.

have applied himself to Scepticism more thoroughly and more conspicuously than his predecessors.

Chapter IV.—What Scepticism is

Scepticism is an ability, or mental attitude, which 8 opposes appearances to judgements in any way whatsoever, with the result that, owing to the equipollence of the objects and reasons thus opposed, we are brought firstly to a state of mental suspense and next to a state of "unperturbedness" or quietude. Now we call it an "ability" not in any subtle sense, 9 but simply in respect of its "being able." By "appearances" we now mean the objects of sense-perception, whence we contrast them with the objects of thought or "judgements." The phrase "in any way whatsoever" can be connected either with the word "ability," to make us take the word "ability," as we said, in its simple sense, or with the phrase "opposing appearances to judgements"; for inasmuch as we oppose these in a variety of ways—appearances to appearances, or judgements to judgements, or *alternando* appearances to judgements,—in order to ensure the inclusion of all these antitheses we employ the phrase "in any way whatsoever." Or, again, we join "in any way whatsoever" to "appearances and judgements" in order that we may not have to inquire how the appearances appear or how the thought-objects are judged, but may take these terms in the simple sense. The phrase "opposed 10 judgements" we do not employ in the sense of negations and affirmations only but simply as equivalent to "conflicting judgements." [a] "Equipollence" we use of equality in respect of probability and improba-

7

ἀπιστίαν ἰσότητα, ὡς μηδένα μηδενὸς προκεῖσθαι
τῶν μαχομένων λόγων ὡς πιστότερον. ἐποχὴ δέ
ἐστι στάσις διανοίας δι᾽ ἣν οὔτε αἴρομέν τι οὔτε
τίθεμεν. ἀταραξία δέ ἐστι ψυχῆς ἀοχλησία καὶ
γαληνότης. πῶς δὲ τῇ ἐποχῇ συνεισέρχεται ἡ
ἀταραξία, ἐν τοῖς περὶ τέλους ὑπομνήσομεν.

Ε΄.—ΠΕΡΙ ΤΟΥ ΣΚΕΠΤΙΚΟΥ

11 Καὶ ὁ Πυρρώνειος δὲ φιλόσοφος δυνάμει τῇ τῆς
σκεπτικῆς ἀγωγῆς ἐννοίᾳ συναποδέδοται· ἔστι γὰρ
ὁ μετέχων ταύτης τῆς δυνάμεως.

ϛ΄.—ΠΕΡΙ ΑΡΧΩΝ ΤΗΣ ΣΚΕΨΕΩΣ

12 Ἀρχὴν δὲ τῆς σκεπτικῆς αἰτιώδη μέν φαμεν
εἶναι τὴν ἐλπίδα τοῦ ἀταρακτήσειν· οἱ γὰρ μεγα-
λοφυεῖς τῶν ἀνθρώπων ταρασσόμενοι διὰ τὴν ἐν
τοῖς πράγμασιν ἀνωμαλίαν, καὶ ἀποροῦντες τίσιν
αὐτῶν χρὴ μᾶλλον συγκατατίθεσθαι, ἦλθον ἐπὶ τὸ
ζητεῖν τί τε ἀληθές ἐστιν ἐν τοῖς πράγμασι καὶ
τί ψεῦδος, ὡς ἐκ τῆς ἐπικρίσεως τούτων ἀταρακ-
τήσοντες. συστάσεως δὲ τῆς σκεπτικῆς ἐστιν
ἀρχὴ μάλιστα τὸ παντὶ λόγῳ λόγον ἴσον ἀντι-
κεῖσθαι· ἀπὸ γὰρ τούτου καταλήγειν δοκοῦμεν εἰς
τὸ μὴ δογματίζειν.

Ζ΄.—ΕΙ ΔΟΓΜΑΤΙΖΕΙ Ο ΣΚΕΠΤΙΚΟΣ

13 Λέγομεν δὲ μὴ δογματίζειν τὸν σκεπτικὸν οὐ
κατ᾽ ἐκεῖνο τὸ σημαινόμενον τοῦ δόγματος καθ᾽ ὃ
καὶ δόγμα εἶναί φασί τινες κοινότερον τὸ εὐδοκεῖν
τινὶ πράγματι (τοῖς γὰρ κατὰ φαντασίαν κατ·

bility, to indicate that no one of the conflicting judgements takes precedence of any other as being more probable. "Suspense" is a state of mental rest owing to which we neither deny nor affirm anything. "Quietude" is an untroubled and tranquil condition of soul. And how quietude enters the soul along with suspension of judgement we shall explain in our chapter (XII.) "Concerning the End."

Chapter V.—Of the Sceptic

In the definition of the Sceptic system there is also 11 implicitly included that of the Pyrrhonean philosopher: he is the man who participates in this "ability."

Chapter VI.—Of the Principles of Scepticism

The originating cause of Scepticism is, we say, the 12 hope of attaining quietude. Men of talent, who were perturbed by the contradictions in things and in doubt as to which of the alternatives they ought to accept, were led on to inquire what is true in things and what false, hoping by the settlement of this question to attain quietude. The main basic principle of the Sceptic system is that of opposing to every proposition an equal proposition ; for we believe that as a consequence of this we end by ceasing to dogmatize.

Chapter VII.—Does the Sceptic dogmatize?

When we say that the Sceptic refrains from dogma- 13 tizing we do not use the term " dogma," as some do, in the broader sense of "approval of a thing" (for the Sceptic gives assent to the feelings which

9

ἠναγκασμένοις πάθεσι συγκατατίθεται ὁ σκεπτικός,
οἷον οὐκ ἂν εἴποι θερμαινόμενος ἢ ψυχόμενος
ὅτι δοκῶ μὴ θερμαίνεσθαι ἢ ψύχεσθαι), ἀλλὰ μὴ
δογματίζειν λέγομεν καθ' ὃ δόγμα εἶναί φασί
τινες τήν τινι πράγματι τῶν κατὰ τὰς ἐπιστήμας
ζητουμένων ἀδήλων συγκατάθεσιν· οὐδενὶ γὰρ τῶν
14 ἀδήλων συγκατατίθεται ὁ Πυρρώνειος. ἀλλ' οὐδὲ
ἐν τῷ προφέρεσθαι περὶ τῶν ἀδήλων τὰς σκεπτικὰς
φωνάς, οἷον τὴν " οὐδὲν μᾶλλον " ἢ τὴν " οὐδὲν
ὁρίζω " ἤ τινα τῶν ἄλλων περὶ ὧν ὕστερον λέξομεν,
δογματίζει. ὁ μὲν γὰρ δογματίζων ὡς ὑπάρχον
τίθεται τὸ πρᾶγμα ἐκεῖνο ὃ λέγεται δογματίζειν,
ὁ δὲ σκεπτικὸς τὰς φωνὰς τίθησι ταύτας οὐχ ὡς
πάντως ὑπαρχούσας· ὑπολαμβάνει γὰρ ὅτι ὥσπερ
ἡ " πάντα ἐστὶ ψευδῆ " φωνὴ μετὰ τῶν ἄλλων
καὶ ἑαυτὴν ψευδῆ εἶναι λέγει, καὶ ἡ " οὐδέν ἐστιν
ἀληθές " ὁμοίως, οὕτως καὶ ἡ " οὐδὲν μᾶλλον "
μετὰ τῶν ἄλλων καὶ ἑαυτὴν φησι μὴ μᾶλλον εἶναι
καὶ διὰ τοῦτο τοῖς ἄλλοις ἑαυτὴν συμπεριγράφει.
τὸ δ' αὐτὸ καὶ ἐπὶ τῶν ἄλλων σκεπτικῶν φωνῶν
15 λέγομεν. πλὴν ἀλλ' εἰ ὁ δογματίζων τίθησιν ὡς
ὑπάρχον τοῦτο ὃ δογματίζει, ὁ δὲ σκεπτικὸς τὰς
φωνὰς αὐτοῦ προφέρεται ὡς δυνάμει ὑφ' ἑαυτῶν
περιγράφεσθαι, οὐκ ἂν ἐν τῇ προφορᾷ τούτων
δογματίζειν λεχθείη. τὸ δὲ μέγιστον, ἐν τῇ προφορᾷ τῶν φωνῶν τούτων τὸ ἑαυτῷ φαινόμενον
λέγει καὶ τὸ πάθος ἀπαγγέλλει τὸ ἑαυτοῦ ἀδοξάστως, μηδὲν περὶ τῶν ἔξωθεν ὑποκειμένων διαβεβαιούμενος.

---

[a] Cf. §§ 187 ff. As there explained, οὐδὲν μᾶλλον is elliptical
for οὐδὲν μᾶλλον τόδε ἢ τόδε.

[b] Lit. " underlying things," i.e. the essences or reals which

are the necessary results of sense-impressions, and he would not, for example, say when feeling hot or cold " I believe that I am not hot or cold ") ; but we say that " he does not dogmatize " using " dogma " in the sense, which some give it, of " assent to one of the non-evident objects of scientific inquiry " ; for the Pyrrhonean philosopher assents to nothing that is non-evident. Moreover, even in the act of 14 enunciating the Sceptic formulae [a] concerning things non-evident—such as the formula " No more (one thing than another)," or the formula " I determine nothing," or any of the others which we shall presently mention,—he does not dogmatize. For whereas the dogmatizer posits the things about which he is said to be dogmatizing as really existent, the Sceptic does not posit these formulae in any absolute sense ; for he conceives that, just as the formula " All things are false " asserts the falsity of itself as well as of everything else, as does the formula " Nothing is true," so also the formula " No more " asserts that itself, like all the rest, is " No more (this than that)," and thus cancels itself along with the rest. And of the other formulae we say the same. If then, 15 while the dogmatizer posits the matter of his dogma as substantial truth, the Sceptic enunciates his formulae so that they are virtually cancelled by themselves, he should not be said to dogmatize in his enunciation of them. And, most important of all, in his enunciation of these formulae he states what appears to himself and announces his own impression in an undogmatic way, without making any positive assertion regarding the external realities.[b]

lie behind, and give rise to, sensations or "appearances": cf. p. 30 note a.

Η΄.—ΕΙ ΑΙΡΕΣΙΝ ΕΧΕΙ Ο ΣΚΕΠΤΙΚΟΣ

16 Ὁμοίως δὲ φερόμεθα καὶ ἐν τῷ ἐρωτᾶσθαι εἰ ἔχει αἵρεσιν ὁ σκεπτικός. εἰ μέν τις αἵρεσιν εἶναι λέγει πρόσκλισιν δόγμασι πολλοῖς ἀκολουθίαν ἔχουσι πρὸς ἄλληλά τε καὶ φαινόμενα, καὶ λέγει δόγμα τινὶ ἀδήλῳ συγκατάθεσιν, φήσομεν μὴ ἔχειν

17 αἵρεσιν. εἰ δέ τις αἵρεσιν εἶναι φάσκει τὴν λόγῳ τινὶ κατὰ τὸ φαινόμενον ἀκολουθοῦσαν ἀγωγήν, ἐκείνου τοῦ λόγου ὡς ἔστιν ὀρθῶς δοκεῖν ζῆν ὑποδεικνύοντος (τοῦ ὀρθῶς μὴ μόνον κατ᾽ ἀρετὴν λαμβανομένου ἀλλ᾽ ἀφελέστερον) καὶ ἐπὶ τὸ ἐπέχειν δύνασθαι διατείνοντος, αἵρεσίν φαμεν ἔχειν· ἀκολουθοῦμεν γάρ τινι λόγῳ κατὰ τὸ φαινόμενον ὑποδεικνύντι ἡμῖν τὸ ζῆν πρὸς τὰ πάτρια ἔθη καὶ τοὺς νόμους καὶ τὰς ἀγωγὰς καὶ τὰ οἰκεῖα πάθη.

Θ΄.—ΕΙ ΦΥΣΙΟΛΟΓΕΙ Ο ΣΚΕΠΤΙΚΟΣ

18 Παραπλήσια δὲ λέγομεν καὶ ἐν τῷ ζητεῖν εἰ φυσιολογητέον τῷ σκεπτικῷ· ἕνεκα μὲν γὰρ τοῦ μετὰ βεβαίου πείσματος ἀποφαίνεσθαι περί τινος τῶν κατὰ τὴν φυσιολογίαν δογματιζομένων οὐ φυσιολογοῦμεν, ἕνεκα δὲ τοῦ παντὶ λόγῳ λόγον ἴσον ἔχειν ἀντιτιθέναι καὶ τῆς ἀταραξίας ἁπτόμεθα τῆς φυσιολογίας. οὕτω δὲ καὶ τὸ λογικὸν μέρος καὶ τὸ ἠθικὸν τῆς λεγομένης φιλοσοφίας ἐπερχόμεθα.

ᵃ Lit. "more smoothly" or "simply"; hence "in a less restricted, more extensive, way."

Chapter VIII.—Has the Sceptic a doctrinal rule?

We follow the same lines in replying to the question 16
" Has the Sceptic a doctrinal rule ? " For if one
defines a " doctrinal rule " as " adherence to a number
of dogmas which are dependent both on one another
and on appearances," and defines " dogma " as
" assent to a non-evident proposition," then we shall
say that he has not a doctrinal rule. But if one 17
defines " doctrinal rule " as " procedure which, in
accordance with appearance, follows a certain line of
reasoning, that reasoning indicating how it is possible
to seem to live rightly (the word ' rightly ' being
taken, not as referring to virtue only, but in a wider
sense [a]) and tending to enable one to suspend judgement," then we say that he has a doctrinal rule.
For we follow a line of reasoning which, in accordance
with appearances, points us to a life conformable to
the customs of our country and its laws and institu-
tions, and to our own instinctive feelings.

Chapter IX.—Does the Sceptic deal with Physics?

We make a similar reply also to the question 18
" Should the Sceptic deal with physical problems ? "
For while, on the one hand, so far as regards making
firm and positive assertions about any of the matters
dogmatically treated in physical theory, we do not
deal with physics ; yet, on the other hand, in respect
of our mode of opposing to every proposition an equal
proposition and of our theory of quietude we do treat
of physics. This, too, is the way in which we approach
the logical and ethical branches of so-called " philosophy."

13

SEXTUS EMPIRICUS

19 Οἱ δὲ λέγοντες ὅτι ἀναιροῦσι τὰ φαινόμενα οἱ σκεπτικοὶ ἀνήκοοί μοι δοκοῦσιν εἶναι τῶν παρ' ἡμῖν λεγομένων· τὰ γὰρ κατὰ φαντασίαν παθητικὴν[1] ἀβουλήτως ἡμᾶς ἄγοντα εἰς συγκατάθεσιν οὐκ ἀνατρέπομεν, ὡς καὶ ἔμπροσθεν ἐλέγομεν· ταῦτα δέ ἐστι τὰ φαινόμενα. ὅταν δὲ ζητῶμεν εἰ τοιοῦτον ἔστι τὸ ὑποκείμενον ὁποῖον φαίνεται, τὸ μὲν ὅτι φαίνεται δίδομεν, ζητοῦμεν δ' οὐ περὶ τοῦ φαινομένου ἀλλὰ περὶ ἐκείνου ὃ λέγεται περὶ τοῦ φαινομένου· τοῦτο δὲ διαφέρει τοῦ ζητεῖν περὶ αὐτοῦ
20 τοῦ φαινομένου. οἷον φαίνεται ἡμῖν γλυκάζειν τὸ μέλι. τοῦτο συγχωροῦμεν· γλυκαζόμεθα γὰρ αἰσθητικῶς. εἰ δὲ καὶ γλυκύ ἐστιν ὅσον ἐπὶ τῷ λόγῳ, ζητοῦμεν· ὃ οὐκ ἔστι τὸ φαινόμενον ἀλλὰ περὶ τοῦ φαινομένου λεγόμενον. ἐὰν δὲ καὶ ἄντικρυς κατὰ τῶν φαινομένων ἐρωτῶμεν λόγους, οὐκ ἀναιρεῖν βουλόμενοι τὰ φαινόμενα τούτους ἐκτιθέμεθα, ἀλλ' ἐπιδεικνύντες τὴν τῶν δογματικῶν προπέτειαν· εἰ γὰρ τοιοῦτος ἀπατεών ἐστιν ὁ λόγος ὥστε καὶ τὰ φαινόμενα μόνον οὐχὶ τῶν ὀφθαλμῶν ἡμῶν ὑφαρπάζειν, πῶς οὐ χρὴ ὑφορᾶσθαι αὐτὸν ἐν τοῖς ἀδήλοις, ὥστε μὴ κατακολουθοῦντας αὐτῷ προπετεύεσθαι;

---

[1] παθητικὴν LMT : παθητικὰ EΛB, Bekk.

---

[a] *i.e.* "impressions" or "presentations" which cause "affections" or "feelings" (πάθη), as described in § 13 *supra.*
[b] *Cf.* § 213.

Chapter X.—Do the Sceptics abolish Appearances ?

Those who say that " the Sceptics abolish appear- 19
ances," or phenomena, seem to me to be unacquainted
with the statements of our School. For, as we said
above, we do not overthrow the affective sense-
impressions[a] which induce our assent involuntarily ;
and these impressions are " the appearances." And
when we question whether the underlying object is
such as it appears, we grant the fact that it appears,
and our doubt does not concern the appearance itself
but the account given of that appearance,—and that
is a different thing from questioning the appearance
itself. For example, honey[b] appears to us to be 20
sweet (and this we grant, for we perceive sweetness
through the senses), but whether it is also sweet in
its essence is for us a matter of doubt, since this is
not an appearance but a judgement regarding the
appearance. And even if we do actually argue
against the appearances, we do not propound such
arguments with the intention of abolishing appearances, but by way of pointing out the rashness of the
Dogmatists ; for if reason is such a trickster as to all
but snatch away the appearances from under our very
eyes, surely we should view it with suspicion in the
case of things non-evident so as not to display rashness
by following it.[c]

[c] *i.e.* the " reason," or logic, which serves to discredit
phenomena may be used *a fortiori* to discredit ultra-sensible
objects. Instead of " abolishing appearances " it really (as
the Sceptics contend) abolishes itself.

ΙΑ΄. — ΠΕΡΙ ΤΟΥ ΚΡΙΤΗΡΙΟΥ ΤΗΣ ΣΚΕΠΤΙΚΗΣ

21 Ὅτι δὲ τοῖς φαινομένοις προσέχομεν, δῆλον ἀπὸ
τῶν λεγομένων ἡμῖν περὶ τοῦ κριτηρίου τῆς σκεπτικῆς ἀγωγῆς. κριτήριον δὲ λέγεται διχῶς, τό τε
εἰς πίστιν ὑπάρξεως ἢ ἀνυπαρξίας λαμβανόμενον,
περὶ οὗ ἐν τῷ ἀντιρρητικῷ λέξομεν λόγῳ, τό τε
τοῦ πράσσειν, ᾧ προσέχοντες κατὰ τὸν βίον τὰ
μὲν πράσσομεν τὰ δ' οὔ, περὶ οὗ νῦν λέγομεν.
22 κριτήριον τοίνυν φαμὲν εἶναι τῆς σκεπτικῆς ἀγωγῆς
τὸ φαινόμενον, δυνάμει τὴν φαντασίαν αὐτοῦ οὕτω
καλοῦντες· ἐν πείσει γὰρ καὶ ἀβουλήτῳ πάθει κει-
μένη ἀζήτητός ἐστιν. διὸ περὶ μὲν τοῦ φαίνεσθαι
τοῖον ἢ τοῖον τὸ ὑποκείμενον οὐδεὶς ἴσως ἀμφισβητεῖ,
περὶ δὲ τοῦ εἰ τοιοῦτόν ἔστιν ὁποῖον φαίνεται ζητεῖται.

23 Τοῖς φαινομένοις οὖν προσέχοντες κατὰ τὴν
βιωτικὴν τήρησιν ἀδοξάστως βιοῦμεν, ἐπεὶ μὴ
δυνάμεθα ἀνενέργητοι παντάπασιν εἶναι. ἔοικε δὲ
αὕτη ἡ βιωτικὴ τήρησις τετραμερὴς εἶναι καὶ τὸ
μέν τι ἔχειν ἐν ὑφηγήσει φύσεως, τὸ δὲ ἐν ἀνάγκῃ
παθῶν, τὸ δὲ ἐν παραδόσει νόμων τε καὶ ἐθῶν,
24 τὸ δὲ ἐν διδασκαλίᾳ τεχνῶν, ὑφηγήσει μὲν φυσικῇ
καθ' ἣν φυσικῶς αἰσθητικοὶ καὶ νοητικοί ἐσμεν,
παθῶν δὲ ἀνάγκῃ καθ' ἣν λιμὸς μὲν ἐπὶ τροφὴν
ἡμᾶς ὁδηγεῖ δίψος δ' ἐπὶ πόμα, ἐθῶν δὲ καὶ νόμων
παραδόσει καθ' ἣν τὸ μὲν εὐσεβεῖν παραλαμβάνομεν βιωτικῶς ὡς ἀγαθὸν τὸ δὲ ἀσεβεῖν ὡς φαῦλον,
τεχνῶν δὲ διδασκαλίᾳ καθ' ἣν οὐκ ἀνενέργητοί
ἐσμεν ἐν αἷς παραλαμβάνομεν τέχναις. ταῦτα δὲ
πάντα φαμὲν ἀδοξάστως.

ᵃ Cf. ii. 14 ff.   **ᵇ** Cf. §§ 226, 237-238.

CHAPTER XI.—OF THE CRITERION OF SCEPTICISM

That we adhere to appearances is plain from what 21 we say about the Criterion of the Sceptic School. The word " Criterion " is used in two senses : in the one it means " the standard regulating belief in reality or unreality," (and this we shall discuss in our refutation [a]) ; in the other it denotes the standard of action by conforming to which in the conduct of life we perform some actions and abstain from others ; and it is of the latter that we are now speaking. The 22 criterion, then, of the Sceptic School is, we say, the appearance, giving this name to what is virtually the sense-presentation. For since this lies in feeling and involuntary affection, it is not open to question. Consequently, no one, I suppose, disputes that the underlying object has this or that appearance ; the point in dispute is whether the object is in reality such as it appears to be.

Adhering, then, to appearances we live in accord- 23 ance with the normal rules of life, undogmatically, seeing that we cannot remain wholly inactive.[b] And it would seem that this regulation of life is fourfold, and that one part of it lies in the guidance of Nature, another in the constraint of the passions, another in the tradition of laws and customs, another in the instruction of the arts. Nature's guidance is that by 24 which we are naturally capable of sensation and thought ; constraint of the passions is that whereby hunger drives us to food and thirst to drink ; tradition of customs and laws, that whereby we regard piety in the conduct of life as good, but impiety as evil ; instruction of the arts, that whereby we are not inactive in such arts as we adopt. But we make all these statements undogmatically.

17

ΙΒ.—ΤΙ ΤΟ ΤΕΛΟΣ ΤΗΣ ΣΚΕΠΤΙΚΗΣ

25 Τούτοις ἀκόλουθον ἂν εἴη καὶ περὶ τοῦ τέλους
τῆς σκεπτικῆς ἀγωγῆς διελθεῖν. ἔστι μὲν οὖν
τέλος τὸ οὗ χάριν πάντα πράττεται ἢ θεωρεῖται,
αὐτὸ δὲ οὐδενὸς ἕνεκα, ἢ τὸ ἔσχατον τῶν ὀρεκτῶν.
φαμὲν δὲ ἄχρι νῦν τέλος εἶναι τοῦ σκεπτικοῦ τὴν
ἐν τοῖς κατὰ δόξαν ἀταραξίαν καὶ ἐν τοῖς κατηναγ-
26 κασμένοις μετριοπάθειαν. ἀρξάμενος γὰρ φιλο-
σοφεῖν ὑπὲρ τοῦ τὰς φαντασίας ἐπικρῖναι καὶ
καταλαβεῖν τίνες μέν εἰσιν ἀληθεῖς τίνες δὲ ψευδεῖς,
ὥστε ἀταρακτῆσαι, ἐνέπεσεν εἰς τὴν ἰσοσθενῆ
διαφωνίαν, ἣν ἐπικρῖναι μὴ δυνάμενος ἐπέσχεν·
ἐπισχόντι δὲ αὐτῷ τυχικῶς παρηκολούθησεν ἡ ἐν
27 τοῖς δοξαστοῖς ἀταραξία. ὁ μὲν γὰρ δοξάζων τι
καλὸν τῇ φύσει ἢ κακὸν εἶναι ταράσσεται διὰ
παντός· καὶ ὅτε μὴ πάρεστιν αὐτῷ τὰ καλὰ εἶναι
δοκοῦντα, ὑπό τε τῶν φύσει κακῶν νομίζει ποινηλατεῖσθαι καὶ διώκει τὰ ἀγαθά, ὡς οἴεται· ἅπερ
κτησάμενος πλείοσι ταραχαῖς περιπίπτει διά τε τὸ
παρὰ λόγον καὶ τὸ ἀμέτρως ἐπαίρεσθαι, καὶ
φοβούμενος τὴν μεταβολὴν πάντα πράσσει ἵνα μὴ
28 ἀποβάλῃ τὰ ἀγαθὰ αὐτῷ δοκοῦντα εἶναι. ὁ δὲ
ἀοριστῶν περὶ τῶν πρὸς τὴν φύσιν καλῶν ἢ κακῶν
οὔτε φεύγει τι οὔτε διώκει συντόνως· διόπερ
ἀταρακτεῖ.

Ὅπερ οὖν περὶ Ἀπελλοῦ τοῦ ζωγράφου λέγεται,
τοῦτο ὑπῆρξε τῷ σκεπτικῷ. φασὶ γὰρ ὅτι ἐκεῖνος

ᵃ Cf. Cic. De fin. i. 12. 42 "vel summum bonum vel
ultimum vel extremum, quod Graeci τέλος nominant, quod
ipsum nullam ad aliam rem, ad id autem res referuntur
omnes." Aristot. Eth. Nic. i. 1. 1 καλῶς ἀπεφήναντο τἀγαθὸν
οὗ πάντ᾽ ἐφίεται; ibid. 5 τέλος ἐστὶ τῶν πρακτῶν ὃ δι᾽ αὐτὸ
βουλόμεθα, τἆλλα δὲ διὰ τοῦτο.

18

CHAPTER XII.—WHAT IS THE END OF SCEPTICISM ?

Our next subject will be the End of the Sceptic 25
system. Now an " End " is " that for which all
actions or reasonings are undertaken, while it exists
for the sake of none " ; or, otherwise, " the ultimate
object of appetency." [a] We assert still that the
Sceptic's End is quietude in respect of matters of
opinion and moderate feeling in respect of things
unavoidable. For the Sceptic, having set out to 26
philosophize with the object of passing judgement
on the sense-impressions and ascertaining which of
them are true and which false, so as to attain quietude
thereby, found himself involved in contradictions of
equal weight, and being unable to decide between
them suspended judgement ; and as he was thus in
suspense there followed, as it happened, the state
of quietude in respect of matters of opinion. For 27
the man who opines that anything is by nature good
or bad is for ever being disquieted : when he is
without the things which he deems good he believes
himself to be tormented by things naturally bad and
he pursues after the things which are, as he thinks,
good ; which when he has obtained he keeps falling
into still more perturbations because of his irrational
and immoderate elation, and in his dread of a change
of fortune he uses every endeavour to avoid losing
the things which he deems good. On the other hand, 28
the man who determines nothing as to what is naturally good or bad neither shuns nor pursues anything
eagerly ; and, in consequence, he is unperturbed.

The Sceptic, in fact, had the same experience which
is said to have befallen the painter Apelles.[b] Once,

[b] Court painter to Alexander the Great (*circa* 350–300 B.C.).

19

ἵππον γράφων καὶ τὸν ἀφρὸν τοῦ ἵππου μιμήσασθαι
τῇ γραφῇ βουληθεὶς οὕτως ἀπετύγχανεν ὡς ἀπ-
ειπεῖν καὶ τὴν σπογγιὰν εἰς ἣν ἀπέμασσε τὰ ἀπὸ
τοῦ γραφείου χρώματα προσρῖψαι τῇ εἰκόνι· τὴν
δὲ προσαψαμένην ἵππου ἀφροῦ ποιῆσαι μίμημα.
29 καὶ οἱ σκεπτικοὶ οὖν ἤλπιζον μὲν τὴν ἀταραξίαν
ἀναλήψεσθαι διὰ τοῦ τὴν ἀνωμαλίαν τῶν φαινομένων τε καὶ νοουμένων ἐπικρῖναι, μὴ δυνηθέντες
δὲ ποιῆσαι τοῦτο ἐπέσχον· ἐπισχοῦσι δὲ αὐτοῖς
οἷον τυχικῶς ἡ ἀταραξία παρηκολούθησεν ὡς
σκιὰ σώματι. οὐ μὴν ἀόχλητον πάντη τὸν σκεπτικὸν εἶναι νομίζομεν, ἀλλ᾿ ὀχλεῖσθαί φαμεν ὑπὸ
τῶν κατηναγκασμένων· καὶ γὰρ ῥιγοῦν ποτὲ ὁμο-
λογοῦμεν καὶ διψῆν καὶ τοιουτότροπά τινα πάσχειν.
30 ἀλλὰ καὶ ἐν τούτοις οἱ μὲν ἰδιῶται δισσαῖς συν-
έχονται περιστάσεσιν, ὑπό τε τῶν παθῶν αὐτῶν
καὶ οὐχ ἧττον ὑπὸ τοῦ τὰς περιστάσεις ταύτας
κακὰς εἶναι φύσει δοκεῖν· ὁ δὲ σκεπτικὸς τὸ προσδοξάζειν ὅτι ἔστι κακὸν τούτων ἕκαστον ὡς πρὸς
τὴν φύσιν περιαιρῶν μετριώτερον καὶ ἐν τούτοις
ἀπαλλάσσει. διὰ τοῦτο οὖν ἐν μὲν τοῖς δοξαστοῖς
ἀταραξίαν τέλος εἶναί φαμεν τοῦ σκεπτικοῦ, ἐν δὲ
τοῖς κατηναγκασμένοις μετριοπάθειαν. τινὲς δὲ
τῶν δοκίμων σκεπτικῶν προσέθηκαν τούτοις καὶ
τὴν ἐν ταῖς ζητήσεσιν ἐποχήν.

ΙʹΓʹ.—ΠΕΡΙ ΤΩΝ ΟΛΟΣΧΕΡΩΝ ΤΡΟΠΩΝ ΤΗΣ ΕΠΟΧΗΣ

31 Ἐπεὶ δὲ τὴν ἀταραξίαν ἀκολουθεῖν ἐφάσκομεν
τῇ περὶ πάντων ἐποχῇ, ἀκόλουθον ἂν εἴη λέγειν

* Viz. Timon and Aenesidemus ; cf. Diog. Laert. ix. 107.

they say, when he was painting a horse and wished to represent in the painting the horse's foam, he was so unsuccessful that he gave up the attempt and flung at the picture the sponge on which he used to wipe the paints off his brush, and the mark of the sponge produced the effect of a horse's foam. So, too, the 29 Sceptics were in hopes of gaining quietude by means of a decision regarding the disparity of the objects of sense and of thought, and being unable to effect this they suspended judgement; and they found that quietude, as if by chance, followed upon their suspense, even as a shadow follows its substance. We do not, however, suppose that the Sceptic is wholly untroubled; but we say that he is troubled by things unavoidable; for we grant that he is cold at times and thirsty, and suffers various affections of that kind. But even in these cases, whereas ordinary people are 30 afflicted by two circumstances,—namely, by the affections themselves and, in no less a degree, by the belief that these conditions are evil by nature,—the Sceptic, by his rejection of the added belief in the natural badness of all these conditions, escapes here too with less discomfort. Hence we say that, while in regard to matters of opinion the Sceptic's End is quietude, in regard to things unavoidable it is " moderate affection." But some notable Sceptics [a] have added the further definition " suspension of judgement in investigations."

CHAPTER XIII.—OF THE GENERAL MODES LEADING TO SUSPENSION OF JUDGEMENT

Now that we have been saying that tranquillity 31 follows on suspension of judgement, it will be our

ὅπως ἡμῖν ἡ ἐποχὴ περιγίνεται. γίνεται τοίνυν
αὕτη, ὡς ἂν ὁλοσχερέστερον εἴποι τις, διὰ τῆς
ἀντιθέσεως τῶν πραγμάτων. ἀντιτίθεμεν δὲ ἢ
φαινόμενα φαινομένοις ἢ νοούμενα νοουμένοις ἢ
32 ἐναλλάξ, οἷον φαινόμενα μὲν φαινομένοις, ὅταν
λέγωμεν " ὁ αὐτὸς πύργος πόρρωθεν μὲν φαίνεται
στρογγύλος ἐγγύθεν δὲ τετράγωνος," νοούμενα δὲ
νοουμένοις, ὅταν πρὸς τὸν κατασκευάζοντα ὅτι
ἔστι πρόνοια ἐκ τῆς τάξεως τῶν οὐρανίων, ἀντιτιθῶμεν τὸ τοὺς μὲν ἀγαθοὺς δυσπραγεῖν πολλάκις
τοὺς δὲ κακοὺς εὐπραγεῖν, καὶ διὰ τούτου συνάγω-
33 μεν τὸ μὴ εἶναι πρόνοιαν· νοούμενα δὲ φαινομένοις,
ὡς ὁ Ἀναξαγόρας τῷ λευκὴν εἶναι τὴν χιόνα
ἀντετίθει ὅτι ἡ χιὼν ὕδωρ ἐστὶ πεπηγός, τὸ δὲ
ὕδωρ ἐστὶ μέλαν, καὶ ἡ χιὼν ἄρα μέλαινά ἐστιν.
καθ' ἑτέραν δὲ ἐπίνοιαν ἀντιτίθεμεν ὁτὲ μὲν
παρόντα παροῦσιν, ὡς τὰ προειρημένα, ὁτὲ δὲ
παρόντα παρεληλυθόσιν ἢ μέλλουσιν, οἷον ὅταν τις
34 ἡμᾶς ἐρωτήσῃ λόγον ὃν λῦσαι οὐ δυνάμεθα, φαμὲν
πρὸς αὐτὸν ὅτι, ὥσπερ πρὸ τοῦ γενέσθαι τὸν
εἰσηγησάμενον τὴν αἵρεσιν ἣν μετέρχῃ, οὐδέπω ὁ
κατ' αὐτὴν λόγος ὑγιὴς ὢν ἐφαίνετο, ὑπέκειτο
μέντοι ὡς πρὸς τὴν φύσιν, οὕτως ἐνδέχεται καὶ
τὸν ἀντικείμενον τῷ ὑπὸ σοῦ ἐρωτηθέντι νῦν λόγῳ
ὑποκεῖσθαι μὲν ὡς πρὸς τὴν φύσιν, μηδέπω δ'
ἡμῖν φαίνεσθαι, ὥστε οὐδέπω χρὴ συγκατατίθεσθαι
ἡμᾶς τῷ δοκοῦντι νῦν ἰσχυρῷ εἶναι λόγῳ.
35 Ὑπὲρ δὲ τοῦ τὰς ἀντιθέσεις ταύτας ἀκριβέστερον
ἡμῖν ὑποπεσεῖν, καὶ τοὺς τρόπους ὑποθήσομαι δι'
ὧν ἡ ἐποχὴ συνάγεται, οὔτε περὶ τοῦ πλήθους

---

[a] Cf. § 118.   [b] See Introd. p. xi ; cf. ii. 244.

next task to explain how we arrive at this suspension. Speaking generally, one may say that it is the result of setting things in opposition. We oppose either appearances to appearances or objects of thought to objects of thought or *alternando*. For instance, we 32 oppose appearances to appearances when we say "The same tower [a] appears round from a distance, but square from close at hand"; and thoughts to thoughts, when in answer to him who argues the existence of Providence from the order of the heavenly bodies we oppose the fact that often the good fare ill and the bad fare well, and draw from this the inference that Providence does not exist. And thoughts 33 we oppose to appearances, as when Anaxagoras [b] countered the notion that snow is white with the argument, "Snow is frozen water, and water is black; therefore snow also is black." With a different idea we oppose things present sometimes to things present, as in the foregoing examples, and sometimes to things past or future, as, for instance, when someone propounds to us a theory which we are unable to refute, we say to him in reply, "Just 34 as, before the birth of the founder of the School to which you belong, the theory it holds was not as yet apparent as a sound theory, although it was really in existence, so likewise it is possible that the opposite theory to that which you now propound is already really existent, though not yet apparent to us, so that we ought not as yet to yield assent to this theory which at the moment seems to be valid."

But in order that we may have a more exact under- 35 standing of these antitheses I will describe the Modes by which suspension of judgement is brought about, but without making any positive assertion regarding

οὔτε περὶ τῆς δυνάμεως αὐτῶν διαβεβαιούμενος·
ἐνδέχεται γὰρ αὐτοὺς καὶ σαθροὺς εἶναι καὶ πλείους
τῶν λεχθησομένων.

ΙΔ΄. ΠΕΡΙ ΤΩΝ ΔΕΚΑ ΤΡΟΠΩΝ

36 Παραδίδονται τοίνυν συνήθως παρὰ τοῖς ἀρχαιο-
τέροις σκεπτικοῖς τρόποι, δι' ὧν ἡ ἐποχὴ συνάγεσθαι δοκεῖ, δέκα τὸν ἀριθμόν, οὓς καὶ λόγους
καὶ τόπους συνωνύμως καλοῦσιν. εἰσὶ δὲ οὗτοι,
πρῶτος ὁ παρὰ τὴν τῶν ζῴων ἐξαλλαγήν, δεύτερος
ὁ παρὰ τὴν τῶν ἀνθρώπων διαφοράν, τρίτος ὁ παρὰ
τὰς διαφόρους τῶν αἰσθητηρίων κατασκευάς, τέ-
ταρτος ὁ παρὰ τὰς περιστάσεις, πέμπτος ὁ παρὰ
τὰς θέσεις καὶ τὰ διαστήματα καὶ τοὺς τόπους,
37 ἕκτος ὁ παρὰ τὰς ἐπιμιξίας, ἕβδομος ὁ παρὰ τὰς
ποσότητας καὶ σκευασίας τῶν ὑποκειμένων, ὄγδοος
ὁ ἀπὸ τοῦ πρός τι, ἔννατος ὁ παρὰ τὰς συνεχεῖς
ἢ σπανίους ἐγκυρήσεις, δέκατος ὁ παρὰ τὰς ἀγωγὰς
καὶ τὰ ἔθη καὶ τοὺς νόμους καὶ τὰς μυθικὰς πίστεις
38 καὶ τὰς δογματικὰς ὑπολήψεις. χρώμεθα δὲ τῇ
τάξει ταύτῃ θετικῶς.

Τούτων δὲ ἐπαναβεβηκότες εἰσὶ τρόποι τρεῖς, ὁ
ἀπὸ τοῦ κρίνοντος, ὁ ἀπὸ τοῦ κρινομένου, ὁ ἐξ
ἀμφοῖν· τῷ μὲν γὰρ ἀπὸ τοῦ κρίνοντος ὑποτάσ-
σονται οἱ πρῶτοι τέσσαρες (τὸ γὰρ κρῖνον ἢ ζῷόν
ἐστιν ἢ ἄνθρωπος ἢ αἴσθησις καὶ ἔν τινι περι-
στάσει), εἰς δὲ τὸν ἀπὸ τοῦ κρινομένου ⟨ἀνάγον-
ται⟩[1] ὁ ἕβδομος καὶ ὁ δέκατος, εἰς δὲ τὸν ἐξ
ἀμφοῖν σύνθετον ὁ πέμπτος καὶ ὁ ἕκτος καὶ ὁ
39 ὄγδοος καὶ ὁ ἔννατος. πάλιν δὲ οἱ τρεῖς οὗτοι

---

[1] ⟨ἀνάγονται⟩ add. Papp.

either their number or their validity ; for it is possible that they may be unsound or there may be more of them than I shall enumerate.

Chapter XIV.—Concerning the Ten Modes

The usual tradition amongst the older Sceptics is 36 that the " modes " by which " suspension " is supposed to be brought about are ten in number ; and they also give them the synonymous names of " arguments " and " positions." They are these : the first, based on the variety in animals ; the second, on the differences in human beings ; the third, on the different structures of the organs of sense ; the fourth, on the circumstantial conditions ; the fifth, on positions and intervals and locations ; the sixth, on intermixtures ; 37 the seventh, on the quantities and formations of the underlying objects ; the eighth, on the fact of relativity ; the ninth, on the frequency or rarity of occurrence ; the tenth, on the disciplines and customs and laws, the legendary beliefs and the dogmatic convictions. This order, however, we adopt without 38 prejudice.

As superordinate to these there stand three Modes —that based on the subject who judges, that on the object judged, and that based on both. The first four of the ten Modes are subordinate to the Mode based on the subject (for the subject which judges is either an animal or a man or a sense, and existent in some condition) : the seventh and tenth Modes are referred to that based on the object judged : the fifth, sixth, eighth and ninth are referred to the Mode based on both subject and object. Furthermore, 39

ἀνάγονται εἰς τὸν πρός τι, ὡς εἶναι γενικώτατον μὲν τὸν πρός τι, εἰδικοὺς δὲ τοὺς τρεῖς, ὑποβεβηκότας δὲ τοὺς δέκα. ταῦτα μὲν περὶ τῆς ποσότητος αὐτῶν κατὰ τὸ πιθανὸν λέγομεν· περὶ δὲ τῆς δυνάμεως τάδε.

40 Πρῶτον ἐλέγομεν εἶναι λόγον καθ᾽ ὃν παρὰ τὴν διαφορὰν τῶν ζώων οὐχ αἱ αὐταὶ ἀπὸ τῶν αὐτῶν ὑποπίπτουσι φαντασίαι. τοῦτο δὲ ἐπιλογιζόμεθα ἔκ τε τῆς περὶ τὰς γενέσεις αὐτῶν διαφορᾶς καὶ ἐκ τῆς περὶ τὰς συστάσεις τῶν σωμάτων παραλ-

41 λαγῆς. περὶ μὲν οὖν τὰς γενέσεις, ὅτι τῶν ζώων τὰ μὲν χωρὶς μίξεως γίνεται τὰ δ᾽ ἐκ συμπλοκῆς. καὶ τῶν μὲν χωρὶς μίξεως γινομένων τὰ μὲν ἐκ πυρὸς γίνεται ὡς τὰ ἐν ταῖς καμίνοις φαινόμενα ζωύφια, τὰ δ᾽ ἐξ ὕδατος φθειρομένου ὡς κώνωπες, τὰ δ᾽ ἐξ οἴνου τρεπομένου ὡς σκνῖπες, τὰ δ᾽ ἐκ γῆς ⟨ὡς τέττιγες⟩,[1] τὰ δ᾽ ἐξ ἰλύος ὡς βάτραχοι, τὰ δ᾽ ἐκ βορβόρου ὡς σκώληκες, τὰ δ᾽ ἐξ ὄνων ὡς κάνθαροι, τὰ δ᾽ ἐκ λαχάνων ὡς κάμπαι, τὰ δ᾽ ἐκ καρπῶν ὡς οἱ ἐκ τῶν ἐρινεῶν ψῆνες, τὰ δ᾽ ἐκ ζώων σηπομένων ὡς μέλισσαι ταύρων καὶ σφῆκες ἵππων·

42 τῶν δ᾽ ἐκ συμπλοκῆς τὰ μὲν ἐξ ὁμοιογενῶν ὡς τὰ πλεῖστα, τὰ δ᾽ ἐξ ἀνομοιογενῶν ὡς ἡμίονοι. πάλιν κοινῇ τῶν ζώων τὰ μὲν ζωοτοκεῖται ὡς ἄνθρωποι, τὰ δ᾽ ᾠοτοκεῖται ὡς ὄρνιθες, τὰ δὲ σαρκοτοκεῖται

43 ὡς ἄρκτοι. εἰκὸς οὖν τὰς περὶ τὰς γενέσεις ἀνομοιότητας καὶ διαφορὰς μεγάλας ποιεῖν ἀντιπαθείας, τὸ ἀσύγκρατον καὶ ἀσυνάρμοστον καὶ μαχόμενον ἐκεῖθεν φερομένας.

44 Ἀλλὰ καὶ ἡ διαφορὰ τῶν κυριωτάτων μερῶν τοῦ σώματος, καὶ μάλιστα τῶν πρὸς τὸ ἐπικρίνειν

[1] ⟨ὡς τέττιγες⟩ addidi: ⟨ὡς μῦς⟩ cj. Fabr.

these three Modes are also referred to that of relation, so that the Mode of relation stands as the highest *genus*, and the three as *species*, and the ten as subordinate *sub-species*. We give this as the probable account of their numbers ; and as to their argumentative force what we say is this :

The *First* argument (or *Trope*), as we said, is that **40** which shows that the same impressions are not produced by the same objects owing to the differences in animals. This we infer both from the differences in their origins and from the variety of their bodily structures. Thus, as to origin, some animals are pro- **41** duced without sexual union, others by coition. And of those produced without coition, some come from fire, like the animalcules which appear in furnaces, others from putrid water, like gnats ; others from wine when it turns sour, like ants ; others from earth, like grasshoppers ; others from marsh, like frogs ; others from mud, like worms ; others from asses, like beetles ; others from greens, like caterpillars ; others from fruits, like the gall-insects in wild figs ; others from rotting animals, as bees from bulls and wasps from horses. Of the animals generated by coition, **42** some—in fact the majority—come from homogeneous parents, others from heterogeneous parents, as do mules. Again, of animals in general, some are born alive, like men ; others are born as eggs, like birds ; and yet others as lumps of flesh, like bears. It is **43** natural, then, that these dissimilar and variant modes of birth should produce much contrariety of sense-affection, and that this is a source of its divergent, discordant and conflicting character.

Moreover, the differences found in the most impor- **44** tant parts of the body, and especially in those of

καὶ πρὸς τὸ αἰσθάνεσθαι πεφυκότων, μεγίστην
δύναται ποιεῖν μάχην τῶν φαντασιῶν [παρὰ τὴν
τῶν ζῴων παραλλαγήν].[1] οἱ γοῦν ἰκτεριῶντες
ὠχρά φασιν εἶναι τὰ ἡμῖν φαινόμενα λευκά, καὶ οἱ
ὑπόσφαγμα ἔχοντες αἱμωπά. ἐπεὶ οὖν καὶ τῶν
ζῴων τὰ μὲν ὠχροὺς ἔχει τοὺς ὀφθαλμοὺς τὰ δ᾽
ὑφαίμους τὰ δὲ λευκανθίζοντας τὰ δ᾽ ἄλλην χροιὰν
ἔχοντας, εἰκός, οἶμαι, διάφορον αὐτοῖς τὴν τῶν
45 χρωμάτων ἀντίληψιν γίγνεσθαι. ἀλλὰ καὶ ἐνατενί-
σαντες ἐπὶ πολὺν χρόνον τῷ ἡλίῳ, εἶτα ἐγκύψαντες
βιβλίῳ τὰ γράμματα χρυσοειδῆ δοκοῦμεν εἶναι καὶ
περιφερόμενα. ἐπεὶ οὖν καὶ τῶν ζῴων τινὰ φύσει
λαμπηδόνα ἐν τοῖς ὀφθαλμοῖς ἔχει καὶ φῶς λεπτο-
μερές τε καὶ εὐκίνητον ἀπ᾽ αὐτῶν ἀποστέλλει, ὡς
καὶ νυκτὸς ὁρᾶν, δεόντως ἂν νομίζοιμεν ὅτι μὴ
46 ὅμοια ἡμῖν τε κἀκείνοις τὰ ἐκτὸς ὑποπίπτει. καὶ
γε οἱ γόητες χρίοντες τὰς θρυαλλίδας ἰῷ χαλκοῦ
καὶ θολῷ σηπίας ποιοῦσιν ὁτὲ μὲν χαλκοῦς ὁτὲ δὲ
μέλανας φαίνεσθαι τοὺς παρόντας διὰ τὴν βραχεῖαν
τοῦ μιχθέντος παρασποράν. πολὺ δήπου εὐλογώ-
τερόν ἐστι, χυμῶν διαφόρων ἀνακεκραμένων τῇ
ὁράσει τῶν ζῴων, διαφόρους τῶν ὑποκειμένων
47 φαντασίας αὐτοῖς γίνεσθαι. ὅταν τε παραθλίψωμεν
τὸν ὀφθαλμόν, ἐπιμήκη καὶ στενὰ φαίνεται τὰ εἴδη
καὶ τὰ σχήματα καὶ τὰ μεγέθη τῶν ὁρατῶν. εἰκὸς
οὖν ὅτι ὅσα τῶν ζῴων λοξὴν ἔχει τὴν κόρην καὶ
προμήκη, καθάπερ αἶγες αἴλουροι καὶ τὰ ἐοικότα,
διάφορα φαντάζεται τὰ ὑποκείμενα εἶναι, καὶ οὐχ
οἷα τὰ περιφερῆ τὴν κόρην ἔχοντα ζῷα εἶναι αὐτὰ
48 ὑπολαμβάνει. τά τε κάτοπτρα παρὰ τὴν διάφορον

[1] [παρὰ . . . παραλλαγήν] secl. Mutsch

28

which the natural function is judging and perceiving, are capable of producing a vast deal of divergence in the sense-impressions [owing to the variety in the animals]. Thus, sufferers from jaundice declare that objects which seem to us white are yellow, while those whose eyes are bloodshot call them blood-red. Since, then, some animals also have eyes which are yellow, others bloodshot, others albino, others of other colours, they probably, I suppose, have different perceptions of colour. Moreover, if we bend down 45 over a book after having gazed long and fixedly at the sun, the letters seem to us to be golden in colour and circling round. Since, then, some animals possess also a natural brilliance in their eyes, and emit from them a fine and mobile stream of light, so that they can even see by night,[a] we seem bound to suppose that they are differently affected from us by external objects. Jugglers, too, by means of smearing lamp- 46 wicks with the rust of copper or with the juice of the cuttle-fish make the bystanders appear now copper-coloured and now black—and that by just a small sprinkling of extra matter. Surely, then, we have much more reason to suppose that when different juices are intermingled in the vision of animals their impressions of the objects will become different. Again, when we press the eyeball at one side the 47 forms, figures and sizes of the objects appear oblong and narrow. So it is probable that all animals which have the pupil of the eye slanting and elongated— such as goats, cats, and similar animals—have impressions of the objects which are different and unlike the notions formed of them by the animals which have round pupils. Mirrors, too, owing to differences in 48

[a] *Cf.* § 84.

κατασκευὴν ὁτὲ μὲν μικρότατα δείκνυσι τὰ ἐκτὸς
ὑποκείμενα, ὡς τὰ κοῖλα, ὁτὲ δ' ἐπιμήκη καὶ
στενά, ὡς τὰ κυρτά· τινὰ δὲ τὴν μὲν κεφαλὴν κάτω
δείκνυσι τοῦ κατοπτριζομένου, τοὺς δὲ πόδας ἄνω.
49 ἐπεὶ οὖν καὶ τῶν περὶ τὴν ὄψιν ἀγγείων τὰ μὲν
ἐξόφθαλμα κομιδῇ πέπτωκεν ὑπὸ κυρτότητος, τὰ
δὲ κοιλότερά ἐστι, τὰ δ' ἐν ὑπτίῳ πλάτει βέβηκεν,
εἰκὸς καὶ διὰ τοῦτο ἀλλοιοῦσθαι τὰς φαντασίας,
καὶ μήτε ἴσα τοῖς μεγέθεσι μήτε ὅμοια ταῖς μορφαῖς ὁρᾶν τὰ αὐτὰ κύνας ἰχθύας λέοντας ἀνθρώπους
πάρνοπας, ἀλλ' οἵαν ἑκάστου ποιεῖ τύπωσιν ἡ
δεχομένη τὸ φαινόμενον ὄψις.

50   Ὁ δὲ αὐτὸς καὶ περὶ τῶν ἄλλων αἰσθήσεων λόγος·
πῶς γὰρ ἂν λεχθείη ὁμοίως κινεῖσθαι κατὰ τὴν
ἁφὴν τά τε ὀστρακόδερμα καὶ τὰ σαρκοφανῆ καὶ
τὰ ἠκανθωμένα καὶ τὰ ἐπτερωμένα ἢ λελεπιδω-
μένα; πῶς δὲ ὁμοίως ἀντιλαμβάνεσθαι κατὰ τὴν
ἀκοὴν τά τε στενώτατον ἔχοντα τὸν πόρον τὸν
ἀκουστικὸν καὶ τὰ εὐρυτάτῳ τούτῳ κεχρημένα,
ἢ τὰ τετριχωμένα τὰ ὦτα καὶ τὰ ψιλὰ ταῦτα
ἔχοντα; ὅπου γε καὶ ἡμεῖς ἄλλως μὲν κινούμεθα
κατὰ τὴν ἀκοὴν παραβύσαντες τὰ ὦτα, ἄλλως δὲ
51 ἢν ἁπλῶς αὐτοῖς χρώμεθα. καὶ ἡ ὄσφρησις δὲ
διαφέροι ἂν παρὰ τὴν τῶν ζώων ἐξαλλαγήν· εἰ γὰρ
καὶ ἡμεῖς ἄλλως μὲν κινούμεθα ἐμψυγέντες καὶ τοῦ
φλέγματος πλεονάσαντος ἐν ἡμῖν, ἄλλως δὲ ἢν τὰ
περὶ τὴν κεφαλὴν ἡμῶν μέρη πλεονασμὸν αἵματος

---

a τὰ ὑποκείμενα (Lat. sub-stantia) is a favourite term with
Sextus for the objective realities which " underlie," or lie
behind, the subjective impressions of sense (phenomena):
they are called ἐκτός as " outside " of and not dependent on

their construction, represent the external objects[a] at one time as very small—as when the mirror is concave, —at another time as elongated and narrow—as when the mirror is convex. Some mirrors, too, show the head of the figure reflected at the bottom and the feet at the top. Since, then, some organs of sight 49 actually protrude beyond the face owing to their convexity, while others are quite concave, and others again lie in a level plane, on this account also it is probable that their impressions differ, and that the same objects, as seen by dogs, fishes, lions, men and locusts, are neither equal in size nor similar in shape, but vary according to the image of each object created by the particular sight that receives the impression.

Of the other sense-organs also the same account 50 holds good. Thus, in respect of touch, how could one maintain that creatures covered with shells, with flesh, with prickles, with feathers, with scales, are all similarly affected ? And as for the sense of hearing, how could we say that its perceptions are alike in animals with a very narrow auditory passage and those with a very wide one, or in animals with hairy ears and those with smooth ears ? For, as regards this sense, even we ourselves find our hearing affected in one way when we have our ears plugged and in another way when we use them just as they are. Smell also will differ because of the variety in animals. 51 For if we ourselves are affected in one way when we have a cold and our internal phlegm is excessive, and in another way when the parts about our head are filled with an excess of blood, feeling an aversion to

the percipient. I render the term indifferently by "objects," "real objects" or "realities," and "underlying objects."

SEXTUS EMPIRICUS

ὑποδέξηται, ἀποστρεφόμενοι τὰ εὐώδη τοῖς ἄλλοις
δοκοῦντα εἶναι καὶ ὥσπερ πλήττεσθαι ὑπ' αὐτῶν
νομίζοντες, ἐπεὶ καὶ τῶν ζῴων τὰ μὲν πλαδαρά τέ
ἐστι φύσει καὶ φλεγματώδη, τὰ δὲ πολύαιμα
σφόδρα, τὰ δ' ἐπικρατοῦσαν καὶ πλεονάζουσαν
ἔχοντα τὴν ξανθὴν χολὴν ἢ τὴν μέλαιναν, εὔλογον
καὶ διὰ τοῦτο διάφορα ἑκάστοις αὐτῶν φαίνεσθαι
52 τὰ ὀσφρητά. καὶ τὰ γευστὰ ὁμοίως τῶν μὲν
τραχεῖαν καὶ ἄνικμον ἐχόντων τὴν γλῶσσαν τῶν
δὲ ἔνυγρον σφόδρα, εἴγε καὶ ἡμεῖς[1] ξηροτέραν ἐν
πυρετοῖς τὴν γλῶτταν σχόντες γεώδη καὶ κακό-
χυμα ἢ πικρὰ τὰ προσφερόμενα εἶναι νομίζομεν,
τοῦτο δὲ πάσχομεν καὶ παρὰ τὴν διάφορον ἐπικράτειαν τῶν ἐν ἡμῖν χυμῶν εἶναι λεγομένων.
ἐπεὶ οὖν καὶ τὰ ζῷα διάφορον τὸ γευστικὸν αἰσθη-
τήριον ἔχει καὶ διαφόροις χυμοῖς πλεονάζον, διαφόρους ἂν καὶ κατὰ τὴν γεῦσιν φαντασίας τῶν
53 ὑποκειμένων λαμβάνοι. ὥσπερ γὰρ ἡ αὐτὴ τροφὴ
ἀναδιδομένη ὅπου μὲν γίνεται φλὲψ ὅπου δὲ
ἀρτηρία ὅπου δὲ ὀστέον ὅπου δὲ νεῦρον καὶ τῶν
ἄλλων ἕκαστον, παρὰ τὴν διαφορὰν τῶν ὑποδεχο-
μένων αὐτὴν μερῶν διάφορον ἐπιδεικνυμένη δύναμιν, καὶ ὥσπερ τὸ ὕδωρ ἓν καὶ μονοειδὲς ἀναδιδό-
μενον εἰς τὰ δένδρα ὅπου μὲν γίνεται φλοιὸς ὅπου
δὲ κλάδος ὅπου δὲ καρπὸς καὶ ἤδη σῦκον καὶ ῥοιὰ
54 καὶ τῶν ἄλλων ἕκαστον, καὶ καθάπερ τὸ τοῦ μουσ-
ουργοῦ πνεῦμα ἓν καὶ τὸ αὐτὸ ἐμπνεόμενον τῷ
αὐλῷ ὅπου μὲν γίνεται ὀξὺ ὅπου δὲ βαρὺ καὶ ἡ
αὐτὴ ἐπέρεισις τῆς χειρὸς ἐπὶ τῆς λύρας ὅπου μὲν
βαρὺν φθόγγον ποιεῖ ὅπου δὲ ὀξύν, οὕτως εἰκὸς
καὶ τὰ ἐκτὸς ὑποκείμενα διάφορα θεωρεῖσθαι

---

[1] εἴγε κ. ἡμεῖς MT: κ. ἡμεῖς εἴγε L, Bekk.

smells which seem sweet to everyone else and regarding them as noxious, it is reasonable to suppose that animals too—since some are flaccid by nature and rich in phlegm, others rich in blood, others marked by a predominant excess of yellow or of black gall—are in each case impressed in different ways by the objects of smell. So too with the objects of taste ; 52 for some animals have rough and dry tongues, others extremely moist tongues. We ourselves, too, when our tongues are very dry, in cases of fever, think the food proffered us to be earthy and ill-flavoured or bitter—an affection due to the variation in the predominating juices which we are said to contain. Since, then, animals also have organs of taste which differ and which have different juices in excess, in respect of taste also they will receive different impressions of the real objects. For just as the same 53 food when digested becomes in one place a vein, in another an artery, in another a bone, in another a sinew, or some other piece of the body, displaying a different potency according to the difference in the parts which receive it;—and just as the same unblended 54 water, when it is absorbed by trees, becomes in one place bark, in another branch, in another blossom, and so finally fig and quince and each of the other fruits ;—and just as the single identical breath of a musician breathed into a flute becomes here a shrill note and there a deep note, and the same pressure of his hand on the lyre produces here a deep note and there a shrill note ;—so likewise it is probable that the external objects appear different owing to differences

33

παρὰ τὴν διάφορον κατασκευὴν τῶν τὰς φαντασίας
ὑπομενόντων ζῴων.

55 Ἐναργέστερον δὲ τὸ τοιοῦτον ἔστι μαθεῖν ἀπὸ
τῶν αἱρετῶν τε καὶ φευκτῶν τοῖς ζῴοις. μύρον
γοῦν ἀνθρώποις μὲν ἥδιστον φαίνεται, κανθάροις
δὲ καὶ μελίσσαις δυσανάσχετον· καὶ τὸ ἔλαιον τοὺς
μὲν ἀνθρώπους ὠφελεῖ, σφῆκας δὲ καὶ μελίσσας
ἀναιρεῖ καταρραινόμενον· καὶ τὸ θαλάττιον· ὕδωρ
ἀνθρώποις μὲν ἀηδές ἐστι πινόμενον καὶ φαρμα-
56 κῶδες, ἰχθύσι δὲ ἥδιστον καὶ πότιμον. σύες δὲ
ἥδιον βορβόρῳ λούονται δυσωδεστάτῳ ἢ ὕδατι
διειδεῖ καὶ καθαρῷ. τῶν τε ζῴων τὰ μέν ἐστι
ποηφάγα τὰ δὲ θαμνοφάγα τὰ δὲ ὑληνόμα τὰ δὲ
σπερμοφάγα τὰ δὲ σαρκοφάγα τὰ δὲ γαλακτοφάγα,
καὶ τὰ μὲν σεσηπυίᾳ χαίρει τροφῇ τὰ δὲ νεαρᾷ,
καὶ τὰ μὲν ὠμῇ τὰ δὲ μαγειρικῶς ἐσκευασμένῃ.
καὶ κοινῶς τὰ ἄλλοις ἡδέα ἄλλοις ἐστὶν ἀηδῆ καὶ
57 φευκτὰ καὶ θανάσιμα. τὸ γοῦν κώνειον πιαίνει
τοὺς ὄρτυγας καὶ ὁ ὑοσκύαμος τὰς ὗς, αἳ δὴ χαί-
ρουσι καὶ σαλαμάνδρας ἐσθίουσαι, ὥσπεροῦν ἔλαφοι
τὰ ἰοβόλα ζῷα καὶ αἱ χελιδόνες κανθαρίδας. οἵ
τε μύρμηκες καὶ οἱ σκνῖπες ἀνθρώποις μὲν ἀηδίας
καὶ στρόφους ἐμποιοῦσι καταπινόμενοι· ἡ δὲ
ἄρκτος ἢν ἀρρωστίᾳ τινὶ περιπέσῃ, τούτους κατα-
58 λιχμωμένη ῥώννυται. ἔχιδνα δὲ θιγόντος αὐτῆς
μόνον φηγοῦ κλάδου καροῦται, καθάπερ καὶ νυ-
κτερὶς πλατάνου φύλλου. φεύγει δὲ κριὸν μὲν
ἐλέφας, λέων δὲ ἀλεκτρυόνα, καὶ θραγμὸν κυάμων
ἐρεικομένων τὰ θαλάττια κήτη, καὶ τίγρις ψόφον
τυμπάνου. καὶ ἄλλα δὲ πλείω τούτων ἔνεστι
λέγειν· ἀλλ' ἵνα μὴ μᾶλλον τοῦ δέοντος ἐνδιατρί-
βειν δοκῶμεν, εἰ τὰ αὐτὰ τοῖς μέν ἐστι ἀηδῆ τοῖς

in the structure of the animals which experience the sense-impressions.

But one may learn this more clearly from the 55 preferences and aversions of animals. Thus, sweet oil seems very agreeable to men, but intolerable to beetles and bees ; and olive oil is beneficial to men, but when poured on wasps and bees it destroys them ; and sea-water is a disagreeable and poisonous potion for men, but fish drink and enjoy it. Pigs, too, enjoy 56 wallowing in the most stinking mire rather than in clear and clean water. And whereas some animals eat grass, others eat shrubs, others feed in woods, others live on seeds or flesh or milk ; some of them, too, prefer their food high, others like it fresh, and while some prefer it raw, others like it cooked. And so generally, the things which are agreeable to some are to others disagreeable, distasteful and deadly. Thus, quails are fattened by hemlock, and pigs by 57 henbane ; and pigs also enjoy eating salamanders, just as deer enjoy poisonous creatures, and swallows gnats. So ants and wood-lice, when swallowed by men, cause distress and gripings, whereas the bear, whenever she falls sick, cures herself by licking them up. The mere touch of an oak-twig paralyses the 58 viper, and that of a plane-leaf the bat. The elephant flees from the ram, the lion from the cock, sea-monsters from the crackle of bursting beans, and the tiger from the sound of a drum. One might, indeed, cite many more examples, but—not to seem unduly prolix—if the same things are displeasing to some

δὲ ἡδέα, τὸ δὲ ἡδὺ καὶ ἀηδὲς ἐν φαντασίᾳ κεῖται,
διάφοροι γίνονται τοῖς ζῴοις ἀπὸ τῶν ὑποκειμένων
φαντασίαι.

59 Εἰ δὲ τὰ αὐτὰ πράγματα ἀνόμοια φαίνεται παρὰ
τὴν τῶν ζῴων ἐξαλλαγήν, ὁποῖον μὲν ἡμῖν θεωρεῖται τὸ ὑποκείμενον ἕξομεν λέγειν, ὁποῖον δὲ ἔστι
πρὸς τὴν φύσιν ἐφέξομεν. οὐδὲ γὰρ ἐπικρίνειν
αὐτοὶ δυνησόμεθα τὰς φαντασίας τάς τε ἡμετέρας
καὶ τὰς τῶν ἄλλων ζῴων, μέρος καὶ αὐτοὶ τῆς
διαφωνίας ὄντες καὶ διὰ τοῦτο τοῦ ἐπικρινοῦντος
60 δεησόμενοι μᾶλλον ἢ αὐτοὶ κρίνειν δυνάμενοι. καὶ
ἄλλως οὔτε ἀναποδείκτως δυνάμεθα προκρίνειν τὰς
ἡμετέρας φαντασίας τῶν παρὰ τοῖς ἀλόγοις ζῴοις
γινομένων οὔτε μετ' ἀποδείξεως. πρὸς γὰρ τῷ
μὴ εἶναι ἀπόδειξιν ἴσως, ὡς ὑπομνήσομεν, αὐτὴ
ἡ λεγομένη ἀπόδειξις ἤτοι φαινομένη ἡμῖν ἔσται
ἢ οὐ φαινομένη. καὶ εἰ μὲν μὴ φαινομένη, οὐδὲ
μετὰ πεποιθήσεως αὐτὴν προσησόμεθα· εἰ δὲ
φαινομένη ἡμῖν, ἐπειδὴ περὶ τῶν φαινομένων τοῖς
ζῴοις ζητεῖται καὶ ἡ ἀπόδειξις ἡμῖν φαίνεται ζῴοις
οὖσι, καὶ αὐτὴ ζητηθήσεται εἰ ἔστιν ἀληθὴς καθό
61 ἐστι φαινομένη. ἄτοπον δὲ τὸ ζητούμενον διὰ
τοῦ ζητουμένου κατασκευάζειν ἐπιχειρεῖν, ἐπεὶ
ἔσται τὸ αὐτὸ πιστὸν καὶ ἄπιστον, ὅπερ ἀμήχανον,
πιστὸν μὲν ᾗ βούλεται ἀποδεικνύειν, ἄπιστον δὲ

---

a See ii. 134 ff. where it is argued that logical demonstration or " proof " is " non-existent."   The argument here is
that, even if we grant the existence of " proof " in the abstract
we cannot prove anything in the particular case before us—
the question as to the superiority of our impressions to those
of animals.   For all proof must be either " apparent " to us,
or " non-apparent " : the latter kind we reject as incompre-

but pleasing to others, and pleasure and displeasure depend upon sense-impression, then animals receive different impressions from the underlying objects.

But if the same things appear different owing to 59 the variety in animals, we shall, indeed, be able to state our own impressions of the real object, but as to its essential nature we shall suspend judgement. For we cannot ourselves judge between our own impressions and those of the other animals, since we ourselves are involved in the dispute and are, therefore, rather in need of a judge than competent to pass judgement ourselves. Besides, we are unable, 60 either with or without proof, to prefer our own impressions to those of the irrational animals. For in addition to the probability that proof is, as we shall show,[a] a non-entity, the so-called proof itself will be either apparent to us or non-apparent. If, then, it is non-apparent, we shall not accept it with confidence; while if it is apparent to us, inasmuch as what is apparent to animals is the point in question and the proof is apparent to us who are animals, it follows that we shall have to question the proof itself as to whether it is as true as it is apparent. It is, indeed, 61 absurd to attempt to establish the matter in question by means of the matter in question,[b] since in that case the same thing will be at once believed and disbelieved,—believed in so far as it purports to prove, but disbelieved in so far as it requires proof,—which

hensible; the former "apparent" proof is indecisive, its "apparency" being relative to us, who are a species of animal, and thus involved in the dispute. Further, as relative to us the "apparent proof" is not absolute, and therefore not necessarily "true."

[b] This would be the fallacy of *petitio principii*, or "arguing in a circle"; *cf.* §§ 117, 164.

ᾗ ἀποδείκνυται. οὐχ ἕξομεν ἄρα ἀπόδειξιν δι᾽ ἧς
προκρινοῦμεν τὰς ἑαυτῶν φαντασίας τῶν παρὰ τοῖς
ἀλόγοις καλουμένοις ζώοις γινομένων. εἰ οὖν διάφοροι γίνονται αἱ φαντασίαι παρὰ τὴν τῶν ζώων
ἐξαλλαγήν, ἃς ἐπικρῖναι ἀμήχανόν ἐστιν, ἐπέχειν
ἀνάγκη περὶ τῶν ἐκτὸς ὑποκειμένων.

62 Ἐκ περιουσίας δὲ καὶ συγκρίνομεν τὰ ἄλογα
καλούμενα ζῷα τοῖς ἀνθρώποις κατὰ φαντασίαν·
καὶ γὰρ καταπαίζειν τῶν δογματικῶν τετυφωμένων
καὶ περιαυτολογούντων οὐκ ἀποδοκιμάζομεν μετὰ
τοὺς πρακτικοὺς τῶν λόγων. οἱ μὲν οὖν ἡμέτε-
ροι τὸ πλῆθος τῶν ἀλόγων ζώων ἁπλῶς εἰώθασι
63 συγκρίνειν τῷ ἀνθρώπῳ· ἐπεὶ δὲ εὑρεσιλογοῦντες
οἱ δογματικοὶ ἄνισον εἶναί φασι τὴν σύγκρισιν,
ἡμεῖς ἐκ πολλοῦ τοῦ περιόντος ἐπὶ πλέον παίζοντες
ἐπὶ ἑνὸς ζώου στήσομεν τὸν λόγον, οἷον ἐπὶ κυνός,
εἰ δοκεῖ, τοῦ εὐτελεστάτου δοκοῦντος εἶναι. εὑρήσομεν γὰρ καὶ οὕτω μὴ λειπόμενα ἡμῶν τὰ ζῷα,
περὶ ὧν ὁ λόγος, ὡς πρὸς τὴν πίστιν τῶν φαινομένων.

64 Ὅτι τοίνυν αἰσθήσει διαφέρει τοῦτο τὸ ζῷον
ἡμῶν, οἱ δογματικοὶ συνομολογοῦσιν· καὶ γὰρ τῇ
ὀσφρήσει μᾶλλον ἡμῶν ἀντιλαμβάνεται, τὰ μὴ
ὁρώμενα αὐτῷ θηρία διὰ ταύτης ἀνιχνεύων, καὶ
τοῖς ὀφθαλμοῖς θᾶττον ἡμῶν ταῦτα ὁρῶν καὶ τῇ
65 ἀκοῇ αἰσθανόμενος ὀξέως. οὐκοῦν ἐπὶ τὸν λόγον
ἔλθωμεν. τούτου δὲ ὁ μέν ἐστιν ἐνδιάθετος ὁ δὲ
προφορικός. ἴδωμεν οὖν πρότερον περὶ τοῦ ἐνδια-

---

[a] *i.e.* as a further, superfluous or jocular, kind of argument,
which serves to " cap " the serious treatment of the questions:
cf. §§ 63, 78.　　　　　[b] Esp. the Stoics.
[c] The Stoic theory of *logos* thus distinguished between its

38

is impossible. Consequently we shall not possess a proof which enables us to give our own sense-impressions the preference over those of the so-called irrational animals. If, then, owing to the variety in animals their sense-impressions differ, and it is impossible to judge between them, we must necessarily suspend judgement regarding the external underlying objects.

By way of super-addition,[a] too, we draw comparisons 62 between mankind and the so-called irrational animals in respect of their sense-impressions. For, after our solid arguments, we deem it quite proper to poke fun at those conceited braggarts, the Dogmatists.[b] As a rule, our School compare the irrational animals in the mass with mankind ; but since the Dogmatists 63 captiously assert that the comparison is unequal, we— super-adding yet more—will carry our ridicule further and base our argument on one animal only, the dog for instance if you like, which is held to be the most worthless of animals. For even in this case we shall find that the animals we are discussing are no wise inferior to ourselves in respect of the credibility of their impressions.

Now it is allowed by the Dogmatists that this 64 animal, the dog, excels us in point of sensation : as to smell it is more sensitive than we are, since by this sense it tracks beasts that it cannot see ; and with its eyes it sees them more quickly than we do ; and with its ears it is keen of perception. Next let 65 us proceed to the reasoning faculty. Of reason one kind is internal, implanted in the soul, the other externally expressed.[c] Let us consider first the

two senses—internal *reason*, or conception, and the enunciation of thought in the uttered *word*.

θέτου. οὗτος τοίνυν κατὰ τοὺς μάλιστα ἡμῖν
ἀντιδοξοῦντας νῦν δογματικούς, τοὺς ἀπὸ τῆς
στοᾶς, ἐν τούτοις ἔοικε σαλεύειν, τῇ αἱρέσει τῶν
οἰκείων καὶ φυγῇ τῶν ἀλλοτρίων, τῇ γνώσει τῶν
εἰς τοῦτο συντεινουσῶν τεχνῶν, τῇ ἀντιλήψει τῶν
κατὰ τὴν οἰκείαν φύσιν ἀρετῶν ⟨καὶ⟩[1] τῶν περὶ
66 τὰ πάθη. ὁ τοίνυν κύων, ἐφ᾽ οὗ τὸν λόγον ἔδοξε
στῆσαι παραδείγματος ἕνεκα, αἵρεσιν ποιεῖται τῶν
οἰκείων καὶ φυγὴν τῶν βλαβερῶν, τὰ μὲν τρόφιμα
διώκων, μάστιγος δὲ ἀνατεθείσης ὑποχωρῶν.
ἀλλὰ καὶ τέχνην ἔχει ποριστικὴν τῶν οἰκείων, τὴν
67 θηρευτικήν. ἔστι δὲ οὐδ᾽ ἀρετῆς ἐκτός· τῆς γέ
τοι δικαιοσύνης οὔσης τοῦ κατ᾽ ἀξίαν ἀποδο-
τικῆς ἑκάστῳ, ὁ κύων τοὺς μὲν οἰκείους τε καὶ εὖ
ποιοῦντας σαίνων καὶ φρουρῶν τοὺς δὲ ἀνοικείους
καὶ ἀδικοῦντας ἀμυνόμενος οὐκ ἔξω ἂν εἴη τῆς
68 δικαιοσύνης. εἰ δὲ ταύτην ἔχει, τῶν ἀρετῶν
ἀντακολουθουσῶν καὶ τὰς ἄλλας ἀρετὰς ἔχει, ἃς
οὔ φασιν ἔχειν τοὺς πολλοὺς ἀνθρώπους οἱ σοφοί.
καὶ ἄλκιμον δὲ αὐτὸν ὄντα ὁρῶμεν ἐν ταῖς ἀμύναις,
καὶ συνετόν, ὡς καὶ Ὅμηρος ἐμαρτύρησεν, ποιή-
σας τὸν Ὀδυσσέα πᾶσι μὲν τοῖς οἰκείοις ἀνθρώποις
ἀγνῶτα ὄντα ὑπὸ μόνου δὲ τοῦ Ἄργου ἐπιγνω-
σθέντα, μήτε ὑπὸ τῆς ἀλλοιώσεως τῆς κατὰ τὸ
σῶμα τἀνδρὸς ἀπατηθέντος τοῦ κυνός, μήτε ἐκ-
στάντος τῆς καταληπτικῆς φαντασίας, ἣν μᾶλλον
69 τῶν ἀνθρώπων ἔχων ἐφάνη. κατὰ δὲ τὸν Χρύσιππον τὸν μάλιστα ὁμιλοῦντα[2] τοῖς ἀλόγοις ζῴοις
καὶ τῆς ἀοιδίμου διαλεκτικῆς μετέχει. φησὶ γοῦν

---

[1] ⟨καὶ⟩ add. T.
[2] ὁμιλοῦντα ego: πολεμοῦντα GT, Bekk.. προσέχοντα Diels.

internal reason. Now according to those Dogmatists who are, at present, our chief opponents—I mean the Stoics—internal reason is supposed to be occupied with the following matters : the choice of things congenial and the avoidance of things alien ; the knowledge of the arts contributing thereto ; the apprehension of the virtues pertaining to one's proper nature and of those relating to the passions. Now 66 the dog—the animal upon which, by way of example, we have decided to base our argument—exercises choice of the congenial and avoidance of the harmful, in that it hunts after food and slinks away from a raised whip. Moreover, it possesses an art which supplies what is congenial, namely hunting. Nor is 67 it devoid even of virtue ; for certainly if justice consists in rendering to each his due,[a] the dog, that welcomes and guards its friends and benefactors but drives off strangers and evil-doers, cannot be lacking in justice. But if he possesses this virtue, then, since 68 the virtues are interdependent, he possesses also all the other virtues ; and these, say the philosophers,[b] the majority of men do not possess. That the dog is also valiant we see by the way he repels attacks, and intelligent as well, as Homer too testified[c] when he sang how Odysseus went unrecognized by all the people of his own household and was recognized only by the dog Argus, who neither was deceived by the bodily alterations of the hero nor had lost his original apprehensive impression, which indeed he evidently retained better than the men. And according to 69 Chrysippus, who shows special interest in irrational animals, the dog even shares in the far-famed " Dia-

---

[a] Cf. [Plato], Deff. 411 E.
[b] i.e. the Stoics.   [c] See Odyss. xvii. 300.

αὐτὸν ὁ προειρημένος ἀνὴρ ἐπιβάλλειν τῷ πέμπτῳ
διὰ πλειόνων ἀναποδείκτῳ,[1] ὅταν ἐπὶ τρίοδον
ἐλθὼν καὶ τὰς δύο ὁδοὺς ἰχνεύσας δι' ὧν οὐ διῆλθε
τὸ θηρίον, τὴν τρίτην μηδ' ἰχνεύσας εὐθέως ὁρμήσῃ
δι' αὐτῆς. δυνάμει γὰρ τοῦτο αὐτὸν λογίζεσθαί
φησιν ὁ ἀρχαῖος " ἤτοι τῇδε ἢ τῇδε ἢ τῇδε διῆλθε
τὸ θηρίον· οὔτε δὲ τῇδε οὔτε τῇδε· τῇδε ἄρα."

70 ἀλλὰ καὶ τῶν ἑαυτοῦ παθῶν ἀντιληπτικός τέ ἐστι
καὶ παραμυθητικός· σκόλοπος γὰρ αὐτῷ καταπαγέντος ἐπὶ τὴν ἆρσιν τούτου ὁρμᾷ τῇ τοῦ ποδὸς
πρὸς τὴν γῆν παρατρίψει καὶ διὰ τῶν ὀδόντων.
ἕλκος τε εἰ ἔχει που, ἐπεὶ τὰ μὲν ῥυπαρὰ ἕλκη
δυσαλθῆ ἐστι τὰ δὲ καθαρὰ ῥᾳδίως θεραπεύεται,

71 πράως ἀποψᾷ τὸν γινόμενον ἰχῶρα. ἀλλὰ καὶ τὸ
Ἱπποκράτειον φυλάσσει μάλα καλῶς· ἐπεὶ γὰρ
ποδὸς ἄκος ἀκινησία, εἴ ποτε τραῦμα ἐν ποδὶ
σχοίη, μετεωρίζει τοῦτον καὶ ὡς οἷόν τε ἄσκυλτον
τηρεῖ. ὀχλούμενός τε ὑπὸ χυμῶν ἀνοικείων πόαν
ἐσθίει, μεθ' ἧς ἀποβλύζων τὸ ἀνοίκειον ὑγιάζεται.

72 εἰ τοίνυν ἐφάνη τὸ ζῷον, ἐφ' οὗ τὸν λόγον ἐστή-
σαμεν παραδείγματος ἕνεκα, καὶ αἱρούμενον τὰ
οἰκεῖα καὶ τὰ ὀχληρὰ φεῦγον, τέχνην τε ἔχον ποριστικὴν τῶν οἰκείων, καὶ τῶν ἑαυτοῦ παθῶν ἀντι-
ληπτικὸν καὶ παραμυθητικόν, καὶ οὐκ ἔξω ἀρετῆς,
ἐν οἷς κεῖται ἡ τελειότης τοῦ ἐνδιαθέτου λόγου,
τέλειος ἂν εἴη κατὰ τοῦτο ὁ κύων· ὅθεν μοι δοκοῦσι

---

[1] ἀναποδείκτῳ T, Prantl: -δείκτων mss., Bekk.

---

[a] *i.e.* the Stoic *logic, cf.* ii. 94.
[b] The Stoics had five syllogisms which they termed
anapodeictic, or "indemonstrable," since they required no
proof themselves but served to prove others. The "com-

lectic.[a] " This person, at any rate, declares that the
dog makes use of the fifth complex indemonstrable
syllogism [b] when, on arriving at a spot where three
ways meet, after smelling at the two roads by which
the quarry did not pass, he rushes off at once by the
third without stopping to smell. For, says the old
writer, the dog implicitly reasons thus : " The creature
went either by this road, or by that, or by the other :
but it did not go by this road or by that : therefore it
went by the other." Moreover, the dog is capable 70
of comprehending and assuaging his own sufferings ;
for when a thorn has got stuck in his foot he hastens
to remove it by rubbing his foot on the ground and
by using his teeth. And if he has a wound anywhere,
because dirty wounds are hard to cure whereas clean
ones heal easily, the dog gently licks off the pus that
has gathered. Nay more, the dog admirably observes 71
the prescription of Hippocrates [c] : rest being what
cures the foot, whenever he gets his foot hurt he lifts
it up and keeps it as far as possible free from pressure.
And when distressed by unwholesome humours he
eats grass, by the help of which he vomits what is
unwholesome and gets well again. If, then, it has 72
been shown that the animal upon which, as an example,
we have based our argument not only chooses the
wholesome and avoids the noxious, but also possesses
an art capable of supplying what is wholesome, and
is capable of comprehending and assuaging its own
sufferings, and is not devoid of virtue, then—these
being the things in which the perfection of internal
reason consists—the dog will be thus far perfect.

plex " syllogism was of the form : " Either A or B or C exists ;
but neither A nor B exists ; therefore C exists."
  [c] The famous physician, of Cos (*circa* 460-400 B.C.).

τινες τῶν κατὰ φιλοσοφίαν ἑαυτοὺς σεμνῦναι τῇ τοῦ ζώου τούτου προσηγορίᾳ.

73 Περὶ δὲ τοῦ προφορικοῦ λόγου τέως μὲν οὐκ ἔστιν ἀναγκαῖον ζητεῖν· τοῦτον γὰρ καὶ τῶν δογματικῶν ἔνιοι παρῃτήσαντο ὡς ἀντιπράττοντα τῇ τῆς ἀρετῆς ἀναλήψει, διὸ καὶ περὶ τὸν τῆς μαθήσεως χρόνον ἤσκησαν σιωπήν· καὶ ἄλλως, εἰ καθ᾽ ὑπόθεσιν εἴη ἄνθρωπος ἐνεός, οὐδεὶς φήσει αὐτὸν εἶναι ἄλογον. ἵνα δὲ καὶ ταῦτα παραλίπωμεν, μάλιστα μὲν ὁρῶμεν τὰ ζῶα, περὶ ὧν ὁ λόγος, καὶ ἀνθρωπίνας προφερόμενα φωνάς, ὡς κίττας καὶ ἄλλα

74 τινά. ἵνα δὲ καὶ τοῦτο ἐάσωμεν, εἰ καὶ μὴ συνίεμεν τὰς φωνὰς τῶν ἀλόγων καλουμένων ζώων, ὅλως οὐκ ἔστιν ἀπεικὸς διαλέγεσθαι μὲν ταῦτα ἡμᾶς δὲ μὴ συνιέναι· καὶ γὰρ τῆς τῶν βαρβάρων φωνῆς ἀκούοντες οὐ συνίεμεν ἀλλὰ μονοειδῆ

75 ταύτην εἶναι δοκοῦμεν. καὶ ἀκούομεν δὲ τῶν κυνῶν ἄλλην μὲν φωνὴν προϊεμένων ὅταν ἀμύνωνταί τινας, ἄλλην δὲ ὅταν ὠρύωνται, καὶ ἄλλην ὅταν τύπτωνται, καὶ διάφορον ἐπὰν σαίνωσιν. καὶ ὅλως εἴ τις εἰς τοῦτο ἀτενίσειεν, εὕροι ἂν πολλὴν παραλλαγὴν τῆς φωνῆς παρὰ τούτῳ καὶ τοῖς ἄλλοις ζώοις ἐν ταῖς διαφόροις περιστάσεσιν, ὥστε διὰ ταῦτα εἰκότως λέγοιτ᾽ ἂν καὶ τοῦ προφορικοῦ μετέχειν λόγου τὰ καλούμενα ἄλογα ζῶα.

76 εἰ δὲ μήτε ἀκριβείᾳ τῶν αἰσθήσεων λείπεται τῶν ἀνθρώπων ταῦτα μήτε τῷ ἐνδιαθέτῳ λόγῳ, ἐκ περιουσίας δὲ εἰπεῖν μηδὲ τῷ προφορικῷ, οὐκ ἂν

---

[a] A sarcastic allusion to the Cynics; cf. Diog. Laert. vi. 13, Introd. p. xvi.

And that, I suppose, is why certain of the professors of philosophy have adorned themselves with the title of this animal.[a]

Concerning external reason, or speech, it is un- 73 necessary for the present to inquire; for it has been rejected even by some of the Dogmatists as being a hindrance to the acquisition of virtue, for which reason they used to practise silence [b] during the period of instruction; and besides, supposing that a man is dumb, no one will therefore call him irrational. But to pass over these cases, we certainly see animals— the subject of our argument—uttering quite human cries,—jays, for instance, and others. And, leaving 74 this point also aside, even if we do not understand the utterances of the so-called irrational animals, still it is not improbable that they converse although we fail to understand them; for in fact when we listen to the talk of barbarians we do not understand it, and it seems to us a kind of uniform chatter. More- 75 over, we hear dogs uttering one sound when they are driving people off, another when they are howling, and one sound when beaten, and a quite different sound when fawning. And so in general, in the case of all other animals as well as the dog, whoever examines the matter carefully will find a great variety of utterance according to the different circumstances, so that, in consequence, the so-called irrational animals may justly be said to participate in external reason. But if they neither fall short of mankind in 76 the accuracy of their perceptions, nor in internal reason, nor yet (to go still further) in external reason, or speech, then they will deserve no less credence

[b] For the Pythagorean rule of silence (ἐχεμυθία) cf. Diog. Laert. viii. 10.

77 ἀπιστότερα ἡμῶν εἴη κατὰ τὰς φαντασίας. καὶ
ἐφ᾽ ἑκάστου δὲ τῶν ἀλόγων ζῴων ἴσως ἱστάντας
τὸν λόγον ταῦτα ἀποδεικνύειν δυνατόν ἐστιν. οἷον
γοῦν τίς οὐκ ἂν εἴποι τοὺς ὄρνιθας ἀγχινοίᾳ τε
διαφέρειν καὶ τῷ προφορικῷ κεχρῆσθαι λόγῳ;
οἵ γε οὐ μόνον τὰ παρόντα ἀλλὰ καὶ τὰ ἐσόμενα
ἐπίστανται καὶ ταῦτα τοῖς συνιέναι δυναμένοις
προδηλοῦσιν, ἄλλως τε σημαίνοντες καὶ τῇ φωνῇ
προαγορεύοντες.

78 Τὴν δὲ σύγκρισιν ἐποιησάμην, ὡς καὶ ἔμπροσθεν
ἐπεσημηνάμην, ἐκ περιόντος, ἱκανῶς, ὡς οἶμαι,
δείξας ἔμπροσθεν ὅτι μὴ δυνάμεθα προκρίνειν τὰς
ἡμετέρας φαντασίας τῶν παρὰ τοῖς ἀλόγοις ζῴοις
γινομένων. πλὴν ἀλλ᾽ εἰ μή ἐστιν ἀπιστότερα τὰ
ἄλογα ζῷα ἡμῶν πρὸς τὴν κρίσιν τῶν φαντασιῶν,
καὶ διάφοροι γίνονται φαντασίαι παρὰ τὴν τῶν
ζῴων παραλλαγήν, ὁποῖον μὲν ἕκαστον τῶν ὑποκειμένων ἐμοὶ φαίνεται δυνήσομαι λέγειν, ὁποῖον
δὲ ἔστι τῇ φύσει διὰ τὰ προειρημένα ἐπέχειν
ἀναγκασθήσομαι.

79 Καὶ ὁ μὲν πρῶτος τῆς ἐποχῆς τρόπος τοιοῦτός
ἐστι, δεύτερον δὲ ἐλέγομεν εἶναι τὸν ἀπὸ τῆς
διαφορᾶς τῶν ἀνθρώπων· ἵνα γὰρ καθ᾽ ὑπόθεσιν
καὶ συγχωρήσῃ τις πιστοτέρους εἶναι τῶν ἀλόγων
ζῴων τοὺς ἀνθρώπους, εὑρήσομεν καὶ ὅσον ἐπὶ τῇ
ἡμετέρᾳ διαφορᾷ τὴν ἐποχὴν εἰσαγομένην. δύο
τοίνυν εἶναι λεγομένων ἐξ ὧν σύγκειται ὁ ἄνθρωπος, ψυχῆς καὶ σώματος, κατ᾽ ἄμφω ταῦτα
διαφέρομεν ἀλλήλων, οἷον κατὰ σῶμα ταῖς τε
80 μορφαῖς καὶ ταῖς ἰδιοσυγκρισίαις. διαφέρει μὲν

─────────────────────

ᵃ Our word "idiosyncrasy" comes from ἰδιοσυγκρασία, a
later form for ἰδιοσυγκρισία. σύγκρισις (or σύμμιξις) is Anax-

than ourselves in respect of their sense-impressions. Probably, too, we may reach this conclusion by basing 77 our argument on each single class of irrational animals. Thus, for example, who would deny that birds excel in quickness of wit or that they employ external reason ? For they understand not only present events but future events as well, and these they fore-show to such as are able to comprehend them by means of prophetic cries as well as by other signs.

I have drawn this comparison (as I previously 78 indicated) by way of super-addition, having already sufficiently proved, as I think, that we cannot prefer our own sense-impressions to those of the irrational animals. If, however, the irrational animals are not less worthy of credence than we in regard to the value of sense-impressions, and their impressions vary according to the variety of animal,—then, although I shall be able to say what the nature of each of the underlying objects appears to me to be, I shall be compelled, for the reasons stated above, to suspend judgement as to its real nature.

Such, then, is the First of the Modes which induce 79 suspense. The *Second Mode* is, as we said, that based on the differences in men ; for even if we grant for the sake of argument that men are more worthy of credence than irrational animals, we shall find that even our own differences of themselves lead to sus-pense. For man, you know, is said to be compounded of two things, soul and body, and in both these we differ one from another.

Thus, as regards the *body*, we differ in our figures and "idiosyncrasies," or constitutional peculiarities.[a]

agoras's term for the process of "composition " by which the world comes into being ; *cf.* Introd. p. xi.

47

γὰρ κατὰ μορφὴν σῶμα Σκύθου Ἰνδοῦ σώματος, τὴν δὲ παραλλαγὴν ποιεῖ, καθάπερ φασίν, ἡ διάφορος τῶν χυμῶν ἐπικράτεια. παρὰ δὲ[1] τὴν διάφορον τῶν χυμῶν ἐπικράτειαν διάφοροι γίνονται καὶ αἱ φαντασίαι, καθάπερ καὶ ἐν τῷ πρώτῳ λόγῳ παρεστήσαμεν. ταῦτά τοι καὶ ἐν τῇ αἱρέσει καὶ φυγῇ τῶν ἐκτὸς διαφορὰ πολλὴ κατ' αὐτούς ἐστιν· ἄλλοις γὰρ χαίρουσιν Ἰνδοὶ καὶ ἄλλοις οἱ καθ' ἡμᾶς, τὸ δὲ διαφόροις χαίρειν τοῦ παρηλλαγμένας ἀπὸ τῶν ὑποκειμένων φαντασίας λαμβάνειν ἐστὶ
81 μηνυτικόν. κατὰ δὲ ἰδιοσυγκρισίας διαφέρομεν ὡς ἐνίους κρέα βόεια πετραίων ἰχθυδίων ῥᾷον πέττειν καὶ ὑπὸ Λεσβίου οἰναρίου εἰς χολέραν περιτρέπεσθαι. ἦν δέ, φασίν, γραῦς Ἀττικὴ τριάκοντα ὁλκὰς κωνείου ἀκινδύνως προσφερομένη, Λῦσις δὲ καὶ μηκωνείου τέσσαρας ὁλκὰς ἀλύπως ἐλάμβανεν.
82 καὶ Δημοφῶν μὲν ὁ Ἀλεξάνδρου τραπεζοποιὸς ἐν ἡλίῳ γινόμενος ἢ ἐν βαλανείῳ ἐρρίγου, ἐν σκιᾷ δὲ ἐθάλπετο, Ἀθηναγόρας δὲ ὁ Ἀργεῖος ὑπὸ σκορπίων καὶ φαλαγγίων ἀλύπως ἐπλήσσετο, οἱ δὲ καλούμενοι Ψυλλαεῖς οὐδ' ὑπὸ ὄφεων ἢ ἀσπίδων
83 δακνόμενοι βλάπτονται, οἱ δὲ Τεντυρῖται τῶν Αἰγυπτίων οὐ βλάπτονται πρὸς [ἄνω κάτω][2] τῶν κροκοδείλων. ἀλλὰ καὶ Αἰθιόπων οἱ ἀντιπέραν τῆς Μερόης παρὰ τὸν Ἀστάπουν[3] ποταμὸν οἰκοῦντες σκορπίους καὶ ὄφεις καὶ τὰ παραπλήσια ἀκινδύνως ἐσθίουσιν. καὶ Ῥουφῖνος δὲ ὁ ἐν Χαλκίδι πίνων ἐλλέβορον οὔτε ἤμει οὔτε ὅλως ἐκαθαίρετο, ἀλλ' ὥς τι τῶν συνήθων προσεφέρετο
84 καὶ ἔπεσσεν. Χρύσερμος δὲ ὁ Ἡροφίλειος εἴ ποτε

---

[1] δὲ MT: om. Bekk.   [2] [ἄνω κάτω] om. T, Apelt.
[3] Ἀστάπουν T, Hercher: Ὑδάσπην mss., Bekk.

48

The body of an Indian differs in shape from that of 80 a Scythian; and it is said that what causes the variation is a difference in the predominant humours. Owing to this difference in the predominant humours the sense-impressions also come to differ, as we indicated in our First Argument.[a] So too in respect of choice and avoidance of external objects men exhibit great differences : thus Indians enjoy some things, our people other things, and the enjoyment of different things is an indication that we receive varying impressions from the underlying objects. In respect 81 of our "idiosyncrasies," our differences are such that some of us digest the flesh of oxen more easily than rock-fish, or get diarrhoea from the weak wine of Lesbos. An old wife of Attica, they say, swallowed with impunity thirty drams of hemlock, and Lysis took four drams of poppy-juice without hurt. Demo- 82 phon, Alexander's butler, used to shiver when he was in the sun or in a hot bath, but felt warm in the shade : Athenagoras the Argive took no hurt from the stings of scorpions and poisonous spiders ; and the Psyllaeans,[b] as they are called, are not harmed by bites from snakes and asps, nor are the Tentyritae[c] of Egypt 83 harmed by the crocodile. Further, those Ethiopians who live beyond Lake Meroë[d] on the banks of the river Astapous eat with impunity scorpions, snakes, and the like. Rufinus of Chalcis when he drank hellebore neither vomited nor suffered at all from purging, but swallowed and digested it just like any ordinary drink. Chrysermus the Herophilean doctor 84

[a] See § 52.
[b] A tribe of N. Africa, cf. Hdt. iv. 173.
[c] Tentyra was a town in Upper Egypt; cf. Juvenal xv. 35.
[d] In S. Egypt. The "Astapous" is the Blue Nile.

πέπερι προσηνέγκατο, καρδιακῶς ἐκινδύνευεν. καὶ
Σωτήριχος δὲ ὁ χειρουργὸς εἴ ποτε σιλούρων
ἤσθετο κνίσσης, χολέρα ἡλίσκετο. "Ανδρων δὲ ὁ
Ἀργεῖος οὕτως ἄδιψος ἦν ὡς καὶ διὰ τῆς ἀνύδρου
Λιβύης ὁδεύειν αὐτὸν μὴ ἐπιζητοῦντα ποτόν.
Τιβέριος δὲ ὁ Καῖσαρ ἐν σκότῳ ἑώρα. Ἀρι-
στοτέλης δὲ ἱστορεῖ Θάσιόν τινα ὃς ἐδόκει ἀν-
θρώπου εἴδωλον προηγεῖσθαι αὐτοῦ διὰ παντός.

85 Τοσαύτης οὖν παραλλαγῆς οὔσης ἐν τοῖς ἀνθρώποις κατὰ τὰ σώματα, ἵνα ὀλίγα ἀπὸ πολλῶν τῶν
παρὰ τοῖς δογματικοῖς κειμένων ἀρκεσθῶμεν εἰπόντες, εἰκός ἐστι καὶ κατ' αὐτὴν τὴν ψυχὴν διαφέρειν ἀλλήλων τοὺς ἀνθρώπους· τύπος γάρ τίς
ἐστι τὸ σῶμα τῆς ψυχῆς, ὡς καὶ ἡ φυσιογνωμονικὴ
σοφία δείκνυσιν. τὸ δὲ μέγιστον δεῖγμα τῆς κατὰ
τὴν διάνοιαν τῶν ἀνθρώπων πολλῆς καὶ ἀπείρου
διαφορᾶς ἡ διαφωνία τῶν παρὰ τοῖς δογματικοῖς
λεγομένων περί τε τῶν ἄλλων καὶ περὶ τοῦ τίνα
86 μὲν αἱρεῖσθαι προσήκει τίνα δὲ ἐκκλίνειν. δεόντως
οὖν καὶ οἱ ποιηταὶ περὶ τούτων ἀπεφήναντο· ὁ μὲν
γὰρ Πίνδαρός φησιν

ἀελλοπόδων μέν τιν' εὐφραίνουσιν ἵππων τιμαὶ
    καὶ στέφανοι,
τοὺς δ' ἐν πολυχρύσοις θαλάμοις βιοτά·
τέρπεται δὲ καί τις ἐπ' οἶδμ' ἅλιον ναΐ θοᾷ [σῶς]¹
    διαστείβων.

ὁ δὲ ποιητὴς λέγει

ἄλλος γάρ τ' ἄλλοισιν ἀνὴρ ἐπιτέρπεται ἔργοις.

ἀλλὰ καὶ ἡ τραγῳδία μεστὴ τῶν τοιούτων ἐστί·
λέγει γοῦν

¹ [σῶς] om. LMT.

was liable to get a heart attack if ever he took pepper ; and Soterichus the surgeon was seized with diarrhoea whenever he smelled fried sprats. Andron the Argive was so immune from thirst that he actually traversed the waterless country of Libya without needing a drink. Tiberius Caesar could see in the dark ; and Aristotle [a] tells of a Thasian who fancied that the image of a man was continually going in front of him.

Seeing, then, that men vary so much in body—to content ourselves with but a few instances of the many collected by the Dogmatists,—men probably also differ from one another in respect of the *soul* itself; for the body is a kind of expression of the soul, as in fact is proved by the science of Physiognomy. But the greatest proof of the vast and endless differences in men's intelligence is the discrepancy in the statements of the Dogmatists concerning the right objects of choice and avoidance, as well as other things. Regarding this the poets, too, have expressed themselves fittingly. Thus Pindar says [b] :

> The crowns and trophies of his storm-foot steeds
> Give joy to one ; yet others find it joy
> To dwell in gorgeous chambers gold-bedeckt ;
> Some even take delight in voyaging
> O'er ocean's billows in a speeding barque.

And the poet [c] says : " One thing is pleasing to one man, another thing to another." Tragedy, too, is full of such sayings ; for example :

---

[a] See Aristot. *Meteorol.* iii. 4.

[b] *Fragm.* 242 (Boeckh), Sandys' *Pindar*, in Loeb Library, p. 610, copied by Horace, *Odes*, i. 1. 3 ff.

[c] See Homer, *Odyss.* xiv. 228. *Cf.* Virgil, *Ecl.* ii. 65 " trahit sua quemque voluntas "; and " quot homines, tot sententiae."

εἰ πᾶσι ταὐτὸν καλὸν ἔφυ σοφόν θ' ἅμα,
οὐκ ἦν ἂν ἀμφίλεκτος ἀνθρώποις ἔρις,

καὶ πάλιν

δεινόν γε ταὐτὸν τοῖς μὲν ἀνδάνειν βροτῶν
τοῖς δ' ἔχθος εἶναι.

87 ἐπεὶ οὖν ἡ αἵρεσις καὶ ἡ φυγὴ ἐν ἡδονῇ καὶ ἀηδισμῷ ἐστίν, ἡ δὲ ἡδονὴ καὶ ὁ ἀηδισμὸς ἐν αἰσθήσει κεῖται καὶ φαντασίᾳ, ὅταν τὰ αὐτὰ οἱ μὲν αἱρῶνται οἱ δὲ φεύγωσιν, ἀκόλουθον ἡμᾶς ἐπιλογίζεσθαι ὅτι οὐδὲ ὁμοίως ὑπὸ τῶν αὐτῶν κινοῦνται, ἐπεὶ ὁμοίως ἂν τὰ αὐτὰ ᾑροῦντο ἢ ἐξέκλινον. εἰ δὲ τὰ αὐτὰ διαφόρως κινεῖ παρὰ τὴν διαφορὰν τῶν ἀνθρώπων, εἰσάγοιτ' ἂν εἰκότως καὶ κατὰ τοῦτο ἡ ἐποχή, ὅ τι μὲν ἕκαστον φαίνεται τῶν ὑποκειμένων ὡς πρὸς ἑκάστην διαφορὰν ἴσως λέγειν ἡμῶν δυναμένων, τί δὲ ἔστι [κατὰ δύναμιν]¹ ὡς πρὸς τὴν φύσιν οὐχ οἷων τε ὄντων ἀποφήνασθαι.

88 ἤτοι γὰρ πᾶσι τοῖς ἀνθρώποις πιστεύσομεν ἢ τισίν. ἀλλ' εἰ μὲν πᾶσιν, καὶ ἀδυνάτοις ἐπιχειρήσομεν καὶ τὰ ἀντικείμενα παραδεξόμεθα· εἰ δὲ τισίν, εἰπάτωσαν ἡμῖν τίσι χρὴ συγκατατίθεσθαι· ὁ μὲν γὰρ Πλατωνικὸς λέξει ὅτι Πλάτωνι, ὁ Ἐπικούρειος δὲ Ἐπικούρῳ, καὶ οἱ ἄλλοι ἀναλόγως, καὶ οὕτως ἀνεπικρίτως στασιάζοντες αὖθις ἡμᾶς

89 εἰς τὴν ἐποχὴν περιστήσουσιν. ὁ δὲ λέγων ὅτι τοῖς πλείστοις δεῖ συγκατατίθεσθαι παιδαριῶδές τι προσίεται, οὐδενὸς δυναμένου πάντας τοὺς ἀνθρώπους ἐπελθεῖν καὶ διαλογίσασθαι τί τοῖς

¹ [κατὰ δύναμιν] secl. Mutsch., Papp.

> Were fair and wise the same thing unto all,
> There had been no contentious quarrelling.[a]

And again :

> 'Tis strange that the same thing abhorr'd by some
> Should give delight to others.[b]

Seeing, then, that choice and avoidance depend on 87 pleasure and displeasure, while pleasure and displeasure depend on sensation and sense-impression, whenever some men choose the very things which are avoided by others, it is logical for us to conclude that they are also differently affected by the same things, since otherwise they would all alike have chosen or avoided the same things. But if the same objects affect men differently owing to the differences in the men, then, on this ground also, we shall reasonably be led to suspension of judgement. For while we are, no doubt, able to state what each of the underlying objects appears to be, relatively to each difference, we are incapable of explaining what it is in reality. For we shall have to believe either all 88 men or some. But if we believe all, we shall be attempting the impossible and accepting contradictories ; and if some, let us be told whose opinions we are to endorse. For the Platonist will say " Plato's " ; the Epicurean, " Epicurus's " ; and so on with the rest ; and thus by their unsettled disputations they will bring us round again to a state of suspense. Moreover, he who maintains that we ought to assent 89 to the majority is making a childish proposal, since no one is able to visit the whole of mankind and determine what pleases the majority of them ; for

[a] From Eurip. *Phoen.* 499 ff.
[b] See *Fragm. Trag. adesp.* 462 (Nauck): perhaps from Eurip.

πλείστοις ἀρέσκει, ἐνδεχομένου τοῦ ἔν τισιν ἔθνεσιν,
ἃ ἡμεῖς οὐκ ἴσμεν, τὰ μὲν παρ' ἡμῖν σπάνια τοῖς
πλείοσι προσεῖναι τὰ δὲ ἡμῶν τοῖς πολλοῖς συμ-
βαίνοντα σπάνια ὑπάρχειν, ὡς τοὺς πολλοὺς μὲν
ὑπὸ φαλαγγίων δακνομένους μὴ ἀλγεῖν τινὰς δὲ
σπανίως ἀλγεῖν, καὶ ἐπὶ τῶν ἄλλων τῶν ἔμπροσθεν
εἰρημένων ἰδιοσυγκρισιῶν τὸ ἀνάλογον. ἀναγκαῖον
οὖν καὶ διὰ τὴν τῶν ἀνθρώπων διαφορὰν εἰσάγεσθαι
τὴν ἐποχήν.

90 Ἐπεὶ δὲ φίλαυτοί τινες ὄντες οἱ δογματικοὶ φασι
δεῖν τῶν ἄλλων ἀνθρώπων ἑαυτοὺς προκρίνειν ἐν
τῇ κρίσει τῶν πραγμάτων, ἐπιστάμεθα μὲν ὅτι
ἄτοπός ἐστιν ἡ ἀξίωσις αὐτῶν (μέρος γάρ εἰσι
καὶ αὐτοὶ τῆς διαφωνίας· καὶ ἐὰν αὐτοὺς προ-
κρίνοντες οὕτω κρίνωσι τὰ φαινόμενα, πρὶν ἄρξασθαι τῆς κρίσεως τὸ ζητούμενον[1] συναρπάζουσιν,
91 ἑαυτοῖς τὴν κρίσιν ἐπιτρέποντες), ὅμως δ' οὖν ἵνα
καὶ ἐπὶ ἑνὸς ἀνθρώπου τὸν λόγον ἱστάντες, οἷον
τοῦ παρ' αὐτοῖς ὀνειροπολουμένου σοφοῦ, ἐπὶ τὴν
ἐποχὴν καταντῶμεν, τὸν τρίτον τῇ τάξει τρόπον
ἐγχειριζόμεθα.

Τοῦτον δὲ λέγομεν τὸν ἀπὸ τῆς διαφορᾶς τῶν
αἰσθήσεων. ὅτι δὲ διαφέρονται αἱ αἰσθήσεις πρὸς
92 ἀλλήλας, πρόδηλον. αἱ γοῦν γραφαὶ τῇ μὲν ὄψει
δοκοῦσιν εἰσοχὰς καὶ ἐξοχὰς ἔχειν, οὐ μὴν καὶ
τῇ ἁφῇ. καὶ τὸ μέλι τῇ μὲν γλώττῃ ἡδὺ φαίνεται
ἐπί τινων, τοῖς δ' ὀφθαλμοῖς ἀηδές· ἀδύνατον οὖν
ἐστιν εἰπεῖν πότερον ἡδύ ἐστιν εἰλικρινῶς ἢ ἀηδές.
καὶ ἐπὶ τοῦ μύρου ὁμοίως· τὴν μὲν γὰρ ὄσφρησιν
93 εὐφραίνει, τὴν δὲ γεῦσιν ἀηδίζει. τό τε εὐφόρβιον

there may possibly be races of whom we know nothing amongst whom conditions rare with us are common, and conditions common with us rare,—possibly, for instance, most of them feel no pain from the bites of spiders, though a few on rare occasions feel such pain ; and so likewise with the rest of the " idiosyncrasies " mentioned above. Necessarily, therefore, the differences in men afford a further reason for bringing in suspension of judgement.

When the Dogmatists—a self-loving class of men— 90 assert that in judging things they ought to prefer themselves to other people, we know that their claim is absurd ; for they themselves are a party to the controversy ; and if, when judging appearances, they have already given the preference to themselves, then, by thus entrusting themselves with the judgement, they are begging the question before the judgement is begun. Nevertheless, in order that we may arrive 91 at suspension of judgement by basing our argument on one person—such as, for example, their visionary " Sage " ᵃ—we adopt the Mode which comes Third in order.

This *Third Mode* is, we say, based on differences in the senses. That the senses differ from one another is obvious. Thus, to the eye paintings 92 seem to have recesses and projections, but not so to the touch. Honey, too, seems to some ᵇ pleasant to the tongue but unpleasant to the eyes ; so that it is impossible to say whether it is absolutely pleasant or unpleasant. The same is true of sweet oil, for it pleases the sense of smell but displeases the taste.

ᵃ The ideal " Wise Man " of the Stoics ; see Introd. p. xxviii.
ᵇ For exceptions see § 101.

¹ τὸ ζητούμενον T : τὰ φαινόμενα MSS., Bekk.

ἐπεὶ τοῖς μὲν ὀφθαλμοῖς λυπηρόν ἐστι τῷ δὲ ἄλλῳ σώματι παντὶ ἄλυπον, οὐχ ἕξομεν εἰπεῖν πότερον ἄλυπόν ἐστιν εἰλικρινῶς τοῖς σώμασιν ὅσον ἐπὶ τῇ ἑαυτοῦ φύσει ἢ λυπηρόν. τό τε ὄμβριον ὕδωρ ὀφθαλμοῖς μέν ἐστιν ὠφέλιμον, ἀρτηρίαν δὲ καὶ πνεύμονα τραχύνει, καθάπερ καὶ τὸ ἔλαιον, καίτοι τὴν ἐπιφάνειαν παρηγοροῦν. καὶ ἡ θαλαττία νάρκη τοῖς μὲν ἄκροις προστεθεῖσα ναρκᾶν ποιεῖ, τῷ δ' ἄλλῳ σώματι ἀλύπως παρατίθεται. διόπερ ὁποῖον μὲν ἔστι πρὸς τὴν φύσιν ἕκαστον τούτων οὐχ ἕξομεν λέγειν, ὁποῖον δὲ φαίνεται ἑκάστοτε δυνατὸν εἰπεῖν.

94 Καὶ ἄλλα δὲ πλείω τούτων ἔνεστι λέγειν· ἀλλ' ἵνα μὴ διατρίβωμεν διὰ τὴν πρόθεσιν [τοῦ τρόπου]¹ τῆς συγγραφῆς, ἐκεῖνο λεκτέον. ἕκαστον τῶν φαινομένων ἡμῖν αἰσθητῶν ποικίλον ὑποπίπτειν δοκεῖ, οἷον τὸ μῆλον λεῖον εὐῶδες γλυκὺ ξανθόν. ἄδηλον οὖν πότερόν ποτε ταύτας μόνας ὄντως ἔχει τὰς ποιότητας, ἢ μονόποιον μέν ἐστιν παρὰ δὲ τὴν διάφορον κατασκευὴν τῶν αἰσθητηρίων διάφορον φαίνεται, ἢ καὶ πλείονας μὲν τῶν φαινομένων ἔχει ποιότητας, ἡμῖν δ' οὐχ ὑποπίπτουσί τινες αὐτῶν.

95 μονόποιον μὲν γὰρ εἶναι τοῦτο ἐνδέχεται λογίζεσθαι ἐκ τῶν ἔμπροσθεν ἡμῖν εἰρημένων περὶ τῆς εἰς τὰ σώματα ἀναδιδομένης τροφῆς καὶ τοῦ ὕδατος τοῦ εἰς τὰ δένδρα ἀναδιδομένου καὶ τοῦ πνεύματος τοῦ ἐν αὐλοῖς καὶ σύριγξι καὶ τοῖς παραπλησίοις ὀργάνοις· δύναται γὰρ καὶ τὸ μῆλον μονοειδὲς μὲν εἶναι, διάφορον δὲ θεωρεῖσθαι παρὰ τὴν διαφορὰν τῶν αἰσθητηρίων περὶ ἃ γίνεται αὐτοῦ ἡ ἀντίληψις.

96 πλείονας δὲ τῶν φαινομένων ἡμῖν ποιοτήτων ἔχειν τὸ μῆλον ποιότητας δύνασθαι οὕτως ἐπιλογιζόμεθα.

So too with spurge [a] : since it pains the eyes but 93
causes no pain to any other part of the body, we cannot
say whether, in its real nature, it is absolutely painful
or painless to bodies. Rain-water, too, is beneficial
to the eyes but roughens the wind-pipe and the lungs;
as also does olive-oil, though it mollifies the epidermis.
The cramp-fish, also, when applied to the extremities
produces cramp, but it can be applied to the rest of
the body without hurt. Consequently we are unable
to say what is the real nature of each of these things,
although it is possible to say what each thing at the
moment appears to be.

A longer list of examples might be given, but to 94
avoid prolixity, in view of the plan of our treatise,
we will say just this. Each of the phenomena perceived by the senses seems to be a complex : the
apple, for example, seems smooth, odorous, sweet and
yellow. But it is non-evident whether it really
possesses these qualities only ; or whether it has but
one quality but appears varied owing to the varying
structure of the sense-organs ; or whether, again, it
has more qualities than are apparent, some of which
elude our perception. That the apple has but one 95
quality might be argued from what we said above [b]
regarding the food absorbed by bodies, and the water
sucked up by trees, and the breath in flutes and pipes
and similar instruments ; for the apple likewise may
be all of one sort but appear different owing to
differences in the sense-organs in which perception
takes place. And that the apple may possibly possess 96
more qualities than those apparent to us we argue in

[a] A species of plants with acrid, milky juice.
[b] See § 53.

---

[1] [τοῦ τρόπου] secl. Mutsch.

ἐννοήσωμέν τινα ἐκ γενετῆς ἁφὴν μὲν ἔχοντα καὶ
ὄσφρησιν καὶ γεῦσιν, μήτε δὲ ἀκούοντα μήτε
ὁρῶντα. οὗτος τοίνυν ὑπολήψεται μήτε ὁρατόν τι
εἶναι τὴν ἀρχὴν μήτε ἀκουστόν, ἀλλὰ μόνα ἐκεῖνα
τὰ τρία γένη τῶν ποιοτήτων ὑπάρχειν ὧν ἀντι-
97 λαμβάνεσθαι δύναται. καὶ ἡμᾶς οὖν ἐνδέχεται τὰς
πέντε μόνας αἰσθήσεις ἔχοντας μόνον ἀντιλαμβάνεσθαι, ἐκ τῶν περὶ τὸ μῆλον ποιοτήτων, ὧν
ἐσμὲν ἀντιληπτικοί· ὑποκεῖσθαι δὲ ἄλλας οἷον τέ
ἐστι ποιότητας, ὑποπιπτούσας ἑτέροις αἰσθητηρίοις,
ὧν ἡμεῖς οὐ μετεσχήκαμεν, διὸ οὐδὲ ἀντιλαμβανόμεθα τῶν κατ' αὐτὰς αἰσθητῶν.

98 Ἀλλ' ἡ φύσις συνεμετρήσατο, φήσει τις, τὰς
αἰσθήσεις πρὸς τὰ αἰσθητά. ποία φύσις, διαφωνίας
τοσαύτης ἀνεπικρίτου παρὰ τοῖς δογματικοῖς
οὔσης περὶ τῆς ὑπάρξεως τῆς κατ' αὐτήν; ὁ γὰρ
ἐπικρίνων αὐτὸ τοῦτο, εἰ ἔστι φύσις, εἰ μὲν ἰδιώτης
εἴη, ἄπιστος ἔσται κατ' αὐτούς, φιλόσοφος δὲ ὢν
μέρος ἔσται τῆς διαφωνίας καὶ κρινόμενος αὐτὸς
99 ἀλλ' οὐ κριτής. πλὴν ἀλλ' εἰ ἐγχωρεῖ[1] καὶ ταύτας
μόνας ὑποκεῖσθαι παρὰ τῷ μήλῳ τὰς ποιότητας
ὧν ἀντιλαμβάνεσθαι δοκοῦμεν, καὶ πλείους τούτων
ἢ πάλιν μηδὲ τὰς ἡμῖν ὑποπιπτούσας, ἄδηλον ἡμῖν
ἔσται ὁποῖόν ἔστι τὸ μῆλον. ὁ δὲ αὐτὸς καὶ ἐπὶ
τῶν ἄλλων αἰσθητῶν λόγος. τῶν αἰσθήσεων μέντοι
μὴ καταλαμβανουσῶν τὰ ἐκτός, οὐδὲ ἡ διάνοια
ταῦτα δύναται καταλαμβάνειν, ὥστε καὶ διὰ τοῦτον
τὸν λόγον ἡ περὶ τῶν ἐκτὸς ὑποκειμένων ἐποχὴ
συνάγεσθαι δόξει.

100 Ἵνα δὲ καὶ ἐπὶ μιᾶς ἑκάστης αἰσθήσεως ἱστάντες

---

[1] εἰ ἐγχωρεῖ Heintz : ἐνεχώρει mss. : εἰ ἐνεχώρει T, Bekk.

this way. Let us imagine a man who possesses from birth the senses of touch, taste and smell, but can neither hear nor see. This man, then, will assume that nothing visible or audible has any existence, but only those three kinds of qualities which he is able to apprehend. Possibly, then, we also, having only 97 our five senses, perceive only such of the apple's qualities as we are capable of apprehending ; and possibly it may possess other underlying qualities which affect other sense-organs, though we, not being endowed with those organs, fail to apprehend the sense-objects which come through them.

"But," it may be objected, "Nature made the 98 senses commensurate with the objects of sense." What kind of " Nature " ? we ask, seeing that there exists so much unresolved controversy amongst the Dogmatists concerning the reality which belongs to Nature. For he who decides the question as to the existence of Nature will be discredited by them if he is an ordinary person, while if he is a philosopher he will be a party to the controversy and therefore himself subject to judgement and not a judge. If, 99 however, it is possible that only those qualities which we seem to perceive subsist in the apple, or that a greater number subsist, or, again, that not even the qualities which affect us subsist, then it will be non-evident to us what the nature of the apple really is. And the same argument applies to all the other objects of sense. But if the senses do not apprehend external objects, neither can the mind apprehend them ; hence, because of this argument also, we shall be driven, it seems, to suspend judgement regarding the external underlying objects.

In order that we may finally reach suspension by 100

SEXTUS EMPIRICUS

τὸν λόγον, ἢ καὶ ἀφιστάμενοι τῶν αἰσθήσεων,
ἔχωμεν καταλήγειν εἰς τὴν ἐποχήν, παραλαμβάνομεν καὶ τὸν τέταρτον τρόπον αὐτῆς. ἔστι δ᾽
οὗτος ὁ παρὰ τὰς περιστάσεις καλούμενος, περιστάσεις λεγόντων ἡμῶν τὰς διαθέσεις. θεωρεῖσθαι δ᾽ αὐτόν φαμεν ἐν τῷ κατὰ φύσιν ἢ παρὰ
φύσιν ⟨ἔχειν⟩,[1] ἐν τῷ ἐγρηγορέναι ἢ καθεύδειν,
παρὰ τὰς ἡλικίας, παρὰ τὸ κινεῖσθαι ἢ ἠρεμεῖν,
παρὰ τὸ μισεῖν ἢ φιλεῖν, παρὰ τὸ ἐνδεεῖς εἶναι ἢ
κεκορεσμένους, παρὰ τὸ μεθύειν ἢ νήφειν, παρὰ
τὰς προδιαθέσεις, παρὰ τὸ θαρρεῖν ἢ δεδιέναι, [ἢ]
101 παρὰ τὸ λυπεῖσθαι ἢ χαίρειν. οἷον παρὰ μὲν τὸ
κατὰ φύσιν ἢ παρὰ φύσιν ἔχειν ἀνόμοια ὑποπίπτει
τὰ πράγματα, ἐπεὶ οἱ μὲν φρενιτίζοντες καὶ οἱ
θεοφορούμενοι δαιμόνων ἀκούειν δοκοῦσιν, ἡμεῖς
δὲ οὔ. ὁμοίως δὲ ἀποφορᾶς στύρακος ἢ λιβανωτοῦ
ἤ τινος τοιούτου καὶ ἄλλων πλειόνων ἀντιλαμβάνεσθαι πολλάκις λέγουσιν, ἡμῶν μὴ αἰσθανο-
μένων. καὶ τὸ αὐτὸ ὕδωρ φλεγμαίνουσι μὲν τόποις
ἐπιχυθὲν ζεστὸν εἶναι δοκεῖ, ἡμῖν δὲ χλιαρόν.
καὶ τὸ αὐτὸ ἱμάτιον τοῖς μὲν ὑπόσφαγμα ἔχουσι
φαίνεται κιρρόν, ἐμοὶ δὲ οὔ. καὶ τὸ αὐτὸ μέλι
ἐμοὶ μὲν φαίνεται γλυκύ, τοῖς δὲ ἰκτερικοῖς πικρόν.
102 εἰ δέ τις λέγει ὅτι χυμῶν τινων παραπλοκὴ ἀνοικείους φαντασίας ἐκ τῶν ὑποκειμένων ποιεῖ
τοῖς παρὰ φύσιν ἔχουσι, λεκτέον ὅτι ἐπεὶ καὶ οἱ
ὑγιαίνοντες χυμοὺς ἔχουσιν ἀνακεκραμένους, δύνανται οὗτοι τὰ ἐκτὸς ὑποκείμενα, τοιαῦτα ὄντα φύσει
ὁποῖα φαίνεται τοῖς παρὰ φύσιν ἔχειν λεγομένοις,
103 ἑτεροῖα φαίνεσθαι ποιεῖν τοῖς ὑγιαίνουσιν. τὸ γὰρ
ἐκείνοις μὲν τοῖς χυμοῖς μεταβλητικὴν τῶν ὑποκει-

[1] ⟨ἔχειν⟩ add. Mutsch.

60

basing our argument on each sense singly, or even by disregarding the senses, we further adopt the *Fourth Mode* of suspension. This is the Mode based, as we say, on the "circumstances," meaning by "circumstances" conditions or dispositions.[a] And this Mode, we say, deals with states that are natural or unnatural, with waking or sleeping, with conditions due to age, motion or rest, hatred or love, emptiness or fulness, drunkenness or soberness, predispositions, confidence or fear, grief or joy. Thus, according as 101 the mental state is natural or unnatural, objects produce dissimilar impressions, as when men in a frenzy or in a state of ecstasy believe they hear daemons' voices, while we do not. Similarly they often say that they perceive an odour of storax or frankincense, or some such scent, and many other things, though we fail to perceive them. Also, the same water which feels very hot when poured on inflamed spots seems lukewarm to us. And the same coat which seems of a bright yellow colour to men with blood-shot eyes does not appear so to me. And the same honey seems to me sweet, but bitter to men with jaundice. Now 102 should anyone say that it is an intermixture of certain humours which produces in those who are in an unnatural state improper impressions from the underlying objects, we have to reply that, since healthy persons also have mixed humours, these humours too are capable of causing the external objects—which really are such as they appear to those who are said to be in an unnatural state—to appear other than they are to healthy persons. For to ascribe the power of 103

---

[a] *i.e.* the mental or physical state of the subject at the moment of perception.

μένων διδόναι δύναμιν, τούτοις δὲ μή, πλασματικόν
ἐστιν, ἐπεὶ καὶ ὥσπερ οἱ ὑγιαίνοντες κατὰ φύσιν
μὲν τὴν τῶν ὑγιαινόντων ἔχουσιν παρὰ φύσιν δὲ
τὴν τῶν νοσούντων, οὕτω καὶ οἱ νοσοῦντες παρὰ
φύσιν μὲν ἔχουσι τὴν τῶν ὑγιαινόντων κατὰ φύσιν
δὲ τὴν τῶν νοσούντων, ὥστε κἀκείνοις πρός τι
κατὰ φύσιν ἔχουσι πιστευτέον.

104   Παρὰ δὲ τὸ ὑπνοῦν ἢ ἐγρηγορέναι διάφοροι γίνονται φαντασίαι, ἐπεὶ ὡς καθ' ὕπνους φανταζόμεθα, οὐ φανταζόμεθα ἐγρηγορότες, οὐδὲ ὡς φανταζόμεθα ἐγρηγορότες, καὶ κατὰ τοὺς ὕπνους
φανταζόμεθα, ὥστε ⟨τὸ⟩[1] εἶναι αὐταῖς[2] ἢ μὴ εἶναι
γίνεται οὐχ ἁπλῶς ἀλλὰ πρός τι· πρὸς γὰρ τὸ
καθ' ὕπνους ἢ πρὸς ἐγρήγορσιν. εἰκότως οὖν καθ'
ὕπνους ὁρῶμεν ταῦτα ἃ ἐστιν ἐν τῷ ἐγρηγορέναι
ἀνύπαρκτα, οὐκ ἐν τῷ καθάπαξ ἀνύπαρκτα ὄντα·
ἔστι γὰρ καθ' ὕπνους, ὥσπερ τὰ ὕπαρ ἔστιν, κἂν
μὴ ᾖ καθ' ὕπνους.

105   Παρὰ δὲ τὰς ἡλικίας, ὅτι ὁ αὐτὸς ἀὴρ τοῖς μὲν
γέρουσι ψυχρὸς εἶναι δοκεῖ τοῖς δὲ ἀκμάζουσιν
εὔκρατος, καὶ τὸ αὐτὸ χρῶμα τοῖς μὲν πρεσ-
βυτέροις ἀμαυρὸν φαίνεται τοῖς δὲ ἀκμάζουσι κατα-
κορές, καὶ φωνὴ ὁμοίως ἡ αὐτὴ τοῖς μὲν ἀμαυρὰ
106 δοκεῖ τυγχάνειν τοῖς δ' ἐξάκουστος. καὶ παρὰ
τὰς αἱρέσεις δὲ καὶ φυγὰς ἀνομοίως κινοῦνται οἱ
ταῖς ἡλικίαις διαφέροντες· παισὶ μὲν γάρ, εἰ τύχοι,
σφαῖραι καὶ τροχοὶ διὰ σπουδῆς εἰσίν, οἱ ἀκμά-
ζοντες δὲ ἄλλα αἱροῦνται, καὶ ἄλλα οἱ γέροντες.
ἐξ ὧν συνάγεται ὅτι διάφοροι γίνονται φαντασίαι
ὑπὸ τῶν αὐτῶν ὑποκειμένων καὶ παρὰ τὰς
διαφόρους ἡλικίας.

---

[1] ⟨τὸ⟩ cj. Mutsch.   [2] αὐταῖς Apelt: αὐτοῖς mss., Bekk.

altering the underlying objects to those humours, and not to these, is purely fanciful ; since just as healthy men are in a state that is natural for the healthy but unnatural for the sick, so also sick men are in a state that is unnatural for the healthy but natural for the sick, so that to these last also we must give credence as being, relatively speaking, in a natural state.[a]

Sleeping and waking, too, give rise to different 104 impressions, since we do not imagine when awake what we imagine in sleep, nor when asleep what we imagine when awake ; so that the existence or non-existence of our impressions is not absolute but relative, being in relation to our sleeping or waking condition. Probably, then, in dreams we see things which to our waking state are unreal,[b] although not wholly unreal ; for they exist in our dreams, just as waking realities exist although non-existent in dreams.

Age is another cause of difference.[c] For the same 105 air seems chilly to the old but mild to those in their prime ; and the same colour appears faint to older men but vivid to those in their prime ; and similarly the same sound seems to the former faint, but to the latter clearly audible. Moreover, those who differ in 106 age are differently moved in respect of choice and avoidance. For whereas children—to take a case— are all eagerness for balls and hoops, men in their prime choose other things, and old men yet others. And from this we conclude that differences in age also cause different impressions to be produced by the same underlying objects.

---

[a] This is aimed against the Stoic view that only the healthy, or normal, is " natural."

[b] ἀνύπαρκτα (from ὑπάρχω, " subsist ") is an Epicurean term for " non-existent."

[c] For age as affecting character cf. Aristot. Rhet. ii. 12 ff.

107 Παρὰ δὲ τὸ κινεῖσθαι ἢ ἠρεμεῖν ἀνόμοια
φαίνεται τὰ πράγματα, ἐπεὶ ἅπερ ἑστῶτες ὁρῶμεν
ἀτρεμοῦντα, ταῦτα παραπλέοντες κινεῖσθαι δοκοῦ-
108 μεν. παρὰ δὲ τὸ φιλεῖν ἢ μισεῖν, ὅτι κρέα ὕεια
τινὲς μὲν ἀποστρέφονται καθ᾽ ὑπερβολὴν τινὲς δὲ
ἥδιστα προσφέρονται. ὅθεν καὶ ὁ Μένανδρος ἔφη

> οἷος δὲ καὶ τὴν ὄψιν εἶναι φαίνεται;
> ἀφ᾽ οὗ τοιοῦτος γέγονεν; οἷον θηρίον.
> τὸ μηδὲν ἀδικεῖν καὶ καλοὺς ἡμᾶς ποιεῖ.

πολλοὶ ⟨δὲ⟩[1] καὶ ἐρωμένας αἰσχρὰς ἔχοντες ὡραιο-
109 τάτας αὐτὰς εἶναι δοκοῦσιν. παρὰ δὲ τὸ πεινῆν
ἢ κεκορέσθαι, ὅτι τὸ αὐτὸ ἔδεσμα τοῖς μὲν
πεινῶσιν ἥδιστον εἶναι δοκεῖ τοῖς δὲ κεκορεσμένοις
ἀηδές. παρὰ δὲ τὸ μεθύειν ἢ νήφειν, ὅτι ἅπερ
νήφοντες αἰσχρὰ εἶναι δοκοῦμεν, ταῦτα ἡμῖν με-
110 θύουσιν οὐκ αἰσχρὰ φαίνεται. παρὰ δὲ τὰς προδιαθέσεις, ὅτι ὁ αὐτὸς οἶνος τοῖς μὲν φοίνικας ἢ
ἰσχάδας προφαγοῦσιν ὀξώδης φαίνεται, τοῖς δὲ
κάρυα ἢ ἐρεβίνθους προσενεγκαμένοις ἡδὺς εἶναι
δοκεῖ, καὶ ἡ τοῦ βαλανείου παραστὰς τοὺς μὲν
ἔξωθεν εἰσιόντας θερμαίνει, ψύχει δὲ τοὺς ἐξιόντας,
111 εἰ ἐν αὐτῇ διατρίβοιεν. παρὰ δὲ τὸ φοβεῖσθαι ἢ
θαρρεῖν, ὅτι τὸ αὐτὸ πρᾶγμα τῷ μὲν δειλῷ φοβερὸν
καὶ δεινὸν εἶναι δοκεῖ, τῷ θαρραλεωτέρῳ δὲ οὐδαμῶς. παρὰ δὲ τὸ λυπεῖσθαι ἢ χαίρειν, ὅτι τὰ
αὐτὰ πράγματα τοῖς μὲν λυπουμένοις ἐστὶν ἐπαχθῆ
τοῖς δὲ χαίρουσιν ἡδέα.

[1] ⟨δὲ⟩ cj. Bekk.

---

* Cf. Lucret. iv. 388.
* Fragm. 518 (Kock). It is supposed that these lines were
spoken by a maiden of her lover who had fallen into evil ways.

Another cause why the real objects appear different 107 lies in motion and rest. For those objects which, when we are standing still, we see to be motionless, we imagine to be in motion when we are sailing past them.[a]

Love and hatred are a cause, as when some have 108 an extreme aversion to pork while others greatly enjoy eating it. Hence, too, Menander said[b]:

> Mark now his visage, what a change is there
> Since he has come to this! How bestial!
> 'Tis actions fair that make the fairest face.

Many lovers, too, who have ugly mistresses think them most beautiful.[c]

Hunger and satiety are a cause; for the same food 109 seems agreeable to the hungry but disagreeable to the sated.

Drunkenness and soberness are a cause; since actions which we think shameful when sober do not seem shameful to us when drunk.

Predispositions are a cause; for the same wine 110 which seems sour to those who have previously eaten dates or figs, seems sweet to those who have just consumed nuts or chick-peas; and the vestibule[d] of the bath-house, which warms those entering from outside, chills those coming out of the bath-room if they stop long in it.

Fear and boldness are a cause; as what seems to 111 the coward fearful and formidable does not seem so in the least to the bold man.

Grief and joy are a cause; since the same affairs are burdensome to those in grief but delightful to those who rejoice.

[c] *Cf.* Horace, *Sat.* i. 3. 38.
[d] *i.e.* the *tepidarium*, of moderate temperature.

112 Τοσαύτης οὖν οὔσης ἀνωμαλίας καὶ παρὰ τὰς διαθέσεις, καὶ ἄλλοτε ἄλλως[1] ἐν ταῖς διαθέσεσι τῶν ἀνθρώπων γινομένων, ὁποῖον μὲν ἕκαστον τῶν ὑποκειμένων ἑκάστῳ φαίνεται ῥᾴδιον ἴσως εἰπεῖν, ὁποῖον δὲ ἔστιν οὐκέτι, ἐπεὶ καὶ ἀνεπίκριτός ἐστιν ἡ ἀνωμαλία. ὁ γὰρ ἐπικρίνων ταύτην ἤτοι ἔν τισι τῶν προειρημένων διαθέσεών ἐστιν ἢ ἐν οὐδεμιᾷ τὸ παράπαν ἐστὶ διαθέσει. τὸ μὲν οὖν λέγειν ὅτι ἐν οὐδεμιᾷ διαθέσει τὸ σύνολόν ἐστιν, οἷον οὔτε ὑγιαίνει οὔτε νοσεῖ, οὔτε κινεῖται οὔτε ἠρεμεῖ, οὔτε ἔν τινι ἡλικίᾳ ἐστίν, ἀπήλλακται δὲ καὶ τῶν ἄλλων διαθέσεων, τελέως ἀπεμφαίνει. εἰ δὲ ἔν τινι διαθέσει ὢν κρινεῖ τὰς φαντασίας,

113 μέρος ἔσται τῆς διαφωνίας, καὶ ἄλλως οὐκ εἰλικρινὴς τῶν ἐκτὸς ὑποκειμένων ἐστὶ κριτὴς διὰ τὸ τεθολῶσθαι ταῖς διαθέσεσιν ἐν αἷς ἔστιν. οὔτε οὖν ὁ ἐγρηγορὼς δύναται συγκρίνειν τὰς τῶν καθευδόντων φαντασίας ταῖς τῶν ἐγρηγορότων, οὔτε ὁ ὑγιαίνων τὰς τῶν νοσούντων ταῖς[2] τῶν ὑγιαινόντων· τοῖς γὰρ παροῦσι καὶ κινοῦσιν ἡμᾶς κατὰ τὸ παρὸν συγκατατιθέμεθα μᾶλλον ἢ τοῖς μὴ παροῦσιν.

114 Καὶ ἄλλως δὲ ἀνεπίκριτός ἐστιν ἡ τῶν τοιούτων φαντασιῶν ἀνωμαλία. ὁ γὰρ προκρίνων φαντασίαν φαντασίας καὶ περίστασιν περιστάσεως ἤτοι ἀκρίτως καὶ ἄνευ ἀποδείξεως τοῦτο ποιεῖ ἢ κρίνων καὶ ἀποδεικνύς. ἀλλ᾽ οὔτε ἄνευ τούτων, ἄπιστος γὰρ ἔσται, οὔτε σὺν τούτοις. εἰ γὰρ κρινεῖ τὰς φαν-

115 τασίας, πάντως κριτηρίῳ κρινεῖ. τοῦτο οὖν τὸ

---

[1] ἄλλως MLT: ἄλλων Bekk.
[2] ταῖς T: καὶ τὰς mss., Bekk.

Seeing then that the dispositions also are the cause 112 of so much disagreement, and that men are differently disposed at different times, although, no doubt, it is easy to say what nature each of the underlying objects appears to each man to possess, we cannot go on to say what its real nature is, since the disagreement admits in itself of no settlement. For the person who tries to settle it is either in one of the afore-mentioned dispositions or in no disposition whatsoever. But to declare that he is in no disposition at all—as, for instance, neither in health nor sickness, neither in motion nor at rest, of no definite age, and devoid of all the other dispositions as well—is the height of absurdity. And if he is to judge the sense-impressions while he is in some one disposition, he will be a party to the disagreement,[a] and, moreover, he will 113 not be an impartial judge of the external underlying objects owing to his being confused by the dispositions in which he is placed. The waking person, for instance, cannot compare the impressions of sleepers with those of men awake, nor the sound person those of the sick with those of the sound; for we assent more readily to things present, which affect us in the present, than to things not present.

In another way, too, the disagreement of such 114 impressions is incapable of settlement. For he who prefers one impression to another, or one " circumstance " to another, does so either uncritically and without proof or critically and with proof; but he can do this neither without these means (for then he would be discredited) nor with them. For if he is to pass judgement on the impressions he must certainly judge them by a criterion; this criterion, then, he 115

[a] *Cf.* § 90.

κριτήριον ἤτοι ἀληθὲς εἶναι λέξει ἢ ψευδές. ἀλλ' εἰ
μὲν ψευδές, ἄπιστος ἔσται. εἰ δὲ ἀληθὲς εἶναι
τοῦτο φήσει, ἤτοι ἄνευ ἀποδείξεως λέξει ὅτι
ἀληθές ἐστι τὸ κριτήριον, ἢ μετὰ ἀποδείξεως.
καὶ εἰ μὲν ἄνευ ἀποδείξεως, ἄπιστος ἔσται· εἰ δὲ
μετὰ ἀποδείξεως, πάντως δεήσει καὶ τὴν ἀπόδειξιν ἀληθῆ εἶναι, ἐπεὶ ἄπιστος ἔσται. ἀληθῆ οὖν
λέξει τὴν ἀπόδειξιν τὴν εἰς τὴν πίστωσιν τοῦ
κριτηρίου λαμβανομένην πότερον κεκρικὼς αὐτὴν
116 ἢ μὴ κεκρικώς; εἰ μὲν γὰρ μὴ κρίνας, ἄπιστος
ἔσται, εἰ δὲ κρίνας, δῆλον ὅτι κριτηρίῳ φήσει
κεκρικέναι, οὗ κριτηρίου ζητήσομεν ἀπόδειξιν,
κἀκείνης κριτήριον. χρῄζει γὰρ ἀεὶ καὶ ἡ ἀπόδειξις κριτηρίου, ἵνα βεβαιωθῇ, καὶ τὸ κριτήριον
ἀποδείξεως, ἵνα ἀληθὲς εἶναι δειχθῇ· καὶ οὔτε
ἀπόδειξις ὑγιὴς εἶναι δύναται μὴ προϋπάρχοντος
κριτηρίου ἀληθοῦς, οὔτε κριτήριον ἀληθὲς μὴ προ-
117 πεπιστωμένης τῆς ἀποδείξεως. καὶ οὕτως ἐμπίπτουσιν εἰς τὸν διάλληλον τρόπον τό τε κριτήριον
καὶ ἡ ἀπόδειξις, ἐν ᾧ ἀμφότερα εὑρίσκεται ἄπιστα·
ἑκάτερον γὰρ τὴν θατέρου πίστιν περιμένον ὁμοίως
τῷ λοιπῷ ἐστιν ἄπιστον. εἰ οὖν μήτε ἄνευ ἀποδείξεως καὶ κριτηρίου μήτε σὺν τούτοις δύναται
τις προκρῖναι φαντασίαν φαντασίας, ἀνεπίκριτοι
ἔσονται αἱ παρὰ τὰς διαφόρους διαθέσεις διάφοροι
γινόμεναι φαντασίαι, ὥστε εἰσάγεται ἡ περὶ τῆς
φύσεως τῶν ἐκτὸς ὑποκειμένων ἐποχὴ καὶ ὡς
ἐπὶ τούτῳ τῷ τρόπῳ.
118   Πέμπτος ἐστὶ λόγος ὁ παρὰ τὰς θέσεις καὶ τὰ
διαστήματα καὶ τοὺς τόπους· καὶ γὰρ παρὰ τούτων
ἕκαστον τὰ αὐτὰ πράγματα διάφορα φαίνεται, οἷον

will declare to be true, or else false. But if false, he will be discredited ; whereas, if he shall declare it to be true, he will be stating that the criterion is true either without proof or with proof. But if without proof, he will be discredited ; and if with proof, it will certainly be necessary for the proof also to be true, to avoid being discredited. Shall he, then, affirm the truth of the proof adopted to establish the criterion after having judged it or without judging it ? If 116 without judging, he will be discredited ; but if after judging, plainly he will say that he has judged it by a criterion ; and of that criterion we shall ask for a proof, and of that proof again a criterion. For the proof always requires a criterion to confirm it, and the criterion also a proof to demonstrate its truth ; and neither can a proof be sound without the previous existence of a true criterion nor can the criterion be true without the previous confirmation of the proof. So in this way both the criterion and the proof are 117 involved in the circular process of reasoning,[a] and thereby both are found to be untrustworthy ; for since each of them is dependent on the credibility of the other, the one is lacking in credibility just as much as the other. Consequently, if a man can prefer one impression to another neither without a proof and a criterion nor with them, then the different impressions due to the differing conditions will admit of no settlement ; so that as a result of this Mode also we are brought to suspend judgement regarding the nature of external realities.

The *Fifth Argument* (or *Trope*) is that based on 118 positions, distances, and locations ; for owing to each of these the same objects appear different ; for

---

[a] *Cf.* §§ 60, 122 ; ii. 34, 121, etc.

ἡ αὐτὴ στοὰ ἀπὸ μὲν τῆς ἑτέρας ἀρχῆς ὁρωμένη
μύουρος φαίνεται ἀπὸ δὲ τοῦ μέσου σύμμετρος
πάντοθεν, καὶ τὸ αὐτὸ πλοῖον πόρρωθεν μὲν μικρὸν
φαίνεται καὶ ἑστὼς ἐγγύθεν δὲ μέγα καὶ κινούμενον,
καὶ ὁ αὐτὸς πύργος πόρρωθεν μὲν φαίνεται στρογγύλος ἐγγύθεν δὲ τετράγωνος.

119 Ταῦτα μὲν παρὰ τὰ διαστήματα, παρὰ δὲ τοὺς
τόπους ὅτι τὸ λυχνιαῖον φῶς ἐν ἡλίῳ μὲν ἀμαυρὸν
φαίνεται ἐν σκότῳ δὲ λαμπρόν, καὶ ἡ αὐτὴ κώπη
ἔναλος μὲν κεκλασμένη ἔξαλος δὲ εὐθεῖα, καὶ τὸ
ᾠὸν ἐν μὲν τῇ ὄρνιθι ἁπαλὸν ἐν ἀέρι δὲ σκληρόν,
καὶ τὸ λυγγούριον ἐν μὲν λυγγὶ ὑγρὸν ἐν ἀέρι δὲ
σκληρόν, καὶ τὸ κοράλιον ἐν θαλάττῃ μὲν ἁπαλὸν
ἐν ἀέρι δὲ σκληρόν, καὶ φωνὴ ἀλλοία μὲν φαίνεται
ἐν σύριγγι γινομένη, ἀλλοία δὲ ἐν αὐλῷ, ἀλλοία δὲ
ἐν ἀέρι ἁπλῶς.

120 Παρὰ δὲ τὰς θέσεις ὅτι ἡ αὐτὴ εἰκὼν ἐξυπτια-
ζομένη μὲν λεία φαίνεται, ποσῶς δὲ ἐπινευομένη
εἰσοχὰς καὶ ἐξοχὰς ἔχειν δοκεῖ. καὶ οἱ τράχηλοι
δὲ τῶν περιστερῶν παρὰ τὰς διαφόρους ἐπικλίσεις
διάφοροι φαίνονται κατὰ χρῶμα.

121 Ἐπεὶ οὖν πάντα τὰ φαινόμενα ἔν τινι θεωρεῖται
καὶ ἀπό τινος διαστήματος ἢ κατά τινα θέσιν, ὧν
ἕκαστον πολλὴν ποιεῖ παραλλαγὴν περὶ τὰς φαντασίας, ὡς ὑπεμνήσαμεν, ἀναγκασθησόμεθα καὶ
διὰ τούτου τοῦ τρόπου καταντᾶν εἰς ἐποχήν. καὶ
γὰρ ὁ βουλόμενος τούτων τῶν φαντασιῶν προ-
122 κρίνειν τινὰς ἀδυνάτοις ἐπιχειρήσει. εἰ μὲν γὰρ
ἁπλῶς καὶ ἄνευ ἀποδείξεως ποιήσεται τὴν ἀπόφασιν,

---

[a] Cf. Lucret. iv. 428 ff.

[b] "Lyngurion," so called from the belief that the stone
was made of the urine of the lynx frozen or crystallized.

example, the same porch [a] when viewed from one of its corners appears curtailed, but viewed from the middle symmetrical on all sides ; and the same ship seems at a distance to be small and stationary, but from close at hand large and in motion ; and the same tower from a distance appears round but from a near point quadrangular.

These effects are due to distances ; among effects 119 due to locations are the following : the light of a lamp appears dim in the sun but bright in the dark ; and the same oar bent when in the water but straight when out of the water ; and the egg soft when inside the fowl but hard when in the air ; and the jacinth [b] fluid when in the lynx but hard when in the air ; and the coral soft when in the sea but hard when in the air ; and sound seems to differ in quality according as it is produced in a pipe, or in a flute, or simply in the air.

Effects due to positions are such as these : the same 120 painting when laid flat appears smooth, but when inclined forward at a certain angle it seems to have recesses and prominences. The necks of doves, also, appear different in hue according to the differences in the angle of inclination.

Since, then, all apparent objects are viewed in a 121 certain place, and from a certain distance, or in a certain position, and each of these conditions produces a great divergency in the sense-impressions, as we mentioned above, we shall be compelled by this Mode also to end up in suspension of judgement. For in fact anyone who purposes to give the preference to any of these impressions will be attempting the impossible. For if he shall deliver his judgement 122 simply and without proof, he will be discredited ; and

71

ἄπιστος ἔσται· εἰ δὲ ἀποδείξει βουλήσεται χρήσασθαι, εἰ μὲν ψευδῆ λέξει τὴν ἀπόδειξιν εἶναι,
ἑαυτὸν περιτρέψει, ἀληθῆ δὲ λέγων εἶναι τὴν ἀπόδειξιν αἰτηθήσεται ἀπόδειξιν τοῦ ἀληθῆ αὐτὴν
εἶναι, κἀκείνης ἄλλην, ἐπεὶ καὶ αὐτὴν ἀληθῆ εἶναι
δεῖ, καὶ μέχρις ἀπείρου. ἀδύνατον δέ ἐστιν ἀ-
123 πείρους ἀποδείξεις παραστῆσαι· οὐκοῦν οὐδὲ μετὰ
ἀποδείξεως δυνήσεται προκρίνειν φαντασίαν φαντασίας. εἰ δὲ μήτε ἄνευ ἀποδείξεως μήτε μετὰ
ἀποδείξεως δυνατὸς ἔσται τις ἐπικρίνειν τὰς προ-
ειρημένας φαντασίας, συνάγεται ἡ ἐποχή, ὁποῖον
μὲν φαίνεται ἕκαστον κατὰ τήνδε τὴν θέσιν ἢ κατὰ
τόδε τὸ διάστημα ἢ ἐν τῷδε εἰπεῖν ἴσως δυναμένων
ἡμῶν, ὁποῖον δέ ἐστιν ὡς πρὸς τὴν φύσιν ἀδυνα-
τούντων ἀποφαίνεσθαι διὰ τὰ προειρημένα.

124 Ἕκτος ἐστὶ τρόπος ὁ παρὰ τὰς ἐπιμιγάς, καθ'
ὃν συνάγομεν ὅτι ἐπεὶ μηδὲν τῶν ὑποκειμένων καθ'
ἑαυτὸ ἡμῖν αὐτὸ ὑποπίπτει ἀλλὰ σύν τινι, ὁποῖον
μέν ἐστι τὸ μῖγμα ἔκ τε τοῦ ἐκτὸς καὶ τοῦ ᾧ συν-
θεωρεῖται τάχα δυνατὸν εἰπεῖν, ὁποῖον δέ ἐστι τὸ
ἐκτὸς ὑποκείμενον εἰλικρινῶς οὐκ ἂν ἔχοιμεν λέγειν.
ὅτι δὲ οὐδὲν τῶν ἐκτὸς καθ' ἑαυτὸ ὑποπίπτει ἀλλὰ
πάντως σύν τινι, καὶ ὅτι παρὰ τοῦτο ἀλλοῖον θεω-
125 ρεῖται, πρόδηλον, οἶμαι. τὸ γοῦν ἡμέτερον χρῶμα
ἀλλοῖον μὲν ὁρᾶται ἐν ἀλεεινῷ ἀέρι ἀλλοῖον δὲ
ἐν τῷ ψυχρῷ, καὶ οὐκ ἂν ἔχοιμεν εἰπεῖν ὁποῖον
ἔστι τῇ φύσει τὸ χρῶμα ἡμῶν, ἀλλ' ὁποῖον σὺν

---

[a] Cf. ii. 128.
[b] i.e. the real (" external ") object of perception (cf. p. 30
note a) plus the physical conditions which accompany the
act of perception; these latter may be either external (e.g.

should he, on the other hand, desire to adduce proof, he will confute himself if he says that the proof is false, while if he asserts that the proof is true he will be asked for a proof of its truth, and again for a proof of this latter proof, since it also must be true, and so on *ad infinitum.*[a] But to produce proofs to infinity is impossible ; so that neither by the use of proofs will 123 he be able to prefer one sense-impression to another. If, then, one cannot hope to pass judgement on the afore-mentioned impressions either with or without proof, the conclusion we are driven to is suspension ; for while we can, no doubt, state the nature which each object appears to possess as viewed in a certain position or at a certain distance or in a certain place, what its real nature is we are, for the foregoing reasons, unable to declare.

The *Sixth Mode* is that based on admixtures, by 124 which we conclude that, because none of the real objects affects our senses by itself but always in conjunction with something else, though we may possibly be able to state the nature of the resultant mixture[b] formed by the external object and that along with which it is perceived, we shall not be able to say what is the exact nature of the external reality in itself. That none of the external objects affects our senses by itself but always in conjunction with something else, and that, in consequence, it assumes a different appearance, is, I imagine, quite obvious. Thus, our own complexion is of one hue 125 in warm air, of another in cold, and we should not be able to say what our complexion really is, but only what it looks like in conjunction with each of

atmospheric) or internal (*e.g.* peculiarities in the sense-organs of the percipient).

SEXTUS EMPIRICUS

ἑκάστῳ τούτων θεωρεῖται. καὶ ἡ αὐτὴ φωνὴ ἀλλοία μὲν φαίνεται σὺν λεπτῷ ἀέρι ἀλλοία δὲ σὺν παχυμερεῖ, καὶ τὰ ἀρώματα ἐν βαλανείῳ καὶ ἡλίῳ πληκτικώτερα μᾶλλόν ἐστιν ἢ ἐν ἀέρι καταψύχρῳ, καὶ τὸ σῶμα ὑπὸ ὕδατος μὲν περιεχόμενον κοῦφόν ἐστιν ὑπὸ δὲ ἀέρος βαρύ.

126 Ἵνα δὲ καὶ τῆς ἔξωθεν ἐπιμιξίας ἀποστῶμεν, οἱ ὀφθαλμοὶ ἡμῶν ἔχουσιν ἐν ἑαυτοῖς καὶ χιτῶνας καὶ ὑγρά. τὰ οὖν ὁρατὰ ἐπεὶ μὴ ἄνευ τούτων θεωρεῖται, οὐ καταληφθήσεται πρὸς ἀκρίβειαν· τοῦ γὰρ μίγματος ἀντιλαμβανόμεθα, καὶ διὰ τοῦτο οἱ μὲν ἰκτερικοὶ πάντα ὠχρὰ ὁρῶσιν, οἱ δ᾽ ὑπόσφαγμα ἔχοντες ὕφαιμα. καὶ ἐπεὶ ἡ φωνὴ ἡ αὐτὴ ἀλλοία μὲν φαίνεται ἐν ἀναπεπταμένοις τόποις ἀλλοία δὲ ἐν στενοῖς καὶ ἑλικοειδέσι, καὶ ἀλλοία μὲν ἐν καθαρῷ ἀέρι ἀλλοία δὲ ἐν τεθολωμένῳ, εἰκός ἐστι μὴ ἀντιλαμβάνεσθαι ἡμᾶς εἰλικρινῶς τῆς φωνῆς· τὰ γὰρ ὦτα σκολιόπορά ἐστι καὶ στενόπορα καὶ ἀτμώδεσιν ἀποφορήσεσιν, αἳ δὴ ἀπὸ τῶν περὶ τὴν κεφαλὴν φέρεσθαι λέγονται τόπων, τεθολωμένα.

127 ἀλλὰ καὶ ἐν τοῖς μυξωτῆρσι καὶ ἐν τοῖς τῆς γεύσεως τόποις ὑλῶν ὑποκειμένων, μετ᾽ ἐκείνων ἀντιλαμβανόμεθα τῶν γευστῶν καὶ τῶν ὀσφρητῶν, ἀλλ᾽ οὐκ εἰλικρινῶς. ὥστε διὰ τὰς ἐπιμιξίας αἱ αἰσθήσεις οὐκ ἀντιλαμβάνονται ὁποῖα πρὸς ἀκρίβειαν τὰ ἐκτὸς ὑποκείμενα ἔστιν.

128 Ἀλλ᾽ οὐδὲ ἡ διάνοια, μάλιστα μὲν ἐπεὶ αἱ ὁδηγοὶ αὐτῆς αἰσθήσεις σφάλλονται· ἴσως δὲ καὶ αὐτὴ ἐπιμιξίαν τινὰ ἰδίαν ποιεῖται πρὸς τὰ ὑπὸ τῶν αἰσθήσεων ἀναγγελλόμενα· περὶ γὰρ ἕκαστον τῶν τόπων ἐν οἷς τὸ ἡγεμονικὸν εἶναι δοκοῦσιν οἱ

74

these conditions. And the same sound appears of one sort in conjunction with rare air and of another sort with dense air; and odours are more pungent in a hot bath-room or in the sun than in chilly air; and a body is light when immersed in water but heavy when surrounded by air.

But to pass on from the subject of external ad- 126 mixture,—our eyes contain within themselves both membranes and liquids. Since, then, the objects of vision are not perceived apart from these, they will not be apprehended with exactness; for what we perceive is the resultant mixture, and because of this the sufferers from jaundice see everything yellow, and those with blood-shot eyes reddish like blood.[a] And since the same sound seems of one quality in open places, of another in narrow and winding places, and different in clear air and in murky air, it is probable that we do not apprehend the sound in its real purity; for the ears have crooked and narrow passages, which are also befogged by vaporous effluvia which are said to be emitted by the regions of the head. Moreover, since there reside substances in the 127 nostrils and in the organs of taste, we apprehend the objects of taste and of smell in conjunction with these and not in their real purity. So that, because of these admixtures, the senses do not apprehend the exact quality of the external real objects.

Nor yet does the mind apprehend it, since, in the 128 first place, its guides, which are the senses, go wrong; and probably, too, the mind itself adds a certain admixture of its own to the messages conveyed by the senses; for we observe that there are certain humours present in each of the regions which the Dogmatists

[a] *Cf.* §§ 44, 101 *supra.*

δογματικοί, χυμούς τινας ὑποκειμένους θεωροῦμεν, εἴτε περὶ ἐγκέφαλον εἴτε περὶ καρδίαν εἴτε περὶ ὁτιδήποτε οὖν μέρος τοῦ ζώου τοῦτο τίθεσθαι βού-λοιτό τις. καὶ κατὰ τοῦτον οὖν τὸν τρόπον ὁρῶμεν ὅτι περὶ τῆς φύσεως τῶν ἐκτὸς ὑποκειμένων οὐδὲν εἰπεῖν ἔχοντες ἐπέχειν ἀναγκαζόμεθα.

129 Ἕβδομον τρόπον ἐλέγομεν εἶναι τὸν παρὰ τὰς ποσότητας καὶ σκευασίας τῶν ὑποκειμένων, σκευα-σίας λέγοντες κοινῶς τὰς συνθέσεις. ὅτι δὲ καὶ κατὰ τοῦτον τὸν τρόπον ἐπέχειν ἀναγκαζόμεθα περὶ τῆς φύσεως τῶν πραγμάτων, δῆλον. οἷον γοῦν τὰ ξέσματα τοῦ κέρατος τῆς αἰγὸς φαίνεται μὲν λευκὰ ἁπλῶς καὶ ἄνευ συνθέσεως θεωρούμενα, συντιθέμενα δὲ ἐν τῇ τοῦ κέρατος ὑπάρξει μέλανα θεωρεῖται. καὶ τοῦ ἀργύρου [τὰ μέρη][1] τὰ ῥινή-ματα κατ' ἰδίαν μὲν ὄντα μέλανα φαίνεται, σὺν δὲ

130 τῷ ὅλῳ ὡς λευκὰ ὑποπίπτει. καὶ τῆς Ταιναρείας λίθου τὰ μὲν μέρη λευκὰ ὁρᾶται ὅταν λεανθῇ, σὺν δὲ τῇ ὁλοσχερεῖ ξανθὰ φαίνεται. καὶ αἱ ἀπ' ἀλλήλων ἐσκεδασμέναι ψάμμοι τραχεῖαι φαίνον-ται, ὡς σωρὸς δὲ συντεθεῖσαι ἁπαλῶς κινοῦσι τὴν αἴσθησιν. καὶ ὁ ἐλλέβορος λεπτὸς μὲν καὶ χνοώδης προσφερόμενος πνιγμὸν ἐπιφέρει, κριμνώδης δὲ ὢν

131 οὐκέτι. καὶ ὁ οἶνος σύμμετρος μὲν πινόμενος ῥώννυσιν ἡμᾶς, πλείων δὲ λαμβανόμενος παραλύει τὸ σῶμα. καὶ ἡ τροφὴ παραπλησίως παρὰ τὴν ποσότητα διάφορον ἐπιδείκνυται δύναμιν· πολλάκις γοῦν διὰ τὸ πολλὴ προσενεχθῆναι καθαιρεῖ τὸ σῶμα

---

[1] [τὰ μέρη] secl. Mutsch.

[a] For the Stoic ἡγεμονικόν see Introd. p. xxv; for the dispute as to its location cf. Adv. Log. i. 313.

regard as the seat of the " Ruling Principle " [a]—
whether it be the brain or the heart, or in whatever
part of the creature one chooses to locate it. Thus,
according to this Mode also we see that, owing to
our inability to make any statement about the real
nature of external objects, we are compelled to
suspend judgement.

The *Seventh Mode* is that based, as we said, on the 129
quantity and constitution of the underlying objects,
meaning generally by " constitution " the manner of
composition. And it is evident that by this Mode
also we are compelled to suspend judgement concerning the real nature of the objects. Thus, for example,
the filings of a goat's horn appear white when viewed
simply by themselves and without combination, but
when combined in the substance of the horn they
look black. And silver filings appear black when they
are by themselves, but when united to the whole
mass they are sensed as white. And chips of the 130
marble of Taenarum [b] seem white when planed, but
in combination with the whole block they appear
yellow. And pebbles when scattered apart appear
rough, but when combined in a heap they produce
the sensation of softness. And hellebore if applied
in a fine and powdery state produces suffocation, but
not so when it is coarse. And wine strengthens us 131
when drunk in moderate quantity, but when too
much is taken it paralyses the body. So likewise
food exhibits different effects according to the quantity consumed ; for instance, it frequently upsets the
body with indigestion and attacks of purging because

[b] Taenarum was the most southerly promontory of
Laconia ; its marble was yellowish green in colour (like
serpentine).

132 διά τε ἀπεψιῶν καὶ χολερικῶν παθῶν. ἕξομεν
οὖν κἀνταῦθα λέγειν ὁποῖόν ἐστι τοῦ κέρατος
τὸ λεπτὸν καὶ ὁποῖον τὸ ἐκ πολλῶν λεπτομερῶν
συγκείμενον, καὶ ὁποῖος μέν ἐστιν ὁ μικρομερὴς
ἄργυρος ὁποῖος δὲ ὁ ἐκ πολλῶν μικρομερῶν συγ-
κείμενος, καὶ ὁποία μὲν ἡ ἀκαριαία Ταιναρεία
λίθος ὁποία δὲ ἡ ἐκ πολλῶν μικρῶν συγκειμένη,
καὶ ἐπὶ τῶν ψάμμων καὶ τοῦ ἐλλεβόρου καὶ τοῦ
οἴνου καὶ τῆς τροφῆς τὸ πρός τι, τὴν μέντοι
φύσιν τῶν πραγμάτων καθ' ἑαυτὴν οὐκέτι διὰ τὴν
παρὰ τὰς συνθέσεις τῶν φαντασιῶν ἀνωμαλίαν.

133 Καθόλου γὰρ δοκεῖ καὶ τὰ ὠφέλιμα λυπηρὰ
γίνεσθαι παρὰ τὴν κατὰ ποσότητα ἄμετρον αὐτῶν
χρῆσιν, καὶ τὰ βλαβερὰ εἶναι δοκοῦντα ἐν τῷ καθ'
ὑπερβολὴν παραλαμβάνεσθαι ἀκαριαῖα μὴ λυπεῖν.
μαρτυρεῖ δὲ τῷ λόγῳ μάλιστα τὸ κατὰ τὰς ἰατρικὰς
δυνάμεις θεωρούμενον, ἐν αἷς ἡ μὲν πρὸς ἀκρίβειαν
μῖξις τῶν ἁπλῶν φαρμάκων ὠφέλιμον ποιεῖ τὸ
συντεθέν, ῥοπῆς δὲ βραχυτάτης ἐνίοτε παροραθείσης
οὐ μόνον οὐκ ὠφέλιμον ἀλλὰ καὶ βλαβερώτατον
134 καὶ δηλητήριον πολλάκις. οὕτως ὁ κατὰ τὰς
ποσότητας καὶ σκευασίας λόγος συγχεῖ τὴν τῶν
ἐκτὸς ὑποκειμένων ὕπαρξιν. διόπερ εἰκότως ἂν
καὶ οὗτος ὁ τρόπος εἰς ἐποχὴν ἡμᾶς περιάγοι
μὴ δυναμένους εἰλικρινῶς ἀποφήνασθαι περὶ τῆς
φύσεως τῶν ἐκτὸς ὑποκειμένων.

135 Ὄγδοός ἐστι τρόπος ὁ ἀπὸ τοῦ πρός τι, καθ' ὃν
συνάγομεν ὅτι ἐπεὶ πάντα ἐστὶ πρός τι, περὶ τοῦ
τίνα ἐστὶν ἀπολύτως καὶ ὡς πρὸς τὴν φύσιν ἐφέξομεν. ἐκεῖνο δὲ χρὴ γινώσκειν ὅτι ἐνταῦθα,
ὥσπερ καὶ ἐν ἄλλοις, τῷ ἔστι καταχρώμεθα ἀντὶ

of the large quantity taken. Therefore in these cases, too, we shall be able to describe the quality of the shaving of the horn and of the compound made up of many shavings, and that of the particle of silver and of the compound of many particles, and that of the sliver of Taenarean marble and of the compound of many such small pieces, and the relative qualities of the pebbles, the hellebore, the wine and the food,— but when it comes to the independent and real nature of the objects, this we shall be unable to describe because of the divergency in the sense-impressions which is due to the combinations.

As a general rule, it seems that wholesome things 133 become harmful when used in immoderate quantities, and things that seem hurtful when taken to excess cause no harm when in minute quantities. What we observe in regard to the effects of medicines is the best evidence in support of our statement ; for there the exact blending of the simple drugs makes the compound wholesome, but when the slightest over- sight is made in the measuring, as sometimes happens, the compound is not only unwholesome but frequently even most harmful and deleterious. Thus the argu- 134 ment from quantities and compositions causes con- fusion as to the real nature of the external sub- stances. Probably, therefore, this Mode also will bring us round to suspension of judgement, as we are unable to make any absolute statement concerning the real nature of external objects.

The *Eighth Mode* is that based on relativity ; and 135 by it we conclude that, since all things are relative, we shall suspend judgement as to what things are absolutely and really existent. But this point we must notice—that here as elsewhere we use the term

τοῦ φαίνεται, δυνάμει τοῦτο λέγοντες " πρός τι
πάντα φαίνεται." τοῦτο δὲ διχῶς λέγεται, ἅπαξ
μὲν ὡς πρὸς τὸ κρῖνον (τὸ γὰρ ἐκτὸς ὑποκείμενον
καὶ κρινόμενον πρὸς τὸ κρῖνον φαίνεται), καθ'
ἕτερον δὲ τρόπον πρὸς τὰ συνθεωρούμενα, ὡς τὸ
136 δεξιὸν πρὸς τὸ ἀριστερόν. ὅτι δὲ πάντα ἐστὶ πρός
τι, ἐπελογισάμεθα μὲν καὶ ἔμπροσθεν, οἷον κατὰ
τὸ κρῖνον ὅτι πρὸς τόδε τὸ ζῷον καὶ τόνδε τὸν
ἄνθρωπον καὶ τήνδε τὴν αἴσθησιν ἕκαστον φαίνεται,
καὶ πρὸς τοιάνδε περίστασιν, κατὰ δὲ τὰ συνθεωρούμενα ὅτι πρὸς τήνδε τὴν ἐπιμιξίαν καὶ τόνδε
τὸν τρόπον καὶ τὴν σύνθεσιν τήνδε καὶ τὴν ποσότητα καὶ τὴν θέσιν ἕκαστον φαίνεται.

137 Καὶ ἰδίᾳ δὲ ἐνδέχεται συνάγειν ὅτι πάντα ἐστὶ
πρός τι, τόνδε τὸν τρόπον. πότερον διαφέρει τῶν
πρός τι τὰ κατὰ διαφορὰν ἢ οὔ; εἰ μὲν οὐ διαφέρει,
καὶ αὐτὰ πρός τι ἐστίν· εἰ δὲ διαφέρει, ἐπεὶ πᾶν τὸ
διαφέρον πρός τι ἐστίν (λέγεται γὰρ πρὸς ἐκεῖνο
138 οὗ διαφέρει), πρός τί ἐστι τὰ κατὰ διαφοράν. τῶν
τε ὄντων τὰ μέν ἐστιν ἀνωτάτω γένη κατὰ τοὺς
δογματικούς, τὰ δ' ἔσχατα εἴδη, τὰ δὲ γένη καὶ
εἴδη· πάντα δὲ ταῦτά ἐστι πρός τι· πάντα ἄρα ἐστὶ

ᵃ The main point urged here is that no object can be
apprehended in its purity. As perceived it is always conditioned by (1) the physical or mental state of the percipient
("the thing which judges"), and (2) by the "concomitant
percepts" which accompany its emergence into the world of
space and time. As thus conditioned, the object is no longer
"absolute" but "relative."

ᵇ Cf. § 39 supra.

ᶜ Or "have a distinct existence of their own," as opposed
to a merely relative existence. This is a technical term for

" are " for the term " appear," and what we virtually mean is " all things appear relative.[a]" And this statement is twofold, implying, firstly, relation to the thing which judges (for the external object which is judged appears in relation to that thing), and, in a second sense, relation to the accompanying percepts, for instance the right side in relation to the left. Indeed, we have already argued [b] that all things are 136 relative—for example, with respect to the thing which judges, it is in relation to some one particular animal or man or sense that each object appears, and in relation to such and such a circumstance ; and with respect to the concomitant percepts, each object appears in relation to some one particular admixture or mode or combination or quantity or position.

There are also special arguments to prove the 137 relativity of all things, in this way : Do things which exist " differentially " [c] differ from relative things or not ? If they do not differ, then they too are relative ; but if they differ, then, since everything which differs is relative to something (for it has its name from its relation to that from which it differs), things which exist differentially are relative. Again,—of existing 138 things some, according to the Dogmatists,[d] are *summa genera*, others *infimae species*, others both genera and species ; and all these are relative ;

the class of objects which are " self-existent," " absolute," or " independent."

[d] Including the Peripatetics, as well as the Stoics. A *summum genus* (*e.g.* " Being ") may be divided into *genera* (*e.g.* " Animals," " Minerals "), and these sub-divided into *species* (*e.g.* " Men," " Dogs," etc.), down to the *infimae species* (*e.g.* " Negroes ") which cannot be further subdivided. The intermediate species (*e.g.* " Men ") are both *genera* (in relation to their sub-species) and *species* (in relation to higher genera).

πρός τι. ἔτι τῶν ὄντων τὰ μέν ἐστι πρόδηλα τὰ
δὲ ἄδηλα, ὡς αὐτοί φασιν, καὶ σημαίνοντα μὲν
τὰ φαινόμενα, σημαινόμενα δὲ ὑπὸ τῶν φαινομένων τὰ ἄδηλα· ὄψις γὰρ κατ' αὐτοὺς τῶν ἀδήλων
τὰ φαινόμενα. τὸ δὲ σημαῖνον καὶ τὸ σημαινό-
139 μενόν ἐστι πρός τι· πρός τι ἄρα ἐστὶ πάντα. πρὸς
τούτοις τῶν ὄντων τὰ μέν ἐστιν ὅμοια τὰ δὲ ἀνόμοια καὶ τὰ μὲν ἴσα τὰ δὲ ἄνισα· ταῦτα δέ ἐστι
πρός τι· πάντα ἄρα ἐστὶ πρός τι. καὶ ὁ λέγων δὲ
μὴ πάντα εἶναι πρός τι βεβαιοῖ τὸ πάντα εἶναι πρός
τι· καὶ αὐτὸ γὰρ τὸ ⟨μὴ⟩[1] εἶναι πάντα πρός τι πρὸς
ἡμᾶς εἶναι δείκνυσι, καὶ οὐ καθόλου, δι' ὧν ἡμῖν
ἐναντιοῦται.

140 Πλὴν ἀλλ' οὕτω παριστάντων ἡμῶν ὅτι πάντα
ἐστὶ πρός τι, δῆλόν ἐστι λοιπὸν ὅτι ὁποῖόν ἐστιν
ἕκαστον τῶν ὑποκειμένων κατὰ τὴν ἑαυτοῦ φύσιν
καὶ εἰλικρινῶς λέγειν οὐ δυνησόμεθα, ἀλλ' ὁποῖον
φαίνεται ἐν τῷ πρός τι. ἀκολουθεῖ τὸ περὶ τῆς
φύσεως τῶν πραγμάτων δεῖν ἡμᾶς ἐπέχειν.

141 Περὶ δὲ τοῦ κατὰ τὰς συνεχεῖς ἢ σπανίους
συγκυρήσεις τρόπου, ὃν ἔννατον εἶναι λέγομεν τῇ
τάξει, τοιαῦτά τινα διέξιμεν. ὁ ἥλιος πολλῷ δήπου
ἐκπληκτικώτερός ἐστιν ἀστέρος κομήτου· ἀλλ'
ἐπεὶ τὸν μὲν ἥλιον συνεχῶς ὁρῶμεν τὸν δὲ κομήτην
ἀστέρα σπανίως, ἐπὶ μὲν τῷ ἀστέρι ἐκπλησσόμεθα
ὥστε καὶ διοσημείαν αὐτὸν εἶναι δοκεῖν, ἐπὶ δὲ
τῷ ἡλίῳ οὐδαμῶς. ἐὰν μέντοι γε ἐννοήσωμεν
τὸν ἥλιον σπανίως μὲν φαινόμενον σπανίως δὲ

[1] ⟨μὴ⟩ add. Papp.

82

therefore all things are relative. Further, some existing things are " pre-evident," [a] as they say, others
non-evident ; and the apparent things are significant,
but the non-evident signified by the apparent ; for
according to them " the things apparent are the
vision of the non-evident." But the significant and
the signified are relative ; therefore all things are
relative. Moreover, some existent things are similar, 139
others dissimilar, and some equal, others unequal ;
and these are relative ; therefore all things are relative. And even he who asserts that not all things
are relative confirms the relativity of all things, since
by his arguments against us he shows that the very
statement " not all things are relative " is relative to
ourselves, and not universal.

When, however, we have thus established that all 140
things are relative, we are plainly left with the conclusion that we shall not be able to state what is the
nature of each of the objects in its own real purity,
but only what nature it appears to possess in its
relative character. Hence it follows that we must
suspend judgement concerning the real nature of the
objects.

The *Mode* which, as we said, comes *Ninth* in order 141
is based on constancy or rarity of occurrence,
and we shall explain it as follows. The sun is, of
course, much more amazing than a comet ; yet
because we see the sun constantly but the comet
rarely we are so amazed by the comet that we even
regard it as a divine portent, while the sun causes
no amazement at all. If, however, we were to conceive of the sun as appearing but rarely and setting

[a] *i.e.* superlatively, or wholly, manifest. *Cf. Adv. Log.*
ii. 141.

δυόμενον, καὶ πάντα μὲν ἀθρόως φωτίζοντα πάντα
δὲ ἐξαίφνης ἐπισκιάζεσθαι ποιοῦντα, πολλὴν ἔκ-
142 πληξιν ἐν τῷ πράγματι θεωρήσομεν. καὶ ὁ σεισ-
μὸς δὲ οὐχ ὁμοίως θορυβεῖ τούς τε πρῶτον αὐτοῦ
πειρωμένους καὶ τοὺς ἐν ἔθει τούτου γεγενημένους.
πόσην δὲ ἔκπληξιν ἀνθρώπῳ φέρει θάλασσα πρῶτον ὀφθεῖσα. ἀλλὰ καὶ κάλλος σώματος ἀνθρω-
πίνου πρῶτον καὶ ἐξαίφνης θεωρούμενον συγκινεῖ
μᾶλλον ἡμᾶς ἢ εἰ ἐν ἔθει τοῦ ὁρᾶσθαι γένοιτο.
143 καὶ τὰ μὲν σπάνια τίμια εἶναι δοκεῖ, τὰ δὲ
σύντροφα ἡμῖν καὶ εὔπορα οὐδαμῶς. ἐὰν γοῦν
ἐννοήσωμεν τὸ ὕδωρ σπανίζον, πόσῳ ἂν τῶν
τιμίων εἶναι δοκούντων ἁπάντων τιμιώτερον ἡμῖν
φανείη. ἢ ἐὰν ἐνθυμηθῶμεν τὸν χρυσὸν ἁπλῶς
ἐπὶ τῆς γῆς ἐρριμμένον πολὺν παραπλησίως τοῖς
λίθοις, τίνι δόξομεν ἔσεσθαι τοῦτον τίμιον ἢ κατά-
κλειστον οὕτως;

144 Ἐπεὶ οὖν τὰ αὐτὰ πράγματα παρὰ τὰς συνεχεῖς
ἢ σπανίους περιπτώσεις ὁτὲ μὲν ἐκπληκτικὰ ἢ
τίμια ὁτὲ δὲ οὐ τοιαῦτα εἶναι δοκεῖ, ἐπιλογιζόμεθα
ὅτι ὁποῖον μὲν φαίνεται τούτων ἕκαστον μετὰ
συνεχοῦς περιπτώσεως ἢ σπανίας ἴσως δυνησόμεθα λέγειν, ψιλῶς δὲ ὁποῖον ἔστιν ἕκαστον τῶν
ἐκτὸς ὑποκειμένων οὐκ ἐσμὲν δυνατοὶ φάσκειν.
καὶ διὰ τοῦτον οὖν τὸν τρόπον περὶ αὐτῶν ἐπέχομεν.

145 Δέκατός ἐστι τρόπος, ὃς καὶ μάλιστα συνέχει
πρὸς τὰ ἠθικά, ὁ παρὰ τὰς ἀγωγὰς καὶ τὰ ἔθη
καὶ τοὺς νόμους καὶ τὰς μυθικὰς πίστεις καὶ τὰς
δογματικὰς ὑπολήψεις. ἀγωγὴ μὲν οὖν ἐστιν
αἵρεσις βίου ἤ τινος πράγματος περὶ ἕνα ἢ πολλοὺς

rarely, and illuminating everything all at once and throwing everything into shadow suddenly, then we should experience much amazement at the sight. An earthquake also does not cause the same alarm 142 in those who experience it for the first time and those who have grown accustomed to such things. How much amazement, also, does the sea excite in the man who sees it for the first time ! And indeed the beauty of a human body thrills us more at the first sudden view than when it becomes a customary spectacle. Rare things too we count as precious, but not what is familiar to us and easily got. Thus, 143 if we should suppose water to be rare, how much more precious it would appear to us than all the things which are accounted precious ! [a] Or if we should imagine gold to be simply scattered in quantities over the earth like stones, to whom do we suppose it would then be precious and worth hoarding ?

Since then, owing to the frequency or rarity of 144 their occurrence, the same things seem at one time to be amazing or precious and at another time nothing of the sort, we infer that though we shall be able perhaps to say what nature appears to belong to each of these things in virtue of its frequent or rare occurrence, we are not able to state what nature absolutely belongs to each of the external objects. So because of this Mode also we suspend judgement regarding them.

There is a *Tenth Mode*, which is mainly concerned 145 with Ethics, being based on rules of conduct, habits, laws, legendary beliefs, and dogmatic conceptions. A rule of conduct is a choice of a way of life, or of a particular action, adopted by one person

---

[a] *Cf.* Plato, *Euthyd.* 304 B.

γινομένη, οἷον περὶ Διογένην ἢ τοὺς Λάκωνας·
146 νόμος δέ ἐστιν ἔγγραφος συνθήκη παρὰ τοῖς πο-
λιτευομένοις, ἣν ὁ παραβαίνων κολάζεται, ἔθος δὲ
ἢ συνήθεια (οὐ διαφέρει γάρ) πολλῶν ἀνθρώπων
κοινὴ πράγματός τινος παραδοχή, ἣν ὁ παραβὰς
οὐ πάντως κολάζεται, οἷον νόμος ἐστὶ τὸ μὴ
μοιχεύειν, ἔθος δὲ ἡμῖν τὸ μὴ δημοσίᾳ γυναικὶ
147 μίγνυσθαι. μυθικὴ δὲ πίστις ἐστὶ πραγμάτων
ἀγενήτων τε καὶ πεπλασμένων παραδοχή, οἷά
ἐστιν ἄλλα τε καὶ τὰ περὶ τοῦ Κρόνου μυθευόμενα·
ταῦτα γὰρ πολλοὺς εἰς πίστιν ἄγει. δογματικὴ δέ
ἐστιν ὑπόληψις παραδοχὴ πράγματος δι' ἀναλογισ-
μοῦ ἤ τινος ἀποδείξεως κρατύνεσθαι δοκοῦσα, οἷον
ὅτι ἄτομα ἔστι τῶν ὄντων στοιχεῖα ἢ ὁμοιομερῆ ἢ
ἐλάχιστα ἤ τινα ἄλλα.
148   Ἀντιτίθεμεν δὲ τούτων ἕκαστον ὁτὲ μὲν ἑαυτῷ
ὁτὲ δὲ τῶν ἄλλων ἑκάστῳ. οἷον ἔθος μὲν ἔθει
οὕτως. τινὲς τῶν Αἰθιόπων στίζουσι τὰ βρέφη,
ἡμεῖς δ' οὔ· καὶ Πέρσαι μὲν ἀνθοβαφεῖ ἐσθῆτι καὶ
ποδήρει χρῆσθαι νομίζουσιν εὐπρεπὲς εἶναι, ἡμεῖς
δὲ ἀπρεπές· καὶ οἱ μὲν Ἰνδοὶ ταῖς γυναιξὶ δημοσίᾳ
μίγνυνται, οἱ δὲ πλεῖστοι τῶν ἄλλων αἰσχρὸν
149 τοῦτο εἶναι ἡγοῦνται. νόμον δὲ νόμῳ οὕτως ἀντιτίθεμεν. παρὰ μὲν τοῖς Ῥωμαίοις ὁ τῆς πατρῴας
ἀποστὰς οὐσίας οὐκ ἀποδίδωσι τὰ τοῦ πατρὸς
χρέα, παρὰ δὲ τοῖς Ῥοδίοις πάντως ἀποδίδωσιν·
καὶ ἐν μὲν Ταύροις τῆς Σκυθίας νόμος ἦν τοὺς
ξένους τῇ Ἀρτέμιδι καλλιερεῖσθαι, παρὰ δὲ ἡμῖν
150 ἄνθρωπον ἀπείρηται πρὸς ἱερῷ φονεύεσθαι. ἀγω-

---

[a] The Cynic philosopher.
[b] Democritus and Epicurus took the first view, Anaxagoras
the second, Diodorus Cronos the third ; cf. iii. 32.

or many — by Diogenes,[a] for instance, or the 146
Laconians. A law is a written contract amongst the
members of a State, the transgressor of which is
punished. A habit or custom (the terms are equivalent) is the joint adoption of a certain kind of action
by a number of men, the transgressor of which is not
actually punished ; for example, the law proscribes
adultery, and custom with us forbids intercourse
with a woman in public. Legendary belief is the 147
acceptance of unhistorical and fictitious events, such
as, amongst others, the legends about Cronos ; for
these stories win credence with many. Dogmatic
conception is the acceptance of a fact which seems
to be established by analogy or some form of demonstration, as, for example, that atoms are the elements
of existing things, or homoeomeries, or *minima*,[b] or
something else.

And each of these we oppose now to itself, and now 148
to each of the others. For example, we oppose habit
to habit in this way : some of the Ethiopians tattoo
their children, but we do not ; and while the Persians
think it seemly to wear a brightly dyed dress reaching to the feet, we think it unseemly ; and whereas
the Indians have intercourse with their women in
public, most other races regard this as shameful. And 149
law we oppose to law in this way : among the Romans
the man who renounces his father's property does
not pay his father's debts, but among the Rhodians
he always pays them ; and among the Scythian
Tauri[c] it was a law that strangers should be sacrificed
to Artemis, but with us it is forbidden to slay a
human being at the altar. And we oppose rule of 150

[c] *i.e.* inhabitants of the Crimea ; *cf.* Hdt. iv. 103, and
Eurip. *Iphigenia in Tauris.*

γὴν δὲ ἀγωγῇ, ὅταν τὴν Διογένους ἀγωγὴν ἀντιτιθῶμεν τῇ τοῦ Ἀριστίππου ἢ τὴν τῶν Λακώνων
τῇ τῶν Ἰταλῶν. μυθικὴν δὲ πίστιν πίστει μυθικῇ, ὅταν ὅπου μὲν ⟨λέγωμεν⟩[1] τὸν Δία μυθεύε-
σθαι πατέρα ἀνδρῶν τε θεῶν τε ὅπου δὲ τὸν
Ὠκεανόν, λέγοντες

Ὠκεανόν τε θεῶν γένεσιν καὶ μητέρα Τηθύν.

151 δογματικὰς δὲ ὑπολήψεις ἀλλήλαις ἀντιτίθεμεν,
ὅταν λέγωμεν τοὺς μὲν ἓν εἶναι στοιχεῖον ἀποφαίνεσθαι τοὺς δὲ ἄπειρα, καὶ τοὺς μὲν θνητὴν
τὴν ψυχὴν τοὺς δὲ ἀθάνατον, καὶ τοὺς μὲν προνοίᾳ
θεῶν διοικεῖσθαι τὰ καθ᾽ ἡμᾶς τοὺς δὲ ἀπρονοήτως.
152 Τὸ ἔθος δὲ τοῖς ἄλλοις ἀντιτίθεμεν, οἷον νόμῳ
μέν, ὅταν λέγωμεν παρὰ μὲν Πέρσαις ἔθος εἶναι
ἀρρενομιξίαις χρῆσθαι, παρὰ δὲ Ῥωμαίοις ἀπαγο-
ρεύεσθαι νόμῳ τοῦτο πράττειν, καὶ παρ᾽ ἡμῖν μὲν
τὸ μοιχεύειν ἀπειρῆσθαι, παρὰ δὲ Μασσαγέταις
ἀδιαφορίας ἔθει παραδεδόσθαι, ὡς Εὔδοξος ὁ
Κνίδιος ἱστορεῖ ἐν τῷ πρώτῳ τῆς περιόδου, καὶ
παρ᾽ ἡμῖν μὲν ἀπηγορεῦσθαι μητράσι μίγνυσθαι,
παρὰ δὲ τοῖς Πέρσαις ἔθος εἶναι μάλιστα οὕτω
γαμεῖν. καὶ παρ᾽ Αἰγυπτίοις δὲ τὰς ἀδελφὰς
153 γαμοῦσιν, ὃ παρ᾽ ἡμῖν ἀπείρηται νόμῳ. ἀγωγῇ
δὲ ἔθος ἀντιτίθεται, ὅταν οἱ μὲν πολλοὶ ἄνθρωποι
ἀναχωροῦντες μίγνυνται ταῖς ἑαυτῶν γυναιξίν, ὁ
δὲ Κράτης τῇ Ἱππαρχίᾳ δημοσίᾳ· καὶ ὁ μὲν
Διογένης ἀπὸ ἐξωμίδος περιῄει, ἡμεῖς δὲ ὡς

---

[1] ⟨λέγωμεν⟩ add. T.

_____

[a] Homer, _Il._ xiv. 201.

conduct to rule of conduct, as when we oppose the rule of Diogenes to that of Aristippus or that of the Laconians to that of the Italians. And we oppose legendary belief to legendary belief when we say that whereas in one story the father of men and gods is alleged to be Zeus, in another he is Oceanos— " Ocean sire of the gods, and Tethys the mother that bare them."[a] And we oppose dogmatic con- 151 ceptions to one another when we say that some declare that there is one element only, others an infinite number ; some that the soul is mortal, others that it is immortal ; and some that human affairs are controlled by divine Providence, others without Providence.

And we oppose habit to the other things, as for 152 instance to law when we say that amongst the Persians it is the habit to indulge in intercourse with males, but amongst the Romans it is forbidden by law to do so ; and that, whereas with us adultery is forbidden, amongst the Massagetae it is traditionally regarded as an indifferent custom, as Eudoxus of Cnidos[b] relates in the first book of his *Travels* ; and that, whereas intercourse with a mother is forbidden in our country, in Persia it is the general custom to form such marriages ; and also among the Egyptians men marry their sisters, a thing forbidden by law amongst us. And habit is opposed to rule of conduct 153 when, whereas most men have intercourse with their own wives in retirement, Crates[c] did it in public with Hipparchia ; and Diogenes went about with one shoulder bare, whereas we dress in the customary

[b] Flourished about 360 B.C., famed as astronomer, geometer, legislator and physician.
[c] A Cynic philosopher, *circa* 320 B.C. ; *cf.* iii. 24.

154 εἰώθαμεν. μυθικῇ δὲ πίστει, ὡς ὅταν λέγωσιν οἱ
μῦθοι ὅτι ὁ Κρόνος κατήσθιεν αὑτοῦ τὰ τέκνα,
ἔθους ὄντος ἡμῖν προνοεῖσθαι παίδων· καὶ παρ'
ἡμῖν μὲν συνήθεια ὡς ἀγαθοὺς καὶ ἀπαθεῖς κακῶν
σέβειν τοὺς θεούς, τιτρωσκόμενοι δὲ καὶ φθονοῦντες
155 ἀλλήλοις ὑπὸ τῶν ποιητῶν εἰσάγονται. δογματικῇ
δὲ ὑπολήψει, ὅταν ἡμῖν μὲν ἔθος ᾖ παρὰ θεῶν
αἰτεῖν τὰ ἀγαθά, ὁ δὲ Ἐπίκουρος λέγῃ μὴ ἐπι-
στρέφεσθαι ἡμῶν τὸ θεῖον, καὶ ὅταν ὁ μὲν
Ἀρίστιππος ἀδιάφορον ἡγῆται τὸ γυναικείαν ἀμφι-
έννυσθαι στολήν, ἡμεῖς δὲ αἰσχρὸν τοῦτο ἡγώ-
μεθα εἶναι.
156 Ἀγωγὴν δὲ ἀντιτίθεμεν νόμῳ μέν, ὅταν νόμου
ὄντος μὴ ἐξεῖναι τύπτειν ἄνδρα ἐλεύθερον καὶ
εὐγενῆ οἱ παγκρατιασταὶ τύπτωσιν ἀλλήλους διὰ
τὴν ἀγωγὴν τοῦ κατ' αὐτοὺς βίου, καὶ ὅταν
ἀπειρημένου τοῦ ἀνδροφονεῖν οἱ μονομάχοι ἀν-
157 αιρῶσιν ἀλλήλους διὰ τὴν αὐτὴν αἰτίαν. μυθικὴν
δὲ πίστιν ἀγωγῇ ἀντιτίθεμεν, ἐπειδὰν λέγωμεν ὅτι
οἱ μὲν μῦθοι παρὰ τῇ Ὀμφάλῃ τὸν Ἡρακλέα
λέγουσιν

εἴριά τε ξαίνειν καὶ δουλοσύνης ἀνέχεσθαι

καὶ ταῦτα ποιῆσαι ἅπερ οὐδ' ἂν μετρίως προῃρη-
μένος ἐποίησεν ἄν τις, ἡ δὲ ἀγωγὴ τοῦ βίου τοῦ
158 Ἡρακλέους ἦν γενναία. δογματικῇ δὲ ὑπολήψει,
ὅταν οἱ μὲν ἀθληταὶ ὡς ἀγαθοῦ τῆς δόξης ἀντι-
ποιούμενοι ἐπίπονον ἀγωγὴν βίου δι' αὐτὴν ἐπ-
αναιρῶνται, πολλοὶ δὲ τῶν φιλοσόφων φαῦλον εἶναι
159 τὴν δόξαν δογματίζωσιν. τὸν δὲ νόμον ἀντιτίθεμεν
μυθικῇ μὲν πίστει, ὅταν οἱ μὲν ποιηταὶ εἰσάγωσι
τοὺς θεοὺς καὶ μοιχεύοντας καὶ ἀρρενομιξίαις

manner. It is opposed also to legendary belief, as 154
when the legends say that Cronos devoured his own
children, though it is our habit to protect our children;
and whereas it is customary with us to revere the
gods as being good and immune from evil, they are
presented by the poets as suffering wounds and
envying one another. And habit is opposed to 155
dogmatic conception when, whereas it is our habit
to pray to the gods for good things, Epicurus[a]
declares that the Divinity pays no heed to us; and
when Aristippus[b] considers the wearing of feminine
attire a matter of indifference, though we consider
it a disgraceful thing.

And we oppose rule of conduct to law when, 156
though there is a law which forbids the striking of
a free or well-born man, the pancratiasts strike
one another because of the rule of life they follow;
and when, though homicide is forbidden, gladiators
destroy one another for the same reason. And we 157
oppose legendary belief to rule of conduct when we
say that the legends relate that Heracles in the house
of Omphale " toiled at the spinning of wool, endur-
ing slavery's burden,"[c] and did things which no one
would have chosen to do even in a moderate degree,
whereas the rule of life of Heracles was a noble one.
And we oppose rule of conduct to dogmatic concep- 158
tion when, whereas athletes covet glory as something
good and for its sake undertake a toilsome rule of
life, many of the philosophers dogmatically assert
that glory is a worthless thing. And we oppose law 159
to legendary belief when the poets represent the gods
as commiting adultery and practising intercourse with

---

[a] *Cf.* iii. 219. [b] *Cf.* iii. 204.
[c] Homer, *Odyss.* x. 423.

χρωμένους, νόμος δὲ παρ᾽ ἡμῖν κωλύῃ ταῦτα πράτ-
160 τειν, δογματικῇ δὲ ὑπολήψει, ὅταν οἱ μὲν περὶ
Χρύσιππον ἀδιάφορον εἶναι λέγωσι τὸ μητράσιν
ἢ ἀδελφαῖς μίγνυσθαι, ὁ δὲ νόμος ταῦτα κωλύῃ.
161 μυθικὴν δὲ πίστιν δογματικῇ ὑπολήψει ἀντιτίθεμεν,
ὅταν οἱ μὲν ποιηταὶ λέγωσι τὸν Δία κατελθόντα
θνηταῖς γυναιξὶ μίγνυσθαι, παρὰ δὲ τοῖς δογματι-
162 κοῖς ἀδύνατον τοῦτο εἶναι νομίζηται, καὶ ὁ μὲν
ποιητὴς λέγῃ ὅτι Ζεὺς διὰ τὸ πένθος τὸ ἐπὶ Σαρ-
πηδόνι αἱματοέσσας ψεκάδας κατέχευεν ἔραζε,
δόγμα μέντοι φιλοσόφων ἀπαθὲς εἶναι τὸ θεῖον,
καὶ ὅταν τὸν τῶν ἱπποκενταύρων μῦθον ἀναιρῶσιν,
ἀνυπαρξίας παράδειγμα τὸν ἱπποκένταυρον ἡμῖν
φέροντες.
163   Πολλὰ μὲν οὖν καὶ ἄλλα ἐνῆν καθ᾽ ἑκάστην τῶν
προειρημένων ἀντιθέσεων λαμβάνειν παραδείγματα·
ὡς ἐν συντόμῳ δὲ λόγῳ ταῦτα ἀρκέσει. πλὴν
τοσαύτης ἀνωμαλίας πραγμάτων καὶ διὰ τούτου
τοῦ τρόπου δεικνυμένης, ὁποῖον μὲν ἔστι τὸ ὑποκείμενον κατὰ τὴν φύσιν οὐχ ἕξομεν λέγειν, ὁποῖον
δὲ φαίνεται πρὸς τήνδε τὴν ἀγωγὴν ἢ πρὸς τόνδε
τὸν νόμον ἢ πρὸς τόδε τὸ ἔθος καὶ τῶν ἄλλων
ἕκαστον. καὶ διὰ τοῦτον οὖν περὶ τῆς φύσεως
τῶν ἐκτὸς ὑποκειμένων πραγμάτων ἐπέχειν ἡμᾶς
ἀνάγκη. οὕτω μὲν οὖν διὰ τῶν δέκα τρόπων
καταλήγομεν εἰς τὴν ἐποχήν.

males, whereas the law with us forbids such actions ; and we oppose it to dogmatic conception when 160 Chrysippus [a] says that intercourse with mothers or sisters is a thing indifferent, whereas the law forbids such things. And we oppose legendary belief to 161 dogmatic conception when the poets say that Zeus came down and had intercourse with mortal women, but amongst the Dogmatists it is held that such a thing is impossible ; and again, when the poet relates[b] 162 that because of his grief for Sarpedon Zeus " let fall upon the earth great gouts of blood," whereas it is a dogma of the philosophers that the Deity is impassive ; and when these same philosophers demolish the legend of the hippocentaurs, and offer us the hippocentaur as a type of unreality.[c]

We might indeed have taken many other examples 163 in connexion with each of the antitheses above mentioned ; but in a concise account like ours, these will be sufficient. Only, since by means of this Mode also so much divergency is shown to exist in objects, we shall not be able to state what character belongs to the object in respect of its real essence, but only what belongs to it in respect of this particular rule of conduct, or law, or habit, and so on with each of the rest. So because of this Mode also we are compelled to suspend judgement regarding the real nature of external objects. And thus by means of all the Ten Modes we are finally led to suspension of judgement.

[a] See Introd. pp. xxvii-xxviii; *cf.* iii. 205.
[b] Homer, *Il.* xvi. 459.
[c] *Cf.* our use of " chimera " (lion+goat+dragon) for what is fantastic.

SEXTUS EMPIRICUS

164 Οἱ δὲ νεώτεροι σκεπτικοὶ παραδιδόασι τρόπους
τῆς ἐποχῆς πέντε τούσδε, πρῶτον τὸν ἀπὸ τῆς
διαφωνίας, δεύτερον τὸν εἰς ἄπειρον ἐκβάλλοντα,
τρίτον τὸν ἀπὸ τοῦ πρός τι, τέταρτον τὸν ὑπο-
165 θετικόν, πέμπτον τὸν διάλληλον. καὶ ὁ μὲν ἀπὸ
τῆς διαφωνίας ἐστὶ καθ᾽ ὃν περὶ τοῦ προτεθέντος
πράγματος ἀνεπίκριτον στάσιν παρά τε τῷ βίῳ
καὶ παρὰ τοῖς φιλοσόφοις εὑρίσκομεν γεγενημένην,
δι᾽ ἣν οὐ δυνάμενοι αἱρεῖσθαί τι ἢ ἀποδοκιμάζειν
166 καταλήγομεν εἰς ἐποχήν. ὁ δὲ ἀπὸ τῆς εἰς
ἄπειρον ἐκπτώσεως ἐστὶν ἐν ᾧ τὸ φερόμενον εἰς
πίστιν τοῦ προτεθέντος πράγματος πίστεως ἑτέρας
χρῄζειν λέγομεν, κἀκεῖνο ἄλλης, καὶ μέχρις ἀπείρου,
ὡς μὴ ἐχόντων ἡμῶν πόθεν ἀρξόμεθα τῆς κατα-
167 σκευῆς τὴν ἐποχὴν ἀκολουθεῖν. ὁ δὲ ἀπὸ τοῦ
πρός τι, καθὼς προειρήκαμεν, ἐν ᾧ πρὸς μὲν τὸ
κρῖνον καὶ τὰ συνθεωρούμενα τοῖον ἢ τοῖον
φαίνεται τὸ ὑποκείμενον, ὁποῖον δὲ ἔστι πρὸς τὴν
168 φύσιν ἐπέχομεν. ὁ δὲ ἐξ ὑποθέσεως ἔστιν ὅταν
εἰς ἄπειρον ἐκβαλλόμενοι οἱ δογματικοὶ ἀπό τινος
ἄρξωνται ὃ οὐ κατασκευάζουσιν ἀλλ᾽ ἁπλῶς καὶ
ἀναποδείκτως κατὰ συγχώρησιν λαμβάνειν ἀξιοῦ-
169 σιν. ὁ δὲ διάλληλος τρόπος συνίσταται ὅταν τὸ
ὀφεῖλον τοῦ ζητουμένου πράγματος εἶναι βεβαιω-
τικὸν χρείαν ἔχῃ τῆς ἐκ τοῦ ζητουμένου πίστεως·
ἔνθα μηδέτερον δυνάμενοι λαβεῖν πρὸς κατασκευὴν
θατέρου, περὶ ἀμφοτέρων ἐπέχομεν.

---

[a] *i.e.* those posterior to Aenesidemus ; but the reference
here is specially to Agrippa (see Introd. p. xl) ; *cf.* Diog.
Laert. ix. 88.

Chapter XV.—Of the Five Modes

The later Sceptics [a] hand down Five Modes leading 164
to suspension, namely these : the first based on discrepancy, the second on regress *ad infinitum*, the
third on relativity, the fourth on hypothesis, the fifth
on circular reasoning. That based on discrepancy 165
leads us to find that with regard to the object
presented there has arisen both amongst ordinary
people and amongst the philosophers an interminable conflict because of which we are unable either
to choose a thing or reject it, and so fall back
on suspension. The Mode based upon regress *ad* 166
infinitum is that whereby we assert that the thing
adduced as a proof of the matter proposed needs a
further proof, and this again another, and so on *ad
infinitum*, so that the consequence is suspension, as
we possess no starting-point for our argument. The 167
Mode based upon relativity, as we have already said,[b]
is that whereby the object has such or such an appearance in relation to the subject judging and to the
concomitant percepts, but as to its real nature we
suspend judgement. We have the Mode based on 168
hypothesis when the Dogmatists, being forced to
recede *ad infinitum*, take as their starting-point something which they do not establish by argument but
claim to assume as granted simply and without
demonstration. The Mode of circular reasoning is 169
the form used when the proof itself which ought to
establish the matter of inquiry requires confirmation
derived from that matter ; in this case, being unable
to assume either in order to establish the other, we
suspend judgement about both.

[b] See §§ 135 ff.

"Ότι δὲ πᾶν τὸ ζητούμενον εἰς τούτους ἀνάγειν
τοὺς τρόπους ἐνδέχεται, διὰ βραχέων ὑποδείξομεν
170 οὕτως. τὸ προτεθὲν ἤτοι αἰσθητόν ἐστιν ἢ νοητόν,
ὁποῖον δ' ἂν ᾖ, διαπεφώνηται· οἱ μὲν γὰρ τὰ
αἰσθητὰ μόνα φασὶν εἶναι ἀληθῆ, οἱ δὲ μόνα τὰ
νοητά, οἱ δὲ τινὰ μὲν αἰσθητὰ τινὰ δὲ νοητά.
πότερον οὖν ἐπικριτὴν εἶναι φήσουσι τὴν διαφωνίαν ἢ ἀνεπίκριτον; εἰ μὲν ἀνεπίκριτον, ἔχομεν
ὅτι δεῖ ἐπέχειν· περὶ γὰρ τῶν ἀνεπικρίτως δια-
φωνουμένων οὐχ οἷόν τέ ἐστιν ἀποφαίνεσθαι. εἰ δὲ
171 ἐπικριτήν, πόθεν ἐπικριθήσεται πυνθανόμεθα. οἷον
τὸ αἰσθητόν (ἐπὶ τούτου γὰρ προτέρου στήσομεν
τὸν λόγον) πότερον ὑπὸ αἰσθητοῦ ἢ ὑπὸ νοητοῦ;
εἰ μὲν γὰρ ὑπὸ αἰσθητοῦ, ἐπεὶ περὶ τῶν αἰσθητῶν
ζητοῦμεν, καὶ ἐκεῖνο ἄλλου δεήσεται πρὸς πίστιν.
εἰ δὲ κἀκεῖνο αἰσθητὸν ἔσται, πάλιν καὶ αὐτὸ ἄλλου
δεήσεται τοῦ πιστώσοντος, καὶ τοῦτο μέχρις
172 ἀπείρου. εἰ δὲ ὑπὸ νοητοῦ ἐπικρίνεσθαι δεήσει τὸ
αἰσθητόν, ἐπεὶ καὶ τὰ νοητὰ διαπεφώνηται, δεήσεται καὶ τοῦτο νοητὸν ὂν κρίσεώς τε καὶ πίστεως.
πόθεν οὖν πιστωθήσεται; εἰ μὲν ὑπὸ νοητοῦ, εἰς
ἄπειρον ἐκπεσεῖται ὁμοίως· εἰ δ' ὑπὸ αἰσθητοῦ,
ἐπεὶ πρὸς μὲν τὴν πίστιν τοῦ αἰσθητοῦ παρελήφθη
νοητὸν πρὸς δὲ τὴν τοῦ νοητοῦ πίστιν αἰσθητόν, ὁ
διάλληλος εἰσάγεται τρόπος.
173 Εἰ δὲ ταῦτα φεύγων, ὁ προσδιαλεγόμενος ἡμῖν

ᵃ Of these views the first was maintained, *e.g.* by Protagoras and Epicurus, the second by Plato and Democritus,
the third by Peripatetics and Stoics.

ᵇ Lit. "the through-one-another mode" (of reasoning).
This is the fallacy known as *circulus in probando*, by which

That every matter of inquiry admits of being brought under these Modes we shall show briefly in this way. The matter proposed is either a sense- 170 object or a thought-object, but whichever it is, it is an object of controversy ; for some say that only sensibles are true, others only intelligibles, others that some sensible and some intelligible objects are true.[a] Will they then assert that the controversy can or cannot be decided? If they say it cannot, we have it granted that we must suspend judgement ; for concerning matters of dispute which admit of no decision it is impossible to make an assertion. But if they say that it can be decided, we ask by what is it to be decided. For example, in the case of the sense- 171 object (for we shall base our argument on it first), is it to be decided by a sense-object or a thought-object? For if they say by a sense-object, since we are inquiring about sensibles that object itself also will require another to confirm it ; and if that too is to be a sense-object, it likewise will require another for its confirmation, and so on *ad infinitum.* And if the sense-object shall have to be decided by 172 a thought-object, then, since thought-objects also are controverted, this being an object of thought will need examination and confirmation. Whence then will it gain confirmation ? If from an intelligible object, it will suffer a similar regress *ad infinitum* ; and if from a sensible object, since an intelligible was adduced to establish the sensible and a sensible to establish the intelligible, the Mode of circular reasoning [b] is brought in.

If, however, our disputant, by way of escape from 173

each of two propositions is used in turn to prove the truth of the other.

κατὰ συγχώρησιν καὶ ἀναποδείκτως ἀξιώσειε λαμβάνειν τι πρὸς ἀπόδειξιν τῶν ἑξῆς, ὁ ὑποθετικὸς
εἰσάγεται τρόπος, ἄπορος ὑπάρχων. εἰ μὲν γὰρ
ὁ ὑποτιθέμενος πιστός ἐστιν, ἡμεῖς ἀεὶ τὸ ἀντικείμενον ὑποτιθέμενοι οὐκ ἐσόμεθα ἀπιστότεροι.
καὶ εἰ μὲν ἀληθές τι ὑποτίθεται ὁ ὑποτιθέμενος,
ὕποπτον αὐτὸ ποιεῖ, καθ᾽ ὑπόθεσιν αὐτὸ λαμβάνων
ἀλλὰ μὴ μετὰ κατασκευῆς· εἰ δὲ ψεῦδος, σαθρὰ
174 ἔσται ἡ ὑποβάθρα τῶν κατασκευαζομένων. καὶ εἰ
μὲν ἀνύει τι τὸ ὑποτίθεσθαι πρὸς πίστιν, αὐτὸ τὸ
ζητούμενον ὑποτιθέσθω, καὶ μὴ ἕτερόν τι δι᾽ οὗ
δὴ κατασκευάσει τὸ πρᾶγμα περὶ οὗ ὁ λόγος· εἰ
δὲ ἄτοπόν ἐστι τὸ ὑποτίθεσθαι τὸ ζητούμενον,
ἄτοπον ἔσται καὶ τὸ ὑποτίθεσθαι τὸ ἐπαναβεβηκός.
175 Ὅτι δὲ καὶ πρός τί ἐστι πάντα τὰ αἰσθητά,
δῆλον· ἔστι γὰρ πρὸς τοὺς αἰσθανομένους. φανερὸν
οὖν ὅτι ὅπερ ἂν ἡμῖν προτεθῇ πρᾶγμα αἰσθητόν,
εἰς τοὺς πέντε τρόπους ἀνάγειν τοῦτο εὐμαρές
ἐστιν. ὁμοίως δὲ καὶ περὶ τοῦ νοητοῦ ἐπιλογιζόμεθα. εἰ μὲν γὰρ ἀνεπικρίτως διαπεφωνῆσθαι
λέγοιτο, δοθήσεται ἡμῖν τὸ δεῖν ἐπέχειν περὶ
176 αὐτοῦ. εἰ δὲ ἐπικριθήσεται ἡ διαφωνία, εἰ μὲν
διὰ νοητοῦ, εἰς ἄπειρον ἐκβαλοῦμεν, εἰ δὲ ὑπὸ
αἰσθητοῦ, εἰς τὸν διάλληλον· τὸ γὰρ αἰσθητὸν
πάλιν διαφωνούμενον, καὶ μὴ δυνάμενον δι᾽ αὑτοῦ
ἐπικρίνεσθαι διὰ τὴν εἰς ἄπειρον ἔκπτωσιν, τοῦ
νοητοῦ δεήσεται ὥσπερ καὶ τὸ νοητὸν τοῦ αἰσθητοῦ.

---

[a] Lit. "without exit (or way of escape)"; *i.e.* it hope-
lessly entangles the opponent.
[b] *i.e.* the super-ordinate, or more universal, proposition.

this conclusion, should claim to assume as granted and without demonstration some postulate for the demonstration of the next steps of his argument, then the Mode of hypothesis will be brought in, which allows no escape.[a] For if the author of the hypothesis is worthy of credence, we shall be no less worthy of credence every time that we make the opposite hypothesis. Moreover, if the author of the hypothesis assumes what is true he causes it to be suspected by assuming it by hypothesis rather than after proof; while if it is false, the foundation of his argument will be rotten. Further, 174 if hypothesis conduces at all to proof, let the subject of inquiry itself be assumed and not some other thing which is merely a means to establish the actual subject of the argument; but if it is absurd to assume the subject of inquiry, it will also be absurd to assume that upon which it depends.[b]

It is also plain that all sensibles are relative; for 175 they are relative to those who have the sensations. Therefore it is apparent that whatever sensible object is presented can easily be referred to one of the Five Modes. And concerning the intelligible object we argue similarly. For if it should be said that it is a matter of unsettled controversy, the necessity of our suspending judgement will be granted. And if, on 176 the other hand, the controversy admits of decision, then if the decision rests on an intelligible object we shall be driven to the regress *ad infinitum*, and to circular reasoning if it rests on a sensible; for since the sensible again is controverted and cannot be decided by means of itself because of the regress *ad infinitum*, it will require the intelligible object, just as also the intelligible will require the sensible. For 177

99

SEXTUS EMPIRICUS

177 διὰ ταῦτα δὲ ἐξ ὑποθέσεως ὁ λαμβάνων τι πάλιν
ἄτοπος ἔσται. ἀλλὰ καὶ πρός τί ἐστι τὰ νοητά·
πρὸς γὰρ τὸν νοοῦντα λέγεται, καὶ εἰ ἦν τῇ φύσει
τοιοῦτον ὁποῖον λέγεται, οὐκ ἂν διεφωνήθη.
ἀνήχθη οὖν καὶ τὸ νοητὸν εἰς τοὺς πέντε τρόπους,
διόπερ ἀνάγκη περὶ τοῦ προτεθέντος πράγματος
πάντως ἡμᾶς ἐπέχειν.

Τοιοῦτοι μὲν καὶ οἱ παρὰ τοῖς νεωτέροις παρα-
διδόμενοι πέντε τρόποι· οὓς ἐκτίθενται οὐκ ἐκ-
βάλλοντες τοὺς δέκα τρόπους, ἀλλ᾽ ὑπὲρ τοῦ
ποικιλώτερον καὶ διὰ τούτων σὺν ἐκείνοις ἐλέγχειν
τὴν τῶν δογματικῶν προπέτειαν.

ιϛ΄.—ΤΙΝΕΣ ΟΙ ΔΥΟ ΤΡΟΠΟΙ

178 Παραδιδόασι δὲ καὶ δύο τρόπους ἐποχῆς
ἑτέρους· ἐπεὶ γὰρ πᾶν τὸ καταλαμβανόμενον ἤτοι
ἐξ ἑαυτοῦ καταλαμβάνεσθαι δοκεῖ ἢ ἐξ ἑτέρου
⟨ὑπομιμνήσκοντες ὅτι οὔτε ἐξ ἑαυτοῦ τι οὔτε ἐξ
ἑτέρου⟩[1] καταλαμβάνεται, τὴν περὶ πάντων ἀπορίαν
εἰσάγειν δοκοῦσιν. καὶ ὅτι μὲν οὐδὲν ἐξ ἑαυτοῦ
καταλαμβάνεται, φασί, δῆλον ἐκ τῆς γεγενημένης
παρὰ τοῖς φυσικοῖς περί τε τῶν αἰσθητῶν καὶ τῶν
νοητῶν ἁπάντων, οἶμαι, διαφωνίας, ἣ δὴ ἀνεπίκριτός ἐστι μὴ δυναμένων ἡμῶν μήτε αἰσθητῷ
μήτε νοητῷ κριτηρίῳ χρῆσθαι διὰ τὸ πᾶν, ὅπερ
179 ἂν λάβωμεν, ἄπιστον εἶναι διαπεφωνημένον. διὰ

---

[1] ⟨ὑπομ. . . . ἑτέρου⟩ add. T.

[a] For this final reduction of the " Tropes " to two—arguing
against the possibility of either (1) immediate or (2) mediate
certitude—see Introd. p. xli.

[b] " Physics," as a branch of philosophy, was treated of by
all the Schools alluded to in § 170 *supra*, which are specially
here in mind.

these reasons, again, he who assumes anything by hypothesis will be acting illogically. Moreover, objects of thought, or intelligibles, are relative ; for they are so named on account of their relation to the person thinking, and if they had really possessed the nature they are said to possess, there would have been no controversy about them. Thus the intelligible also is referred to the Five Modes, so that in all cases we are compelled to suspend judgement concerning the object presented.

Such then are the Five Modes handed down amongst the later Sceptics ; but they propound these not by way of superseding the Ten Modes but in order to expose the rashness of the Dogmatists with more variety and completeness by means of the Five in conjunction with the Ten.

Chapter XVI.—Of the Two Modes

They hand down also *Two* other *Modes* leading 178 to suspension of judgement.[a] Since every object of apprehension seems to be apprehended either through itself or through another object, by showing that nothing is apprehended either through itself or through another thing, they introduce doubt, as they suppose, about everything. That nothing is apprehended through itself is plain, they say, from the controversy which exists amongst the physicists [b] regarding, I imagine, all things, both sensibles and intelligibles ; which controversy admits of no settlement because we can neither employ a sensible nor an intelligible criterion, since every criterion we may adopt is controverted and therefore discredited. And the reason why they do not allow 179

δὲ τοῦτο οὐδ' ἐξ ἑτέρου τι καταλαμβάνεσθαι συγ-
χωροῦσιν. εἰ μὲν γὰρ τὸ ἐξ οὗ τι καταλαμβάνεται
ἀεὶ ἐξ ἑτέρου καταλαμβάνεσθαι δεήσει, εἰς τὸν
διάλληλον ἢ τὸν ἄπειρον ἐμβάλλουσι τρόπον. εἰ
δὲ βούλοιτό τις λαβεῖν ὡς ἐξ ἑαυτοῦ καταλαμ-
βανόμενόν τι ἐξ οὗ τι καταλαμβάνεται[1] ἕτερον,
ἀντιπίπτει τὸ μηδὲν ἐξ ἑαυτοῦ καταλαμβάνεσθαι
διὰ τὰ προειρημένα. τὸ δὲ μαχόμενον πῶς ἂν
δύναιτο καταληφθῆναι ⟨ἢ⟩[2] ἀφ' ἑαυτοῦ ἢ ἀφ'
ἑτέρου, ἀπορῦμεν, τοῦ κριτηρίου τῆς ἀληθείας ἢ
τῆς καταλήψεως μὴ φαινομένου, σημείων δὲ καὶ
δίχα ἀποδείξεως διατρεπομένων, καθάπερ ἐν τοῖς
ἑξῆς εἰσόμεθα.

Τοσαῦτα μὲν οὖν καὶ περὶ τῶν τρόπων τῆς
ἐποχῆς ἐπὶ τοῦ παρόντος ἀρκέσει λελέχθαι.

ΙΖ'.—ΤΙΝΕΣ ΤΡΟΠΟΙ ΤΗΣ ΤΩΝ ΑΙΤΙΟΛΟΓΙΚΩΝ ΑΝΑΤΡΟΠΗΣ

180 Ὥσπερ δὲ τοὺς τρόπους τῆς ἐποχῆς παραδίδομεν,
οὕτω καὶ τρόπους ἐκτίθενταί τινες καθ' οὓς ἐν ταῖς
κατὰ μέρος αἰτιολογίαις διαποροῦντες ἐφιστῶμεν
τοὺς δογματικοὺς διὰ τὸ μάλιστα ἐπὶ ταύταις
αὐτοὺς μέγα φρονεῖν. καὶ δὴ Αἰνησίδημος ὀκτὼ
τρόπους παραδίδωσι καθ' οὓς οἴεται πᾶσαν δογματικὴν αἰτιολογίαν ὡς μοχθηρὰν ἐλέγχων ἀποφή-
181 νασθαι, ὧν πρῶτον μὲν εἶναί φησι καθ' ὃν τρόπον
τὸ τῆς αἰτιολογίας γένος ἐν ἀφανέσιν ἀναστρεφό-
μενον οὐχ ὁμολογουμένην ἔχει τὴν ἐκ τῶν φαινο-

---

[1] καταλαμβάνεται TM : λαμβάνειν mss., Bekk.
[2] ⟨ἢ⟩ add. T.

---

[a] See ii. 96 ff.

that anything is apprehended through something else is this : If that through which an object is apprehended must always itself be apprehended through some other thing, one is involved in a process of circular reasoning or in regress *ad infinitum*. And if, on the other hand, one should choose to assume that the thing through which another object is apprehended is itself apprehended through itself, this is refuted by the fact that, for the reasons already stated, nothing is apprehended through itself. But as to how what conflicts with itself can possibly be apprehended either through itself or through some other thing we remain in doubt, so long as the criterion of truth or of apprehension is not apparent, and signs, even apart from demonstration, are rejected, as we shall discover in our next Book.[a]

For the present, however, it will suffice to have said thus much concerning the Modes leading to suspension of judgement.

CHAPTER XVII.—OF THE MODES BY WHICH THE AETIOLOGISTS ARE CONFUTED

Just as we teach the traditional Modes leading to 180 suspense of judgement, so likewise some Sceptics propound Modes by which we express doubt about the particular " aetiologies," or theories of causation, and thus pull up the Dogmatists because of the special pride they take in these theories. Thus Aenesidemus furnishes us with *Eight Modes* by which, as he thinks, he tests and exposes the unsoundness of every dogmatic theory of causation. Of these the First, he 181 says, is that which shows that, since aetiology as a whole deals with the non-apparent, it is unconfirmed

μένων ἐπιμαρτύρησιν· δεύτερον δὲ καθ᾽ ὃν πολλάκις εὐεπιφορίας οὔσης δαψιλοῦς ὥστε πολυτρόπως αἰτιολογῆσαι τὸ ζητούμενον, καθ᾽ ἕνα μόνον τρό-
182 πον τοῦτό τινες αἰτιολογοῦσιν· τρίτον καθ᾽ ὃν τῶν τεταγμένως γινομένων αἰτίας ἀποδιδόασιν οὐδεμίαν τάξιν ἐπιφαινούσας· τέταρτον καθ᾽ ὃν τὰ φαινόμενα λαβόντες ὡς γίνεται, καὶ τὰ μὴ φαινόμενα νομί-ζουσιν ὡς γίνεται κατειληφέναι, τάχα μὲν ὁμοίως τοῖς φαινομένοις τῶν ἀφανῶν ἐπιτελουμένων, τάχα
183 δ᾽ οὐχ ὁμοίως ἀλλ᾽ ἰδιαζόντως· πέμπτον καθ᾽ ὃν πάντες ὡς ἔπος εἰπεῖν κατὰ τὰς ἰδίας τῶν στοι-χείων ὑποθέσεις ἀλλ᾽ οὐ κατά τινας κοινὰς καὶ ὁμολογουμένας ἐφόδους αἰτιολογοῦσιν· ἕκτον καθ᾽ ὃν πολλάκις τὰ μὲν φωρατὰ ταῖς ἰδίαις ὑποθέσεσι παραλαμβάνουσιν, τὰ δὲ ἀντιπίπτοντα καὶ τὴν
184 ἴσην ἔχοντα πιθανότητα παραπέμπουσιν· ἕβδομον καθ᾽ ὃν πολλάκις ἀποδιδόασιν αἰτίας οὐ μόνον τοῖς φαινομένοις ἀλλὰ καὶ ταῖς ἰδίαις ὑποθέσεσι μαχο-μένας· ὄγδοον καθ᾽ ὃν πολλάκις ὄντων ἀπόρων ὁμοίως τῶν τε φαίνεσθαι δοκούντων καὶ τῶν ἐπι-ζητουμένων, ἐκ τῶν ὁμοίως ἀπόρων περὶ τῶν
185 ὁμοίως ἀπόρων ποιοῦνται τὰς διδασκαλίας. οὐκ ἀδύνατον δέ φησι καὶ κατά τινας ἐπιμίκτους τρό-πους, ἠρτημένους ἐκ τῶν προειρημένων, διαπίπτειν ἐνίους ἐν ταῖς αἰτιολογίαις.

Τάχα δ᾽ ἂν καὶ οἱ πέντε τρόποι τῆς ἐποχῆς ἀπαρ-κοῦσι πρὸς τὰς αἰτιολογίας. ἤτοι γὰρ σύμφωνον πάσαις ταῖς κατὰ φιλοσοφίαν αἱρέσεσι καὶ τῇ

ᵃ See §§ 164 ff. supra.

by any agreed evidence derived from appearances. The Second Mode shows how often, when there is ample scope for ascribing the object of investigation to a variety of causes, some of them account for it in one way only. The Third shows how to orderly 182 events they assign causes which exhibit no order. The Fourth shows how, when they have grasped the way in which appearances occur, they assume that they have also apprehended how non-apparent things occur, whereas, though the non-apparent may possibly be realized in a similar way to the appearances, possibly they may not be realized in a similar way but in a peculiar way of their own. In the Fifth Mode it 183 is shown how practically all these theorists assign causes according to their own particular hypotheses about the elements, and not according to any commonly agreed methods. In the Sixth it is shown how they frequently admit only such facts as can be explained by their own theories, and dismiss facts which conflict therewith though possessing equal probability. The Seventh shows how they 184 often assign causes which conflict not only with appearances but also with their own hypotheses. The Eighth shows that often, when there is equal doubt about things seemingly apparent and things under investigation, they base their doctrine about things equally doubtful upon things equally doubtful. Nor is it impossible, he adds, that the overthrow of 185 some of their theories of causation should be referred to certain mixed Modes which are dependent on the foregoing.

Possibly, too, the Five Modes of suspension *a* may suffice as against the aetiologies. For if a person propounds a cause, it will either be or not be in accord

SEXTUS EMPIRICUS

σκέψει καὶ τοῖς φαινομένοις αἰτίαν ἐρεῖ τις ἢ οὔ.
καὶ σύμφωνον μὲν ἴσως οὐκ ἐνδέχεται· τά τε γὰρ
186 φαινόμενα καὶ τὰ ἄδηλα πάντα διαπεφώνηται. εἰ
δὲ διαφωνεῖ, ἀπαιτηθήσεται καὶ ταύτης τὴν αἰτίαν,
καὶ φαινομένην μὲν φαινομένης ἢ ἄδηλον ἀδήλου
λαμβάνων εἰς ἄπειρον ἐκπεσεῖται, ἐναλλὰξ δὲ
αἰτιολογῶν εἰς τὸν διάλληλον. ἱστάμενος δέ που,
ἢ ὅσον ἐπὶ τοῖς εἰρημένοις λέξει τὴν αἰτίαν συνεστάναι, καὶ εἰσάγει τὸ πρός τι, ἀναιρῶν τὸ πρὸς
τὴν φύσιν, ἢ ἐξ ὑποθέσεώς τι λαμβάνων ἐπι-
σχεθήσεται. ἔστιν οὖν καὶ διὰ τούτων ἐλέγχειν
ἴσως τὴν τῶν δογματικῶν ἐν ταῖς αἰτιολογίαις
προπέτειαν.

ΙΗ΄.—ΠΕΡΙ ΤΩΝ ΣΚΕΠΤΙΚΩΝ ΦΩΝΩΝ

187 Ἐπεὶ δὲ ἑκάστῳ χρώμενοι τούτων τε καὶ τῶν
τῆς ἐποχῆς τρόπων ἐπιφθεγγόμεθα φωνάς τινας
τῆς σκεπτικῆς διαθέσεως καὶ τοῦ περὶ ἡμᾶς
πάθους μηνυτικάς, οἷον λέγοντες " οὐ μᾶλλον "
" οὐδὲν ὁριστέον " καὶ ἄλλας τινάς, ἀκόλουθον ἂν
εἴη καὶ περὶ τούτων ἑξῆς διαλαβεῖν. ἀρξώμεθα
δὲ ἀπὸ τῆς " οὐ μᾶλλον."

with all the philosophical systems and with Scepticism and with appearances. Probably, however, it is impracticable to propound a cause in accord with all these, since all things, whether apparent or non-evident, are matters of controversy. But if, on the 186 other hand, the cause propounded be not in accord therewith, the theorist will be asked in turn for the cause of this cause, and if he assumes an apparent cause for an apparent, or a non-evident for a non-evident, he will be involved in the regress *ad infinitum*, or reduced to arguing in a circle if he grounds each cause in turn on another. And if at any point he makes a stand, either he will state that the cause is well-grounded so far as relates to the previous admissions, thus introducing relativity and destroying its claim to absolute reality, or he will make some assumption *ex hypothesi* and will be stopped by us. So by these Modes also it is, no doubt, possible to expose the rashness of the Dogmatists in their aetiologies.

Chapter XVIII.—Of the Sceptic Expressions or Formulae

And because when we make use of these Modes 187 and those which lead to suspension of judgement we give utterance to certain expressions [a] indicative of our sceptical attitude and tone of mind—such as "Not more," "Nothing must be determined," and others of the kind—it will be our next task to discuss these in order. So let us begin with the expression "Not more."

[a] *Cf.* §§ 14, 15 *supra.*

SEXTUS EMPIRICUS

ΙΘ΄.—ΠΕΡΙ ΤΗΣ "ΟΥ ΜΑΛΛΟΝ" ΦΩΝΗΣ

188 Ταύτην τοίνυν ὀτὲ μὲν ὡς ἔφην προφερόμεθα, ὀτὲ δὲ οὕτως "οὐδὲν μᾶλλον"· οὐ γάρ, ὥς τινες ὑπολαμβάνουσι, τὴν μὲν "οὐ μᾶλλον" ἐν ταῖς εἰδικαῖς ζητήσεσι παραλαμβάνομεν, τὴν δὲ "οὐδὲν μᾶλλον" ἐν ταῖς γενικαῖς, ἀλλ᾽ ἀδιαφόρως τήν τε "οὐ μᾶλλον" καὶ τὴν "οὐδὲν μᾶλλον" προφερόμεθα, καὶ νῦν ὡς περὶ μιᾶς διαλεξόμεθα. ἔστι μὲν οὖν αὕτη ἡ φωνὴ ἐλλιπής. ὡς γὰρ ὅταν λέγωμεν διπλῆ, δυνάμει φαμὲν ἑστία διπλῆ, καὶ ὅταν λέγωμεν πλατεῖα, δυνάμει λέγομεν πλατεῖα ὁδός,[1] οὕτως ὅταν εἴπωμεν "οὐ μᾶλλον," δυνάμει φαμὲν
189 "οὐ μᾶλλον τόδε ἢ τόδε, ἄνω κάτω." τινὲς μέντοι τῶν σκεπτικῶν παραλαμβάνουσιν ἀντὶ [τοῦ πύσματος][2] τοῦ οὗ τὸ τί μᾶλλον τόδε ἢ τόδε, τὸ τί παραλαμβάνοντες νῦν ἀντὶ αἰτίας, ἵν᾽ ἦ τὸ λεγόμενον "διὰ τί μᾶλλον τόδε ἢ τόδε;" σύνηθες δέ ἐστι καὶ πύσμασιν ἀντὶ ἀξιωμάτων χρῆσθαι, οἷον

τίς τὸν Διὸς σύλλεκτρον οὐκ οἶδε βροτῶν;

καὶ ἀξιώμασιν ἀντὶ πυσμάτων, οἷον "ζητῶ ποῦ οἰκεῖ Δίων" καὶ "πυνθάνομαι τίνος ἕνεκα χρὴ θαυμάζειν ἄνδρα ποιητήν." ἀλλὰ καὶ τὸ τί ἀντὶ τοῦ διὰ τί παραλαμβάνεται παρὰ Μενάνδρῳ·

τί γὰρ ἐγὼ κατελειπόμην;

190 δηλοῖ δὲ τὸ "οὐ μᾶλλον τόδε ἢ τόδε" καὶ πάθος

[1] πλατεῖα ... πλατεῖα ὁδός Diels: πλατεῖαν ... πλατεῖαν ὁδόν MSS., Bekk.
[2] [τοῦ πύσματος] del. ego.

[a] *i.e.* (perhaps) a two-storied house (taking ἑστία as meaning οἰκία). Fabric. proposed ἐσθής, διπλῆ then being = διπλοῖς, "a double cloak." πλατεῖα, "square," lit. "broad, open, place."

108

CHAPTER XIX.—OF THE EXPRESSION " NOT MORE "

This expression, then, we sometimes enunciate 188
in the form I have stated but sometimes in the form
" Nowise more." For we do not, as some suppose,
adopt the form " Not more " in specific inquiries
and " Nowise more " in generic inquiries, but we
enunciate both " Not more " and " Nowise more " indifferently, and we shall discuss them now as identical
expressions. This expression, then, is elliptical. For
just as when we say " a double " we are implicitly
saying " a double hearth," [a] and when we say " a
square " we are implicitly saying " a square road-
way," so when we say " Not more " we are implicitly
saying " Not this more than that, up than down."
Some of the Sceptics, however, in place of the " Not " 189
adopt the form " (For) what this more than that,"
taking the " what " to denote, in this case, cause,
so that the meaning is " For what reason this more
than that ? " [b] And it is a common practice to use
questions instead of assertions, as for example—" The
bride of Zeus, what mortal knows her not ? " [c] And
also assertions in the place of questions ; for instance
—" I am inquiring where Dion lives," and " I ask
you what reason there is for showing surprise at a
poet." And further, the use of " What " instead of
" For what reason " is found in Menander,[d] " (For)
what was I left behind ? " And the expression " Not 190
more this than that" indicates also our feeling, where-

---

[b] The τί, here substituted for οὐ, is capable of meaning
either "what" (or "in what respect") or "why," "for what
cause or reason" (= διὰ τί). Thus τί gives an interrogative
form (πύσμα) to the formula, as distinct from the affirmative
form (ἀξίωμα) with οὐ.

[c] Eurip. *Herc. Fur.* 1.   [d] *Fragm.* 900 (Kock).

ἡμέτερον, καθ' ὃ διὰ τὴν ἰσοσθένειαν τῶν ἀντικειμένων πραγμάτων εἰς ἀρρεψίαν καταλήγομεν,
ἰσοσθένειαν¹ μὲν λεγόντων ἡμῶν τὴν ⟨ἰσότητα
τὴν⟩² κατὰ τὸ φαινόμενον ἡμῖν πιθανόν, ἀντικείμενα δὲ κοινῶς τὰ μαχόμενα, ἀρρεψίαν δὲ τὴν πρὸς
μηδέτερον συγκατάθεσιν.

191 Ἡ γοῦν "οὐδὲν μᾶλλον" φωνὴ κἂν ἐμφαίνῃ
χαρακτῆρα συγκαταθέσεως ἢ ἀρνήσεως, ἡμεῖς οὐχ
οὕτως αὐτῇ χρώμεθα, ἀλλ' ἀδιαφόρως αὐτὴν παραλαμβάνομεν καὶ καταχρηστικῶς, ἤτοι ἀντὶ πύσ-
ματος ἢ ἀντὶ τοῦ λέγειν "ἀγνοῶ τίνι μὲν τούτων
χρὴ συγκατατίθεσθαι τίνι δὲ μὴ συγκατατίθεσθαι."
πρόκειται ἡμῖν δηλῶσαι τὸ φαινόμενον ἡμῖν· κατὰ
δὲ τὴν φωνὴν δι' ἧς αὐτὸ δηλοῦμεν ἀδιαφοροῦμεν.
κἀκεῖνο δὲ χρὴ γινώσκειν ὅτι προφερόμεθα τὴν
"οὐδὲν μᾶλλον" φωνὴν οὐ διαβεβαιούμενοι περὶ
τοῦ πάντως ὑπάρχειν αὐτὴν ἀληθῆ καὶ βεβαίαν,
ἀλλὰ κατὰ τὸ φαινόμενον ἡμῖν καὶ περὶ αὐτῆς
λέγοντες.

Κ'.—ΠΕΡΙ ΑΦΑΣΙΑΣ

192 Περὶ δὲ τῆς ἀφασίας λέγομεν τάδε. φάσις
καλεῖται διχῶς, κοινῶς τε καὶ ἰδίως, κοινῶς μὲν
ἡ δηλοῦσα θέσιν ἢ ἄρσιν φωνή, οἷον "ἡμέρα ἔστιν,
οὐχ ἡμέρα ἔστιν," ἰδίως δὲ ἡ δηλοῦσα θέσιν μόνον,
καθ' ὃ σημαινόμενον τὰ ἀποφατικὰ οὐ καλοῦσι
φάσεις. ἡ οὖν ἀφασία ἀπόστασίς ἐστι τῆς κοινῶς
λεγομένης φάσεως, ᾗ ὑποτάσσεσθαι λέγομεν τήν
τε κατάφασιν καὶ τὴν ἀπόφασιν, ὡς εἶναι ἀφασίαν

¹ ἰσοσθένειαν Papp.: ἰσότητα mss., Bekk.
² ⟨ἰσότητα τὴν⟩ add. Papp.

by we come to end in equipoise because of the equipollence of the opposed objects; and by "equipollence" we mean equality in respect of what seems probable to us, and by "opposed" we mean in general conflicting, and by "equipoise"[a] refusal of assent to either alternative.

Then as to the formula "Nowise more," even 191 though it exhibits the character of a form of assent or of denial, we do not employ it in this way, but we take it in a loose and inexact sense, either in place of a question or in place of the phrase "I know not to which of these things I ought to assent, and to which I ought not." For our aim is to indicate what appears to us; while as to the expression by which we indicate this we are indifferent. This point, too, should be noticed—that we utter the expression "Nowise more" not as positively affirming that it really is true and certain, but as stating in regard to it also what appears to us.

CHAPTER XX.—OF "APHASIA" OR NON-ASSERTION

Concerning non-assertion what we say is this. The 192 term "assertion" has two senses, general and special; used in the general sense it indicates affirmation or negation, as for example "It is day," "It is not day"; in its special sense it indicates affirmation only, and in this sense negations are not termed assertions. Non-assertion, then, is avoidance of assertion in the general sense in which it is said to include both affirmation and negation, so that non-assertion

[a] This is the typical Sceptic's attitude of complete mental neutrality, or "state of even balance" (ἀρρεψία, Diog. Laert. ix. 74).

πάθος ἡμέτερον δι' ὃ οὔτε τιθέναι τι οὔτε ἀναιρεῖν
193 φαμέν. ὅθεν δῆλόν ἐστιν ὅτι καὶ τὴν ἀφασίαν
παραλαμβάνομεν οὐχ ὡς πρὸς τὴν φύσιν τοιούτων
ὄντων τῶν πραγμάτων ὥστε πάντως ἀφασίαν
κινεῖν, ἀλλὰ δηλοῦντες ὅτι ἡμεῖς νῦν, ὅτε προφερόμεθα αὐτήν, ἐπὶ τῶνδε τῶν ζητουμένων τοῦτο
πεπόνθαμεν. κἀκεῖνο χρὴ μνημονεύειν ὅτι μηδὲν
τιθέναι μηδὲ ἀναιρεῖν φαμὲν τῶν κατὰ τὸ ἄδηλον
δογματικῶς λεγομένων· τοῖς γὰρ κινοῦσιν ἡμᾶς
παθητικῶς καὶ ἀναγκαστικῶς ἄγουσιν εἰς συγκατάθεσιν εἴκομεν.

ΚΑ΄.—ΠΕΡΙ ΤΟΥ "ΤΑΧΑ," ΚΑΙ ΤΟΥ "ΕΞΕΣΤΙ," ΚΑΙ
ΤΟΥ "ΕΝΔΕΧΕΤΑΙ"

194 Τὸ δὲ " τάχα " καὶ " οὐ τάχα " καὶ " ἔξεστι "
καὶ " οὐκ ἔξεστι " καὶ " ἐνδέχεται " καὶ " οὐκ
ἐνδέχεται " παραλαμβάνομεν ἀντὶ τοῦ τάχα μὲν
ἔστιν τάχα δ' οὐκ ἔστιν, καὶ ἔξεστι μὲν εἶναι
ἔξεστι δὲ μὴ εἶναι, καὶ ἐνδέχεται μὲν εἶναι ἐνδέχεται δὲ μὴ εἶναι, ὡς παραλαμβάνειν ἡμᾶς συντομίας χάριν τὸ μὴ ἐξεῖναι ἀντὶ τοῦ ἐξεῖναι μὴ
εἶναι, καὶ τὸ μὴ ἐνδέχεσθαι ἀντὶ τοῦ ἐνδέχεσθαι μὴ
εἶναι, καὶ τὸ οὐ τάχα ἀντὶ τοῦ τάχα μὴ εἶναι.
195 πάλιν δὲ ἐνταῦθα οὐ φωνομαχοῦμεν, οὐδὲ εἰ φύσει
ταῦτα δηλοῦσιν αἱ φωναὶ ζητοῦμεν, ἀλλ' ἀδιαφόρως αὐτάς, ὡς εἶπον, παραλαμβάνομεν. ὅτι
μέντοι αὗται αἱ φωναὶ ἀφασίας εἰσὶ δηλωτικαί,
πρόδηλον, οἶμαι. ὁ γοῦν λέγων " τάχα ἔστιν "
δυνάμει τίθησι καὶ τὸ μάχεσθαι δοκοῦν αὐτῷ, τὸ

is a mental condition of ours because of which we refuse either to affirm or to deny anything. Hence 193 it is plain that we adopt non-assertion also not as though things are in reality of such a kind as wholly to induce non-assertion, but as indicating that we now, at the time of uttering it, are in this condition regarding the problems now before us. It must also be borne in mind that what, as we say, we neither posit nor deny, is some one of the dogmatic statements made about what is non-apparent ; for we yield to those things which move us emotionally and drive us compulsorily to assent.

CHAPTER XXI.—OF THE EXPRESSIONS " PERHAPS,"
" POSSIBLY," AND " MAYBE "

The formulae " perhaps " and " perhaps not," and 194 " possibly " and " possibly not," and " maybe " and " maybe not," we adopt in place of " perhaps it is and perhaps it is not," and " possibly it is and possibly it is not," and " maybe it is and maybe it is not," so that for the sake of conciseness we adopt the phrase " possibly not " instead of " possibly it is not," and " maybe not " instead of " maybe it is not," and " perhaps not " instead of " perhaps it is not." But here again we do not fight 195 about phrases nor do we inquire whether the phrases indicate realities, but we adopt them, as I said,[a] in a loose sense. Still it is evident, as I think, that these expressions are indicative of non-assertion. Certainly the person who says " perhaps it is " is implicitly affirming also the seemingly contradictory

* *Cf.* §§ 13, 191 *supra.*

τάχα μὴ εἶναι, τῷ μὴ διαβεβαιοῦσθαι περὶ τοῦ
εἶναι αὐτό. ὁμοίως δὲ καὶ ἐπὶ τῶν λοιπῶν ἔχει.

ΚΒʹ.—ΠΕΡΙ ΤΟΥ "ΕΠΕΧΩ"

196 Τὸ δὲ "ἐπέχω" παραλαμβάνομεν ἀντὶ τοῦ οὐκ
ἔχω εἰπεῖν τίνι χρὴ τῶν προκειμένων πιστεῦσαι
ἢ τινι ἀπιστῆσαι, δηλοῦντες ὅτι ἴσα ἡμῖν φαίνεται
τὰ πράγματα πρὸς πίστιν καὶ ἀπιστίαν. καὶ εἰ
μὲν ἴσα ἐστίν, οὐ διαβεβαιούμεθα· τὸ δὲ φαινόμενον
ἡμῖν περὶ αὐτῶν, ὅτε ἡμῖν ὑποπίπτει, λέγομεν.
καὶ ἡ ἐποχὴ δὲ εἴρηται ἀπὸ τοῦ ἐπέχεσθαι τὴν
διάνοιαν ὡς μήτε τιθέναι τι μήτε ἀναιρεῖν διὰ τὴν
ἰσοσθένειαν τῶν ζητουμένων.

ΚΓʹ.—ΠΕΡΙ ΤΟΥ "ΟΥΔΕΝ ΟΡΙΖΩ"

197 Περὶ δὲ τοῦ "οὐδὲν ὁρίζω" ταῦτα φαμέν.
ὁρίζειν εἶναι νομίζομεν οὐχὶ τὸ ἁπλῶς λέγειν τι,
ἀλλὰ τὸ πρᾶγμα ἄδηλον προφέρεσθαι μετὰ συγκαταθέσεως. οὕτω γὰρ οὐδὲν ὁρίζων ὁ σκεπτικὸς
τάχα εὑρεθήσεται, οἰδὲ αὐτὸ τὸ "οὐδὲν ὁρίζω"·
οὐ γάρ ἐστι δογματικὴ ὑπόληψις, τουτέστιν ἀδήλῳ
συγκατάθεσις, ἀλλὰ φωνὴ πάθους ἡμετέρου δηλωτική. ὅταν οὖν εἴπῃ ὁ σκεπτικὸς "οὐδὲν ὁρίζω,"
τοῦτό φησιν "ἐγὼ οὕτω πέπονθα νῦν ὡς μηδὲν

* Cf. §§ 7, 10 supra.

phrase " perhaps it is not " by his refusal to make the positive assertion that " it is." And the same applies to all the other cases.

Chapter XXII.—Of the Expression " I suspend Judgement "

The phrase " I suspend judgement " [a] we adopt in 196 place of " I am unable to say which of the objects presented I ought to believe and which I ought to disbelieve," indicating that the objects appear to us equal as regards credibility and incredibility. As to whether they are equal we make no positive assertion ; but what we state is what appears to us in regard to them at the time of observation. And the term " suspension " is derived from the fact of the mind being held up or " suspended " so that it neither affirms nor denies anything owing to the equipollence of the matters in question.

Chapter XXIII.—Of the Expression " I determine Nothing "

Regarding the phrase " I determine nothing " this 197 is what we say. We hold that " to determine " is not simply to state a thing but to put forward something non-evident combined with assent. For in this sense, no doubt, it will be found that the Sceptic determines nothing, not even the very proposition " I determine nothing " ; for this is not a dogmatic assumption, that is to say assent to something non-evident, but an expression indicative of our own mental condition. So whenever the Sceptic says " I determine nothing," what he means is " I am now in such a state of mind as neither to affirm

115

τῶν ὑπὸ τὴν ζήτησιν τήνδε πεπτωκότων τιθέναι δογματικῶς ἢ ἀναιρεῖν." τοῦτο δέ φησι λέγων τὸ ἑαυτῷ φαινόμενον περὶ τῶν προκειμένων [οὐκ] ἀπαγγελτικῶς, ⟨οὐ δογματικῶς⟩[1] μετὰ πεποιθήσεως ἀποφαινόμενος, ἀλλ' ὃ πάσχει διηγούμενος.

ΚΔ'.—ΠΕΡΙ ΤΟΥ "ΠΑΝΤΑ ΕΣΤΙΝ ΑΟΡΙΣΤΑ"

198 Καὶ ἡ ἀοριστία δὲ πάθος διανοίας ἐστί, καθ' ὃ οὔτε αἴρομέν τι οὔτε τίθεμεν τῶν δογματικῶς ζητουμένων, τουτέστι τῶν ἀδήλων. ὅταν οὖν λέγῃ ὁ σκεπτικός " πάντα ἐστὶν ἀόριστα," τὸ μὲν ἔστι λαμβάνει ἀντὶ τοῦ φαίνεσθαι αὐτῷ, πάντα δὲ λέγει οὐ τὰ ὄντα ἀλλ' ἅπερ διεξῆλθε τῶν παρὰ τοῖς δογματικοῖς ζητουμένων ἀδήλων, ἀόριστα δὲ μὴ προύχοντα τῶν ἀντικειμένων ἢ κοινῶς μαχομένων
199 κατὰ πίστιν ἢ ἀπιστίαν. καὶ ὥσπερ ὁ λέγων " περιπατῶ " δυνάμει φησὶν " ἐγὼ περιπατῶ," οὕτως ὁ λέγων " πάντα ἐστὶν ἀόριστα " συσσημαίνει καθ' ἡμᾶς τὸ ὡς πρὸς ἐμέ ἢ ὡς ἐμοὶ φαίνεται, ὡς εἶναι τὸ λεγόμενον τοιοῦτον " ὅσα ἐπῆλθον τῶν δογματικῶς ζητουμένων, τοιαῦτά μοι φαίνεται ὡς μηδὲν αὐτῶν τοῦ μαχομένου προύχειν μοι δοκεῖν κατὰ πίστιν ἢ ἀπιστίαν."

ΚΕ'.—ΠΕΡΙ ΤΟΥ "ΠΑΝΤΑ ΕΣΤΙΝ ΑΚΑΤΑΛΗΠΤΑ"

200 Οὕτω δὲ φερόμεθα καὶ ὅταν λέγωμεν " πάντα ἐστὶν ἀκατάληπτα"· καὶ γὰρ τὸ πάντα ὁμοίως

---

[1] [οὐκ] . . . ⟨οὐ δογματικῶς⟩ om. et add. T.

---

[a] For " opposed " and " conflicting " see § 10 above.
[b] i.e. the personal pronoun " I " is potentially, or implicitly, expressed in the ending of the Greek verb (first person singular).   [c] Cf. § 1.

dogmatically nor deny any of the matters now in question." And this he says simply by way of announcing undogmatically what appears to himself regarding the matters presented, not making any confident declaration, but just explaining his own state of mind.

CHAPTER XXIV.—OF THE EXPRESSION
" ALL THINGS ARE UNDETERMINED "

Indetermination is a state of mind in which we neither deny nor affirm any of the matters which are subjects of dogmatic inquiry, that is to say, non-evident. So whenever the Sceptic says " All things are undetermined," he takes the word " are " in the sense of " appear to him," and by " all things " he means not existing things but such of the non-evident matters investigated by the Dogmatists as he has examined, and by " undetermined " he means not superior in point of credibility or incredibility to things opposed, or in any way conflicting.[a] And just as the man who says " (I) walk about"[b] is potentially saying " I walk about," so he who says " All are undetermined " conveys also, as we hold, the meaning " so far as relates to me," or " as appears to me," so that the statement amounts to this—" All the matters of dogmatic inquiry which I have examined appear to me to be such that no one of them is preferable to the one in conflict with it in respect of credibility or incredibility."

CHAPTER XXV.—OF THE EXPRESSION
" ALL THINGS ARE NON-APPREHENSIBLE "

We adopt a similar attitude when we say " All things are non-apprehensible."[c] For we give a

117

ἐξηγούμεθα καὶ τὸ ἐμοί συνεκδεχόμεθα, ὡς εἶναι
τὸ λεγόμενον τοιοῦτον " πάντα ὅσα ἐφώδευσα τῶν
δογματικῶς ζητουμένων ἀδήλων φαίνεταί μοὶ
ἀκατάληπτα." τοῦτο δέ ἐστιν οὐ διαβεβαιουμένου
περὶ τοῦ τὰ παρὰ τοῖς δογματικοῖς ζητούμενα
φύσεως εἶναι τοιαύτης ὡς εἶναι ἀκατάληπτα, ἀλλὰ
τὸ ἑαυτοῦ πάθος ἀπαγγέλλοντος, καθ' ὅ, φησίν,
ὑπολαμβάνω ὅτι ἄχρι νῦν οὐδὲν κατέλαβον ἐκείνων
ἐγὼ διὰ τὴν τῶν ἀντικειμένων ἰσοσθένειαν· ὅθεν
καὶ τὰ εἰς περιτροπὴν φερόμενα πάντα ἀπάδοντα
εἶναι δοκεῖ μοι τῶν ὑφ' ἡμῶν ἀπαγγελλομένων.

Κϛ'.—ΠΕΡΙ ΤΟΥ "ΑΚΑΤΑΛΗΠΤΩ" ΚΑΙ "ΟΥ
ΚΑΤΑΛΑΜΒΑΝΩ"

201 Καὶ ἡ " ἀκαταλήπτω " δὲ καὶ ἡ " οὐ καταλαμβάνω " φωνὴ πάθους οἰκείου ἐστὶ δηλωτική, καθ'
ὃ ἀφίσταται ὁ σκεπτικὸς ὡς πρὸς τὸ παρὸν τοῦ
τιθέναι τι τῶν ζητουμένων ἀδήλων ἢ ἀναιρεῖν, ὡς
ἔστι δῆλον ἐκ τῶν προειρημένων ἡμῖν περὶ τῶν
ἄλλων φωνῶν.

Κζ'.—ΠΕΡΙ ΤΟΥ ΠΑΝΤΙ ΛΟΓΩΙ ΛΟΓΟΝ ΙΣΟΝ
ΑΝΤΙΚΕΙΣΘΑΙ

202 Ὅταν δὲ λέγωμεν " παντὶ λόγῳ λόγος ἴσος
ἀντίκειται," παντὶ μὲν λέγομεν τῷ ὑφ' ἡμῶν διεξ-
ωδευμένῳ, λόγον δέ φαμεν οὐχ ἁπλῶς ἀλλὰ τὸν
κατασκευάζοντά τι δογματικῶς, τουτέστι περὶ
118

similar explanation of the word "all," and we similarly supply the words "to me," so that the meaning conveyed is this—"All the non-apparent matters of dogmatic inquiry which I have investigated appear to me non-apprehensible." And this is the utterance not of one who is positively asserting that the matters investigated by the Dogmatists are really of such a nature as to be non-apprehensible, but of one who is announcing his own state of mind, "wherein," he says, "I conceive that up till now I myself have apprehended nothing owing to the equipollence of the opposites ; and therefore also nothing that is brought forward to overthrow our position seems to me to have any bearing on what we announce."

Chapter XXVI.—Of the Expressions "I am Non-apprehensive" and "I apprehend not"

Both the expressions "I am non-apprehensive" 201 and "I apprehend not" are indicative of a personal state of mind, in which the Sceptic, for the time being, avoids affirming or denying any non-evident matter of inquiry, as is obvious from what we have said above concerning the other expressions.

Chapter XXVII.—Of the Phrase "To every Argument an Equal Argument is Opposed"

When we say "To every argument an equal argu 202 ment is opposed," we mean "to every argument" that has been investigated by us, and the word "argument" we use not in its simple sense, but of that which establishes a point dogmatically (that is to say with reference to what is non-evident) and estab-

119

ἀδήλου, καὶ οὐ πάντως τὸν ἐκ λημμάτων καὶ ἐπιφορᾶς ἀλλὰ τὸν ὁπωσοῦν κατασκευάζοντα. ἴσον δέ φαμεν κατὰ πίστιν ἢ ἀπιστίαν, τό τε ἀντίκειται λαμβάνομεν ἀντὶ τοῦ μάχεται κοινῶς, καὶ τὸ "ὡς ἐμοὶ φαίνεται" συνεκδεχόμεθα.

203 ὅταν οὖν εἴπω "παντὶ λόγῳ λόγος ἴσος ἀντίκειται," δυνάμει τοῦτό φημι "παντὶ τῷ ὑπ' ἐμοῦ ἐξητασμένῳ[1] λόγῳ, ὃς κατασκευάζει τι δογματικῶς, ἕτερος λόγος κατασκευάζων τι δογματικῶς, ἴσος αὐτῷ κατὰ πίστιν καὶ ἀπιστίαν, ἀντικεῖσθαι φαίνεταί μοι," ὡς εἶναι τὴν τοῦ λόγου προφορὰν οὐ δογματικὴν ἀλλ' ἀνθρωπείου πάθους ἀπαγγελίαν, ὅ ἐστι φαινόμενον τῷ πάσχοντι.

204 Προφέρονται δέ τινες καὶ οὕτω τὴν φωνήν "παντὶ λόγῳ λόγον ἀντικεῖσθαι τὸν ἴσον," ἀξιοῦντες παραγγελματικῶς τοῦτο "παντὶ λόγῳ δογματικῶς τι κατασκευάζοντι λόγον δογματικῶς ζητοῦντα, ἴσον κατὰ πίστιν καὶ ἀπιστίαν, μαχόμενον αὐτῷ ἀντιτιθῶμεν," ἵνα ὁ μὲν λόγος αὐτοῖς ᾖ πρὸς τὸν σκεπτικόν, χρῶνται δὲ ἀπαρεμφάτῳ ἀντὶ προστακτικοῦ, τῷ ἀντικεῖσθαι ἀντὶ τοῦ ἀντιτιθῶμεν.

205 παραγγέλλουσι δὲ τοῦτο τῷ σκεπτικῷ, μή πως ὑπὸ τοῦ δογματικοῦ παρακρουσθεὶς ἀπείπῃ τὴν περὶ αὐτοὺς[2] ζήτησιν, καὶ τῆς φαινομένης αὐτοῖς ἀταραξίας, ἣν νομίζουσι παρυφίστασθαι τῇ περὶ πάντων ἐποχῇ, καθὼς ἔμπροσθεν ὑπεμνήσαμεν, σφαλῇ προπετευσάμενος.

---

[1] ἐξητασμένῳ Heintz : ἐξητημένῳ ML : ζητουμένῳ Bekk.
[2] αὐτοὺς cj. Heintz : αὐτοῦ Bekk. : αὐτῆς EAB.

---

[a] i.e. by the use of syllogisms.
[b] As with Protagoras, who seems to have originated it.

lishes it by any method, and not necessarily by means of premises and a conclusion.[a] We say "equal" with reference to credibility or incredibility, and we employ the word "opposed" in the general sense of "conflicting"; and we supply therewith in thought the phrase "as appears to me." So whenever I say 203 "To every argument an equal argument is opposed," what I am virtually saying is "To every argument investigated by me which establishes a point dogmatically, it seems to me there is opposed another argument, establishing a point dogmatically, which is equal to the first in respect of credibility and incredibility"; so that the utterance of the phrase is not a piece of dogmatism,[b] but the announcement of a human state of mind which is apparent to the person experiencing it.

But some also utter the expression in the form 204 "To every argument an equal argument is to be opposed,"[c] intending to give the injunction "To every argument which establishes a point dogmatically let us oppose an argument which investigates dogmatically, equal to the former in respect of credibility and incredibility, and conflicting therewith"; for they mean their words to be addressed to the Sceptic, although they use the infinitive form "to be opposed" instead of the imperative "let us oppose." And they 205 address this injunction to the Sceptic lest haply, through being misled by the Dogmatist, he may give up the Sceptic search, and through precipitancy miss the "quietude"[d] approved by the Sceptics, which they—as we said above[e]—believe to be dependent on universal suspension of judgement.

[c] The infinite is here used in a jussive sense.
[d] Cf. §§ 10, 25 ff.   [e] Cf. § 29.

SEXTUS EMPIRICUS

206 Περὶ τοσούτων ἀρκέσει τῶν φωνῶν ὡς ἐν ὑποτυπώσει διεξελθεῖν, ἄλλως τε καὶ ἐπεὶ ἐκ τῶν
νῦν ἡμῖν εἰρημένων δυνατόν ἐστι λέγειν καὶ περὶ
τῶν παραλελειμμένων. περὶ πασῶν γὰρ τῶν σκεπτικῶν φωνῶν ἐκεῖνο χρὴ προειληφέναι ὅτι περὶ
τοῦ ἀληθεῖς αὐτὰς εἶναι πάντως οὐ διαβεβαιούμεθα, ὅπου γε καὶ ὑφ᾽ ἑαυτῶν αὐτὰς ἀναιρεῖσθαι
λέγομεν δύνασθαι, συμπεριγραφομένας ἐκείνοις
περὶ ὧν λέγονται, καθάπερ τὰ καθαρτικὰ τῶν φαρμάκων οὐ μόνον τοὺς χυμοὺς ὑπεξαιρεῖ τοῦ σώματος ἀλλὰ καὶ ἑαυτὰ τοῖς χυμοῖς συνεξάγει.
207 φαμὲν δὲ καὶ ὡς οὐ κυρίως δηλοῦντες τὰ πράγματα, ἐφ᾽ ὧν παραλαμβάνονται, τίθεμεν αὐτάς,
ἀλλ᾽ ἀδιαφόρως καὶ εἰ βούλονται καταχρηστικῶς·
οὔτε γὰρ πρέπει τῷ σκεπτικῷ φωνομαχεῖν, ἄλλως
τε ἡμῖν συνεργεῖ τὸ μηδὲ ταύτας τὰς φωνὰς
εἰλικρινῶς σημαίνειν λέγεσθαι, ἀλλὰ πρός τι καὶ
208 πρὸς τοὺς σκεπτικούς. πρὸς τούτοις κἀκείνου δεῖ
μεμνῆσθαι ὅτι οὐ περὶ πάντων τῶν πραγμάτων
καθόλου φαμὲν αὐτάς, ἀλλὰ περὶ τῶν ἀδήλων καὶ
τῶν δογματικῶς ζητουμένων, καὶ ὅτι τὸ φαινόμενον ἡμῖν φαμὲν καὶ οὐχὶ διαβεβαιωτικῶς περὶ
τῆς φύσεως τῶν ἐκτὸς ὑποκειμένων ἀποφαινόμεθα·
ἐκ γὰρ τούτων πᾶν σόφισμα πρὸς φωνὴν ἐνεχθὲν
σκεπτικὴν οἴομαι δύνασθαι διατρέπεσθαι.
209 Ἐπεὶ δὲ τὴν ἔννοιαν καὶ τὰ μέρη καὶ τὸ κριτήριον καὶ τὸ τέλος, ἔτι δὲ τοὺς τρόπους τῆς
ἐποχῆς ἐφοδεύσαντες, καὶ περὶ τῶν σκεπτικῶν

---

[a] Cf. § 195 supra.
[b] Suggesting that such attacks must involve the fallacy
of *ignoratio elenchi*.

CHAPTER XXVIII.—SUPPLEMENTARY NOTES ON
THE SCEPTIC EXPRESSIONS

In a preliminary outline it will be sufficient to have 206
explained the expressions now set forth, especially
since it is possible to explain the rest by deductions
from the foregoing. For, in regard to all the Sceptic
expressions, we must grasp first the fact that we make
no positive assertion respecting their absolute truth,
since we say that they may possibly be confuted by
themselves, seeing that they themselves are included
in the things to which their doubt applies, just as
aperient drugs do not merely eliminate the humours
from the body, but also expel themselves along with
the humours. And we also say that we employ them 207
not by way of authoritatively explaining the things
with reference to which we adopt them, but without
precision and, if you like, loosely ; for it does not
become the Sceptic to wrangle over expressions,[a] and
besides it is to our advantage that even to these expressions no absolute significance should be ascribed,
but one that is relative and relative to the Sceptics.
Besides this we must also remember that we do not 208
employ them universally about all things, but about
those which are non-evident and are objects of dogmatic inquiry ; and that we state what appears to us
and do not make any positive declarations as to the
real nature of external objects ; for I think that, as
a result of this, every sophism [b] directed against a
Sceptic expression can be refuted.

And now that we have reviewed the idea or purpose 209
of Scepticism and its divisions, and the criterion and
the end, and the modes, too, of suspension, and have
discussed the Sceptic expressions, and have thus made

φωνῶν εἰπόντες, τὸν χαρακτῆρα τῆς σκέψεως
ἐμπεφανίκαμεν, ἀκόλουθον ἡγούμεθα εἶναι καὶ τῶν
παρακειμένων αὐτῇ φιλοσοφιῶν τὴν πρὸς αὐτὴν
διάκρισιν συντόμως ἐπελθεῖν, ἵνα σαφέστερον τὴν
ἐφεκτικὴν ἀγωγὴν κατανοήσωμεν. ἀρξώμεθα δὲ
ἀπὸ τῆς Ἡρακλειτείου φιλοσοφίας.

ΚΘ΄.—ΟΤΙ ΔΙΑΦΕΡΕΙ Η ΣΚΕΠΤΙΚΗ ΑΓΩΓΗ ΤΗΣ
ΗΡΑΚΛΕΙΤΕΙΟΥ ΦΙΛΟΣΟΦΙΑΣ

210   Ὅτι μὲν οὖν αὕτη διαφέρει τῆς ἡμετέρας ἀγωγῆς,
πρόδηλον· ὁ μὲν γὰρ Ἡράκλειτος περὶ πολλῶν
ἀδήλων ἀποφαίνεται δογματικῶς, ἡμεῖς δ᾽ οὐχί,
καθάπερ εἴρηται. ἐπεὶ δὲ οἱ περὶ τὸν Αἰνησίδημον
ἔλεγον ὁδὸν εἶναι τὴν σκεπτικὴν ἀγωγὴν ἐπὶ τὴν
Ἡρακλείτειον φιλοσοφίαν, διότι προηγεῖται τοῦ
τἀναντία περὶ τὸ αὐτὸ ὑπάρχειν τὸ τἀναντία περὶ
τὸ αὐτὸ φαίνεσθαι, καὶ οἱ μὲν σκεπτικοὶ φαίνεσθαι
λέγουσι τὰ ἐναντία περὶ τὸ αὐτό, οἱ δὲ Ἡρακλείτειοι ἀπὸ τούτου καὶ ἐπὶ τὸ ὑπάρχειν αὐτὰ
μετέρχονται, φαμὲν πρὸς τούτους ὅτι τὸ τὰ ἐναντία
περὶ τὸ αὐτὸ φαίνεσθαι οὐ δόγμα ἐστὶ τῶν σκεπτικῶν ἀλλὰ πρᾶγμα οὐ μόνον τοῖς σκεπτικοῖς ἀλλὰ
καὶ τοῖς ἄλλοις φιλοσόφοις καὶ πᾶσιν ἀνθρώποις
211 ὑποπῖπτον· οὐδεὶς γοῦν τολμήσαι ἂν εἰπεῖν ὅτι τὸ
μέλι οὐ γλυκάζει τοὺς ὑγιαίνοντας ἢ ὅτι τοὺς

ᵃ For Heracleitus see Introd. p. viii; cf. ii. 59, 63.   For
Aenesidemus see Introd. pp. xxxvii ff.
  ᵇ i.e. the Sceptic view that the same thing apparently
possesses opposite attributes or qualities is regarded as a
step on the road to the Heracleitean view that it really
possesses such qualities.   But, as Sextus proceeds to argue,

clear the character of Scepticism, our next task is, we suppose, to explain briefly the distinction which exists between it and the philosophic systems which lie next to it, in order that we may more clearly understand the " suspensive " Way of thought. Let us begin with the Heracleitean philosophy.

CHAPTER XXIX.—THAT THE SCEPTIC WAY OF THOUGHT DIFFERS FROM THE HERACLEITEAN PHILOSOPHY

Now that this latter differs from our Way of thought 210 is plain at once ; for Heracleitus [a] makes dogmatic statements about many non-evident things, whereas we, as has been said, do not. It is true that Aenesidemus and his followers used to say that the Sceptic Way is a road leading up to the Heracleitean philosophy, since to hold that the same thing is the subject of opposite appearances is a preliminary to holding that it is the subject of opposite realities, and while the Sceptics say that the same thing is the subject of opposite appearances, the Heracleiteans go on from this to assert their reality.[b] But in reply to them we declare that the view about the same thing having opposite appearances is not a dogma of the Sceptics but a fact which is experienced not by the Sceptics alone but also by the rest of philosophers and by all mankind ; for certainly no one would venture to 211 say that honey [c] does not taste sweet to people in sound health or that it does not taste bitter to those

the ascription of *apparently* contradictory attributes to a thing is not peculiar to the Sceptics but common to all men, so that all others might equally well be regarded as Heracleiteans in the making. For the opposition of " appearances " *cf.* §§ 32, 91 ff., 101 ff.   *Cf.* § 101 *supra.*

SEXTUS EMPIRICUS

ἰκτερικοὺς οὐ πικράζει, ὥστε ἀπὸ κοινῆς τῶν ἀνθρώπων προλήψεως ἄρχονται οἱ Ἡρακλείτειοι,
καθάπερ καὶ ἡμεῖς, ἴσως δὲ καὶ αἱ ἄλλαι φιλοσοφίαι.
διόπερ εἰ μὲν ἀπό τινος τῶν σκεπτικῶς λεγομένων
ἐλάμβανον τὸ τἀναντία περὶ τὸ αὐτὸ ὑποκεῖσθαι,
οἷον τοῦ "πάντα ἐστὶν ἀκατάληπτα" ἢ τοῦ
"οὐδὲν ὁρίζω" ἢ τινος τῶν παραπλησίων, ἴσως
ἂν συνῆγον ὃ λέγουσιν· ἐπεὶ δὲ ἀρχὰς ἔχουσιν οὐ
μόνον ἡμῖν ἀλλὰ καὶ τοῖς ἄλλοις φιλοσόφοις καὶ
τῷ βίῳ ὑποπιπτούσας, τί μᾶλλον τὴν ἡμετέραν
ἀγωγὴν ἢ ἑκάστην τῶν ἄλλων φιλοσοφιῶν ἢ καὶ
τὸν βίον ὁδὸν ἐπὶ τὴν Ἡρακλείτειον φιλοσοφίαν
εἶναι λέγοι τις ἄν, ἐπειδὴ πάντες κοιναῖς ὕλαις
κεχρήμεθα;

212   Μήποτε δὲ οὐ μόνον οὐ συνεργεῖ πρὸς τὴν γνῶσιν
τῆς Ἡρακλειτείου φιλοσοφίας ἡ σκεπτικὴ ἀγωγή,
ἀλλὰ καὶ ἀποσυνεργεῖ, εἴγε ὁ σκεπτικὸς πάντα τὰ
ὑπὸ τοῦ Ἡρακλείτου δογματιζόμενα ὡς προπετῶς
λεγόμενα διαβάλλει, ἐναντιούμενος μὲν τῇ ἐκπυ-
ρώσει ἐναντιούμενος δὲ τῷ τὰ ἐναντία περὶ τὸ
αὐτὸ ὑπάρχειν, καὶ ἐπὶ παντὸς δόγματος τοῦ Ἡρακλείτου τὴν μὲν δογματικὴν προπέτειαν διασύρων,
τὸ δὲ "οὐ καταλαμβάνω" καὶ τὸ "οὐδὲν ὁρίζω"
ἐπιφθεγγόμενος, ὡς ἔφην ἔμπροσθεν· ὅπερ μάχεται
τοῖς Ἡρακλειτείοις. ἄτοπον δέ ἐστι τὸ τὴν μαχο-
μένην ἀγωγὴν ὁδὸν εἶναι λέγειν τῆς αἱρέσεως
ἐκείνης ᾗ μάχεται· ἄτοπον ἄρα τὸ τὴν σκεπτικὴν
ἀγωγὴν ἐπὶ τὴν Ἡρακλείτειον φιλοσοφίαν ὁδὸν
εἶναι λέγειν.

---

[a] *i.e.* general human experience and observation, derived
from sense-impressions.

suffering from jaundice; so that the Heracleiteans start from the general preconception of mankind, just as we also do and probably all the other philosophies. Consequently, if they had derived their theory that the same thing is the subject of opposite realities from one of the Sceptic formulae, such as " All things are non-apprehensible," or " I determine nothing," or some similar expression, probably they would have reached the conclusion they assert ; but since their starting-points are impressions experienced not by us only but by all the other philosophers and by ordinary people, why should anyone declare that our Way of thought is a road to the Heracleitean philosophy any more than any of the other philosophies or even than the ordinary view, since we all make use of the same common material [a] ?

Rather it is the case that the Sceptic Way so far 212 from being an aid to the knowledge of the Heracleitean philosophy is actually an obstacle thereto, seeing that the Sceptic decries all the dogmatic statements of Heracleitus as rash utterances, contradicting his " Ecpyrosis," [b] and contradicting his view that the same thing is the subject of opposite realities, and in respect of every dogma of Heracleitus scoffing at his dogmatic precipitancy, and constantly repeating, as I said before, his own " I apprehend not " and " I determine nothing," which are in conflict with the Heracleiteans. Now it is absurd to say that a conflicting Way is a road to the system with which it is in conflict ; therefore it is absurd to say that the Sceptic Way is a road leading to the Heracleitean philosophy.

[b] *i.e.* " world-conflagration," by which all things are resolved into the primal Fire.

Λ'.—ΤΙΝΙ ΔΙΑΦΕΡΕΙ Η ΣΚΕΠΤΙΚΗ ΑΓΩΓΗ ΤΗΣ
ΔΗΜΟΚΡΙΤΕΙΟΥ ΦΙΛΟΣΟΦΙΑΣ

213   Ἀλλὰ καὶ ἡ Δημοκρίτειος φιλοσοφία λέγεται
κοινωνίαν ἔχειν πρὸς τὴν σκέψιν, ἐπεὶ δοκεῖ τῇ
αὐτῇ ὕλῃ ἡμῖν κεχρῆσθαι· ἀπὸ γὰρ τοῦ τοῖς μὲν
γλυκὺ φαίνεσθαι τὸ μέλι τοῖς δὲ πικρὸν τὸν Δημό-
κριτον ἐπιλογίζεσθαί φασι τὸ μήτε γλυκὺ αὐτὸ
εἶναι μήτε πικρόν, καὶ διὰ τοῦτο ἐπιφθέγγεσθαι
τὴν " οὐ μᾶλλον " φωνὴν σκεπτικὴν οὖσαν. διαφόρως μέντοι χρῶνται τῇ " οὐ μᾶλλον " φωνῇ οἵ
τε σκεπτικοὶ καὶ οἱ ἀπὸ τοῦ Δημοκρίτου· ἐκεῖνοι
μὲν γὰρ ἐπὶ τοῦ μηδέτερον εἶναι τάττουσι τὴν
φωνήν, ἡμεῖς δὲ ἐπὶ τοῦ ἀγνοεῖν πότερον ἀμφότερα
214 ἢ οὐθέτερόν τι ἔστι τῶν φαινομένων. ὥστε καὶ
κατὰ τοῦτο μὲν διαφέρομεν, προδηλοτάτη δὲ
γίνεται ἡ διάκρισις ὅταν ὁ Δημόκριτος λέγῃ " ἐτεῇ
δὲ ἄτομα καὶ κενόν ''· ἐτεῇ μὲν γὰρ λέγει ἀντὶ
τοῦ ἀληθείᾳ· κατ' ἀλήθειαν δὲ ὑφεστάναι λέγων
τάς τε ἀτόμους καὶ τὸ κενὸν ὅτι διενήνοχεν ἡμῶν,
εἰ καὶ ἀπὸ τῆς ἀνωμαλίας τῶν φαινομένων ἄρχεται, περιττόν, οἶμαι, λέγειν.

ΛΑ'.—ΤΙΝΙ ΔΙΑΦΕΡΕΙ ΤΗΣ ΚΥΡΗΝΑΙΚΗΣ Η ΣΚΕΨΙΣ

215   Φασὶ δέ τινες ὅτι ἡ Κυρηναϊκὴ ἀγωγὴ ἡ αὐτή ἐστι
τῇ σκέψει, ἐπειδὴ κἀκείνη τὰ πάθη μόνα φησὶ καταλαμβάνεσθαι.[1]   διαφέρει δὲ αὐτῆς, ἐπειδὴ ἐκείνη
μὲν τὴν ἡδονὴν καὶ τὴν λείαν τῆς σαρκὸς κίνησιν
τέλος εἶναι λέγει, ἡμεῖς δὲ τὴν ἀταραξίαν, ᾗ ἐναντιοῦται τὸ κατ' ἐκείνους τέλος· καὶ γὰρ παρούσης

---

[1] καταλαμβάνεσθαι Pohlenz, Mutsch.: καταλαμβάνειν mss.,
Bekk.

CHAPTER XXX.—WHEREIN THE SCEPTIC WAY
DIFFERS FROM THE DEMOCRITEAN PHILOSOPHY

But it is also said that the Democritean [a] philo- 213
sophy has something in common with Scepticism,
since it seems to use the same material as we ; for
from the fact that honey appears sweet to some and
bitter to others, Democritus, as they say, infers that
it really is neither sweet nor bitter, and pronounces
in consequence the formula " Not more," which is
a Sceptic formula. The Sceptics, however, and the
School of Democritus employ the expression " Not
more " in different ways ; for while they use it to
express the unreality of either alternative, we express
by it our ignorance as to whether both or neither of
the appearances is real. So that in this respect 214
also we differ, and our difference becomes specially
evident when Democritus says " But in verity atoms
and void " (for he says " In verity " in place of " In
truth ") ; and that he differs from us when he says
that the atoms and the void are in truth subsistent,
although he starts out from the incongruity of appearances, it is superfluous, I think, to state.

CHAPTER XXXI.—WHEREIN SCEPTICISM DIFFERS
FROM CYRENAICISM

Some assert that the Cyrenaic [b] doctrine is identical 215
with Scepticism since it too affirms that only mental
states are apprehended. But it differs from Scepticism
inasmuch as it says that the End is pleasure and the
smooth motion of the flesh, whereas we say it is
" quietude," which is the opposite of their End ; for

[a] See Introd. pp. xi ff.
[b] See Introd. p. xvii; cf. *Adv. Log.* i. 191 ff.

τῆς ἡδονῆς καὶ μὴ παρούσης ταραχὰς ὑπομένει
ὁ διαβεβαιούμενος τέλος εἶναι τὴν ἡδονήν, ὡς ἐν
τῷ περὶ τοῦ τέλους ἐπελογισάμην. εἶτα ἡμεῖς
μὲν ἐπέχομεν ὅσον ἐπὶ τῷ λόγῳ περὶ τῶν ἐκτὸς
ὑποκειμένων, οἱ δὲ Κυρηναϊκοὶ ἀποφαίνονται φύσιν
αὐτὰ ἔχειν ἀκατάληπτον.

ΛΒ΄.—ΤΙΝΙ ΔΙΑΦΕΡΕΙ ΤΗΣ ΠΡΩΤΑΓΟΡΕΙΟΤ ΑΓΩΓΗΣ
Η ΣΚΕΨΙΣ

216   Καὶ ὁ Πρωταγόρας δὲ βούλεται πάντων χρημάτων εἶναι μέτρον τὸν ἄνθρωπον, τῶν μὲν ὄντων
ὡς ἔστιν, τῶν δὲ οὐκ ὄντων ὡς οὐκ ἔστιν, μέτρον
μὲν λέγων τὸ κριτήριον, χρημάτων δὲ τῶν πραγμάτων, ὡς δυνάμει φάσκειν πάντων πραγμάτων
κριτήριον εἶναι τὸν ἄνθρωπον, τῶν μὲν ὄντων ὡς
ἔστιν, τῶν δὲ οὐκ ὄντων ὡς οὐκ ἔστιν. καὶ διὰ
τοῦτο τίθησι τὰ φαινόμενα ἑκάστῳ μόνα, καὶ οὕτως
217 εἰσάγει τὸ πρός τι. διὸ καὶ δοκεῖ κοινωνίαν ἔχειν
πρὸς τοὺς Πυρρωνείους. διαφέρει δὲ αὐτῶν, καὶ
εἰσόμεθα τὴν διαφοράν, ἐξαπλώσαντες συμμέτρως
τὸ δοκοῦν τῷ Πρωταγόρᾳ.

Φησὶν οὖν ὁ ἀνὴρ τὴν ὕλην ῥευστὴν εἶναι, ῥεού-
σης δὲ αὐτῆς συνεχῶς προσθέσεις ἀντὶ τῶν ἀπο-
φορήσεων γίγνεσθαι καὶ τὰς αἰσθήσεις μετακοσ-
μεῖσθαί τε καὶ ἀλλοιοῦσθαι παρά τε ἡλικίας καὶ
218 παρὰ τὰς ἄλλας κατασκευὰς τῶν σωμάτων. λέγει
δὲ καὶ τοὺς λόγους πάντων τῶν φαινομένων ὑποκεῖσθαι ἐν τῇ ὕλῃ, ὡς δύνασθαι τὴν ὕλην ὅσον
ἐφ᾽ ἑαυτῇ πάντα εἶναι ὅσα πᾶσι φαίνεται. τοὺς

―――――――――――――――――――――――――

ᵃ §§ 25 ff. supra.

whether pleasure be present or not present the man who positively affirms pleasure to be the End undergoes perturbations, as I have argued in my chapter " Of the End." [a] Further, whereas we suspend judgement, so far as regards the essence of external objects, the Cyrenaics declare that those objects possess a real nature which is inapprehensible.

Chapter XXXII.—Wherein Scepticism differs from the Protagorean Doctrine

Protagoras [b] also holds that " Man is the measure 216 of all things, of existing things that they exist, and of non-existing things that they exist not " ; and by " measure " he means the criterion, and by " things " the objects, so that he is virtually asserting that " Man is the criterion of all objects, of those which exist that they exist, and of those which exist not that they exist not." And consequently he posits only what appears to each individual, and thus he introduces relativity. And for this reason he seems also 217 to have something in common with the Pyrrhoneans. Yet he differs from them, and we shall perceive the difference when we have adequately explained the views of Protagoras.

What he states then is this—that matter is in flux, and as it flows additions are made continuously in the place of the effluxions, and the senses are transformed and altered according to the times of life and to all the other conditions of the bodies. He says also 218 that the " reasons " of all the appearances subsist in matter, so that matter, so far as depends on itself, is capable of being all those things which appear to

[b] See Introd. p. xiv. In his physical theory Protagoras follows Heracleitus

δὲ ἀνθρώπους ἄλλοτε ἄλλων ἀντιλαμβάνεσθαι παρὰ
τὰς διαφόρους αὐτῶν διαθέσεις· τὸν μὲν γὰρ κατὰ
φύσιν ἔχοντα ἐκεῖνα τῶν ἐν τῇ ὕλῃ καταλαμβάνειν
ἃ τοῖς κατὰ φύσιν ἔχουσι φαίνεσθαι δύναται, τοὺς
219 δὲ παρὰ φύσιν ἃ τοῖς παρὰ φύσιν. καὶ ἤδη παρὰ
τὰς ἡλικίας καὶ κατὰ τὸ ὑπνοῦν ἢ ἐγρηγορέναι καὶ
καθ' ἕκαστον εἶδος τῶν διαθέσεων ὁ αὐτὸς λόγος.
γίνεται τοίνυν κατ' αὐτὸν τῶν ὄντων κριτήριον ὁ
ἄνθρωπος· πάντα γὰρ τὰ φαινόμενα τοῖς ἀνθρώποις
καὶ ἔστι, τὰ δὲ μηδενὶ τῶν ἀνθρώπων φαινόμενα
οὐδὲ ἔστιν.

Ὁρῶμεν οὖν ὅτι καὶ περὶ τοῦ τὴν ὕλην ῥευστὴν
εἶναι καὶ περὶ τοῦ τοὺς λόγους τῶν φαινομένων
πάντων ἐν αὐτῇ ὑποκεῖσθαι δογματίζει, ἀδήλων
ὄντων καὶ ἡμῖν ἐφεκτῶν.

ΑΓ.—ΤΙΝΙ ΔΙΑΦΕΡΕΙ ΤΗΣ ΑΚΑΔΗΜΑΪΚΗΣ ΦΙΛΟΣΟΦΙΑΣ Η ΣΚΕΨΙΣ

220 Φασὶ μέντοι τινὲς ὅτι ἡ Ἀκαδημαϊκὴ φιλοσοφία
ἡ αὐτή ἐστι τῇ σκέψει· διόπερ ἀκόλουθον ἂν εἴη
καὶ περὶ τούτου διεξελθεῖν.

Ἀκαδήμιαι δὲ γεγόνασιν, ὡς ⟨οἱ μὲν πλείους⟩
φασί, [πλείους μὲν ἢ]¹ τρεῖς, μία μὲν καὶ ἀρχαιο-
τάτη ἡ τῶν περὶ Πλάτωνα, δευτέρα δὲ καὶ μέση
ἡ τῶν περὶ Ἀρκεσίλαον τὸν ἀκουστὴν Πολέμωνος,
τρίτη δὲ καὶ νέα ἡ τῶν περὶ Καρνεάδην καὶ
Κλειτόμαχον· ἔνιοι δὲ καὶ τετάρτην προστιθέασι
τῶν περὶ Φίλωνα καὶ Χαρμίδαν, τινὲς δὲ καὶ

¹ add. et om. e conj. Bekk.

ᵃ i.e., in brief, all "appearances" (sensations, opinions,
etc.) are due to inter-action between the matter of the

all.[a] And men, he says, apprehend different things at different times owing to their differing dispositions; for he who is in a natural state apprehends those things subsisting in matter which are able to appear to those in a natural state, and those who are in a non-natural state the things which can appear to those in a non-natural state. Moreover, precisely the same 219 account applies to the variations due to age, and to the sleeping or waking state, and to each several kind of condition. Thus, according to him, Man becomes the criterion of real existences; for all things that appear to men also exist, and things that appear to no man have no existence either.

We see, then, that he dogmatizes about the fluidity of matter and also about the subsistence therein of the " reasons " of all appearances, these being non-evident matters about which we suspend judgement.

CHAPTER XXXIII.—WHEREIN SCEPTICISM DIFFERS FROM THE ACADEMIC PHILOSOPHY

Some indeed say that the Academic philosophy [b] is 220 identical with Scepticism; consequently it shall be our next task to discuss this statement.

According to most people there have been three Academies—the first and most ancient that of Plato and his School, the second or middle Academy that of Arcesilaus, the pupil of Polemo, and his School, the third or New Academy that of the School of Carneades and Cleitomachus. Some, however, add as a fourth that of the School of Philo and Charmidas; and some

percipient subject and the matter of the objective world, both of which are in constant flux. Thus " matter " is potentially the " phenomenon."

[b] See Introd. pp. xxxii f.

πέμπτην καταλέγουσι τὴν τῶν περὶ τὸν Ἀντίοχον.
221 ἀρξάμενοι τοίνυν ἀπὸ τῆς ἀρχαίας ἴδωμεν τὴν
διαφορὰν τῶν εἰρημένων φιλοσοφιῶν.

Τὸν Πλάτωνα οὖν οἱ μὲν δογματικὸν ἔφασαν
εἶναι, οἱ δὲ ἀπορητικόν, οἱ δὲ κατὰ μέν τι ἀπορητικὸν κατὰ δέ τι δογματικόν· ἐν μὲν γὰρ τοῖς
γυμναστικοῖς [φασὶ] λόγοις, ἔνθα ὁ Σωκράτης
εἰσάγεται ἤτοι παίζων πρός τινας ἢ ἀγωνιζόμενος
πρὸς σοφιστάς, γυμναστικόν τε καὶ ἀπορητικὸν
φασιν ἔχειν αὐτὸν χαρακτῆρα, δογματικὸν δὲ
ἔνθα σπουδάζων ἀποφαίνεται ἤτοι διὰ Σωκράτους
222 ἢ Τιμαίου ἤ τινος τῶν τοιούτων.   περὶ μὲν οὖν
τῶν δογματικὸν αὐτὸν εἶναι λεγόντων, ἢ κατὰ μέν
τι δογματικὸν κατὰ δέ τι ἀπορητικόν, περισσὸν ἂν
εἴη λέγειν νῦν· αὐτοὶ γὰρ ὁμολογοῦσι τὴν πρὸς
ἡμᾶς διαφοράν· περὶ δὲ τοῦ εἰ ἔστιν εἰλικρινῶς
σκεπτικὸς πλατύτερον μὲν ἐν τοῖς ὑπομνήμασι
διαλαμβάνομεν, νῦν δὲ ὡς ἐν ὑποτυπώσει λέγομεν[1]
κατὰ τῶν περὶ[2] Μηνόδοτον καὶ Αἰνησίδημον (οὗτοι
γὰρ μάλιστα ταύτης προέστησαν τῆς στάσεως) ὅτι
ὅταν ὁ Πλάτων ἀποφαίνηται περὶ ἰδεῶν ἢ περὶ
τοῦ πρόνοιαν εἶναι ἢ περὶ τοῦ τὸν ἐνάρετον βίον
αἱρετώτερον εἶναι τοῦ μετὰ κακιῶν, εἴτε ὡς ὑπ-
άρχουσι τούτοις συγκατατίθεται, δογματίζει, εἴτε
ὡς πιθανωτέροις προστίθεται, ἐπεὶ προκρίνει τι
κατὰ πίστιν ἢ ἀπιστίαν, ἐκπέφευγε τὸν σκεπτικὸν
χαρακτῆρα· ὡς γὰρ καὶ τοῦτο ἡμῖν ἐστιν ἀλλό-
τριον, ἐκ τῶν ἔμπροσθεν εἰρημένων πρόδηλον.

---

[1] λέγομεν T, cj. Bekk.: διαλαμβάνομεν mss.
[2] ⟨τῶν⟩ περὶ M. Heintz: περμηδοτον mss.: κατὰ M. Fabr.,
Bekk.

---

[a] i.e. those which aim at training the mind—subdivided

even count the School of Antiochus as a fifth. Be- 221
ginning, then, with the Old Academy let us consider
how the philosophies mentioned differ ⟨from ours⟩.

Plato has been described by some as " dogmatic," by
others as " dubitative," and by others again as partly
dogmatic and partly dubitative. For in his exercitatory discourses,[a] where Socrates is introduced either
as talking playfully with his auditors or as arguing
against sophists, he shows, they say, an exercitatory
and dubitative character ; but a dogmatic character
when he is speaking seriously by the mouth either
of Socrates or of Timaeus or of some similar personage.
Now as regards those who describe him as a dogmatist, 222
or as partly dogmatic and partly dubitative, it would
be superfluous to say anything now ; for they themselves acknowledge his difference from us. But the
question whether Plato is a genuine Sceptic is one
which we discuss more fully in our " Commentaries "[b] ;
but now, in opposition to Menodotus[c] and Aenesidemus (these being the chief champions of this view),
we declare in brief that when Plato makes statements about Ideas or about the reality of Providence
or about the virtuous life being preferable to the
vicious, he is dogmatizing if he is assenting to these as
actual truths, while if he is accepting them as more
probable than not, since thereby he gives a preference
to one thing over another in point of probability or
improbability, he throws off the character of a Sceptic ;
for that such an attitude is foreign to us is quite plain
from what has been said above.

(in Diog. Laert. iii. 49 ff.) into " maeeutic " (" akin to the
midwife's art " or " mental obstetrics ") and " peirastic " (or
" tentative," *e.g. Lysis, Laches, Euthyphro, Meno*).
  [b] *i.e.* the five books *Against the Dogmatists* ; see Introd.
p. xli.   [c] See Introd. p. xl.

223 Εἰ δέ τινα καὶ σκεπτικῶς προφέρεται, ὅταν, ὡς
φασί, γυμνάζηται, οὐ παρὰ τοῦτο ἔσται σκεπτικός·
ὁ γὰρ περὶ ἑνὸς δογματίζων, ἢ προκρίνων φαντασίαν φαντασίας ὅλως κατὰ πίστιν ἢ ἀπιστίαν
⟨ἢ ἀποφαινόμενος⟩[1] περί τινος τῶν ἀδήλων, τοῦ
δογματικοῦ γίνεται χαρακτῆρος, ὡς δηλοῖ καὶ ὁ
Τίμων διὰ τῶν περὶ Ξενοφάνους αὐτῷ λεγομένων.
224 ἐν πολλοῖς γὰρ αὐτὸν ἐπαινέσας [τὸν Ξενοφάνην],[2]
ὡς καὶ τοὺς σίλλους αὐτῷ ἀναθεῖναι, ἐποίησεν
αὐτὸν ὀδυρόμενον καὶ λέγοντα

ὡς καὶ ἐγὼν ὄφελον πυκινοῦ νόου ἀντιβολῆσαι
ἀμφοτερόβλεπτος· δολίῃ δ᾽ ὁδῷ ἐξαπατήθην
πρεσβυγενὴς ἔτ᾽ ἐὼν καὶ ἀμενθήριστος[3] ἁπάσης
σκεπτοσύνης. ὅππῃ γὰρ ἐμὸν νόον εἰρύσαιμι,
εἰς ἓν ταὐτό τε πᾶν ἀνελύετο· πᾶν δ᾽ ἐὸν αἰεὶ
πάντῃ ἀνελκόμενον μίαν εἰς φύσιν ἵσταθ᾽ ὁμοίην.

διὰ τοῦτο γοῦν καὶ ὑπάτυφον αὐτὸν λέγει, καὶ οὐ
τέλειον ἄτυφον, δι᾽ ὧν φησὶ

Ξεινοφάνης ὑπάτυφος, ὁμηραπάτης ἐπισκώπτης,
ἐκτὸς ἀπ᾽ ἀνθρώπων θεὸν ἐπλάσατ᾽ ἴσον ἁπάντῃ,
⟨ἀτρεμῆ⟩[4] ἀσκηθῆ, νοερώτερον[5] ἠὲ νόημα.

ὑπάτυφον μὲν γὰρ εἶπε τὸν κατά τι ἄτυφον, ὁμηραπάτης δὲ ἐπισκώπτην, ἐπεὶ τὴν παρ᾽ Ὁμήρῳ
225 ἀπάτην διέσυρεν. ἐδογμάτιζε δὲ ὁ Ξενοφάνης παρὰ
τὰς τῶν ἄλλων ἀνθρώπων προλήψεις ἓν εἶναι τὸ
πᾶν, καὶ τὸν θεὸν συμφυῆ τοῖς πᾶσιν, εἶναι δὲ
σφαιροειδῆ καὶ ἀπαθῆ καὶ ἀμετάβλητον καὶ λογι-

---

[1] ⟨ἢ ἀποφαινόμενος⟩ add. Papp.
[2] [τὸν Ξ.] del. Kayser, Mutsch.
[3] ἀμενθήριστος Bergk : ἀπενθ. mss., Bekk.
[4] ⟨ἀτρεμῆ⟩ add. Diels.
[5] νοερώτερον Diels : νοερωτὸν mss., Bekk.

And if Plato does really utter some statements in a 223
sceptical way when he is, as they say, " exercising,"
that will not make him a Sceptic ; for the man that
dogmatizes about a single thing, or ever prefers one
impression to another in point of credibility or incredibility, or makes any assertion about any non-evident
object, assumes the dogmatic character, as Timon [a]
also shows by his remarks about Xenophanes.   For 224
after praising him repeatedly, so that he even
dedicated to him his *Satires*, he represented him as
uttering this lamentation—

Would that I too had attained a mind compacted of wisdom,
Both ways casting my eyes ; but the treacherous pathway
    deceived me,
Old that I was, and as yet unversed in the doubts of the
    Sceptic.
For in whatever direction I turned my mind in its questing
All was resolved into One and the Same ; All ever-existing
Into one self-same nature returning shaped itself all ways.

So on this account he also calls him " semi-vain," and
not perfectly free from vanity, where he says—

Xenophanes semi-vain, derider of Homer's deceptions,
Framed him a God far other than Man, self-equal in all ways,
Safe from shaking or scathe, surpassing thought in his
    thinking.

He called him " semi-vain " as being in some degree
free from vanity, and " derider of Homer's deceptions " because he censured the deceit mentioned in
Homer.[b] Xenophanes, contrary to the preconceptions 225
of all other men, asserted dogmatically that the All
is one, and that God is consubstantial with all things,
and is of spherical form and passionless and unchange-

<hr>

[a] See Introd. p. xxxi; and for Xenophanes, *ibid.* p. viii.
[b] *e.g.* Homer, *Il.* ii. 114 where Agamemnon says of Zeus
νῦν δὲ κακὴν ἀπάτην βουλεύσατ'.   *Cf.* Plato, *Rep.* 380 D ff.

SEXTUS EMPIRICUS

κόν· ὅθεν καὶ ῥᾴδιον τὴν Ξενοφάνους πρὸς ἡμᾶς
διαφορὰν ἐπιδεικνύναι. πλὴν ἀλλ᾽ ἐκ τῶν εἰρημένων πρόδηλον ὅτι κἂν περί τινων ἐπαπορῇ ὁ
Πλάτων, ἀλλ᾽ ἐπεὶ ἔν τισι φαίνεται ἢ περὶ ὑπάρξεως ἀποφαινόμενος πραγμάτων ἀδήλων ἢ προκρίνων ἄδηλα κατὰ πίστιν, οὐκ ἂν εἴη σκεπτικός.

226 Οἱ δὲ ἀπὸ τῆς νέας Ἀκαδημίας, εἰ καὶ ἀκατάληπτα εἶναι πάντα φασί, διαφέρουσι τῶν σκεπτικῶν
ἴσως μὲν καὶ κατ᾽ αὐτὸ τὸ λέγειν πάντα εἶναι
ἀκατάληπτα (διαβεβαιοῦνται γὰρ περὶ τούτου, ὁ
δὲ σκεπτικὸς ἐνδέχεσθαι καὶ καταληφθῆναί τινα
προσδοκᾷ), διαφέρουσι δὲ ἡμῶν προδήλως ἐν τῇ
τῶν ἀγαθῶν καὶ τῶν κακῶν κρίσει. ἀγαθὸν γάρ
τί φασιν εἶναι οἱ Ἀκαδημαϊκοὶ καὶ κακὸν οὐχ ὡς
ἡμεῖς, ἀλλὰ μετὰ τοῦ πεπεῖσθαι ὅτι πιθανόν ἐστι
μᾶλλον ὃ λέγουσιν εἶναι ἀγαθὸν ὑπάρχειν ἢ τὸ
ἐναντίον, καὶ ἐπὶ τοῦ κακοῦ ὁμοίως, ἡμῶν ἀγαθόν
τι ἢ κακὸν εἶναι λεγόντων οὐδὲν μετὰ τοῦ πιθανὸν
εἶναι νομίζειν ὅ φαμεν, ἀλλ᾽ ἀδοξάστως ἑπομένων
227 τῷ βίῳ, ἵνα μὴ ἀνενέργητοι ὦμεν. τάς τε φαντασίας ἡμεῖς μὲν ἴσας λέγομεν εἶναι κατὰ πίστιν
ἢ ἀπιστίαν ὅσον ἐπὶ τῷ λόγῳ, ἐκεῖνοι δὲ τὰς μὲν
πιθανὰς εἶναί φασι τὰς δὲ ἀπιθάνους.

Καὶ τῶν πιθανῶν δὲ λέγουσι διαφοράς· τὰς μὲν
γὰρ αὐτὸ μόνον πιθανὰς ὑπάρχειν ἡγοῦνται, τὰς
δὲ πιθανὰς καὶ διεξωδευμένας, τὰς δὲ πιθανὰς καὶ

---

[a] Carneades was the chief exponent of this " probabilism ";
see Introd. pp. xxxiii-xxxiv.

able and rational ; and from this it is easy to show how Xenophanes differs from us. However, it is plain from what has been said that even if Plato evinces doubt about some matters, yet he cannot be a Sceptic inasmuch as he shows himself at times either making assertions about the reality of non-evident objects or preferring one non-evident thing to another in point of credibility.

The adherents of the New Academy, although they 226 affirm that all things are non-apprehensible, yet differ from the Sceptics even, as seems probable, in respect of this very statement that all things are non-apprehensible (for they affirm this positively, whereas the Sceptic regards it as possible that some things may be apprehended) ; but they differ from us quite plainly in their judgement of things good and evil. For the Academicians do not describe a thing as good or evil in the way we do ; for they do so with the conviction that it is more probable [a] that what they call good is really good rather than the opposite, and so too in the case of evil, whereas when we describe a thing as good or evil we do not add it as our opinion that what we assert is probable, but simply conform to life undogmatically that we may not be precluded from activity.[b] And as regards 227 sense-impressions, we say [c] that they are equal in respect of probability and improbability, so far as their essence is concerned, whereas they assert that some impressions are probable, others improbable.

And respecting the probable impressions they make distinctions : some they regard as just simply probable, others as probable and tested, others as

[b] Cf. §§ 15, 23 f. ; ii. 13.   [c] Cf. § 117.

περιωδευμένας καὶ ἀπερισπάστους. οἷον ἐν οἴκῳ
σκοτεινῷ ποσῶς κειμένου σχοινίου ἐσπειραμένου
πιθανὴ ἁπλῶς φαντασία γίνεται ἀπὸ τούτου ὡς
228 ἀπὸ ὄφεως τῷ ἀθρόως ἐπεισελθόντι· τῷ μέντοι
περισκοπήσαντι ἀκριβῶς καὶ διεξοδεύσαντι τὰ περὶ
αὐτό, οἷον ὅτι οὐ κινεῖται, ὅτι τὸ χρῶμα τοῖόν
ἐστι, καὶ τῶν ἄλλων ἕκαστον, φαίνεται σχοινίον
κατὰ τὴν φαντασίαν τὴν πιθανὴν καὶ περιωδευμένην. ἡ δὲ καὶ ἀπερίσπαστος φαντασία τοιάδε
ἐστίν. λέγεται ὁ Ἡρακλῆς ἀποθανοῦσαν τὴν
Ἄλκηστιν αὖθις ἐξ ᾅδου ἀναγαγεῖν καὶ δεῖξαι
τῷ Ἀδμήτῳ, ὃς[1] πιθανὴν ἐλάμβανε φαντασίαν τῆς
Ἀλκήστιδος καὶ περιωδευμένην· ἐπεὶ μέντοι ᾔδει
ὅτι τέθνηκεν, περιεσπᾶτο αὐτοῦ ἡ διάνοια ἀπὸ
τῆς συγκαταθέσεως καὶ πρὸς ἀπιστίαν ἔκλινεν.
229 προκρίνουσιν οὖν οἱ ἐκ τῆς νέας Ἀκαδημίας τῆς
μὲν πιθανῆς ἁπλῶς τὴν πιθανὴν καὶ περιωδευμένην
φαντασίαν, ἀμφοτέρων δὲ τούτων τὴν πιθανὴν καὶ
περιωδευμένην καὶ ἀπερίσπαστον.

Εἰ δὲ καὶ πείθεσθαί τισιν οἵ τε ἀπὸ τῆς Ἀκαδημίας καὶ οἱ ἀπὸ τῆς σκέψεως λέγουσι, πρόδηλος καὶ ἡ κατὰ τοῦτο διαφορὰ τῶν φιλοσοφιῶν.
230 τὸ γὰρ πείθεσθαι λέγεται διαφόρως, τό τε μὴ
ἀντιτείνειν ἀλλ' ἁπλῶς ἕπεσθαι ἄνευ σφοδρᾶς
προσκλίσεως καὶ προσπαθείας, ὡς ὁ παῖς λέγεται
πείθεσθαι τῷ παιδαγωγῷ· ἅπαξ δὲ τὸ μετὰ
αἱρέσεως καὶ οἱονεὶ συμπαθείας κατὰ τὸ σφόδρα
βούλεσθαι συγκατατίθεσθαί τινι, ὡς ὁ ἄσωτος

---

[1] ὃς T: καὶ mss., Bekk.

---

[a] διεξωδευμένας and περιωδευμένας mean literally "gone all
through" (or "all over"), hence "thoroughly inspected,"

probable, tested, and "irreversible."[a] For example, when a rope is lying coiled up in a dark room, to one who enters hurriedly it presents the simply "probable" appearance of being a serpent; but to the 228 man who has looked carefully round and has investigated the conditions — such as its immobility and its colour, and each of its other peculiarities—it appears as a rope, in accordance with an impression that is probable and tested. And the impression that is also "irreversible" or incontrovertible is of this kind. When Alcestis had died, Heracles, it is said, brought her up again from Hades and showed her to Admetus, who received an impression of Alcestis that was probable and tested; since, however, he knew that she was dead his mind recoiled from its assent and reverted to unbelief.[b] So then the philosophers 229 of the New Academy prefer the probable and tested impression to the simply probable, and to both of these the impression that is probable and tested and irreversible.

And although both the Academics and the Sceptics say that they believe some things, yet here too the difference between the two philosophies is quite plain. For the word "believe" has different meanings: it 230 means not to resist but simply to follow without any strong impulse or inclination, as the boy is said to believe his tutor; but sometimes it means to assent to a thing of deliberate choice and with a kind of sympathy due to strong desire, as when the incontinent man believes him who approves of

---

"scrutinized": ἀπερισπάστους, "not able to be drawn round" (or "stripped off"), hence "indubitable."

[b] This is a curious example of an "irreversible" impression. If the text is right, it looks as if Sextus was nodding.

πείθεται τῷ δαπανητικῶς βιοῦν ἀξιοῦντι. διόπερ
ἐπειδὴ οἱ μὲν περὶ Καρνεάδην καὶ Κλειτόμαχον
μετὰ προσκλίσεως σφοδρᾶς πείθεσθαί τε καὶ
πιθανὸν εἶναί τι φασίν, ἡμεῖς δὲ κατὰ τὸ ἁπλῶς
εἴκειν ἄνευ προσπαθείας, καὶ κατὰ τοῦτο ἂν αὐτῶν
διαφέροιμεν.

231 Ἀλλὰ καὶ ἐν τοῖς πρὸς τὸ τέλος διαφέρομεν τῆς
νέας Ἀκαδημίας· οἱ μὲν γὰρ κατ' αὐτὴν κοσ-
μεῖσθαι λέγοντες ἄνδρες τῷ πιθανῷ προσχρῶνται
κατὰ τὸν βίον, ἡμεῖς δὲ τοῖς νόμοις καὶ τοῖς ἔθεσι
καὶ τοῖς φυσικοῖς πάθεσιν ἑπόμενοι βιοῦμεν ἀδοξάστως. καὶ πλείω δ' ἂν εἴπομεν πρὸς τὴν διάκρισιν,
εἰ μὴ τῆς συντομίας ἐστοχαζόμεθα.

232 Ὁ μέντοι Ἀρκεσίλαος, ὃν τῆς μέσης Ἀκαδημίας ἐλέγομεν εἶναι προστάτην καὶ ἀρχηγόν,
πάνυ μοι δοκεῖ τοῖς Πυρρωνείοις κοινωνεῖν λόγοις,
ὡς μίαν εἶναι σχεδὸν τὴν κατ' αὐτὸν ἀγωγὴν καὶ
τὴν ἡμετέραν· οὔτε γὰρ περὶ ὑπάρξεως ἢ ἀνυπαρξίας τινὸς ἀποφαινόμενος εὑρίσκεται, οὔτε κατὰ
πίστιν ἢ ἀπιστίαν προκρίνει τι ἕτερον ἑτέρου, ἀλλὰ
περὶ πάντων ἐπέχει. καὶ τέλος μὲν εἶναι τὴν
ἐποχήν, ᾗ συνεισέρχεσθαι τὴν ἀταραξίαν ἡμεῖς
233 ἐφάσκομεν. λέγει δὲ καὶ ἀγαθὰ μὲν εἶναι τὰς κατὰ
μέρος ἐποχάς, κακὰ δὲ τὰς κατὰ μέρος συγκατα-
θέσεις. [ἤτοι] πλὴν εἰ μὴ λέγοι τις ὅτι ἡμεῖς μὲν
κατὰ τὸ φαινόμενον ἡμῖν ταῦτα λέγομεν καὶ οὐ
διαβεβαιωτικῶς, ἐκεῖνος δὲ ὡς πρὸς τὴν φύσιν,
ὥστε καὶ ἀγαθὸν μὲν εἶναι αὐτὴν λέγειν τὴν ἐποχήν,
234 κακὸν δὲ τὴν συγκατάθεσιν. εἰ δὲ δεῖ καὶ τοῖς
περὶ αὐτοῦ λεγομένοις πιστεύειν, φασὶν ὅτι κατὰ

---

[a] Cf. §§ 22, 27 ff. supra.   [b] See §§ 25 supra.
[c] Cf. § 226.   [d] Cf. §§ 23, 24.   [e] Cf. § 220 supra.

an extravagant mode of life. Since, therefore, Carneades and Cleitomachus declare that a strong inclination accompanies their credence and the credibility of the object, while we [a] say that our belief is a matter of simple yielding without any consent, here too there must be a difference between us and them.

Furthermore, as regards the End (or aim of life) [b] we differ from the New Academy; for whereas the men who profess to conform to its doctrine [c] use probability as the guide of life, we [d] live in an undogmatic way by following the laws, customs, and natural affections. And we might say still more about this distinction had it not been that we are aiming at conciseness.

Arcesilaus, however, who was, as we said, [e] the president and founder of the Middle Academy, certainly seems to me to have shared the doctrines of Pyrrho, so that his Way of thought is almost identical with ours. For we do not find him making any assertion about the reality or unreality of anything, nor does he prefer any one thing to another in point of probability or improbability, but suspends judgement about all. He also says that the End is suspension—which is accompanied, as we have said, by " quietude." He declares, too, that suspension regarding particular objects is good, but assent regarding particulars bad. Only one might say that whereas we make these statements not positively but in accordance with what appears to us, he makes them as statements of real facts, so that he asserts that suspension in itself really is good and assent bad. And if one ought to credit also what is said about him, he appeared at the first

231

232

233

234

143

μὲν τὸ πρόχειρον Πυρρώνειος ἐφαίνετο εἶναι, κατὰ
δὲ τὴν ἀλήθειαν δογματικὸς ἦν· καὶ ἐπεὶ τῶν
ἑταίρων ἀπόπειραν ἐλάμβανε διὰ τῆς ἀπορητικῆς
εἰ εὐφυῶς ἔχουσι πρὸς τὴν ἀνάληψιν τῶν Πλατω-
νικῶν δογμάτων, δόξαι αὐτὸν ἀπορητικὸν εἶναι,
τοῖς μέντοι γε εὐφυέσι τῶν ἑταίρων τὰ Πλάτωνος
παρεγχειρεῖν. ἔνθεν καὶ τὸν Ἀρίστωνα εἰπεῖν περὶ
αὐτοῦ

πρόσθε Πλάτων, ὄπιθεν Πύρρων, μέσσος Διό-
    δωρος,

διὰ τὸ προσχρῆσθαι τῇ διαλεκτικῇ τῇ κατὰ τὸν
Διόδωρον, εἶναι δὲ ἄντικρυς Πλατωνικόν.
235 Οἱ δὲ περὶ Φιλωνά φασιν ὅσον μὲν ἐπὶ τῷ
στωικῷ κριτηρίῳ, τουτέστι τῇ καταληπτικῇ φαντασίᾳ, ἀκατάληπτα εἶναι τὰ πράγματα, ὅσον δὲ
ἐπὶ τῇ φύσει τῶν πραγμάτων αὐτῶν καταληπτά.
ἀλλὰ καὶ ὁ Ἀντίοχος τὴν στοὰν μετήγαγεν εἰς
τὴν Ἀκαδήμιαν, ὡς καὶ εἰρῆσθαι ἐπ' αὐτῷ ὅτι ἐν
Ἀκαδημίᾳ φιλοσοφεῖ τὰ στωικά· ἐπεδείκνυε γὰρ
ὅτι παρὰ Πλάτωνι κεῖται τὰ τῶν στωικῶν δόγματα.
ὡς πρόδηλον εἶναι τὴν τῆς σκεπτικῆς ἀγωγῆς
διαφορὰν πρός τε τὴν τετάρτην καὶ τὴν πέμπτην
καλουμένην Ἀκαδήμιαν.

ΛΔ΄.—ΕΙ Η ΚΑΤΑ ΤΗΝ ΙΑΤΡΙΚΗΝ ΕΜΠΕΙΡΙΑ Η ΑΥΤΗ
ΕΣΤΙ ΤΗ ΣΚΕΨΕΙ

236 Ἐπεὶ δὲ καὶ τῇ ἐμπειρίᾳ τῇ κατὰ τὴν ἰατρικὴν
αἱρέσει τὴν αὐτὴν λέγουσί τινες εἶναι τὴν σκεπ-

---

[a] Ariston of Chios, a pupil of Zeno the Stoic.
[b] The verse is a parody of Homer, *Il.* vi. 181 (*cf.* Hesiod,

glance, they say, to be a Pyrrhonean, but in reality he was a dogmatist; and because he used to test his companions by means of dubitation to see if they were fitted by nature for the reception of the Platonic dogmas, he was thought to be a dubitative philosopher, but he actually passed on to such of his companions as were naturally gifted the dogmas of Plato. And this was why Ariston [a] described him as " Plato the head of him, Pyrrho the tail, in the midst Diodorus " [b]; because he employed the dialectic of Diodorus, although he was actually a Platonist.

Philo [c] asserts that objects are inapprehensible 235 so far as concerns the Stoic criterion, that is to say " apprehensive impression," but are apprehensible so far as concerns the real nature of the objects themselves. Moreover, Antiochus [c] actually transferred the Stoa to the Academy, so that it was even said of him that " In the Academy he teaches the Stoic philosophy " ; for he tried to show that the dogmas of the Stoics are already present in Plato. So that it is quite plain how the Sceptic " Way " differs from what is called the Fourth Academy and the Fifth.

CHAPTER XXXIV.—WHETHER MEDICAL EMPIRICISM
IS THE SAME AS SCEPTICISM

Since some allege that the Sceptic philosophy 236 is identical with the Empiricism of the Medical

Theog. 323), who thus describes the Chimaera: πρόσθε λέων, ὄπιθεν δὲ δράκων, μέσση δὲ χίμαιρα (" Lion the head of her, Dragon the tail of her, trunk of a She-goat"). Diodorus Cronos was a Megaric philosopher (*circa* 300 B.C.).
  [b] See Introd. pp. xxxvi f.

SEXTUS EMPIRICUS

τικὴν φιλοσοφίαν, γνωστέον ὅτι εἴπερ ἡ ἐμπειρία
ἐκείνη περὶ τῆς ἀκαταληψίας τῶν ἀδήλων δια-
βεβαιοῦται, οὔτε ἡ αὐτή ἐστι τῇ σκέψει οὔτε
ἁρμόζοι ἂν τῷ σκεπτικῷ τὴν αἵρεσιν ἐκείνην
ἀναλαμβάνειν. μᾶλλον δὲ τὴν καλουμένην μέθοδον,
237 ὡς ἐμοὶ δοκεῖ, δύναιτο ἂν μετιέναι· αὕτη γὰρ μόνη
τῶν κατὰ ἰατρικὴν αἱρέσεων περὶ μὲν τῶν ἀδήλων
δοκεῖ μὴ προπετεύεσθαι, πότερον καταληπτὰ ἐστιν
ἢ ἀκατάληπτα λέγειν αὐθαδειαζομένη, τοῖς δὲ
φαινομένοις ἑπομένη ἀπὸ τούτων λαμβάνει τὸ συμ-
φέρειν δοκοῦν κατὰ τὴν τῶν σκεπτικῶν ἀκολουθίαν. καὶ ἐλέγομεν γὰρ ἐν τοῖς ἔμπροσθεν ὅτι ὁ
βίος ὁ κοινός, ᾧ καὶ ὁ σκεπτικὸς χρῆται, τετρα-
μερής ἐστιν, τὸ μέν τι ἔχων ἐν ὑφηγήσει φύσεως,
τὸ δ' ἐν ἀνάγκῃ παθῶν, τὸ δ' ἐν παραδόσει νόμων
238 τε καὶ ἐθῶν, τὸ δ' ἐν διδασκαλίᾳ τεχνῶν. ὥσπερ
οὖν κατὰ τὴν ἀνάγκην τῶν παθῶν ὁ σκεπτικὸς
ὑπὸ μὲν δίψους ἐπὶ ποτὸν ὁδηγεῖται ὑπὸ δὲ λιμοῦ
ἐπὶ τροφήν, καὶ ἐπί τι τῶν ἄλλων ὁμοίως, οὕτω
καὶ ὁ μεθοδικὸς ἰατρὸς ὑπὸ τῶν παθῶν ἐπὶ τὰ
κατάλληλα ὁδηγεῖται, ὑπὸ μὲν στεγνώσεως ἐπὶ
τὴν χαύνωσιν, ὡς καταφεύγει τις ἀπὸ τῆς διὰ
ψύχος ἐπιτεταμένον πυκνώσεως ἐπὶ ἀλέαν, ὑπὸ
δὲ ῥύσεως ἐπὶ τὴν ἐποχὴν αὐτῆς, ὡς καὶ οἱ ἐν
βαλανείῳ ἱδρῶτι πολλῷ περιρρεόμενοι καὶ ἐκλυό-
μενοι ἐπὶ τὴν ἐποχὴν αὐτοῦ παραγίνονται καὶ διὰ
τοῦτο ἐπὶ τὸν ψυχρὸν ἀέρα καταφεύγουσιν. ὅτι
δὲ καὶ τὰ φύσει ἀλλότρια ἐπὶ τὴν λύσιν[1] αὐτῶν

---

[1] λύσιν ego : φύσιν mss., Bekk.: ἄρσιν Papp.

---

[a] The later schools of Medicine were three: (1) the
Dogmatic or Logical, which theorized about the "non-

sect,[a] it must be recognized that inasmuch as that Empiricism positively affirms the inapprehensibility of what is non-evident it is not identical with Scepticism nor would it be consistent in a Sceptic to embrace that doctrine. He could more easily, in my opinion, adopt the so-called " Method " ; for it alone of the Medical 237 systems appears to avoid rash treatment of things non-evident by arbitrary assertions as to their apprehensibility or non-apprehensibility, and following appearances derives from them what seems beneficial, in accordance with the practice of the Sceptics. For we stated above [b] that the common life, in which the Sceptic also shares, is four-fold, one part depending on the directing force of Nature, another on the compulsion of the affections, another on the tradition of laws and customs, and another on the training of the arts. So then, just as the Sceptic, in virtue of the 238 compulsion of the affections, is guided by thirst to drink and by hunger to food, and in like manner to other such objects, in the same way the Methodical physician is guided by the pathological affections to the corresponding remedies—by contraction to dilatation, as when one seeks refuge in heat from the contraction due to the application of cold, or by fluxion to the stoppage of it, as when persons in a hot bath, dripping with perspiration and in a relaxed condition, seek to put a stop to it and for this reason rush off into the cool air. It is plain, too, that conditions which are naturally alien compel us to take measures for their

evident " causes of health and disease; (2) the Empiric, which regarded such causes as indiscoverable and confined itself to observation of evident facts ; (3) the Methodic, which adopted an intermediate position, refusing either to affirm or deny " non-evident " causes; cf. Introd. p. xl.
   [b] § 23.

ἰέναι καταναγκάζει, πρόδηλον, ὅπου γε καὶ ὁ κύων
σκόλοπος αὐτῷ καταπαγέντος ἐπὶ τὴν ἆρσιν αὐτοῦ
239 παραγίνεται. καὶ ἵνα μὴ καθ' ἕκαστον λέγων
ἐκβαίνω τὸν ὑποτυπωτικὸν τρόπον τῆς συγγραφῆς,
πάντα οἶμαι τὰ ὑπὸ τῶν μεθοδικῶν οὕτω λεγόμενα
ὑποτάσσεσθαι δύνασθαι τῇ ἐκ τῶν παθῶν ἀνάγκῃ,
τῶν τε κατὰ φύσιν καὶ τῶν παρὰ φύσιν, πρὸς τῷ
καὶ τὸ ἀδόξαστόν τε καὶ ἀδιάφορον τῆς χρήσεως
240 τῶν ὀνομάτων κοινὸν εἶναι τῶν ἀγωγῶν. ὡς γὰρ ὁ
σκεπτικὸς ⟨ἀδοξάστως⟩[1] χρῆται τῇ " οὐδὲν ὁρίζω "
φωνῇ καὶ τῇ " οὐδὲν καταλαμβάνω," καθάπερ εἰρήκαμεν, οὕτω καὶ ὁ μεθοδικὸς κοινότητα λέγει καὶ
διήκειν καὶ τὰ παραπλήσια ἀπεριέργως. οὕτω δὲ καὶ
τὸ τῆς ἐνδείξεως ὄνομα ἀδοξάστως παραλαμβάνει
ἀντὶ τῆς ἀπὸ τῶν φαινομένων παθῶν τῶν τε κατὰ
φύσιν καὶ τῶν παρὰ φύσιν ὁδηγήσεως ἐπὶ τὰ κατάλληλα εἶναι δοκοῦντα, ὡς καὶ ἐπὶ δίψους καὶ ἐπὶ
241 λιμοῦ καὶ τῶν ἄλλων ὑπεμιμνήσκον. ὅθεν οἰκειό-
τητά τινα ἔχειν τὴν ἀγωγὴν τὴν κατὰ ἰατρικὴν
τῶν μεθοδικῶν πρὸς τὴν σκέψιν, μᾶλλον τῶν ἄλλων
κατὰ ἰατρικὴν αἱρέσεων καὶ ὡς πρὸς σύγκρισιν
ἐκείνων, οὐχ ἁπλῶς, ῥητέον ἐκ τούτων καὶ τῶν
παραπλησίων τούτοις τεκμαιρομένοις.

Τοσαῦτα καὶ περὶ τῶν παρακεῖσθαι δοκούντων
τῇ κατὰ τοὺς σκεπτικοὺς ἀγωγῇ διεξελθόντες, ἐν
τούτοις ἀπαρτίζομεν τόν τε καθόλου τῆς σκέψεως
λόγον καὶ τὸ πρῶτον τῶν ὑποτυπώσεων σύνταγμα.

---

[1] ⟨ἀδοξάστως⟩ add. Mutsch. e T.

[a] Or "generic character." All diseases being referred to
one or other of the two "general" morbid states, over-
contraction or over-dilatation of the pores or passages of the

removal, seeing that even the dog when it is pricked
by a thorn proceeds to remove it. And in short—to 239
avoid exceeding the limits proper to an outline of this
kind by a detailed enumeration—I suppose that all
the facts described by the Methodic School can be
classed as instances of the compulsion of the affections,
whether natural or against nature.

Besides, the use of terms in an undogmatic and
indeterminate sense is common to both systems. For 240
just as the Sceptic uses the expressions " I determine
nothing " and " I apprehend nothing," as we have
said, in an undogmatic sense, even so the Methodic
speaks of " generality " a and " pervade " and the like
in a non-committal way. So also he employs the
term " indication " in an undogmatic sense to denote
the guidance derived from the apparent affections, or
symptoms, both natural and contra-natural, for the
discovery of the seemingly appropriate remedies—
as, in fact, I mentioned in regard to hunger and thirst
and the other affections. Consequently, judging 241
from these and similar indications, we should say that
the Methodic School of Medicine has some affinity
with Scepticism ; and, when viewed not simply by
itself, but in comparison with the other Medical
Schools, it has more affinity than they.

And now that we have said thus much concerning
the Schools which seem to stand nearest to that of
the Sceptics, we here bring to a conclusion both our
general account of Scepticism and the First Book of
our " Outlines."

body, each of these " general " states was said to " pervade "
all the cases which exhibited the symptoms of that state.
The " genus " " pervades " (its characteristics run through)
its " species " and " particulars."

B

Α΄.—ΕΙ ΔΥΝΑΤΑΙ ΖΗΤΕΙΝ Ο ΣΚΕΠΤΙΚΟΣ ΠΕΡΙ ΤΩΝ ΛΕΓΟΜΕΝΩΝ ΠΑΡΑ ΤΟΙΣ ΔΟΓΜΑΤΙΚΟΙΣ

1 Ἐπεὶ δὲ τὴν ζήτησιν τὴν πρὸς τοὺς δογματικοὺς μετήλθομεν, ἕκαστον τῶν μερῶν τῆς καλουμένης φιλοσοφίας συντόμως καὶ ὑποτυπωτικῶς ἐφοδεύσωμεν, πρότερον ἀποκρινάμενοι πρὸς τοὺς ἀεὶ θρυλοῦντας ὡς μήτε ζητεῖν μήτε νοεῖν ὅλως οἷός τέ ἐστιν ὁ σκεπτικὸς περὶ τῶν δογματιζομένων 2 παρ᾽ αὐτοῖς. φασὶ γὰρ ὡς ἤτοι καταλαμβάνει ὁ σκεπτικὸς τὰ ὑπὸ τῶν δογματικῶν λεγόμενα ἢ οὐ καταλαμβάνει· καὶ εἰ μὲν καταλαμβάνει, πῶς ἂν ἀποροίη περὶ ὧν κατειληφέναι λέγει; εἰ δ᾽ οὐ καταλαμβάνει, ἄρα περὶ ὧν οὐ κατείληφεν οὐδὲ 3 οἶδε λέγειν. ὥσπερ γὰρ ὁ μὴ εἰδώς, εἰ τύχοι, τί ἐστι τὸ καθ᾽ ὃ περιαιρουμένου ἢ τὸ διὰ δύο τροπικῶν θεώρημα, οὐδὲ εἰπεῖν τι δύναται περὶ αὐτῶν, οὕτως ὁ μὴ γινώσκων ἕκαστον τῶν λεγομένων παρὰ τοῖς δογματικοῖς οὐ δύναται ζητεῖν πρὸς

---

[a] *i.e.* the "special" section of this Sceptical treatise, as distinguished from the "general" exposition contained in Bk. I.; *cf.* i. 5, 6, 21.

[b] *i.e.* Stoics and Epicureans.

[c] This argument is not elsewhere mentioned; possibly it refers to some form of the "Sorites"; *cf.* § 253. But T has

BOOK II

Chapter I.—Can the Sceptic investigate the Statements of the Dogmatists?

Since we have undertaken this inquiry in criticism 1 of the Dogmatists,[a] let us review briefly and in outline the several divisions of so-called philosophy, when we have first made reply to those who keep constantly repeating that the Sceptic is incapable of either investigating or in any way cognizing the objects about which they dogmatize. For they [b] maintain 2 that the Sceptic either apprehends or does not apprehend the statements made by the Dogmatists; if, then, he apprehends, how can he be perplexed about things which he has, as he says, apprehended? Whereas if he apprehends not, then neither does he know how to discuss matters which he has not apprehended. For just as he who is ignorant, for instance, 3 of the arguments known as " How far reduced " [c] or " By two hypotheses," [d] is unable also to say anything about them, so the man who does not know each of the statements made by the Dogmatists is unable to

"qui non novit . . . quid est omnis triangulus habet tres angulos equales duobus rectis."

[d] The hypothetical syllogism " by two hypotheses " has its major premiss in double form; *e.g.* " If A is, B is, and if A is not, B is; but A either is or is not; therefore B is." *Cf.* §§ 131, 186 *infra.*

151

αὐτοὺς περὶ ὧν οὐκ οἶδεν. οὐδαμῶς ἄρα δύναται
ζητεῖν ὁ σκεπτικὸς περὶ τῶν λεγομένων παρὰ τοῖς
4 δογματικοῖς. οἱ δὴ ταῦτα λέγοντες ἀποκρινάσθωσαν ἡμῖν πῶς λέγουσι νῦν τὸ καταλαμβάνειν,
πότερον τὸ νοεῖν ἁπλῶς ἄνευ τοῦ καὶ ὑπὲρ τῆς
ὑπάρξεως ἐκείνων περὶ ὧν ποιούμεθα τοὺς λόγους
διαβεβαιοῦσθαι, ἢ μετὰ τοῦ [νοεῖν]¹ καὶ τὴν ὕπαρξιν
ἐκείνων τιθέναι περὶ ὧν διαλεγόμεθα. εἰ μὲν γὰρ
καταλαμβάνειν εἶναι λέγουσιν ἐν τῷ λόγῳ τὸ
καταληπτικῇ φαντασίᾳ συγκατατίθεσθαι, τῆς καταληπτικῆς φαντασίας οὔσης ἀπὸ ὑπάρχοντος, κατ'
αὐτὸ τὸ ὑπάρχον ἐναπομεμαγμένης καὶ ἐναπεσφρα-
γισμένης, οἷα οὐκ ἂν γένοιτο ἀπὸ μὴ ὑπάρχοντος, οὐδὲ αὐτοὶ βουλήσονται τάχα μὴ δύνασθαι
ζητεῖν περὶ ἐκείνων ἃ μὴ κατειλήφασιν οὕτως.
5 οἷον γοῦν ὅταν ὁ στωικὸς πρὸς τὸν Ἐπικούρειον
ζητῇ λέγοντα ὅτι διήρηται ἡ οὐσία ἢ ὡς ὁ θεὸς
οὐ προνοεῖ τῶν ἐν κόσμῳ ἢ ὅτι ἡ ἡδονὴ ἀγαθόν,
πότερον κατείληφεν ἢ οὐ κατείληφεν; καὶ εἰ μὲν
κατείληφεν, ὑπάρχειν αὐτὰ λέγων ἄρδην ἀναιρεῖ
τὴν στοάν· εἰ δ' οὐ κατείληφεν, οὐ δύναταί τι πρὸς
αὐτὰ λέγειν.
6 Τὰ δὲ παραπλήσια καὶ πρὸς τοὺς ἀπὸ τῶν ἄλλων
αἱρέσεων ἀναγομένους λεκτέον, ὅταν τι ζητεῖν περὶ
τῶν δοκούντων τοῖς ἑτεροδόξοις αὐτῶν ἐθέλωσιν.

¹ [νοεῖν] del. Heintz.

<hr>

ᵃ For this term in the Stoic epistemology see Introd. p. xxv.
The argument is, in brief, that the Stoic cannot consistently
criticize the Epicurean unless he allows that his " apprehensive impression " of their dogmas is an impression of
things which have no basis in reality, and this contradicts
the Stoic definition of " apprehensive impression."
ᵇ It is uncertain to what " division " this refers—whether

criticize them concerning matters of which he has no knowledge. Thus the Sceptic is wholly incapable of investigating the statements made by the Dogmatists.

Now let those who speak thus make answer and 4 tell us in what sense they are now using the term "apprehend," whether simply of mental conception without the further affirmation of the reality of the objects under discussion, or with the further assumption of the reality of the objects discussed. For if they say that "to apprehend" means, in their argument, to assent to an "apprehensive impression," [a] the apprehensive impression being derived from a real object and being an imprint or stamp upon the mind corresponding to the actual object, such as would not result from what is unreal, then probably not even they themselves will wish to allow their inability to investigate things which, in this sense, they have not apprehended. Thus, for example, when the 5 Stoic criticizes the statement of the Epicurean that "Being is divided," [b] or that "God does not foreknow events in the Universe," or that "Pleasure is the Good," has he apprehended or has he not apprehended? If he has apprehended these dogmas, by asserting their real truth he entirely overthrows the Porch; while if he has not apprehended them, he is unable to say anything against them.

And we must use a like argument against those 6 who issue from any of the other Sects, whenever they desire to make any critical investigation of the tenets of those who differ from them in doctrine. Con-

that of God from the world (Fabricius), of Body from Void (Zimmermann), of the "numberless worlds" from one another (Pappenheim), or (as seems simplest) of Body into numberless atomic fractions. For the *dicta* about "God" and "Pleasure" *cf.* iii. 219.

ὥστε οὐ δύνανται περί τινος ζητεῖν πρὸς ἀλλήλους.
μᾶλλον δέ, εἰ χρὴ μὴ ληρεῖν, συγχυθήσεται μὲν
αὐτῶν ἅπασα ὡς ἔπος εἰπεῖν ἡ δογματική, συν-
τόνως δὲ προσαχθήσεται ἡ σκεπτικὴ φιλοσοφία,
διδομένου τοῦ μὴ δύνασθαι ζητεῖν περὶ τοῦ μὴ
7 οὕτως κατειλημμένου. ὁ γὰρ περί τινος ἀδήλου
πράγματος ἀποφαινόμενός τε καὶ δογματίζων ἤτοι
κατειληφὼς αὐτὸ ἀποφαίνεσθαι περὶ αὐτοῦ λέξει
ἢ μὴ κατειληφώς. ἀλλ᾽ εἰ μὲν μὴ κατειληφώς,
ἄπιστος ἔσται· εἰ δὲ κατειληφώς, ἤτοι αὐτόθεν καὶ
ἐξ ἑαυτοῦ καὶ κατ᾽ ἐνάργειαν ὑποπεσὸν αὐτῷ
τοῦτο λέξει κατειληφέναι ἢ διά τινος ἐρεύνης καὶ
8 ζητήσεως. ἀλλ᾽ εἰ μὲν ἐξ ἑαυτοῦ περιπτωτικῶς
κατ᾽ ἐνάργειαν λέγοιτο ὑποπεσεῖν αὐτῷ καὶ κατειλῆφθαι τὸ ἄδηλον, οὕτως ἂν οὐδὲ ἄδηλον εἴη
ἀλλὰ πᾶσιν ἐπ᾽ ἴσης φαινόμενον καὶ ὁμολογούμενον
καὶ μὴ διαπεφωνημένον. περὶ ἑκάστου δὲ τῶν
ἀδήλων ἀνήνυτος γέγονε παρ᾽ αὐτοῖς διαφωνία·
οὐκ ἄρα ἐξ ἑαυτοῦ καὶ κατ᾽ ἐνάργειαν ὑποπεσὸν
αὐτῷ κατειληφὼς ἂν εἴη τὸ ἄδηλον ὁ περὶ τῆς
ὑπάρξεως αὐτοῦ διαβεβαιούμενός τε καὶ ἀποφαινό-
9 μενος δογματικός. εἰ δὲ διά τινος ἐρεύνης, πῶς
οἷός τε ἦν ζητεῖν πρὸ τοῦ καταλαβεῖν ἀκριβῶς
αὐτὸ κατὰ τὴν προκειμένην ὑπόθεσιν; τῆς μὲν
γὰρ ζητήσεως χρῃζούσης τοῦ πρότερον ἀκριβῶς
κατειλῆφθαι τὸ μέλλον ζητεῖσθαι καὶ οὕτω ζητεῖσθαι, τῆς δὲ καταλήψεως τοῦ ζητουμένου πράγ-

---

^a For this distinction cf. i. 178 ff.

sequently they are debarred from indulging in any criticism of one another. Or rather—to avoid talking nonsense—practically the whole of Dogmatism will be confounded and the Sceptic philosophy will be firmly established once it is granted that it is impossible to inquire regarding an object which is not, in this sense, apprehended. For he who makes a **7** dogmatic statement about a non-evident object will declare that he is making it either after having apprehended or after having not apprehended it. But if he has not apprehended it he will not gain credence ; while if he has apprehended it, he will say that he has apprehended the object directly and through itself and owing to the clear impression it has made on him, or else by means of some kind of search and inquiry.[a] But if he shall say that the **8** non-evident object has impressed him and has been apprehended through itself, immediately and clearly, in this case the object would not be non-evident but apparent to all men equally, an acknowledged and uncontroverted fact. But about every single object that is non-evident there exists amongst them endless controversy ; so that the Dogmatist who makes positive assertions about the reality of a non-evident object cannot have apprehended it because of its having made on him a direct and clear impression. If, on the other hand, his apprehension is a result of **9** search, how was he in a position to make inquiry before he had accurately apprehended the object, without violating our present assumption ? For since the inquiry necessitates as a preliminary the existence of an accurate apprehension of that which is to be the subject of inquiry, while the apprehension of the subject of inquiry demands, in its turn, the previous

ματος δεομένης πάλιν αὐτῆς τοῦ προεζητῆσθαι
πάντως αὐτό, κατὰ τὸν διάλληλον τρόπον τῆς
ἀπορίας ἀδύνατον αὐτοῖς γίγνεται καὶ τὸ ζητεῖν
περὶ τῶν ἀδήλων καὶ τὸ δογματίζειν, ἤν τε ἀπὸ
τῆς καταλήψεως ἄρχεσθαι βούλωνταί τινες, μετ-
αγόντων ἡμῶν αὐτοὺς ἐπὶ τὸ δεῖν αὐτὸ προ-
εζητηκέναι πρὸ τοῦ κατειληφέναι, ἤν τε ἀπὸ τῆς
ζητήσεως, ἐπὶ τὸ δεῖν πρὸ τοῦ ζητεῖν κατειληφέναι
τὸ μέλλον ζητεῖσθαι. ὥστε διὰ ταῦτα μήτε καταλαμβάνειν αὐτοὺς δύνασθαί τι τῶν ἀδήλων μήτε
ἀποφαίνεσθαι διαβεβαιωτικῶς ὑπὲρ αὐτῶν. ἐξ ὧν
ἀναιρεῖσθαι μὲν τὴν δογματικὴν εὑρεσιλογίαν αὐτόθεν, οἶμαι, συμβήσεται, τὴν ἐφεκτικὴν δὲ εἰσάγεσθαι φιλοσοφίαν.

10   Εἰ δὲ φήσουσι μὴ τοιαύτην λέγειν κατάληψιν
ἡγεῖσθαι ζητήσεως προσήκειν, νόησιν δὲ ἁπλῶς,
οὐκ ἔστιν ἀδύνατον [ἐν] τοῖς ἐπέχουσι περὶ τῆς
ὑπάρξεως τῶν ἀδήλων ζητεῖν. νοήσεως γὰρ οὐκ
ἀπείργεται ὁ σκεπτικός, οἶμαι, ἀπό τε τῶν παθη-
ματικῶς ὑποπιπτόντων κατ' ἐνάργειαν φαινομένων
αὐτῷ λόγῳ γινομένης καὶ μὴ πάντως εἰσαγούσης
τὴν ὕπαρξιν τῶν νοουμένων· οὐ γὰρ μόνον τὰ
ὑπάρχοντα νοοῦμεν, ὥς φασιν, ἀλλ' ἤδη καὶ τὰ
ἀνύπαρκτα. ὅθεν καὶ ζητῶν καὶ νοῶν ἐν τῇ
σκεπτικῇ διαθέσει μένει ὁ ἐφεκτικός· ὅτι γὰρ τοῖς
κατὰ φαντασίαν παθητικὴν ὑποπίπτουσιν αὐτῷ,
καθὸ φαίνεται αὐτῷ, συγκατατίθεται, δεδήλωται.

11 ὅρα δὲ μὴ καὶ νῦν οἱ δογματικοὶ ζητήσεως ἀπείρ-
γονται. οὐ γὰρ τοῖς ἀγνοεῖν τὰ πράγματα ὡς

---

[a] Cf. i. 61.   [b] Cf. i. 63, ii. 84.

existence of a complete inquiry into that subject, owing to this circular process of reasoning [a] it becomes impossible for them either to inquire concerning things non-evident or to dogmatize; for if some of them wish to make apprehension their starting-point we force them to grant that the object must be investigated before it is apprehended, while if they start from inquiry we make them admit that before inquiring they must apprehend the object of the inquiry, so that for these reasons they can neither apprehend any non-evident object nor make positive statements about them. From this there will follow automatically, as I think, the demolition of the Dogmatic sophistry [b] and the establishment of the Suspensive philosophy.

If, however, they say that it is not this kind of 10 apprehension that ought, in their view, to precede inquiry, but simply mental conception, then it is no longer impossible for those who suspend judgement to inquire about the reality of things non-evident. For the Sceptic is not, I suppose, prohibited from mental conception which arises through the reason itself as a result of passive impressions and clear appearances and does not at all involve the reality of the objects conceived; for we conceive, as they say, not only of real things but also of unreal. Hence both while inquiring and while conceiving the Suspensive person continues in the Sceptical state of mind. For, as has been shown, he assents to what he experiences by way of subjective impression, according as that impression appears to him. But consider whether, even in this case, the 11 Dogmatists are not precluded from inquiry. For to continue the investigation of problems is not

SEXTUS EMPIRICUS

ἔχει πρὸς τὴν φύσιν ὁμολογοῦσι τὸ ζητεῖν ἔτι περὶ
αὐτῶν ἀνακόλουθον, τοῖς δ' ἐπ' ἀκριβὲς οἰομένοις
ταῦτα γινώσκειν· οἷς μὲν γὰρ ἐπὶ πέρας ἤδη
πάρεστιν ἡ ζήτησις, ὡς ὑπειλήφασιν, οἷς δὲ τὸ
δι' ὃ πᾶσα συνίσταται ζήτησις ἀκμὴν ὑπάρχει,
τὸ νομίζειν ὡς οὐχ εὑρήκασιν.

12   Οὐκοῦν ζητητέον ἡμῖν περὶ ἑκάστου μέρους
τῆς καλουμένης φιλοσοφίας συντόμως ἐπὶ τοῦ
παρόντος. καὶ ἐπεὶ πολλὴ γέγονε παρὰ τοῖς δογματικοῖς διαφωνία περὶ τῶν μερῶν τῆς φιλοσοφίας,
τῶν μὲν ἓν τῶν δὲ δύο τῶν δὲ τρία εἶναι λεγόντων,
περὶ ἧς οὐκ ἂν εἴη προσῆκον πλείω νῦν διεξιέναι,
τὴν δόξαν τῶν δοκούντων τελειότερον ἀνεστράφθαι
κατὰ τὸ ἴσον ἐκθέμενοι κατ' αὐτὴν προσάξομεν
τὸν λόγον.

Β'.—ΠΟΘΕΝ ΑΡΚΤΕΟΝ ΤΗΣ ΠΡΟΣ ΤΟΥΣ ΔΟΓΜΑΤΙΚΟΥΣ
ΖΗΤΗΣΕΩΣ

13   Οἱ στωικοὶ τοίνυν καὶ ἄλλοι τινὲς τρία μέρη τῆς
φιλοσοφίας εἶναι λέγουσι, λογικὸν φυσικὸν ἠθικόν·
καὶ ἄρχονταί γε τῆς διδασκαλίας ἀπὸ τοῦ λογικοῦ,
καίτοι πολλῆς καὶ περὶ τοῦ πόθεν ἄρχεσθαι δεῖ
στάσεως γεγενημένης. οἷς ἀκολουθήσαντες ἀδοξάστως, ἐπεὶ τὰ ἐν τοῖς τρισὶ μέρεσι λεγόμενα
κρίσεως χρῄζει καὶ κριτηρίου, ὁ δὲ περὶ κριτηρίου
λόγος ἐμπεριέχεσθαι δοκεῖ τῷ λογικῷ μέρει, ἀρξώμεθα ἀπὸ τοῦ περὶ τοῦ κριτηρίου λόγου καὶ τοῦ
λογικοῦ μέρους.

ª Cf. Adv. Log. i. ad init.
ᵇ The others mentioned in Adv. Log. i. 16 are Plato,
Xenocrates, and the Peripatetics; so too the Epicureans.

inconsistent in those who confess their ignorance of their real nature, but only in those who believe they have an exact knowledge of them ; since for the latter the inquiry has already, as they suppose, reached its goal, whereas for the former the ground on which all inquiry is based—namely, the belief that they have not found the truth—still subsists.

Thus we have to inquire briefly, on the present 12 occasion, concerning each several division of philosophy so called. And since there exists much dispute amongst the Dogmatists regarding the divisions of philosophy [a]—some saying there is one division, some two, some three—and it would not now be convenient to discuss the question at length, we will explain fairly and impartially the view of those who seem to have treated it most fully, and take their view as the subject of our discourse.

CHAPTER II.—THE STARTING-POINT FOR CRITICISM OF THE DOGMATISTS

The Stoics, then, and several others,[b] say that there 13 are three divisions of philosophy, namely, Logic, Physics, and Ethics ; and they begin their teaching with Logic,[c] although the question of the right starting-point is also a matter of much controversy. So we shall follow them in an undogmatic way ; and since the subject matter of all three divisions requires testing and a criterion, and the doctrine of the criterion seems to be included in the division of Logic, we shall begin with the doctrine of the criterion and the division of Logic.

[c] So Chrysippus. Sextus treats of Logic in this Bk. ii., Physics in iii. 1-167, Ethics in iii. 167-278.

159

Γ'.—ΠΕΡΙ ΚΡΙΤΗΡΙΟΥ

14 Ἐκεῖνο προειπόντες ὅτι κριτήριον μὲν λέγεται
τό τε ᾧ κρίνεσθαί φασιν ὕπαρξιν καὶ ἀνυπαρξίαν
καὶ τὸ ᾧ προσέχοντες βιοῦμεν, πρόκειται δὲ ἡμῖν
νῦν περὶ τοῦ κριτηρίου τῆς ἀληθείας εἶναι λεγομένου διαλαβεῖν· περὶ γὰρ τοῦ κατὰ τὸ ἕτερον
σημαινόμενον ἐν τῷ περὶ τῆς σκέψεως λόγῳ διεξ-
ήλθομεν.

15 Τὸ κριτήριον τοίνυν περὶ οὗ ὁ λόγος ἐστὶν
λέγεται τριχῶς, κοινῶς ἰδίως ἰδιαίτατα, κοινῶς
μὲν πᾶν μέτρον καταλήψεως, καθ' ὃ σημαινόμενον
καὶ τὰ φυσικὰ οὕτω προσαγορεύεται κριτήρια, ὡς
ὅρασις, ἰδίως δὲ πᾶν μέτρον καταλήψεως τεχνικὸν
ὡς κανὼν καὶ διαβήτης, ἰδιαίτατα δὲ πᾶν μέτρον
καταλήψεως τεχνικὸν ἀδήλου πράγματος, καθ' ὃ
τὰ μὲν βιωτικὰ οὐ λέγεται κριτήρια, μόνα δὲ τὰ
λογικὰ καὶ ἅπερ οἱ δογματικοὶ φέρουσι πρὸς τὴν
16 τῆς ἀληθείας κρίσιν. φαμὲν οὖν προηγουμένως
περὶ τοῦ λογικοῦ κριτηρίου διεξιέναι. ἀλλὰ καὶ
τὸ λογικὸν κριτήριον λέγοιτ' ἂν τριχῶς, τὸ ὑφ'
οὗ καὶ τὸ δι' οὗ καὶ τὸ καθ' ὅ, οἷον ὑφ' οὗ μὲν
ἄνθρωπος, δι' οὗ δὲ ἤτοι αἴσθησις ἢ διάνοια, καθ' ὃ
δὲ ἡ προσβολὴ τῆς φαντασίας, καθ' ἣν ὁ ἄνθρωπος
ἐπιβάλλει κρίνειν διά τινος τῶν προειρημένων.

17 Ταῦτα μὲν οὖν ἁρμόζον ἦν ἴσως προειπεῖν, ἵνα
ἐννοήσωμεν περὶ οὗ ἡμῖν ἐστιν ὁ λόγος· λοιπὸν δὲ

---

[a] See i. chap. xi.
[b] i.e. standards of weight and measure (e.g. pound, pint, yard).
[c] Cf. Adv. Log. i. 261.
[d] Examples of these three criteria are—the carpenter, his rule, the " applying " of his rule ; cf. Adv. Log. i. 35 f.

Chapter III.—Of the Criterion

But first we must notice that the word " criterion " 14
is used both of that by which, as they say, we judge
of reality and non-reality, and of that which we use
as the guide of life ; and our present task is to discuss
the so-called criterion of truth, since we have already
dealt with the criterion in its other sense in our
discourse " On Scepticism." [a]

The criterion, then, with which our argument is 15
concerned, has three several meanings—the general,
the special, and the most special. In the " general "
sense it is used of every standard of apprehension,
and in this sense we speak even of physical organs,
such as sight, as criteria. In the " special " sense
it includes every technical standard of apprehension, such as the rule and compass. In the " most
special " sense it includes every technical standard
of apprehension of a non-evident object ; but in this
application ordinary standards [b] are not regarded as
criteria but only logical standards and those which
the Dogmatists employ for the judging of truth. We 16
propose, therefore, in the first place to discuss the
logical criterion. But the logical criterion also may
be used in three senses [c]—of the agent, or the
instrument, or the " according to what " ; the agent,
for instance, may be a man, the instrument either
sense-perception or intelligence, and the " according
to what " the application of the impression " according to " which the man proceeds to judge by means
of one of the aforesaid instruments. [d]

It was appropriate, I consider, to make these pre- 17
fatory observations so that we may realize what is
the exact subject of our discourse ; and it remains

ἐπὶ τὴν ἀντίρρησιν χωρῶμεν τὴν πρὸς τοὺς λέγοντας προπετῶς κατειληφέναι τὸ κριτήριον τῆς
ἀληθείας, ἀπὸ τῆς διαφωνίας[1] ἀρξάμενοι.

Δ΄.—ΕΙ ΥΠΑΡΧΕΙ ΤΙ ΚΡΙΤΗΡΙΟΝ ΑΛΗΘΕΙΑΣ

18 Τῶν διαλαβόντων τοίνυν περὶ κριτηρίου οἱ μὲν
εἶναι τοῦτο ἀπεφήναντο, ὡς οἱ στωικοὶ καὶ ἄλλοι
τινές, οἱ δὲ μὴ εἶναι, ὡς ἄλλοι τε καὶ ὁ Κορίνθιος
Ξενιάδης καὶ Ξενοφάνης ὁ Κολοφώνιος, λέγων
δόκος δ᾽ ἐπὶ πᾶσι τέτυκται·
ἡμεῖς δ᾽ ἐπέσχομεν[2] πότερον ἔστιν ἢ οὐκ ἔστιν.
19 ταύτην οὖν τὴν διαφωνίαν ἤτοι ἐπικριτὴν εἶναι
φήσουσιν ἢ ἀνεπίκριτον· καὶ εἰ μὲν ἀνεπίκριτον,
αὐτόθεν εἶναι δώσουσι τὸ δεῖν ἐπέχειν, εἰ δὲ ἐπι-
κρίνεται, τίνι κριθήσεται λεγέτωσαν, μήτε κριτήριον ὁμολογούμενον ἡμῶν ἐχόντων, μήθ᾽ ὅλως εἰ
20 ἔστιν εἰδότων ἀλλὰ ζητούντων. καὶ ἄλλως, ἵνα
ἡ γενομένη περὶ τοῦ κριτηρίου διαφωνία ἐπικριθῇ,
δεῖ κριτήριον ἡμᾶς ἔχειν ὡμολογημένον, δι᾽ οὗ
δυνησόμεθα κρίνειν αὐτήν· καὶ ἵνα κριτήριον ὁμολογούμενον ἔχωμεν, δεῖ πρότερον ἐπικριθῆναι τὴν
περὶ τοῦ κριτηρίου διαφωνίαν. οὕτω δὲ εἰς τὸν
διάλληλον ἐμπίπτοντος τρόπον τοῦ λόγου ἄπορος
ἡ εὕρεσις τοῦ κριτηρίου γίνεται, μήτε ἐξ ὑποθέσεως
ἡμῶν ἐώντων αὐτοὺς κριτήριον λαμβάνειν, ἐάν τε
κριτηρίῳ τὸ κριτήριον κρίνειν ἐθέλωσιν, εἰς ἀπει-

---

[1] διαφωνίας T: ἀληθείας mss., Bekk.
[2] ἐπέσχομεν Kayser: ἐπίσχωμεν mss., Bekk.

---

[a] Earlier than Democritus ; cf. Adv. Log. i. 53, 388.
[b] Cf. i. 224 ; Adv. Log. i. 48, 110.
[c] Cf. i. 164 ff., 115 ff.

for us to proceed to our counter-statement aimed against those who rashly assert that they have apprehended the criterion of truth, and we will begin with the dispute which exists about this question.

Chapter IV.—Does a Criterion of Truth really exist ?

Of those, then, who have treated of the criterion 18 some have declared that a criterion exists—the Stoics, for example, and certain others—while by some its existence is denied, as by the Corinthian Xeniades,[a] amongst others, and by Xenophanes [b] of Colophon, who says—" Over all things opinion bears sway " ; while we have adopted suspension of judgement as to whether it does or does not exist. This dispute,[c] 19 then, they will declare to be either capable or incapable of decision ; and if they shall say it is incapable of decision they will be granting on the spot the propriety of suspension of judgement, while if they say it admits of decision, let them tell us whereby it is to be decided, since we have no accepted criterion, and do not even know, but are still inquiring, whether any criterion exists. Besides, in order to decide the 20 dispute which has arisen about the criterion, we must possess an accepted criterion by which we shall be able to judge the dispute ; and in order to possess an accepted criterion, the dispute about the criterion must first be decided. And when the argument thus reduces itself to a form of circular reasoning the discovery of the criterion becomes impracticable, since we do not allow them to adopt a criterion by assumption, while if they offer to judge the criterion by a

ρίαν αὐτοὺς ἐκβαλλόντων. ἀλλὰ καὶ ἐπεὶ ἡ μὲν
ἀπόδειξις δεῖται κριτηρίου ἀποδεδειγμένου τὸ δὲ
κριτήριον ἀποδείξεως κεκριμένης, εἰς τὸν διάλληλον
ἐκβάλλονται τρόπον.

21 Οἰόμενοι οὖν ἱκανὰ καὶ ταῦτα εἶναι δεικνύναι
τὴν τῶν δογματικῶν προπέτειαν κατὰ τὸν περὶ
τοῦ κριτηρίου λόγον, ἵνα καὶ ποικίλως αὐτοὺς ἐλέγχειν ἔχωμεν, οὐκ ἄτοπον προσκαρτερῆσαι τῷ
τόπῳ. οὐ μὴν ἑκάστῃ τῶν περὶ κριτηρίου δοξῶν
ἁμιλληθῆναι προαιρούμεθα εἰδικῶς (ἀμύθητος γὰρ
ἡ διαφωνία γέγονεν, καὶ οὕτως εἰς ἀμέθοδον καὶ
ἡμᾶς λόγον ἐμπεσεῖν ἀναγκαῖον ἔσται), ἀλλ᾽ ἐπεὶ
τὸ κριτήριον περὶ οὗ ζητοῦμεν τρισσὸν εἶναι δοκεῖ,
τό τε ὑφ᾽ οὗ καὶ τὸ δι᾽ οὗ καὶ τὸ καθ᾽ ὅ, ἕκαστον
τούτων ἐπελθόντες ἐν μέρει τὴν ἀκαταληψίαν αὐτοῦ
παραστήσομεν· οὕτω γὰρ ἐμμέθοδος ἅμα καὶ
τέλειος ἡμῖν ὁ λόγος ἔσται. ἀρξώμεθα δὲ ἀπὸ
τοῦ ὑφ᾽ οὗ· δοκεῖ γάρ πως συναπορεῖσθαι τούτῳ
καὶ τὰ λοιπά.

Ε΄. ΠΕΡΙ ΤΟΥ ΥΦ᾽ ΟΥ

22 Ὁ ἄνθρωπος τοίνυν δοκεῖ μοι, ὅσον ἐπὶ τοῖς
λεγομένοις ὑπὸ τῶν δογματικῶν, οὐ μόνον ἀκατάληπτος ἀλλὰ καὶ ἀνεπινόητος εἶναι. ἀκούομεν γοῦν
τοῦ παρὰ Πλάτωνι Σωκράτους διαρρήδην ὁμο-
λογοῦντος μὴ εἰδέναι πότερον ἄνθρωπός ἐστιν ἢ
ἕτερόν τι. παριστάναι τε βουλόμενοι τὴν ἔννοιαν

criterion we force them to a regress *ad infinitum.*
And furthermore, since demonstration requires a
demonstrated criterion, while the criterion requires
an approved demonstration, they are forced into
circular reasoning.

We suppose, then, that this is sufficient to expose 21
the rashness of the Dogmatists in respect of their
doctrine of the Criterion ; but in order to enable us
to confute them in detail, it will not be out of place
to dwell at length upon this topic. We do not,
however, desire to oppose their opinions about the
criterion severally, one by one—for their controversy is endless, and to do so would necessarily involve
us as well in a confused discussion,—but inasmuch as
the criterion in question is three-fold (the agent, the
instrument, and the " according to what "), we shall
discuss each of these in turn and establish the non-
apprehensibility of each, since in this way our exposition will be at once both methodical and complete.
Let us begin with the agent ; for the perplexity
which attaches to this seems somehow to involve the
rest as well.

Chapter V.—Of the Criterion " By whom," or Agent

Now " Man " (if he is " the agent ") seems to me, 22
so far as regards the statements made by the Dogmatists, to be not only non-apprehensible but also inconceivable. At least we hear the Platonic Socrates[a]
expressly confessing that he does not know whether
he is a man or something else. And when they wish
to establish the concept of " Man " they disagree in

---

[a] *Cf.* Plato, *Phaedr.* 229 e f., *Theaet.* 174 b.

αὐτοῦ πρῶτον μὲν διαφωνοῦσιν, εἶτα καὶ ἀσύνετα
λέγουσιν.

23 Ὁ μὲν γὰρ Δημόκριτός φησιν ὅτι ἄνθρωπός
ἐστιν ὃ πάντες ἴσμεν. ὅσον δ' ἐπὶ τούτῳ οὐ γνωσόμεθα τὸν ἄνθρωπον, ἐπεὶ καὶ κύνα ἴσμεν, καὶ παρὰ
τοῦτο ἔσται καὶ ὁ κύων ἄνθρωπος. τινάς τε
ἀνθρώπους οὐκ ἴσμεν· διὸ οὐκ ἔσονται ἄνθρωποι.
μᾶλλον δέ, ὅσον ἐπὶ τῇ ἐννοίᾳ ταύτῃ, οὐδεὶς ἔσται
ἄνθρωπος· εἰ γὰρ ἐκεῖνος μέν φησι δεῖν ὑπὸ πάντων
γινώσκεσθαι τὸν ἄνθρωπον, οὐδένα δὲ ἄνθρωπον
ἴσασι πάντες ἄνθρωποι, οὐδεὶς ἔσται κατ' αὐτὸν
24 ἄνθρωπος. καὶ ὅτι ταῦτα οὐ σοφιζόμενοι λέγομεν,
ἐκ τῆς πρὸς αὐτὸν ἀκολουθίας φαίνεται. μόνα γὰρ
κατ' ἀλήθειαν ὑπάρχειν φησὶν ὁ ἀνὴρ τὰ ἄτομα
καὶ τὸ κενόν, ἅπερ φησὶν οὐ μόνον τοῖς ζῴοις
ἀλλὰ καὶ πᾶσι τοῖς συγκρίμασιν ὑπάρχειν, ὥστε
ὅσον μὲν ἐπὶ τούτοις οὐκ ἐπινοήσομεν τὴν τοῦ
ἀνθρώπου ἰδιότητα, ἐπειδὴ κοινὰ πάντων ἐστίν.
ἀλλ' οὐδὲ ἄλλο τι ὑπόκειται παρὰ ταῦτα· οὐκ ἄρα
ἕξομεν δι' οὗ τὸν ἄνθρωπον διακρῖναί τε ἀπὸ τῶν
ἄλλων ζῴων καὶ εἰλικρινῶς νοῆσαι δυνησόμεθα.

25 Ὁ δ' Ἐπίκουρός φησιν ἄνθρωπον εἶναι τὸ
τοιουτοὶ μόρφωμα μετὰ ἐμψυχίας. καὶ κατὰ τοῦτον δέ, ἐπεὶ ὁ ἄνθρωπος δείξει ἐμφανίζεται, ὁ μὴ
δεικνύμενος οὐκ ἔστιν ἄνθρωπος. καὶ εἰ μὲν
γυναῖκα δείκνυσί τις, ὁ ἀνὴρ οὐκ ἔσται ἄνθρωπος,
εἰ δὲ ἄνδρα, ἡ γυνὴ ἄνθρωπος οὐκ ἔσται. τὰ δὲ
αὐτὰ ἐπιχειρήσομεν καὶ ἀπὸ τῆς διαφορᾶς τῶν

---

[a] Cf. i. 213 ff. ; Adv. Log. i. 265.
[b] Cf. Adv. Log. i. 267. Epicurus taught that truth is given

the first place, and in the second place they speak unintelligibly.

Thus Democritus [a] declares that " Man is that which we all know." Then, so far as his opinion goes, we shall not know Man, since we also know a dog, and consequently Dog too will be Man. And some men we do not know, therefore they will not be men. Or rather, if we are to judge by this concept, no one will be a man ; for since Democritus says that Man must be known by all, and all men know no one man, no one, according to him, will be a man. And it is evident from the relevance of this criticism that we are not now arguing sophistically. For this thinker proceeds to say that " Only the atoms and the void truly exist," and these he says " form the substrate not only of animals but of all compound substances," so that, so far as depends on these, we shall not form a concept of the particular essence of " Man," seeing that they are common to all things. But besides these there is no existing substrate ; so that we shall possess no means whereby we shall be able to distinguish Man from the other animals and form a precise conception of him.

Again, Epicurus says that Man is " This sort of a shape combined with vitality." [b] According to him, then, since Man is shown by pointing out, he that is not pointed out is not a man, and if anyone points out a female, the male will not be Man, while if he points out a male the female will not be Man. And we shall also draw the same inferences from the

by sense-perception : the percept is the real " thing in itself " ; hence we have no general concepts which can be logically " defined " but only particular phenomena which are " indicated " or pointed out as " such and such, look you " (τοιουτοί); cf. Introd. p. xxiii.

περιστάσεων ἃς ἴσμεν ἐκ τοῦ τετάρτου τρόπου τῆς ἐποχῆς.

26 Ἄλλοι ἔφασκον ἄνθρωπον εἶναι ζῷον λογικὸν θνητόν, νοῦ καὶ ἐπιστήμης δεκτικόν. ἐπεὶ οὖν δείκνυται ἐν τῷ πρώτῳ τῆς ἐποχῆς τρόπῳ ὅτι οὐδέν ἐστι ζῷον ἄλογον, ἀλλὰ καὶ νοῦ καὶ ἐπιστήμης δεκτικά ἐστι πάντα, ὅσον ἐπὶ τοῖς ὑπ' αὐτῶν λεγομένοις οὐ γνωσόμεθα τί ποτε λέγουσιν.

27 τά τε κείμενα ἐν τῷ ὅρῳ συμβεβηκότα ἤτοι κατ' ἐνέργειαν λέγουσιν ἢ δυνάμει. εἰ μὲν οὖν κατ' ἐνέργειαν, οὐκ ἔστιν ἄνθρωπος ὁ μὴ ἐπιστήμην ἤδη τελείαν ἀπειληφὼς καὶ ἐν τῷ λόγῳ τέλειος ὢν καὶ ἐν αὐτῷ τῷ ἀποθνήσκειν καθεστώς· τοῦτο γὰρ τὸ ἐνεργείᾳ θνητόν ἐστιν. εἰ δὲ δυνάμει, οὐκ ἔσται ἄνθρωπος οὔτε ὁ τὸν λόγον ἔχων τέλειον οὔτε ὁ νοῦν καὶ ἐπιστήμην ἀνειληφώς· [καὶ] τοῦτο δὲ τοῦ προτέρου ἐστὶν ἀτοπώτερον.

Καὶ ταύτῃ ἄρα ἀσύστατος πέφηνεν ἡ ἐπίνοια τοῦ

28 ἀνθρώπου. ὁ γὰρ Πλάτων ὅταν ἀξιοῖ τὸν ἄνθρωπον εἶναι ζῷον ἄπτερον δίπουν πλατυώνυχον, ἐπιστήμης πολιτικῆς δεκτικόν, οὐδὲ αὐτὸς ἀξιοῖ διαβεβαιωτικῶς τοῦτο ἐκτίθεσθαι· εἰ γὰρ καὶ ὁ ἄνθρωπος ἕν τί ἐστι τῶν κατ' αὐτὸν γινομένων μὲν ὄντως δὲ οὐδέποτε ὄντων, ἀδύνατον δὲ περὶ τῶν μηδέποτε ὄντων διαβεβαιωτικῶς ἀποφαίνεσθαι κατ' αὐτόν, οὐδὲ ὁ Πλάτων ἀξιώσει τὸν ὅρον

---

[a] Cf. i. 100.
[b] Stoics and Peripatetics, cf. § 211 infra.
[c] See i. 40 ff.

168

difference in the circumstances which we learn from the Fourth Mode of Suspension.[a]

Others [b] used to assert that " Man is a rational 26 mortal animal, receptive of intelligence and science." Now since it is shown by the First Mode of Suspension [c] that no animal is irrational but all are receptive of intelligence and science, so far as their statements go, we shall be unable to perceive what they mean. And the attributes contained 27 in this definition are used either in an " actual," or full, or in a potential sense [d] ; if in a full sense, he that has not already acquired complete science and is not rationally perfect and in the very act of dying—for this is to be mortal in the full sense of the word—is not a man. And if the sense is to be potential, then he will not be a man who possesses reason in perfection or who has acquired intelligence and science ; but this conclusion is even more absurd than the former.

In this way, then, the concept of Man is shown to be one which it is impossible to frame. For when Plato [e] 28 declares that " Man is a featherless two-footed animal with broad nails, receptive of political science," not even he himself claims to affirm this positively ; for if Man is one of the class of things which, as he puts it,[f] come into being but never possess absolute being, and if it is impossible, in his view, to make a positive declaration about things which never really exist, then even Plato will not claim to be taken as

[d] The familiar Aristotelian distinction between " actuality" and " potentiality " is here used by Sextus to confute the Peripatetics, *cf.* Introd. p. xx.

[e] *Cf. Adv. Log.* i. 281 ; Diog. Laert. vi. 40 ; [Plato], *Deff.* 415 A.

[f] *Cf. Theaet.* 152 D, *Tim.* 27 D.

169

ἐκτίθεσθαι δοκεῖν ὡς διαβεβαιούμενος, ἀλλ᾽ ὥσπερ εἴωθεν κατὰ τὸ πιθανὸν λέγων.

29 Εἰ μέντοι καὶ δοίημεν κατὰ συγχώρησιν ὅτι ἐπινοεῖσθαι δύναται ὁ ἄνθρωπος, ἀκατάληπτος εὑρεθήσεται. συνέστηκε μὲν γὰρ ἐκ ψυχῆς καὶ σώματος, οὔτε δὲ τὸ σῶμα καταλαμβάνεται τάχα
30 οὔτε ἡ ψυχή· οὐδὲ ὁ ἄνθρωπος ἄρα. καὶ ὅτι μὲν τὸ σῶμα οὐ καταλαμβάνεται, δῆλον ἐντεῦθεν· τὰ συμβεβηκότα τινὶ ἕτερά ἐστιν ἐκείνου ᾧ συμβέβηκεν. ὅταν οὖν χρῶμα ἤ τι παραπλήσιον ἡμῖν ὑποπίπτῃ, τὰ συμβεβηκότα τῷ σώματι εἰκὸς ἡμῖν ὑποπίπτειν, ἀλλ᾽ οὐκ αὐτὸ τὸ σῶμα. τό γέ τοι[1] σῶμα τριχῇ διαστατὸν εἶναι λέγουσιν· ὀφείλομεν οὖν τὸ μῆκος καὶ τὸ πλάτος καὶ τὸ βάθος καταλαμβάνειν, ἵνα τὸ σῶμα καταλάβωμεν. εἰ γὰρ τοῦτο ἡμῖν ὑπέπιπτεν, ἐγινώσκομεν ἂν καὶ τὰ ὑπάργυρα χρυσία. οὐδὲ τὸ σῶμα ἄρα.
31 Ἵνα δὲ καὶ τὴν περὶ τοῦ σώματος ἀμφισβήτησιν παρῶμεν, πάλιν ὁ ἄνθρωπος εὑρίσκεται ἀκατάληπτος διὰ τὸ ἀκατάληπτον εἶναι τὴν ψυχήν. ὅτι δὲ ἀκατάληπτός ἐστιν αὕτη, δῆλον ἐντεῦθεν· τῶν περὶ ψυχῆς διαλαβόντων, ἵνα τὴν πολλὴν καὶ ἀνήνυτον μάχην παραλίπωμεν, οἱ μὲν μὴ εἶναι τὴν ψυχὴν ἔφασαν, ὡς οἱ περὶ τὸν Μεσσήνιον Δικαί-
32 αρχον, οἱ δὲ εἶναι, οἱ δὲ ἐπέσχον. ταύτην οὖν τὴν διαφωνίαν εἰ μὲν ἀνεπίκριτον εἶναι λέξουσιν οἱ

[1] τό γέ τοι: the particles seem out of place here; read perhaps αὐτό τε τό.

[a] "Perchance," one of the Sceptic formulae, cf. i. 194.
[b] i.e. a "substance" in the Aristotelian sense, as distinguished from its "attributes," "properties," or "accidents"; cf. Adv. Log. i. 283 ff.

putting forward this definition positively, but rather as making, in his usual way, a probable statement.

But even if we should grant, by way of concession, 29 that Man can be conceived, yet he will be found to be non-apprehensible. For he is compounded of soul and body, and neither body nor soul perchance [a] is apprehended ; so that Man is not apprehended. Now that body is not apprehended is easily shown 30 thus : the attributes of an object [b] are different from the object whereof they are attributes. So when colour or any similar quality is perceived by us, what we perceive is probably the attributes of the body but not the body itself. Certainly the body, they say, exists in three dimensions ; we ought therefore to apprehend its length and breadth and depth in order to apprehend the body. For if we perceived depth [c] we should also discern silver pieces under their coating of gold. Therefore we do not apprehend the body either.

But, not to dwell on the controversy about the 31 body, Man is also found to be non-apprehensible owing to the fact that his soul is non-apprehensible. That it is non-apprehensible is plain from this : of those who have treated of the soul—so that we may avoid dwelling on the long and endless controversy —some have asserted, as did Dicaearchus [d] the Messenian, that the soul has no existence, others that it has existence, and others have suspended judgement. If, then, the Dogmatists shall maintain 32

[c] Lit. "this" (τοῦτο: Mutsch. suggests ταῦτα). The argument would be clearer if we inserted the words "But we do not apprehend depth" after "body"; the text as it stands is too obscure to be sound.

[d] A pupil of Aristotle, cf. Adv. Log. i. 349 ; Cicero, Tusc. i. 10. 22.

δογματικοί, δώσουσιν αὐτόθεν τὴν τῆς ψυχῆς
ἀκαταληψίαν, εἰ δὲ ἐπικριτήν, τίνι ἐπικρινοῦσιν
αὐτὴν εἰπάτωσαν. αἰσθήσει μὲν γὰρ οὐ δύνανται
διὰ τὸ νοητὴν ὑπ᾽ αὐτῶν εἶναι λέγεσθαι· εἰ δὲ
λέξουσιν ὅτι διανοίᾳ, ἐροῦμεν ὅτι ἐπεὶ τῆς ψυχῆς
τὸ ἀδηλότατόν ἐστιν ἡ διάνοια, ὡς δεικνύουσιν οἱ
περὶ μὲν τῆς ὑπάρξεως τῆς ψυχῆς ὁμοφωνοῦντες
33 περὶ δὲ τῆς διανοίας διαφερόμενοι, εἰ τῇ διανοίᾳ
τὴν ψυχὴν ἐθέλουσι καταλαμβάνειν καὶ τὴν περὶ
αὐτῆς διαφωνίαν ἐπικρίνειν, τῷ μᾶλλον ζητουμένῳ
τὸ ἧττον ζητούμενον ἐπικρίνειν τε καὶ βεβαιοῦν
ἐθελήσουσιν, ὅπερ ἄτοπον. οὐδὲ τῇ διανοίᾳ τοίνυν
ἐπικριθήσεται ἡ περὶ τῆς ψυχῆς διαφωνία. οὐδενὶ
ἄρα. εἰ δὲ τοῦτο, καὶ ἀκατάληπτός ἐστιν. ὅθεν
οὐδὲ ὁ ἄνθρωπος καταλαμβάνοιτ᾽ ἄν.
34 Ἵνα δὲ καὶ δῶμεν ὅτι καταλαμβάνεται ὁ ἄνθρωπος, μήποτε οὐκ ἂν ἐνδέχοιτο δεῖξαι ὅτι ὑπ᾽
αὐτοῦ κρίνεσθαι δεῖ τὰ πράγματα. ὁ γὰρ λέγων
ὅτι ὑπ᾽ ἀνθρώπου δεῖ κρίνεσθαι τὰ πράγματα, ἤτοι
ἄνευ ἀποδείξεως τοῦτο λέξει ἢ μετὰ ἀποδείξεως.
οὔτε δὲ μετὰ ἀποδείξεως· δεῖ γὰρ τὴν ἀπόδειξιν
ἀληθῆ εἶναι καὶ κεκριμένην, διὰ δὲ τοῦτο καὶ ὑπό
τινος κεκριμένην. ἐπεὶ οὖν οὐκ ἔχομεν εἰπεῖν ὁμολογουμένως ὑφ᾽ οὗ κριθῆναι δυνήσεται αὐτὴ ἡ
ἀπόδειξις (ζητοῦμεν γὰρ τὸ κριτήριον τὸ ὑφ᾽ οὗ),
οὐ δυνησόμεθα τὴν ἀπόδειξιν ἐπικρίνειν, διὰ δὲ
τοῦτο οὐδὲ τὸ κριτήριον περὶ οὗ ὁ λόγος ἀπο-
35 δεικνύαι. εἰ δὲ ἀναποδείκτως λεχθήσεται ὅτι ὑπὸ
τοῦ ἀνθρώπου δεῖ κριθῆναι τὰ πράγματα, ἄπιστον

---

[a] Cf. i. 115, 164 ff. Note that, in the context, the words
"test," "judge," "decide," are various renderings of κρίνω
(whence κριτήριον).

that this dispute is incapable of decision, they will be admitting thereby the non-apprehensibility of the soul, while if they say it is capable of decision, let them tell us by what means they will decide it. For they cannot say " by sense-perception," since the soul is said by them to be an object of intelligence ; and if they shall say " by the intellect," we will say that inasmuch as the intellect is the least evident part of the soul—as is shown by those who agree about the real existence of the soul, though differing about the intellect,—if they propose to apprehend the soul and 33 to decide the dispute about it by means of the intellect, they will be proposing to decide and establish the less questionable matter by the more questionable, which is absurd. Thus, neither by the intellect will the dispute about the soul be decided ; therefore there is no means to decide it. And this being so, it is non-apprehensible ; and, in consequence, Man too will not be apprehended.

But even supposing we grant that Man is appre- 34 hended, it would not, probably, be possible to show that objects ought to be judged by him. For he who asserts that objects ought to be judged by Man will be asserting this either without proof or with proof.[a] Not with proof ; for the proof must be true and tested, and therefore tested by some standard. Since, then, we are unable to make an agreed statement as to the standard by which the proof itself can be tested (for we are still inquiring about the criterion " By whom "), we shall be unable to pronounce judgement on the proof, and therefore also to prove the criterion, which is the subject of discussion. And 35 if it shall be asserted without proof that objects ought to be judged by Man, the assertion will be

ἔσται, ὥστε οὐχ ἕξομεν διαβεβαιοῦσθαι ὅτι τὸ ὑφ'
οὗ κριτήριόν ἐστιν ὁ ἄνθρωπος. ὑπὸ τίνος δὲ καὶ
κριθήσεται ὅτι τὸ ὑφ' οὗ κριτήριον ὁ ἄνθρωπος
ἐστίν; οὐ γὰρ δὴ ἀκρίτως τοῦτο λέγοντες πιστευ-
θήσονται. ἀλλ' εἰ μὲν ὑπ' ἀνθρώπου, τὸ ζητού-
36 μενον συναρπασθήσεται. εἰ δ' ὑπὸ ἑτέρου ζώου,
πῶς ἐκεῖνο πρὸς τὴν κρίσιν τοῦ ἄνθρωπον εἶναι τὸ
κριτήριον παραλαμβάνεται; εἰ μὲν γὰρ ἀκρίτως,
οὐ πιστευθήσεται, εἰ δὲ μετὰ κρίσεως, πάλιν ἐκεῖνο
ὑπό τινος ὀφείλει κριθῆναι. ἀλλ' εἰ μὲν ὑφ' ἑαυτοῦ,
μένει ἡ αὐτὴ ἀτοπία (τὸ ζητούμενον γὰρ διὰ τοῦ
ζητουμένου κριθήσεται), εἰ δὲ ὑπὸ ἀνθρώπου, ὁ
διάλληλος εἰσάγεται τρόπος· εἰ δὲ ὑπό τινος παρὰ
ταῦτα ἄλλου, πάλιν ἐκείνου τὸ κριτήριον ἀπαιτή-
σομεν τὸ ὑφ' οὗ, καὶ μέχρις ἀπείρου. καὶ διὰ
τοῦτο ἄρα οὐχ ἕξομεν λέγειν ὡς ὑπὸ ἀνθρώπου δεῖ
κρίνεσθαι τὰ πράγματα.

37 Ἔστω δὲ καὶ πεπιστώσθω τὸ δεῖν ὑπὸ τοῦ
ἀνθρώπου κρίνεσθαι τὰ πράγματα. οὐκοῦν ἐπεὶ
πολλὴ τῶν ἀνθρώπων ἐστὶ διαφορά, πρότερον οἱ
δογματικοὶ συμφωνησάτωσαν ὅτι τῷδε τῷ ἀνθρώπῳ δεῖ προσέχειν, εἶθ' οὕτω καὶ ἡμᾶς αὐτῷ
θέσθαι κελευέτωσαν. εἰ δ'

ἔστ' ἂν ὕδωρ τε νάῃ καὶ δένδρεα μακρὰ τεθήλῃ,

τοῦτο δὴ τὸ τοῦ λόγου, περὶ αὐτοῦ διαφωνήσουσιν,
πῶς ἡμᾶς ἐπείγουσι προπετῶς τινι συγκατα-
38 τίθεσθαι; ἢν γὰρ καὶ λέγωσιν ὅτι τῷ σοφῷ πιστευτέον, ἐρωτήσομεν αὐτοὺς ποίῳ σοφῷ, πότερον
τῷ κατὰ Ἐπίκουρον ἢ τῷ κατὰ τοὺς Στωικοὺς ἢ

ᵃ The fallacy of *petitio principii*, *cf.* §§ 57, 60, 67 *infra*.

disbelieved, so that we shall be unable to affirm positively that the criterion " By whom " (or Agent) is Man. Moreover, who is to be the judge that the criterion of the Agent is Man ? For if they assert this without a judgement (or criterion) they will surely not be believed. Yet if they say that a man is to be the 36 judge, that will be assuming the point at issue [a] ; while if they make another animal the judge, in what way do they come to adopt that animal for the purpose of judging whether Man is the criterion ? If they do so without a judgement, it will not be believed, and if with a judgement, it in turn needs to be judged by something. If, then, it is judged by itself, the same absurdity remains (for the object of inquiry will be judged by the object of inquiry) ; and if by Man, circular reasoning is introduced ; and if by some judge other than these two, we shall once again in his case demand the criterion " By whom," and so on *ad infinitum*. Consequently we shall not be in a position to declare that objects ought to be judged by Man.

But let it be granted and established that objects 37 ought to be judged by Man. Then, since there exists great difference amongst men, let the Dogmatists first agree together that this is the particular man to whom we must attend, and then, and only then, let them bid us also to yield him our assent. But if they are going to dispute about this " long as the waters flow on and the tall trees cease not to burgeon " (to quote the familiar saying),[b] how can they urge us to assent rashly to anyone ? For if they declare that 38 we must believe the Sage, we shall ask them " What Sage ? " Is it the Sage of Epicurus or of the Stoics,

[b] From the inscription on the tomb of Midas quoted in Plato, *Phaedr.* 264 D ; *cf.* Tibullus i. 4. 60.

τῷ ⟨Κυρηναϊκῷ ἢ τῷ⟩[1] Κυνικῷ· οὐχ ἕξουσι γὰρ συμφώνως εἰπεῖν.

39 Εἰ δὲ ἀξιώσει τις ἡμᾶς τῆς περὶ τοῦ σοφοῦ ζητήσεως ἀποστάντας ἁπλῶς τῷ συνετωτέρῳ τῶν ὄντων ἁπάντων πιστεύειν, πρῶτον μὲν καὶ περὶ τοῦ τίς συνετώτερός ἐστι τῶν ἄλλων διαφωνήσουσιν, εἶτα κἂν δοθῇ συμφώνως δύνασθαι ληφθῆναι τίς ἐστι τῶν τε ὄντων καὶ τῶν γεγονότων συνετώτερος, οὐδ᾽ οὕτως ἔσται πίστεως οὗτος ἄξιος.

40 ἐπεὶ γὰρ πολλὴ καὶ σχεδὸν ἄπειρός ἐστιν ἐπίτασίς τε καὶ ἄνεσις κατὰ σύνεσιν, φαμὲν ὅτι τούτου τοῦ ἀνθρώπου ὃν λέγομεν εἶναι τῶν γεγονότων τε καὶ ὄντων συνετώτερον, ἕτερον συνετώτερον ἐνδέχεται γενέσθαι. ὥσπερ οὖν τῷ νῦν εἶναι λεγομένῳ φρονιμωτέρῳ τῶν τε ὄντων καὶ τῶν γεγονότων διὰ τὴν σύνεσιν αὐτοῦ πιστεύειν ἀξιούμεθα, οὕτω καὶ τῷ μετ᾽ αὐτὸν ἐσομένῳ τούτου συνετωτέρῳ μᾶλλον τούτου χρὴ πιστεύειν. καὶ ἐκείνου γενομένου πάλιν ἄλλον ἐλπίζειν χρὴ συνετώτερον αὐτοῦ γενήσεσθαι, κἀκείνου ἄλλον, καὶ μέχρις ἀπείρου.

41 καὶ ἄδηλον πότερόν ποτε συμφωνήσουσιν ἀλλήλοις οὗτοι ἢ διάφωνα λέξουσιν. διόπερ κἂν τῶν γεγονότων τε καὶ ὄντων συνετώτερος εἶναι ὁμολογηθῇ τις, ἐπεὶ οὐκ ἔχομεν εἰπεῖν διαβεβαιωτικῶς ὅτι οὐδεὶς ἔσται τούτου ἀγχινούστερος (ἄδηλον γάρ), ἀεὶ δεήσει τὴν τοῦ μετὰ ταῦτα ἐσομένου συνετωτέρου κρίσιν περιμένειν καὶ μηδέποτε συγκατατίθεσθαι τῷ κρείττονι.

42 Ἵνα δὲ καὶ κατὰ συγχώρησιν δῶμεν ὅτι οὐδεὶς τοῦ ὑποτιθεμένου συνετοῦ συνετώτερος οὔτε ἔστιν

---

[1] ⟨Κ. ἢ τῷ⟩ add. T.

the Cyrenaic Sage or the Cynic? For they will be unable to return a unanimous answer.

And if anyone shall demand that we should desist 39 from our inquiry about the Sage and simply believe the man who is more sagacious than all others, then, in the first place, they will dispute as to who is more sagacious than the rest, and in the next place, even if it be granted that it can be unanimously agreed who the man is who is more sagacious than those of the present and the past, even so this man will not deserve credence. For inasmuch as sagacity is liable 40 to a great, indeed almost incalculable, advance or decline in intensity, we assert that it is possible for another man to arise who is more sagacious than this man who, we say, is more sagacious than those of the past and present. So, then, just as we are requested to believe the man who is now said to be wiser than .those of the present and the past because of his sagacity, so it is still more proper to believe his successor in the future who will be more sagacious than he. And when that successor has arisen, then it is right to expect that yet another will arise more sagacious than he, and so on *ad infinitum.* Nor is it 41 evident whether all these men will agree with one another or contradict one another. And consequently, even when one of them is acknowledged to be more sagacious than those of the past and present, seeing that we are unable to affirm positively that no man will be more clever than he (this being non-evident), we shall always have to wait for the judgement of the more sagacious man of the future, and never give our assent to this superior person.

And even should we grant, by way of concession, 42 that no one either is, was, or will be more sagacious

οὔτε ἐγένετο οὔτε ἔσται, οὐδὲ ὡς πιστεύειν αὐτῷ
προσήκει. ἐπεὶ γὰρ μάλιστα οἱ συνετοὶ φιλοῦσιν
ἐν τῇ τῶν πραγμάτων κατασκευῇ τοῖς σαθροῖς
παριστάμενοι πράγμασιν ὑγιῆ καὶ ἀληθῆ ταῦτα
δοκεῖν εἶναι ποιεῖν, ὅταν τι λέγῃ οὗτος ὁ ἀγχίνους,
οὐκ εἰσόμεθα πότερόν ποτε, ὡς ἔχει τὸ πρᾶγμα
φύσεως, οὕτω λέγει, ἢ ψεῦδος αὐτὸ ὑπάρχον ὡς
ἀληθὲς παρίστησι καὶ ἡμᾶς πείθει φρονεῖν ὡς περὶ
ἀληθοῦς, ἅτε δὴ συνετώτερος τῶν ἀνθρώπων ἁπάντων ὑπάρχων καὶ διὰ τοῦτο ὑφ' ἡμῶν ἐλέγχεσθαι
μὴ δυνάμενος. οὐδὲ τούτῳ τοίνυν συγκαταθησόμεθα ὡς ἀληθῶς τὰ πράγματα κρίνοντι, διὰ τὸ
οἴεσθαι μὲν αὐτὸν ἀληθῆ ⟨ἐνεῖναι⟩[1] λέγειν, οἴεσθαι
δ' ὅτι δι' ὑπερβολὴν ἀγχινοίας τὰ ψευδῆ τῶν πραγμάτων ὡς ἀληθῆ βουλόμενος παριστᾶν ἃ φησι
λέγει. διὰ ταῦτα μὲν οὖν οὐδὲ τῷ τῶν ἁπάντων
ἀγχινουστάτῳ δοκοῦντι ὑπάρχειν ἐν τῇ κρίσει τῶν
πραγμάτων χρὴ πιστεύειν.

43   Εἰ δὲ φήσει τις ὅτι τῇ τῶν πολλῶν συμφωνίᾳ δεῖ
προσέχειν, λέξομεν ὅτι τοῦτ' ἔστι μάταιον. πρῶτον
μὲν γὰρ σπάνιον ἴσως ἐστὶ τὸ ἀληθές, καὶ διὰ τοῦτο
ἐνδέχεται ἕνα τῶν πολλῶν φρονιμώτερον εἶναι.
εἶτα καὶ παντὶ κριτηρίῳ πλείους ἀντιδοξοῦσι τῶν
κατ' αὐτὸ συμφωνούντων· οἱ γὰρ ὁποιονοῦν ἀπο-
λιπόντες κριτήριον ἕτερον τοῦ συμφωνεῖσθαι δοκοῦντος παρά τισιν ἀντιδοξοῦσί τε αὐτῷ καὶ κατὰ
πολὺ πλείους εἰσὶ τῶν περὶ αὐτοῦ συμφωνούντων.
44   χωρὶς δὲ τούτων, οἱ συμφωνοῦντες ἤτοι ἐν διαφόροις εἰσὶ διαθέσεσιν ἢ ἐν μιᾷ. ἐν διαφόροις μὲν
οὖν οὐδαμῶς ὅσον ἐπὶ τῷ λεγομένῳ· πῶς γὰρ ἂν

---

[1] ⟨ἐνεῖναι⟩ addidi: ⟨εἶναι⟩ add. EBA.

than our hypothetical Sage, not even so is it proper to believe him. For since it is the sagacious above all who, in the construction of their doctrines, love to champion unsound doctrines and to make them appear sound and true, whenever this sharp-witted person makes a statement we shall not know whether he is stating the matter as it really is, or whether he is defending as true what is really false and persuading us to think of it as something true, on the ground that he is more sagacious than all other men and therefore incapable of being refuted by us. So not even to this man will we assent, as one who judges matters truly, since, though we suppose it possible that he speaks the truth, we also suppose that owing to his excessive cleverness he makes his statements with the object of defending false propositions as true. Consequently, in the judgement of propositions we ought not to believe even the man who is thought to be the most clever of all.

And if anyone shall say that we ought to attend to **43** the consensus of the majority, we shall reply that this is idle.[a] For, in the first place, truth is a rare thing, and on this account it is possible for one man to be wiser than the majority. And, next, the opponents of any criterion are more numerous than those who agree about it ; for those who admit any kind of criterion different from that which seems to some to be generally agreed upon oppose this latter, and they are much more numerous than those who agree about it. And besides all this, those who agree are either **44** in diverse dispositions [b] or in one and the same. Now they certainly are not in diverse dispositions so far as regards the matter under discussion ; else how could

[a] Cf. *Adv. Log.* i. 327 ff.   [b] Cf. i. 100 ; *Adv. Log.* i. 333.

τὰ αὐτὰ ἔλεγον περὶ αὐτοῦ; εἰ δὲ ἐν μιᾷ, ἐπεὶ
καὶ ὁ εἷς ὁ λέγων ἕτερόν τι μίαν ἔχει διάθεσιν καὶ
οὗτοι πάντες οἱ συμφωνοῦντες μίαν, ὅσον ἐπὶ ταῖς
διαθέσεσιν αἷς προσέχομεν οὐδὲ κατὰ πλῆθος
45 εὑρίσκεται διαφορά τις. διόπερ οὐ χρὴ τοῖς πολλοῖς προσέχειν μᾶλλον ἢ τῷ ἑνί, πρὸς τῷ καὶ
ἀκατάληπτον εἶναι, καθάπερ ἐν τῷ τετάρτῳ τρόπῳ
τῆς σκέψεως ὑπεμνήσαμεν, τὴν κατὰ πλῆθος διαφορὰν τῶν κρίσεων, ἀπείρων τῶν κατὰ μέρος
ἀνθρώπων ὑπαρχόντων καὶ ἡμῶν μὴ δυναμένων
ἁπάντων αὐτῶν τὰς κρίσεις ἐπελθεῖν καὶ ἀποφήνασθαι τί μὲν οἱ πλείους τῶν ἀνθρώπων ἁπάντων
ἀποφαίνονται τί δὲ οἱ ἐλάττους. καὶ κατὰ τοῦτο
οὖν ἄτοπος ἡ κατὰ τὸ πλῆθος πρόκρισις τῶν
κρινόντων.

46 Εἰ δ' οὐδὲ τῷ πλήθει προσέξομεν, οὐχ εὑρήσομεν
οὐδένα ὑφ' οὗ κριθήσεται τὰ πράγματα, καίτοι
τοσαῦτα κατὰ συγχώρησιν διδόντες. διόπερ ἐξ
ἁπάντων τούτων ἀκατάληπτον εὑρίσκεται τὸ κριτήριον ὑφ' οὗ κριθήσεται τὰ πράγματα.

47 Συμπεριγραφομένων δὲ τούτῳ καὶ τῶν ἄλλων
κριτηρίων, ἐπεὶ ἕκαστον αὐτῶν ἤτοι μέρος ἢ πάθος
ἢ ἐνέργημά ἐστι τοῦ ἀνθρώπου, ἀκόλουθον μὲν ἦν
ἴσως ἐπί τι τῶν ἑξῆς ἰέναι τῷ λόγῳ ὡς καὶ περὶ
ἐκείνων ἱκανῶς εἰρημένον ἐν τούτοις· ἵνα δὲ μηδὲ
τὴν εἰδικὴν ὡς πρὸς ἕκαστον ἀντίρρησιν φεύγειν
δοκῶμεν, ὀλίγα καὶ περὶ αὐτῶν ἐξ ἐπιμέτρου λέξο-

---

[a] Cf. i. 100 ff. for the fourth trope ; but the reference ought
rather to be to the second, in i. 89.

[b] ἐξ ἐπιμέτρου, lit. " as extra-measure " or "overplus";
" into the bargain."

they have made identical statements about it ? And if they are in one disposition, inasmuch as both the one man who makes a different statement is in one disposition and all these who agree together are also in one, so far as regards the dispositions in which we find ourselves, no difference is found even on the ground of numbers. Consequently we ought not to pay heed to the many more than to the one ; besides the 45 further fact that—as we pointed out in " The Fourth Mode of Scepticism "[a]—the difference in judgements that is based on numbers is non-apprehensible, since individual men are innumerable and we are incapable of investigating and expounding the judgements of all of them—what it is the majority of all mankind affirm and what the minority. Thus, on this showing also, the preference given to men's judgements on the ground of their numbers is absurd.

But if we are not even to give heed to numbers, 46 we shall not find anyone by whom objects are to be judged, in spite of our having granted so much by way of concession. Therefore, on all these grounds, the criterion " By whom " objects are to be judged is found to be non-apprehensible.

And seeing that the other criteria are included in 47 this one, since each of them is either a part or an affection or an activity of Man, our next task might perhaps have been to proceed in our discussion to one of the subjects which follows next in order, supposing that those criteria also have been sufficiently dealt with in what we have now said ; yet in order that we may not seem to be shirking the specific counter-statement proper to each case, we will exceed our brief[b] and deal with them also shortly. And we shall

181

μεν. πρότερον δὲ περὶ τοῦ κριτηρίου τοῦ δι' οὗ καλουμένου διαλεξόμεθα.

ϛ'.—ΠΕΡΙ ΤΟΥ ΔΙ' ΟΥ

48 Πολλὴ μὲν οὖν καὶ ἄπειρος σχεδὸν ἡ περὶ αὐτὸ γέγονε διαφωνία παρὰ τοῖς δογματικοῖς· ἡμεῖς δὲ πάλιν τοῦ ἐμμεθόδου προνοούμενοι φαμὲν ὅτι, ἐπεὶ κατ' αὐτοὺς ἄνθρωπός ἐστι τὸ ὑφ' οὗ κρίνεται τὰ πράγματα, οὐδὲν δὲ οὗτος ἔχοι ἂν δι' οὗ κρίνειν δυνήσεται, καθάπερ καὶ αὐτοὶ συνομολογοῦσιν, ἢ αἴσθησιν καὶ διάνοιαν, ἐὰν δείξωμεν ὅτι οὔτε δι' αἰσθήσεως μόνης δύναται κρίνειν οὔτε διὰ μόνης τῆς διανοίας οὔτε δι' ἀμφοτέρων αὐτῶν, συντόμως πρὸς ἁπάσας τὰς κατὰ μέρος δόξας εἰρήκαμεν· πᾶσαι γὰρ δοκοῦσιν εἰς τὰς τρεῖς ταύτας ἀναφέρεσθαι 49 στάσεις. ἀρξώμεθα δὲ ἀπὸ τῶν αἰσθήσεων.

Οὐκοῦν ἐπεὶ τινὲς μὲν κενοπαθεῖν τὰς αἰσθήσεις φασίν (οὐδὲν γὰρ ὑποκεῖσθαι ὧν ἀντιλαμβάνεσθαι δοκοῦσιν), οἱ δὲ πάντα ὑποκεῖσθαι ὑφ' ὧν οἴονται κινεῖσθαι λέγουσιν, οἱ δὲ τὰ μὲν ὑποκεῖσθαι τὰ δὲ μὴ ὑποκεῖσθαι, τίνι συγκαταθησόμεθα οὐχ ἕξομεν· οὔτε γὰρ τῇ αἰσθήσει τὴν διαφωνίαν ἐπικρινοῦμεν, ἐπεὶ περὶ αὐτῆς ζητοῦμεν πότερον κενοπαθεῖ ἢ ἀληθῶς καταλαμβάνει, οὔτε ἑτέρῳ τινί, ἐπεὶ μηδὲ ἔστιν ἄλλο τι κριτήριον δι' οὗ χρὴ κρίνειν κατὰ 50 τὴν προκειμένην ὑπόθεσιν. ἀνεπίκριτον ἄρα καὶ

---

[a] Cf. *Adv. Log.* i. 343.

[b] *e.g.* Heracleitus, Parmenides, Democritus; *cf. Adv. Log.* i. 126 ff.

[c] Epicurus and Protagoras; *cf. Adv. Log.* i. 204, 369.

[d] Peripatetics, Stoics, and Academics; *cf. Adv. Log.* i. 369, 388.

discuss first the criterion " By means of which " (or Instrument) as it is called.

Chapter VI.—Of the Criterion " By means of which " (or Instrument)

Concerning this criterion [a] the controversy which 48 exists amongst the Dogmatists is fierce and, one may say, unending. We, however,—with a view here also to a systematic treatment,—maintain that inasmuch as Man is, according to them, the criterion " By whom " matters are judged, and Man (as they also themselves agree) can have no other instrument by means of which he will be able to judge except sense and intellect, then if we shall show that he is unable to judge by means of either sense alone or intellect alone or both conjoined, we shall have given a concise answer to all the individual opinions ; for they can all, as it seems, be referred to these three rival theories. Let us begin with the senses. 49

Since, then, some [b] assert that the senses have " empty " impressions (none of the objects they seem to apprehend having any real existence), and others [c] say that all the objects by which they suppose them to be moved are really existent, and others again [d] say that some of the objects are real, some unreal, we shall not know whom we should assent to. For we shall not decide the controversy by sense-perception, since it is regarding this that we are making our inquiry whether it is illusory or apprehends truly, nor yet by anything else, seeing that there does not even exist any other criterion " by means of which " one ought to judge, according to the present hypothesis. So then the question whether the senses have 50

ἀκατάληπτον ἔσται πότερον κενοπαθεῖ ἡ αἴσθησις
ἢ καταλαμβάνει τι· ᾧ συνεισέρχεται τὸ μὴ δεῖν
ἡμᾶς τῇ αἰσθήσει μόνῃ προσέχειν ἐν τῇ κρίσει τῶν
πραγμάτων, περὶ ἧς οὐκ ἔχομεν εἰπεῖν εἰ καὶ τὴν
ἀρχὴν καταλαμβάνει τι.

51 Ἀλλ' ἔστω κατὰ συγχώρησιν τὰς αἰσθήσεις
ἀντιληπτικὰς εἶναι· οὐδὲν γὰρ ἧττον καὶ οὕτως
ἄπιστοι εὑρεθήσονται πρὸς τὴν κρίσιν τῶν ἐκτὸς
ὑποκειμένων πραγμάτων. αἱ γοῦν αἰσθήσεις ὑπ-
εναντίως κινοῦνται ὑπὸ τῶν ἐκτός, οἷον ἡ γεῦσις
ὑπὸ τοῦ αὐτοῦ μέλιτος ὁτὲ μὲν πικράζεται ὁτὲ δὲ
γλυκάζεται, καὶ ἡ ὅρασις τὸ αὐτὸ χρῶμα ὁτὲ μὲν
52 αἱμωπὸν ὁτὲ δὲ λευκὸν εἶναι ⟨δοκεῖ⟩.[1] ἀλλ' οὐδὲ
ἡ ὄσφρησις ἑαυτῇ συμφωνεῖ· τὸ γοῦν μύρον ὁ μὲν
κεφαλαλγικὸς ἀηδὲς εἶναί φησιν, ὁ δὲ μὴ οὕτως
ἔχων ἡδύ. καὶ οἱ θεόληπτοι δὲ καὶ οἱ φρενιτίζοντες ἀκούειν δοκοῦσί τινων διαλεγομένων αὐτοῖς,
ὧν ἡμεῖς οὐκ ἐπακούομεν. καὶ τὸ αὐτὸ ὕδωρ τοῖς
μὲν φλεγμαίνουσιν ἀηδὲς εἶναι δοκεῖ δι' ὑπερβολὴν
53 θερμότητος, τοῖς δ' ἄλλοις χλιαρόν. πότερον οὖν
πάσας τὰς φαντασίας ἀληθεῖς εἶναι φήσει τις, ἢ
τάσδε μὲν ἀληθεῖς τάσδε δὲ ψευδεῖς, ἢ καὶ ψευδεῖς
ἁπάσας, εἰπεῖν ἀμήχανον, μηδὲν ἡμῶν ἐχόντων
κριτήριον ὡμολογημένον δι' οὗ κρινοῦμεν ὃ προκρίνειν μέλλομεν, ἀλλὰ μηδὲ ἀποδείξεως εὐπο-
ρούντων ἀληθοῦς τε καὶ κεκριμένης, διὰ τὸ μέχρι
νῦν ζητεῖσθαι τὸ τῆς ἀληθείας κριτήριον, δι' οὗ
καὶ τὴν ἀληθῆ ἀπόδειξιν ἐπικρίνεσθαι προσήκει.
54 διὰ ταῦτα καὶ ὁ ἀξιῶν τοῖς μὲν κατὰ φύσιν ἔχουσιν
[ἐν τούτοις][2] πιστεύειν, τοῖς δὲ παρὰ φύσιν δια-
κειμένοις μηδαμῶς, ἄτοπος ἔσται· οὔτε γὰρ

---

[1] ⟨δοκεῖ⟩ add. T.   [2] ἐν τούτοις om. Stephanus.

illusory affections or apprehend some real object will be incapable of either decision or apprehension ; and there follows the corollary, that we must not attend to sensation alone in our judgement of matters, since regarding it we cannot so much as affirm that it apprehends anything at all.

But let it be granted, by way of concession, that 51 the senses are apprehensive ; yet, even so they will not be found any the less unreliable for judging the external real objects. For certainly the senses are affected in diverse ways by external objects—taste, for instance, perceives the same honey now as bitter and now as sweet ; and vision pronounces the same colour now blood-red and now white.[a] Nay, even 52 smell is not consistent with itself ; for certainly the sufferer from headache declares myrrh to be unpleasant, while one who does not so suffer calls it pleasant. And those who are possessed or in a frenzy fancy they hear persons conversing with them whom we do not hear. And the same water seems to those in a fever to be unpleasant because of its excessive heat, but to all others tepid. Whether, then, one is to call 53 all the appearances true, or some true and some false, or all false, it is impossible to say since we possess no agreed criterion whereby we shall judge the question we are proposing to decide, nor are we even provided with a proof that is true and approved, because we are still in search of the criterion of truth " By means of which " the true proof itself ought to be tested. For these reasons he also who asks us to 54 believe those who are in a natural state, but not those whose disposition is non-natural, will be acting absurdly ; for he will not gain credence if he says

[a] *Cf.* i. 100 ff.

ἀναποδείκτως τοῦτο λέγων πιστευθήσεται, οὔτε ἀπόδειξιν ἀληθῆ καὶ κεκριμένην ἕξει διὰ τὰ προειρημένα.

55 Εἰ μέντοι καὶ συγχωρήσειέ τις τὰς μὲν τῶν κατὰ φύσιν ἐχόντων φαντασίας εἶναι πιστὰς τὰς δὲ τῶν παρὰ φύσιν διακειμένων ἀπίστους, καὶ οὕτως ἀδύνατος εὑρεθήσεται ἡ διὰ τῶν αἰσθήσεων μόνων κρίσις τῶν ἐκτὸς ὑποκειμένων. ἡ ὅρασις γοῦν καὶ ἡ κατὰ φύσιν ἔχουσα τὸν ⟨αὐτὸν⟩[1] πύργον ὁτὲ μὲν στρογγύλον ὁτὲ δὲ τετράγωνον εἶναι λέγει, καὶ ἡ γεῦσις τὰ αὐτὰ σιτία ἐπὶ μὲν τῶν κεκορεσμένων ἀηδῆ ἐπὶ δὲ τῶν πεινώντων ἡδέα φησὶν εἶναι, καὶ ἡ ἀκοὴ παραπλησίως τῆς αὐτῆς φωνῆς νυκτὸς μὲν ὡς εὐμεγέθους ἀντιλαμβάνεται ἡμέρας

56 δὲ ⟨ὡς⟩[2] ἀμαυρᾶς, καὶ ἡ ὄσφρησις ἐπὶ μὲν τῶν πολλῶν δυσώδη ἐπὶ δὲ τῶν βυρσοδεψῶν οὐδαμῶς τὰ αὐτὰ εἶναι δοκεῖ, καὶ ἡ αὐτὴ ἁφὴ εἰσιόντων μὲν ἡμῶν εἰς τὸ βαλανεῖον θερμαίνεται ὑπὸ τῆς παραστάδος, ἐξιόντων δὲ ψύχεται. διόπερ ἐπεὶ καὶ κατὰ φύσιν ἔχουσαι αἱ αἰσθήσεις ἑαυταῖς μάχονται, καὶ ἡ διαφωνία ἐστὶν ἀνεπίκριτος, ἐπεὶ μὴ ἔχομεν ὡμολογημένον ⟨κριτήριον⟩[3] δι' οὗ κρίνεσθαι δύναται, τὰς αὐτὰς ἀπορίας ἀκολουθεῖν ἀνάγκη. καὶ ἄλλα δὲ πλείω μεταφέρειν πρὸς τὴν τούτου κατασκευὴν ἐνδέχεται ἐκ τῶν προειρημένων ἡμῖν περὶ τῶν τῆς ἐποχῆς τρόπων. διόπερ οὐκ ἂν εἴη ἀληθὲς ἴσως τὸ τὴν αἴσθησιν μόνην δύνασθαι κρίνειν τὰ ἐκτὸς ὑποκείμενα.

57 Οὐκοῦν ἐπὶ τὴν διάνοιαν μετέλθωμεν τῷ λόγῳ. οἱ τοίνυν ἀξιοῦντες τῇ διανοίᾳ μόνῃ προσέχειν ἐν

---

[1] ⟨αὐτὸν⟩ add. Mutsch.
[2] ⟨ὡς⟩ add. cj. Bekk. [3] ⟨κριτήριον⟩ add. T.

this without proof, and, for the reasons given above, he will not possess a true and approved proof.

And even were one to concede that the sense- 55 impressions of those in a natural state are reliable, and those of men in a non-natural condition unreliable, even so the judgement of external real objects by means of the senses alone will be found to be impossible. For certainly the sense of sight, even when it is in a natural state, pronounces the same tower [a] to be at one time round, at another square ; and the sense of taste declares the same food to be unpleasant in the case of those full-fed, but pleasant in the case of those who are hungry ; and the sense of hearing likewise perceives the same sound as loud by night but as faint by day ; and the sense of smell 56 regards the same objects as malodorous in the case of most people, but not so in the case of tanners ; and the same sense of touch feels warmth in the outer hall,[b] when we enter the bath-rooms, but cold when we leave them. Therefore, since even when in a natural state the senses contradict themselves, and their dispute is incapable of decision, seeing that we possess no accepted criterion by means of which it can be judged, the same perplexities must necessarily follow. Moreover, for the establishment of this conclusion we may derive still further arguments from our previous discussion of the Modes of Suspension.[c] Hence it would probably be untrue to say that sense-perception alone is able to judge real external objects.

Let us, then, proceed in our exposition to the in- 57 tellect. Now those who claim [d] that we should attend

[a] *Cf.* i. 118.
[b] *Cf.* i. 110.
[c] See i. 36 ff.
[d] *Cf. Adv. Log.* i. 89 ff.

τῇ κρίσει τῶν πραγμάτων πρῶτον μὲν ἐκεῖνο οὐχ
ἕξουσιν δεικνύναι ὅτι καταληπτόν ἐστι τὸ εἶναι
διάνοιαν. ἐπεὶ γὰρ ὁ μὲν Γοργίας οὐδὲν εἶναι
φάσκων οὐδὲ διάνοιαν εἶναί φησι, τινὲς δὲ ταύτην
ἀποφαίνονται ὑπάρχειν, πῶς οὖν ἐπικρινοῦσι τὴν
διαφωνίαν; οὔτε γὰρ διανοίᾳ, ἐπεὶ τὸ ζητούμενον
συναρπάσουσιν, οὔτε ἄλλῳ τινί· οὐδὲν γὰρ ἄλλο
εἶναί φασι κατὰ τὴν ὑπόθεσιν τὴν νῦν ὑποκειμένην,
δι' οὗ κρίνεται τὰ πράγματα. ἀνεπίκριτον ἄρα
καὶ ἀκατάληπτον ἔσται πότερον ἔστι διάνοια ἢ
οὐκ ἔστιν· ᾧ συνεισέρχεται τὸ μὴ δεῖν μόνῃ τῇ
διανοίᾳ προσέχειν ἐν τῇ τῶν πραγμάτων κρίσει,
τῇ μηδέπω κατειλημμένῃ.

58 Ἀλλὰ κατειλήφθω ἡ διάνοια, καὶ ὡμολογήσθω
τὸ εἶναι ταύτην καθ' ὑπόθεσιν· λέγω ὅτι οὐ
δύναται κρίνειν τὰ πράγματα. εἰ γὰρ μηδ' ἑαυτὴν ἀκριβῶς ὁρᾷ, ἀλλὰ διαφωνεῖ περί τε τῆς
οὐσίας αὐτῆς καὶ τοῦ τρόπου τῆς γενέσεως καὶ
τοῦ τόπου ἐν ᾧ ἔστιν, πῶς ἂν δυνηθείη τῶν ἄλλων
59 τι ἀκριβῶς καταλαμβάνειν; διδομένου δὲ καὶ τοῦ
τὴν διάνοιαν κριτικὴν εἶναι τῶν πραγμάτων, οὐχ
εὑρήσομεν πῶς κατ' αὐτὴν κρινοῦμεν. πολλῆς γὰρ
οὔσης τῆς κατὰ διάνοιαν διαφορᾶς, ἐπειδὴ ἑτέρα
μέν ἐστιν ἡ Γοργίου διάνοια, καθ' ἣν φησι μηδὲν
εἶναι, ἑτέρα δὲ ἡ Ἡρακλείτου, καθ' ἣν λέγει πάντα
εἶναι, ἑτέρα δὲ ἡ τῶν λεγόντων τάδε μὲν εἶναι τάδε
δὲ μὴ εἶναι, πῶς ἐπικρίνωμεν τὴν τῶν διανοιῶν
διαφορὰν οὐχ ἕξομεν, οὐδὲ δυνησόμεθα εἰπεῖν ὅτι

---

[a] See Introd. p. xv; cf. Adv. Log. i. 65.
[b] i.e. whether in the head or breast or elsewhere; cf. Adv.
Log. i. 313, 348.

to the intellect only in our judgement of things will, in the first place, be unable to show that the existence of intellect is apprehensible. For when Gorgias,[a] in denying that anything exists, denies also the existence of intellect, while some declare that it has real existence, how will they decide this contradiction? Not by the intellect, for so they will be assuming the matter in question; nor yet by anything else, since, as they assert, according to our present assumption there exists nothing else by means of which objects are judged. So then the problem as to whether intellect does or does not exist will not admit of decision or apprehension; and from this it follows, as a corollary, that in the judgement of objects we ought not to attend to the intellect alone, which has not as yet been apprehended.

But let it be granted that the intellect has been 58 apprehended, and let us agree, by way of assumption, that it really exists; I still affirm that it cannot judge objects. For if it does not even discern itself accurately but contradicts itself about its own existence and the mode of its origin and the position in which it is placed,[b] how can it be able to apprehend anything else accurately? And even if it be granted 59 that the intellect is capable of judging objects, we shall not discover how to judge according to it. For since there exists great divergence in respect of the intellect—for the intellect of Gorgias, according to which he states that nothing exists, is one kind, and another kind is that of Heracleitus, according to which he declares that all things exist, and another that of those who say that some things do and others do not exist—we shall have no means of deciding between these divergent intellects, nor shall we be able to

τῇ μὲν τοῦδε διανοίᾳ κατακολουθεῖν προσήκει τῇ
60 τοῦδε δὲ οὐδαμῶς. ἤν τε γὰρ διανοίᾳ τινὶ κρίνειν
τολμῶμεν, τῆς διαφωνίας μέρει συγκατατιθέμενοι
τὸ ζητούμενον συναρπάσομεν· ἤν τε ἑτέρῳ τινί,
ψευσόμεθα ὅτι μόνῃ τῇ διανοίᾳ δεῖ κρίνειν τὰ
πράγματα.

61 Λοιπὸν ἐκ τῶν περὶ κριτηρίου τοῦ ὑφ' οὗ λεγομένου ῥηθέντων δεικνύναι δυνησόμεθα ὅτι μήτε
τὴν ἀγχινουστέραν τῶν ἄλλων διάνοιαν εὑρεῖν
δυνάμεθα, ὅτι τε ἂν εὕρωμεν τῶν τε γεγενημένων
καὶ οὐσῶν διανοιῶν ἀγχινουστέραν διάνοιαν, ἐπεὶ
ἄδηλόν ἐστιν εἰ πάλιν ταύτης ἑτέρα ἔσται ἀγχι-
62 νουστέρα, οὐ δεῖ προσέχειν αὐτῇ, ὅτι τε κἂν ὑπο-
θώμεθα διάνοιαν ἧς ἐντρεχεστέρα οὐκ ἂν γένοιτο,
οὐ συγκαταθησόμεθα τῷ δι' αὐτῆς κρίνοντι, εὐλα-
βούμενοι μὴ ψευδῆ τινὰ λόγον προφερόμενος διὰ
τὸ ὀξυτάτης διανοίας μετεσχηκέναι δύναται ἡμᾶς
πείθειν ὅτι ἀληθής ἐστιν. οὐκοῦν οὐδὲ τῇ διανοίᾳ
μόνῃ δεῖ κρίνειν τὰ πράγματα.

63 Λείπεται λέγειν ὅτι δι' ἀμφοτέρων. ὃ πάλιν ἐστὶν
ἀδύνατον· οὐ μόνον γὰρ οὐχ ὁδηγοῦσιν αἱ αἰσθήσεις τὴν διάνοιαν πρὸς κατάληψιν, ἀλλὰ καὶ
ἐναντιοῦνται αὐτῇ. ἀμέλει γοῦν ἐκ τοῦ τὸ μέλι
τοῖσδε μὲν πικρὸν τοῖσδε δὲ γλυκὺ φαίνεσθαι ὁ
μὲν Δημόκριτος ἔφη μήτε γλυκὺ αὐτὸ εἶναι μήτε
πικρόν, ὁ δὲ Ἡράκλειτος ἀμφότερα. καὶ ἐπὶ τῶν
ἄλλων αἰσθήσεών τε καὶ αἰσθητῶν ὁ αὐτὸς λόγος.
οὕτως ἀπὸ τῶν αἰσθήσεων ὁρμωμένη ἡ διάνοια
διάφορά τε καὶ μαχόμενα ἀποφαίνεσθαι ἀναγκά-

assert that it is right to take this man's intellect as
our guide but not that man's. For if we venture 60
to judge by any one intellect, by thus agreeing to
assent to one side in the dispute we shall be assuming
the matter in question ; while if we judge by anything else, we shall be falsifying the assertion that
one ought to judge objects by the intellect alone.

Further, we shall be able to show, from the state- 61
ments made concerning the criterion " By whom "
(as it is called), that we are unable to discover the
intellect that is cleverer than all others ; and also
that if we should discover the intellect that is cleverer
than past and present intellects we ought not to 62
attend to it, since it is not evident whether yet
another intellect may not arise which is cleverer than
it ; and further, that even if we assume an intellect
which none could possibly surpass, we shall not
assent to the man who judges by means of it, dread-
ing lest he may put forward some false statement
and succeed in persuading us of its truth because
he possesses the keenest intellect. Neither, then, by
the intellect alone ought we to judge objects.

The only remaining alternative is judgement by 63
means of both senses and intellect.[a] But this again is
impossible ; for not only do the senses not guide the
intellect to apprehension, but they even oppose it. For
it is certain, at any rate, that from the fact that honey
appears bitter to some and sweet to others, Democritus declared that it is neither sweet nor bitter,
while Heracleitus said that it is both. And the same
account may be given of all the other senses and
sensibles. Thus, when it starts out from the senses,
the intellect is compelled to make diverse and con-

* *Cf. Adv. Log.* i. 354 ff.

SEXTUS EMPIRICUS

ζεται. τοῦτο δὲ ἀλλότριόν ἐστι κριτηρίου κατα-
ληπτικοῦ.

64 Εἶτα κἀκεῖνο λεκτέον· ἤτοι πάσαις ταῖς αἰσθήσεσι καὶ ταῖς πάντων διανοίαις κρινοῦσι τὰ πράγματα ἢ τισίν. ἀλλ' εἰ μὲν πάσαις λέξει τις, ἀ-
δύνατα ἀξιώσει τοσαύτης μάχης ἐν ταῖς αἰσθήσεσι
καὶ ἐν ταῖς διανοίαις ἐμφαινομένης, ἄλλως τε καὶ
ἐπεὶ τῆς Γοργίου διανοίας ἀπόφασίς ἐστι τὸ μὴ
δεῖν μήτε αἰσθήσει μήτε διανοίᾳ προσέχειν, περιτραπήσεται ὁ λόγος. εἰ δὲ τισίν, πῶς κρινοῦσιν
ὅτι ταῖσδε μὲν ταῖς αἰσθήσεσι καὶ ⟨τῇδε⟩[1] τῇ
διανοίᾳ προσέχειν δεῖ ταῖσδε δὲ οὔ, μὴ ἔχοντες
κριτήριον ὡμολογημένον δι' οὗ τὰς διαφόρους
65 αἰσθήσεις τε καὶ διανοίας ἐπικρινοῦσιν; ἢν δὲ
λέγωσιν ὅτι τὰς αἰσθήσεις καὶ τὰς διανοίας τῇ
διανοίᾳ καὶ ταῖς αἰσθήσεσι κρινοῦμεν, τὸ ζητούμενον συναρπάζουσιν· περὶ γὰρ τοῦ εἰ δύναταί τις
διὰ τούτων κρίνειν ζητοῦμεν.

66 Εἶτα κἀκεῖνο ῥητέον ὅτι ἤτοι ταῖς αἰσθήσεσι τάς
τε αἰσθήσεις καὶ τὰς διανοίας κρινεῖ τις,[2] ἢ ταῖς
διανοίαις τάς τε αἰσθήσεις καὶ τὰς διανοίας, ἢ
ταῖς τε αἰσθήσεσι τὰς αἰσθήσεις καὶ ταῖς διανοίαις
τὰς διανοίας, ἢ ταῖς μὲν αἰσθήσεσι τὰς διανοίας
τῇ δὲ διανοίᾳ τὰς αἰσθήσεις. εἰ μὲν οὖν ταῖς
αἰσθήσεσιν ἢ τῇ διανοίᾳ ἀμφότερα κρίνειν ἐθελήσουσιν, οὐκέτι δι' αἰσθήσεως καὶ διανοίας κρινοῦσιν
ἀλλὰ δι' ἑνὸς τούτων, ὅπερ ἂν ἕλωνται· καὶ παρακολουθήσουσιν αὐτοῖς αἱ ἔμπροσθεν εἰρημέναι
67 ἀπορίαι. εἰ δὲ ταῖς αἰσθήσεσι τὰς αἰσθήσεις καὶ

---

[1] ⟨τῇδε⟩ add. cj. Bekk.
[2] κρινεῖ τις ego: κρίνεται L: κρίνετε MEAB, Bekk.: κρινοῦσιν
T, Mutsch.

192

flicting statements ; and this is alien to a criterion of apprehension.

Then there is this also to be said : they will judge 64 objects either by all the senses and by all men's intellects or by some. But if a man shall say " by all," he will be claiming what is impossible in view of the immense discrepancy which obviously exists amongst the senses and the intellects ; and moreover, by reason of the assertion of Gorgias's intellect that " we must not give heed either to sense or to intellect," the man's statement will be demolished. And if they shall say " by some," how will they decide that we ought to give heed to these senses and this intellect and not to those, seeing that they possess no accepted criterion by which to judge the differing senses and intellects ? And if they shall say that we will judge 65 the senses and the intellects by the intellect and the senses, they are assuming the matter in question ; for what we are questioning is the possibility of judging by means of these.

Another point we must make is this : either one 66 will judge both the senses and the intellects by the senses, or both the senses and the intellects by the intellects, or the senses by the senses and the intellect by the intellects, or the intellects by the senses and the senses by the intellect. If then they shall propose to judge both objects by the senses or by the intellect, they will no longer be judging by sense and intellect but by one of these two, whichever one they may choose, and thus they will be entangled in the perplexities previously mentioned. And if they shall 67 judge the senses by the senses and the intellects by

τῇ διανοίᾳ τὰς διανοίας ἐπικρινοῦσιν, ἐπειδὴ
μάχονται καὶ αἰσθήσεις αἰσθήσεσι καὶ διάνοιαι
διανοίαις, ἥντινα ἂν λάβωσιν ἀπὸ τῶν μαχομένων
αἰσθήσεων πρὸς τὴν κρίσιν τῶν ἄλλων αἰσθήσεων,
τὸ ζητούμενον συναρπάσουσιν· μέρος γὰρ τῆς
διαφωνίας ὡς πιστὸν ἤδη λήψονται πρὸς τὴν τῶν
68 ἐπ᾿ ἴσης αὐτῷ ζητουμένων ἐπίκρισιν. ὁ δὲ αὐτὸς
καὶ ἐπὶ τῶν διανοιῶν λόγος. εἰ δὲ ταῖς μὲν
αἰσθήσεσι τὰς διανοίας ἐπικρινοῦσι τῇ διανοίᾳ δὲ
τὰς αἰσθήσεις, ὁ διάλληλος εὑρίσκεται τρόπος,
καθ᾿ ὃν ἵνα μὲν αἱ αἰσθήσεις ἐπικριθῶσι δεῖ προκεκρίσθαι τὰς διανοίας, ἵνα δὲ αἱ διάνοιαι δοκιμα-
69 σθῶσι, χρὴ προδιακρίνεσθαι τὰς αἰσθήσεις. ἐπεὶ
οὖν μήτε ὑπὸ τῶν ὁμογενῶν τὰ ὁμογενῆ κριτήρια
δύναται ἐπικρίνεσθαι μήτε ὑπὸ ἑνὸς γένους ἀμφότερα τὰ γένη μήτε ὑπὸ τῶν ἑτερογενῶν ἐναλλάξ,
οὐ δυνησόμεθα προκρίνειν διάνοιαν διανοίας ἢ
αἴσθησιν αἰσθήσεως. διὰ δὲ τοῦτο οὐδὲ ἕξομεν
διὰ τίνος κρινοῦμεν· εἰ γὰρ μήτε πάσαις ταῖς
αἰσθήσεσι καὶ ταῖς διανοίαις κρίνειν δυνησόμεθα,
μήτε εἰσόμεθα ποίαις μὲν δεῖ κρίνειν ποίαις δὲ μή,
οὐχ ἕξομεν δι᾿ οὗ κρινοῦμεν τὰ πράγματα.

Ὥστε καὶ διὰ ταῦτα ἀνύπαρκτον ἂν εἴη τὸ
κριτήριον τὸ δι᾿ οὗ.

Ζ΄.—ΠΕΡΙ ΤΟΥ ΚΑΘ᾿ Ο

70 Ἴδωμεν οὖν ἑξῆς περὶ τοῦ κριτηρίου καθ᾿ ὃ
κρίνεσθαι λέγουσι τὰ πράγματα. πρῶτον τοίνυν
ἐκεῖνο ἔστιν εἰπεῖν περὶ αὐτοῦ ὅτι ἀνεπινόητός

ᵃ i.e. the Stoics, cf. § 16; Adv. Log. i. 35, 370. For the
Stoic doctrine of " presentation " and the " Criterion " see
Introd. p. xxv.

the intellect, then, since both senses conflict with senses and intellects with intellects, whichever of the conflicting senses they shall adopt for judging the rest of the senses, they will be assuming the matter in question ; for they will be adopting one section of the series in dispute, as being already reliable, to decide about the others which, equally with it, are in question. And the same argument applies to the 68 intellects. And if they shall judge the intellects by the senses, and the senses by the intellect, this involves circular reasoning inasmuch as it is required that the intellects should be judged first in order that the senses may be judged, and the senses be first scrutinized in order that the intellects may be tested. Since, therefore, criteria of the one species cannot be 69 judged by those of a like species, nor those of both the species by those of one species, nor conversely by those of an unlike species, we shall not be able to prefer intellect to intellect or sense to sense. And because of this we shall have nothing by which to judge ; for if we shall be unable to judge by all the senses and intellects, and shall not know either by which of them we ought and by which we ought not to judge, then we shall possess no means by which to judge objects.

Consequently, for these reasons also the criterion " By means of which " will have no real existence.

CHAPTER VII.—OF THE CRITERION " ACCORDING TO WHICH "

Let us consider next the Criterion " According to 70 which," as they [a] say, objects are judged. In the first place, then, we may say this of it, that " presentation "

195

ἐστιν ἡ φαντασία. λέγουσι γὰρ φαντασίαν εἶναι
τύπωσιν ἐν ἡγεμονικῷ. ἐπεὶ οὖν ἡ ψυχὴ καὶ τὸ
ἡγεμονικὸν πνεῦμά ἐστιν ἢ λεπτομερέστερόν τι
πνεύματος, ὡς φασίν, οὐ δυνήσεταί τις τύπωσιν
ἐπινοεῖν ἐν αὐτῷ οὔτε κατ᾽ εἰσοχὴν καὶ ἐξοχήν,
ὡς ἐπὶ τῶν σφραγίδων ὁρῶμεν, οὔτε κατὰ τὴν
τερατολογουμένην ἑτεροιωτικήν· οὐ γὰρ ἂν μνήμην
τοσούτων ἀναδέξαιτο θεωρημάτων ὅσα συνίστησι
τέχνην, ἐν ταῖς ἐπιγινομέναις ἑτεροιώσεσι τῶν
71 προϋποκειμένων ἀπαλειφομένων. εἰ μέντοι καὶ
ἐπινοηθῆναι δύναιτο ἡ φαντασία, ἀκατάληπτος
ἔσται· ἐπεὶ γὰρ πάθος ἐστὶν ἡγεμονικοῦ, τὸ δὲ
ἡγεμονικὸν οὐ καταλαμβάνεται, ὡς ἐδείξαμεν,
οὐδὲ τὸ πάθος αὐτοῦ καταληψόμεθα.

72 Εἶτα εἰ καὶ δοίημεν ὅτι καταλαμβάνεται ἡ φαντασία, οὐ δύναται κρίνεσθαι [καὶ] κατ᾽ αὐτὴν τὰ
πράγματα· οὐ γὰρ δι᾽ ἑαυτῆς ἐπιβάλλει τοῖς ἐκτὸς
καὶ φαντασιοῦται ἡ διάνοια, ὡς φασίν, ἀλλὰ διὰ
τῶν αἰσθήσεων, αἱ δὲ αἰσθήσεις τὰ μὲν ἐκτὸς
ὑποκείμενα οὐ καταλαμβάνουσιν, μόνα δέ, εἰ ἄρα,
τὰ ἑαυτῶν πάθη. καὶ ἡ φαντασία οὖν τοῦ πάθους
τῆς αἰσθήσεως ἔσται, ὅπερ διαφέρει τοῦ ἐκτὸς
ὑποκειμένου· οὐ γὰρ τὸ αὐτό ἐστι τὸ μέλι τῷ
γλυκάζεσθαί με καὶ τὸ ἀψίνθιον τῷ πικράζεσθαι,
73 ἀλλὰ διαφέρει. εἰ δὲ διαφέρει τοῦτο τὸ πάθος τοῦ
ἐκτὸς ὑποκειμένου, ἡ φαντασία ἔσται οὐχὶ τοῦ
ἐκτὸς ὑποκειμένου ἀλλ᾽ ἑτέρου τινὸς διαφέροντος
αὐτοῦ. εἰ οὖν κατὰ ταύτην κρίνει ἡ διάνοια,

---

[a] Or "ruling principle," cf. i. 128, Adv. Log. i. 380 ; Introd.
p. xxv.   [b] Cf. § 81 infra, iii. 188: Introd. p. xxv.
[c] The first of these views is ascribed to Cleanthes, the second
to Chrysippus, cf. Adv. Log. i. 228, 372 : Introd. p. xxv.

is inconceivable. They declare that "presentation" is an impression on "the regent part."[a] Since, then, the soul, and the regent part, is breath or something more subtle than breath,[b] as they affirm, no one will be able to conceive of an impression upon it either by way of depression and eminence, as we see in the case of seals, or by way of the magical "alteration" they talk about[c]; for the soul will not be able to conserve the remembrance of all the concepts that compose an art, since the pre-existing concepts are obliterated by the subsequent "alterations." Yet 71 even if "presentation" could be conceived, it would still be non-apprehensible; for since it is an affection of the regent part, and the regent part, as we have shown,[d] is not apprehended, neither shall we apprehend its affection.

Further, even were we to grant that the "presenta- 72 tion" is apprehended, objects cannot be judged according to it; for the intellect, as they assert, does not make contact with external objects and receive presentations by means of itself but by means of the senses, and the senses do not apprehend external real objects but only, if at all, their own affections.[e] So then the presentation will be that of the affection of the sense, which is different from the external reality; for honey is not the same as my feeling of sweetness nor gall the same as my feeling of bitterness, but a different thing. And if this affection differs 73 from the external real object, the presentation will not be that of the external reality but of something else which is different therefrom. If, therefore, the intellect judges according to this, it judges badly and

[d] See §§ 57 ff. *supra*.
[e] *i.e.* sensations or feelings.

φαύλως κρίνει καὶ οὐ κατὰ τὸ ὑποκείμενον. διόπερ
ἄτοπόν ἐστι τὸ κατὰ τὴν φαντασίαν τὰ ἐκτὸς
κρίνεσθαι λέγειν.

74 Ἀλλ᾽ οὐδὲ τοῦτο ἔστιν εἰπεῖν ὅτι ἡ ψυχὴ καταλαμβάνει διὰ τῶν αἰσθητικῶν παθῶν τὰ ἐκτὸς
ὑποκείμενα διὰ τὸ ὅμοια τὰ πάθη τῶν αἰσθήσεων
εἶναι τοῖς ἐκτὸς ὑποκειμένοις. πόθεν γὰρ εἴσεται
ἡ διάνοια εἰ ὅμοιά ἐστι τὰ πάθη τῶν αἰσθήσεων
τοῖς αἰσθητοῖς, μήτε αὐτὴ τοῖς ἐκτὸς ἐντυγχάνουσα,
μήτε τῶν αἰσθήσεων αὐτῇ τὴν φύσιν αὐτῶν δη-
λουσῶν ἀλλὰ τὰ ἑαυτῶν πάθη, καθάπερ ἐκ τῶν
75 τρόπων τῆς ἐποχῆς ἐπελογισάμην. ὥσπερ γὰρ ὁ
ἀγνοῶν μὲν Σωκράτην εἰκόνα δὲ τούτου θεασάμενος
οὐκ οἶδεν εἰ ὁμοία ἐστὶν ἡ εἰκὼν τῷ Σωκράτει,
οὕτω καὶ ἡ διάνοια τὰ μὲν πάθη τῶν αἰσθήσεων
ἐποπτεύουσα τὰ δὲ ἐκτὸς μὴ θεωροῦσα οὐδὲ εἰ
ὅμοιά ἐστι τὰ τῶν αἰσθήσεων πάθη τοῖς ἐκτὸς
ὑποκειμένοις εἴσεται. οὐδὲ καθ᾽ ὁμοίωσιν ἄρα
δυνήσεται ταῦτα κρίνειν κατὰ τὴν φαντασίαν.

76 Ἀλλὰ δῶμεν κατὰ συγχώρησιν, πρὸς τῷ ἐπινοεῖσθαι τὴν φαντασίαν καὶ καταλαμβάνεσθαι, ἔτι
καὶ ἐπιδεκτικὴν εἶναι τοῦ κρίνεσθαι κατ᾽ αὐτὴν τὰ
πράγματα, καίτοι τοῦ λόγου πᾶν τὸ ἐναντίον
ὑπομνήσαντος. οὐκοῦν ἤτοι πάσῃ φαντασίᾳ πιστεύσομεν ⟨καὶ κατ᾽ αὐτὴν ἐπικρινοῦμεν, ἤ τινι·
ἀλλ᾽ εἰ μὲν πάσῃ, δῆλον ὅτι καὶ τῇ Ξενιάδου
φαντασίᾳ πιστεύσομεν⟩¹ καθ᾽ ἣν ἔλεγε πάσας τὰς
φαντασίας ἀπίστους εἶναι, καὶ περιτραπήσεται ὁ
λόγος εἰς τὸ μὴ εἶναι πάσας τὰς φαντασίας ὥστε

¹ ⟨καὶ . . . πιστεύσομεν⟩ add. T.

_____

ᵃ See i. 100 ff.   ᵇ Cf. § 18 supra.

not according to reality. Consequently, it is absurd to say that external objects are judged according to the presentation.

Nor, again, is it possible to assert that the soul 74 apprehends external realities by means of the affections of sense owing to the similarity of the affections of the senses to the external real objects. For how is the intellect to know whether the affections of the senses are similar to the objects of sense when it has not itself encountered the external objects, and the senses do not inform it about their real nature but only about their own affections, as I have argued from the Modes of Suspension? [a] For just as the man 75 who does not know Socrates but has seen a picture of him does not know whether the picture is like Socrates, so also the intellect when it gazes on the affections of the senses but does not behold the external objects will not so much as know whether the affections of the senses are similar to the external realities. So that not even on the ground of resemblance will he be able to judge these objects according to the presentation.

But let us grant by way of concession that in 76 addition to being conceived and apprehended the presentation is also such that it admits of objects being judged according to it, although the argument points to an entirely opposite conclusion. In this case we shall either believe every presentation, or impression, and judge according thereto, or some one impression. But if we are to believe every impression, clearly we shall believe also that of Xeniades [b] according to which he asserted that all impressions are untrustworthy, and our statement will be reversed and made to say that all impressions are not of such a sort

199

καὶ κατ' αὐτὰς κρίνεσθαι δύνασθαι τὰ πράγματα·
77 εἰ δέ τισίν, πῶς ἐπικρινοῦμεν ὅτι ταῖσδε μὲν ταῖς
φαντασίαις πιστεύειν προσήκει ταῖσδε δὲ ἀπιστεῖν;
εἰ μὲν γὰρ ἄνευ φαντασίας, δώσουσιν ὅτι παρέλκει
ἡ φαντασία πρὸς τὸ κρίνειν, εἴγε χωρὶς αὐτῆς
κρίνεσθαι δύνασθαι τὰ πράγματά [τινα] λέξουσιν·
εἰ δὲ μετὰ φαντασίας, πῶς λήψονται τὴν φαντασίαν ἣν παραλαμβάνουσι πρὸς τὴν τῶν ἄλλων φαν-
78 τασιῶν κρίσιν; ἢ πάλιν αὐτοῖς ἄλλης φαντασίας
δεήσει πρὸς τὴν κρίσιν [τῶν ἄλλων φαντασιῶν],[1]
καὶ εἰς τὴν ἐκείνης κρίσιν ἄλλης, καὶ εἰς ἄπειρον.
ἀδύνατον δὲ ἄπειρα ἐπικρῖναι· ἀδύνατον ἄρα εὑρεῖν
ποίαις μὲν φαντασίαις ὡς κριτηρίοις δεῖ χρῆσθαι
ποίαις δὲ οὐδαμῶς. ἐπεὶ οὖν κἂν δῶμεν ὅτι κατὰ
τὰς φαντασίας δεῖ κρίνειν τὰ πράγματα, ἑκατέρωθεν περιτρέπεται ὁ λόγος, καὶ ἐκ τοῦ πάσῃ
πιστεύειν καὶ ἐκ τοῦ τισὶ μὲν πιστεύειν ὡς κριτηρίοις τισὶ δὲ ἀπιστεῖν, συνάγεται τὸ μὴ δεῖν
τὰς φαντασίας πρὸς τὴν κρίσιν τῶν πραγμάτων
ὡς κριτήρια παραλαμβάνειν.
79 Ταῦτα μὲν ἀρκεῖ νῦν εἰπεῖν ὡς ἐν ὑποτυπώσει
καὶ πρὸς τὸ κριτήριον καθ' ὃ κρίνεσθαι τὰ πράγματα ἐλέγετο. εἰδέναι δὲ χρὴ ὅτι οὐ πρόκειται
ἡμῖν ἀποφήνασθαι ὅτι ἀνύπαρκτόν ἐστι τὸ κριτήριον τὸ τῆς ἀληθείας (τοῦτο γὰρ δογματικόν)·
ἀλλ' ἐπεὶ οἱ δογματικοὶ πιθανῶς δοκοῦσι κατ-
εσκευακέναι ὅτι ἔστι τι κριτήριον ἀληθείας, ἡμεῖς
αὐτοῖς πιθανοὺς δοκοῦντας εἶναι λόγους ἀντεθή-
καμεν, οὔτε ὅτι ἀληθεῖς εἰσι διαβεβαιούμενοι οὔτε
ὅτι πιθανώτεροι τῶν ἐναντίων, ἀλλὰ διὰ τὴν φαινο-

———
[1] [τῶν ἄ. φ.] del. Papp.

[a] Cf. § 103 infra, Adv. Log. i. 443.

that objects can be judged according to them. And 77
if we are to believe some, how shall we decide that
it is proper to believe these and disbelieve those?
For if they say we are to do so without presentation,
they will be granting that presentation is superfluous
for judging, inasmuch as they will be stating that
objects can be judged without it; while if they say
"by the aid of presentation," how will they select
the presentation which they are adopting for the
purpose of judging all the other presentations? Once 78
again they will need a second presentation to judge
the first, and a third to judge the second, and so on
ad infinitum. But it is impossible to judge an infinite
series; and therefore it is impossible to discover what
sort of presentations we ought to employ as criteria,
and what we ought not. Seeing, then, that, even
should we grant that one ought to judge objects
according to presentations, whether we adopt the
alternative of trusting all as criteria or that of trusting
some and distrusting others, in either case the argument is overthrown, and we are forced to conclude
that we ought not to adopt presentations as criteria
for the judging of objects.

This is enough to say now, in our outline sketch, 79
with reference to the criterion "According to which,"
as it was said, objects are judged. But one should
notice that we do not propose to assert that the
criterion of truth is unreal [a] (for that would be dogmatism); but since the Dogmatists appear to have
established plausibly that there really is a criterion of
truth, we have set up counter-arguments which appear
to be plausible; and though we do not positively
affirm either that they are true or that they are more
plausible than their opposites, yet because of the

μένην ἴσην πιθανότητα τούτων τε τῶν λόγων καὶ
τῶν παρὰ τοῖς δογματικοῖς κειμένων τὴν ἐποχὴν
συνάγοντες.

Η΄.—ΠΕΡΙ ΑΛΗΘΟΥΣ ΚΑΙ ΑΛΗΘΕΙΑΣ

80 Εἰ μέντοι καὶ δοίημεν καθ᾽ ὑπόθεσιν εἶναί τι
τῆς ἀληθείας κριτήριον, ἄχρηστον εὑρίσκεται καὶ
μάταιον, ἐὰν ὑπομνήσωμεν ὅτι, ὅσον ἐπὶ τοῖς
λεγομένοις ὑπὸ τῶν δογματικῶν, ἀνύπαρκτος μέν
81 ἐστιν ἡ ἀλήθεια ἀνυπόστατον δὲ τὸ ἀληθές. ὑπο-
μιμνήσκομεν δὲ οὕτως. λέγεται διαφέρειν τῆς
ἀληθείας τὸ ἀληθὲς τριχῶς, οὐσίᾳ συστάσει δυνά-
μει· οὐσίᾳ μὲν ἐπεὶ τὸ μὲν ἀληθὲς ἀσώματόν ἐστιν
(ἀξίωμα γάρ ἐστι καὶ λεκτόν), ἡ δὲ ἀλήθεια σῶμα
(ἔστι γὰρ ἐπιστήμη πάντων ἀληθῶν ἀποφαντική,
ἡ δὲ ἐπιστήμη πῶς ἔχον ἡγεμονικὸν ὥσπερ καὶ ἡ
πῶς ἔχουσα χεὶρ πυγμή, τὸ δὲ ἡγεμονικὸν σῶμα·
82 ἔστι γὰρ κατ᾽ αὐτοὺς πνεῦμα), συστάσει δὲ ἐπεὶ
τὸ μὲν ἀληθὲς ἁπλοῦν τί ἐστιν, οἷον " ἐγὼ διαλέγομαι," ἡ δὲ ἀλήθεια ἀπὸ [τῆς] πολλῶν ἀληθῶν
83 γνώσεων[1] συνίσταται, δυνάμει δὲ ἐπεὶ ἡ μὲν ἀλήθεια
ἐπιστήμης ἔχεται, τὸ δὲ ἀληθὲς οὐ πάντως.
διόπερ τὴν μὲν ἀλήθειαν ἐν μόνῳ σπουδαίῳ φασὶν
εἶναι, τὸ δὲ ἀληθὲς καὶ ἐν φαύλῳ· ἐνδέχεται γὰρ
τὸν φαῦλον ἀληθές τι εἰπεῖν.

---

[1] γνώσεων T: γνώσεως mss. (τῆς . . . γν. Bekk.).

---

[a] Cf. Adv. Log. i. 38 ff. S. argues that, to go by the
Stoics' own statement, neither "truth" (which is "corporeal") nor "the true" (particular "judgement," which is
"incorporeal") has any real existence: he terms the former
"unreal," or "non-existent" (ἀνύπαρκτος), the latter "non-
substantial" (ἀνυπόστατον).

apparently equal plausibility of these arguments and of those propounded by the Dogmatists we deduce suspension of judgement.

CHAPTER VIII.—OF THE TRUE AND TRUTH

Even were we to grant, by way of hypothesis, that 80 a criterion of truth exists, it is found to be useless and vain if we recall that, so far as the statements of the Dogmatists go, truth is unreal and the true non-substantial.[a]   The passage we recall is this : " The 81 true is said to differ from truth in three ways—in essence, composition, potency.   In essence, since the true is incorporeal (for it is judgement and " expression "[b]), while truth is a body (for it is knowledge declaratory of all true things, and knowledge is a particular state of the regent part, just as the fist is a particular state of the hand, and the regent part is a body ; for according to them it is breath).   In com- 82 position, because the true is a simple thing, as for example ' I converse,' whereas truth is a compound of many true cognitions.[c]   In potency, since truth 83 depends on knowledge but the true does not alto-gether so depend.   Consequently, as they say, truth exists only in the good man, but the true in the bad man as well ; for it is possible for the bad man to utter something true."

[b] Literally "the utterable" (*lekton*), or thought in its relation to speech ; *i.e.* the meaning or significance of a word or name (the idea or mental picture evoked by it) as distinguished from (1) the name itself, as uttered ($\phi\omega\nu\dot\eta$), and (2) the real object, existing outside the mind ($\dot{\epsilon}\kappa\tau\dot{o}s$), denoted by the name: these two last were said (by the Stoics) to be "corporeal."

[c] *Cf. Adv. Log.* i. 41 ff.

84 Ταῦτα μὲν οἱ δογματικοί· ἡμεῖς δὲ πάλιν τῆς
κατὰ τὴν συγγραφὴν προαιρέσεως στοχαζόμενοι
πρὸς μόνον τὸ ἀληθὲς νῦν τοὺς λόγους ποιησόμεθα,
ἐπεὶ συμπεριγράφεται τούτῳ καὶ ἡ ἀλήθεια, σύστημα τῆς τῶν ἀληθῶν γνώσεως εἶναι λεγομένη.
πάλιν δὲ ἐπεὶ τῶν λόγων οἱ μέν εἰσι καθολικώ-
τεροι, δι᾽ ὧν αὐτὴν τὴν ὑπόστασιν τοῦ ἀληθοῦς
κινοῦμεν, οἱ δὲ εἰδικοί, δι᾽ ὧν δείκνυμεν ὅτι οὐκ
ἔστιν ἐν φωνῇ τὸ ἀληθὲς ἢ ἐν λεκτῷ ἢ ἐν τῇ
κινήσει τῆς διανοίας, τοὺς καθολικωτέρους ἐκ-
θέσθαι μόνους ὡς πρὸς τὸ παρὸν ἀρκεῖν ἡγούμεθα.
ὥσπερ γὰρ τείχους θεμελίῳ κατενεχθέντι καὶ τὰ
ὑπερκείμενα πάντα συγκαταφέρεται, οὕτω τῇ τοῦ
ἀληθοῦς ὑποστάσει διατρεπομένῃ καὶ αἱ κατὰ
μέρος τῶν δογματικῶν εὑρεσιλογίαι συμπεριγρά-
φονται.

Θ΄.—ΕΙ ΕΣΤΙ ΤΙ ΦΥΣΕΙ ΑΛΗΘΕΣ

85 Διαφωνίας τοίνυν οὔσης περὶ τοῦ ἀληθοῦς παρὰ
τοῖς δογματικοῖς, ἐπεὶ τινὲς μέν φασιν εἶναί τι
ἀληθὲς τινὲς δὲ μηδὲν εἶναι ἀληθές, οὐκ ἐνδέχεται
τὴν διαφωνίαν ἐπικρῖναι, ἐπειδὴ ὁ λέγων εἶναί τι
ἀληθὲς οὔτε ἄνευ ἀποδείξεως τοῦτο λέγων πιστευθήσεται διὰ τὴν διαφωνίαν· ἤν τε καὶ ἀπόδειξιν
βούληται φέρειν, ἢν μὲν ψευδῆ ταύτην εἶναι συν-
ομολογήσῃ, ἄπιστος ἔσται, ἀληθῆ δὲ τὴν ἀπόδειξιν
εἶναι λέγων εἰς τὸν διάλληλόν τε ἐμπίπτει λόγον
καὶ ἀπόδειξιν αἰτηθήσεται τοῦ ἀληθῆ αὐτὴν ὑπάρχειν, καὶ ἐκείνης ἄλλην, καὶ μέχρις ἀπείρου.
ἀδύνατον δὲ ἄπειρα ἀποδεῖξαι· ἀδύνατον ἄρα
γνῶναι καὶ ὅτι ἔστι τι ἀληθές.

Such are the statements of the Dogmatists. But 84 we,—having regard here again to the plan of our treatise,—shall confine our present discussion to the true, since its refutation entails that of truth as well, it being defined as the "system of the knowledge of things true." Again, since some of our arguments, whereby we dispute the very existence of the true, are more general, others of a specific kind, whereby we prove that the true does not exist in utterance or in expression or in the movement of the intellect, we deem it sufficient for the present to set forth only those of the more general kind. For just as, when the foundation of a wall collapses, all the super-structure collapses along with it, so also, when, the substantial existence of the true is refuted, all the particular inventions of the logic of the Dogmatists are included in the refutation.

CHAPTER IX.—DOES ANYTHING TRUE REALLY EXIST?

Seeing, then, that there is a controversy amongst 85 the Dogmatists regarding "the true," since some assert that something true exists, others that nothing true exists, it is impossible to decide the controversy, because the man who says that something true exists will not be believed without proof, on account of the controversy; and if he wishes to offer proof, he will be disbelieved if he acknowledges that his proof is false, whereas if he declares that his proof is true he becomes involved in circular reasoning and will be required to show proof of the real truth of his proof, and another proof of that proof, and so on *ad infinitum.* But it is impossible to prove an infinite series; and so it is impossible also to get to know that something true exists.

86 Καὶ μὴν τό τι, ὅπερ φασὶν εἶναι πάντων γενικώτατον, ἤτοι ἀληθὲς ἢ ψεῦδός ἐστιν ἢ οὔτε ἀληθὲς
οὔτε ψεῦδος ἢ καὶ ψεῦδος καὶ ἀληθές. εἰ μὲν οὖν
ψεῦδος αὐτὸ εἶναι φήσουσιν, ὁμολογήσουσιν ὅτι
ἔστι πάντα ψευδῆ. ὥσπερ γὰρ ἐπεὶ τὸ ζῷον
ἔμψυχόν ἐστι, καὶ πάντα τὰ ζῷα τὰ κατὰ μέρος
ἔμψυχά ἐστι, οὕτως εἰ τὸ γενικώτατον πάντων
τό τι ψεῦδός ἐστι, καὶ πάντα τὰ κατὰ μέρος ἔσται
ψευδῆ καὶ οὐδὲν ἀληθές. ᾧ συνεισάγεται τὸ μηδὲν
εἶναι ψεῦδος· καὶ γὰρ αὐτὸ τὸ " πάντα ἐστὶ ψευδῆ "
καὶ τὸ " ἔστι τι ψεῦδος " τῶν πάντων καθεστὼς
ψεῦδος ἔσται. εἰ δὲ ἀληθές ἐστι τό τι, πάντα ἔσται
ἀληθῆ· ᾧ συνεισάγεται πάλιν τὸ μηδὲν εἶναι ἀληθές,
εἴγε καὶ αὐτὸ τοῦτο τὶ ὑπάρχον, λέγω δὲ τὸ μηδὲν
87 εἶναι ἀληθές, ἀληθές ἐστιν. εἰ δὲ καὶ ψεῦδός ἐστι
καὶ ἀληθὲς τό τι, ἕκαστον τῶν κατὰ μέρος καὶ
ψεῦδος ἔσται καὶ ἀληθές. ἐξ οὗ συνάγεται τὸ
μηδὲν φύσει ἀληθὲς εἶναι· τὸ γὰρ φύσιν ἔχον
τοιαύτην ὥστε εἶναι ἀληθές, πάντως οὐκ ἂν εἴη
ψεῦδος. εἰ δ' οὔτε ψεῦδός ἐστιν οὔτε ἀληθὲς τό
τι, ὁμολογεῖται ὅτι καὶ πάντα τὰ ἐπὶ μέρους μήτε
ψευδῆ μήτε ἀληθῆ εἶναι λεγόμενα οὐκ ἔσται ἀληθῆ.
καὶ διὰ ταῦτα μὲν οὖν ἄδηλον ἡμῖν ἔσται εἰ ἔστιν
ἀληθές.

88 Πρὸς τούτοις ἤτοι φαινόμενά ἐστι μόνον τὰ
ἀληθῆ, ἢ ἄδηλα μόνον, ἢ τῶν ἀληθῶν τὰ μὲν
ἄδηλά ἐστι τὰ δὲ φαινόμενα· οὐδὲν δὲ τούτων ἐστὶν
ἀληθές, ὡς δείξομεν· οὐδὲν ἄρα ἐστὶν ἀληθές. εἰ
μὲν οὖν φαινόμενα μόνον ἐστὶ τὰ ἀληθῆ, ἤτοι
πάντα τὰ φαινόμενα λέξουσιν εἶναι ἀληθῆ ἢ τινά.
καὶ εἰ μὲν πάντα, περιτρέπεται ὁ λόγος· φαίνεται

---

^a Cf. Adv. Log. ii. 32 ff.; Introd. p. xxvi.

Moreover, the " something," which is, they declare, 86 the highest genus of all,[a] is either true or false or neither false nor true or both false and true. If, then, they shall assert that it is false they will be confessing that all things are false. For just as it follows because " animal " is animate that all particular animals also are animate, so too if the highest genus of all (" something ") is false all the particulars also will be false and nothing true. And this involves also the conclusion that nothing is false ; for the very statements " all things are false," and " something false exists," being themselves included in the " all," will be false. And if the " something " is true, all things will be true ; and from this again it follows that nothing is true, since this statement itself (I mean that " nothing is true ") being " something " is true. And if the " something " is both false and 87 true, each of its particulars will be both false and true. From which we conclude that nothing is really true ; for that which has its real nature such that it is true will certainly not be false. And if the " something " is neither false nor true, it is acknowledged that all the particulars also, being declared to be neither false nor true, will not be true. So for these reasons it will be non-evident to us whether the true exists.

Furthermore, the true things are either apparent 88 only, or non-evident only, or in part non-evident and in part apparent ; [b] but none of these alternatives is true, as we shall show ; therefore nothing is true. If, however, the true things are apparent only, they will assert either that all or that some of the apparent are true. And if they say " all," the argument is over-

[b] *Cf. Adv. Log.* ii. 17 ff. By "true things" are meant judgements or propositions which conform to fact.

γάρ τισι τὸ μηδὲν εἶναι ἀληθές. εἰ δὲ τινά, ἀνεπικρίτως μὲν οὐ δύναταί τις λέγειν ὅτι τάδε μέν
ἐστιν ἀληθῆ τάδε δὲ ψευδῆ, κριτηρίῳ δὲ χρώμενος
ἤτοι φαινόμενον εἶναι λέξει τοῦτο τὸ κριτήριον ἢ
ἄδηλον.   καὶ ἄδηλον μὲν οὐδαμῶς· μόνα γὰρ
89 ὑπόκειται νῦν ἀληθῆ τὰ φαινόμενα. εἰ δὲ φαινόμενον, ἐπεὶ ζητεῖται τίνα μὲν φαινόμενά ἐστιν
ἀληθῆ τίνα δὲ ψευδῆ, καὶ τὸ λαμβανόμενον φαινόμενον πρὸς τὴν κρίσιν τῶν φαινομένων πάλιν
ἑτέρου δεήσεται κριτηρίου φαινομένου, κἀκεῖνο
ἄλλου, καὶ μέχρις ἀπείρου. ἀδύνατον δὲ ἄπειρα
ἐπικρίνειν· ἀδύνατον ἄρα καταλαβεῖν εἰ φαινόμενά
ἐστι μόνον τὰ ἀληθῆ.

90   Ὁμοίως δὲ καὶ ὁ λέγων τὰ ἄδηλα μόνον εἶναι
ἀληθῆ πάντα μὲν οὐ λέξει εἶναι ἀληθῆ (οὐ γὰρ
καὶ τὸ ἀρτίους εἶναι τοὺς ἀστέρας ἀληθὲς εἶναι
λέξει καὶ[1] τὸ περιττοὺς τούτους ὑπάρχειν)· εἰ δὲ
τινά, τίνι κρινοῦμεν ὅτι τάδε μὲν τὰ ἄδηλά ἐστιν
ἀληθῆ τάδε δὲ ψευδῆ;   φαινομένῳ μὲν γὰρ οὐ-
δαμῶς· εἰ δὲ ἀδήλῳ, ἐπεὶ ζητοῦμεν[2] τίνα τῶν
ἀδήλων ἐστὶν ἀληθῆ καὶ τίνα ψευδῆ, δεήσεται καὶ
τοῦτο τὸ ἄδηλον ἀδήλου ἑτέρου τοῦ ἐπικρινοῦντος
αὐτό, κἀκεῖνο ἄλλου, καὶ μέχρις ἀπείρου. διόπερ
οὐδὲ ἄδηλα μόνον ἐστὶ τἀληθῆ.

91   Λείπεται λέγειν ὅτι τῶν ἀληθῶν τὰ μέν ἐστι
φαινόμενα τὰ δὲ ἄδηλα· ἔστι δὲ καὶ τοῦτο ἄτοπον.
ἤτοι γὰρ πάντα τά τε φαινόμενα καὶ τὰ ἄδηλά

---

[1] καὶ Heintz : ἢ mss., Bekk.
[2] ἐπεὶ ζητοῦμεν T : ἐπιζητοῦμεν mss., Bekk.

---

* This is incorrect ; on the hypothesis, non-evidents may
also be true.

thrown; for it is apparent to some that nothing is true. If, again, they say " some," no one can assert without testing that these phenomena are true, those false, while if he employs a test or criterion he will say either that this criterion is apparent or that it is non-evident. But it is certainly not non-evident; for it is now being assumed[a] that the apparent objects only are true. And if it is apparent, since the matter 89 in question is what apparent things are true and what false, that apparent thing which is adopted for the purpose of judging the apparent objects will itself in turn require an apparent criterion, and this again another, and so on *ad infinitum.* But it is impossible to judge an infinite series; and hence it is impossible to apprehend whether the true things are apparent only.

Similarly also he who declares that the non-evident 90 only are true will not imply that they are all true (for he will not say that it is true that the stars[b] are even in number and that they are also odd); while if some are true, whereby shall we decide that these non-evident things are true and those false? Certainly not by an apparent criterion; and if by a non-evident one, then since our problem is which of the non-evident things are true and which false, this non-evident criterion will itself also need another to judge it, and this again a third, and so on *ad infinitum.* Neither, then, are the true things non-evident only.

The remaining alternative is to say that of the true 91 some are apparent, some non-evident; but this too is absurd. For either all the apparent and all the non-evident are true, or some of the apparent and

[b] A favourite example of the " non-evident," *cf.* § 97 *infra*, *Adv. Log.* ii. 147, etc.

ἐστιν ἀληθῆ, ἢ τινὰ φαινόμενα καὶ τινὰ ἄδηλα. εἰ
μὲν οὖν πάντα, πάλιν περιτραπήσεται ὁ λόγος,
ἀληθοῦς εἶναι διδομένου καὶ τοῦ μηδὲν εἶναι ἀληθές,
λεχθήσεταί τε ἀληθὲς καὶ τὸ ἀρτίους εἶναι τοὺς
92 ἀστέρας καὶ τὸ περιττοὺς τούτους ὑπάρχειν. εἰ
δὲ τινὰ τῶν φαινομένων καὶ τινὰ τῶν ἀδήλων
ἐστὶν ἀληθῆ, πῶς ἐπικρινοῦμεν ὅτι τῶν φαινομένων
τάδε μέν ἐστιν ἀληθῆ τάδε δὲ ψευδῆ; εἰ μὲν διὰ
φαινομένου, εἰς ἄπειρον ἐκβάλλεται ὁ λόγος· εἰ
δὲ δι᾿ ἀδήλου, ἐπεὶ καὶ τὰ ἄδηλα δεῖται κρίσεως,
πάλιν τοῦτο τὸ ἄδηλον διά τινος κριθήσεται; εἰ
μὲν διὰ φαινομένου, ὁ διάλληλος εὑρίσκεται τρόπος,
93 εἰ δὲ δι᾿ ἀδήλου, ὁ εἰς ἄπειρον ἐκβάλλων. ὁμοίως
δὲ καὶ περὶ τῶν ἀδήλων λεκτέον· ὁ μὲν γὰρ ἀδήλῳ
τινὶ κρίνειν αὐτὰ ἐπιχειρῶν εἰς ἄπειρον ἐκβάλλεται,
ὁ δὲ φαινομένῳ ἢ ἀεὶ φαινόμενον προσλαμβάνων
εἰς ἄπειρον, ἢ ἐπὶ ἄδηλον μεταβαίνων εἰς τὸν
διάλληλον. ψεῦδος ἄρα ἐστὶ τὸ λέγειν τῶν ἀληθῶν
τὰ μὲν εἶναι φαινόμενα τὰ δὲ ἄδηλα.

94 Εἰ οὖν μήτε τὰ φαινόμενά ἐστιν ἀληθῆ μήτε τὰ
ἄδηλα μόνα, μήτε τινὰ μὲν φαινόμενα τινὰ δὲ
ἄδηλα, οὐδέν ἐστιν ἀληθές. εἰ δὲ μηδέν ἐστιν
ἀληθές, τὸ δὲ κριτήριον δοκεῖ πρὸς τὴν κρίσιν τοῦ
ἀληθοῦς χρησιμεύειν, ἄχρηστον καὶ μάταιόν ἐστι
τὸ κριτήριον, κἂν δῶμεν αὐτὸ κατὰ συγχώρησιν
ἔχειν τινὰ ὑπόστασιν. καὶ εἴγε ἐφεκτέον περὶ τοῦ
εἰ ἔστι τι ἀληθές, ἀκόλουθόν ἐστι τοὺς λέγοντας
ὡς διαλεκτική ἐστιν ἐπιστήμη ψευδῶν καὶ ἀληθῶν
καὶ οὐδετέρων προπετεύεσθαι.

---

* For this Stoic definition *cf.* §§ 229, 247 ; *Adv. Eth.* 187;
it is ascribed to Poseidonius by Diog. Laert. vii. 62.

some of the non-evident. If, then, we say " all," the argument will again be overthrown, since the truth is granted of the statement " nothing is true," and the truth will be asserted of both the statements " the stars are even in number " and " they are odd." But if some of the apparent are true and some of the 92 non-evident, how shall we judge that of the apparent these are true but those false? For if we do so by means of an apparent thing, the argument is thrown back *ad infinitum* ; and if by means of a thing non-evident, then, since the non-evidents also require to be judged, by what means is this non-evident thing to be judged? If by an apparent thing, we fall into circular reasoning ; and if by a thing non-evident, into the regress *ad infinitum*. And about the non- 93 evident we must make a similar statement ; for he who attempts to judge them by something non-evident is thrown back *ad infinitum*, while he who judges by a thing apparent or with the constant assistance of a thing apparent falls back *ad infinitum*, or, if he passes over to the apparent, is guilty of circular reasoning. It is false, therefore, to say that of the true some are apparent, some non-evident.

If, then, neither the apparent nor the non-evident 94 alone are true, nor yet some apparent and some non-evident things, nothing is true. But if nothing is true, and the criterion seems to require the true for the purpose of judging, the criterion is useless and vain, even if we grant, by way of concession, that it possesses some substantial reality. And if we have to suspend judgement as to whether anything true exists, it follows that those who declare that " dialectic is the science of things true and false and neither " [a] speak rashly.

SEXTUS EMPIRICUS

95 Ἀπόρου δὲ τοῦ κριτηρίου τῆς ἀληθείας φανέντος,
οὔτε περὶ τῶν ἐναργῶν εἶναι δοκούντων, ὅσον ἐπὶ
τοῖς λεγομένοις ὑπὸ τῶν δογματικῶν, ἔτι οἷόν τέ
ἐστι διισχυρίζεσθαι, οὔτε περὶ τῶν ἀδήλων· ἐπεὶ
γὰρ ἀπὸ τῶν ἐναργῶν ταῦτα καταλαμβάνειν οἱ
δογματικοὶ νομίζουσιν, ἐὰν ἐπέχειν περὶ τῶν ἐναργῶν καλουμένων ἀναγκαζώμεθα, πῶς ἂν περὶ τῶν
96 ἀδήλων ἀποφαίνεσθαι τολμήσαιμεν; ἐκ πολλοῦ
δὲ τοῦ περιόντος καὶ πρὸς τὰ ἄδηλα τῶν πραγμάτων ἰδίως ἐνστησόμεθα. καὶ ἐπειδὴ ταῦτα διὰ
σημείου τε καὶ ἀποδείξεως καταλαμβάνεσθαι καὶ
κρατύνεσθαι δοκεῖ, διὰ βραχέων ὑπομνήσομεν ὅτι
καὶ περὶ τοῦ σημείου καὶ περὶ τῆς ἀποδείξεως
ἐπέχειν προσήκει. ἀρξώμεθα δὲ ἀπὸ σημείου·
καὶ γὰρ ἡ ἀπόδειξις τῷ γένει σημεῖον εἶναι δοκεῖ.

Ι΄.—ΠΕΡΙ ΣΗΜΕΙΟΥ

97 Τῶν πραγμάτων τοίνυν κατὰ τοὺς δογματικοὺς
τὰ μέν ἐστι πρόδηλα τὰ δὲ ἄδηλα, καὶ τῶν ἀδήλων
τὰ μὲν καθάπαξ ἄδηλα τὰ δὲ πρὸς καιρὸν ἄδηλα
τὰ δὲ φύσει ἄδηλα. καὶ πρόδηλα μὲν εἶναί φασι
τὰ ἐξ ἑαυτῶν εἰς γνῶσιν ἡμῖν ἐρχόμενα, οἷόν ἐστι
τὸ ἡμέραν εἶναι, καθάπαξ δὲ ἄδηλα ἃ μὴ πέφυκεν
εἰς τὴν ἡμετέραν πίπτειν κατάληψιν, ὡς τὸ ἀρτίους
98 εἶναι τοὺς ἀστέρας, πρὸς καιρὸν δὲ ἄδηλα ἅπερ τὴν
φύσιν ἔχοντα ἐναργῆ παρά τινας ἔξωθεν περιστάσεις κατὰ καιρὸν ἡμῖν ἀδηλεῖται, ὡς ἐμοὶ νῦν ἡ

---

[a] Cf. i. 62-63.
[b] i.e. the Stoics. " Pre-evident "=evident of themselves,
self-manifesting ; cf. i. 138.
[c] Cf. Adv. Log. ii. 141, 144, 316.   [d] Cf. § 90 supra.

And since the criterion of truth has appeared to be 95 unattainable, it is no longer possible to make positive assertions either about those things which (if we may depend on the statements of the Dogmatists) seem to be evident or about those which are non-evident ; for since the Dogmatists suppose they apprehend the latter from the things evident, if we are forced to suspend judgement about the evident, how shall we dare to make pronouncements about the non-evident ? Yet, by way of super-addition,[a] we shall 96 also raise separate objections against the non-evident class of objects. And since they seem to be apprehended and confirmed by means of sign and proof, we shall show briefly that it is proper to suspend judgement also about sign and proof. We will begin with sign ; for indeed proof seems to be a kind of sign.

CHAPTER X.—CONCERNING SIGN

Of objects, then, some, according to the Dogma- 97 tists,[b] are pre-evident, some non-evident ; and of the non-evident, some are altogether non-evident, some occasionally non-evident, some naturally non-evident. Pre-evident are, as they assert, those which come to our knowledge of themselves,[c] as for example the fact that it is day-time ; altogether non-evident are those which are not of a nature to fall within our apprehension, as that the stars [d] are even in number ; occasionally non-evident are those which, though 98 patent in their nature, are occasionally rendered non-evident to us owing to certain external circumstances,[e]

[e] *i.e.* distance in space. From this we infer that Sextus was not then residing at Athens.

SEXTUS EMPIRICUS

τῶν Ἀθηναίων πόλις, φύσει δὲ ἄδηλα τὰ μὴ ἔχοντα
φύσιν ὑπὸ τὴν ἡμετέραν πίπτειν ἐνάργειαν, ὡς οἱ
νοητοὶ πόροι· οὗτοι γὰρ οὐδέποτε ἐξ ἑαυτῶν φαίνονται, ἀλλ᾽ εἰ ἄρα, ἐξ ἑτέρων καταλαμβάνεσθαι
ἂν νομισθεῖεν, οἷον τῶν ἱδρώτων ἤ τινος παρα-
99 πλησίου. τὰ μὲν οὖν πρόδηλα μὴ δεῖσθαι σημείου
φασίν· ἐξ ἑαυτῶν γὰρ αὐτὰ καταλαμβάνεσθαι.
ἀλλ᾽ οὐδὲ τὰ καθάπαξ ἄδηλα ἅτε δὴ μηδὲ τὴν ἀρχὴν
καταλαμβανόμενα. τὰ δὲ πρὸς καιρὸν ἄδηλα καὶ
τὰ φύσει ἄδηλα διὰ σημείων μὲν καταλαμβάνεσθαι,
οὐ μὴν διὰ τῶν αὐτῶν, ἀλλὰ τὰ μὲν πρὸς καιρὸν
ἄδηλα διὰ τῶν ὑπομνηστικῶν, τὰ δὲ φύσει ἄδηλα
διὰ τῶν ἐνδεικτικῶν.

100 Τῶν οὖν σημείων τὰ μέν ἐστιν ὑπομνηστικὰ
κατ᾽ αὐτοὺς τὰ δ᾽ ἐνδεικτικά. καὶ ὑπομνηστικὸν
μὲν σημεῖον καλοῦσιν ὃ συμπαρατηρηθὲν τῷ σημειωτῷ δι᾽ ἐναργείας ἅμα τῷ ὑποπεσεῖν, ἐκείνου
ἀδηλουμένου, ἄγει ἡμᾶς εἰς ὑπόμνησιν τοῦ συμ-
παρατηρηθέντος αὐτῷ καὶ νῦν ἐναργῶς μὴ ὑπο-
πίπτοντος, ὡς ἔχει ἐπὶ τοῦ καπνοῦ καὶ τοῦ πυρός.
101 ἐνδεικτικὸν δέ ἐστι σημεῖον, ὡς φασίν, ὃ μὴ συμπαρατηρηθὲν τῷ σημειωτῷ δι᾽ ἐναργείας, ἀλλ᾽ ἐκ
τῆς ἰδίας φύσεως καὶ κατασκευῆς σημαίνει τὸ οὗ
ἐστι σημεῖον, ὡσπεροῦν αἱ περὶ τὸ σῶμα κινήσεις
σημεῖά εἰσι τῆς ψυχῆς. ὅθεν καὶ ὁρίζονται τοῦτο
τὸ σημεῖον οὕτως " σημεῖόν ἐστιν ἐνδεικτικὸν
ἀξίωμα ἐν ὑγιεῖ συνημμένῳ προκαθηγούμενον,

---

[a] Cf. §§ 146, 318. For the " pores " (or excretory " ducts,"
or " passages ") as " intelligible " (νοητοί), or objects of thought
as opposed to sense, cf. § 140, Adv. Log. ii. 306.
[b] The Stoic doctrine. Cf. Adv. Log. ii. 151 ff., 156.
[c] Cf. § 104 infra. As smoke "indicates" fire, so in the

214

as the city of Athens is now to me ; naturally non-evident are those which are not of such a nature [a] as to fall within our clear perception, like the intelligible pores ; for these never appear of themselves but may be thought to be apprehended, if at all, owing to other things, such as perspirations or something of the sort. Now the pre-evident objects, they say, do 99 not require a sign, for they are apprehended of themselves. And neither do the altogether non-evident, since of course they are not even apprehended at all. But such objects as are occasionally or naturally non-evident are apprehended by means of signs—not of course by the same signs, but by "suggestive" signs in the case of the occasionally non-evident and by "indicative" signs in the case of the naturally non-evident.

Of the signs, then, according to them, some are 100 suggestive, some indicative.[b] They term a sign "suggestive" when, being mentally associated with the thing signified, it by its clearness at the time of its perception, though the thing signified remains non-evident, suggests to us the thing associated with it, which is not clearly perceived at the moment—as for instance in the case of smoke and fire. An 101 "indicative" sign, they say, is that which is not clearly associated with the thing signified, but signifies that whereof it is a sign by its own particular nature and constitution, just as, for instance, the bodily motions are signs of the soul. Hence, too, they define this sign as follows : "An indicative sign is an antecedent judgement, in a sound hypothetical syllogism,[c]

hypothetical syllogism—"If there is smoke, there is fire; but in fact there is smoke; therefore there is fire "—the "antecedent" (or "if"-clause) "reveals" (or is a "sign" of) the "consequent" judgement "there is fire."

215

102 ἐκκαλυπτικὸν τοῦ λήγοντος.'' διττῆς οὖν οὔσης
τῶν σημείων διαφορᾶς, ὡς ἔφαμεν, οὐ πρὸς πᾶν
σημεῖον ἀντιλέγομεν, ἀλλὰ πρὸς μόνον τὸ ἐνδεικτικὸν ὡς ὑπὸ τῶν δογματικῶν πεπλάσθαι δοκοῦν.
τὸ γὰρ ὑπομνηστικὸν πεπίστευται ὑπὸ τοῦ βίου,
ἐπεὶ καπνὸν ἰδών τις σημειοῦται πῦρ καὶ οὐλὴν
θεασάμενος τραῦμα γεγενῆσθαι λέγει. ὅθεν οὐ
μόνον οὐ μαχόμεθα τῷ βίῳ ἀλλὰ καὶ συναγωνιζό-
μεθα, τῷ μὲν ὑπ’ αὐτοῦ πεπιστευμένῳ ἀδοξάστως
συγκατατιθέμενοι, τοῖς δὲ ⟨ὑπὸ⟩[1] τῶν δογματικῶν
ἰδίως ἀναπλαττομένοις ἀνθιστάμενοι.

103 Ταῦτα μὲν οὖν ἥρμοζεν ἴσως προειπεῖν ὑπὲρ
τῆς σαφηνείας τοῦ ζητουμένου· λοιπὸν δὲ ἐπὶ τὴν
ἀντίρρησιν χωρῶμεν, οὐκ ἀνύπαρκτον δεῖξαι τὸ
ἐνδεικτικὸν σημεῖον πάντως ἐσπουδακότες, ἀλλὰ
τὴν φαινομένην ἰσοσθένειαν τῶν φερομένων λόγων
πρός τε τὴν ὕπαρξιν αὐτοῦ καὶ τὴν ἀνυπαρξίαν
ὑπομιμνήσκοντες.

ΙΑ΄.—ΕΙ ΕΣΤΙ ΤΙ ΣΗΜΕΙΟΝ ΕΝΔΕΙΚΤΙΚΟΝ

104 Τὸ σημεῖον τοίνυν, ὅσον ἐπὶ τοῖς λεγομένοις περὶ
αὐτοῦ παρὰ τοῖς δογματικοῖς, ἀνεπινόητόν ἐστιν.
αὐτίκα γοῦν οἱ ἀκριβῶς περὶ αὐτοῦ διειληφέναι
δοκοῦντες, οἱ στωικοί, βουλόμενοι παραστῆσαι
τὴν ἔννοιαν τοῦ σημείου, φασὶ σημεῖον εἶναι
ἀξίωμα ἐν ὑγιεῖ συνημμένῳ προκαθηγούμενον,
ἐκκαλυπτικὸν τοῦ λήγοντος. καὶ τὸ μὲν ἀξίωμά
φασιν εἶναι λεκτὸν αὐτοτελὲς ἀποφαντὸν ὅσον ἐφ’
ἑαυτῷ, ὑγιὲς δὲ συνημμένον τὸ μὴ ἀρχόμενον

---

[1] ⟨ὑπὸ⟩ add. T, cj. Bekk.

which serves to reveal the consequent." Seeing, 102
then, that there are, as we have said, two different
kinds of sign, we do not argue against every sign
but only against the indicative kind as it seems to
be invented by the Dogmatists. For the suggestive
sign is relied on by living experience, since when a
man sees smoke fire is signified, and when he beholds
a scar he says that there has been a wound. Hence,
not only do we not fight against living experience,
but we even lend it our support by assenting undogmatically to what it relies on, while opposing the
private inventions of the Dogmatists.

These prefatory remarks it was, perhaps, fitting to 103
make for the sake of elucidating the object of our
inquiry. It remains for us to proceed to our refutation, not in any anxiety to show that the indicative
sign is wholly unreal, but reminding ourselves of the
apparent equivalence of the arguments adduced for
its reality and for its unreality.

Chapter XI.—Does an Indicative Sign exist ?

Now the sign, judging by the statements of the 104
Dogmatists about it, is inconceivable. Thus, for
instance, the Stoics, who seem to have defined it
exactly, in attempting to establish the conception of
the sign, state that "A sign is an antecedent judgement in a valid hypothetical syllogism, which serves
to reveal the consequent " ; and " judgement " they
define as " A self-complete expression [a] which is of
itself declaratory " ; and " valid hypothetical syllo-

---

[a] An " expression," *lekton* (see p. 203 note *b*), may be
either " deficient " (*e.g.* " writes ") or " complete " (*e.g.* " he
writes ") ; *cf.* § 81, *Adv. Log.* ii. 71.

105 ἀπὸ ἀληθοῦς καὶ λῆγον ἐπὶ ψεῦδος. τὸ γὰρ συνημμένον ἤτοι ἄρχεται ἀπὸ ἀληθοῦς καὶ λήγει ἐπὶ
ἀληθές, οἷον " εἰ ἡμέρα ἔστι, φῶς ἔστιν," ἢ ἄρχεται
ἀπὸ ψεύδους καὶ λήγει ἐπὶ ψεῦδος, οἷον " εἰ
πέταται ἡ γῆ, πτερωτή ἐστιν ἡ γῆ," ἢ ἄρχεται
ἀπὸ ἀληθοῦς καὶ λήγει ἐπὶ ψεῦδος, οἷον " εἰ ἔστιν
ἡ γῆ, πέταται ἡ γῆ," ἢ ἄρχεται ἀπὸ ψεύδους καὶ
λήγει ἐπὶ ἀληθές, οἷον " εἰ πέταται ἡ γῆ, ἔστιν ἡ
γῆ." τούτων δὲ μόνον τὸ ἀπὸ ἀληθοῦς ἀρχόμενον
καὶ λῆγον ἐπὶ ψεῦδος μοχθηρὸν εἶναί φασιν, τὰ
106 δ' ἄλλα ὑγιῆ. προκαθηγούμενον δὲ λέγουσι τὸ ἐν
συνημμένῳ ἀρχομένῳ ἀπὸ ἀληθοῦς καὶ λήγοντι
ἐπὶ ἀληθές ἡγούμενον. ἐκκαλυπτικὸν δέ ἐστι τοῦ
λήγοντος, ἐπεὶ τὸ " γάλα ἔχει αὕτη " τοῦ " κεκύηκεν αὕτη " δηλωτικὸν εἶναι δοκεῖ ἐν τούτῳ τῷ
συνημμένῳ " εἰ γάλα ἔχει αὕτη, κεκύηκεν αὕτη."
107 Ταῦτα μὲν οὗτοι, ἡμεῖς δὲ λέγομεν πρῶτον ὅτι
ἄδηλόν ἐστιν εἰ ἔστι τι λεκτόν. ἐπεὶ γὰρ τῶν
δογματικῶν οἱ μὲν Ἐπικούρειοί φασι μὴ εἶναί τι
λεκτὸν οἱ δὲ στωικοὶ εἶναι, ὅταν λέγωσιν οἱ στωικοὶ
εἶναί τι λεκτόν, ἤτοι μόνῃ φάσει χρῶνται ἢ καὶ
ἀποδείξει. ἀλλ' εἰ μὲν φάσει, ἀντιθήσουσιν αὐτοῖς
οἱ Ἐπικούρειοι φάσιν τὴν λέγουσαν ὅτι οὐκ ἔστι
τι λεκτόν· εἰ δὲ ἀπόδειξιν παραλήψονται, ἐπεὶ ἐξ
ἀξιωμάτων συνέστηκε λεκτῶν ἡ ἀπόδειξις, ἐκ τῶν
λεκτῶν δὲ συνεστῶσα οὐ δυνήσεται πρὸς πίστιν τοῦ
λεκτὸν εἶναι παραλαμβάνεσθαι (ὁ γὰρ μὴ διδοὺς
εἶναι λεκτὸν πῶς συγχωρήσει σύστημα λεκτῶν

---

[a] *i.e.* with a true antecedent, or " if " clause. *Cf.* generally
Adv. Log. ii. 112, 245 ff., 449.

[b] For this stock example *cf.* Aristot. *Anal. pr.* ii. 27, *Rhet.*
i. 2. 18 ; Plato, *Menex.* 237 ε.

gism " as one " which does not begin with truth [a] and end with a false consequent." For either the 105 syllogism begins with the true and ends with the true (*e.g.* " If there is day, there is light "), or it begins with what is false and ends in falsehood (like " If the earth flies, the earth is winged "), or it begins with truth and ends in falsehood (like " If the earth exists, the earth flies "), or it begins with falsehood and ends in truth (like " If the earth flies, the earth exists "). And they say that of these only that which begins with truth and ends in falsehood is invalid, and the rest valid. " Antecedent," they say, is " the precedent 106 clause in a hypothetical syllogism which begins in truth and ends in truth." And it " serves to reveal the consequent," since in the syllogism " If this woman has milk, she has conceived," the clause " If this woman has milk " seems to be evidential of the clause " she has conceived." [b]

Such is the Stoic doctrine. But we assert, firstly, 107 that it is non-evident whether any " expression " exists. For since some of the Dogmatists, the Epicureans, declare that expression does not exist, others, the Stoics, that it does exist, when the Stoics assert its existence they are employing either mere assertion or demonstration as well. If assertion, then the Epicureans will confute them with the assertion which states that no expression exists. But if they shall adduce demonstration, then since demonstration is composed of expressed judgements, and because it is composed of expressions will be unable to be adduced to confirm the existence of expression (for how will he who refuses to allow the existence of expression grant the reality of a system compounded

108 ὑπάρχειν;)—διὰ τοῦ ζητουμένου τοίνυν τὸ ζητούμενον πιστοῦσθαι βούλεται ὁ ἐκ τῆς ὑπάρξεως τοῦ
συστήματος τῶν λεκτῶν εἶναί τι λεκτὸν πειρώμενος
κατασκευάζειν. εἰ οὖν μήτε ἁπλῶς μήτε δι' ἀποδείξεως ἐνδέχεται παριστᾶν ὅτι ἔστι τι λεκτόν,
ἄδηλόν ἐστιν ὅτι ἔστι τι λεκτόν.

Ὁμοίως δὲ καὶ εἰ ἔστιν ἀξίωμα· λεκτὸν γάρ
109 ἐστι τὸ ἀξίωμα. μήποτε δὲ καὶ εἰ καθ' ὑπόθεσιν
εἶναί τι λεκτὸν δοθείη, τὸ ἀξίωμα ἀνύπαρκτον εὑρίσκεται, συνεστηκὸς ἐκ λεκτῶν μὴ συνυπαρχόντων
ἀλλήλοις. οἷον γοῦν ἐπὶ τοῦ " εἰ ἡμέρα ἔστι,
φῶς ἔστιν," ὅτε λέγω τὸ " ἡμέρα ἔστιν," οὐδέπω
ἔστι τὸ " φῶς ἔστιν," καὶ ὅτε λέγω τὸ " φῶς
ἔστιν," οὐκέτι ἔστι τὸ " ἡμέρα ἔστιν." εἰ οὖν
τὰ μὲν συγκείμενα ἔκ τινων ἀδύνατον ὑπάρχειν μὴ
συνυπαρχόντων ἀλλήλοις τῶν μερῶν αὐτῶν, τὰ
δὲ ἐξ ὧν σύγκειται τὸ ἀξίωμα οὐ συνυπάρχει
ἀλλήλοις, οὐχ ὑπάρξει τὸ ἀξίωμα.

110 Ἵνα δὲ καὶ ταῦτα παραλίπωμεν, τὸ ὑγιὲς συνημμένον ἀκατάληπτον εὑρεθήσεται. ὁ μὲν γὰρ Φίλων
φησὶν ὑγιὲς εἶναι συνημμένον τὸ μὴ ἀρχόμενον ἀπὸ
ἀληθοῦς καὶ λῆγον ἐπὶ ψεῦδος, οἷον ἡμέρας οὔσης
καὶ ἐμοῦ διαλεγομένου τὸ " εἰ ἡμέρα ἔστιν, ἐγὼ
διαλέγομαι," ὁ δὲ Διόδωρος, ὁ μήτε ἐνεδέχετο μήτε
ἐνδέχεται ἀρχόμενον ἀπὸ ἀληθοῦς λήγειν ἐπὶ ψεῦ-
δος· καθ' ὃν τὸ μὲν εἰρημένον συνημμένον ψεῦδος
εἶναι δοκεῖ, ἐπεὶ ἡμέρας μὲν οὔσης ἐμοῦ δὲ σιωπή-
σαντος ἀπὸ ἀληθοῦς ἀρξάμενον ἐπὶ ψεῦδος κατα-

---

[a] Cf. Adv. Log. ii. 80 ff.
[b] A Megaric philosopher (circa 300 B.C.), not the Academic
mentioned in i. 235, and Introd. pp. xxxvi f.; cf. Adv. Log.
ii. 113 ff.   [c] Cf. i. 234, Adv. Log. ii. 115.

of expressions ?),—it follows that the man who 108 attempts to establish the existence of expression from the reality of the system of expressions is proposing to confirm the problematic by the problematic. If, then, it is impossible to establish either simply or by means of demonstration that any expression exists, it is non-evident that any expression exists.

So, too, with the question whether judgement exists ; for the judgement is a form of expression. And very possibly, even should it be granted by 109 way of assumption that expression exists, judgement will be found to be non-existent, it being compounded of expressions not mutually co-existent.[a] Thus, for example, in the case of " If day exists, light exists," when I say " day exists " the clause " light exists " is not yet in existence, and when I say " light exists " the clause " day exists " is no longer in existence. If then it is impossible for things compounded of certain parts to be really existent if those parts do not mutually co-exist, and if the parts whereof the judgement is composed do not mutually co-exist, then the judgement will have no real existence.

But passing over this objection, it will be found that 110 the valid hypothetical syllogism is non-apprehensible. For Philo [b] says that a valid hypothetical syllogism is " that which does not begin with a truth and end with a falsehood," as for instance the syllogism " If it is day, I converse," when in fact it is day and I am conversing ; but Diodorus [c] defines it as " that which neither was nor is capable of beginning with a truth and ending with a falsehood " ; so that according to him the syllogism now mentioned seems to be false, since if it is in fact day but I have remained silent it will begin with a truth but end with a falsehood,

111 λήξει, ἐκεῖνο δὲ ἀληθές " εἰ οὐκ ἔστιν ἀμερῆ τῶν
ὄντων στοιχεῖα, ἔστιν ἀμερῆ τῶν ὄντων στοιχεῖα "·
ἀεὶ γὰρ ἀπὸ ψεύδους ἀρχόμενον τοῦ " οὐκ ἔστιν
ἀμερῆ τῶν ὄντων στοιχεῖα " εἰς ἀληθὲς καταλήξει
κατ' αὐτὸν τὸ " ἔστιν ἀμερῆ τῶν ὄντων στοιχεῖα."
οἱ δὲ τὴν συνάρτησιν εἰσάγοντες ὑγιὲς εἶναί φασι
συνημμένον ὅταν τὸ ἀντικείμενον τῷ ἐν αὐτῷ
λήγοντι μάχηται τῷ ἐν αὐτῷ ἡγουμένῳ· καθ' οὓς
τὰ μὲν εἰρημένα συνημμένα ἔσται μοχθηρά, ἐκεῖνο
112 δὲ ἀληθές " εἰ ἡμέρα ἔστιν, ἡμέρα ἔστιν." οἱ δὲ
τῇ ἐμφάσει κρίνοντές φασιν ὅτι ἀληθές ἐστι συνημμένον οὗ τὸ λῆγον ἐν τῷ ἡγουμένῳ περιέχεται
δυνάμει· καθ' οὓς τὸ " εἰ ἡμέρα ἔστιν, ἡμέρα
ἔστι " καὶ πᾶν διαφορούμενον [ἀξίωμα] συνημμένον ἴσως ψεῦδος ἔσται· αὐτὸ γάρ τι ἐν ἑαυτῷ περιέχεσθαι ἀμήχανον.

113 Ταύτην τοίνυν τὴν διαφωνίαν ἐπικριθῆναι ἀμήχανον ἴσως ἂν εἶναι δόξει. οὔτε γὰρ ἀναποδείκτως
προκρίνοντές τινα τῶν στάσεων τῶν προειρημένων
πιστοὶ ἐσόμεθα οὔτε μετὰ ἀποδείξεως. καὶ γὰρ
ἡ ἀπόδειξις ὑγιὴς εἶναι δοκεῖ ὅταν ἀκολουθῇ
τῇ διὰ τῶν λημμάτων αὐτῆς συμπλοκῇ τὸ συμπέρασμα αὐτῆς ὡς λῆγον ἡγουμένῳ, οἷον οὕτως
" εἰ ἡμέρα ἔστιν, φῶς ἔστιν· ἀλλὰ μὴν ἡμέρα ἔστιν·
φῶς ἄρα ἔστιν. [εἴπερ ἡμέρα ἔστι, φῶς ἔστιν· καὶ
114 ἡμέρα ἔστι καὶ φῶς ἔστιν.]"[1] ζητουμένου δὲ περὶ

---

[1] [εἴπερ . . . ἔστιν] secl. Papp.: T om. καὶ ἡμέρα . . .
ἔστιν.

---

[a] The opposite is " diartesis," incoherence or incompati-
bility, §§ 146, 152, 238 infra, Adv. Log. ii. 430.
[b] " Implication " (emphasis) is power of signifying more

whereas the syllogism " If atomic elements of things 111
do not exist, atomic elements exist," seems true,
since it begins with the false clause " atomic elements
do not exist " and will end, according to him, with
the true clause " atomic elements exist." And
those who introduce " connexion," or " coherence," [a]
assert that it is a valid hypothetical syllogism whenever the opposite of its consequent contradicts its
antecedent clause ; so that, according to them, the
above-mentioned syllogisms are invalid, whereas the
syllogism " If day exists, day exists " is true.
And those who judge by " implication " [b] declare 112
that a hypothetical syllogism is true when its consequent is potentially included in its antecedent ;
and according to them the syllogism " If day exists,
day exists," and every such duplicated syllogism,
will probably be false ; for it is not feasible that any
object should itself be included in itself.

Probably, then, it will not seem feasible to get this 113
controversy resolved. For whether we prefer any one
of the above-mentioned rival views without proof or
by the aid of proof, in neither case shall we gain
credence. For proof itself is held to be valid whenever its conclusion follows the combination of its
premisses as the consequent follows the antecedent ;
thus, for example—" If it is day it is light ; but in
fact it is day ; therefore it is light " : [" If it is day it
is light," " it is day and also it is light."][c] But when 114

than is explicitly expressed. An example of this " potential
inclusion " is " If a man exists, a beast exists."

[a] The words bracketed give an unintelligible form of
syllogism, and the Greek text is evidently corrupt. Possibly
we should read—" It is day ; and if it is day it is light ;
therefore it is light "—thus merely transposing the premisses
of the preceding syllogism (cf. § 137).

SEXTUS EMPIRICUS

τοῦ πῶς κρινοῦμεν τὴν ἀκολουθίαν τοῦ λήγοντος
πρὸς τὸ ἡγούμενον, ὁ διάλληλος εὑρίσκεται τρόπος.
ἵνα μὲν γὰρ ἡ κρίσις τοῦ συνημμένου ἀποδειχθῇ,
τὸ συμπέρασμα τοῖς λήμμασι τῆς ἀποδείξεως
ἀκολουθεῖ, ὡς προειρήκαμεν· ἵνα δὲ πάλιν τοῦτο
πιστευθῇ, δεῖ τὸ συνημμένον καὶ τὴν ἀκολουθίαν
115 ἐπικεκρίσθαι. ὅπερ ἄτοπον. ἀκατάληπτον ἄρα τὸ
ὑγιὲς συνημμένον.

Ἀλλὰ καὶ τὸ προκαθηγούμενον ἄπορόν ἐστιν.
τὸ μὲν γὰρ προκαθηγούμενον, ὡς φασίν, ἐστὶ τὸ
ἡγούμενον ἐν τοιούτῳ συνημμένῳ, ὃ ἄρχεται ἀπὸ
116 ἀληθοῦς καὶ λήγει ἐπὶ ἀληθές. εἰ δὲ ἐκκαλυπτικόν
ἐστι τοῦ λήγοντος τὸ σημεῖον, ἤτοι πρόδηλόν ἐστι
τὸ λῆγον ἢ ἄδηλον. εἰ μὲν οὖν πρόδηλον, οὐδὲ
τοῦ ἐκκαλύψοντος δεήσεται, ἀλλὰ συγκαταληφθή-
σεται αὐτῷ, καὶ οὐκ ἔστιν αὐτοῦ σημειωτόν,
διόπερ οὐδὲ ἐκεῖνο τούτου σημεῖον. εἰ δὲ ἄδηλον,
ἐπεὶ περὶ τῶν ἀδήλων διαπεφώνηται ἀνεπικρίτως
ποῖα μέν ἐστιν αὐτῶν ἀληθῆ ποῖα δὲ ψευδῆ, καὶ
ὅλως εἰ ἔστι τι αὐτῶν ἀληθές, ἄδηλον ἔσται εἰ εἰς
ἀληθὲς λήγει τὸ συνημμένον. ᾧ συνεισέρχεται
καὶ τὸ ἄδηλον εἶναι εἰ προκαθηγεῖται τὸ ἐν αὐτῷ
117 ἡγούμενον. ἵνα δὲ καὶ ταῦτα παραλίπωμεν, οὐ
δύναται ἐκκαλυπτικὸν εἶναι τοῦ λήγοντος, εἴγε
πρὸς τὸ σημεῖόν ἐστι τὸ σημειωτὸν καὶ διὰ τοῦτο
συγκαταλαμβάνεται αὐτῷ. τὰ γὰρ πρός τι ἀλλήλοις συγκαταλαμβάνεται· καὶ ὥσπερ τὸ δεξιὸν πρὸ
τοῦ ἀριστεροῦ ὡς δεξιὸν ἀριστεροῦ καταληφθῆναι

---

[a] Cf. §§ 105 f. supra.

224

we inquire how we are to judge the logical sequence of the consequent in its relation to the antecedent, we are met with the argument in a circle. For in order to prove the judgement upon the hypothetical syllogism, the conclusion of the proof must follow logically from its premisses, as we said above; and, in turn, in order to establish this, the hypothetical syllogism and its logical sequence must be tested; and this is absurd. So then the valid hypothetical 115 syllogism is non-apprehensible.

But the " antecedent " also is unintelligible. For the antecedent, as they assert, is " the leading clause in a hypothetical syllogism of the kind which begins with a truth and ends in a truth." [a] But if the sign 116 serves to reveal the consequent, the consequent is either pre-evident or non-evident. If, then, it is pre-evident, it will not so much as need the thing which is to reveal it but will be apprehended along with it and will not be the object signified thereby, and hence also the thing mentioned will not be a " sign " of the object. But if the consequent is non-evident, seeing that there exists an unsettled controversy about things non-evident, as to which of them are true, which false, and in general whether any of them is true, it will be non-evident whether the hypothetical syllogism ends in a true consequent. And this involves the further fact that it is non-evident whether the leading clause in the syllogism is the logical antecedent. But to pass over this 117 objection also, the sign cannot serve to reveal the consequent, if the thing signified is relative to the sign and is, therefore, apprehended along with it. For relatives are apprehended along with each other; and just as " right " cannot be apprehended as " right

225

οὐ δύναται, οὐδὲ ἀνάπαλιν, καὶ ἐπὶ τῶν ἄλλων τῶν
πρός τι παραπλησίως, οὕτως οὐδὲ τὸ σημεῖον πρὸ
τοῦ σημειωτοῦ ⟨ὡς σημειωτοῦ⟩[1] καταληφθῆναι
118 δυνατὸν ἔσται. εἰ δ' οὐ προκαταλαμβάνεται τὸ
σημεῖον τοῦ σημειωτοῦ, οὐδὲ ἐκκαλυπτικὸν αὐτοῦ
δύναται ὑπάρχειν τοῦ ἅμα αὐτῷ καὶ μὴ μετ' αὐτὸ
καταλαμβανομένου.

Οὐκοῦν καὶ ὅσον ἐπὶ τοῖς κοινότερον λεγομένοις
ὑπὸ τῶν ἑτεροδόξων ἀνεπινόητόν ἐστι τὸ σημεῖον.
καὶ γὰρ πρός τι καὶ ἐκκαλυπτικὸν τοῦ σημειωτοῦ,
πρὸς ᾧ φασιν αὐτὸ εἶναι, τοῦτο εἶναι λέγουσιν.
119 ὅθεν εἰ μὲν πρός τί ἐστι καὶ πρὸς τῷ σημειωτῷ,
συγκαταλαμβάνεσθαι πάντως ὀφείλει τῷ σημειωτῷ,
καθάπερ τὸ ἀριστερὸν τῷ δεξιῷ καὶ τὸ ἄνω τῷ
κάτω καὶ τὰ ἄλλα πρός τι. εἰ δὲ ἐκκαλυπτικόν ἐστι
τοῦ σημειωτοῦ, προκαταλαμβάνεσθαι αὐτοῦ πάντως ὀφείλει, ἵνα προεπιγνωσθὲν εἰς ἔννοιαν ἡμᾶς
ἀγάγῃ τοῦ ἐξ αὐτοῦ γινωσκομένου πράγματος.
120 ἀδύνατον δὲ ἐννοῆσαι πρᾶγμα μὴ δυνάμενον πρὸ
ἐκείνου γνωσθῆναι οὗ προκαταλαμβάνεσθαι ἀνάγκην
ἔχει· ἀδύνατον ἄρα ἐπινοεῖν τι καὶ πρός τι ὂν καὶ
ἐκκαλυπτικὸν ἐκείνου ὑπάρχον πρὸς ᾧ νοεῖται. τὸ
δὲ σημεῖον καὶ πρός τί φασιν εἶναι καὶ ἐκκαλυπτικὸν
τοῦ σημειωτοῦ· ἀδύνατον ἄρα ἐστὶν ἐπινοῆσαι τὸ
σημεῖον.

121   Πρὸς τούτοις κἀκεῖνο λεκτέον. διαφωνία γέγονε
παρὰ τοῖς πρὸ ἡμῶν, τῶν μὲν λεγόντων εἶναί τι

---

[1] ⟨ὡς σημειωτοῦ⟩ add. T, ML corr.

of left " before " left," nor *vice versa*—and the same
holds good of all other relative terms,—so neither will
it be possible for the sign, as " sign of signified," to be
apprehended before the thing signified.[a]   And if the 118
sign is not apprehended before the thing signified,
neither can it really serve to reveal the actual thing
which is apprehended along with itself and not after
itself.

Thus also, so far as we may judge by the usual
statements of the dissenting philosophers (the
Stoics), the sign is inconceivable.   For they assert
that it is both relative and serving to reveal the
thing signified, in relation to which they say it was.
Accordingly, if it is relative and in relation to the 119
thing signified it certainly ought to be apprehended
along with the thing signified, as is " left " with
" right," " up " with " down," and the rest of the
relative terms.   Whereas, if it serves to reveal the
thing signified, it certainly ought to be apprehended
before it, in order that by being foreknown it may
lead us to a conception of the object which comes to
be known by means of it.   But it is impossible to form 120
a conception of an object which cannot be known
before the thing before which it must necessarily be
apprehended ; and so it is impossible to conceive of
an object which is both relative and also really serves
to reveal the thing in relation to which it is thought.
But the sign is, as they affirm, both relative and
serving to reveal the thing signified ; wherefore it is
impossible to conceive of the sign.

Furthermore, there is this also to be said.   Amongst 121
our predecessors there existed a controversy, some

[a] *Cf. Adv. Log.* ii. 163 ff.

227

SEXTUS EMPIRICUS

σημεῖον ἐνδεικτικόν, τῶν δὲ μηδὲν εἶναι σημεῖον ἐνδεικτικὸν φασκόντων. ὁ λέγων οὖν εἶναί τι σημεῖον
ἐνδεικτικὸν ἤτοι ἁπλῶς ἐρεῖ καὶ ἀναποδείκτως,
ψιλῇ φάσει χρώμενος, ἢ μετὰ ἀποδείξεως. ἀλλ᾽
εἰ μὲν φάσει μόνῃ χρήσεται, ἄπιστος ἔσται,
εἰ δὲ ἀποδεῖξαι βουλήσεται, τὸ ζητούμενον συν-
122 αρπάσει. ἐπεὶ γὰρ ἡ ἀπόδειξις τῷ γένει σημεῖον
εἶναι λέγεται, ἀμφισβητουμένου τοῦ πότερον
ἔστι τι σημεῖον ἢ οὐκ ἔστιν, ἀμφισβήτησις ἔσται
καὶ περὶ τοῦ πότερον ἔστιν ἀπόδειξις ἢ οὐδαμῶς, ὥσπερ καθ᾽ ὑπόθεσιν ζητουμένου εἰ ἔστι
ζῶον, ζητεῖται καὶ περὶ τοῦ εἰ ἔστιν ἄνθρωπος·
ζῶον γὰρ ὁ ἄνθρωπος. ἄτοπον δὲ τὸ ζητούμενον
διὰ τοῦ ἐπ᾽ ἴσης ζητουμένου ἢ δι᾽ ἑαυτοῦ ἀπο-
δεικνύναι· οὐδὲ δι᾽ ἀποδείξεως ἄρα δυνήσεταί τις
123 διαβεβαιοῦσθαι ὅτι ἔστι σημεῖον. εἰ δὲ μήτε
ἁπλῶς μήτε μετὰ ἀποδείξεως οἷόν τέ ἐστι περὶ
τοῦ σημείου διαβεβαιωτικῶς ἀποφαίνεσθαι, ἀδύνατόν ἐστι περὶ αὐτοῦ καταληπτικὴν ἀπόφασιν
ποιήσασθαι· εἰ δὲ μὴ καταλαμβάνεται μετὰ ἀκρι-
βείας τὸ σημεῖον, οὐδὲ σημαντικὸν εἶναι λεχθήσεταί τινος ἅτε δὴ μηδὲ αὐτὸ ὁμολογούμενον· διὰ
δὲ τοῦτο οὐδὲ σημεῖον ἔσται. ὅθεν καὶ κατὰ τοῦτον τὸν ἐπιλογισμὸν ἀνύπαρκτον ἔσται τὸ σημεῖον
καὶ ἀνεπινόητον.

124 Ἔτι μέντοι κἀκεῖνο ῥητέον. ἤτοι φαινόμενα
μόνον ἐστὶ τὰ σημεῖα ἢ ἄδηλα μόνον, ἢ τῶν σημείων
τὰ μέν ἐστι φαινόμενα τὰ δὲ ἄδηλα. οὐδὲν δὲ
τούτων ἐστὶν ὑγιές· οὐκ ἄρα ἔστι σημεῖον.

---

[a] Cf. § 99 : the " others " include some of the Academics
and medical Empirics (cf. i. 236).
[b] Cf. § 96 ; Adv. Log. ii. 178 ff.

declaring that an indicative sign exists, others maintaining that no indicative sign exists.[a] He, then, who asserts the existence of an indicative sign will assert it either simply and without proof, making a bald assertion, or by the aid of proof. But if he shall employ mere assertion he will not gain credence; while if he shall propose to prove it he will be assuming the matter in question. For since proof is stated 122 to come under the genus sign,[b] seeing that it is disputed whether or not a sign exists, there will also be a dispute as to whether proof does or does not all exist—just as, when we make, let us suppose, the inquiry " Does animal exist ? " we are inquiring also " Does man exist ? " But it is absurd to try to prove the matter in question either by means of what is equally in question or by means of itself. So that neither will one be able by means of proof to affirm positively that sign exists. And if it is not possible 123 either simply or with the aid of proof to make a positive declaration about the sign, it is impossible to make an apprehensive affirmation[c] concerning it; and if the sign is not apprehended with exactness, neither will it be said to be significant of anything, inasmuch as there is no agreement even about itself; and because of this it will not even be a sign. Hence, according to this line of reasoning also, the sign will be unreal and inconceivable.

But there is this further to be said. Either the signs 124 are apparent only or non-evident only, or some are apparent and some non-evident.[d] But none of these alternatives is valid; therefore sign does not exist.

[c] A curious expression, only used here by Sextus; it seems to mean " an affirmation which treats the thing as though it were apprehended."
[d] Cf. § 88 ; Adv. Log. ii. 171 ff.

Ὅτι μὲν οὖν ἄδηλα οὐκ ἔστι πάντα τὰ σημεῖα,
ἐντεῦθεν δείκνυται. τὸ ἄδηλον οὐκ ἐξ ἑαυτοῦ φαίνεται, ὡς οἱ δογματικοί φασιν, ἀλλὰ δι᾽ ἑτέρου ὑποπίπτει. καὶ τὸ σημεῖον οὖν, εἰ ἄδηλον εἴη, ἑτέρου
δεήσεται σημείου ἀδήλου, ἐπεὶ μηδὲν φαινόμενόν
ἐστι σημεῖον κατὰ τὴν προκειμένην ὑπόθεσιν,
κἀκεῖνο ἄλλου, καὶ μέχρις ἀπείρου. ἀδύνατον
δὲ ἄπειρα σημεῖα λαμβάνειν· ἀδύνατον ἄρα τὸ
σημεῖον καταληφθῆναι ἄδηλον ὄν. διὰ δὲ τοῦτο
καὶ ἀνύπαρκτον ἔσται, μὴ δυνάμενον σημαίνειν
τι καὶ σημεῖον εἶναι διὰ τὸ μὴ καταλαμβάνεσθαι.

125 Εἰ δὲ πάντα τὰ σημεῖα φαινόμενά ἐστιν, ἐπεὶ
καὶ πρός τί ἐστι τὸ σημεῖον καὶ πρὸς τῷ σημειωτῷ,
τὰ δὲ πρός τι συγκαταλαμβάνεται ἀλλήλοις, τὰ
σημειωτὰ εἶναι λεγόμενα σὺν τοῖς φαινομένοις
καταλαμβανόμενα φαινόμενα ἔσται· ὥσπερ γὰρ
ἅμα ὑποπιπτόντων τοῦ τε δεξιοῦ καὶ τοῦ ἀριστεροῦ
οὐ μᾶλλον τὸ δεξιὸν τοῦ ἀριστεροῦ ἢ τὸ ἀριστερὸν
τοῦ δεξιοῦ φαίνεσθαι λέγεται, οὕτω συγκαταλαμ-
βανομένων τοῦ τε σημείου καὶ τοῦ σημειωτοῦ οὐ
μᾶλλον τὸ σημεῖον ἢ τὸ σημειωτὸν φαίνεσθαι
126 ῥητέον. εἰ δὲ φαινόμενόν ἐστι τὸ σημειωτόν, οὐδὲ
σημειωτὸν ἔσται μὴ δεόμενον τοῦ σημανοῦντος
αὐτὸ καὶ ἐκκαλύψοντος. ὅθεν ὥσπερ ἀναιρουμένου
δεξιοῦ οὐδὲ ἀριστερὸν ἔστιν, οὕτως ἀναιρουμένου
τοῦ σημειωτοῦ οὐδὲ σημεῖον εἶναι δύναται, ὥστε
ἀνύπαρκτον εὑρίσκεται τὸ σημεῖον, εἴπερ φαινόμενα μόνα εἶναι λέγοι τις τὰ σημεῖα.

127 Λείπεται λέγειν ὅτι τῶν σημείων τὰ μέν ἐστι
φαινόμενα τὰ δὲ ἄδηλα· καὶ οὕτως δὲ αἱ ἀπορίαι

Now that all the signs are not non-evident is shown by the following argument. The non-evident does not become apparent of itself, as the Dogmatists assert, but is perceived by means of something else. The sign, therefore, if it were non-evident, would require another non-evident sign—since, according to the hypothesis assumed, there is no apparent sign —and this again a third, and so on *ad infinitum.* But it is impossible to grasp an infinite series of signs ; and so it is impossible for the sign to be apprehended when it is non-evident. And for this reason it will also be unreal, as it is unable to signify anything and to be a sign owing to its not being apprehended.

And if all the signs are apparent, then, because 125 the sign is a relative thing and in relation to the thing signified, and relatives are apprehended conjointly,[a] the things said to be signified, being apprehended along with what is apparent, will be apparent. For just as when the right and left are perceived together, the right is not said to appear more than the left nor the left than the right, so when the sign and the thing signified are apprehended together the sign should not be said to appear any more than the thing signified. And if the thing signified is apparent, 126 it will not even be signified, as it requires nothing to signify and reveal it. Hence, just as when " right " is abolished there exists no " left," so when the thing signified is abolished there can exist no sign, so that the sign is found to be unreal, if one should declare that the signs are apparent only.

It remains to declare that of the signs some are 127 apparent, others non-evident ; but even so the diffi-

---

[a] *Cf.* §§ 119, 169.

μένουσιν. τῶν τε γὰρ φαινομένων σημείων τὰ σημειωτὰ εἶναι λεγόμενα φαινόμενα ἔσται, καθὰ προειρήκαμεν, καὶ μὴ δεόμενα τοῦ σημανοῦντος οὐδὲ σημειωτὰ ὅλως ὑπάρξει, ὅθεν οὐδὲ ἐκεῖνα 128 σημεῖα ἔσται, μηδὲν σημαίνοντα· τά τε ἄδηλα σημεῖα χρῄζοντα τῶν ἐκκαλυψόντων αὐτά, ἐὰν μὲν ὑπὸ ἀδήλων σημαίνεσθαι λέγηται, εἰς ἄπειρον ἐκπίπτοντος τοῦ λόγου ἀκατάληπτα εὑρίσκεται καὶ διὰ τοῦτο ἀνύπαρκτα, ὡς προειρήκαμεν· ἐὰν δὲ ὑπὸ φαινομένων, φαινόμενα ἔσται σὺν τοῖς φαινομένοις αὐτῶν σημείοις καταλαμβανόμενα, διὰ δὲ τοῦτο καὶ ἀνύπαρκτα. ἀδύνατον γὰρ εἶναί τι πρᾶγμα ὃ καὶ ἄδηλόν ἐστι φύσει καὶ φαίνεται, τὰ δὲ σημεῖα περὶ ὧν ἐστιν ὁ λόγος, ἄδηλα ὑποτεθέντα, φαινόμενα εὑρέθη κατὰ τὴν περιτροπὴν τοῦ λόγου.

129 Εἰ οὖν μήτε πάντα τὰ σημεῖα φαινόμενά ἐστι μήτε πάντα ἄδηλα, μήτε τῶν σημείων τινὰ μέν ἐστι φαινόμενα τινὰ δὲ ἄδηλα, καὶ παρὰ ταῦτα οὐδὲν ἔστιν, ὡς καὶ αὐτοί φασιν, ἀνύπαρκτα ἔσται τὰ λεγόμενα σημεῖα.

130 Ταῦτα μὲν οὖν ὀλίγα ἀπὸ πολλῶν ἀρκέσει νῦν εἰρῆσθαι πρὸς ὑπόμνησιν τοῦ μὴ εἶναι σημεῖον ἐνδεικτικόν· ἑξῆς δὲ καὶ τὰς ὑπομνήσεις τοῦ εἶναί τι σημεῖον ἐκθησόμεθα, ἵνα τὴν ἰσοσθένειαν τῶν ἀντικειμένων λόγων παραστήσωμεν.

Ἤτοι οὖν σημαίνουσί τι αἱ κατὰ τοῦ σημείου

culties remain. For the things said to be signified
by the apparent signs will, as we said before, be
apparent and require nothing to signify them, and
will not even be things signified at all, so that neither
will the signs be signs, as not signifying anything.
And as to the non-evident signs which need things 128
to reveal them, if we say that they are signified by
things non-evident, the argument will be involved in
a regress *ad infinitum*, rendering them non-apprehensible and therefore unreal, as we said before [a];
whereas, if they are to be signified by things apparent,
they will be apparent, because apprehended along
with their apparent signs, and therefore also unreal.
For it is impossible for any object really to exist
which is by nature both non-evident and apparent ;
but the signs which we are discussing though assumed
to be non-evident have been found to be apparent
owing to the reversal of the argument.[b]

If, therefore, the signs are neither all apparent nor 129
all non-evident, nor yet some of the signs apparent
and some non-evident, and besides these there is no
other alternative, as they themselves affirm, then the
so-called signs will be unreal.

So then these few arguments out of many will be 130
enough for the present to suggest to us the non-
existence of an indicative sign. Next, we shall set
forth those which go to suggest the existence of a
sign, in order that we may exhibit the equipollence
of the counter-balancing arguments.

Either, then, the phrases used in criticism of the

[a] *Cf.* § 124 *supra.*
[b] *Cf.* §§ 185, 187.

SEXTUS EMPIRICUS

φωναὶ φερόμεναι ἢ οὐδὲν σημαίνουσιν. καὶ εἰ μὲν
ἄσημοί εἰσιν, πῶς ἂν κινήσειαν τὴν ὕπαρξιν τοῦ
131 σημείου; εἰ δὲ σημαίνουσί τι, ἔστι σημεῖον. ἔτι
ἤτοι ἀποδεικτικοί εἰσιν οἱ λόγοι οἱ κατὰ τοῦ
σημείου ἢ οὐκ ἀποδεικτικοί. ἀλλ' εἰ μὲν οὐκ ἀποδεικτικοί, οὐκ ἀποδεικνύουσι τὸ μὴ εἶναι σημεῖον·
εἰ δὲ ἀποδεικτικοί, ἐπεὶ ἡ ἀπόδειξις τῷ γένει
σημεῖόν ἐστιν, ἐκκαλυπτικὴ οὖσα τοῦ συμπεράσματος, ἔσται σημεῖον. ὅθεν καὶ συνερωτᾶται λόγος
τοιοῦτος. εἰ ἔστι τι σημεῖον, ἔστι σημεῖον, καὶ εἰ
μὴ ἔστι σημεῖον, ἔστι σημεῖον· τὸ γὰρ μὴ εἶναι
σημεῖον δι' ἀποδείξεως, ἢ δὴ ἔστι σημεῖον, δείκνυται. ἤτοι δὲ ἔστι σημεῖον ἢ οὐκ ἔστι σημεῖον·
132 ἔστιν ἄρα σημεῖον. τούτῳ δὲ τῷ λόγῳ παρά-
κειται τοιοῦτος λόγος· εἰ οὐκ ἔστι τι σημεῖον,
οὐκ ἔστι σημεῖον· καὶ εἰ ἔστι σημεῖον ὃ φασιν οἱ
δογματικοὶ σημεῖον εἶναι, οὐκ ἔστι σημεῖον· τὸ
γὰρ σημεῖον περὶ οὗ ὁ λόγος, κατὰ τὴν ἐπίνοιαν
αὐτοῦ καὶ πρός τι εἶναι λεγόμενον καὶ ἐκκαλυπτικὸν τοῦ σημειωτοῦ, ἀνύπαρκτον εὑρίσκεται, ὡς
133 παρεστήσαμεν. ἤτοι δὲ ἔστι σημεῖον ἢ οὐκ ἔστι
σημεῖον· οὐκ ἄρα ἔστι σημεῖον.

Καὶ περὶ τῶν φωνῶν δὲ τῶν ὑπὲρ τοῦ σημείου
αὐτοὶ ἀποκρινάσθωσαν οἱ δογματικοί, πότερον

---

a Cf. *Adv. Log.* ii. 279. The meaning of these sections,
130-133, is briefly this: The Dogmatists argue (§§ 130-131)
(1) that the Sceptics' objections to "sign" must signify either
something or nothing; if nothing, they have no force against
it, while if they signify something they are signs themselves
and so prove sign's existence; (2) the arguments (λόγοι)
against "sign" prove either something or nothing; if
nothing, they fail to prove the non-existence of "sign,"
while if they prove something, they are "proofs," *i.e.* a
species of "sign," and thus prove sign's existence. Hence,

sign signify something or they signify nothing.[a] But if they are non-significant how could they affect the reality of the sign ? While if they signify something, there exists a sign. Further, the arguments against 131 the sign are either probative or non-probative ; but if they are non-probative they do not prove the non-existence of a sign ; while if they are probative, since proof, as serving to reveal the conclusion, belongs to the genus sign, sign will exist. Whence this argument also is propounded : " If sign exists, sign exists ; and if sign exists not, sign exists ; for the non-existence of sign is shown by proof, which is a form of sign. But sign either exists or exists not ; therefore sign exists." And this argument is counter- 132 balanced by the following argument : " If any sign does not exist, sign does not exist ; and if sign is that which the Dogmatists declare sign to be, sign does not exist (for the sign under discussion, according to the conception of it and as stated to be both relative and serving to reveal the thing signified, is found to be unreal, as we have shown). But sign 133 either exists or exists not ; therefore sign does not exist."

Regarding also the phrases used in support of the sign,[b] let the Dogmatists themselves say in reply to our argument whether they signify something or signify

whichever view we take—the Dogmatists' that "sign exists," or the Sceptics' that "sign exists not "—we arrive at the same conclusion that "sign exists." In § 132 we have the counter-argument of the Sceptics, "reversing" that of the Dogmatists.

[b] In this § 133 the Sceptics are replying to the first argument of the Dogmatists (in § 130) ; the conclusion that "the existence of sign" proves its "non-existence" is based on the arguments in § 132, which "reverses" that of the Dogmatists.

σημαίνουσί τι ἢ οὐδὲν σημαίνουσιν. εἰ μὲν γὰρ
οὐδὲν σημαίνουσιν, οὐ πιστοῦται τὸ εἶναι σημεῖον·
εἰ δὲ σημαίνουσιν, ἀκολουθήσει αὐταῖς τὸ σημειωτόν. τοῦτο δὲ ἦν τὸ εἶναί τι σημεῖον· ᾧ ἔπεται τὸ
⟨μὴ⟩[1] εἶναι σημεῖον, ὡς ὑπεμνήσαμεν, κατὰ τὴν
τοῦ λόγου περιτροπήν.

Πλὴν ἀλλ' οὕτω πιθανῶν καὶ πρὸς τὸ εἶναι
σημεῖον καὶ πρὸς τὸ μὴ εἶναι λόγων φερομένων,
οὐ μᾶλλον εἶναι σημεῖον ἢ μὴ εἶναι ῥητέον.

ΙΒ'.—ΠΕΡΙ ΑΠΟΔΕΙΞΕΩΣ

134 Φανερὸν μὲν οὖν ἐκ τούτων ὅτι οὐδὲ ἡ ἀπόδειξις
ὁμολογούμενόν τι πρᾶγμα ἐστίν· εἰ γὰρ περὶ τοῦ
σημείου ἐπέχομεν, καὶ ἡ ἀπόδειξις δὲ σημεῖόν τί
ἐστι, καὶ περὶ τῆς ἀποδείξεως ἐπέχειν ἀνάγκη.
καὶ γὰρ εὑρήσομεν τοὺς περὶ τοῦ σημείου λόγους
ἠρωτημένους ἐφαρμόζεσθαι δυναμένους καὶ κατὰ
τῆς ἀποδείξεως, ἐπεὶ καὶ πρός τι εἶναι δοκεῖ καὶ
ἐκκαλυπτικὴ τοῦ συμπεράσματος, οἷς ἠκολούθει
τὰ πρὸς τὸ σημεῖον ἡμῖν εἰρημένα σχεδὸν ἅπαντα.
135 εἰ δὲ δεῖ καὶ ἰδίως περὶ ἀποδείξεως εἰπεῖν, συντόμως ἐπελεύσομαι τὸν περὶ αὐτῆς λόγον, πρότερον σαφηνίσαι πειραθεὶς διὰ βραχέων τί φασιν
εἶναι τὴν ἀπόδειξιν.

Ἔστιν οὖν, ὡς φασίν, ἡ ἀπόδειξις λόγος δι' ὁμολογουμένων λημμάτων κατὰ συναγωγὴν ἐπιφορὰν
ἐκκαλύπτων ἄδηλον. σαφέστερον δὲ ὃ λέγουσιν
ἔσται διὰ τούτων. λόγος ἐστὶ σύστημα ἐκ λημμά-

---

[1] ⟨μὴ⟩ add. Kayser, Papp.

[a] For this Sceptic formula cf. i. 188.

nothing. For if they signify nothing, the existence of sign is not confirmed ; whereas if they signify something, the thing signified will follow them ; and it was " the existence of a sign." And from this follows, as we have shown, the non-existence of sign, because of the reversal of the argument.

In short, then, since such plausible arguments are adduced both for the existence and for the non-existence of sign, we must declare that sign is " no more " [a] existent than non-existent.

Chapter XII.—Of Proof

Now it is plain from this that neither is proof a matter upon which there is agreement ; for if we suspend judgement about the sign, and proof also is a sign,[b] we must necessarily suspend judgement about proof likewise. And in fact we shall find that the arguments propounded concerning the sign can be adapted to apply to proof as well, since it seems to be both relative and serving to reveal the conclusion, and from these properties followed nearly all the results we mentioned in the case of the sign. If, however, one ought to devote a separate discussion to proof, I shall proceed to treat of it concisely after endeavouring first to explain shortly the definition they give of proof.

Proof is, as they assert, " an argument which, by means of agreed premisses, reveals by way of deduction a non-evident inference." What their statement means will be made clearer by what follows. " An argument is a system composed of premisses and an

[b] *Cf.* §§ 96, 122, 131 *supra* ; and for the next ten sections *cf. Adv. Log.* ii. 299 ff.

136 τῶν καὶ ἐπιφορᾶς· τούτου δὲ λήμματα μὲν εἶναι
λέγεται τὰ πρὸς κατασκευὴν τοῦ συμπεράσματος
συμφώνως λαμβανόμενα ἀξιώματα, ἐπιφορὰ δὲ [ἢ
συμπέρασμα]¹ τὸ ἐκ τῶν λημμάτων κατασκευα-
ζόμενον ἀξίωμα. οἷον ἐν τούτῳ " εἰ ἡμέρα ἔστι,
φῶς ἔστιν· ἀλλὰ μὴν ἡμέρα ἔστιν· φῶς ἄρα ἔστιν "
τὸ μὲν " φῶς ἄρα ἔστιν " συμπέρασμά ἐστι, τὰ
137 δὲ λοιπὰ λήμματα. τῶν δὲ λόγων οἱ μέν εἰσι
συνακτικοὶ οἱ δὲ ἀσύνακτοι, συνακτικοὶ μὲν ὅταν
τὸ συνημμένον τὸ ἀρχόμενον μὲν ἀπὸ τοῦ διὰ τῶν
τοῦ λόγου λημμάτων συμπεπλεγμένου, λῆγον δὲ
εἰς τὴν ἐπιφορὰν αὐτοῦ, ὑγιὲς ᾖ, οἷον ὁ προειρημένος λόγος συνακτικός ἐστιν, ἐπεὶ τῇ διὰ τῶν
λημμάτων αὐτοῦ συμπλοκῇ ταύτῃ " ἡμέρα ἔστι,
καὶ εἰ ἡμέρα ἔστι, φῶς ἔστιν " ἀκολουθεῖ τὸ " φῶς
ἔστιν " ἐν τούτῳ τῷ συνημμένῳ " [εἰ]² ἡμέρα ἔστι,
καὶ εἰ ἡμέρα ἔστι, φῶς ἔστιν < · φῶς ἄρα ἔστιν >.³ "
ἀσύνακτοι δὲ οἱ μὴ οὕτως ἔχοντες.

138 Τῶν δὲ συνακτικῶν οἱ μέν εἰσιν ἀληθεῖς οἱ δὲ
οὐκ ἀληθεῖς, ἀληθεῖς μὲν ὅταν μὴ μόνον τὸ συνημμένον ἐκ τῆς τῶν λημμάτων συμπλοκῆς καὶ τῆς
ἐπιφορᾶς, ὡς προειρήκαμεν, ὑγιὲς ᾖ, ἀλλὰ καὶ τὸ
συμπέρασμα καὶ τὸ διὰ τῶν λημμάτων αὐτοῦ συμπεπλεγμένον ἀληθὲς ὑπάρχῃ, ὅ ἐστιν ἡγούμενον
ἐν τῷ συνημμένῳ. ἀληθὲς δὲ συμπεπλεγμένον ἐστὶ
τὸ πάντα ἔχον ἀληθῆ, ὡς τὸ " ἡμέρα ἔστι, καὶ εἰ
ἡμέρα ἔστι, φῶς ἔστιν." οὐκ ἀληθεῖς δὲ οἱ μὴ
139 οὕτως ἔχοντες. ὁ γὰρ τοιοῦτος λόγος ἡμέρας
οὔσης " εἰ νὺξ ἔστι, σκότος ἔστιν· ἀλλὰ μὴν νὺξ
ἔστιν· σκότος ἄρα ἔστιν " συνακτικὸς μέν ἐστιν,

---

¹ ἢ om. mss., συμπέρασμα om. T.
² [εἰ] secl. Rüstow.   ³ < φῶς ἄρα ἔστιν > add. Papp.

inference. The premisses of it are (it is said) the 136
judgements adopted by consent for the establishment
of the inference, and the inference is the judgement
established by the premisses." For example, in the
argument " If it is day, it is light ; but it is in truth
day ; therefore it is light," the clause " therefore it
is light " is a conclusion, and the rest are premisses.
And of arguments some are conclusive, some incon- 137
clusive—conclusive when the hypothetical syllogism [a]
which begins with the combination made by the
premisses of the argument and ends with its inference is valid ; thus, for example, the argument
just stated is conclusive since the combination of its
premisses—" it is day " and " if it is day, it is light "
—is followed by " it is light " in the syllogism " it is
day, and if it is day it is light ; therefore it is light."
But arguments that are not like this are inconclusive.

And of the conclusive arguments some are true, 138
some not true—true when not only the syllogism
formed by the combination of the premisses and the
inference is valid,[b] as we said above, but the conclusion also and the combination of the premisses,
which is the antecedent in the syllogism, is really
true. And a combination is true when it has all its
parts true, as in the case of " It is day, and if it is
day, it is light " ; but those of a different kind are
not true. For an argument such as this—" If it is 139
night, it is dark ; but in fact it is night ; therefore
it is dark "—is indeed conclusive, since the syllogism

---

[a] τὸ συνημμένον, lit. " the combination " ; cf. p. 246 note a.
[b] " Valid " refers only to logical form ; " true " to content;
cf. § 139 ; Adv. Log. ii. 413.

ἐπεὶ τὸ συνημμένον τοῦτο ὑγιές ἐστιν " [εἰ]¹ νὺξ ἔστι, καὶ εἰ νὺξ ἔστι, ⟨σκότος ἔστι,⟩² σκότος ἄρα ἔστιν," οὐ μέντοι ἀληθής. τὸ γὰρ ἡγούμενον συμπεπλεγμένον ψεῦδός ἐστι, τὸ " νὺξ ἔστι, καὶ εἰ νὺξ ἔστι, σκότος ἔστι," ψεῦδος ἔχον ἐν ἑαυτῷ τὸ " νὺξ ἔστιν "· ψεῦδος γάρ ἐστι συμπεπλεγμένον τὸ ἔχον ἐν ἑαυτῷ ψεῦδος. ἔνθεν καὶ ἀληθῆ λόγον εἶναί φασι τὸν δι' ἀληθῶν λημμάτων ἀληθὲς συνάγοντα συμπέρασμα.

140 Πάλιν δὲ τῶν ἀληθῶν λόγων οἱ μέν εἰσιν ἀποδεικτικοὶ οἱ δ' οὐκ ἀποδεικτικοί, καὶ ἀποδεικτικοὶ μὲν οἱ διὰ προδήλων ἄδηλόν τι συνάγοντες, οὐκ ἀποδεικτικοὶ δὲ οἱ μὴ τοιοῦτοι. οἷον ὁ μὲν τοιοῦτος λόγος " εἰ ἡμέρα ἔστι, φῶς ἔστιν· ἀλλὰ μὴν ἡμέρα ἔστιν· φῶς ἄρα ἔστιν " οὐκ ἔστιν ἀποδεικτικός· τὸ γὰρ φῶς εἶναι, ὅπερ ἐστὶν αὐτοῦ συμπέρασμα, πρόδηλόν ἐστιν. ὁ δὲ τοιοῦτος " εἰ ἱδρῶτες ῥέουσι διὰ τῆς ἐπιφανείας, εἰσὶ νοητοὶ πόροι· ἀλλὰ μὴν ἱδρῶτες ῥέουσι διὰ τῆς ἐπιφανείας· εἰσὶν ἄρα νοητοὶ πόροι " ἀποδεικτικός ἐστι, τὸ συμπέρασμα ἔχων ἄδηλον, τὸ " εἰσὶν ἄρα νοητοὶ πόροι."

141 Τῶν δὲ ἄδηλόν τι συναγόντων οἱ μὲν ἐφοδευτικῶς μόνον ἄγουσιν ἡμᾶς διὰ τῶν λημμάτων ἐπὶ τὸ συμπέρασμα, οἱ δὲ ἐφοδευτικῶς ἅμα καὶ ἐκκαλυπτικῶς. οἷον ἐφοδευτικῶς μὲν οἱ ἐκ πίστεως καὶ μνήμης ἠρτῆσθαι δοκοῦντες, οἷός ἐστιν ὁ τοιοῦτος " εἴ τίς σοι θεῶν εἶπεν ὅτι πλουτήσει οὗτος, πλουτήσει οὗτος· οὑτοσὶ δὲ ὁ θεός " (δείκνυμι δὲ καθ' ὑπόθεσιν τὸν Δία) " εἶπέ σοι ὅτι

---

¹ [εἰ] secl. Rüstow.
² ⟨σκότος ἔστι⟩ add. Rüstow.

" it is night, and if it is night it is dark, therefore it is dark " is a valid one, but, when it is day-time, it is not true. For the antecedent combination—" it is night, and if it is night it is dark "—is false since it contains the falsehood " it is night "; for the combination which contains a falsehood is false. Hence they also say that a true argument is that which deduces a true conclusion from true premises.

Of true arguments, again, some are " probative," 140 some " non-probative "; and the probative are those which deduce something non-evident by means of pre-evident premises, the non-probative those not of this sort.[a] For example, an argument such as this— " If it is day it is light; but in fact it is day; therefore it is light " is not probative; for its conclusion, that " it is light," is pre-evident. But an argument like this—" If sweat pours through the surface, there are insensible pores[b]; but in fact sweat does pour through the surface; therefore there are insensible pores "—is a probative one, as its conclusion (" there are therefore insensible pores ") is non-evident.

And of arguments which deduce something non- 141 evident, some conduct us through the premises to the conclusion by way of progression only, others both by way of progression and by way of discovery as well. By progression, for instance, are those which seem to depend on belief and memory, such as the argument " If a god has said to you that this man will be rich, this man will be rich; but this god (assume that I point to Zeus) has said to you that

---

[a] For this and the following sections cf. *Adv. Log.* ii. 305 ff.
[b] Cf. § 98 *supra*.

πλουτήσει οὗτος· πλουτήσει ἄρα οὗτος ''· συγκατατιθέμεθα γὰρ τῷ συμπεράσματι οὐχ οὕτως
διὰ τὴν τῶν λημμάτων ἀνάγκην ὡς πιστεύοντες
142 τῇ τοῦ θεοῦ ἀποφάσει. οἱ δὲ οὐ μόνον ἐφοδευτικῶς ἀλλὰ καὶ ἐκκαλυπτικῶς ἄγουσιν ἡμᾶς ἐπὶ
τὸ συμπέρασμα, ὡς ὁ τοιοῦτος '' εἰ ῥέουσι διὰ τῆς
ἐπιφανείας ἱδρῶτες, εἰσὶ νοητοὶ πόροι· ἀλλὰ μὴν
τὸ πρῶτον· τὸ δεύτερον ἄρα ''· τὸ γὰρ ῥεῖν τοὺς
ἱδρῶτας ἐκκαλυπτικόν ἐστι τοῦ πόρους εἶναι, διὰ
τὸ προειλῆφθαι ὅτι διὰ ναστοῦ σώματος ὑγρὸν οὐ
δύναται φέρεσθαι.
143 Ἡ οὖν ἀπόδειξις καὶ λόγος εἶναι ὀφείλει καὶ
συνακτικὸς καὶ ἀληθὴς καὶ ἄδηλον ἔχων συμπέρασμα [καὶ]¹ ἐκκαλυπτόμενον ὑπὸ τῆς δυνάμεως
τῶν λημμάτων, καὶ διὰ τοῦτο εἶναι λέγεται ἀπόδειξις λόγος δι' ὁμολογουμένων λημμάτων κατὰ
συναγωγὴν ἐπιφορὰν ἐκκαλύπτων ἄδηλον.
   Διὰ τούτων μὲν οὖν σαφηνίζειν εἰώθασι τὴν
ἔννοιαν τῆς ἀποδείξεως.

ΙΓ΄.—ΕΙ ΕΣΤΙΝ ΑΠΟΔΕΙΞΙΣ

144 Ὅτι δὲ ἀνύπαρκτός ἐστιν ἡ ἀπόδειξις, ἀπ' αὐτῶν
ὧν λέγουσιν ἐπιλογίζεσθαι δυνατόν, ἕκαστον τῶν
περιεχομένων ἐν τῇ ἐννοίᾳ διατρέποντα. οἷον γοῦν
ὁ λόγος σύγκειται ἐξ ἀξιωμάτων, τὰ δὲ σύνθετα
πράγματα οὐ δύναται ὑπάρχειν ἐὰν μὴ τὰ ἐξ
ὧν συνέστηκεν ἀλλήλοις συνυπάρχῃ, ὡς πρόδηλον
ἀπὸ κλίνης καὶ τῶν παραπλησίων, τὰ δὲ μέρη τοῦ

____
¹ [καὶ] om. T.

____
ᵃ See the definition of '' proof '' in §§ 135-136.   It is with
'' hypothetical syllogisms '' that Sextus here concerned.   The
242

this man will be rich ; therefore he will be rich " ;
for we assent to the conclusion not so much on account
of the logical force of the premisses as because of our
belief in the statement of the god. But some argu- 142
ments conduct us to the conclusion by way of discovery as well as of progression, like the following : " If sweat pours through the surface, there are
insensible pores ; but the first is true, therefore also
the second " ; for the pouring of the sweat makes
discovery of the fact of the existence of pores,
because of the prior assumption that moisture cannot
pass through a solid body.

So, then, proof ought to be an argument which 143
is deductive and true and has a non-evident conclusion which is discovered by the potency of the
premisses ; and because of this, proof is defined as
" an argument which by means of agreed premisses discovers by way of deduction a non-evident
inference." It is in these terms, then, that they are
in the habit of explaining the conception of proof.

CHAPTER XIII.—DOES PROOF EXIST ?

That proof has no real existence may be inferred 144
from their own statements, by refuting each of the
assumptions implied in its conception.[a] Thus, for
instance, the argument is compounded of judgements,
but compound things cannot exist unless its component
elements mutually co-exist, as is pre-evident from
the case of a bed and similar objects ; but the parts

" component elements " of the syllogism (or " argument ")
are the " judgements " (or propositions) which go to form
its " premisses."

SEXTUS EMPIRICUS

λόγου ἀλλήλοις οὐ συνυπάρχει. ὅτε γὰρ λέγομεν
τὸ πρῶτον λῆμμα, οὐδέπω ὑπάρχει οὔτε τὸ ἕτερον
λῆμμα οὔτε ἡ ἐπιφορά· ὅτε δὲ τὸ δεύτερόν φαμεν,
τὸ μὲν πρότερον λῆμμα οὐκέτι ὑπάρχει, ἡ δὲ
ἐπιφορὰ οὐδέπω ἔστιν· ὅτε δὲ τὴν ἐπιφορὰν προφερόμεθα, τὰ λήμματα αὐτῆς οὐκέτι ὑφέστηκεν.
οὐ συνυπάρχει ἄρα ἀλλήλοις τὰ μέρη τοῦ λόγου·
ὅθεν οὐδὲ ὁ λόγος ὑπάρχειν δόξει.

145 Χωρὶς δὲ τούτων ὁ συνακτικὸς λόγος ἀκατάληπτός ἐστιν· εἰ γὰρ οὗτος κρίνεται ἀπὸ τῆς τοῦ
συνημμένου ἀκολουθίας, ἡ δὲ κατὰ τὸ συνημμένον
ἀκολουθία ἀνεπικρίτως διαπεφώνηται καὶ ἔστιν
ἴσως ἀκατάληπτος, ὡς ἐν τῷ περὶ σημείου λόγῳ
ὑπεμνήσαμεν, καὶ ὁ συνακτικὸς λόγος ἀκατάληπτος
146 ἔσται. οἵ γε μὴν διαλεκτικοί φασιν ἀσύνακτον
λόγον γίγνεσθαι ἤτοι παρὰ διάρτησιν ἢ παρὰ
ἔλλειψιν ἢ παρὰ τὸ κατὰ μοχθηρὸν ἠρωτῆσθαι
σχῆμα ἢ κατὰ παρολκήν. οἷον κατὰ διάρτησιν
μὲν ὅταν μὴ ἔχῃ τὰ λήμματα ἀκολουθίαν πρὸς
ἄλληλά τε καὶ τὴν ἐπιφοράν, ὡς ὁ τοιοῦτος " εἰ
ἡμέρα ἔστι, φῶς ἔστιν· ἀλλὰ μὴν πυροὶ ἐν ἀγορᾷ
147 πωλοῦνται· Δίων ἄρα περιπατεῖ." παρὰ δὲ παρολκὴν ὅταν εὑρίσκηται λῆμμα παρέλκον πρὸς τὴν
τοῦ λόγου συναγωγήν, οἷον " εἰ ἡμέρα ἔστι, φῶς
ἔστιν· ἀλλὰ μὴν ἡμέρα ἔστιν, ἀλλὰ καὶ Δίων περι-
πατεῖ· φῶς ἄρα ἔστιν." παρὰ δὲ τὸ ἐν μοχθηρῷ
ἠρωτῆσθαι σχήματι ὅταν μὴ ᾖ τὸ σχῆμα τοῦ λόγου
συνακτικόν, οἷον ὄντων συλλογισμῶν, ὥς φασί,
τούτων " εἰ ἡμέρα ἔστι, φῶς ἔστιν· ἀλλὰ μὴν
ἡμέρα ἔστιν· φῶς ἄρα ἔστιν," " εἰ ἡμέρα ἔστι, φῶς
ἔστιν· οὐχὶ δὲ φῶς ἔστιν· οὐκ ἄρα ἡμέρα ἔστιν,"

---

[a] i.e. the Stoics, cf. §§ 166, 235.

of an argument do not mutually co-exist. For when we are stating the first premiss, neither the second premiss nor the inference is as yet in existence ; and when we are stating the second premiss, the first is no longer existent and the inference is not yet existent ; and when we announce the inference, its premisses are no longer in being. Therefore the parts of the argument do not mutually co-exist ; and hence the argument too will seem to be non-existent.

But apart from this, the conclusive argument is 145 non-apprehensible; for if it is judged by the coherence of the hypothetical premiss, and the coherence in that premiss is a matter of unsettled dispute and is probably non-apprehensible, as we suggested in our chapter (xi.) " On the Sign," then the conclusive argument also will be non-apprehensible. Now the 146 Dialecticians [a] assert that an argument is inconclusive owing to inconsistency or to deficiency or to its being propounded in a bad form or to redundancy. An example of inconsistency is when the premisses are not logically coherent with each other and with the inference, as in the argument " If it is day, it is light ; but in fact wheat is being sold in the market ; therefore Dion is walking." And it is a case of redundancy 147 when we find a premiss that is superfluous for the logic of the argument, as for instance " If it is day, it is light ; but in fact it is day and Dion also is walking ; therefore it is light." And it is due to the bad form in which it is propounded when the form of the argument is not conclusive ; for whereas the really syllogistic arguments are, they say, such as these : " If it is day, it is light ; but in fact it is day ; therefore it is light " ; and " If it is day, it is light ; but it is not light ; therefore it is not day,"—the inconclusive

245

ὁ λόγος ἀσύνακτός ἐστιν οὗτος " εἰ ἡμέρα ἔστι,
φῶς ἔστιν· ἀλλὰ μὴν φῶς ἔστιν· ἡμέρα ἄρα ἔστιν."

148 ἐπεὶ γὰρ ἐπαγγέλλεται τὸ συνημμένον ὄντος[1] τοῦ
ἐν αὐτῷ ἡγουμένου εἶναι καὶ τὸ λῆγον, εἰκότως
τοῦ ἡγουμένου προσλαμβανομένου ἐπάγεται καὶ τὸ
λῆγον, καὶ τοῦ λήγοντος ἀναιρουμένου ἀναιρεῖται
καὶ τὸ ἡγούμενον· εἰ γὰρ ἦν τὸ ἡγούμενον, ἦν ἂν
καὶ τὸ λῆγον. τοῦ δὲ λήγοντος προσλαμβανομένου
οὐ πάντως τίθεται καὶ τὸ ἡγούμενον· οὐδὲ γὰρ
ὑπισχνεῖτο τὸ συνημμένον τῷ λήγοντι ἀκολουθεῖν
τὸ ἡγούμενον, ἀλλὰ τῷ ἡγουμένῳ τὸ λῆγον μόνον.

149 διὰ τοῦτο οὖν ὁ μὲν ἐκ συνημμένου καὶ τοῦ ἡγουμένου τὸ λῆγον συνάγων συλλογιστικὸς εἶναι λέγεται, καὶ ὁ ἐκ συνημμένου καὶ τοῦ ἀντικειμένου
τοῦ λήγοντος τὸ ἀντικείμενον τῷ ἡγουμένῳ συν-
άγων· ὁ δὲ ἐκ συνημμένου καὶ τοῦ λήγοντος τὸ
ἡγούμενον συνάγων ἀσύνακτος, ὡς ὁ προειρημένος,
παρὸ καὶ ἀληθῶν ὄντων τῶν λημμάτων αὐτοῦ
ψεῦδος συνάγει, ὅταν λυχνιαίου φωτὸς ὄντος νυκτὸς
λέγηται. τὸ μὲν γὰρ " εἰ ἡμέρα ἔστι, φῶς ἔστι "
συνημμένον ἀληθές ἐστιν, καὶ ἡ " ἀλλὰ μὴν φῶς
ἔστι " πρόσληψις, ἡ δὲ " ἡμέρα ἄρα " ἐπιφορὰ

150 ψευδής. κατὰ παράλειψιν δέ ἐστι μοχθηρὸς λόγος
ἐν ᾧ παραλείπεταί τι τῶν πρὸς τὴν συναγωγὴν
τοῦ συμπεράσματος χρησιμευόντων· οἷον ὑγιοῦς
ὄντος, ὡς οἴονται, τοῦ λόγου τούτου " ἤτοι ἀγαθός
ἐστιν ὁ πλοῦτος ἢ κακὸς ἢ ἀδιάφορος· οὔτε δὲ
κακός ἐστιν οὔτε ἀδιάφορος· ἀγαθὸς ἄρα ἐστίν,"

[1] ὄντος Heintz: ἐντὸς MSS. Bekk.

[a] *i.e.* (in Stoic terminology) definitely valid and conclusive ; *cf.* § 163 *infra.* Note that the term συνημμένον
(" combination ") mostly means the " hypothetical, or major,

246

argument runs thus : " If it is day, it is light ; but in fact it is light ; therefore it is day." For since the **148** major premiss announces that if its antecedent exists its consequent also exists, naturally when the antecedent is admitted the consequent also is inferred, and when the consequent is denied the antecedent also is denied ; for if the antecedent had existed, the consequent also would have existed. But when the consequent is admitted, the antecedent is not necessarily admitted as well ; for the major premiss did not promise that the antecedent should follow the consequent, but only the consequent the antecedent.

Hence, the argument which deduces the conse- **149** quent from the major premiss and the antecedent is said to be syllogistic,[a] and also that which deduces the opposite of the antecedent from the major premiss and the opposite of the consequent ; but the argument which, like that stated above, deduces the antecedent from the major premiss and the consequent is inconclusive, so that it makes a false deduction, even though its premisses are true, whenever it is uttered by lamplight at night. For though the major premiss " If it is day, it is light " is true, and also the minor premiss, " but in fact it is light," the inference " therefore it is day " is false. And the **150** argument is faulty by deficiency, when it suffers from the omission of some factor needed for the deducing of the conclusion : thus, for instance, while we have, as they think, a valid argument in " Wealth is either good or bad or indifferent ; but it is neither bad nor indifferent ; therefore it is good," [b] the following

premiss of a hypothetical syllogism," but sometimes the whole syllogism.   [b] *Cf.* iii. 177 ff.

φαῦλός ἐστι παρὰ ἔλλειψιν οὗτος ὁ λόγος " ἤτοι
ἀγαθός ἐστιν ὁ πλοῦτος ἢ κακός· οὐκ ἔστι δὲ κακός·
151 ἀγαθὸς ἄρα ἐστίν." ἐὰν οὖν δείξω ὅτι οὐδεμία
διαφορὰ τῶν ἀσυνάκτων διακρίνεσθαι δύναται κατ'
αὐτοὺς ἀπὸ τῶν συνακτικῶν, ἔδειξα ὅτι ἀκατάληπτός ἐστιν ὁ συνακτικὸς λόγος, ὡς περιττὰς εἶναι
τὰς κατὰ διαλεκτικὴν αὐτοῖς φερομένας ἀπειρο-
λογίας. δείκνυμι δὲ οὕτως.
152 Ὁ κατὰ διάρτησιν ἀσύνακτος λόγος ἐλέγετο
ἐγνωρίσθαι ἐκ τοῦ μὴ ἔχειν ἀκολουθίαν τὰ λήμματα
αὐτοῦ πρὸς ἄλληλα καὶ τὴν ἐπιφοράν. ἐπεὶ οὖν
τῆς γνώσεως τῆς ἀκολουθίας ταύτης δεῖ προηγεῖσθαι τὴν κρίσιν τοῦ συνημμένου, ἀνεπίκριτον
δέ ἐστι τὸ συνημμένον, ὡς ἐπελογισάμην, ἀδιά-
κριτος ἔσται καὶ ὁ κατὰ διάρτησιν ἀσύνακτος
153 λόγος. καὶ γὰρ ὁ λέγων κατὰ διάρτησιν ἀσύνακτον εἶναί τινα λόγον, φάσιν μὲν προφερόμενος
μόνην ἀντιτιθεμένην αὐτῷ φάσιν ἕξει τὴν ἀντι-
κειμένην τῇ προειρημένῃ· ἀποδεικνὺς δὲ διὰ λόγου
ἀκούσεται ὅτι δεῖ τὸν λόγον τοῦτον πρότερον
συνακτικὸν εἶναι, εἶθ' οὕτως ἀποδεικνύειν ὅτι ἀ-
συνάρτητα τὰ λήμματα τοῦ διηρτῆσθαι λεγομένου
λόγου. οὐ γνωσόμεθα δὲ εἰ ἔστιν ἀποδεικτικός,
μὴ ἔχοντες συνημμένου σύμφωνον κρίσιν, ᾗ κρινοῦμεν εἰ ἀκολουθεῖ τῇ διὰ τῶν λημμάτων τοῦ
λόγου συμπλοκῇ τὸ συμπέρασμα. καὶ κατὰ τοῦτο
οὖν οὐχ ἕξομεν διακρίνειν τῶν συνακτικῶν τὸν
κατὰ διάρτησιν μοχθηρὸν εἶναι λεγόμενον.

---

[a] Over 300 volumes, dealing with grammar and logic
("dialectic"), are ascribed to Chrysippus.
[b] With §§ 152-156 cf. Adv. Log. ii. 435 ff.
[c] i.e. the syllogism as a whole, which is a " combination "

is faulty by way of deficiency : " Wealth is either good or bad ; but it is not bad ; therefore it is good." If, then, I shall show that, according to them, it is 151 impossible to distinguish any difference between the inconclusive and the conclusive arguments, I shall have shown that the conclusive argument is non-apprehensible, so that their endless disquisitions on " dialectic "[a] are superfluous.   And I show it in this wise.

It was said that the argument which is inconclusive 152 owing to inconsistency is recognized by the want of coherence which marks its premisses in their relation both to each other and to the inference.[b]   Since, then, the recognition of this coherence ought to be preceded by the judgement on the hypothetical syllogism,[c] and that syllogism, as I have argued, does not admit of judgement, the argument that is inconclusive through inconsistency will likewise be incapable of being distinguished.   For he who declares that any particular 153 argument is inconclusive through inconsistency will, if he is merely uttering a statement, find himself opposed by a statement which contradicts his own ; while if he tries to prove it by argument, he will be told that this argument of his must itself be conclusive before he can prove that the premisses of the argument said to be inconsistent are devoid of consistency. But we shall not know whether it is probative, since we have no agreed test of the syllogism whereby to judge whether the conclusion follows the logical connexion formed by the premisses.   And thus, also, we shall be unable to distinguish the argument that is faulty through inconsistency from those that are conclusive.

of premisses and conclusion, *cf.* § 137 ; for another sense of the word *cf.* note on § 149.

154 Τὰ δὲ αὐτὰ ἐροῦμεν πρὸς τὸν λέγοντα μοχθηρὸν
εἶναι λόγον τινὰ παρὰ τὸ ἐν φαύλῳ σχήματι ἠρω-
τῆσθαι· ὁ γὰρ κατασκευάζων ὅτι μοχθηρόν τι
σχῆμά ἐστιν, οὐχ ἕξει ὁμολογούμενον συνακτικὸν
155 λόγον δι' οὗ δυνήσεται συνάγειν ὃ φησιν. δυνάμει
δὲ ἀντειρήκαμεν[1] διὰ τούτων[2] καὶ πρὸς τοὺς πειρωμένους παρ' ἔλλειψιν ἀσυνάκτους λόγους εἶναι
δεικνύναι. εἰ γὰρ ὁ ἐντελὴς ⟨καὶ⟩[3] ἀπηρτισμένος
ἀδιάκριτός ἐστι, καὶ ὁ ἐν ἐλλείψει ἄδηλος ἔσται.
καὶ ἔτι ὁ διὰ λόγου δεικνύναι τινὰ ἐλλιπῆ βουλόμενος λόγον, μὴ ἔχων συνημμένου κρίσιν ὡμο-
λογημένην, δι' ἧς κρίνειν δυνήσεται τὴν ἀκολουθίαν
τοῦ ὑπ' αὐτοῦ λεγομένου λόγου, οὐ δυνήσεται
κεκριμένως καὶ ὀρθῶς λέγειν ὅτι ἐλλιπής ἐστιν.

156 Ἀλλὰ καὶ ὁ κατὰ παρολκὴν λεγόμενος εἶναι
μοχθηρὸς ἀδιάκριτός ἐστιν ἀπὸ τῶν ἀποδεικτικῶν.
ὅσον γὰρ ἐπὶ τῇ παρολκῇ καὶ οἱ θρυλούμενοι παρὰ
τοῖς στωικοῖς ἀναπόδεικτοι ἀσύνακτοι εὑρεθήσονται, ὧν ἀναιρουμένων ἡ πᾶσα διαλεκτικὴ ἀνα-
τρέπεται· οὗτοι γάρ εἰσιν οὓς φασιν ἀποδείξεως
μὲν μὴ δεῖσθαι πρὸς τὴν ἑαυτῶν σύστασιν, ἀποδεικτικοὺς δὲ ὑπάρχειν τοῦ καὶ τοὺς ἄλλους συνάγειν λόγους. ὅτι δὲ παρέλκουσιν, ἔσται σαφὲς
ἐκθεμένων ἡμῶν τοὺς ἀναποδείκτους καὶ οὕτως ὃ
φαμεν ἐπιλογιζομένων.

157 Πολλοὺς μὲν ἀναποδείκτους ὀνειροπολοῦσιν, πέντε
δὲ τούτους μάλιστα ἐκτίθενται, εἰς οὓς οἱ λοιποὶ

---

[1] ἀντειρήκαμεν T: ἀντειρήσομεν EAB: ἀντειρήσθω L, Bekk.
[2] τούτων T, cj. Bekk.: τοῦτο mss.   [3] ⟨καὶ⟩ add. T.

---

[a] i.e. those which need no proof as being self-evident;
cf. Aristotle's " perfect syllogisms," and i. 69; Adv. Log. ii.
223 ff.

And we will make the same reply to the man who 154
says that an argument is unsound owing to its being
propounded in a faulty form ; for he who maintains
that a form is unsound will have no argument agreed
to be conclusive whereby he will be able to draw the
conclusion he states. And hereby we have also 155
potentially refuted those who try to show that there
are arguments which are inconclusive through deficiency. For if the complete and finished argument
is indistinguishable ⟨from others⟩, the deficient also
will be non-evident. And, further, he who proposes
to prove by argument that a certain argument is
deficient, seeing that he has no agreed test of a
hypothetical syllogism whereby he can judge the
coherence of the argument he is talking about, will
be unable to make a tested and true pronouncement
that it is deficient.

Moreover, the argument that is said to be faulty 156
through redundancy is indistinguishable from those
that are probative. For, so far as concerns redundancy, even the " non-demonstrable " arguments [a] so
much talked of by the Stoics will be found to be
inconclusive, and if they are demolished the whole of
dialectic is overturned ; for they are the arguments
which, they say, need no proof to establish them,
and themselves serve as proofs of the conclusiveness
of the other arguments. And that they are redundant will be clear when we have set forth these
non-probative arguments and thus confirm our statement by reasoning.

Now there are, in their imaginings, many non- 157
demonstrable arguments, but the five which they
chiefly propound, and to which all the rest can, it

πάντες ἀναφέρεσθαι δοκοῦσιν, πρῶτον τὸν ἐκ
συνημμένου καὶ τοῦ ἡγουμένου τὸ λῆγον συνάγοντα, οἷον " εἰ ἡμέρα ἔστι, φῶς ἔστιν· ἀλλὰ μὴν
ἡμέρα ἔστιν· φῶς ἄρα ἔστιν." δεύτερον τὸν ἐκ
συνημμένου καὶ τοῦ ἀντικειμένου τοῦ λήγοντος τὸ
ἀντικείμενον τοῦ ἡγουμένου συνάγοντα, οἷον " εἰ
ἡμέρα ἔστι, φῶς ἔστιν· οὐκ ἔστι δὲ φῶς· οὐκ ἄρα
158 ἡμέρα ἔστιν." τρίτον τὸν ἐξ ἀποφατικοῦ συμπλοκῆς καὶ ἑνὸς τῶν ἐκ τῆς συμπλοκῆς τὸ ἀντικείμενον τοῦ λοιποῦ συνάγοντα, οἷον " οὐχὶ ἡμέρα
ἔστι καὶ νὺξ ἔστιν· ἡμέρα δὲ ἔστιν· οὐκ ἄρα νὺξ
ἔστιν." τέταρτον τὸν ἐκ διεζευγμένου καὶ ἑνὸς
τῶν ἐπεζευγμένων τὸ ἀντικείμενον τοῦ λοιποῦ
συνάγοντα, οἷον " ἤτοι ἡμέρα ἔστιν ἢ νὺξ ἔστιν·
ἡμέρα δὲ ἔστιν· οὐκ ἄρα νὺξ ἔστιν." πέμπτον τὸν
ἐκ διεζευγμένου καὶ τοῦ ἀντικειμένου ἑνὸς τῶν
ἐπεζευγμένων τὸ λοιπὸν συνάγοντα, οἷον " ἤτοι
ἡμέρα ἔστιν ἢ νὺξ ἔστιν· οὐχὶ δὲ νὺξ ἔστιν· ἡμέρα
ἄρα ἔστιν."

159 Οὗτοι μὲν οὖν εἰσὶν οἱ θρυλούμενοι ἀναπόδεικτοι,
πάντες δέ μοι δοκοῦσιν ἀσύνακτοι εἶναι κατὰ παρολκήν. αὐτίκα γοῦν, ἵνα ἀπὸ τοῦ πρώτου ἀρξώμεθα,
ἤτοι ὁμολογεῖται ὅτι ἀκολουθεῖ τὸ " φῶς ἔστιν " τῷ
" ἡμέρα ἔστιν " ἡγουμένῳ αὐτῷ ἐν τῷ " εἰ ἡμέρα
ἔστι, φῶς ἔστιν " συνημμένῳ, ἢ ἄδηλόν ἐστιν.
ἀλλ' εἰ μὲν ἄδηλόν ἐστιν, οὐ δώσομεν τὸ συνημμένον ὡς ὁμολογούμενον· εἰ δὲ πρόδηλόν ἐστιν
ὅτι ὄντος τοῦ " ἡμέρα ἔστιν " ἐξ ἀνάγκης ἔστι καὶ

---

^a Literally, the " combination," which here (as in § 104)
means the hypothetical major premiss, of which the "if,"
clause is the " antecedent," the other clause the "consequent."

seems, be referred, are these. The first is that which deduces the consequent from the major premiss [a] and the antecedent, as for example " If it is day, it is light ; but in fact it is day ; therefore it is light." The second is that which deduces the opposite of the antecedent from the major premiss and the opposite of the consequent, as for example " If it is day, it is light ; but it is not light ; therefore it is not day." The third deduces from the negation of a coupled 158 premiss [b] and ⟨the affirmation of⟩ one of its clauses the opposite of the other clause, as for example " It is not both night and day ; but it is day ; therefore it is not night." The fourth deduces from a disjunctive premiss and one of its alternative clauses the opposite of the other, as for example " Either it is day or it is night ; but it is day ; therefore it is not night." The fifth [c] deduces from a disjunctive premiss and the opposite of one of its clauses the other clause, as for example " Either it is day or it is night ; but it is not night ; therefore it is day."

These, then, are the much talked of non-demon- 159 strable arguments, but they all seem to me to be inconclusive through redundancy. Thus for instance, to begin with the first, either it is agreed, or else it is non-evident, that in the major premiss " If it is day, it is light," the clause " it is light " follows from its antecedent " it is day." But if this is non-evident, we shall not grant the major premiss as agreed ; if, however, it is pre-evident that if the clause " it is day " be true, the clause " it is light " will necessarily

[b] *i.e.* a premiss consisting of two clauses "coupled" by " and " (or " both . . . and "); a "conjunctive" premiss (as opposed to a " disjunctive," coupled by " either . . . or ").
[c] *Cf.* i. 69.

SEXTUS EMPIRICUS

τὸ " φῶς ἔστιν," εἰπόντων ἡμῶν ὅτι ἡμέρα ἔστιν,
συνάγεται καὶ τὸ φῶς ἔστιν, ὡς ἀρκεῖν τὸν τοιοῦτον
λόγον " ἡμέρα ἔστι, φῶς ἄρα ἔστιν," καὶ παρέλκειν
τὸ " εἰ ἡμέρα ἔστι, φῶς ἔστιν " συνημμένον.

160 Ὁμοίως δὲ φερόμεθα καὶ ἐπὶ τοῦ δευτέρου ἀναποδείκτου. ἤτοι γὰρ ἐνδέχεται τοῦ λήγοντος μὴ
ὄντος εἶναι τὸ ἡγούμενον, ἢ οὐκ ἐνδέχεται. ἀλλ'
εἰ μὲν ἐνδέχεται, οὐκ ἔσται ὑγιὲς τὸ συνημμένον·
εἰ δὲ οὐκ ἐνδέχεται, ἅμα τῷ τεθῆναι τὸ " οὐχὶ τὸ
λῆγον " τίθεται καὶ τὸ " οὐχὶ τὸ ἡγούμενον," καὶ
παρέλκει πάλιν τὸ συνημμένον, τῆς συνερωτήσεως
τοιαύτης γινομένης " οὐχὶ φῶς ἔστιν, οὐκ ἄρα
ἡμέρα ἔστιν."

161 Ὁ δὲ αὐτὸς λόγος καὶ ἐπὶ τοῦ τρίτου ἀναποδείκτου. ἤτοι γὰρ πρόδηλόν ἐστιν ὅτι οὐκ ἐνδέχεται τὰ ἐν τῇ συμπλοκῇ συνυπάρξαι ἀλλήλοις, ἢ
ἄδηλον. καὶ εἰ μὲν ἄδηλον, οὐ δώσομεν τὸ ἀποφατικὸν τῆς συμπλοκῆς· εἰ δὲ πρόδηλον, ἅμα τῷ
τεθῆναι τὸ ἕτερον ἀναιρεῖται τὸ λοιπόν, καὶ
παρέλκει τὸ ἀποφατικὸν τῆς συμπλοκῆς, οὕτως
ἡμῶν ἐρωτώντων " ἡμέρα ἔστιν, οὐκ ἄρα νὺξ
ἔστιν."

162 Τὰ δὲ παραπλήσια λέγομεν καὶ ἐπὶ τοῦ τετάρτου
καὶ ἐπὶ τοῦ πέμπτου ἀναποδείκτου. ἤτοι γὰρ
πρόδηλόν ἐστιν ὅτι ἐν τῷ διεζευγμένῳ τὸ μὲν
ἀληθές ἐστι τὸ δὲ ψεῦδος μετὰ μάχης τελείας, ὅπερ
ἐπαγγέλλεται τὸ διεζευγμένον, ἢ ἄδηλον. καὶ εἰ
μὲν ἄδηλον, οὐ δώσομεν τὸ διεζευγμένον· εἰ δὲ
πρόδηλον, τεθέντος ἑνὸς ἀπ' αὐτῶν φανερόν ἐστιν
ὅτι τὸ λοιπὸν οὐκ ἔστιν, καὶ ἀναιρεθέντος ἑνὸς

---

^a An example of the *syllogismus decurtatus*, which has but
one premiss; *cf.* § 167.

254

be true also, then, once we have asserted that " it is day," the statement " it is light " is also inferred, so that an argument in the form " It is day, therefore it is light " is sufficient,[a] and the major premiss " If it is day, it is light " is redundant.

And in the case of the second non-demonstrable argument we make a similar objection. For it is either possible or impossible for the antecedent to be true when the consequent is not true. But if this is possible, the major premiss will not be valid ; while if it is impossible, at the moment of positing " Not the consequent " we posit also " Not the antecedent," and the major premiss is redundant once again, the argument propounded being " It is not light, therefore it is not day."

The same reasoning applies also to the third non-demonstrable argument. For either it is pre-evident that it is impossible for the clauses in the coupled premiss mutually to co-exist, or else it is non-evident. And if it is non-evident we shall not grant the negative of the coupled premiss ; but if it is pre-evident, at the moment of positing the one clause the other is annulled, and the negative of the coupled premiss is redundant when we propound the argument in the form " It is day, therefore it is not night."

And we deal in like manner with the fourth non-demonstrable argument and the fifth. For either it is pre-evident or it is non-evident that in the disjunctive premiss one clause is true, the other false, in complete contradiction, as the disjunctive proclaims. And if this is non-evident, we shall not grant the disjunctive ; but if it is pre-evident, if one of its clauses be affirmed it is apparent that the other is not true, and if one is negated it is pre-evident that the other is true, so

πρόδηλον ὅτι τὸ λοιπὸν ἔστιν, ὡς ἀρκεῖν συνερωτᾶν οὕτως " ἡμέρα ἔστιν, οὐκ ἄρα νὺξ ἔστιν," " οὐχὶ ἡμέρα ἔστιν, νὺξ ἄρα ἔστιν," καὶ παρέλκειν τὸ διεζευγμένον.

163 Παραπλήσια δὲ λέγειν ἔνεστι καὶ περὶ τῶν κατηγορικῶν καλουμένων συλλογισμῶν, οἷς μάλιστα χρῶνται οἱ ἀπὸ τοῦ περιπάτου. οἷον γοῦν ἐν τούτῳ τῷ λόγῳ " τὸ δίκαιον καλόν, τὸ καλὸν ἀγαθόν, τὸ δίκαιον ἄρα ἀγαθόν " ἤτοι ὁμολογεῖται καὶ πρόδηλόν ἐστιν ὅτι τὸ καλὸν ἀγαθόν ἐστιν, ἢ ἀμφισβητεῖται καὶ ἔστιν ἄδηλον. ἀλλ' εἰ μὲν ἄδηλόν ἐστιν, οὐ δοθήσεται κατὰ τὴν τοῦ λόγου συνερώτησιν, καὶ διὰ τοῦτο οὐ συνάξει ὁ συλλογισμός· εἰ δὲ πρόδηλόν ἐστιν ὅτι πᾶν ὅπερ ἂν ᾖ καλόν, τοῦτο πάντως καὶ ἀγαθόν ἐστιν, ἅμα τῷ λεχθῆναι ὅτι τόδε τι καλόν ἐστι συνεισάγεται καὶ τὸ ἀγαθὸν αὐτὸ εἶναι, ὡς ἀρκεῖν τὴν τοιαύτην συνερώτησιν " τὸ δίκαιον καλόν, τὸ δίκαιον ἄρα ἀγαθόν," καὶ παρέλκειν τὸ ἕτερον λῆμμα ἐν ᾧ τὸ 164 καλὸν ἀγαθὸν εἶναι ἐλέγετο. ὁμοίως δὲ καὶ ἐν τῷ τοιούτῳ λόγῳ " Σωκράτης ἄνθρωπος, πᾶς ἄνθρωπος ζῷον, Σωκράτης ἄρα ζῷον," εἰ μὲν οὐκ ἔστι πρόδηλον αὐτόθεν ὅτι πᾶν ὅ τι περ ἂν ᾖ ἄνθρωπος, τοῦτο καὶ ζῷόν ἐστιν, οὐχ ὁμολογεῖται ἡ καθόλου πρότασις, οὐδὲ δώσομεν αὐτὴν ἐν τῇ 165 συνερωτήσει. εἰ δὲ ἕπεται τῷ ἄνθρωπόν τινα εἶναι τὸ καὶ ζῷον αὐτὸν ὑπάρχειν, καὶ διὰ τοῦτο ἀληθής ἐστιν ὁμολογουμένως ἡ " πᾶς ἄνθρωπος ζῷον " πρότασις, ἅμα τῷ λεχθῆναι ὅτι Σωκράτης ἄνθρωπος συνεισάγεται καὶ τὸ ζῷον αὐτὸν εἶναι, ὡς ἀρκεῖν τὴν τοιαύτην συνερώτησιν " Σωκράτης ἄνθρωπος, Σωκράτης ἄρα ζῷον," καὶ παρέλκειν

that it is sufficient to frame the argument thus—" It is day, therefore it is not night," or " It is not day, therefore it is night " ; and the disjunctive premiss is redundant.

One may also make similar observations on the so-163 called " categorical " syllogisms, which are chiefly used by the Peripatetics.[a] Thus, for example, in the argument—" The just is fair, but the fair is good, therefore the just is good," [b] either it is agreed and pre-evident that " the fair is good," or it is disputed and is non-evident. But if it is non-evident, it will not be granted in the process of deduction, and consequently the syllogism will not be conclusive ; while if it is pre-evident that whatsoever is fair is also without exception good, at the moment of stating that this particular thing is fair the fact that it is good is likewise implied, so that it is enough to put the argument in the form " The just is fair, therefore the just is good," and the other premiss, in which it was stated that " the fair is good," is redundant. So 164 too in an argument such as this—" Socrates is a man ; every man is an animal ; therefore Socrates is an animal,"—if it is not at once pre-evident that whatsoever is man is always also animal, the universal premiss is not agreed, and neither will we admit it in the process of deduction. But if the fact that he is a 165 man is logically followed by the fact that he is also an animal, and in consequence the premiss " Every man is an animal " is by agreement true, at the moment of stating that " Socrates is a man " we admit therewith that he is also an animal, so that an argument in the form " Socrates is a man, therefore Socrates is an

[a] Aristotle dealt only with this form of proof ; later Peripatetics with the hypothetical and disjunctive forms as well.
[b] Cf. Plato, Alcib. I. 116.

SEXTUS EMPIRICUS

166 τὴν " πᾶς ἄνθρωπος ζῷον " πρότασιν. παρα-
πλησίαις δὲ μεθόδοις καὶ ἐπὶ τῶν ἄλλων πρώτων
κατηγορικῶν λόγων χρῆσθαι δυνατόν ἐστιν, ἵνα μὴ
νῦν ἐνδιατρίβωμεν.

Πλὴν ἐπεὶ παρέλκουσιν οὗτοι οἱ λόγοι ἐν οἷς τὴν
ὑποβάθραν τῶν συλλογισμῶν οἱ διαλεκτικοὶ τίθεν-
ται, ὅσον ἐπὶ τῇ παρολκῇ διατρέπεται πᾶσα ἡ
διαλεκτική, μὴ δυναμένων ἡμῶν διακρῖναι τοὺς
παρέλκοντας καὶ διὰ τοῦτο ἀσυνάκτους λόγους ἀπὸ
167 τῶν συνακτικῶν καλουμένων συλλογισμῶν. εἰ δὲ
οὐκ ἀρέσκει τισὶ λόγους μονολημμάτους εἶναι, οὐκ
εἰσὶν ἀξιοπιστότεροι Ἀντιπάτρου, ὃς οὐδὲ τοὺς
τοιούτους λόγους ἀποδοκιμάζει.

Διὰ ταῦτα μὲν οὖν ἀνεπίκριτός ἐστιν ὁ παρὰ τοῖς
διαλεκτικοῖς συνακτικὸς καλούμενος λόγος. ἀλλὰ
καὶ ὁ ἀληθὴς λόγος ἀνεύρετός ἐστι διά τε τὰ
προειρημένα καὶ ἐπεὶ πάντως ὀφείλει εἰς ἀληθὲς
λήγειν. τὸ γὰρ συμπέρασμα τὸ ἀληθὲς εἶναι λεγό-
168 μενον ἤτοι φαινόμενόν ἐστιν ἢ ἄδηλον. καὶ φαινόμενον μὲν οὐδαμῶς· οὐ γὰρ ἂν δέοιτο τοῦ διὰ τῶν
λημμάτων ἐκκαλύπτεσθαι δι᾽ ἑαυτοῦ προσπῖπτον
καὶ οὐχ ἧττον τῶν λημμάτων αὐτοῦ φαινόμενον.
εἰ δὲ ἄδηλον, ἐπεὶ περὶ τῶν ἀδήλων ἀνεπικρίτως
διαπεφώνηται, καθάπερ ἔμπροσθεν ὑπεμνήσαμεν,
διόπερ καὶ ἀκατάληπτά ἐστιν, ἀκατάληπτον ἔσται
καὶ τὸ συμπέρασμα τοῦ ἀληθοῦς εἶναι λεγομένου
λόγου. εἰ δὲ [καὶ] τοῦτο ἀκατάληπτόν ἐστιν, οὐ

---

[a] i.e. of the First Figure: the previous examples are cases of
Barbara and *Darii*, so " the others " would belong to
Celarent and *Ferio*. But Heintz's suggestion, τρόπων τῶν
(for πρώτων), " the other figures," may well be right.
[b] i.e. Stoics and Peripatetics, cf. § 146 supra.

animal " is sufficient, and the premiss " Every man is an animal " is redundant. And (not to dwell on the **166** matter now) in the case of the other primary *a* categorical arguments also it is possible to employ similar methods of reasoning.

Since, however, these arguments which the Dialecticians *b* lay down as the foundations of their syllogisms are redundant, by reason of this redundancy the whole of Dialectic is thus far overthrown, seeing that we cannot distinguish the redundant, and consequently inconclusive, arguments from what are called the conclusive syllogisms. But if some persons disapprove of arguments being of a " one-premiss form," **167** they deserve no more credence than does Antipater *c* who does not reject such arguments.

For these reasons, then, the argument named by the Dialecticians " conclusive " is not judged acceptable. But further, the " true " *d* argument is indiscoverable both for the foregoing reasons *e* and because it ought in all cases to end in truth. For the conclusion which is said to be true is either apparent or non-evident. And it is certainly not apparent ; **168** for it would not need to be disclosed by means of the premisses if it were perceptible of itself and no less apparent than its premisses. But if it is non-evident, then, since there is an unsettled dispute concerning things non-evident, as we mentioned above,*f* and they are in consequence non-apprehensible, the conclusion also of the argument said to be true will be nonapprehensible. And if this is non-apprehensible,

c A. of Tarsus was head of the Stoic School *circa* 150-30 B.C.; *cf. Adv. Log.* ii. 443 for Chrysippus on the " curtailed syllogism."

d *Cf.* § 143.

e See §§ 85-94 *supra*, and § 138.   *f* *Cf.* § 116.

γνωσόμεθα πότερον ἀληθές ἐστι τὸ συναγόμενον ἢ
ψεῦδος. ἀγνοήσομεν οὖν πότερον ἀληθής ἐστιν ὁ
λόγος ἢ ψευδής, καὶ ἀνεύρετος ἔσται ὁ ἀληθὴς
λόγος.

169 Ἵνα δὲ καὶ ταῦτα παρῶμεν, ὁ διὰ προδήλων
ἄδηλον συνάγων ἀνεύρετός ἐστιν. εἰ γὰρ ἔπεται
τῇ διὰ τῶν λημμάτων αὐτοῦ συμπλοκῇ ἡ ἐπιφορά,
τὸ δ᾽ ἑπόμενον καὶ τὸ λῆγον πρός τί ἐστι καὶ πρὸς
τὸ ἡγούμενον, τὰ δὲ πρός τι συγκαταλαμβάνεται
ἀλλήλοις, ὡς παρεστήσαμεν, εἰ μὲν ἄδηλόν ἐστι
τὸ συμπέρασμα, ἄδηλα ἔσται καὶ τὰ λήμματα, εἰ
δὲ πρόδηλά ἐστι τὰ λήμματα, πρόδηλον ἔσται καὶ
τὸ συμπέρασμα ἅτε συγκαταλαμβανόμενον αὐτοῖς
προδήλοις οὖσιν, ὡς μηκέτι ἐκ προδήλων ἄδηλον
170 συνάγεσθαι. διὰ δὲ ταῦτα οὐδὲ ἐκκαλύπτεται ὑπὸ
τῶν λημμάτων ἡ ἐπιφορά, ἤτοι ἄδηλος οὖσα καὶ
μὴ καταλαμβανομένη, ἢ πρόδηλος καὶ μὴ δεομένη
τοῦ ἐκκαλύψοντος. εἰ τοίνυν ἡ ἀπόδειξις λόγος
εἶναι λέγεται κατὰ συναγωγήν, τουτέστι συνακτι-
κῶς, διά τινων ὁμολογουμένως ἀληθῶν ἐπιφορὰν
ἐκκαλύπτων ἄδηλον, ὑπεμνήσαμεν δὲ ἡμεῖς ὅτι
οὔτε λόγος τις ἔστιν οὔτε συνακτικὸς οὔτε ἀληθὴς
οὔτε διά τινων προδήλων ἄδηλον συνάγων οὔτε
ἐκκαλυπτικὸς τοῦ συμπεράσματος, φανερόν ἐστιν
ὅτι ἀνυπόστατός ἐστιν ἡ ἀπόδειξις.

171 Καὶ κατ᾽ ἐκείνην δὲ τὴν ἐπιβολὴν ἀνύπαρκτον ἢ
καὶ ἀνεπινόητον εὑρήσομεν τὴν ἀπόδειξιν. ὁ γὰρ
λέγων εἶναι ἀπόδειξιν ἤτοι γενικὴν τίθησιν ἀπόδειξιν ἢ εἰδικήν τινα· ἀλλ᾽ οὔτε τὴν γενικὴν οὔτε
εἰδικὴν ἀπόδειξιν τιθέναι δυνατόν, ὡς ὑπομνήσο-

ᵃ Cf. §§ 117 ff., 125.
ᵇ Cf. §§ 135, 143 ff.   ᶜ Cf. Adv. Log. ii. 382 ff.
260

we shall not know whether the deduction is true or false. Thus we shall be in ignorance as to whether the argument is true or false, and the " true " argument will be indiscoverable.

But, to pass over these objections also, the argu- 169 ment which deduces what is non-evident by means of pre-evident premisses is indiscoverable. For if the inference follows from the combination of its premisses, and what follows and forms the consequent is relative and relative to the antecedent, and relatives are apprehended, as we have shown,[a] simultaneously,— then, if the conclusion is non-evident, the premisses also will be non-evident, while if the premisses are pre-evident the conclusion also will be pre-evident, as being apprehended along with the pre-evident premisses, so that no longer is there a deduction of what is non-evident from pre-evident premisses. And 170 for these reasons, neither is the inference revealed by the premisses, as it is either non-evident and not apprehended, or pre-evident and not in need of anything to reveal it. So that if proof is defined[b] as "an argument which by deduction, that is conclusively, reveals a non-evident inference by means of certain premisses agreed to be true," while we have shown that there exists no argument either conclusive or true or which deduces a non-evident conclusion by means of evident premisses or serves to reveal its conclusion,—then it is apparent that proof is without real existence.

That proof is unreal, or even inconceivable, we shall 171 discover also from the following line of attack.[c] He who asserts the existence of proof posits either a general or a particular proof ; but, as we shall suggest, it is not possible to posit either the general or the

μεν· παρὰ δὲ ταύτας ἄλλο τι νοεῖν οὐκ ἐνδέχεται·
οὐκ ἄρα δύναταί τις ὡς ὑπάρχουσαν τιθέναι τὴν
172 ἀπόδειξιν. ἡ μὲν οὖν γενικὴ ἀπόδειξις ἀνυπόστατός ἐστι διὰ τάδε. ἤτοι ἔχει λήμματά τινα
καί τινα ἐπιφορὰν ἢ οὐκ ἔχει. καὶ εἰ μὲν οὐκ ἔχει,
οὐδὲ ἀπόδειξίς ἐστίν· εἰ δὲ λήμματά τινα ἔχει καὶ
ἐπιφοράν τινα, ἐπεὶ πᾶν τὸ ἀποδεικνύμενον οὕτω
καὶ ἀποδεικνύον ἐπὶ μέρους ἐστίν, εἰδικὴ ἔσται
ἀπόδειξις· οὐκ ἄρα ἔστι τις γενικὴ ἀπόδειξις.
173 ἀλλ' οὐδὲ εἰδική. ἤτοι γὰρ τὸ ἐκ τῶν λημμάτων
καὶ τῆς ἐπιφορᾶς σύστημα ἀπόδειξιν ἐροῦσιν, ἢ
τὸ σύστημα τῶν λημμάτων μόνον· οὐθέτερον δὲ
τούτων ἐστὶν ἀπόδειξις, ὡς παραστήσω· οὐκ ἄρα
174 ἔστιν εἰδικὴ ἀπόδειξις. τὸ μὲν οὖν σύστημα τὸ
ἐκ τῶν λημμάτων καὶ τῆς ἐπιφορᾶς οὐκ ἔστιν
ἀπόδειξις πρῶτον μὲν ὅτι μέρος τι ἔχουσα ἄδηλον,
τουτέστι τὴν ἐπιφοράν, ἄδηλος ἔσται, ὅπερ ἄ-
τοπον· εἰ γὰρ ἄδηλός ἐστιν ἡ ἀπόδειξις, αὐτὴ
δεήσεται τοῦ ἀποδείξοντος αὐτὴν μᾶλλον ἢ
ἑτέρων ἔσται ἀποδεικτική.
175 Εἶτα καὶ ἐπεὶ πρός τί φασιν εἶναι τὴν ἀπόδειξιν
καὶ πρὸς τὴν ἐπιφοράν, τὰ δὲ πρός τι πρὸς ἑτέροις
νοεῖται, ὡς αὐτοί φασιν, ἕτερον εἶναι δεῖ τὸ ἀποδεικνύμενον τῆς ἀποδείξεως· εἰ οὖν τὸ συμπέρασμά
ἐστι τὸ ἀποδεικνύμενον, οὐ νοηθήσεται ἡ ἀπόδειξις σὺν τῷ συμπεράσματι. καὶ γὰρ ἤτοι συμ-
βάλλεταί τι πρὸς τὴν ἀπόδειξιν ἑαυτοῦ τὸ συμπέρασμα ἢ οὐδαμῶς· ἀλλ' εἰ μὲν συμβάλλεται,
ἑαυτοῦ ἔσται ἐκκαλυπτικόν, εἰ δὲ οὐ συμβάλλεται
ἀλλὰ παρέλκει, οὐδὲ μέρος τῆς ἀποδείξεως ἔσται,
262

particular proof; and besides these no other can be conceived; no one, therefore, can posit proof as really existing. Now the general proof is unreal for the 172 following reasons. It either has or has not certain premisses and a certain inference. And if it has them not, it is not even proof; while if it has premisses and an inference, then, since everything which proves or is proved in this way belongs to the class of " particulars," [a] proof will be particular; therefore no general proof exists. Nor yet any particular proof. For they 173 will describe as proof either the system made up of the premisses and the inference [b] or only the system of the premisses; but neither of these is proof, as I shall show; therefore particular proof does not exist. Now the system composed of the premisses and the 174 inference is not proof because, firstly, it contains a non-evident part—that is to say, the inference—and so will be non-evident, which is absurd; for if the proof is non-evident, instead of serving to prove other things it will itself be in need of something to prove it.

Moreover, since they assert that proof is a relative 175 thing and relative to the inference, and relatives, as they themselves affirm, are conceived in relation to other things, the thing proved must be other than the proof; if, then, the thing proved is the conclusion, the proof will not be conceived along with the conclusion. For the conclusion either contributes something to its own proof or does not do so; but if it contributes, it will serve to reveal itself, while if it does not contribute but is redundant it will not be even a part of the proof, since we shall declare the

---

[a] Cf. τὰ ἐπὶ μέρους, § 87 supra; "things of a partial character" as opposed to "wholes" or genera.

[b] Cf. § 135 supra.

ἐπεὶ κἀκείνην κατὰ παρολκὴν ἐροῦμεν εἶναι μοχ-
176 θηράν. ἀλλ' οὐδὲ τὸ σύστημα τῶν λημμάτων
μόνων ἀπόδειξις ἂν εἴη· τίς γὰρ ἂν εἴποι τὸ οὕτω
λεγόμενον " εἰ ἡμέρα ἔστι, φῶς ἔστιν· ἀλλὰ μὴν
ἡμέρα ἔστιν " ἢ λόγον εἶναι ἢ διάνοιαν ὅλως
ἀπαρτίζειν; οὐκ ἄρα οὐδὲ τὸ σύστημα τῶν λημμάτων μόνον ἀπόδειξίς ἐστιν. οὐδὲ ἡ εἰδικὴ ἄρα
ἀπόδειξις ὑπόστασιν ἔχει. εἰ δὲ μήτε ἡ εἰδικὴ
ἀπόδειξις ὑφέστηκε μήτε ἡ γενική, παρὰ δὲ ταύτας
οὐκ ἔστιν ἐννοεῖν ἀπόδειξιν, ἀνυπόστατός ἐστιν ἡ
ἀπόδειξις.

177 Ἔτι ἐκ τούτων τὸ ἀνυπόστατον τῆς ἀποδείξεως
ἔνεστιν ὑπομιμνήσκειν. εἰ γὰρ ἔστιν ἀπόδειξις,
ἤτοι φαινομένη φαινομένου ἐστὶν ἐκκαλυπτικὴ ἢ
ἄδηλος ἀδήλου ἢ ἄδηλος φαινομένου ἢ φαινομένη
ἀδήλου· οὐδενὸς δὲ τούτων ἐκκαλυπτικὴ δύναται
178 ἐπινοεῖσθαι· ἀνεπινόητος ἄρα ἐστί. εἰ μὲν γὰρ
φαινομένη φαινομένου ἐκκαλυπτική ἐστιν, ἔσται
τὸ ἐκκαλυπτόμενον ἅμα φαινόμενόν τε καὶ ἄδηλον,
φαινόμενον μὲν ἐπεὶ τοιοῦτον εἶναι ὑπετέθη, ἄδηλον
δὲ ἐπεὶ δεῖται τοῦ ἐκκαλύψοντος καὶ οὐκ ἐξ ἑαυτοῦ
ὑποπίπτει ἡμῖν σαφῶς. εἰ δὲ ἄδηλος ἀδήλου, αὐτὴ
δεήσεται τοῦ ἐκκαλύψοντος αὐτὴν καὶ οὐκ ἔσται
ἐκκαλυπτικὴ ἑτέρων, ὅπερ ἀφέστηκε τῆς ἐννοίας
179 τῆς ἀποδείξεως. διὰ δὲ ταῦτα οὐδὲ ἄδηλος προδήλου δύναται εἶναι ἀπόδειξις. ἀλλ' οὐδὲ πρόδηλος ἀδήλου· ἐπεὶ γὰρ πρός τι ἐστίν, τὰ δὲ πρός
τι ἀλλήλοις συγκαταλαμβάνεται, συγκαταλαμβανόμενον τῇ προδήλῳ ἀποδείξει τὸ ἀποδείκνυσθαι
λεγόμενον πρόδηλον ἔσται, ὡς περιτρέπεσθαι τὸν
λόγον καὶ μὴ εὑρίσκεσθαι πρόδηλον τὴν ἀδήλου ἀπο-

proof to be faulty by reason of redundance. Nor yet 176 will the system composed of the premisses by itself be proof ; for who would maintain that a statement in the form " If it is day, it is light ; but in fact it is day," either is an argument or completely expresses a piece of reasoning ? So then, neither does the system of the premisses alone constitute proof. There-fore the particular proof has no real existence either. But if neither the particular nor the general proof has real existence, and besides these one can conceive no other proof, then proof is without real existence.

And it is possible to show the unreality of proof 177 from these further considerations. If proof exists, either as apparent it serves to reveal what is apparent, or as non-evident what is non-evident, or as non-evident what is apparent, or as apparent what is non-evident ; but it cannot be conceived as serving to reveal any of these ; therefore it is inconceivable. For if it as apparent serves to reveal the apparent, 178 the thing revealed will be at once both apparent and non-evident—apparent because it was assumed to be such, and non-evident because it needs a revealer and is not clearly perceived by us of itself. And if as non-evident it reveals the non-evident, it will itself need something to reveal it and will not serve to reveal other things, which is foreign to the conception of proof. And for these reasons neither can there 179 be a non-evident proof of the pre-evident ; nor yet a pre-evident proof of the non-evident ; for since they are relatives, and relatives are apprehended together, that which is said to be proved, being apprehended together with its pre-evident proof, will be pre-evident, so that the argument is reversed and the proof probative of the non-evident is not found

265

δεικτικήν. εἰ οὖν μήτε φαινομένη φαινομένου ἐστὶν
ἡ ἀπόδειξις μήτε ἄδηλος ἀδήλου μήτε ἄδηλος προδήλου μήτε πρόδηλος ἀδήλου, παρὰ δὲ ταῦτα οὐδὲν
εἶναι λέγουσιν, λεκτέον μηδὲν εἶναι τὴν ἀπόδειξιν.

180 Πρὸς τούτοις κἀκεῖνο λεκτέον. διαπεφώνηται
περὶ τῆς ἀποδείξεως· οἱ μὲν γὰρ μηδὲ εἶναι λέγουσιν
αὐτήν, ὡς οἱ μηδὲν ὅλως εἶναι φάσκοντες, οἱ δὲ
εἶναι, ὡς οἱ πολλοὶ τῶν δογματικῶν· ἡμεῖς δὲ μὴ
181 μᾶλλον εἶναι αὐτὴν ἢ μὴ εἶναι φαμέν. καὶ ἄλλως
ἡ ἀπόδειξις δόγμα πάντως περιέχει, περὶ παντὸς
δὲ δόγματος διαπεφωνήκασιν, ὥστε περὶ πάσης
ἀποδείξεως ἀνάγκη εἶναι διαφωνίαν. εἰ γὰρ τῆς
ἀποδείξεως τοῦ εἶναι κενὸν λόγου ἕνεκεν ὁμολογου-
μένης καὶ τὸ εἶναι κενὸν συνομολογεῖται, δῆλον
ὅτι οἱ ἀμφισβητοῦντες περὶ τοῦ εἶναι κενὸν καὶ
περὶ τῆς ἀποδείξεως αὐτοῦ ἀμφισβητοῦσιν· καὶ
περὶ τῶν ἄλλων δογμάτων, ὧν εἰσὶν αἱ ἀποδείξεις,
ὁ αὐτὸς λόγος. πᾶσα τοίνυν ἀπόδειξις ἀμφισβητεῖται καὶ ἐν διαφωνίᾳ ἐστίν.

182 Ἐπεὶ οὖν ἄδηλός ἐστιν ἡ ἀπόδειξις διὰ τὴν διαφωνίαν τὴν περὶ αὐτῆς (τὰ γὰρ διάφωνα, καθὸ
διαπεφώνηται, ἄδηλά ἐστιν), οὐκ ἔστιν ἐξ ἑαυτῆς
πρόϋπτος ἀλλ' ἐξ ἀποδείξεως ὀφείλει ἡμῖν συνίστα-
σθαι. ἡ οὖν ἀπόδειξις δι' ἧς κατασκευάζεται ἡ
ἀπόδειξις, ὁμολογουμένη μὲν καὶ πρόϋπτος οὐκ
ἔσται (ζητοῦμεν γὰρ νῦν εἰ ἔστιν ἀπόδειξις ὅλως),
διαφωνουμένη δὲ καὶ ἄδηλος οὖσα δεήσεται ἀποδείξεως ἄλλης, κἀκείνη ἄλλης, καὶ μέχρις ἀπείρου.

---

[a] *i.e.* is real, as opposed to phenomenal ; so Xenophanes,
Xeniades, Gorgias, *cf.* § 18.

[b] For this Sceptic formula *cf.* i. 188.

[c] The Epicurean proof of Void ran thus : " If motion

to be pre-evident. If, therefore, proof is neither apparent of the apparent, nor non-evident of the non-evident, nor non-evident of the pre-evident, nor pre-evident of the non-evident, and besides these, as they say, there is no other alternative, then we must declare that proof is nothing.

Furthermore, there is this also to be said. Proof 180 is a matter of controversy ; for some declare that it does not even exist, as do those who assert that nothing at all exists,[a] but others, including the majority of the Dogmatists, that it does exist ; and we affirm that it is " no more "[b] existent than non-existent. And besides, proof always contains a 181 dogma, and they are in dispute about every dogma, so that there must necessarily be dispute about every proof. For if (for the sake of argument) when the proof for the existence of void is accepted the existence of void is likewise accepted,[c] it is plain that those who dispute the existence of void dispute its proof also ; and the same argument applies to all the other dogmas with which the proofs are concerned. Therefore every proof is questioned and is in dispute.

Since, then, proof is non-evident, owing to the 182 controversy which exists concerning it (for things controverted, in so far as controverted, are non-evident), its existence is not self-evident but needs to be established for us by proof. The proof, then, by which proof is established will not be evident and agreed (for we are now inquiring whether proof in general exists), and being thus in dispute and non-evident it will need another proof, and this again a third, and so on *ad infinitum.* But it is impossible to

exists, Void exists ; but motion does exist ; therefore Void exists." *Cf.* § 245, *Adv. Log.* ii. 329 ff.

ἀδύνατον δὲ ἄπειρα ἀποδεῖξαι· ἀδύνατον ἄρα παραστῆσαι ὅτι ἔστιν ἀπόδειξις.

183 'Αλλ' οὐδὲ διὰ σημείου δύναται ἐκκαλύπτεσθαι.
ζητουμένου γὰρ τοῦ εἰ ἔστι σημεῖον, καὶ ἀποδείξεως
τοῦ σημείου δεομένου πρὸς τὴν ἑαυτοῦ ὕπαρξιν, ὁ
δι' ἀλλήλων εὑρίσκεται τρόπος, τῆς μὲν ἀποδείξεως
σημείου δεομένης, τοῦ δὲ σημείου πάλιν ἀπο-
δείξεως· ὅπερ ἄτοπον. διὰ δὲ ταῦτα οὐδὲ ἐπικρῖναι δυνατόν ἐστι τὴν περὶ τῆς ἀποδείξεως
διαφωνίαν, ἐπεὶ χρῄζει μὲν κριτηρίου ἡ ἐπίκρισις,
ζητήσεως δὲ οὔσης περὶ τοῦ εἰ ἔστι κριτήριον, ὡς
παρεστήσαμεν, καὶ διὰ τοῦτο ἀποδείξεως τοῦ
κριτηρίου δεομένου τῆς δεικνυούσης ὅτι ἔστι τι
κριτήριον, ὁ διάλληλος τρόπος τῆς ἀπορίας εὑρί-
184 σκεται πάλιν. εἰ οὖν μήτε δι' ἀποδείξεως μήτε
διὰ σημείου μήτε διὰ κριτηρίου ἔστιν ὑπομνῆσαι
ὅτι ἔστιν ἀπόδειξις, ἀλλ' οὐδ' ἐξ ἑαυτῆς πρόδηλός
ἐστιν, ὡς παρεστήσαμεν, ἀκατάληπτον ἔσται εἰ
ἔστιν ἀπόδειξις. διὰ δὲ τοῦτο καὶ ἀνύπαρκτος
ἔσται ἡ ἀπόδειξις· νενόηται μὲν γὰρ σὺν τῷ ἀποδεικνύναι, ἀποδεικνύναι δὲ οὐκ ἂν δύναιτο μὴ
καταλαμβανομένη. διόπερ οὐδὲ ἀπόδειξις ἔσται.

185 Ταῦτα μὲν ὡς ἐν ὑποτυπώσει καὶ πρὸς τὴν ἀπόδειξιν ἀρκέσει λελέχθαι. οἱ δὲ δογματικοὶ τοὐναντίον κατασκευάζοντές φασιν ὅτι ἤτοι ἀποδεικτικοί
εἰσιν οἱ κατὰ τῆς ἀποδείξεως ἠρωτημένοι λόγοι ἢ
οὐκ ἀποδεικτικοί. καὶ εἰ μὲν οὐκ ἀποδεικτικοί,
οὐ δύνανται δεικνύναι ὅτι οὐκ ἔστιν ἡ ἀπόδειξις· εἰ
δὲ ἀποδεικτικοί εἰσιν, αὐτοὶ οὗτοι τὴν ὑπόστασιν

---

[a] Cf. §§ 104 ff., 121.
[b] Cf. §§ 48 ff. supra.   [c] Cf. §§ 144 supra.
268

prove an infinite series; therefore it is impossible to show that proof exists.

But neither can it be revealed by means of a sign. 183 For since it is a matter of inquiry whether sign exists,[a] and since the sign needs proof to ensure its reality, we find ourselves involved in circular reasoning—the proof requiring a sign, and the sign in turn a proof; which is absurd. And for these reasons neither is it possible to decide the controversy regarding proof, seeing that the decision requires a criterion, but—because it is a matter of inquiry, as we have shown,[b] whether a criterion exists, and consequently the criterion needs a proof showing the existence of a criterion—we are again involved in the perplexity of circular reasoning. If, then, neither 184 by proof nor by sign nor by criterion it is possible to show that proof exists, and it is not evident of itself either, as we have shown,[c] then it will be non-apprehensible whether proof exists. Consequently, proof will also be unreal; for it is conceived together with the act of proving, and were it not apprehended it would be unable to prove.[d] Wherefore proof will not exist.

Thus much it will be enough to say by way of 185 outline and in criticism of proof. The Dogmatists, however, maintaining the opposite view assert that the arguments propounded against proof are either probative or not probative; and if they are not probative, they are incapable of showing that proof does not exist; while if they are probative, they

[d] *i.e.* if "proof" is non-apprehensible it must also be unreal or non-existent, because non-apprehensible "proof" is incapable of "proving" anything, and "proof" apart from "proving" is inconceivable—the "conception" of the one necessarily implying the other.

186 τῆς ἀποδείξεως ἐκ περιτροπῆς εἰσάγουσιν. ὅθεν
καὶ τοιοῦτον συνερωτῶσι λόγον· "εἰ ἔστιν ἀπόδειξις,
ἔστιν ἀπόδειξις· εἰ οὐκ ἔστιν ἀπόδειξις, ἔστιν ἀπό-
δειξις· ἤτοι δὲ ἔστιν ἀπόδειξις ἢ οὐκ ἔστιν ἀπό-
δειξις· ἔστιν ἄρα ἀπόδειξις." ἀπὸ δὲ τῆς αὐτῆς
δυνάμεως καὶ τοῦτον ἐρωτῶσι τὸν λόγον· "τὸ τοῖς
ἀντικειμένοις ἑπόμενον οὐ μόνον ἀληθές ἐστιν ἀλλὰ
καὶ ἀναγκαῖον· ἀντίκειται δὲ ταῦτα ἀλλήλοις
'ἔστιν ἀπόδειξις—οὐκ ἔστιν ἀπόδειξις,' ὧν ἑκα-
τέρῳ ἀκολουθεῖ τὸ εἶναι ἀπόδειξιν· ἔστιν ἄρα
ἀπόδειξις."

187 Ἔνεστι μὲν οὖν πρὸς ταῦτα ἀντιλέγειν, οἷον
γοῦν, ἐπεὶ μὴ νομίζομέν τινα λόγον εἶναι ἀποδεικ-
τικόν, καὶ τοὺς κατὰ τῆς ἀποδείξεως λόγους οὐ
πάντως φαμὲν ἀποδεικτικοὺς εἶναι ἀλλὰ φαίνεσθαι
ἡμῖν πιθανούς· οἱ δὲ πιθανοὶ οὐκ ἐξ ἀνάγκης εἰσὶν
ἀποδεικτικοί. εἰ δὲ ἄρα καὶ ἀποδεικτικοί εἰσιν,
ὅπερ οὐ διαβεβαιούμεθα, πάντως καὶ ἀληθεῖς.
ἀληθεῖς δέ εἰσι λόγοι δι᾽ ἀληθῶν ἀληθὲς συνάγοντες·
οὐκοῦν ἀληθής ἐστιν αὐτῶν ἡ ἐπιφορά. ἦν δέ γε
αὕτη " οὐκ ἔστιν ἄρα ἀπόδειξις"· ἀληθὲς ἄρα ἔστι

188 τὸ " οὐκ ἔστιν ἀπόδειξις " ἐκ περιτροπῆς. δύνανται δὲ οἱ λόγοι καὶ καθάπερ τὰ καθαρτικὰ φάρ-
μακα ταῖς ἐν τῷ σώματι ὑποκειμέναις ὕλαις ἑαυτὰ
συνεξάγει, οὕτω καὶ αὐτοὶ τοῖς ἄλλοις λόγοις τοῖς
ἀποδεικτικοῖς εἶναι λεγομένοις καὶ ἑαυτοὺς συμ-
περιγράφειν. τοῦτο γὰρ οὐκ ἔστιν ἀπεμφαῖνον,
ἐπεὶ καὶ ἡ φωνὴ αὕτη ἡ " οὐδέν ἐστιν ἀληθές "

ᵃ Lit. " reversal " of the argument; *cf.* § 128, *Adv. Log.*
ii. 463.

themselves involve the reality of proof by self-refutation.[a] Hence also they propound an argument 186 in this form [b] : " If proof exists, proof exists ; if proof exists not, proof exists ; but proof either exists or exists not ; therefore proof exists." With the same intention they propound also this argument : " That which follows logically from contradictories is not only true but necessary ; ' proof exists ' and ' proof exists not ' are contradictories, and the existence of proof follows from each of them ; therefore proof exists."

Now to this we may reply, for instance, that, because 187 we do not believe that any argument is probative, we do not assert either that the arguments against proof are absolutely probative but that they appear to us plausible ; but those that are plausible are not necessarily probative. Yet if they actually are probative (which we do not positively affirm) they certainly are also true. And true arguments are those which deduce what is true by means of true premisses ; wherefore their inference is true. Now the inference was this—" therefore proof does not exist " ; therefore the statement " proof does not exist " is true by reversing the argument. And just 188 as purgative medicines expel themselves together with the substances already present in the body, so these arguments are capable of cancelling themselves along with the other arguments which are said to be probative.[c] Nor is this preposterous, since in fact

[b] *Cf.* § 131 for this hypothetical syllogism with double major premiss. Here, as there, the Dogmatists argue that the Sceptics' proof that " proof exists not " refutes itself, the very proof they employ being itself an " existent " proof.

[c] *Cf.* i. 206, *Adv. Log.* ii. 480.

οὐ μόνον τῶν ἄλλων ἕκαστον ἀναιρεῖ, ἀλλὰ καὶ ἑαυτὴν ἐκείνοις συμπεριτρέπει.

Ὅ τε λόγος οὗτος δύναται δείκνυσθαι ἀσύνακτος " εἰ ἔστιν ἀπόδειξις, ἔστιν ἀπόδειξις· εἰ οὐκ ἔστιν ἀπόδειξις, ἔστιν ἀπόδειξις· ἤτοι δὲ ἔστιν ἢ οὐκ ἔστιν· ἔστιν ἄρα," καὶ διὰ πλειόνων μέν, ὡς δὲ πρὸς τὸ παρὸν ἀρκούντως διὰ τοῦδε τοῦ ἐπιχειρή-
189 ματος. εἰ ὑγιές ἐστι τὸ συνημμένον τοῦτο " εἰ ἔστιν ἀπόδειξις, ἔστιν ἀπόδειξις," δεῖ τὸ ἀντικεί-μενον τοῦ ἐν αὐτῷ λήγοντος, τουτέστι τὸ " οὐκ ἔστιν ἀπόδειξις," μάχεσθαι τῷ " ἔστιν ἀπόδειξις"· τοῦτο γάρ ἐστι τοῦ συνημμένου τὸ ἡγούμενον. ἀδύνατον δέ ἐστι κατ' αὐτοὺς συνημμένον ὑγιὲς εἶναι ἐκ μαχομένων ἀξιωμάτων συνεστώς. τὸ μὲν γὰρ συνημμένον ἐπαγγέλλεται ὄντος τοῦ ἐν αὐτῷ ἡγουμένου εἶναι καὶ τὸ λῆγον, τὰ δὲ μαχόμενα τοὐναντίον, ὄντος τοῦ ἑτέρου αὐτῶν ὁποιουδήποτε ἀδύνατον εἶναι τὸ λοιπὸν ὑπάρχειν. ὄντος ἄρα ὑγιοῦς τοῦδε τοῦ συνημμένου " εἰ ἔστιν ἀπόδειξις, ἔστιν ἀπόδειξις " οὐ δύναται ὑγιὲς εἶναι τοῦτο τὸ συνημμένον " εἰ οὐκ ἔστιν ἀπόδειξις, ἔστιν ἀπό-
190 δειξις." πάλιν δ' αὖ συγχωρούντων ἡμῶν καθ' ὑπόθεσιν ὑγιὲς εἶναι τόδε τὸ συνημμένον " εἰ οὐκ ἔστιν ἀπόδειξις, ἔστιν ἀπόδειξις," δύναται συν-υπάρχειν τὸ " εἰ ἔστιν ἀπόδειξις" τῷ " οὐκ ἔστιν ἀπόδειξις." εἰ δὲ δύναται αὐτῷ συνυπάρχειν, οὐ μάχεται αὐτῷ. ἐν ἄρα τῷ " εἰ ἔστιν ἀπόδειξις, ἔστιν ἀπόδειξις " συνημμένῳ οὐ μάχεται τὸ ἀντι-κείμενον τοῦ ἐν αὐτῷ λήγοντος τῷ ἐν αὐτῷ ἡγουμένῳ, ὥστε οὐκ ἔσται ὑγιὲς πάλιν τοῦτο τὸ συνημμένον, ἐκείνου κατὰ συγχώρησιν ὡς ὑγιοῦς
191 τιθεμένου. μὴ μαχομένου δὲ τοῦ " οὐκ ἔστιν

the saying " nothing is true " not only refutes every other saying but also nullifies itself as well.

And as regards this argument—" If proof exists, proof exists ; if proof does not exist, proof exists ; but it either exists or exists not ; therefore it exists " —there are a number of ways by which it can be shown to be inconclusive, but for the moment the following method may suffice. If the hypothetical 188 premiss " If proof exists, proof exists " is valid, the contradictory of its consequent, namely " proof does not exist," must conflict with " proof exists," for this is the antecedent of the hypothetical premiss. But, according to them, it is impossible for a hypothetical premiss to be valid when composed of conflicting clauses. For the hypothetical premiss promises that when its antecedent is true its consequent is also true, whereas conflicting clauses contrariwise promise that if either one of them is true the other cannot possibly be true. If therefore the premiss " If proof exists, proof exists " is valid, the premiss " If proof exists not, proof exists " cannot be valid. And again, conversely, if we grant by way of 190 assumption that the premiss " If proof exists not, proof exists " is valid, then the clause " If proof exists " can co-exist with " proof exists not." But if it can co-exist with it, it is not in conflict with it. Therefore, in the premiss " If proof exists, proof exists," the contrary of its consequent is not in conflict with its antecedent, so that, conversely, this premiss will not be valid, as the former was posited, by agreement, as valid. And as the clause 191 " proof exists not " is not in conflict with " proof

ἀπόδειξις " τῷ " ἔστιν ἀπόδειξις " οὐδὲ τὸ διεζευγμένον ὑγιὲς ἔσται τὸ " ἤτοι ἔστιν ἀπόδειξις ἢ
οὐκ ἔστιν ἀπόδειξις"· τὸ γὰρ ὑγιὲς διεζευγμένον
ἐπαγγέλλεται ἓν τῶν ἐν αὐτῷ ὑγιὲς εἶναι, τὸ δὲ
λοιπὸν ἢ τὰ λοιπὰ ψεῦδος ἢ ψευδῆ μετὰ μάχης. ἢ
εἴπερ ὑγιές ἐστι τὸ διεζευγμένον, πάλιν φαῦλον
εὑρίσκεται τὸ " εἰ οὐκ ἔστιν ἀπόδειξις, ἔστιν
ἀπόδειξις " συνημμένον, ἐκ μαχομένων συνεστώς.
οὐκοῦν ἀσύμφωνά τέ ἐστι καὶ ἀλλήλων ἀναιρετικὰ
192 τὰ ἐν τῷ λόγῳ τῷ προειρημένῳ λήμματα· διόπερ
οὐκ ἔστιν ὑγιὴς ὁ λόγος. ἀλλ' οὐδὲ ὅτι ἀκολουθεῖ
τι τοῖς ἀντικειμένοις δύνανται δεικνύναι, μὴ ἔχοντες
κριτήριον ἀκολουθίας, ὡς ἐπελογισάμεθα.

Ταῦτα δὲ ἐκ περιουσίας λέγομεν. εἰ γὰρ πιθανοὶ
μέν εἰσιν οἱ ὑπὲρ τῆς ἀποδείξεως λόγοι (ἔστωσαν
γάρ), πιθαναὶ δὲ καὶ αἱ πρὸς τὴν ἀπόδειξιν λεγό-
μεναι ἐπιχειρήσεις, ἐπέχειν ἀνάγκη καὶ περὶ τῆς
ἀποδείξεως, μὴ μᾶλλον εἶναι ἀπόδειξιν ἢ μὴ εἶναι
λέγοντας.

ΙΔ'.—ΠΕΡΙ ΣΥΛΛΟΓΙΣΜΩΝ

193 Διὸ καὶ περὶ τῶν θρυλουμένων συλλογισμῶν ἴσως
περιττόν ἐστι διεξιέναι, τοῦτο μὲν συμπεριτρεπο-
μένων αὐτῶν τῇ ὑπάρξει τῆς ἀποδείξεως (δῆλον
γὰρ ὅτι ἐκείνης μὴ οὔσης οὐδὲ ἀποδεικτικὸς λόγος
χώραν ἔχει), τοῦτο δὲ καὶ δυνάμει διὰ τῶν ἔμπροσθεν ἡμῖν λελεγμένων ἀντειρηκότων ἡμῶν πρὸς
αὐτούς, ὅτε περὶ τῆς παρολκῆς διαλεγόμενοι μέθ-
οδόν τινα ἐλέγομεν δι' ἧς ἐνδέχεται δεικνύναι ὅτι

---

[a] See §§ 145 ff.
[b] Cf. §§ 159-162 against the Stoics, and 163-166 against
the Peripatetics.

exists," the disjunctive "Either proof exists or proof exists not" will not be valid; for the valid disjunctive promises that one of its clauses is valid, but the other or others false and contradictory. Or else, if the disjunctive be valid, the hypothetical premiss "If proof exists not, proof exists" is, in turn, found to be fallacious, as composed of conflicting clauses. So then the premisses in the foregoing argument are discordant and mutually destructive; wherefore the argument is not valid. And further, 192 they are unable even to show that anything follows logically from the contradictories, since, as we have argued,[a] they possess no criterion of logical consequence or deduction.

But this discussion is, in fact, superfluous. For if, on the one hand, the arguments in defence of proof are (let it be granted) plausible, while, on the other hand, the criticisms directed against proof are also plausible, then we must necessarily suspend judgement concerning proof also, and declare that proof is "no more" existent than non-existent.

Chapter XIV.—Concerning Syllogisms

So then it is also superfluous, perhaps, to discuss 193 in detail the much vaunted "syllogisms," since, for one thing, they are included in the refutation of the existence of "proof" (for it is plain that if this is non-existent there is no place either for probative argument), and for another, we have implicitly contradicted them in our previous statements, when in discussing redundancy[b] we mentioned a certain method by which it is possible to show that all the

πάντες οἱ ἀποδεικτικοὶ λόγοι τῶν τε στωικῶν καὶ
τῶν περιπατητικῶν ἀσύνακτοι τυγχάνουσιν ὄντες.

194 ἐξ ἐπιμέτρου δὲ οὐ χεῖρον ἴσως καὶ ἰδίᾳ περὶ αὐτῶν
διαλαβεῖν, ἐπεὶ μάλιστα ἐπ᾽ αὐτοῖς μέγα φρονοῦσιν.
πολλὰ μὲν οὖν ἔστι λέγειν τὸ ἀνυπόστατον αὐτῶν
ὑπομιμνήσκοντας· ὡς ἐν ὑποτυπώσει δὲ ἀρκεῖ τῇδε
τῇ μεθόδῳ χρῆσθαι κατὰ αὐτῶν. λέξω δὲ καὶ νῦν
περὶ τῶν ἀναποδείκτων· τούτων γὰρ ἀναιρουμένων
καὶ οἱ λοιποὶ σύμπαντες λόγοι διατρέπονται, τὴν
ἀπόδειξιν τοῦ συνάγειν ἀπ᾽ αὐτῶν ἔχοντες.

195 Ἡ πρότασις τοίνυν αὕτη " πᾶς ἄνθρωπος ζῷον "
ἐκ τῶν κατὰ μέρος ἐπαγωγικῶς βεβαιοῦται· ἐκ
γὰρ τοῦ Σωκράτην ἄνθρωπον ὄντα καὶ ζῷον εἶναι,
καὶ Πλάτωνα ὁμοίως καὶ Δίωνα καὶ ἕκαστον τῶν
κατὰ μέρος, δυνατὸν εἶναι δοκεῖ διαβεβαιοῦσθαι
καὶ ὅτι πᾶς ἄνθρωπος ζῷόν ἐστιν, ὡς εἰ κἂν ἕν
τι τῶν κατὰ μέρος ἐναντιούμενον φαίνοιτο τοῖς
ἄλλοις, οὐκ ἔστιν ὑγιὴς ἡ καθόλου πρότασις, οἷον
γοῦν, ἐπεὶ τὰ μὲν πλεῖστα τῶν ζῴων τὴν κάτω
γένυν κινεῖ, μόνος δὲ ὁ κροκόδειλος τὴν ἄνω, οὐκ
ἔστιν ἀληθὴς ἡ " πᾶν ζῷον τὴν κάτω γένυν κινεῖ "

196 πρότασις. ὅταν οὖν λέγωσι " πᾶς ἄνθρωπος ζῷον,
Σωκράτης δ᾽ ἄνθρωπος, Σωκράτης ἄρα ζῷον,"
ἐκ τῆς καθόλου προτάσεως τῆς " πᾶς ἄνθρωπος
ζῷον " τὴν κατὰ μέρος πρότασιν συνάγειν βουλόμενοι, τὴν " Σωκράτης ἄρα ζῷον," ἣ δὴ βεβαιω-
τικὴ τῆς καθολικῆς προτάσεώς ἐστι κατὰ τὸν
ἐπαγωγικὸν τρόπον, ὡς ὑπεμνήσαμεν, εἰς τὸν

ᵃ For the phrase ἐξ ἐπιμέτρου, "into the bargain," cf. § 47
supra.

probative arguments of the Stoics and the Peripatetics are really inconclusive. Yet perhaps it will not **194** be amiss to go further[a] and deal with them separately, especially since these thinkers pride themselves upon them. Now there is much that one can say by way of suggesting their unreality, but in an outline sketch it is sufficient to treat of them by the method which follows. And I will deal at present with the axiomatic[b] arguments ; for if these are destroyed all the rest of the arguments are overthrown as well, since it is from these that they derive the proof of their deductions.

Well then, the premiss " Every man is an animal " **195** is established by induction from the particular instances ; for from the fact that Socrates, who is a man, is also an animal, and Plato likewise, and Dion and each one of the particular instances,[c] they think it possible to assert that every man is an animal ; so that if even a single one of the particulars should apparently conflict with the rest the universal premiss is not valid ; thus, for example, when most animals move the lower jaw, and only the crocodile the upper,[d] the premiss " Every animal moves the lower jaw " is not true. So whenever they argue " Every man is an **196** animal, and Socrates is a man, therefore Socrates is an animal," proposing to deduce from the universal proposition " Every man is an animal " the particular proposition " Socrates therefore is an animal," which in fact goes (as we have mentioned) to establish by way of induction the universal proposition, they fall into the

---

[b] Or " non-demonstrable," including here categorical syllogisms as well as those mentioned in § 157 *supra*.

[c] *Cf.* Aristot. *Anal. pr.* ii. 23 on logical " induction."

[d] *Cf.* Hdt. ii. 68 ; Aristot. *Hist. An.* iii. 7.

διάλληλον ἐμπίπτουσι λόγον, τὴν μὲν καθολικὴν
πρότασιν δι' ἑκάστης τῶν κατὰ μέρος ⟨ἐπαγωγικῶς
βεβαιοῦντες, τὴν δὲ κατὰ μέρος⟩[1] ἐκ τῆς καθολικῆς
197 συλλογιστικῶς. παραπλησίως δὲ καὶ ἐπὶ τοῦ
τοιούτου λόγου " Σωκράτης ἄνθρωπος, οὐδεὶς δὲ
ἄνθρωπος τετράπους, Σωκράτης ἄρα οὐκ ἔστι
τετράπους " τὴν μὲν " οὐδεὶς ἄνθρωπος τετράπους " πρότασιν ἐκ τῶν κατὰ μέρος ἐπαγωγικῶς
βουλόμενοι βεβαιοῦν, ἑκάστην δὲ τῶν κατὰ μέρος
ἐκ τῆς " οὐδεὶς ἄνθρωπος τετράπους " συλλογί-
ζεσθαι θέλοντες, τῇ κατὰ τὸν διάλληλον ἀπορίᾳ
περιπίπτουσιν.

198 Ὁμοίως δὲ ἐφοδευτέον καὶ τοὺς λοιποὺς τῶν
παρὰ τοῖς περιπατητικοῖς λεγομένων ἀναποδείκτων. ἀλλὰ καὶ τοὺς τοιούτους " εἰ ἡμέρα ἔστι,
φῶς ἔστι "· τό τε γὰρ " εἰ ἡμέρα ἔστι, φῶς ἔστι "
συνακτικόν ἐστιν, ὥς φασί, τοῦ " φῶς ἔστι," τό
τε " φῶς ἔστι " μετὰ τοῦ " ἡμέρα ἔστι " βεβαιωτι-
κόν ἐστι τοῦ " εἰ ἡμέρα ἔστι, φῶς ἔστιν "· οὐ γὰρ
ἂν ὑγιὲς ἐνομίσθη τὸ προειρημένον συνημμένον
εἶναι, εἰ μὴ πρότερον τεθεώρητο συνυπάρχον ἀεὶ
199 τὸ " φῶς ἔστι " τῷ " ἡμέρα ἔστιν." εἰ οὖν δεῖ
προκατειληφέναι ὅτι ἡμέρας οὔσης πάντως ἔστι
καὶ φῶς εἰς τὸ συνθεῖναι τὸ " εἰ ἡμέρα ἔστι, φῶς
ἔστι " συνημμένον, διὰ δὲ τοῦ συνημμένου τούτου
συνάγεται τὸ [ὅτι] ἡμέρας οὔσης φῶς εἶναι, τὴν
μὲν συνύπαρξιν τοῦ ἡμέραν εἶναι καὶ τοῦ φῶς εἶναι
συνάγοντος τοῦ " εἰ ἡμέρα ἔστι, φῶς ἔστι " συνημμένου ὅσον ἐπὶ τῷ προκειμένῳ ἀναποδείκτῳ, τὸ
δὲ συνημμένον τῆς συνυπάρξεως τῶν προειρημένων

---

[1] ⟨ἐπαγωγικῶς βεβαιοῦντες, τὴν δὲ κατὰ μέρος⟩ supplevi:
lacunam indic. Bekk.

error of circular reasoning, since they are establishing the universal proposition inductively by means of each of the particulars and deducing the particular proposition from the universal syllogistically. So likewise in 197 the case of such an argument as "Socrates is a man, but no man is four-footed, therefore Socrates is not four-footed," by proposing to establish the premiss " No man is four-footed " by induction from the particular instances while wishing to deduce each several particular from the premiss " No man is four-footed," they become involved in the perplexity of the circular fallacy.

And a similar criticism may be passed upon the 198 rest of the " axiomatic " arguments, as they are called by the Peripatetics ; and also upon arguments in the form " If it is day, it is light." For the proposition " If it is day, it is light " is capable, they say, of proving that " it is light," and the clause " it is light " in conjunction with " it is day " serves to establish the proposition " If it is day, it is light." For the hypothetical premiss stated above would not have been considered valid unless the constant co-existence of "it is light" with "it is day" had already been observed. If, then, one has to apprehend 199 beforehand that when there is day there certainly is light also, in order to construct the hypothetical premiss " If it is day, it is light," while by means of this premiss we deduce that when it is day it is light, the co-existence of the being of day and of night being proved (so far as depends on the axiomatic argument before us) by the premiss " If it is day, it is light," and that premiss in turn being established by the co-existence of the facts aforesaid,

βεβαιούσης, κἀνταῦθα ὁ διάλληλος τρόπος τῆς
ἀπορίας ἀνατρέπει τὴν ὑπόστασιν τοῦ λόγου.

200 Ὁμοίως δὲ καὶ ἐπὶ τοῦ τοιούτου λόγου " εἰ
ἡμέρα ἔστι, φῶς ἔστιν· οὐχὶ δὲ φῶς ἔστιν· οὐκ ἄρα
ἡμέρα ἔστιν." ἐκ μὲν γὰρ τοῦ μὴ ἄνευ φωτὸς
ἡμέραν θεωρεῖσθαι ὑγιὲς ἂν εἶναι νομισθείη τὸ " εἰ
ἡμέρα ἔστι, φῶς ἔστι " συνημμένον, ὡς εἴγε καθ'
ὑπόθεσιν ἡμέρα μὲν φανείη ποτὲ φῶς δὲ μή,
ψεῦδος ἂν λεχθείη τὸ συνημμένον εἶναι· ὅσον δὲ
ἐπὶ τῷ προειρημένῳ ἀναποδείκτῳ τὸ μὴ εἶναι
ἡμέραν φωτὸς μὴ ὄντος διὰ τοῦ " εἰ ἡμέρα ἔστι,
φῶς ἔστι " συνάγεται, ὥστε ἑκάτερον αὐτῶν πρὸς
τὴν ἑαυτοῦ βεβαίωσιν χρήζειν τοῦ τὸ ἕτερον βε-
βαίως εἰλῆφθαι, ἵνα δι' αὐτοῦ πιστὸν γένηται κατὰ
201 τὸν διάλληλον τρόπον. ἀλλὰ καὶ ἐκ τοῦ μὴ δύνασθαι ἀλλήλοις συνυπάρχειν τινά, οἷον ἡμέραν, εἰ
τύχοι, καὶ νύκτα, τό τε ἀποφατικὸν τῆς συμπλοκῆς,
τὸ " οὐχ ἡμέρα ἔστι καὶ νὺξ ἔστι, καὶ τὸ διεζευγμένον, τὸ " ἤτοι ἡμέρα ἔστιν ἢ νὺξ ἔστιν,"
ὑγιῆ νομίζοιτο ἂν εἶναι. ἀλλὰ τὸ μὴ συνυπάρχειν
αὐτὰ βεβαιοῦσθαι νομίζουσι διά τε τοῦ ἀποφατικοῦ
τῆς συμπλοκῆς καὶ τοῦ διεζευγμένου, λέγοντες
" οὐχὶ ἡμέρα ἔστι καὶ νὺξ ἔστιν· ἀλλὰ μὴν νὺξ
ἔστιν· οὐκ ἄρα ἡμέρα ἔστιν." " ἤτοι ἡμέρα ἔστιν
ἢ νὺξ ἔστιν· ἀλλὰ μὴν νὺξ ἔστιν· οὐκ ἄρα ἡμέρα
ἔστιν," ἢ " οὐχὶ δὲ νὺξ ἔστιν· ἡμέρα ἄρα ἔστιν."
202 ὅθεν ἡμεῖς πάλιν ἐπιλογιζόμεθα ὅτι εἰ μὲν πρὸς
τὴν βεβαίωσιν τοῦ διεζευγμένου καὶ τοῦ τῆς συμπλοκῆς ἀποφατικοῦ χρήζομεν τοῦ προκατειληφέναι
ὅτι τὰ ἐν αὐτοῖς περιεχόμενα ἀξιώματά ἐστιν
ἀσυνύπαρκτα, τὸ δὲ ἀσυνύπαρκτα ταῦτα εἶναι συν-

—in this case also the fallacy of circular reasoning overthrows the substance of the argument.

So likewise with an argument in the form " If it is 200 day, it is light ; but it is not light ; therefore it is not day." For from the fact that we do not observe day without light the hypothetical premiss " If it is day, it is light " might be considered to be valid ; just as if, should day, let us suppose, at some time appear, without the appearance of light, the premiss would be said to be false ; but, so far as concerns the axiomatic argument aforesaid, the non-existence of day when light is non-existent is proved by the premiss " If it is day, it is light," so that each of these statements needs for its confirmation the secure grasp of the other in order thereby to become credible by means of circular reasoning. Moreover, from the fact that some things are 201 unable to co-exist—take, for instance, if you like, day and night—both the conjunctive [a] negation " Not day exists and night exists " and the disjunctive " Either day exists or night exists " might be considered to be valid. But they consider that their non-co-existence is established both by the negative of the conjunctive and by the disjunctive, arguing " Not day exists and night exists ; but in fact night exists ; day therefore exists not " ; and " Either it is day or it is night ; but in fact it is night ; therefore it is not day," or " it is not night, therefore it is day." Whence we argue again 202 that if for establishing the disjunctive proposition and the negative of the conjunctive we require to apprehend beforehand the fact that the judgements they contain are incapable of co-existence, while they believe that they are deducing this incapacity for

[a] For the " conjunctive " or " coupled " premiss see § 158, note.

ἄγειν δοκοῦσι διά τε τοῦ διεζευγμένου καὶ τοῦ τῆς
συμπλοκῆς ἀποφατικοῦ, ὁ δι᾽ ἀλλήλων εἰσάγεται
τρόπος, μὴ δυναμένων ἡμῶν μήτε τοῖς προειρημένοις τροπικοῖς πιστεύειν ἄνευ τοῦ τὸ ἀσυνύπαρκτον τῶν ἐν αὐτοῖς περιεχομένων ἀξιωμάτων
καταλαβεῖν, μήτε τὸ ἀσυνύπαρκτον αὐτῶν διαβεβαιοῦσθαι πρὸ τῆς τῶν συλλογισμῶν διὰ τῶν
203 τροπικῶν συνερωτήσεως. διόπερ οὐκ ἔχοντες πόθεν
ἀρξόμεθα τῆς πίστεως διὰ τὸ παλίνδρομον, λέξομεν
μήτε τὸν τρίτον μήτε τὸν τέταρτον μήτε τὸν
πέμπτον τῶν ἀναποδείκτων ὅσον ἐπὶ τούτοις
ὑπόστασιν ἔχειν.

Τοσαῦτα μὲν καὶ περὶ συλλογισμῶν ἐπὶ τοῦ
παρόντος ἀρκέσει λελέχθαι.

ΙΕ΄.—ΠΕΡΙ ΕΠΑΓΩΓΗΣ

204 Εὐπαραίτητον δὲ εἶναι νομίζω καὶ τὸν περὶ
ἐπαγωγῆς τρόπον. ἐπεὶ γὰρ ἀπὸ τῶν κατὰ μέρος
πιστοῦσθαι βούλονται δι᾽ αὐτῆς τὸ καθόλου, ἤτοι
πάντα ἐπιόντες τὰ κατὰ μέρος τοῦτο ποιήσουσιν
ἢ τινά. ἀλλ᾽ εἰ μὲν τινά, ἀβέβαιος ἔσται ἡ ἐπ-
αγωγή, ἐνδεχομένου τοῦ ἐναντιοῦσθαι τῷ καθόλου
τινὰ τῶν παραλειπομένων κατὰ μέρος ἐν τῇ ἐπ-
αγωγῇ· εἰ δὲ πάντα, ἀδύνατα μοχθήσουσιν, ἀπείρων
ὄντων τῶν κατὰ μέρος καὶ ἀπεριορίστων. ὥσθ᾽
οὕτως ἑκατέρωθεν, οἶμαι, συμβαίνει σαλεύεσθαι
τὴν ἐπαγωγήν.

co-existence by means of both the disjunctive and the negative conjunctive, we involve ourselves in circular reasoning, seeing that we are unable either to give credence to the aforesaid premisses without having apprehended the incapacity for co-existence of the judgements they contain, or to affirm positively that incapacity before concluding the syllogisms based on these premisses. Consequently, 203 as we possess no principle on which to ground belief owing to the circular style of the argument, we shall declare that, so far as depends on these statements, neither the third nor the fourth nor the fifth of the " axiomatic " syllogisms [a] possesses valid substance.

For the present, then, it will suffice to have said thus much concerning syllogisms.

CHAPTER XV.—CONCERNING INDUCTION

It is also easy, I consider, to set aside the method 204 of induction. For, when they propose to establish the universal from the particulars by means of induction, they will effect this by a review either of all or of some of the particular instances. But if they review some, the induction will be insecure, since some of the particulars omitted in the induction may contravene the universal; while if they are to review all, they will be toiling at the impossible, since the particulars are infinite and indefinite. Thus on both grounds, as I think, the consequence is that induction is invalidated.

[a] For the " five non-demonstrable (or axiomatic) syllogisms " see §§ 157-158 *supra.*

SEXTUS EMPIRICUS

205 Ἀλλὰ καὶ ἐπὶ τῇ περὶ ὅρων δὴ τεχνολογίᾳ μέγα
φρονοῦσιν οἱ δογματικοί, ἣν τῷ λογικῷ μέρει τῆς
καλουμένης φιλοσοφίας ἐγκαταλέγουσιν. φέρε οὖν
καὶ περὶ ὅρων ὀλίγα ἐπὶ τοῦ παρόντος εἴπωμεν.

Πρὸς πολλὰ τοίνυν χρησιμεύειν τοὺς ὅρους τῶν
δογματικῶν δοκούντων, δύο τὰ ἀνωτάτω κεφάλαια
⟨ἃ⟩[1] περιληπτικὰ πάσης [ἧς][2] λέγουσιν ἀναγ-
206 καιότητος αὐτῶν ἴσως εὑρήσεις· ἢ γὰρ ὡς πρὸς
κατάληψιν ἢ ὡς πρὸς διδασκαλίαν ἐν πᾶσι παρα-
δεικνύουσι τοὺς ὅρους ἀναγκαίους. ἐὰν οὖν ὑπομνήσωμεν ὅτι πρὸς οὐδέτερον τούτων χρησιμεύουσι,
περιτρέψομεν, οἶμαι, πᾶσαν τὴν γεγενημένην περὶ
αὐτῶν παρὰ τοῖς δογματικοῖς ματαιοπονίαν.

207 Εὐθέως οὖν, εἰ ὁ μὲν ἀγνοῶν τὸ ὁριστὸν οὐχ
οἷός τέ ἐστι τὸ μὴ γινωσκόμενον αὐτῷ ὁρίσασθαι,
ὁ δὲ γινώσκων, εἶθ' ὁριζόμενος οὐκ ἐκ τοῦ ὅρου
τὸ ὁριστὸν κατείληφεν ἀλλ' ἐπὶ προκατειλημμένῳ
τούτῳ τὸν ὅρον ἐπισυντέθεικεν, πρὸς κατάληψιν
τῶν πραγμάτων ὁ ὅρος οὐκ ἔστιν ἀναγκαῖος. καὶ
γὰρ ἐπεὶ πάντα μὲν ὁρίζεσθαι θέλοντες καθάπαξ
οὐδὲν ὁριζόμεθα διὰ τὴν εἰς ἄπειρον ἔκπτωσιν,
τινὰ δὲ καταλαμβάνεσθαι καὶ δίχα τῶν ὅρων ὁμο-
λογοῦντες οὐκ ἀναγκαίους πρὸς κατάληψιν τοὺς
ὅρους ἀποφαίνομεν, καθ' ὃν τρόπον τὰ μὴ ὁρισθέντα
κατελήφθη δυναμένων ἡμῶν πάντα χωρὶς τῶν
208 ὅρων καταλαμβάνειν, ἢ καθάπαξ οὐδὲν ὁρισόμεθα
[διὰ τὴν εἰς ἄπειρον ἔκπτωσιν] ἢ οὐκ ἀναγκαίους
τοὺς ὅρους ἀποφανοῦμεν.

---

[1] ⟨ἃ⟩ add. T. [2] [ἧς] om. mss.

[a] Cf. § 4 supra.

CHAPTER XVI.—CONCERNING DEFINITIONS

Further, the Dogmatists take great pride in their 205 systematic treatment of definitions, which they include in the logical division of their Philosophical System, as they call it. So come and let us now make a few observations on definitions.

Now while the Dogmatists hold that definitions have many uses, you will probably find that these fall under two main heads which, as they say, include all their necessary uses ; for, as they explain, definitions 206 are necessary in all cases either for apprehension *a* or for instruction. If, then, we shall show that they are of use for neither of these purposes, we shall, I think, bring to naught all the labour so vainly spent on them by the Dogmatists.

So then, without preliminary, if, on the one hand, 207 the man who knows not the object of definition is unable to define the object unknown to him, while, on the other hand, the man who knows and proceeds to define has not apprehended the object from its definition but has put together his definition to fit the object already apprehended, then the definition is not necessary for the apprehension of objects. And since, if we propose to define absolutely all things, we shall define nothing, because of the regress *ad infinitum* ; while if we allow that some things are apprehended even without definitions, we are declaring that definitions are not necessary for apprehension, seeing that we are able to apprehend all things apart from definitions in the same way as the undefined objects were apprehended,—then we shall 208 either define absolutely nothing or we shall declare that definitions are not necessary.

Διὰ δὲ ταῦτα οὐδὲ πρὸς διδασκαλίαν αὐτοὺς
εὕροιμεν ἂν ἀναγκαίους· ὡς γὰρ ὁ πρῶτος τὸ
πρᾶγμα γνοὺς ἔγνω τοῦτο χωρὶς ὅρου, κατὰ τὸ
παραπλήσιον καὶ ὁ διδασκόμενος αὐτὸ δύναται
209 χωρὶς ὅρου διδαχθῆναι. ἔτι ἀπὸ τῶν ὁριστῶν
ἐπικρίνουσι τοὺς ὅρους, καί φασι μοχθηροὺς ὅρους
εἶναι τοὺς περιέχοντάς τι τῶν μὴ προσόντων τοῖς
ὁριστοῖς, ἤτοι πᾶσιν ἢ τισίν. διόπερ ὅταν εἴπῃ
τις τὸν ἄνθρωπον εἶναι ζῷον λογικὸν ἀθάνατον ἢ
ζῷον λογικὸν θνητὸν γραμματικόν, ὅπου μὲν μηδενὸς ὄντος ἀνθρώπου ἀθανάτου, ὅπου δὲ τινῶν
μὴ γραμματικῶν ὄντων, φασὶ μοχθηρὸν εἶναι τὸν
210 ὅρον. τάχα μὲν καὶ ἀνεπίκριτοί εἰσιν οἱ ὅροι διὰ
τὴν ἀπειρίαν τῶν κατὰ μέρος, ἐξ ὧν ἐπικρίνεσθαι
ὀφείλουσιν· εἶτα οὐκ ἂν καταληπτικοί τε καὶ δι-
δακτικοὶ τούτων εἶεν ἐξ ὧν ἐπικρίνονται δηλονότι
προεπεγνωσμένων, εἴγε ἄρα, καὶ προκατειλημμέ-
νων.

Πῶς δὲ οὐκ ἂν εἴη γελοῖον τὸ λέγειν ὡς οἱ ὅροι
χρησιμεύουσι πρὸς κατάληψιν ἢ διδασκαλίαν ἢ
σαφήνειαν ὅλως, ἀσάφειαν ἡμῖν ἐπεισκυκλοῦντες
211 τοσαύτην; οἷον γοῦν, ἵνα τι καὶ παίξωμεν, εἴ τις
παρά του βουλόμενος πυθέσθαι εἰ ἀπήντηται αὐτῷ
ἄνθρωπος ἐπὶ ἵππου ὀχούμενος καὶ κύνα ἐφελκό-
μενος, τὴν ἐρώτησιν οὕτω ποιήσαιτο " ὦ ζῷον
λογικὸν θνητόν, νοῦ καὶ ἐπιστήμης δεκτικόν,
ἀπήντητό σοι ζῷον γελαστικὸν πλατυώνυχον,
ἐπιστήμης πολιτικῆς δεκτικόν, ζῴῳ θνητῷ χρε-
μετιστικῷ τὰ σφαιρώματα ἐφηδρακός, ἐφ-
ελκόμενον ζῷον τετράπουν ὑλακτικόν;" πῶς οὐκ
ἂν εἴη καταγέλαστος, εἰς ἀφασίαν οὕτω γνωρίμου

---

^a Cf. §§ 26, 28 for this definition of Man.

And for these reasons they are not necessary for instruction either, as we shall discover. For just as the man who first perceived the object perceived it apart from definition, so likewise the man who receives instruction about it can be instructed without definition. Moreover, they judge the definitions by 209 the objects defined and declare those definitions to be faulty which include any attributes not belonging either to all or to some of the objects defined. Hence, whenever one states that man is " a rational immortal animal " or " a rational mortal literary animal," whereas no man is immortal, and some are not literary, such a definition they say is faulty. And it may be 210 also that the definitions do not admit of judgement owing to the infinity of the particulars by which they ought to be judged ; and consequently they will not convey apprehension and instruction regarding the objects whereby they are judged, which evidently have been known beforehand, if at all, and apprehended beforehand.

And how could it be other than absurd to assert that definitions are of use for apprehension or instruction or elucidation of any kind, when they involve us in such a fog of uncertainty ? Thus, for instance, to take 211 a ridiculous case, suppose that one wished to ask someone whether he had met a man riding a horse and leading a dog and put the question in this form— " O rational mortal animal, receptive of intelligence and science, have you met with an animal capable of laughter, with broad nails and receptive of political science,^{a} with his (posterior) hemispheres seated on a mortal animal capable of neighing, and leading a four-footed animal capable of barking ? "—how would one be otherwise than ridiculous, in thus reducing the

πράγματος ἐμβαλὼν τὸν ἄνθρωπον διὰ τοὺς ὅρους;

Οὐκοῦν ἄχρηστον εἶναι τὸν ὅρον ὅσον ἐπὶ τούτοις
212 λεκτέον, εἴτ' οὖν λόγος εἶναι λέγοιτο διὰ βραχείας ὑπομνήσεως εἰς ἔννοιαν ἡμᾶς ἄγων τῶν ὑποτεταγμένων ταῖς φωναῖς πραγμάτων, ὡς δῆλόν γε (οὐ γάρ;) ἐκ τῶν μικρῷ πρόσθεν ἡμῖν εἰρημένων, εἴτε λόγος ὁ τὸ τί ἦν εἶναι δηλῶν, εἴτε ὃ βούλεταί τις. καὶ γὰρ τί ἐστιν ὁ ὅρος βουλόμενοι παριστᾶν εἰς ἀνήνυτον ἐμπίπτουσι διαφωνίαν, ἣν διὰ τὴν προαίρεσιν τῆς γραφῆς παρίημι νῦν, εἰ καὶ δοκεῖ διατρέπειν τοὺς ὅρους.

Τοσαῦτα μὲν καὶ περὶ ὅρων ἀπόχρη μοι νῦν λελέχθαι.

ΙΖ'.—ΠΕΡΙ ΔΙΑΙΡΕΣΕΩΣ

213 Ἐπεὶ δέ τινες τῶν δογματικῶν τὴν διαλεκτικὴν εἶναί φασιν ἐπιστήμην συλλογιστικὴν ἐπαγωγικὴν ὁριστικὴν διαιρετικήν, διελέχθημεν δὲ ἡμεῖς ἤδη μετὰ τοὺς περὶ τοῦ κριτηρίου καὶ τοῦ σημείου καὶ τῆς ἀποδείξεως λόγους περί τε συλλογισμῶν καὶ ἐπαγωγῆς καὶ περὶ ὅρων, οὐκ ἄτοπον ἡγούμεθα εἶναι καὶ περὶ διαιρέσεως βραχέα διαλαβεῖν. γίνεσθαι τοίνυν τὴν διαίρεσίν φασι τετραχῶς· ἢ γὰρ ὄνομα εἰς σημαινόμενα διαιρεῖσθαι ἢ ὅλον εἰς μέρη ἢ γένος εἰς εἴδη ἢ εἶδος εἰς τὰ καθ' ἕκαστον.

---

[a] The Aristotelian definition of " Definition," the previous definition being probably Stoic.

[b] The definition of " Dialectic," and also the four kinds of " Division," here mentioned are given by Alcinous, a second-century (A.D.) Eclectic. As used by Plato and Aristotle, " Division " includes only the 3rd and 4th kinds (*i.e.* " logical " as distinguished from grammatical (§ 214) and

man to speechlessness concerning so familiar an object because of one's definitions ?

So then we must declare that, so far as we may judge by this, the definition is useless, whether it be **212** described as " a statement which by a brief reminder brings us to a conception of the objects which underlie the terms,"—as is plain (is it not ?) from what we have said just a moment ago,—or as " a statement declaratory of the essence," [a] or what you like. For in fact, in their desire to propound a definition of the definition they plunge into an endless controversy which I now pass over, because of the plan of my present treatise, although it seems to overthrow definitions.

So what I have said about definitions is enough for the present.

Chapter XVII.—Concerning Division

Inasmuch as some of the Dogmatists [b] affirm that 213 " Dialectic " is " a science dealing with syllogism, induction, definition and division," and, after our arguments concerning the criterion and the sign and proof, we have already discussed syllogisms and induction as well as definitions, we deem that it will not be amiss to treat shortly of " division " also. Division then, as they allege, is effected in four ways : either a name, or word, is divided into its significations, or a whole into parts, or a genus into species, or a

arithmetical (§§ 215-218) division). Logical " division " is the process of defining a class-name by splitting it up into its component parts—the " genus " into " species," the " species " into particulars. By it we enumerate the classes of objects denoted by the name or term which is " divided."

ὅτι δὲ οὐδενὸς τούτων ἔστιν ἐπιστήμη διαιρετική, ῥᾴδιον ἴσως ἐπελθεῖν.

ΙΗ'.—ΠΕΡΙ ΤΗΣ ΟΝΟΜΑΤΟΣ ΕΙΣ ΣΗΜΑΙΝΟΜΕΝΑ ΔΙΑΙΡΕΣΕΩΣ

214 Εὐθέως οὖν τὰς ἐπιστήμας τῶν φύσει φασὶν εἶναι, τῶν θέσει δὲ οὐδαμῶς. καὶ εἰκότως· ἡ μὲν γὰρ ἐπιστήμη βέβαιόν τι καὶ ἀμετάπτωτον πρᾶγμα εἶναι θέλει, τὰ δὲ θέσει ῥᾳδίαν ἔχει καὶ εὐμετάπτωτον τὴν μεταβολήν, ταῖς ἐναλλαγαῖς τῶν θέσεων, αἵ εἰσιν ἐφ' ἡμῖν, ἑτεροιούμενα. ἐπεὶ οὖν τὰ ὀνόματα θέσει σημαίνει καὶ οὐ φύσει (πάντες γὰρ ἂν συνίεσαν πάντα τὰ ὑπὸ τῶν φωνῶν σημαινόμενα, ὁμοίως Ἕλληνές τε καὶ βάρβαροι, πρὸς τῷ καὶ ἐφ' ἡμῖν εἶναι τὰ σημαινόμενα οἷς ἂν βουλώμεθα ὀνόμασιν ἑτέροις ἀεὶ δηλοῦν τε καὶ σημαίνειν), πῶς ἂν δυνατὸν εἴη διαιρετικὴν ὀνόματος εἰς σημαινόμενα ἐπιστήμην εἶναι; ἢ πῶς ἐπιστήμη σημαινόντων τε καὶ σημαινομένων, ὡς οἴονταί τινες, ἡ διαλεκτικὴ δύναιτ' ἂν ὑπάρχειν;

ΙΘ'.—ΠΕΡΙ ΟΛΟΥ ΚΑΙ ΜΕΡΟΥΣ

215 Περὶ δὲ ὅλου καὶ μέρους διαλεξόμεθα μὲν καὶ ἐν τοῖς φυσικοῖς δὴ λεγομένοις, ἐπὶ δὲ τοῦ παρόντος περὶ τῆς λεγομένης διαιρέσεως τοῦ ὅλου εἰς τὰ μέρη αὐτοῦ τάδε λεκτέον. ὅταν λέγῃ τις διαιρεῖσθαι

---

[a] That " names " exist " by nature " was held by Heracleitus, Cratylus, Stoics and Epicureans ; Aristotle and the Sceptics took the other view. θέσει, " by convention " (or human ordinance), like the more usual νόμῳ, is opposed to

species into particulars. But it is probably easy to show that, on the contrary, in respect of none of these does a divisive science exist.

CHAPTER XVIII.—CONCERNING THE DIVISION OF A NAME INTO THINGS SIGNIFIED

Now they at once assert that the sciences of natural **214** objects exist whereas those of conventional objects have no existence, and that with reason. For science claims to be a thing that is firm and invariable, but the conventional objects are easily liable to change and variation, because their character is altered by the shifting of the conventions which depend upon ourselves. Since, then, the significance of names is based on convention and not on nature [a] (for otherwise all men, barbarians as well as Greeks, would understand all the things signified by the terms, besides the fact that it is in our power at any time to point out and signify the objects by any other names we may choose), how would it be possible for a science capable of dividing a name into its significations to exist ? Or how could Dialectic really be, as some imagine, a " science of things which signify and are signified " ?

CHAPTER XIX.—CONCERNING WHOLE AND PART

Whole and part we shall discuss in what we call **215** our physical treatise,[b] but at present we have to deal with the so-called division of the whole into its parts. When a man says that the decad is being divided into

φύσει, "by nature," much as we contrast the "artificial" with the "natural."

[b] *Cf.* iii. 82 ff.; *Adv. Phys.* i. 297 ff., 330 ff., ii. 304.

τὴν δεκάδα εἰς μονάδα[1] καὶ δύο καὶ τρία καὶ τέσσαρα, οὐ διαιρεῖται εἰς ταῦτα ἡ δεκάς. ἅμα γὰρ τῷ τὸ πρῶτον αὐτῆς ἀρθῆναι μέρος, ἵνα κατὰ συγχώρησιν νῦν τοῦτο δῶμεν, οἷον τὴν μονάδα, οὐκέτι ὑπόκειται ἡ δεκάς, ἀλλ' ἐννέα καὶ ὅλως 216 ἕτερόν τι παρὰ τὴν δεκάδα. ἡ οὖν τῶν λοιπῶν ἀφαίρεσίς τε καὶ διαίρεσις οὐκ ἀπὸ τῆς δεκάδος γίνεται ἀλλ' ἀπό τινων ἄλλων, καθ' ἑκάστην ἀφαίρεσιν ἑτεροιουμένων.

Τάχα οὖν οὐκ ἐνδέχεται τὸ ὅλον διαιρεῖν εἰς τὰ λεγόμενα εἶναι αὐτοῦ μέρη. καὶ γὰρ εἰ διαιρεῖται τὸ ὅλον εἰς μέρη, ὀφείλει[2] τὰ μέρη ἐμπεριέχεσθαι τῷ ὅλῳ πρὸ τῆς διαιρέσεως, οὐ περιέχεται δὲ ἴσως. οἷον γοῦν, ἵνα ἐπὶ τῆς δεκάδος στήσωμεν πάλιν τὸν λόγον, τῆς δεκάδος μέρος φασὶ πάντως εἶναι τὰ ἐννέα· διαιρεῖται γοῦν εἰς ἓν καὶ ἐννέα. ἀλλὰ καὶ τὰ ὀκτὼ ὁμοίως· διαιρεῖται γὰρ εἰς ὀκτὼ καὶ δύο. καὶ τὰ ἑπτὰ ὁμοίως καὶ ἓξ καὶ πέντε καὶ τέσσαρα 217 καὶ τρία καὶ δύο καὶ ἕν. εἰ οὖν ταῦτα πάντα ἐν τῇ δεκάδι περιέχεται καὶ συντιθέμενα μετ' αὐτῆς πεντεκαιπεντήκοντα γίνεται, ἐν τοῖς δέκα περιέχεται πεντεκαιπεντήκοντα· ὅπερ ἄτοπον. οὐκοῦν οὔτε περιέχεται ἐν τῇ δεκάδι τὰ λεγόμενα αὐτῆς εἶναι μέρη, οὔτε ἡ δεκὰς εἰς ἐκεῖνα διαιρεῖσθαι δύναται ὡς ὅλον εἰς μέρη, ἃ μηδὲ ὅλως ἐν αὐτῇ θεωρεῖται.

218   Τὰ δὲ αὐτὰ ἀπαντήσεται καὶ ἐπὶ τῶν μεγεθῶν, ὅταν τὸ δεκάπηχυ μέγεθος, εἰ τύχοι, διαιρεῖν ἐθέλοι τις. οὐκ ἐνδέχεται οὖν ἴσως διαιρεῖν οὐδὲ ὅλον εἰς μέρη.

---

[1] μονάδα T, cj. Bekk. : μίαν mss.
[2] ὀφείλει Heintz : φιλεῖ mss., Bekk.

one and two and three and four, the decad is not being divided into these. For as soon as its first part, say one, is subtracted—granting for the moment that this can be done—there no longer subsists the decad but the number nine, something quite different from the decad. Hence the division and the subtraction 216 of the other parts is not made from the decad but from some other numbers, and these vary with each subtraction.

Probably then it is impracticable to divide the whole into what are called its parts. For, in fact, if the whole is divided into parts, the parts ought to be comprised in the whole before the act of division, but probably they are not so comprised. Thus for example—to base our argument once more on the decad—they say that nine is certainly a part of the decad, since it is divided into one plus nine. But so likewise is the number eight, since it is divided into eight plus two ; and so also are the numbers seven, six, five, four, three, two and one. If then all these 217 numbers are included in the decad, and when added together with it make up fifty-five, then fifty-five is included in the number ten, which is absurd. Therefore neither are its so-called parts included in the decad nor can the decad be divided into them, as a whole into parts, since they are not even seen in it at all.

And the same objections will confront us in the case 218 of magnitudes *a* also, supposing one should wish, for example, to divide the magnitude of ten cubits. Probably, then, it is not practicable to divide a whole into parts.

a The subject of geometry, as numbers are of arithmetic.

SEXTUS EMPIRICUS

Κ΄.—ΠΕΡΙ ΓΕΝΩΝ ΚΑΙ ΕΙΔΩΝ

219 Οὐκοῦν ὁ περὶ τῶν γενῶν καὶ τῶν εἰδῶν ὑπο-
λείπεται λόγος, περὶ οὗ πλατύτερον μὲν ἐν ἄλλοις
διαλεξόμεθα, ὡς ἐν συντόμῳ δὲ νῦν ταῦτα λέξομεν.
εἰ μὲν ἐννοήματα εἶναι τὰ γένη καὶ τὰ εἴδη λέγουσιν, αἱ κατὰ τοῦ ἡγεμονικοῦ καὶ τῆς φαντασίας
ἐπιχειρήσεις αὐτοὺς διατρέπουσιν· εἰ δὲ ἰδίαν
ὑπόστασιν αὐτοῖς ἀπολείπουσιν, τί πρὸς τοῦτο
220 ἐροῦσιν; εἰ ἔστι τὰ γένη, ἤτοι τοσαῦτά ἐστιν ὅσα
τὰ εἴδη, ἢ ἕν ἐστι κοινὸν πάντων τῶν εἰδῶν αὐτοῦ
λεγομένων εἶναι γένος. εἰ μὲν οὖν τοσαῦτά ἐστι
τὰ γένη ὅσα τὰ εἴδη αὐτῶν, οὐκέτ᾽ ἂν εἴη κοινὸν
γένος, ὃ εἰς αὐτὰ διαιρεθήσεται. εἰ δὲ ἓν εἶναι
λέγοιτο ἐν πᾶσι τοῖς εἴδεσιν αὐτοῦ τὸ γένος, ἤτοι
ὅλου αὐτοῦ ἕκαστον εἶδος αὐτοῦ μετέχει ἢ μέρους
αὐτοῦ. ἀλλ᾽ ὅλου μὲν οὐδαμῶς· ἀμήχανον γάρ
ἐστιν ἕν τι ὑπάρχον ἄλλῳ καὶ ἄλλῳ κατὰ ταὐτὸ
περιέχεσθαι οὕτως ὡς ὅλον ἐν ἑκάστῳ θεωρεῖσθαι
τῶν ἐν οἷς εἶναι λέγεται. εἰ δὲ μέρους, πρῶτον
μὲν οὐκ ἀκολουθήσει τῷ εἴδει τὸ γένος πᾶν, ὡς
ὑπολαμβάνουσιν, οὐδὲ ὁ ἄνθρωπος ἔσται ζῷον ἀλλὰ
μέρος ζῴου, οἷον οὐσία, οὔτε δὲ ἔμψυχος οὔτε
221 αἰσθητική. εἶτα μέντοι καὶ ἤτοι ταὐτοῦ λέγοιτο
ἂν μετεσχηκέναι πάντα τὰ εἴδη μέρους τοῦ γένους
αὐτῶν, ἢ ἑτέρου καὶ ἑτέρου. ἀλλὰ ταὐτοῦ μὲν οὐκ
ἐνδέχεται διὰ τὰ προειρημένα. εἰ δὲ ἄλλου καὶ

ᵃ No such discussion is to be found in the extant works of
Sextus.
ᵇ i.e. the Stoics ; cf. §§ 29 ff., 70 ff., Adv. Log. i. 370 ff. for
the Sceptic criticisms.
ᶜ This view is Plato's, the former Aristotle's. The following
objections are like those brought against the Platonic theory

Chapter XX.—Of Genera and Species

There still remains, then, the subject of genera and 219
species, which we shall discuss more at large elsewhere,[a] but here we shall deal with them concisely.
If, on the one hand, they[b] assert that genera and
species are mental concepts, our criticisms of the
" regent part " and of " presentation " refute them ;
whereas if they assign to them a substantiality of
their own, how will they reply to this objection ? If 220
the genera exist, either they are equal in number to
the species or else there is one genus common to all
the species which are said to belong to it. If, then,
the genera are equal in number to their species, there
will no longer be a common genus to be divided into
the species ; while if it shall be said that the genus
exists as one in all its species, then each species partakes
of either the whole or a part of it.[c] But it certainly
does not partake of the whole ; for it is impossible
that what is one real object should be equally included
in separate things in such a way as to appear as a
whole in each of those things in which it is said to
exist. And if it partakes of a part, then, in the first
place, all the genus will not, as they suppose, accompany the species, nor will " man " be " an animal "
but a part of an animal—he will be substance, for
example, but neither animate nor sensitive.[d] Then, 221
in the next place, all the species will be said to partake
either of the same part of their genus or of different
parts ; but to partake of the same part is impossible
for the reasons stated above ; while if they partake

of " participation " by Aristotle and in the *Parmenides* of
Plato.
   [d] *i.e.* a part of the Genus is taken as meaning a part of its
definition ; *cf.* § 224 for this definition of the genus " animal."

ἄλλου, οὔτε ὅμοια ἀλλήλοις ἔσται τὰ εἴδη κατὰ
γένος, ὅπερ οὐ προσδέξονται, ἄπειρόν τε ἔσται
γένος ἕκαστον εἰς ἄπειρα τεμνόμενον οὐ μόνον τὰ
εἴδη ἀλλὰ καὶ τὰ καθ' ἕκαστον, ἐν οἷς καὶ αὐτοῖς
μετὰ τῶν εἰδῶν αὐτοῦ θεωρεῖται· οὐ γὰρ μόνον
ἄνθρωπος ἀλλὰ καὶ ζῶον ὁ Δίων εἶναι λέγεται. εἰ
δὲ ταῦτα ἄτοπα, οὐδὲ κατὰ μέρος μετέσχηκε τὰ
εἴδη τοῦ γένους αὐτῶν ἑνὸς ὄντος.

222 Εἰ δὲ μήτε ὅλου μετέσχηκεν ἕκαστον εἶδος τοῦ
γένους μήτε μέρους αὐτοῦ, πῶς ἂν λέγοιτο ἓν
εἶναι γένος ἐν πᾶσι τοῖς εἴδεσιν αὐτοῦ, ὥστε καὶ
εἰς αὐτὰ διαιρεῖσθαι; τάχα οὐκ ἂν ἔχοι τις λέγειν
μὴ οὐχὶ ἀναπλάσσων τινὰς εἰδωλοποιήσεις, αἳ ταῖς
ἐκείνων αὐτῶν ἀνεπικρίτοις διαφωνίαις κατὰ τὰς
σκεπτικὰς ἐφόδους περιτραπήσονται.

223 Πρὸς δὲ τούτοις κἀκεῖνο λεκτέον. τὰ εἴδη τοῖα
ἢ τοῖά ἐστιν· τούτων τὰ γένη ἤτοι καὶ τοῖα καὶ
τοῖα ἢ τοῖα μὲν τοῖα δὲ οὔ ἢ οὔτε τοῖα οὔτε τοῖα.
οἷον ἐπεὶ τῶν τινῶν τὰ μέν ἐστι σώματα τὰ δὲ
ἀσώματα, καὶ τὰ μὲν ἀληθῆ τὰ δὲ ψευδῆ, καὶ ἔνια
μὲν λευκά, εἰ τύχοι, ἔνια δὲ μέλανα, καὶ ἔνια μὲν
μέγιστα ἔνια δὲ σμικρότατα, καὶ τὰ ἄλλα ὁμοίως,
τό τι λόγου ἕνεκεν, ὅ φασιν εἶναί τινες γενικώτατον,
224 ἢ πάντα ἔσται ἢ τὰ ἕτερα ἢ οὐδέν. ἀλλ' εἰ μὲν
οὐδέν ἐστιν ὅλως τό τι, οὐδὲ τὸ γένος, πέρας ἔχει

---

[a] The stock name for a specimen of " Man," cf. i. 189,
and §§ 227 ff.

[b] e.g. the Platonic Ideas, cf. iii. 189.

[c] The argument here is that it is impossible to conceive a
number of opposite qualities, such as are possessed by the
multitude of species and particulars included in the " genus,"
co-existing in the unity of the genus; while if they do not
all co-exist in it, the " genus" ceases to be inclusive of all

of different parts, the species will be generically dissimilar one to another (which they will not admit), and each genus will be infinite because cut up into infinite sections (not into the species only but also into the particulars, since it is actually seen in these along with its species ; for Dion [a] is said to be an animal as well as a man). But if these consequences are absurd, then not even by way of parts do the species partake of their genus, it being a unity.

If, then, each several species partakes neither of 222 the whole genus nor of a part of it, how can it be said that the one genus exists in all its parts so as to be actually divided into them ? No one, probably, could make such a statement unless by concocting some imaginary entities,[b] which will be overturned, as the attacks of the Sceptics show, by the unsettled disputes of the Dogmatists themselves.

Furthermore, there is this to be said.[c] The species 223 are of this kind or of that kind : the genera of these species either are of both this kind and that kind, or of this kind but not of that kind, or neither of this kind nor of that kind. When, for instance, of the " somethings " (or particulars) some are corporeal others incorporeal, and some true others false, and some (it may be) white others black, and some very large others very small, and so on with the rest, the genus " something " (to take it for the sake of argument), which some regard as the *summum genus*,[d] will either be all these or some of them or none. But 224 if the " something," and the genus too, is absolutely

its proper species and particulars ; and if it includes *none* of the opposites, it is wholly unrelated to its particulars, and has no claim to be termed a " genus."

[d] The Stoic view, *cf.* §§ 86 f. *supra.*

ἡ ζήτησις. εἰ δὲ πάντα εἶναι ῥηθείη, πρὸς τῷ
ἀδύνατον εἶναι τὸ λεγόμενον, ἕκαστον¹ τῶν εἰδῶν
καὶ τῶν καθ' ἕκαστον ἐν οἷς ἐστὶ δεήσει πάντα
εἶναι. ὡς γάρ, ἐπεὶ τὸ ζῶον, ὡς φασίν, οὐσία
ἐστὶν ἔμψυχος αἰσθητική, ἕκαστον τῶν εἰδῶν αὐτοῦ
καὶ οὐσία εἶναι λέγεται καὶ ἔμψυχος καὶ αἰσθητική,
οὕτως εἰ τὸ γένος καὶ σῶμά ἐστι καὶ ἀσώματον
καὶ ψευδὲς καὶ ἀληθὲς καὶ μέλαν, εἰ τύχοι, καὶ
λευκὸν καὶ σμικρότατον καὶ μέγιστον καὶ τἆλλα
πάντα, ἕκαστον τῶν εἰδῶν καὶ τῶν καθ' ἕκαστον
πάντα ἔσται· ὅπερ οὐ θεωρεῖται. ψεῦδος οὖν καὶ
225 τοῦτο. εἰ δὲ τὰ ἕτερα μόνα ἐστί, τούτων τὸ γένος
τῶν λοιπῶν οὐκ ἔσται γένος, οἷον εἰ σῶμα τό τι,
τῶν ἀσωμάτων, καὶ εἰ λογικὸν τὸ ζῶον, τῶν
ἀλόγων, ὡς μήτε ἀσώματον τὶ εἶναι μήτε ἄλογον
ζῶον,² καὶ ἐπὶ τῶν ἄλλων ὁμοίως· ὅπερ ἄτοπον.
οὐκοῦν οὔτε καὶ τοῖον καὶ τοῖον τὸ γένος, οὔτε
τοῖον μὲν τοῖον δὲ οὔ, οὔτε μὴν οὔτε τοῖον οὔτε
τοῖον δύναται εἶναι [γένος]· εἰ δὲ τοῦτο, οὐδὲ ἔστιν
ὅλως τὸ γένος.

Εἰ δὲ λέγοι τις ὅτι δυνάμει πάντα ἐστὶ τὸ γένος,
λέξομεν ὡς τὸ δυνάμει τι ὂν δεῖ τι καὶ ἐνεργείᾳ
εἶναι, οἷον οὐ δύναταί τις γραμματικὸς εἶναι εἰ μὴ
καὶ³ ἐνεργείᾳ. καὶ τὸ γένος οὖν εἰ δυνάμει πάντα
ἐστίν, ἐρωτῶμεν αὐτοὺς τί ἐστιν ἐνεργείᾳ, καὶ

---

¹ ἕκαστον cj. Bekk.: καὶ MSS.
² ζῶον post εἶναι MSS., edd., transp. Papp.
³ εἰ μὴ καὶ T: μή τις MSS., ὢν add. Bekk.

ᵃ Aristotle regarded the relation of Genus to Species as
that of Potentiality to Actuality, *i.e.* of unrealized possibility

none of them, the inquiry comes to an end. And if we should say that it is all of them, then, besides the impossibility of such a statement, each of the species and of the particulars wherein it exists will have to be all. For just as when the genus " animal " is, as they assert, " an animate sensitive substance," each of its species is said to be substance and animate and sensitive, so likewise if the genus is both corporeal and incorporeal and false and true and black, it may be, and white and very small and very large, and all the rest, each of the species and of the particulars will be all these—which is contrary to observation. So this too is false. But if the genus is some of them 225 only, the genus of these will not be the genus of the rest ; if, for instance, the genus " something " is corporeal it will not be that of the incorporeal, and if the genus " animal " is rational it will not be that of the irrational, so that there is neither an incorporeal " something " nor an irrational animal, and so likewise with all other cases ; and this is absurd. Therefore the genus cannot be either of both this and that kind, or of this kind but not of that, or of neither this kind nor that ; and if this be so, neither does the genus exist at all.

And if one should say that the genus is potentially all things,[a] we shall reply that what is potentially something must also be actually something, as, for instance, no one can be potentially literary without being so actually. So too, if the genus is potentially all things, what, we ask them, is it actually ? And

to what is real and determinate, or of the germinal to the fully evolved. As the " actuality " of the oak is implicit in the " potency " of the acorn, so the plurality of " actual " particulars are implicit in the " potency " of the unitary " genus."

οὕτω μένουσιν αἱ αὐταὶ ἀπορίαι. τἀναντία μὲν
226 γὰρ πάντα ἐνεργείᾳ εἶναι οὐ δύναται. ἀλλ' οὐδὲ
τὰ μὲν καὶ ἐνεργείᾳ τὰ δὲ δυνάμει μόνον, οἷον σῶμα
μὲν ἐνεργείᾳ, δυνάμει δὲ ἀσώματον. δυνάμει γάρ
ἐστιν ὃ οἷόν τέ ἐστιν ἐνεργείᾳ ὑποστῆναι, τὸ δὲ
σῶμα ἐνεργείᾳ ἀδύνατόν ἐστιν ἀσώματον γενέσθαι
κατ' ἐνέργειαν, ὥστε εἰ <τό τι>¹ λόγου χάριν σῶμά
ἐστιν ἐνεργείᾳ, οὐκ ἔστιν ἀσώματον δυνάμει, καὶ
τὸ ἀνάπαλιν. οὐκοῦν οὐκ ἐνδέχεται τὸ γένος τὰ
μὲν ἐνεργείᾳ εἶναι τὰ δὲ δυνάμει μόνον. εἰ δὲ
οὐδὲν ὅλως ἐστὶν ἐνεργείᾳ, οὐδὲ ὑφέστηκεν.
οὐκοῦν οὐδέν ἐστι τὸ γένος, ὃ διαιρεῖν εἰς τὰ εἴδη
λέγουσιν.

227 Ἔτι καὶ τοῦτο θεάσασθαι ἄξιον. ὥσπερ γὰρ
ἐπεὶ ὁ αὐτός ἐστιν Ἀλέξανδρος καὶ Πάρις, οὐκ
ἐνδέχεται τὸ μὲν '' Ἀλέξανδρος περιπατεῖ '' ἀληθὲς
εἶναι, τὸ δὲ '' Πάρις περιπατεῖ '' ψεῦδος, οὕτως
εἰ τὸ αὐτό ἐστι τὸ ἀνθρώπῳ² εἶναι Θέωνι καὶ
Δίωνι, εἰς σύνταξιν ἀξιώματος ἀγομένη ἡ ἄνθρωπος προσηγορία ἢ ἀληθὲς ἢ ψεῦδος ἐπ' ἀμφοτέρων
ποιήσει τὸ ἀξίωμα. οὐ θεωρεῖται δὲ τοῦτο· τοῦ
μὲν γὰρ Δίωνος καθημένου Θέωνος δὲ περιπα-
τοῦντος τὸ '' ἄνθρωπος περιπατεῖ '' ἐφ' οὗ μὲν
λεγόμενον ἀληθές ἐστιν ἐφ' οὗ δὲ ψεῦδος. οὐκ ἄρα
κοινή ἐστιν ἀμφοτέρων ἡ ἄνθρωπος προσηγορία,
καὶ ἡ αὐτὴ ἀμφοῖν, ἀλλ' εἰ ἄρα, ἰδία ἑκατέρου.

¹ <τό τι> add. Heintz.
² τὸ ἀνθρώπῳ cj. R. Philippson : τὸ ἄνθρωπον Τ, cj. Papp. :
τῷ ἀνθρώπῳ mss., Bekk.

thus we find that the same difficulties remain. For it cannot actually be all the contraries ; nor yet can it be some of them actually and some only potentially —corporeal, for instance, actually and incorporeal potentially. For it is potentially that which it is capable of really being actually, but that which is actually corporeal is incapable of becoming incorporeal in actuality, so that if, for example, the genus " something " is actually corporeal it is not potentially incorporeal, and *vice versa.* It is impossible, therefore, for the genus to be some things actually and some only potentially. But if it is absolutely nothing actually, it has no substantial existence. Hence the genus, which they say they divide into the species, is nothing.

And further, here is another point worthy of notice. Just as, because Alexander and Paris [a] are identical, it is impossible that the statement "Alexander walks " should be true when " Paris walks " is false, so also if " manhood " is identical for both Theon and Dion, the term " man " when introduced as an element in a judgement will cause the judgement to be equally true or false in the case of both. But this is not what we find ; for when Dion is sitting and Theon walking, the judgement " man walks " is true when used of the one, but false of the other. Therefore the term [b] " man " is not common to them both and the same for both but, if applicable at all, it is peculiar to one of the two.

[a] Two names of the son of Priam who carried off Helen to Troy.
[b] " Term," *i.e.* (in Stoic usage) " common noun or appellative " (Diog. Laert. vii. 58).

ΚΑ΄.—ΠΕΡΙ ΚΟΙΝΩΝ ΣΥΜΒΕΒΗΚΟΤΩΝ

228 Παραπλήσια δὲ λέγεται καὶ περὶ τῶν κοινῶν
συμβεβηκότων. εἰ γὰρ ἓν καὶ τὸ αὐτὸ συμβέβηκε
Δίωνί τε καὶ Θέωνι τὸ ὁρᾶν, ἐὰν καθ᾽ ὑπόθεσιν
φθαρῇ μὲν Δίων, Θέων δὲ περιῇ καὶ ὁρᾷ, ἤτοι τὴν
ὅρασιν τοῦ ἐφθαρμένου Δίωνος ἄφθαρτον μένειν
ἐροῦσιν, ὅπερ ἀπεμφαίνει, ἢ τὴν αὐτὴν ὅρασιν
ἐφθάρθαι τε καὶ μὴ ἐφθάρθαι λέξουσιν, ὅπερ ἄτοπον·
οὐκ ἄρα ἡ Θέωνος ὅρασις ἡ αὐτή ἐστι τῇ Δίωνος,
ἀλλ᾽ εἰ ἄρα, ἰδία ἑκατέρου. καὶ γὰρ εἰ ταὐτὸν
συμβέβηκε Δίωνί τε καὶ Θέωνι τὸ ἀναπνεῖν, οὐκ
ἐνδέχεται τὴν ἐν Θέωνι ἀναπνοὴν εἶναι, τὴν ἐν
Δίωνι δὲ μὴ εἶναι· ἐνδέχεται δὲ τοῦ μὲν φθαρέντος
τοῦ δὲ περιόντος· οὐκ ἄρα ἡ αὐτή ἐστιν.

Περὶ μὲν οὖν τούτων ἐπὶ τοσοῦτον νῦν ἀρκέσει
συντόμως λελέχθαι.

ΚΒ΄.—ΠΕΡΙ ΣΟΦΙΣΜΑΤΩΝ

229 Οὐκ ἄτοπον δὲ ἴσως καὶ τῷ περὶ τῶν σοφισμάτων ἐπιστῆσαι λόγῳ διὰ βραχέων, ἐπεὶ καὶ εἰς
τὴν τούτων διάλυσιν ἀναγκαίαν εἶναι λέγουσι τὴν
διαλεκτικὴν οἱ σεμνύνοντες αὐτήν. εἰ γὰρ τῶν τε
ἀληθῶν καὶ ψευδῶν λόγων, φασίν, ἐστὶν αὕτη
διαγνωστική, ψευδεῖς δὲ λόγοι καὶ τὰ σοφίσματα,
καὶ τούτων ἂν εἴη διακριτικὴ λυμαινομένων τὴν
ἀλήθειαν φαινομέναις πιθανότησιν. ὅθεν ὡς βοη-
θοῦντες οἱ διαλεκτικοὶ σαλεύοντι τῷ βίῳ καὶ τὴν
ἔννοιαν καὶ τὰς διαφορὰς καὶ τὰς ἐπιλύσεις δὴ τῶν

---

[a] The Stoics ; cf. § 94 supra for the definition of Dialectic.

CHAPTER XXI.—CONCERNING COMMON PROPERTIES

Similar arguments apply also to the " common 228
properties." For if vision is one and the same
property in Dion and in Theon, then, suppose that
Dion should perish and Theon survive and retain his
sight, either they will assert that the vision of the
perished Dion remains unperished, which is incredible,
or they will declare that the same vision has both
perished and not perished, which is absurd ; therefore
the vision of Theon is not identical with Dion's but,
if anything, the vision of each is peculiar to himself.
And if breathing is an identical property in Dion and
Theon, it is impossible that breathing should exist
in Theon and not exist in Dion ; but this is possible
when the one has perished and the other survives ;
therefore it is not identical.

However, as regards this subject, this concise statement will be sufficient for the present.

CHAPTER XXII.—CONCERNING SOPHISMS

It will not, perhaps, be amiss to give our attention 229
for a moment to the subject of Sophisms, seeing that
those who glorify Dialectic [a] declare that it is indis-
pensable for exposing sophisms. For, they say, if
Dialectic is capable of distinguishing true and false
arguments, and sophisms are false arguments, it will
also be capable of discerning these, which distort the
truth by apparent plausibilities. Hence the dialecticians, by way of assisting life [b] when it totters, strive
earnestly to teach us the conception of sophisms, their

[b] *i.e.* the views and conduct of ordinary people, *cf.* i. 23,
165.

σοφισμάτων μετὰ σπουδῆς ἡμᾶς πειρῶνται διδάσκειν, λέγοντες σόφισμα εἶναι λόγον πιθανὸν καὶ
δεδολιευμένον ὥστε προσδέξασθαι τὴν ἐπιφορὰν
ἤτοι ψευδῆ ἢ ὡμοιωμένην ψευδεῖ ἢ ἄδηλον ἢ
230 ἄλλως ἀπρόσδεκτον, οἷον ψευδῆ μὲν ὡς ἐπὶ τούτου
τοῦ σοφίσματος ἔχει " οὐδεὶς δίδωσι κατηγόρημα
πιεῖν· κατηγόρημα δέ ἐστι τὸ ἀψίνθιον πιεῖν·
οὐδεὶς ἄρα δίδωσιν ἀψίνθιον πιεῖν," ἔτι δὲ ὅμοιον
ψευδεῖ ὡς ἐπὶ τούτου " ὃ μήτε ἐνεδέχετο μήτε
ἐνδέχεται, τοῦτο οὐκ ἔστιν ἄτοπον· οὔτε δὲ ἐνεδέχετο οὔτε ἐνδέχεται τὸ ὁ ἰατρός, καθὸ ἰατρός ἐστι,
φονεύει <οὐκ ἄρα ἄτοπόν ἐστι τὸ ὁ ἰατρός, καθὸ
231 ἰατρός ἐστι, φονεύει>.[1]" ἔτι δὲ ἄδηλον οὕτως
" οὐχὶ καὶ ἠρώτηκά τί σε πρῶτον, καὶ οὐχὶ οἱ
ἀστέρες ἄρτιοί εἰσιν· ἠρώτηκα δέ τί σε πρῶτον·
οἱ ἄρα ἀστέρες ἄρτιοί εἰσιν." ἔτι δὲ ἀπρόσδεκτον
ἄλλως, ὡς οἱ λεγόμενοι σολοικίζοντες λόγοι, οἷον
" ὃ βλέπεις, ἔστιν· βλέπεις δὲ φρενιτικόν· ἔστιν
ἄρα φρενιτικόν." " ὃ ὁρᾷς, ἔστιν· ὁρᾷς δὲ φλεγμαίνοντα τόπον· ἔστιν ἄρα φλεγμαίνοντα τόπον."
232 Εἶτα μέντοι καὶ τὰς ἐπιλύσεις αὐτῶν [ὁρᾶν ἤτοι]
παριστᾶν ἐπιχειροῦσι, λέγοντες ἐπὶ μὲν τοῦ πρώτου
σοφίσματος ὅτι ἄλλο διὰ τῶν λημμάτων συγκεχώρηται καὶ ἄλλο ἐπενήνεκται. συγκεχώρηται
γὰρ τὸ μὴ πίνεσθαι κατηγόρημα, καὶ εἶναι κατηγόρημα τὸ ἀψίνθιον πίνειν, οὐκ αὐτὸ τὸ ἀψίνθιον.
διὸ δέον ἐπιφέρειν " οὐδεὶς ἄρα πίνει τὸ ἀψίνθιον

---

[1] <οὐκ . . . φονεύει> add. cj. Bekk.

---

[a] Or " meaningless." The Stoics held that every " judgement " or " proposition " (ἀξίωμα) was significant; so the

differences and their solutions. They declare that a sophism is " a plausible argument cunningly framed to induce acceptance of the inference, it being either false or resembling what is false or non-evident or otherwise unacceptable." It is false, for example, 230 in the case of the sophism " Nobody offers one a predicate to drink ; but ' to drink absinth ' is a predicate ; nobody therefore offers one absinth to drink." Or again, it may resemble the false, as in this case—" What neither was nor is possible is not absurd[a] ; but it neither was nor is possible for a doctor, *qua* doctor, to murder ; therefore it is not absurd that a doctor, *qua* doctor, should murder." Or again, it 231 may be non-evident, as thus—" It is not true both that I have asked you a question first and that the stars are not even in number ; but I have asked you a question first ; therefore the stars are even." Or again, it may be otherwise unacceptable, like the so-called solecistic [b] arguments, such as—" That at which you look exists ; but you have a frenzied look ; therefore ' frenzied ' exists " ; or " What you gaze at exists ; but you gaze at an inflamed spot ; therefore ' at an inflamed spot ' exists."

Moreover, they attempt also to set forth solutions 232 of the sophisms, saying in the case of the first sophism that one thing is established by the premisses and another inferred in the conclusion. For it is established that a predicate is not drunk and that " to drink absinth " is a predicate, but not " absinth " by itself. Hence, whereas one ought to infer " Nobody

proposition " this is not possible " is not ἄτοπον, in this sense of the word.

[b] *i.e.* ungrammatical, involving the use of an adjective for a noun, the accusative for the nominative case (as here τόπον for τόπος), and the like. *Cf.* Aristot. *Soph. El.* cc. 14, 32.

πίνειν," ὅπερ ἐστὶν ἀληθές, ἐπενήνεκται " οὐδεὶς
ἄρα ἀψίνθιον πίνει," ὅπερ ἐστὶ ψεῦδος, οὐ συναγό-
233 μενον ἐκ τῶν συγκεχωρημένων λημμάτων. ἐπὶ
δὲ τοῦ δευτέρου ὅτι δοκεῖ μὲν ἐπὶ ψεῦδος ἀπάγειν
ὡς ποιεῖν τοὺς ἀνεπιστάτους ὀκνεῖν αὐτῷ συγκατατίθεσθαι, συνάγει δὲ ἀληθές, τὸ " οὐκ ἄρα
ἄτοπόν ἐστι τὸ ὁ ἰατρός, καθὸ ἰατρός ἐστι,
φονεύει." οὐδὲν γὰρ ἀξίωμα ἄτοπόν ἐστιν, ἀξίωμα
δέ ἐστι τὸ " ὁ ἰατρός, καθὸ ἰατρός ἐστι, φονεύει"·
234 διὸ οὐδὲ τοῦτο ἄτοπον. ἡ δὲ ἐπὶ τὸ ἄδηλον
ἀπαγωγή φασιν ὅτι ἐκ τοῦ γένους τῶν μεταπιπ-
τόντων ἐστίν. μηδενὸς γὰρ προηρωτημένου κατὰ
τὴν ὑπόθεσιν τὸ ἀποφατικὸν τῆς συμπλοκῆς ἀληθὲς
γίνεται, ψευδοῦς τῆς συμπλοκῆς οὔσης παρὰ τὸ
ἐμπεπλέχθαι ψεῦδος τὸ " ἠρώτηκά τί σε πρῶτον "
ἐν αὐτῇ. μετὰ δὲ τὸ ἐρωτηθῆναι τὸ ἀποφατικὸν
τῆς συμπλοκῆς, τῆς προσλήψεως ἀληθοῦς γινομένης, " ἠρώτηκα δέ τί σε πρῶτον," διὰ τὸ
ἠρωτῆσθαι πρὸ τῆς προσλήψεως τὸ ἀποφατικὸν
τῆς συμπλοκῆς ἡ τοῦ ἀποφατικοῦ τῆς συμπλοκῆς
πρότασις γίνεται ψευδὴς τοῦ ἐν τῷ συμπεπλεγμένῳ
ψεύδους γενομένου ἀληθοῦς· ὡς μηδέποτε δύνασθαι
συναχθῆναι τὸ συμπέρασμα μὴ συνυπάρχοντος τοῦ
235 ἀποφατικοῦ τῆς συμπλοκῆς τῇ προσλήψει. τοὺς
δὲ τελευταίους, φασὶν ἔνιοι,[1] τοὺς σολοικίζοντας
λόγους ἀτόπως ἐπάγεσθαι[2] παρὰ τὴν συνήθειαν.

Τοιαῦτα μὲν οὖν τινὲς διαλεκτικοί φασι περὶ
σοφισμάτων (καὶ γὰρ ἄλλοι ἄλλα λέγουσιν)· ταῦτα

---

[1] ἔνιοι MT : ἔνθα L, Bekk.
[2] ἐπάγεσθαι T : ἐπάγειν mss., Bekk.

---

[a] i.e. meaningless—a Stoic dictum.
[b] i.e. the third Sophism, in § 231.

therefore drinks the 'to drink absinth,'" which is true, the inference drawn is "Nobody therefore drinks absinth," which is false, as not deduced from the established premisses. And as regards the 233 second sophism, they explain that while it seems to lead in a false direction, so that it makes the inattentive hesitate in assenting to it, its conclusion is true, namely "It is not therefore absurd that the doctor, *qua* doctor, should murder." For no judgement is absurd,[a] and "the doctor, *qua* doctor, murders" is a judgement, so that neither is it absurd. And 234 the method of leading up to the non-evident [b] deals, they say, with the class of things that are variable.[c] For when, according to the assumption, no previous question has been asked, the negation of the conjunctive premiss is true, the conjunctive or major premiss being false because of its inclusion of the false clause "I have asked you a question first." But after the negation of the major has been asked, as the minor premiss "I have asked you a question first" has become true, owing to the fact that the negation of the major has been asked before the minor premiss, the first clause in the negation of the major becomes false while the false clause in the major has become true; so that it is never possible for the conclusion to be deduced if the negation of the major premiss does not co-exist with the minor premiss. And as 235 to the last class—the solecistic arguments—some declare that they are introduced absurdly, contrary to linguistic usage.

Such are the statements made by some of the Dialecticians concerning sophisms—though others

[c] *i.e.* judgements which change from truth to falsehood; *cf.* Diog. Laert. vii. 76.

δὲ τὰς μὲν τῶν εἰκαιοτέρων ἀκοὰς ἴσως δύναται
γαργαλίζειν, περιττὰ δέ ἐστι καὶ μάτην αὐτοῖς
πεπονημένα. καὶ τοῦτο δυνατὸν μὲν ἴσως καὶ ἀπὸ
τῶν ἤδη λελεγμένων ἡμῖν ὁρᾶν· ὑπεμνήσαμεν γὰρ
ὅτι μὴ δύναται τὸ ἀληθὲς καὶ τὸ ψεῦδος κατὰ τοὺς
διαλεκτικοὺς καταλαμβάνεσθαι, ποικίλως τε ἄλλως
καὶ τῷ τὰ μαρτύρια τῆς συλλογιστικῆς δυνάμεως
αὐτῶν, τὴν ἀπόδειξιν καὶ τοὺς ἀναποδείκτους δια-
236 τρέπεσθαι λόγους. εἰς δὲ τὸν προκείμενον τόπον
ἰδίως καὶ ἄλλα μὲν πολλὰ λέγειν ἔνεστιν, ὡς δὲ
ἐν συντόμῳ νῦν τόδε λεκτέον.

Ὅσα μὲν σοφίσματα ἰδίως ἡ διαλεκτικὴ δύνασθαι
δοκεῖ διελέγχειν, τούτων ἡ διάλυσις ἄχρηστός
ἐστιν· ὅσων δὲ ἡ διάλυσις χρησιμεύει, ταῦτα ὁ μὲν
διαλεκτικὸς οὐκ ἂν διαλύσειεν, οἱ δὲ ἐν ἑκάστῃ
τέχνῃ τὴν ἐπὶ τῶν πραγμάτων παρακολούθησιν
237 ἐσχηκότες. εὐθέως γοῦν, ἵνα ἑνὸς ἢ δευτέρου
μνησθῶμεν παραδείγματος, ἐρωτηθέντος ἰατρῷ
τοιούτου σοφίσματος '' κατὰ τὰς νόσους ἐν ταῖς
παρακμαῖς τήν τε ποικίλην δίαιταν καὶ τὸν οἶνον
δοκιμαστέον· ἐπὶ πάσης δὲ τυπώσεως νόσου πρὸ
τῆς πρώτης διατρίτου πάντως γίνεται παρακμή·
ἀναγκαῖον ἄρα πρὸ τῆς πρώτης διατρίτου τήν τε
ποικίλην δίαιταν καὶ τὸν οἶνον ὡς τὸ πολὺ παραλαμβάνειν '' ὁ μὲν διαλεκτικὸς οὐδὲν ἂν εἰπεῖν ἔχοι
πρὸς διάλυσιν τοῦ λόγου, καίτοι χρησίμην οὖσαν,
238 ὁ δὲ ἰατρὸς διαλύσεται τὸ σόφισμα, εἰδὼς ὅτι
παρακμὴ λέγεται διχῶς ἥ τε τοῦ ὅλου νοσήματος
καὶ ἡ ἑκάστης ἐπιτάσεως μερικῆς ἀπὸ τῆς ἀκμῆς

---

[a] Cf. §§ 80 ff. supra.   [b] Cf. §§ 144 ff., 156 ff.
[c] The '' Methodic '' School of medicine held that the pro-
gress of a disease was marked by three-day periods of increas-

indeed make other statements ; and what they say may be able, perhaps, to tickle the ears of the casual hearer, superfluous though it is and the result of vain labour on their part. Probably this can be seen from what we have said already [a] ; for we have shown that truth and falsehood, according to the Dialecticians, cannot be apprehended, and that by a variety of arguments as well as by the refutation of their evidences for the validity of the syllogism, namely proof and axiomatic arguments.[b] And there are 236 many other special objections bearing on the topic before us which we might mention, but now, for brevity's sake, we mention only this one.

As regards all the sophisms which dialectic seems peculiarly able to expose, their exposure is useless ; whereas in all cases where the exposure is useful, it is not the dialectician who will expose them but the experts in each particular art who grasp the connexion of the facts. Thus, for instance, to mention 237 one or two examples, if a sophism such as this were propounded—" In diseases, at the stages of abatement, a varied diet and wine are to be approved ; but in every type of disease an abatement inevitably occurs before the first third day [c] ; it is necessary, therefore, to take for the most part a varied diet and wine before the first third day,"—in this case the dialectician would be unable to assist in exposing the argument, useful though the exposure would be, but the doctor will expose the sophism, since he 238 knows that the term " abatement " is used in two senses, of the general " abatement " in the disease and of the tendency to betterment after the crisis in

ing (up to the crisis) or decreasing severity ; for the former they prescribed a light diet.

ῥοπὴ πρὸς τὸ κρεῖσσον, καὶ πρὸ μὲν τῆς πρώτης
διατρίτου ὡς τὸ πολὺ γίνεται παρακμὴ ἡ τῆς ἐπιτάσεως τῆς μερικῆς, τὴν δὲ ποικίλην δίαιταν οὐκ
ἐν ταύτῃ δοκιμάζομεν ἀλλ' ἐν τῇ παρακμῇ τοῦ
ὅλου νοσήματος. ὅθεν καὶ διῃρῆσθαι λέξει τὰ
λήμματα τοῦ λόγου, ἑτέρας μὲν παρακμῆς ἐν τῷ
προτέρῳ λήμματι λαμβανομένης, τουτέστι τῆς τοῦ
ὅλου πάθους, ἑτέρας δὲ ἐν τῷ δευτέρῳ, τουτέστι
τῆς μερικῆς.

239   Πάλιν τε ἐπί τινος πυρέσσοντος κατὰ πύκνωσιν
ἐπιτεταμένην ἐρωτηθέντος τοῦ τοιούτου λόγου " τὰ
ἐναντία τῶν ἐναντίων ἰάματά ἐστιν· ἐναντίον δὲ
τῇ ὑποκειμένῃ πυρώσει τὸ ψυχρόν· κατάλληλον
ἄρα τῇ ὑποκειμένῃ πυρώσει τὸ ψυχρόν" ὁ μὲν
240 διαλεκτικὸς ἡσυχάσει, ὁ δὲ ἰατρὸς εἰδὼς τίνα μέν
ἐστιν προηγουμένως προσεχῆ πάθη, τίνα δὲ συμ-
πτώματα τούτων, ἐρεῖ μὴ ἐπὶ τῶν συμπτωμάτων
προκόπτειν τὸν λόγον (ἀμέλει γοῦν πρὸς τὴν ἐπί-
χυσιν τοῦ ψυχροῦ πλείονα γίνεσθαι συμβαίνειν τὴν
πύρωσιν) ἀλλ' ἐπὶ τῶν προσεχῶν παθῶν, καὶ τὴν
μὲν στέγνωσιν εἶναι προσεχῆ, ἥτις οὐ τὴν πύκνωσιν
ἀλλὰ τὸν χαλαστικὸν τρόπον τῆς ἐπιμελείας ἀπαιτεῖ,
τὸ δὲ τῆς ἐπακολουθούσης θερμασίας οὐ προηγουμένως προσεχές, ὅθεν μηδὲ τὸ κατάλληλον εἶναι
δοκοῦν αὐτῇ.

241   Καὶ οὕτως μὲν ἐπὶ τοῖς σοφίσμασι τοῖς χρησίμως
ἀπαιτοῦσι τὴν διάλυσιν οὐδὲν ἕξει λέγειν ὁ διαλεκ-

_____

ᵃ Cf. Hippocrates, De flat. 2 ; for morbid " contraction "
counteracted by "dilatation" or "relaxation" cf. i. 238.

the strained local conditions, and this improvement in the local strain generally occurs before the first third day, but it is not for this but for the general abatement in the disease that we recommend the varied diet. Consequently he will say that the premisses are discordant, since one kind of " abatement " is adopted in the first premiss, namely that of the general condition, and another—that of the local condition—in the second premiss.

Again, in the case of one who suffers from fever 239 due to aggravated " contraction " or obstruction, if an argument is propounded in the form—" Opposites are cures of opposites [a] ; cold is the opposite of the present feverish condition ; therefore cold is the treatment which corresponds to the present feverish condition,"—here again the dialectician will keep silence, but the doctor, since he knows what morbid 240 states are fundamentally persistent and what are symptoms of such states, will declare that the argument does not apply to the symptoms (not to mention the fact that the result of the application of cold is to aggravate the feverish condition) but to the persistent morbid states, and that the constipation is persistent but requires an expansive method of treatment rather than contraction, whereas the resultant symptom of inflammation is not fundamentally persistent, nor (consequently) is the state of cold which seems to correspond thereto.

Thus, as regards sophisms the exposure of which 241 is useful, the dialectician will not have a word to say,

By " corresponding " is meant the appropriate " counteracting " remedy. The " persistent " or " deep-seated " (προσεχῆ) morbid states are distinguished from the superficial " symptoms " which the Methodic School disregarded as accidentals.

τικός, ἐρωτήσας δὲ ἡμῖν τοιούτους λόγους " εἰ
οὐχὶ καὶ καλὰ κέρατα ἔχεις καὶ κέρατα ἔχεις,
κέρατα ἔχεις· οὐχὶ δὲ καλὰ κέρατα ἔχεις καὶ κέρατα
242 ἔχεις· κέρατα ἄρα ἔχεις." " εἰ κινεῖταί τι, ἤτοι
ἐν ᾧ ἔστι τόπῳ κινεῖται, ἢ ἐν ᾧ οὐκ ἔστιν· οὔτε
δὲ ἐν ᾧ ἔστιν, μένει γάρ, οὔτε ἐν ᾧ μὴ ἔστιν·
πῶς γὰρ ἂν ἐνεργοίη τι ἐν ἐκείνῳ ἐν ᾧ μηδὲ τὴν
243 ἀρχὴν ἔστιν; οὐκ ἄρα κινεῖταί τι." " ἤτοι τὸ ὂν
γίνεται ἢ τὸ μὴ ὄν. τὸ μὲν οὖν ὂν οὐ γίνεται,
ἔστι γάρ· ἀλλ᾽ οὐδὲ τὸ μὴ ὄν· τὸ μὲν γὰρ γινόμενον πάσχει τι, τὸ δὲ μὴ ὂν οὐ πάσχει. οὐδὲν
244 ἄρα γίνεται." " ἡ χιὼν ὕδωρ ἐστὶ πεπηγός· μέλαν
δὲ τὸ ὕδωρ ἐστίν· μέλαινα ἄρα ἐστὶν ἡ χιών."

Καὶ τοιούτους τινὰς ἀθροίσας ὕθλους συνάγει
τὰς ὀφρῦς, καὶ προχειρίζεται τὴν διαλεκτικήν, καὶ
πάνυ σεμνῶς ἐπιχειρεῖ κατασκευάζειν ἡμῖν δι᾽
ἀποδείξεων συλλογιστικῶν ὅτι γίνεταί τι καὶ ὅτι
κινεῖταί τι καὶ ὅτι ἡ χιών ἐστι λευκὴ καὶ ὅτι κέρατα
οὐκ ἔχομεν, καίτοι γε ἀρκοῦντος ἴσως τοῦ τὴν
ἐνάργειαν αὐτοῖς ἀντιτιθέναι πρὸς τὸ θραύεσθαι τὴν
διαβεβαιωτικὴν θέσιν αὐτῶν διὰ τῆς ἐκ τῶν
φαινομένων ἰσοσθενοῦς αὐτῶν ἀντιμαρτυρήσεως.
ταῦτά τοι καὶ ἐρωτηθεὶς φιλόσοφος τὸν κατὰ τῆς
κινήσεως λόγον σιωπῶν περιεπάτησεν, καὶ οἱ κατὰ
τὸν βίον ἄνθρωποι πεζάς τε καὶ διαποντίους στέλ-
λονται πορείας κατασκευάζουσί τε ναῦς καὶ οἰκίας

---

[a] The *ceratinē* or " Horn-fallacy " (invented by the
Megarics, *cf.* Diog. Laert. ii. 111, vi. 39) is generally put in
a simpler form—" If you have not lost anything, you have
it ; you have not lost horns, therefore you have horns " (a
joke aimed at cuckolds, thinks Fabricius). Sextus's complex syllogism seems much more clumsy (if the text is right).

but he will propound for us arguments such as these [a]
—" If it is not so that you both have fair horns and
have horns, you have horns ; but it is not so that
you have fair horns and have horns ; therefore you
have horns." " If a thing moves, it moves either in 242
the spot where it is or where it is not ; but it moves
neither in the spot where it is (for it is at rest) nor
in that where it is not (for how could a thing be
active in a spot where it does not so much as exist ?) ;
therefore nothing moves." [b] " Either the existent 243
becomes or the non-existent ; now the existent does
not become (for it exists) ; nor yet does the non-
existent (for the becoming is passive but the non-
existent is not passive) ; therefore nothing becomes." [c]
" Snow is frozen water ; but water is black ; there- 244
fore snow is black." [d]

And when he has made a collection of such trash
he draws his eyebrows together, and expounds
Dialectic and endeavours very solemnly to establish
for us by syllogistic proofs that a thing becomes, a
thing moves, snow is white, and we do not have
horns, although it is probably sufficient to confront
the trash with the plain fact in order to smash up
their positive affirmation by means of the equipollent
contradictory evidence derived from appearances.
Thus, in fact, a certain philosopher,[e] when the argument against motion was put to him, without a word
started to walk about ; and people who follow the usual
way of life proceed on journeys by land and sea and

[b] Cf. § 245, iii. 7, and *Adv. Gramm.* 311, where this argument is ascribed to Diodorus the Megaric.
[c] In *Adv. Log.* i. 71 this argument is ascribed to Gorgias.
[d] Anaxagoras held this notion about snow, cf. i. 33.
[e] Diogenes the Cynic (Diog. Laert. vi. 39) ; see iii. 66.
Cf. Boswell's story of how Dr. Johnson refuted Berkeley.

καὶ παιδοποιοῦνται τῶν κατὰ τῆς κινήσεως καὶ
245 γενέσεως ἀμελοῦντες λόγων. φέρεται δὲ καὶ
Ἡροφίλου τοῦ ἰατροῦ χαρίεν ἀπομνημόνευμα·
συνεχρόνισε γὰρ οὗτος Διοδώρῳ, ὃς ἐναπειροκαλῶν
τῇ διαλεκτικῇ λόγους διεξῄει σοφιστικοὺς κατά
τε ἄλλων πολλῶν καὶ τῆς κινήσεως. ὡς οὖν ἐκ-
βαλών ποτε ὦμον ὁ Διόδωρος ἧκε θεραπευθησόμενος
ὡς τὸν Ἡρόφιλον, ἐχαριεντίσατο ἐκεῖνος πρὸς
αὐτὸν λέγων " ἤτοι ἐν ᾧ ἦν τόπῳ ὁ ὦμος ὢν ἐκπέπτωκεν, ἢ ἐν ᾧ οὐκ ἦν· οὔτε δὲ ἐν ᾧ ἦν οὔτε
ἐν ᾧ οὐκ ἦν· οὐκ ἄρα ἐκπέπτωκεν," ὡς τὸν σοφι-
στὴν λιπαρεῖν ἐᾶν μὲν τοὺς τοιούτους λόγους, τὴν
δὲ ἐξ ἰατρικῆς ἁρμόζουσαν αὐτῷ προσάγειν θερα-
246 πείαν. ἀρκεῖ γάρ, οἶμαι, τὸ ἐμπείρως τε καὶ ἀδοξάστως κατὰ τὰς κοινὰς τηρήσεις τε καὶ προλήψεις
βιοῦν, περὶ τῶν ἐκ δογματικῆς περιεργίας καὶ
μάλιστα ἔξω τῆς βιωτικῆς χρείας λεγομένων
ἐπέχοντας. εἰ οὖν ὅσα μὲν εὐχρήστως ἂν ἐπιλυθείη,
ταῦτα οὐκ ἂν διαλύσαιτο ἡ διαλεκτική, ὅσα δὲ
ἐπιλύεσθαι δοίη τις ἂν ἴσως ὑπ' αὐτῆς σοφίσματα,
τούτων ἡ διάλυσις ἄχρηστός ἐστιν, ἄχρηστός ἐστι
κατὰ τὴν ἐπίλυσιν τῶν σοφισμάτων ἡ διαλεκτική.
247 Καὶ ἀπ' αὐτῶν δὲ τῶν παρὰ τοῖς διαλεκτικοῖς
λεγομένων ὁρμώμενός τις οὕτως ἂν συντόμως
ὑπομνήσειε περιττὰ εἶναι τὰ περὶ τῶν σοφισμάτων
παρ' αὐτοῖς δὴ τεχνολογούμενα. ἐπὶ τὴν τέχνην
τὴν διαλεκτικὴν φασιν ὡρμηκέναι οἱ διαλεκτικοὶ
οὐχ ἁπλῶς ὑπὲρ τοῦ γνῶναι τί ἐκ τίνος συνάγεται,

---

[a] A famous anatomist of Cos, *circa* 300 B.C. For Diodorus
Cronos *cf.* i. 234.

[b] This refers back to the end of § 244, § 245 being paren-
thetic.

build ships and houses and beget children without paying any attention to the arguments against motion and becoming.   And we are told of an amusing retort 245 made by the physician Herophilus [a] : he was a contemporary of Diodorus who, being given to juggling with dialectic, used to promulgate sophistical arguments against motion as well as many other things. So when Diodorus had dislocated his shoulder he came to Herophilus to get treated, and the latter jestingly said to him—" Your shoulder has been put out either in the place where it was or where it was not ; but it was put out neither where it was nor where it was not ; therefore it has not been put out " ; so that the Sophist begged him to leave such arguments alone and apply the treatment prescribed by medical art as suitable to his case.   For [b] it is, I 246 think, sufficient to conduct one's life empirically and undogmatically in accordance with the rules and beliefs that are commonly accepted, suspending judgement regarding the statements derived from dogmatic subtlety and furthest removed from the usage of life.[c]   If, then, dialectic would fail to expose any of the sophisms which might usefully be exposed, while the exposure of all the sophisms which we might perhaps grant it capable of exposing is useless, then in respect of the exposure of sophisms dialectic is useless.

Starting even from the actual statements made by 247 the dialecticians one might show concisely in this wise that their technical arguments about sophisms are superfluous.   The dialecticians assert that they have resorted to the art of dialectic not simply for the sake of ascertaining what is deduced from what but chiefly

[c] The traditional Sceptic attitude, cf. i. 15, 23 ff., etc.

ἀλλὰ προηγουμένως ὑπὲρ τοῦ δι᾽ ἀποδεικτικῶν
λόγων τὰ ἀληθῆ καὶ τὰ ψευδῆ κρίνειν ἐπίστασθαι·
λέγουσι γοῦν εἶναι τὴν διαλεκτικὴν ἐπιστήμην ἀλη-
248 θῶν καὶ ψευδῶν καὶ οὐδετέρων. ἐπεὶ τοίνυν αὐτοί
φασιν ἀληθῆ λόγον εἶναι τὸν δι᾽ ἀληθῶν λημμάτων
ἀληθὲς συνάγοντα συμπέρασμα, ἅμα τῷ ἐρωτηθῆναι λόγον ψεῦδος ἔχοντα τὸ συμπέρασμα
εἰσόμεθα ὅτι ψευδής ἐστιν καὶ οὐ συγκαταθησόμεθα
αὐτῷ. ἀνάγκη γὰρ καὶ αὐτὸν τὸν λόγον ἤτοι μὴ
εἶναι συνακτικὸν ἢ μηδὲ τὰ λήμματα ἔχειν ἀληθῆ.
249 καὶ τοῦτο δῆλον ἐκ τῶνδε. ἤτοι ἀκολουθεῖ τὸ ἐν
τῷ λόγῳ ψευδὲς συμπέρασμα τῇ διὰ τῶν λημμάτων αὐτοῦ συμπλοκῇ ἢ οὐκ ἀκολουθεῖ. ἀλλ᾽
εἰ μὲν οὐκ ἀκολουθεῖ, οὐδὲ συνακτικὸς λόγος ἔσται·
λέγουσι γὰρ συνακτικὸν γίνεσθαι λόγον ὅταν ἀκολουθῇ τῇ διὰ τῶν λημμάτων αὐτοῦ συμπλοκῇ τὸ
ἐν αὐτῷ συμπέρασμα. εἰ δὲ ἀκολουθεῖ, ἀνάγκη
καὶ τὴν διὰ τῶν λημμάτων συμπλοκὴν εἶναι ψευδῆ
κατὰ τὰς αὐτῶν ἐκείνων τεχνολογίας· φασὶ γὰρ
ὅτι τὸ ψεῦδος ψεύδει μὲν ἀκολουθεῖ, ἀληθεῖ δὲ
250 οὐδαμῶς. ὅτι δὲ ὁ μὴ συνακτικὸς ἢ μὴ ἀληθὴς
λόγος κατὰ αὐτοὺς οὐδὲ ἀποδεικτικός ἐστιν, δῆλον
ἐκ τῶν ἔμπροσθεν εἰρημένων.

Εἰ τοίνυν ἐρωτηθέντος λόγου ἐν ᾧ ψεῦδός ἐστι
τὸ συμπέρασμα, αὐτόθεν γινώσκομεν ὅτι οὐκ ἔστιν
ἀληθὴς οὐδὲ συνακτικὸς ὁ λόγος, ἐκ τοῦ συμπέρασμα ἔχειν ψευδές, οὐ συγκαταθησόμεθα αὐτῷ,
κἂν μὴ γινώσκωμεν παρὰ τί τὸ ἀπατηλὸν ἔχει.
ὥσπερ γὰρ οὐδ᾽ ὅτι ἀληθῆ ἐστὶ τὰ ὑπὸ τῶν ψηφο-
παικτῶν γινόμενα συγκατατιθέμεθα, ἀλλ᾽ ἴσμεν

for the sake of knowing how to discern the true and the false by means of probative arguments. Thus they declare that dialectic is " the science of what is true and false and neither." Since, then, they assert 248 that a true argument is one which draws a true conclusion by means of true premisses,[a] when an argument is propounded which has a false conclusion we shall at once know that it is false and shall not yield it assent. For the argument itself must either be illogical or contain premisses that are not true. The 249 following considerations show this clearly : The false conclusion in the argument either follows from the combination formed by its premisses, or it does not so follow. But if it does not so follow, neither will the argument be logically sound ; for an argument, they say, is logically sound when its conclusion follows from the combination formed by its premisses. If, again, it does so follow, then—according to their own technical treatises—the combination formed by its premisses must necessarily be false; for they say that the false follows from the false and nohow from the true.[b] And from what we have already said[c] it is plain that 250 according to them the argument which is not logically sound or not true is not probative either.

If, then, when an argument is propounded with a false conclusion we know at once that the argument is neither true nor logically sound, because of its false conclusion, we shall not assent to it, even if we fail to see wherein the fallacy lies. For just as we refuse our assent to the truth of the tricks performed by jugglers and know that they are deluding us, even

[a] *Cf.* §§ 137 ff.
[b] *Cf.* Aristot. *Anal. pr.* ii. 2 ; Diog. Laert. vii. 81.
[c] *Cf.* § 139.

ὅτι ἀπατῶσιν κἂν μὴ γινώσκωμεν ὅπως ἀπατῶσιν,
οὕτως οὐδὲ τοῖς ψευδέσι μὲν πιθανοῖς δὲ εἶναι
δοκοῦσι λόγοις πειθόμεθα, κἂν μὴ γινώσκωμεν
ὅπως παραλογίζονται.

251 Ἢ ἐπεὶ οὐ μόνον ἐπὶ ψεῦδος ἀπάγειν τὸ σόφισμά
φασιν[1] ἀλλὰ καὶ ἐπὶ ἄλλας ἀτοπίας, κοινότερον
οὕτω συνερωτητέον. ὁ ἐρωτώμενος λόγος ἤτοι
ἐπί τι ἀπρόσδεκτον ἡμᾶς ἄγει ἢ ἐπί τι τοιοῦτον
ὡς χρῆναι αὐτὸ προσδέχεσθαι. ἀλλ' εἰ μὲν τὸ
δεύτερον, οὐκ ἀτόπως αὐτῷ συγκαταθησόμεθα·
εἰ δὲ ἐπί τι ἀπρόσδεκτον, οὐχ ἡμᾶς τῇ ἀτοπίᾳ
δεήσει συγκατατίθεσθαι προπετῶς διὰ τὴν πιθανότητα, ἀλλ' ἐκείνους ἀφίστασθαι τοῦ λόγου τοῦ
τοῖς ἀτόποις ἀναγκάζοντος συγκατατίθεσθαι, εἴγε
μὴ ληρεῖν παιδαριωδῶς ἀλλὰ τἀληθῆ ζητεῖν, ὡς
252 ὑπισχνοῦνται, προῄρηνται. ὥσπερ γὰρ εἰ ὁδὸς
εἴη ἐπί τινα κρημνὸν φέρουσα, οὐκ ὠθοῦμεν αὐτοὺς
εἰς τὸν κρημνὸν διὰ τὸ ὁδόν τινα εἶναι φέρουσαν
ἐπ' αὐτόν, ἀλλ' ἀφιστάμεθα τῆς ὁδοῦ διὰ τὸν
κρημνόν, οὕτω καὶ εἰ λόγος εἴη ἐπί τι ὁμολογουμένως ἄτοπον ἡμᾶς ἀπάγων, οὐχὶ τῷ ἀτόπῳ συγκαταθησόμεθα διὰ τὸν λόγον, ἀλλ' ἀποστησόμεθα
253 τοῦ λόγου διὰ τὴν ἀτοπίαν. ὅταν οὖν οὕτως ἡμῖν
συνερωτᾶται λόγος, καθ' ἑκάστην πρότασιν ἐφέξομεν, εἶτα τοῦ ὅλου συνερωτηθέντος λόγου τὰ
δοκοῦντα ἐπάξομεν.

Καὶ εἴγε οἱ περὶ τὸν Χρύσιππον δογματικοὶ ἐν
τῇ συνερωτήσει τοῦ σωρίτου προϊόντος τοῦ λόγου

---

[1] τὸ σόφισμά φασιν T : τοῖς σοφίσμασιν mss., Bekk.

[a] The fallacy of the " Heap " (acervalis), so-called because
commonly framed thus : " This is a heap of grain : take away
one grain—two grains—three grains, and so on—is it still a

if we do not know how they do it, so likewise we
refuse to believe arguments which, though seemingly
plausible, are false, even when we do not know how
they are fallacious.

Further, since the sophism leads, they say, not only 251
to falsehood but also to other absurdities, we must
discuss it more at large. The argument propounded
leads us either to an inadmissible conclusion or to one
of such a sort that we must needs admit it. In the
latter case we shall assent to it without absurdity ;
but if it leads to what is inadmissible, it is not we that
ought to yield hasty assent to the absurdity because
of its plausibility, but it is they that ought to abstain
from the argument which constrains them to assent
to absurdities, if they really choose to seek truth, as
they profess, rather than drivel like children. Thus, 252
suppose there were a road leading up to a chasm, we
do not push ourselves into the chasm just because there
is a road leading to it but we avoid the road because
of the chasm ; so, in the same way, if there should be
an argument which leads us to a confessedly absurd
conclusion, we shall not assent to the absurdity just
because of the argument but avoid the argument
because of the absurdity. So whenever such an 253
argument is propounded to us we shall suspend
judgement regarding each premiss, and when finally
the whole argument is propounded we shall draw
what conclusions we approve.

And if the Dogmatists of the School of Chrysippus
declare that when the "Sorites"[a] is being propounded

heap?" Or "Does one grain make a heap? Or, if not,
2, 3, . . . x grains?" The essence of the fallacy is that "aliquid
minutatim et gradatim additur aut demitur" (Cicero, *Lucull.*
16). In modern Logic "Sorites" denotes a chain of syllogisms
in which all the conclusions save the last are suppressed.

φασὶ δεῖν ἵστασθαι καὶ ἐπέχειν, ἵνα μὴ ἐκπέσωσιν
εἰς ἀτοπίαν, πολὺ δήπου μᾶλλον ἂν ἡμῖν ἁρμόζον
εἴη σκεπτικοῖς οὖσιν, ὑποπτεύουσιν ἀτοπίαν, μὴ
προπίπτειν κατὰ τὰς συνερωτήσεις τῶν λημμάτων,
ἀλλ' ἐπέχειν καθ' ἕκαστον ἕως τῆς ὅλης συνερω-
254 τήσεως τοῦ λόγου. καὶ ἡμεῖς μὲν ἀδοξάστως ἀπὸ
τῆς βιωτικῆς τηρήσεως ὁρμώμενοι τοὺς ἀπατηλοὺς
οὕτως ἐκκλίνομεν λόγους, οἱ δογματικοὶ δὲ
ἀδυνάτως ἕξουσι διακρῖναι τὸ σόφισμα ἀπὸ τοῦ
δεόντως δοκοῦντος ἐρωτᾶσθαι λόγου, εἴγε χρὴ
δογματικῶς αὐτοὺς ἐπικρῖναι καὶ ὅτι συνακτικόν
ἐστι τὸ σχῆμα τοῦ λόγου καὶ ὅτι τὰ λήμματά ἐστιν
255 ἀληθῆ ἢ οὐχ οὕτως ἔχει· ὑπεμνήσαμεν γὰρ ἔμπροσθεν ὅτι οὔτε τοὺς συνακτικοὺς λόγους δύνανται
καταλαμβάνειν οὔτε ἀληθές εἶναί τι κρίνειν οἱοί
τέ εἰσι, μήτε κριτήριον μήτε ἀπόδειξιν ὁμολογουμένως ἔχοντες, ὡς ἐκ τῶν λεγομένων ὑπ' αὐτῶν
ἐκείνων ὑπεμνήσαμεν. παρέλκει οὖν ὅσον ἐπὶ
τούτοις ἡ θρυλουμένη παρὰ τοῖς διαλεκτικοῖς περὶ
τῶν σοφισμάτων τεχνολογία.
256 Παραπλήσια δὲ καὶ ἐπὶ τῆς διαστολῆς τῶν
ἀμφιβολιῶν λέγομεν. εἰ γὰρ ἡ ἀμφιβολία λέξις
ἐστὶ δύο καὶ πλείω σημαίνουσα καὶ αἱ λέξεις
σημαίνουσι θέσει, ὅσας μὲν χρήσιμόν ἐστιν ἀμφιβολίας διαλύεσθαι, τουτέστι τὰς ἔν τινι τῶν ἐμπειριῶν, ταύτας οἱ καθ' ἑκάστην τέχνην ἐγγεγυμ-
νασμένοι διαλύσονται, τὴν ἐμπειρίαν ἔχοντες αὐτοὶ
τῆς ὑπ' αὐτῶν πεποιημένης θετικῆς χρήσεως τῶν
ὀνομάτων κατὰ τῶν σημαινομένων, ὁ δὲ διαλεκ-
257 τικὸς οὐδαμῶς, οἷον ὡς ἐπὶ ταύτης τῆς ἀμφιβολίας

• Cf. § 214.

they ought to halt while the argument is still proceeding and suspend judgement, to avoid falling into absurdity, much more, surely, would it be fitting for us, who are Sceptics, when we suspect absurdity, to give no hasty approval of the premises propounded but rather to suspend judgement about each until the completion of the whole series which forms the argument. And 254 whereas we, by starting undogmatically from the observation of practical life, thus avoid these fallacious arguments, the Dogmatists will not be in a position to distinguish the Sophism from the argument which seems to be correctly propounded, seeing that they have to pronounce dogmatically that the form of the argument is, or is not, logically sound and also that the premises are, or are not, true. For we have 255 shown above that they are neither able to apprehend the logically valid arguments nor yet capable of deciding that a thing is true, since—as we have shown from their own statements—they possess neither a Criterion nor a Demonstration that commands general agreement. Thus far, then, the technical treatment of Sophisms so much talked of amongst the Dialecticians is otiose.

And we say much the same regarding the distin- 256 guishing of ambiguities. For if the Ambiguity is a word or phrase having two or more meanings, and it is by convention [a] that words have meaning, then all such ambiguities as can be usefully cleared up—such, that is, as occur in the course of some practical affair—will be cleared up, not certainly by the dialectician, but by the craftsmen trained in each several art, as they have personal experience of the conventional way adopted by themselves of using the terms to denote the objects signified—as, for example, in the 257

SEXTUS EMPIRICUS

" ἐν ταῖς παρακμαῖς τὴν ποικίλην δίαιταν καὶ τὸν οἶνον δοκιμαστέον." ἤδη δὲ καὶ κατὰ τὸν βίον ἄχρι καὶ τοὺς παῖδας ὁρῶμεν διαστελλομένους ἀμφιβολίας, ὧν ἡ διαστολὴ χρησιμεύειν αὐτοῖς δοκεῖ. εἰ γοῦν τις ὁμωνύμους οἰκέτας ἔχων κελεύοι παιδίον κληθῆναι αὐτῷ τὸν Μάνην, εἰ τύχοι, (τοῦτο γὰρ τοὔνομα τοῖς οἰκέταις ἔστω κοινόν) πεύσεται ὁ παῖς ποῖον. καὶ εἰ πλείονας καὶ διαφόρους τις οἴνους ἔχων λέγοι τῷ παιδίῳ " ἔγχεόν μοι τοῦ οἴνου πιεῖν," ὁμοίως ὁ παῖς πεύσεται ποίου.
258 οὕτως ἡ ἐν ἑκάστοις ἐμπειρία τοῦ χρησίμου τὴν διαστολὴν εἰσάγει.

Ὅσαι μέντοι μὴ ἔν τινι τῶν βιωτικῶν ἐμπειριῶν εἰσιν ἀμφιβολίαι, ἀλλ' ἐν δογματικαῖς οἰήσεσι κεῖνται καὶ εἰσὶν ἴσως ἄχρηστοι πρὸς τὸ ἀδοξάστως βιοῦν, περὶ ταύτας ἰδίως ὁ διαλεκτικὸς ἔχων ἀναγκασθήσεται καὶ ἐν αὐταῖς ὁμοίως ἐπέχειν κατὰ τὰς σκεπτικὰς ἐφόδους, καθὸ πράγμασιν ἀδήλοις καὶ ἀκαταλήπτοις ἢ καὶ ἀνυποστάτοις ἴσως εἰσὶ
259 συνεζευγμέναι. ἀλλὰ περὶ μὲν τούτων καὶ εἰσαῦθις διαλεξόμεθα· εἰ δέ τις δογματικὸς πρός τι τούτων ἀντιλέγειν ἐπιχειροίη, κρατυνεῖ τὸν σκεπτικὸν λόγον, ἐκ τῆς ἑκατέρωθεν ἐπιχειρήσεως καὶ τῆς ἀνεπικρίτου διαφωνίας τὴν περὶ τῶν ζητουμένων ἐποχὴν καὶ αὐτὸς βεβαιῶν.

Τοσαῦτα καὶ περὶ ἀμφιβολιῶν εἰπόντες αὐτοῦ που περιγράφομεν καὶ τὸ δεύτερον τῶν ὑποτυπώσεων σύνταγμα.

---

* Cf. § 237.
^b i.e. his special attitude, as a Dogmatist, towards ambiguities.

322

case of the ambiguity " In periods of abatement one should sanction a varied diet and wine." [a] And in the ordinary affairs of life we see already how people —ay, and even the slave-boys—distinguish ambiguities when they think such distinction is of use. Certainly, if a master who had servants named alike were to bid a boy called, say, " Manes " (supposing this to be common name for a servant) to be summoned, the slave-boy will ask " Which one ? " And if a man who had several different wines were to say to his boy " Pour me out a draught of wine," then too the boy will ask " Which one ? " Thus it 258 is the experience of what is useful in each affair that brings about the distinguishing of ambiguities.

All such ambiguities, however, as are not involved in the practical experiences of life but in dogmatic opinions, and are no doubt useless for a life void of dogmatism,—concerning these the Dialectician, in his own peculiar position,[b] will be similarly forced, in view of the Sceptic attacks, to suspend judgement, in so far as they are probably linked up with matters that are non-evident and non-apprehensible, or even non-substantial. This subject, however, we 259 shall discuss later on[c]; and if any Dogmatist should attempt to refute any of our statements he will be strengthening the Sceptic argument by adding support to their suspension of judgement about the matters in question as a result of our mutual antagonism and interminable dissension.

Having said thus much concerning ambiguities we now conclude therewith our Second Book of Outlines.

[c] No such discussion is to be found in the extant works of Sextus.

Γ

1 Περὶ μὲν τοῦ λογικοῦ μέρους τῆς λεγομένης φιλοσοφίας ὡς ἐν ὑποτυπώσει τοσαῦτα ἀρκούντως λέγοιτο ἄν.

Α΄.—ΠΕΡΙ ΤΟΥ ΦΥΣΙΚΟΥ ΜΕΡΟΥΣ

Κατὰ δὲ τὸν αὐτὸν τρόπον τῆς συγγραφῆς καὶ τὸ φυσικὸν μέρος αὐτῆς ἐπιόντες οὐ πρὸς ἕκαστον τῶν λεγομένων αὐτοῖς κατὰ τόπον ἀντεροῦμεν, ἀλλὰ τὰ καθολικώτερα κινεῖν ἐπιχειρήσομεν, οἷς συμπεριγράφεται καὶ τὰ λοιπά. ἀρξόμεθα δὲ ἀπὸ τοῦ περὶ ἀρχῶν λόγου.

Β΄.—ΠΕΡΙ ΑΡΧΩΝ ΔΡΑΣΤΙΚΩΝ

Καὶ ἐπειδὴ παρὰ τοῖς πλείστοις συμπεφώνηται τῶν ἀρχῶν τὰς μὲν ὑλικὰς εἶναι τὰς δὲ δραστικάς, ἀπὸ τῶν δραστικῶν τὴν ἀρχὴν τοῦ λόγου ποιησόμεθα· ταύτας γὰρ καὶ κυριωτέρας τῶν ὑλικῶν φασὶν εἶναι.

Γ΄.—ΠΕΡΙ ΘΕΟΥ

2 Οὐκοῦν ἐπεὶ θεὸν εἶναι δραστικώτατον αἴτιον οἱ πλείους ἀπεφήναντο, πρότερον περὶ θεοῦ σκοπή-

---

[a] For the Stoic division of " Philosophy " into three parts —logic, physics and ethics—see ii. 13.   [b] *Cf.* ii. 84.

BOOK III

Concerning the logical division of what is called **1** " Philosophy " [a] the foregoing account may suffice by way of outline.

Chapter I.—Of the Physical Division

Pursuing the same method of exposition in our investigation of the Physical division of Philosophy, we shall not refute each of their statements in order, but we shall endeavour to overthrow those of a more general character [b] wherein the rest also are included.

Let us begin with their doctrine of Principles.[c]

Chapter II.—Of Efficient Principles

Since it is agreed by most that of Principles some are material and some efficient, we shall make our argument start with the efficient ; for these, as they assert, are superior to the material.

Chapter III.—Concerning God

Since, then, the majority have declared that God **2** is a most efficient Cause, let us begin by inquiring

[c] " Principles," or " origins " (ἀρχαί), which are assumed to explain existence: fundamental realities: here used practically as a synonym for " Causes " (αἰτία).

σωμεν, ἐκεῖνο προειπόντες ὅτι τῷ μὲν βίῳ κατακολουθοῦντες ἀδοξάστως φαμὲν εἶναι θεοὺς καὶ
σέβομεν θεοὺς καὶ προνοεῖν αὐτοὺς φαμέν, πρὸς
δὲ τὴν προπέτειαν τῶν δογματικῶν τάδε λέγομεν.

Τῶν ἐννοουμένων ἡμῖν πραγμάτων τὰς οὐσίας
ἐπινοεῖν ὀφείλομεν, οἷον εἰ σώματά ἐστιν ἢ ἀσώματα. ἀλλὰ καὶ τὰ εἴδη· οὐ γὰρ ἄν τις ἵππον
ἐννοῆσαι δύναιτο μὴ οὐχὶ πρότερον τὸ εἶδος τοῦ
ἵππου μαθών. τό τε ἐννοούμενον ἐννοεῖσθαί που
3 ὀφείλει. ἐπεὶ οὖν τῶν δογματικῶν οἱ μὲν σῶμά
φασιν εἶναι τὸν θεὸν οἱ δὲ ἀσώματον, καὶ οἱ μὲν
ἀνθρωποειδῆ οἱ δὲ οὔ, καὶ οἱ μὲν ἐν τόπῳ οἱ δὲ
οὔ, καὶ τῶν ἐν τόπῳ οἱ μὲν ἐντὸς κόσμου οἱ δὲ
ἐκτός, πῶς δυνησόμεθα ἔννοιαν θεοῦ λαμβάνειν
μήτε οὐσίαν ἔχοντες αὐτοῦ ὁμολογουμένην μήτε
εἶδος μήτε τόπον ἐν ᾧ εἴη; πρότερον γὰρ ἐκεῖνοι
ὁμολογησάτωσάν τε καὶ συμφωνησάτωσαν ὅτι
τοιόσδε ἐστὶν ὁ θεός· εἶτα ἡμῖν αὐτὸν ὑποτυπω-
σάμενοι οὕτως ἀξιούτωσαν ἡμᾶς ἔννοιαν θεοῦ λαμβάνειν. ἐς ὅσον δὲ ἀνεπικρίτως διαφωνοῦσιν, τί
νοήσομεν ἡμεῖς ὁμολογουμένως παρ' αὐτῶν οὐκ
ἔχομεν.

4 Ἀλλ' ἄφθαρτόν τι, φασί, καὶ μακάριον ἐννοήσας,
τὸν θεὸν εἶναι τοῦτο νόμιζε. τοῦτο δέ ἐστιν εὔηθες·
ὡς γὰρ ὁ μὴ εἰδὼς τὸν Δίωνα οὐδὲ τὰ συμβεβηκότα αὐτῷ ὡς Δίωνι δύναται νοεῖν, οὕτως ἐπεὶ

---

[a] Cf. Adv. Phys. i. 13 ff. It is argued here (1) that God is
not "conceived," §§ 2-5 ; nor (2) "apprehended," §§ 6-11.
Cf. § 218 infra.

[b] Literally "life" ; cf. i. 23 f.

[c] "Substances" in the logical sense, as opposed to
"properties."

[d] The Stoics held God to be "corporeal," not "of human

about God,[a] first premising that although, following
the ordinary view,[b] we affirm undogmatically that
Gods exist and reverence Gods and ascribe to them
foreknowledge, yet as against the rashness of the
Dogmatists we argue as follows.

When we conceive objects we ought to form conceptions of their substances [c] as well, as, for instance,
whether they are corporeal or incorporeal. And also
of their forms ; for no one could conceive " Horse "
unless he had first learnt the horse's form. And
of course the object conceived must be conceived
⟨as existing⟩ somewhere. Since, then, some of the [3]
Dogmatists assert that God is corporeal, others that
he is incorporeal, and some that he has human form,
others not, and some that he exists in space, others
not ; and of those who assert that he is in space some
put him inside the world, others outside [d] ; how shall
we be able to reach a conception of God when we have
no agreement about his substance or his form or his
place of abode ? Let them first agree and consent
together that God is of such and such a nature, and
then, when they have sketched out for us that nature,
let them require that we should form a conception of
God. But so long as they disagree interminably, we
cannot say what agreed notion we are to derive
from them.

But, say they,[e] when you have conceived of a Being [4]
imperishable and blessed, regard this as God. But
this is foolish ; for just as one who does not know Dion
is unable also to conceive the properties which belong
to him as Dion, so also when we do not know the

form," " inside the world " ; the Epicureans, " corporeal,"
" of human form," " outside the world " ; Aristotle, " incorporeal " and " not in space." *Cf.* § 218 *infra.*
   [e] *i.e.* the Stoics and Epicurus, *cf.* § 219 *infra.*

οὐκ ἴσμεν τὴν οὐσίαν τοῦ θεοῦ, οὐδὲ τὰ συμβεβηκότα αὐτῷ μαθεῖν τε καὶ ἐννοῆσαι δυνησόμεθα.
5 χωρὶς δὲ τούτων εἰπάτωσαν ἡμῖν τί ἐστι τὸ
μακάριον, πότερον τὸ ἐνεργοῦν κατὰ ἀρετὴν καὶ
προνοούμενον τῶν ὑφ᾽ ἑαυτὸ τεταγμένων, ἢ τὸ
ἀνενέργητον καὶ μήτε αὐτὸ πράγματα ἔχον μήτε
ἑτέρῳ παρέχον· καὶ γὰρ καὶ περὶ τούτου διαφωνή-
σαντες ἀνεπικρίτως ἀνεννόητον ἡμῖν πεποιήκασι τὸ
μακάριον, διὰ δὲ τοῦτο καὶ τὸν θεόν.
6 ῞Ινα δὲ καὶ ἐπινοῆται ὁ θεός, ἐπέχειν ἀνάγκη
περὶ τοῦ πότερον ἔστιν ἢ οὐκ ἔστιν ὅσον ἐπὶ τοῖς
δογματικοῖς. τὸ γὰρ εἶναι τὸν θεὸν πρόδηλον μὲν
οὐκ ἔστιν. εἰ γὰρ ἐξ ἑαυτοῦ προσέπιπτεν, συν-
εφώνησαν ἂν οἱ δογματικοὶ τίς ἐστι καὶ ποδαπὸς
καὶ ποῦ· ἡ ἀνεπίκριτος δὲ διαφωνία πεποίηκεν
αὐτὸν ἄδηλον ἡμῖν εἶναι δοκεῖν καὶ ἀποδείξεως
7 δεόμενον. ὁ μὲν οὖν ἀποδεικνύων[1] ὅτι ἔστι θεός,
ἤτοι διὰ προδήλου τοῦτο ἀποδείκνυσιν ἢ δι᾽ ἀδήλου.
διὰ προδήλου μὲν οὖν οὐδαμῶς· εἰ γὰρ ἦν πρόδηλον
τὸ ἀποδεικνύον ὅτι ἔστι θεός, ἐπεὶ τὸ ἀποδεικνύμενον πρὸς τῷ ἀποδεικνύντι νοεῖται, διὸ καὶ συγκαταλαμβάνεται αὐτῷ, καθὼς καὶ παρεστήσαμεν,
πρόδηλον ἔσται καὶ τὸ εἶναι θεόν, συγκαταλαμβανόμενον τῷ ἀποδεικνύντι αὐτὸ προδήλῳ ὄντι.
οὐκ ἔστι δὲ πρόδηλον, ὡς ὑπεμνήσαμεν· οὐδὲ ἀπο-
8 δείκνυται ἄρα διὰ προδήλου. ἀλλ᾽ οὐδὲ δι᾽ ἀδήλου.

---

[1] ἀποδεικνύων T: λέγων Steph., Bekk.: om. mss.

---

^a The Epicurean Deity as contrasted with the Platonic
and Stoic. *Cf.* Lucretius ii. 646 ff. :

> omnis enim per se divom natura necessest
> inmortali aevo summa cum pace fruatur
> semota ab nostris rebus seiunctaque longe.

substance of God we shall also be unable to learn and conceive his properties. And apart from this, let 5 them tell us what a " blessed " thing is—whether it is that which energizes according to virtue and fore-knows what is subject to itself, or that which is void of energy and neither performs any work itself nor provides work for another.[a] For indeed about this also they disagree interminably and thus render " the blessed " something we cannot conceive, and therefore God also.

Further, in order to form a conception of God one 6 must necessarily—so far as depends on the Dog-matists—suspend judgement as to his existence or non-existence. For the existence of God is not pre-evident.[b] For if God impressed us automatically, the Dogmatists would have agreed together regard-ing his essence, his character, and his place ; whereas their interminable disagreement has made him seem to us non-evident and needing demonstration. Now 7 he that demonstrates the existence of God does so by means of what is either pre-evident or non-evident. Certainly not, then, by means of the pre-evident ; for if what demonstrates God's existence were pre-evident, then—since the thing proved is conceived together with that which proves it, and therefore is apprehended along with it as well, as we have estab-lished [c]—God's existence also will be pre-evident, it being apprehended along with the pre-evident fact which proves it. But, as we have shown, it is not pre-evident ; therefore it is not proved, either, by a pre-evident fact. Nor yet by what is non-evident. For 8

[b] *i.e.* plainly manifest, self-evident, *cf.* i. 178.
[c] *Cf.* ii. 179, 128.

τὸ γὰρ ἄδηλον τὸ ἀποδεικτικὸν τοῦ εἶναι θεόν,
ἀποδείξεως χρῇζον, εἰ μὲν διὰ προδήλου λέγοιτο
ἀποδείκνυσθαι, οὐκέτι ἄδηλον ἔσται ἀλλὰ πρόδηλον
[τὸ εἶναι θεόν].[1] οὐκ ἄρα τὸ ἀποδεικτικὸν αὐτοῦ
ἄδηλον διὰ προδήλου ἀποδείκνυται. ἀλλ' οὐδὲ δι'
ἀδήλου· εἰς ἄπειρον γὰρ ἐκπεσεῖται ὁ τοῦτο λέγων,
αἰτούντων ἡμῶν ἀεὶ ἀπόδειξιν τοῦ φερομένου
ἀδήλου πρὸς ἀπόδειξιν τοῦ προκειμένου. οὐκ ἄρα
9 ἐξ ἑτέρου δύναται ἀποδείκνυσθαι τὸ εἶναι θεόν. εἰ
δὲ μήτε ἐξ ἑαυτοῦ ἐστι πρόδηλον μήτε ἐξ ἑτέρου
ἀποδείκνυται, ἀκατάληπτον ἔσται εἰ ἔστι θεός.

Ἔτι καὶ τοῦτο λεκτέον. ὁ λέγων εἶναι θεὸν ἤτοι
προνοεῖν αὐτὸν τῶν ἐν κόσμῳ φησὶν ἢ οὐ προνοεῖν,
καὶ εἰ μὲν προνοεῖ, ἤτοι πάντων ἢ τινῶν. ἀλλ' εἰ
μὲν πάντων προυνόει, οὐκ ἦν ἂν οὔτε κακόν τι
οὔτε κακία ἐν τῷ κόσμῳ· κακίας δὲ πάντα μεστὰ
εἶναι λέγουσιν· οὐκ ἄρα πάντων προνοεῖν λεχθή-
10 σεται ὁ θεός. εἰ δὲ τινῶν προνοεῖ, διὰ τί τῶνδε
μὲν προνοεῖ τῶνδε δὲ οὔ; ἤτοι γὰρ καὶ βούλεται
καὶ δύναται πάντων προνοεῖν, ἢ βούλεται μὲν οὐ
δύναται δέ, ἢ δύναται μὲν οὐ βούλεται δέ, ἢ οὔτε
βούλεται οὔτε δύναται. ἀλλ' εἰ μὲν καὶ ἠβούλετο
καὶ ἠδύνατο, πάντων ἂν προυνόει· οὐ προνοεῖ δὲ
πάντων διὰ τὰ προειρημένα· οὐκ ἄρα καὶ βούλεται
καὶ δύναται πάντων προνοεῖν. εἰ δὲ βούλεται μὲν
οὐ δύναται δέ, ἀσθενέστερός ἐστι τῆς αἰτίας δι' ἣν
11 οὐ δύναται προνοεῖν ὧν οὐ προνοεῖ· ἔστι δὲ παρὰ

---

[1] [τὸ . . . θεόν] del. l'app.

if the non-evident fact which is capable of proving God's existence, needing proof as it does, shall be said to be proved by means of a pre-evident fact, it will no longer be non-evident but pre-evident. Therefore the non-evident fact which proves his existence is not proved by what is pre-evident. Nor yet by what is non-evident; for he who asserts this will be driven into circular reasoning when we keep demanding proof every time for the non-evident fact which he produces as proof of the one last propounded. Consequently, the existence of God cannot be proved from any other fact. But if God's existence is neither 9 automatically pre-evident nor proved from another fact, it will be inapprehensible.

There is this also to be said. He who affirms that God exists either declares that he has, or that he has not, forethought for the things in the universe, and in the former case that such forethought is for all things or for some things. But if he had forethought for all, there would have been nothing bad and no badness in the world; yet all things, they say, are full of badness; hence it shall not be said that God forethinks all things. If, again, he forethinks some, why 10 does he forethink these things and not those? For either he has both the will and the power to forethink all things, or else he has the will but not the power, or the power but not the will, or neither the will nor the power. But if he had had both the will and the power he would have had forethought for all things; but for the reasons stated above he does not forethink all; therefore he has not both the will and the power to forethink all. And if he has the will but not the power, he is less strong than the cause which renders him unable to forethink what he does not forethink:

τὴν θεοῦ ἐπίνοιαν τὸ ἀσθενέστερον εἶναί τινος
αὐτόν. εἰ δὲ δύναται μὲν πάντων προνοεῖν, οὐ
βούλεται δέ, βάσκανος ἂν εἴη νομισθείη. εἰ δὲ
οὔτε βούλεται οὔτε δύναται, καὶ βάσκανός ἐστι
καὶ ἀσθενής, ὅπερ λέγειν περὶ θεοῦ ἀσεβούντων
ἐστίν. οὐκ ἄρα προνοεῖ τῶν ἐν κόσμῳ ὁ θεός.

Εἰ δὲ οὐδενὸς πρόνοιαν ποιεῖται οὐδὲ ἔστιν αὐτοῦ
ἔργον οὐδὲ ἀποτέλεσμα, οὐχ ἕξει τις εἰπεῖν πόθεν
καταλαμβάνει ὅτι ἔστι θεός, εἴγε μήτε ἐξ ἑαυτοῦ
φαίνεται μήτε δι᾽ ἀποτελεσμάτων τινῶν καταλαμβάνεται. καὶ διὰ ταῦτα ἄρα ἀκατάληπτόν ἐστιν εἰ
12 ἔστι θεός. ἐκ δὲ τούτων ἐπιλογιζόμεθα ὅτι ἴσως
ἀσεβεῖν ἀναγκάζονται οἱ διαβεβαιωτικῶς λέγοντες
εἶναι θεόν· πάντων μὲν γὰρ αὐτὸν προνοεῖν λέγοντες
κακῶν αἴτιον τὸν θεὸν εἶναι φήσουσιν, τινῶν δὲ ἢ
καὶ μηδενὸς προνοεῖν αὐτὸν λέγοντες ἤτοι βάσκανον
τὸν θεὸν ἢ ἀσθενῆ λέγειν ἀναγκασθήσονται, ταῦτα
δέ ἐστιν ἀσεβούντων προδήλως.

Δ᾽.—ΠΕΡΙ ΑΙΤΙΟΥ

13 Ἵνα δὲ μὴ καὶ ἡμᾶς βλασφημεῖν ἐπιχειρήσωσιν
οἱ δογματικοὶ δι᾽ ἀπορίαν τοῦ πραγματικῶς ἡμῖν
ἀντιλέγειν, κοινότερον περὶ τοῦ ἐνεργητικοῦ αἰτίου
διαπορήσομεν, πρότερον ἐπιστῆσαι πειραθέντες τῇ
τοῦ αἰτίου ἐπινοίᾳ. ὅσον μὲν οὖν ἐπὶ τοῖς λεγομένοις ὑπὸ τῶν δογματικῶν οὐδ᾽ ἂν ἐννοῆσαί τις τὸ
αἴτιον δύναιτο, εἴγε πρὸς τῷ διαφώνους καὶ ἀλλο-
κότους ἐννοίας τοῦ αἰτίου ⟨ἀποδιδόναι⟩,[1] ἔτι καὶ
τὴν ὑπόστασιν αὐτοῦ πεποιήκασιν ἀνεύρετον διὰ

---

[1] ⟨ἀποδιδόναι⟩ add. T, Bekk. cj.

---

[a] *i.e.* by charging us with atheism.

but it is contrary to our notion of God that he should 11
be weaker than anything. And if, again, he has the
power but not the will to have forethought for all, he
will be held to be malignant ; while if he has neither
the will nor the power, he is both malignant and weak
—an impious thing to say about God. Therefore
God has no forethought for the things in the universe.

But if he exercises no forethought for anything, and
there exists no work nor product of his, no one will be
able to name the source of the apprehension of God's
existence, inasmuch as he neither appears of himself
nor is apprehended by means of any of his products.
So for these reasons we cannot apprehend whether
God exists. And from this we further conclude that 12
those who positively affirm God's existence are probably compelled to be guilty of impiety ; for if they
say that he forethinks all things they will be declaring
that God is the cause of what is evil, while if they say
that he forethinks some things or nothing they will
be forced to say that God is either malignant or weak,
and obviously this is to use impious language.

Chapter IV.—Concerning Cause

To prevent the Dogmatists attempting also to 13
slander us,[a] because of their inability to refute us
in a practical way, we shall discuss the question of
the efficient Cause more at large when we have first
tried to give attention to the conception of Cause.
Now so far as the statements of the Dogmatists are
concerned, it would be impossible for anyone even to
conceive Cause, since, in addition to offering dis-
crepant and contradictory conceptions of Cause, they
have rendered its substance also indiscoverable by

14 τὴν περὶ αὐτὸ διαφωνίαν. οἱ μὲν γὰρ σῶμα οἱ δὲ ἀσώματον τὸ αἴτιον εἶναί φασιν. δόξαι δ' ἂν αἴτιον εἶναι κοινότερον κατ' αὐτοὺς δι' ὃ ἐνεργοῦν γίνεται τὸ ἀποτέλεσμα, οἷον ὡς ὁ ἥλιος ἢ ἡ τοῦ ἡλίου θερμότης τοῦ χεῖσθαι τὸν κηρὸν ἢ τῆς χύσεως τοῦ κηροῦ. καὶ γὰρ ἐν τούτῳ διαπεφωνήκασιν, οἱ μὲν προσηγοριῶν αἴτιον εἶναι τὸ αἴτιον φάσκοντες, οἷον τῆς χύσεως, οἱ δὲ κατηγορημάτων, οἷον τοῦ χεῖσθαι. διό, καθάπερ εἶπον, κοινότερον ἂν εἴη τὸ αἴτιον τοῦτο δι' ὃ ἐνεργοῦν γίνεται τὸ ἀποτέλεσμα.

15 Τούτων δὲ τῶν αἰτίων οἱ μὲν πλείους ἡγοῦνται τὰ μὲν συνεκτικὰ εἶναι τὰ δὲ συναίτια τὰ δὲ συνεργά, καὶ συνεκτικὰ μὲν ὑπάρχειν ὧν παρόντων πάρεστι τὸ ἀποτέλεσμα καὶ αἰρομένων αἴρεται καὶ μειουμένων μειοῦται (οὕτω γὰρ τὴν περίθεσιν τῆς στραγγάλης αἴτιον εἶναί φασι τοῦ πνιγμοῦ), συναίτιον δὲ ὃ τὴν ἴσην εἰσφέρεται δύναμιν ἑτέρῳ συναιτίῳ πρὸς τὸ εἶναι τὸ ἀποτέλεσμα (οὕτως ἕκαστον τῶν ἑλκόντων τὸ ἄροτρον βοῶν αἴτιον εἶναί φασι τῆς ὁλκῆς τοῦ ἀρότρου), συνεργὸν δὲ ὃ βραχεῖαν εἰσφέρεται δύναμιν καὶ πρὸς τὸ μετὰ ῥᾳστώνης ὑπάρχειν τὸ ἀποτέλεσμα, οἷον ὅταν δυοῖν βάρος τι βασταζόντων μόλις τρίτος τις προσελθὼν συγκουφίσῃ τοῦτο.

16 Ἔνιοι μέντοι καὶ παρόντα μελλόντων αἴτια ἔφασαν εἶναι, ὡς τὰ προκαταρκτικά, οἷον τὴν ἐπιτεταμένην ἡλίωσιν πυρετοῦ. τινὲς δὲ ταῦτα παρῃτήσαντο, ἐπειδὴ τὸ αἴτιον πρός τι ὑπάρχον καὶ

---

[a] e.g. Plato's " Ideas " and the Pythagorean " Numbers "; cf. § 32, Adv. Phys. i. 364.

[b] Cf. Plato, Cratyl. 413 A, Phileb. 26 E ; Adv. Phys. i. 228.

their disagreement about it. For some affirm Cause **14**
to be corporeal, others incorporeal.[a] In the broad
sense, a Cause would seem to be, according to them,
"That by whose energizing the effect comes about";[b]
as, for example, the sun or the sun's heat is the cause
of the wax being melted or of the melting of the
wax. For even on this point they are at variance,
some declaring that Cause is causal of nouns, such as
"the melting," others of predicates, such as "being
melted." Hence, as I said, in the broad sense Cause
will be "that by whose energizing the effect comes
about."

The majority of them hold that of these Causes **15**
some are immediate,[c] some associate, some co-
operant; and that causes are "immediate" when
their presence involves the presence, and their removal the removal, and their decrease the decrease,
of the effect (it is thus, they say, that the fixing on
of the halter causes the strangling); and that an
"associate" cause is one which contributes a force
equal to that of its fellow-cause towards the production of the effect (it is thus, they say, that each of the
oxen which draw the plough is a cause of the drawing
of the plough); and that a "co-operant" cause is
one which contributes a slight force towards the easy
production of the effect, as in the case when two men
are lifting a heavy load with difficulty the assistance
of a third helps to lighten it.

Some of them, however, have asserted further that **16**
things present are causes of things future, being
"antecedents"; as when intense exposure to the
sun causes fever. But this view is rejected by some,
on the ground that, since the Cause is relative to

[a] *Cf. Adv. Phys.* i. 1, 243.

πρὸς τὸ ἀποτέλεσμα ὂν οὐ δύναται προηγεῖσθαι
αὐτοῦ ὡς αἴτιον.

Ἐν δὲ τῇ περὶ αὐτῶν διαπορήσει τοιάδε λέγομεν.

Ε΄.—ΕΙ ΕΣΤΙ ΤΙ ΤΙΝΟΣ ΑΙΤΙΟΝ

17 Πιθανόν ἐστιν εἶναι τὸ αἴτιον· πῶς γὰρ ἂν
αὔξησις γένοιτο, μείωσις, γένεσις, φθορά, καθόλου
κίνησις, τῶν φυσικῶν τε καὶ ψυχικῶν ἀποτελεσμάτων ἕκαστον, ἡ τοῦ παντὸς κόσμου διοίκησις,
τὰ ἄλλα πάντα, εἰ μὴ κατά τινα αἰτίαν; καὶ γὰρ
εἰ μηδὲν τούτων ὡς πρὸς τὴν φύσιν ὑπάρχει,
λέξομεν ὅτι διά τινα αἰτίαν πάντως φαίνεται ἡμῖν
18 τοιαῦτα ὁποῖα οὐκ ἔστιν. ἀλλὰ καὶ πάντα ἐκ
πάντων καὶ ὡς ἔτυχεν ἂν ἦν μὴ οὔσης αἰτίας.
οἷον ἵπποι μὲν ἐκ μυῶν, εἰ τύχοι, γεννηθήσονται,
ἐλέφαντες δὲ ἐκ μυρμήκων· καὶ ἐν μὲν ταῖς
Αἰγυπτίαις Θήβαις ὄμβροι ποτὲ ἐξαίσιοι καὶ χιόνες
ἂν ἐγίνοντο, τὰ δὲ νότια ὄμβρων οὐ μετεῖχεν, εἰ
μὴ αἰτία τις ἦν, δι' ἣν τὰ μὲν νότιά ἐστι δυσχείμερα,
19 αὐχμηρὰ δὲ τὰ πρὸς τὴν ἕω. καὶ περιτρέπεται
δὲ ὁ λέγων μηδὲν αἴτιον εἶναι· εἰ μὲν γὰρ ἁπλῶς
καὶ ἄνευ τινὸς αἰτίας τοῦτό φησι λέγειν, ἄπιστος
ἔσται, εἰ δὲ διά τινα αἰτίαν, βουλόμενος ἀναιρεῖν τὸ
αἴτιον τίθησιν, ἀποδιδοὺς[1] αἰτίαν δι' ἣν οὐκ ἔστιν
αἴτιον.

---

[1] ἀποδιδοὺς Kayser, Papp.: ἀποδιδόσθω mss., Bekk.

[a] Cf. § 25 infra.

[b] To mark the distinction between αἴτιον and αἰτία, I
render the former by "Cause," the latter by "cause."
The latter seems used mostly of the particular instance,
the former of the general notion; or (as in §§ 19, 23, 24)
the former of the cause of existence, the latter of the cause
of cognition.

something existent and to a real effect, it cannot precede it as its cause.[a]

As regards this controversy, our position is as follows:

CHAPTER V.—DOES ANYTHING CAUSE ANYTHING?

That Cause exists is plausible; for how could 17 there come about increase, decrease, generation, corruption, motion in general, each of the physical and mental effects, the ordering of the whole universe, and everything else, except by reason of some cause[b]? For even if none of these things has real existence,[c] we shall affirm that it is due to some cause that they appear to us other than they really are. Moreover, if 18 cause were non-existent everything would have been produced by everything and at random. Horses, for instance, might be born, perchance, of flies, and elephants of ants; and there would have been severe rains and snow in Egyptian Thebes, while the southern districts would have had no rain, unless there had been a cause which makes the southern parts stormy, the eastern dry. Also, he who asserts 19 that there is no Cause is refuted; for if he says that he makes this assertion absolutely and without any cause, he will not win credence; but if he says that he makes it owing to some cause, he is positing Cause while wishing to abolish it, since he offers us a cause to prove the non-existence of Cause.

[c] *Cf. Adv. Phys.* i. 201. "These things," being "appearances" (or phenomena), may not really exist in the form in which they "appear" to us: the "real" may differ from the "phenomenal," but even so a "Cause" of that difference must be assumed.

SEXTUS EMPIRICUS

Διὰ ταῦτα μὲν οὖν πιθανόν ἐστιν εἶναι τὸ αἴτιον·
20 ὅτι δὲ καὶ τὸ λέγειν μὴ εἶναί τινός τι αἴτιον
πιθανόν ἐστι, φανερὸν ἔσται λόγους ἡμῶν ἐκθεμένων ὀλίγους ἀπὸ πολλῶν ἐπὶ τοῦ παρόντος πρὸς
τὴν τούτου ὑπόμνησιν. οἷον γοῦν ἀδύνατόν ἐστι
τὸ αἴτιον ἐννοῆσαι πρὶν τὸ ἀποτέλεσμα τούτου
καταλαβεῖν ὡς ἀποτέλεσμα αὐτοῦ· τότε γὰρ γνω-
ρίζομεν ὅτι αἴτιόν ἐστι τοῦ ἀποτελέσματος, ὅταν
21 ἐκεῖνο ὡς ἀποτέλεσμα καταλαμβάνωμεν. ἀλλ' οὐδὲ
τὸ ἀποτέλεσμα τοῦ αἰτίου ὡς ἀποτέλεσμα αὐτοῦ
καταλαβεῖν δυνάμεθα, ἐὰν μὴ καταλάβωμεν τὸ
αἴτιον τοῦ ἀποτελέσματος ὡς αἴτιον αὐτοῦ· τότε
γὰρ καὶ ὅτι ἀποτέλεσμά ἐστιν αὐτοῦ γινώσκειν
δοκοῦμεν, ὅταν τὸ αἴτιον αὐτοῦ ὡς αἴτιον αὐτοῦ
22 καταλάβωμεν. εἰ οὖν ἵνα μὲν ἐννοήσωμεν τὸ
αἴτιον, δεῖ προεπιγνῶναι τὸ ἀποτέλεσμα, ἵνα δὲ
τὸ ἀποτέλεσμα γνῶμεν, ὡς ἔφην, δεῖ προεπίστασθαι
τὸ αἴτιον, ὁ διάλληλος τῆς ἀπορίας τρόπος ἄμφω
δείκνυσιν ἀνεπινόητα, μήτε τοῦ αἰτίου ὡς αἰτίου
μήτε τοῦ ἀποτελέσματος ὡς ἀποτελέσματος ἐπινοεῖσθαι δυναμένου· ἑκατέρου γὰρ αὐτῶν δεομένου
τῆς παρὰ θατέρου πίστεως, οὐχ ἕξομεν ἀπὸ τίνος
αὐτῶν ἀρξόμεθα τῆς ἐννοίας. διόπερ οὐδὲ ἀποφαίνεσθαι δυνησόμεθα ὅτι ἔστι τί τινος αἴτιον.
23 Ἵνα δὲ καὶ ἐννοεῖσθαι δύνασθαι τὸ αἴτιον συγχωρήσῃ τις, ἀκατάληπτον ἂν εἶναι νομισθείη διὰ
τὴν διαφωνίαν. ὃς μὲν γάρ φησιν εἶναί τί τινος
αἴτιον, ἤτοι ἁπλῶς καὶ ἀπὸ μηδεμιᾶς ὁρμώμενος
αἰτίας εὐλόγου τοῦτό φησι λέγειν, ἢ διά τινας
αἰτίας ἐπὶ τὴν συγκατάθεσιν ταύτην ἰέναι λέξει.
καὶ εἰ μὲν ἁπλῶς, οὐκ ἔσται πιστότερος τοῦ λέγον-

For these reasons, then, the existence of Cause is plausible. But that it is also plausible to say that nothing is the Cause of anything will be evident when we have set forth, to suit the occasion, a few of the many arguments which go to prove this case. Thus it is, for example, impossible to conceive the Cause before apprehending its effect as *its* effect ; for we only recognize that it is causative of the effect when we apprehend the latter as an effect. But we cannot either apprehend the effect of the Cause as *its* effect unless we apprehend the Cause of the effect as *its* Cause ; for we think we know that it is its effect only when we have apprehended the Cause of it as its Cause. If, then, in order to conceive the Cause, we must first know the effect, while in order to know the effect we must, as I said, have previous knowledge of the Cause, the fallacy of this circular mode of reasoning proves both to be inconceivable, the Cause being incapable of being conceived as Cause, and the effect as effect. For since each of them needs the evidence of the other, we shall not be able to say which conception is to have the precedence. Hence we shall be unable to declare that anything is the Cause of anything.

And even were one to grant that Cause can be conceived, it might be held to be inapprehensible because of the divergency of opinion. For he who says that there is some Cause of something either asserts that he makes this statement absolutely and without basing it on any rational cause, or else he will declare that he has arrived at his conviction owing to certain causes.[a] If, then, he says that he states it " absolutely," he will be no more worthy of credence

---

[a] *Cf.*, for the following arguments, i. 164.

τος ἁπλῶς μηδὲν εἶναι μηδενὸς αἴτιον· εἰ δὲ καὶ
αἰτίας λέξει δι' ἃς εἶναί τί τινος αἴτιον νομίζει,
τὸ ζητούμενον διὰ τοῦ ζητουμένου παριστᾶν ἐπι-
χειρήσει· ζητούντων γὰρ ἡμῶν εἰ ἔστι τί τινος
αἴτιον, αὐτὸς ὡς αἰτίας οὔσης τοῦ εἶναι αἴτιον
24 αἴτιον εἶναι φησίν. καὶ ἄλλως, ἐπεὶ περὶ τῆς
ὑπάρξεως τοῦ αἰτίου ζητοῦμεν, δεήσει πάντως
αὐτὸν καὶ τῆς αἰτίας τοῦ εἶναί τι αἴτιον αἰτίαν
παρασχεῖν, κἀκείνης ἄλλην, καὶ μέχρις ἀπείρου.
ἀδύνατον δὲ ἀπείρους αἰτίας παρασχεῖν· ἀδύνατον
ἄρα διαβεβαιωτικῶς ἀποφῆναι ὅτι ἔστι τί τινος
αἴτιον.

25 Πρὸς τούτοις ἤτοι ὂν καὶ ὑφεστὼς ἤδη αἴτιον τὸ
αἴτιον ποιεῖ τὸ ἀποτέλεσμα, ἢ μὴ ὂν αἴτιον. καὶ
μὴ ὂν μὲν οὐδαμῶς· εἰ δὲ ὄν, δεῖ αὐτὸ πρότερον
ὑποστῆναι καὶ προγενέσθαι αἴτιον, εἶθ' οὕτως
ἐπάγειν τὸ ἀποτέλεσμα, ὅπερ ὑπ' αὐτοῦ ἀποτελεῖσθαι λέγεται ὄντος ἤδη αἰτίου. ἀλλ' ἐπεὶ πρός
τί ἐστι τὸ αἴτιον καὶ πρὸς τὸ ἀποτέλεσμα, σαφὲς
ὅτι μὴ δύναται τούτου ὡς αἴτιον προϋποστῆναι·
οὐδὲ ὂν ἄρα αἴτιον τὸ αἴτιον ἀποτελεῖν δύναται τὸ
26 οὗ ἐστιν αἴτιον. εἰ δὲ μήτε μὴ ὂν αἴτιον ἀποτελεῖ
τι μήτε ὄν, οὐδὲ ἀποτελεῖ τι. διὸ οὐδὲ αἴτιον ἔσται·
ἄνευ γὰρ τοῦ ἀποτελεῖν τι τὸ αἴτιον οὐ δύναται ὡς
αἴτιον νοεῖσθαι.

Ὅθεν κἀκεῖνο λέγουσί τινες. τὸ αἴτιον ἤτοι
συνυφίστασθαι δεῖ τῷ ἀποτελέσματι ἢ προϋφίστασθαι τούτου ἢ μετ' αὐτὸ γίγνεσθαι. τὸ μὲν
οὖν λέγειν ὅτι τὸ αἴτιον εἰς ὑπόστασιν ἄγεται μετὰ

than the man who asserts " absolutely " that nothing
is a cause of anything ; whereas if he shall mention
causes on account of which he holds that something
causes something, he will be attempting to support
the matter in question by means of that matter itself ;
for when we are examining the question whether
anything is the Cause of anything, he asserts that
Cause exists since there exists a cause for the existence
of Cause. Besides, since we are inquiring about the 24
reality of Cause, it will certainly be necessary for him
to produce a cause for the cause of the existence of
Cause, and of that cause yet another, and so on *ad
infinitum*. But it is impossible to produce causes
infinite in number. It is impossible, therefore, to
affirm positively that anything is Cause of anything.

Moreover, the Cause, when it produces the effect, 25
either is and subsists already as causal or is non-causal.
Certainly it is not non-causal ; while if it is causal, it
must first have subsisted and become causal, and
thereafter produces the effect which is said to be
brought about by it as already existing Cause. But
since the Cause is relative and relative to the effect,
it is clear that it cannot be prior in existence to the
latter ; therefore not even as being causal can the
Cause bring about that whereof it is Cause. And if it 26
does not bring about anything either as being or as
not being causal, then it does not bring anything
about ; and hence it will not be a Cause ; for apart
from its effecting something the Cause cannot be
conceived as Cause.

Hence some people argue thus : The Cause must
either subsist along with its effect or before it or must
come into being after it. Now to say that the Cause
is brought into existence after the appearance of its

τὴν γένεσιν τοῦ ἀποτελέσματος αὐτοῦ μὴ καὶ
γελοῖον ᾖ. ἀλλ' οὐδὲ προϋφίστασθαι δύναται τού-
27 του· πρὸς αὐτὸ γὰρ νοεῖσθαι λέγεται, τὰ δὲ πρός
τι φασὶν αὐτοί, καθὸ πρός τι ἐστίν, συνυπάρχειν
καὶ συννοεῖσθαι ἀλλήλοις. ἀλλ' οὐδὲ συνυφίστα-
σθαι· εἰ γὰρ ἀποτελεστικὸν αὐτοῦ ἐστί, τὸ δὲ
γινόμενον ὑπὸ ὄντος ἤδη γίνεσθαι χρή, πρότερον
δεῖ τὸ αἴτιον γενέσθαι αἴτιον, εἶθ' οὕτως ποιεῖν τὸ
ἀποτέλεσμα. εἰ οὖν τὸ αἴτιον μήτε προϋφίσταται
τοῦ ἀποτελέσματος αὐτοῦ μήτε συνυφίσταται
τούτῳ, ἀλλ' οὐδὲ ⟨τὸ ἀποτέλεσμα⟩[1] πρὸ αὐτοῦ
γίνεται, μήποτε οὐδὲ ὑποστάσεως ὅλως μετέχει.
28 σαφὲς δὲ ἴσως ὅτι καὶ διὰ τούτων ἡ ἐπίνοια τοῦ
αἰτίου πάλιν περιτρέπεται. εἰ γὰρ τὸ αἴτιον ὡς
μὲν πρός τι οὐ δύναται τοῦ ἀποτελέσματος αὐτοῦ
προεπινοηθῆναι, ἵνα δὲ ὡς αἴτιον τοῦ ἀποτελέσματος αὐτοῦ νοηθῇ, δεῖ αὐτὸ προεπινοεῖσθαι τοῦ
ἀποτελέσματος αὐτοῦ, ἀδύνατον δὲ προεπινοηθῆναί
τι ἐκείνου οὗ προεπινοηθῆναι [τι] οὐ δύναται,
ἀδύνατον ἄρα ἐστὶν ἐπινοηθῆναι τὸ αἴτιον.
29 Ἐκ τούτων οὖν λοιπὸν ἐπιλογιζόμεθα ὅτι εἰ[2]
πιθανοὶ μέν εἰσιν οἱ λόγοι καθ' οὓς ὑπεμνήσαμεν
ὡς χρὴ λέγειν αἴτιον εἶναι, πιθανοὶ δὲ καὶ οἱ παρ-
ιστάντες ὅτι μὴ προσήκει αἴτιον εἶναί τι ἀποφαίνεσθαι, καὶ τούτων προκρίνειν τινὰς οὐκ ἐνδέχεται
μήτε · σημεῖον μήτε κριτήριον μήτε ἀπόδειξιν
ὁμολογουμένως ἡμῶν ἐχόντων, ὡς ἔμπροσθεν
παρεστήσαμεν, ἐπέχειν ἀνάγκη καὶ περὶ τῆς ὑποστάσεως τοῦ αἰτίου, μὴ μᾶλλον εἶναι ἢ μὴ εἶναί

---

[1] ⟨τὸ ἀποτέλεσμα⟩ add. T, Kayser: μετ' αὐτὸ cj. Steph.
[2] εἰ T: ἐπεὶ Bekk.: om. mss.

effect would seem ridiculous. But neither can it subsist before the effect; for it is said to be conceived in relation thereto, and they affirm that relatives, in so far as 27 they are relative, co-exist with each other and are conceived together. Nor, again, can it subsist along with its effect; for if it is productive of the effect, and what comes into existence must so come by the agency of what exists already, the Cause must have become causal first, and this done, then produces its effect. If, then, the Cause neither subsists before its effect, nor subsists along with it, nor does the effect precede the Cause, it would seem that it has no substantial existence at all. And it is clear probably 28 that by these arguments the conception of Cause is overthrown again. For if Cause as a relative notion cannot be conceived before its effect, and yet, if it is to be conceived as causative of its effect, it must be conceived before its effect, while it is impossible for anything to be conceived before that which the conception of it cannot precede,—then it is impossible for the Cause to be conceived.

From all this we conclude finally that—if the 29 arguments by which it was shown [a] that we ought to affirm the existence of Cause are plausible, and if the arguments which go to prove that it is improper to declare that any Cause exists are likewise plausible, and if it is inadmissible to prefer any of these arguments to the others, since, as we have shown above,[b] we confessedly possess neither sign nor criterion nor proof,—we are compelled to suspend judgement concerning the real existence of Cause, declaring that a Cause is "no more" existent than non-existent,

[a] *Cf.* §§ 17 ff.
[b] *Cf.* ii. 18, 104, 134 ff.

τι αἴτιον λέγοντας ὅσον ἐπὶ τοῖς λεγομένοις ὑπὸ
τῶν δογματικῶν.

ϛʹ.—ΠΕΡΙ ΥΛΙΚΩΝ ΑΡΧΩΝ

30 Περὶ μὲν οὖν τῆς δραστικῆς τοσαῦτα νῦν ἀρκέσει λελέχθαι· συντόμως δὲ καὶ περὶ τῶν ὑλικῶν
καλουμένων ἀρχῶν λεκτέον. ὅτι τοίνυν αὗταί
εἰσιν ἀκατάληπτοι, ῥᾴδιον συνιδεῖν ἐκ τῆς περὶ
αὐτῶν γεγενημένης διαφωνίας παρὰ τοῖς δογματικοῖς. Φερεκύδης μὲν γὰρ ὁ Σύριος γῆν εἶπε
τὴν πάντων εἶναι ἀρχήν, Θαλῆς δὲ ὁ Μιλήσιος
ὕδωρ, Ἀναξίμανδρος δὲ ὁ ἀκουστὴς τούτου τὸ
ἄπειρον, Ἀναξιμένης δὲ καὶ Διογένης ὁ Ἀπολ-
λωνιάτης ἀέρα, Ἵππασος δὲ ὁ Μεταποντῖνος πῦρ,
Ξενοφάνης δὲ ὁ Κολοφώνιος γῆν καὶ ὕδωρ, Οἰνο-
πίδης δὲ ὁ Χῖος πῦρ καὶ ἀέρα, Ἵππων δὲ ὁ Ῥη-
γῖνος πῦρ καὶ ὕδωρ, Ὀνομάκριτος δὲ ἐν τοῖς
31 Ὀρφικοῖς πῦρ καὶ ὕδωρ καὶ γῆν, οἱ δὲ περὶ τὸν
Ἐμπεδοκλέα πρὸς τοῖς στωικοῖς πῦρ ἀέρα ὕδωρ
γῆν—περὶ γὰρ τῆς τερατολογουμένης ἀποίου παρά
τισιν ὕλης, ἣν οὐδὲ αὐτοὶ καταλαμβάνειν διαβεβαιοῦνται, τί δεῖ καὶ λέγειν; οἱ δὲ περὶ Ἀρισ-
τοτέλη τὸν περιπατητικὸν πῦρ ἀέρα ὕδωρ γῆν,
32 τὸ κυκλοφορητικὸν σῶμα, Δημόκριτος δὲ καὶ
Ἐπίκουρος ἀτόμους, Ἀναξαγόρας δὲ ὁ Κλαζο-
μένιος ὁμοιομερείας, Διόδωρος δὲ ὁ ἐπικληθεὶς

---

[a] With the following sections *cf. Adv. Phys.* i. 360 ff.,
ii. 310 ff. ; and for the arguments employed, i. 164.

[b] Pherecydes, *circa* 650 B.C., was a semi-scientific cosmo-
gonist ; Oenopides was an astronomer and mathematician of
the fifth century B.C. ; Onomacritus was an Athenian religious
poet, said to be the author of some of the Orphic hymns.
For the other names see Introd.

if we are to judge by the statements made by the Dogmatists.

CHAPTER VI.—CONCERNING MATERIAL PRINCIPLES

So far, then, as concerns the efficient Principle this 30 account will suffice for the present. But we must also give a brief account of what are called the Material Principles.[a] Now that these are inapprehensible may easily be gathered from the disagreement which exists about them amongst the Dogmatists. For Pherecydes of Syros[b] declared earth to be the Principle of all things ; Thales of Miletus, water ; Anaximander (his pupil), the Unlimited ; Anaximenes and Diogenes of Apollonia, air ; Hippasus of Metapontum, fire ; Xenophanes of Colophon, earth and water ; Oenopides of Chios, fire and air ; Hippo of Rhegium, fire and water ; Onomacritus, in his *Orphica*, fire and water and earth ; the School of 31 Empedocles as well as the Stoics, fire, air, water and earth—for why should one even mention that mysterious " indeterminate matter " which some of them talk about,[c] when not even they themselves are positive that they apprehend it ? Aristotle the Peripatetic ⟨takes as his Principles⟩ fire, air, water, earth, and the "revolving body"[d] ; Democritus 32 and Epicurus, atoms ; Anaxagoras of Clazomenae, homoeomeries[e] ; Diodorus, surnamed Cronos, minimal

---

[c] For this " formless " or " unqualified " primary matter of the Stoics *cf. Adv. Phys.* i. 11, ii. 312.

[d] *i.e.* the *quinta essentia*, aether (αἰθήρ fr. ἀεὶ θεῖν, " ever-speeding," Plato, *Cratyl.* 410 B, Aristot. *De Caelo* i. 3).

[e] *i.e.* " things with like parts," or " homogeneous substances," is Aristotle's name for Anaxagoras's " seeds of things," or material " elements " ; *cf.* Introd. p. xi.

SEXTUS EMPIRICUS

Κρόνος ἐλάχιστα καὶ ἀμερῆ σώματα, Ἡρακλείδης
δὲ ὁ Ποντικὸς καὶ Ἀσκληπιάδης ὁ Βιθυνὸς ἀνάρ-
μους ὄγκους, οἱ δὲ περὶ Πυθαγόραν τοὺς ἀριθμούς,
οἱ δὲ μαθηματικοὶ τὰ πέρατα τῶν σωμάτων,
Στράτων δὲ ὁ φυσικὸς τὰς ποιότητας.

33 Τοσαύτης τοίνυν καὶ ἔτι πλείονος διαφωνίας
γεγενημένης περὶ τῶν ὑλικῶν ἀρχῶν παρ' αὐτοῖς,
ἤτοι πάσαις συγκαταθησόμεθα ταῖς κειμέναις στάσεσι καὶ ταῖς ἄλλαις ἢ τισίν. ἀλλὰ πάσαις μὲν οὐ
δυνατόν· οὐ γὰρ δήπου δυνησόμεθα καὶ τοῖς περὶ
Ἀσκληπιάδην συγκατατίθεσθαι, θραυστὰ εἶναι τὰ
στοιχεῖα λέγουσι καὶ ποιά, καὶ τοῖς περὶ Δημό-
κριτον, ἄτομα ταῦτα εἶναι φάσκουσι καὶ ἄποια,
καὶ τοῖς περὶ Ἀναξαγόραν, πᾶσαν αἰσθητὴν ποιό-
34 τητα περὶ ταῖς ὁμοιομερείαις ἀπολείπουσιν. εἰ δέ
τινα στάσιν τῶν ἄλλων προκρινοῦμεν, ἤτοι ἁπλῶς
καὶ ἄνευ ἀποδείξεως προκρινοῦμεν ἢ μετὰ ἀποδείξεως. ἄνευ μὲν οὖν ἀποδείξεως οὐ συνθησόμεθα·
εἰ δὲ μετὰ ἀποδείξεως, ἀληθῆ δεῖ τὴν ἀπόδειξιν
εἶναι. ἀληθὴς δὲ οὐκ ἂν δοθείη μὴ οὐχὶ κεκριμένη
κριτηρίῳ ἀληθεῖ, ἀληθὲς δὲ κριτήριον εἶναι δεί-
35 κνυται δι' ἀποδείξεως κεκριμένης. εἰ τοίνυν ἵνα
μὲν ἡ ἀπόδειξις ἡ προκρίνουσά τινα στάσιν ἀληθὴς
εἶναι δειχθῇ, δεῖ τὸ κριτήριον αὐτῆς ἀποδεδεῖχθαι,
ἵνα δὲ τὸ κριτήριον ἀποδειχθῇ, δεῖ τὴν ἀπόδειξιν
αὐτοῦ προκεκρίσθαι, ὁ διάλληλος εὑρίσκεται τρόπος,
ὃς οὐκ ἐάσει προβαίνειν τὸν λόγον, τῆς μὲν ἀποδείξεως ἀεὶ κριτηρίου δεομένης ἀποδεδειγμένου,
36 τοῦ κριτηρίου δὲ ἀποδείξεως κεκριμένης. εἰ δὲ

---

[a] Asclepiades (first century B.C.), a physician at Rome,
held a theory of non-sensible, frangible " molecules " (ὄγκοι)
of matter always in motion ; by collision with one another

346

and non-composite bodies; Heracleides Ponticus and Asclepiades the Bithynian,[a] homogeneous masses; the School of Pythagoras, the numbers; the Mathematicians, the limits of bodies; Strato the Physicist, the qualities.

Since, then, there exists amongst them as much 33 divergence as this, and even more, regarding the Material Principles, we shall give assent either to all the positions stated, and all others as well, or to some of them. But to assent to all is not possible; for we certainly shall not be able to assent both to Asclepiades, who says that the elements can be broken up and possess qualities, and to Democritus, who asserts that they are indivisible and void of quality, and to Anaxagoras, who leaves every sensible quality attached to the homoeomeries. Yet if we shall prefer any one standpoint. or view, 34 to the rest, we shall be preferring it either absolutely and without proof or with proof.[b] Now without proof we shall not yield assent; and if it is to be with proof, the proof must be true. But a true proof can only be given when approved by a true criterion, and a criterion is shown to be true by means of an approved proof. If, then, in order 35 to show the truth of the proof which prefers any one view, its criterion must be proved, and to prove the criterion in turn its proof must be pre-established, the argument is found to be the circular one which will not allow the reasoning to go forward, since the proof keeps always requiring a proved criterion, and the criterion an approved proof. And 36

these " molecules " break in pieces, and when re-united become objects of sense.
    [b] For this form of argument cf. ii. 183.

ἀεὶ τὸ κριτήριον κριτηρίῳ κρίνειν καὶ τὴν ἀπόδειξιν
ἀποδείξει[1] ἀποδεικνύναι βούλοιτό τις, εἰς ἄπειρον
ἐκβληθήσεται.[2] εἰ τοίνυν μήτε πάσαις ταῖς περὶ
στοιχείων στάσεσι δυνάμεθα συγκατατίθεσθαι μήτε
τινὶ τούτων, ἐπέχειν προσήκει περὶ αὐτῶν.

37 Δυνατὸν μὲν οὖν ἴσως ἐστὶ καὶ διὰ τούτων μόνων
ὑπομιμνήσκειν τὴν τῶν στοιχείων καὶ τῶν ὑλικῶν
ἀρχῶν ἀκαταληψίαν· ἵνα δὲ καὶ ἀμφιλαφέστερον
τοὺς δογματικοὺς ἐλέγχειν ἔχωμεν, ἐνδιατρίψομεν
συμμέτρως τῷ τόπῳ. καὶ ἐπεὶ πολλαὶ καὶ σχεδὸν
ἄπειροί τινές εἰσιν αἱ περὶ στοιχείων δόξαι, καθὼς
ὑπεμνήσαμεν, τὸ μὲν πρὸς ἑκάστην λέγειν εἰδικῶς
νῦν παραιτησόμεθα διὰ τὸν χαρακτῆρα τῆς συγγραφῆς, δυνάμει δὲ πρὸς πάσας ἀντεροῦμεν. ἐπεὶ
γὰρ ἦν ἄν τις εἴπῃ περὶ στοιχείων στάσιν, ἤτοι
ἐπὶ σώματα κατενεχθήσεται ἢ ἐπὶ ἀσώματα, ἀρκεῖν
ἡγούμεθα ὑπομνῆσαι ὅτι ἀκατάληπτα μέν ἐστι τὰ
σώματα ἀκατάληπτα δὲ τὰ ἀσώματα· διὰ γὰρ
τούτου σαφὲς ἔσται ὅτι καὶ τὰ στοιχεῖά ἐστιν
ἀκατάληπτα.

Ζ΄.—ΕΙ ΚΑΤΑΛΗΠΤΑ ΤΑ ΣΩΜΑΤΑ

38 Σῶμα τοίνυν λέγουσιν εἶναί τινες ὃ οἷόν τε
ποιεῖν ἢ πάσχειν. ὅσον δὲ ἐπὶ ταύτῃ τῇ ἐπινοίᾳ
ἀκατάληπτόν ἐστι τοῦτο. τὸ μὲν γὰρ αἴτιον ἀ-
κατάληπτόν ἐστι, καθὼς ὑπεμνήσαμεν· μὴ ἔχοντες
δὲ εἰπεῖν εἰ ἔστι τι αἴτιον, οὐδὲ εἰ ἔστι τι πάσχον
εἰπεῖν δυνάμεθα· τὸ γὰρ πάσχον πάντως ὑπὸ

---

[1] ἀποδείξει MLT: δι' ἀποδείξεως Bekk.
[2] ἐκβληθήσεται T, Nauck: ἐμβλ. mss., Bekk.

---

[a] A favourite classification of the Stoics, cf. Adv. Phys.
ii. 218.

should any one propose to approve the criterion by a criterion and to prove the proof by a proof, he will be driven to a regress *ad infinitum*. Accordingly, if we are unable to assent either to all the views held about the elements or to any one of them, it is proper to suspend judgement about them.

Now though it is, perhaps, possible to show by 37 these arguments alone the inapprehensibility of the elements and of the Material Principles, yet in order that we may be able to refute the Dogmatists in a more comprehensive manner we shall dwell on this topic at appropriate length. And since the opinions about the elements are, as we have shown, numerous and well-nigh infinite, we will excuse ourselves—because of the character of our present treatise—from discussing each opinion in detail, but will make answer to them all implicitly. For since the elements, whatever view one takes of them, must be finally regarded either as corporeal or incorporeal,[a] we think it enough to show that corporeal things are inapprehensible and incorporeal things inapprehensible; for thus it will be clear that the elements also are inapprehensible.

CHAPTER VII.—ARE BODIES APPREHENSIBLE?

Some say that Body is that which is capable of 38 being active or passive.[b] But so far as this conception goes it is inapprehensible. For, as we have shown, Cause is inapprehensible; and if we cannot say whether any Cause exists, neither can we say whether anything passive exists; for what is passive

[a] This definition is ascribed to Pythagoras in *Adv. Phys.* i. 366.

αἰτίου πάσχει. ἀκαταλήπτου δὲ ὄντος καὶ τοῦ
αἰτίου καὶ τοῦ πάσχοντος, διὰ ταῦτα ἀκατάληπτον
39 ἔσται καὶ τὸ σῶμα. τινὲς δὲ σῶμα εἶναι λέγουσι
τὸ τριχῇ διαστατὸν μετὰ ἀντιτυπίας. σημεῖον μὲν
γάρ φασιν οὗ μέρος οὐθέν, γραμμὴν δὲ μῆκος
ἀπλατές, ἐπιφάνειαν δὲ μῆκος μετὰ πλάτους· ὅταν
δὲ αὕτη καὶ βάθος προσλάβῃ καὶ ἀντιτυπίαν,
σῶμα εἶναι, περὶ οὗ νῦν ἐστὶν ἡμῖν ὁ λόγος, συνεστὼς ἔκ τε μήκους καὶ πλάτους καὶ βάθους καὶ
40 ἀντιτυπίας. εὐμαρὴς μέντοι καὶ ὁ πρὸς τούτους
λόγος. τὸ γὰρ σῶμα ἤτοι οὐδὲν παρὰ ταῦτα εἶναι
λέξουσιν ἢ ἕτερόν τι παρὰ τὴν συνέλευσιν τῶν
προειρημένων. καὶ ἔξωθεν μὲν τοῦ μήκους τε καὶ
τοῦ πλάτους καὶ τοῦ βάθους καὶ τῆς ἀντιτυπίας
οὐδὲν ἂν εἴη τὸ σῶμα· εἰ δὲ ταῦτά ἐστι τὸ σῶμα,
ἐὰν δείξῃ τις ὅτι ἀνύπαρκτά ἐστιν, ἀναιροίη ἂν
καὶ τὸ σῶμα· τὰ γὰρ ὅλα συναναιρεῖται τοῖς
ἑαυτῶν πᾶσι μέρεσιν.

Ποικίλως μὲν οὖν ἔστι ταῦτα ἐλέγχειν· τὸ δὲ νῦν
ἀρκέσει λέγειν ὅτι εἰ ἔστι τὰ πέρατα, ἤτοι γραμμαί
41 εἰσιν ἢ ἐπιφάνειαι ἢ σώματα. εἰ μὲν οὖν ἐπι-
φάνειάν τινα ἢ γραμμὴν εἶναι λέγοι τις, καὶ τῶν
προειρημένων ἕκαστον ἤτοι κατὰ ἰδίαν ὑφεστάναι
δύνασθαι λεχθήσεται ἢ μόνον περὶ τοῖς λεγομένοις
σώμασι θεωρεῖσθαι. ἀλλὰ καθ᾽ ἑαυτὴν μὲν ὑπάρχουσαν ἤτοι γραμμὴν ἢ ἐπιφάνειαν ὀνειροπολεῖν
ἴσως εὔηθες. εἰ δὲ περὶ τοῖς σώμασι θεωρεῖσθαι
λέγοιτο μόνον καὶ μὴ καθ᾽ ἑαυτὸ ὑφεστάναι τούτων

[a] Cf. ii. 30, Adv. Phys. i. 367, ii. 12.
[b] In geometry "Limits" (or "boundaries") was used to

is certainly made passive by a Cause. And when both the Cause and the passive object are inapprehensible, the result will be that Body also is inapprehensible. But some define Body as what has three dimensions 39 combined with resistance or solidity.[a] For they describe the point as that which has no parts, the line as length without breadth, the surface as length with breadth ; and when this takes on both depth and resistance there is formed Body—the object of our present discussion—it being composed of length and breadth and depth and resistance. The answer, 40 however, to these people is simple. For they will say either that Body is nothing more than these qualities, or that it is something else than the combination of the qualities already mentioned. Now apart from length and breadth and depth and solidity the Body would be nothing ; but if these things are the Body, anyone who shall prove that they are unreal will likewise abolish the Body ; for wholes are abolished along with the sum of their parts.

Now it is possible to disprove these dimensions in a variety of ways ; but for the present it will be enough to say that if the Limits [b] exist, they are either lines or surfaces or bodies. If, then, one should affirm the 41 existence of a surface or a line, then it will be affirmed that each of the afore-mentioned objects either can subsist of itself or is cognized solely in connexion with so-called Bodies. But to imagine either a line or a surface as existing of itself is doubtless silly. While if it should be said that each of these objects is cognized solely in connexion with the Bodies and has no independent existence, it will thereby be

denote the lines or surfaces by which any magnitude is " bounded."

ἕκαστον, πρῶτον μὲν αὐτόθεν δοθήσεται τὸ μὴ ἐξ
αὐτῶν γεγονέναι τὰ σώματα (ἐχρῆν γάρ, οἶμαι,
ταῦτα πρότερον ὑπόστασιν καθ᾽ ἑαυτὰ ἐσχηκέναι,
καὶ οὕτω συνελθόντα πεποιηκέναι τὰ σώματα),
42 εἶτα οὐδὲ ἐν τοῖς καλουμένοις σώμασιν ὑφέστηκεν.

Καὶ τοῦτο διὰ πλειόνων μὲν ἔστιν ὑπομιμνήσκειν,
ἀρκέσει δὲ νῦν τὰ ἐκ τῆς ἁφῆς ἀπορούμενα λέγειν.
εἰ γὰρ ἅπτεται ἀλλήλων τὰ παρατιθέμενα σώματα,
τοῖς πέρασιν αὐτῶν, οἷον ταῖς ἐπιφανείαις, ψαύει
ἀλλήλων. αἱ οὖν ἐπιφάνειαι ὅλαι μὲν δι᾽ ὅλων
ἀλλήλαις οὐχ ἑνωθήσονται κατὰ τὴν ἁφήν, ἐπεὶ
σύγχυσις ἔσται ἡ ἁφὴ καὶ ὁ χωρισμὸς τῶν ἁπτο-
43 μένων διασπασμός· ὅπερ οὐ θεωρεῖται. εἰ δὲ ἄλλοις
μὲν μέρεσιν ἡ ἐπιφάνεια ἅπτεται τῆς τοῦ παρα-
τιθεμένου αὐτῇ σώματος ἐπιφανείας, ἄλλοις δὲ
συνήνωται τῷ σώματι οὗ ἐστι πέρας, * * *[1] οὐκ ἄρα
οὐδὲ περὶ σώματι θεωρῆσαι δύναταί τις μῆκος καὶ
πλάτος ἀβαθές, ὅθεν οὐδὲ ἐπιφάνειαν.

Ὁμοίως δὲ καὶ δύο ἐπιφανειῶν καθ᾽ ὑπόθεσιν
παρατιθεμένων ἀλλήλαις κατὰ τὰ πέρατα αὐτῶν
εἰς ἃ λήγουσι, κατὰ τὸ λεγόμενον αὐτῶν μῆκος
εἶναι, τουτέστι κατὰ γραμμάς, αἱ γραμμαὶ αὗται,
δι᾽ ὧν ἅπτεσθαι λέγονται ἀλλήλων αἱ ἐπιφάνειαι,
οὐχ ἑνωθήσονται μὲν ἀλλήλαις (συγχυθεῖεν γὰρ
ἄν)· εἰ δὲ ἑκάστη αὐτῶν ἄλλοις μὲν μέρεσι τοῖς

---

[1] The lacuna marked here is to denote that there is probably an omission in the MSS. (and Bekk.) of something
corresponding to the insertion of T—" (terminus) non erit sine
profunditate differentibus eius partibus intellectis secundum
profunditatem hac quidem cui opponitur tangenti hac autem
secundum ⟨quod⟩ coniungitur corpori cuius est terminus."
Mutsch. inserts a Greek version of this in his text, and I give
an English version between brackets.

granted, in the first place, that the Bodies are not generated from them (for if so, I suppose, these objects ought to have had independent existence first, and then have combined to form the Bodies) ; and 42 further, they have no real existence even in the so-called Bodies.

This can be shown by several arguments, but for the present it will suffice to mention the difficulties which arise from ⟨the fact of⟩ touch.[a] For if juxtaposed Bodies touch one another they are in contact with their Limits—for example, with their surfaces. The surfaces, then, will not be completely unified one with another as a result of touching, since otherwise touch would be fusion and the separation of things touching a rending apart ; and this is not what we find. And if the surface touches the surface of the 43 juxtaposed Body with some of its parts, and with other parts is united with the Body of which it is a limit, ⟨it will not be without depth, since its parts are conceived as different in respect of depth, one part touching the juxtaposed Body, the other being that which effects its union with the Body whereof it is a limit⟩. Hence, even in connexion with Body one cannot imagine length and breadth without depth, nor, consequently, surface.

So likewise when two surfaces are, let us imagine, juxtaposed along the limits where they come to an end, by way of what is called their " length," that is to say by way of their " lines," then these lines, by means of which the surfaces are said to touch each other, will not be unified (else they would be fused together) ; yet if each of them touches the line which

[a] For arguments based on " touch," or contact, cf. Adv. Phys. i. 258 ff., Adv. Geom. 34 ff.

κατὰ πλάτος ἅπτεται τῆς παρατιθεμένης αὐτῇ
γραμμῆς, ἄλλοις δὲ συνήνωται τῇ ἐπιφανείᾳ ἧς
ἐστὶ πέρας, οὐκ ἔσται ἀπλατής, ὅθεν οὐδὲ γραμμή.
εἰ δὲ μήτε γραμμὴ ἔστιν ἐν σώματι μήτε ἐπιφάνεια, οὐδὲ μῆκος ἢ πλάτος ἢ βάθος ἔσται ἐν
σώματι.

44 Εἰ δέ τις σώματα εἶναι τὰ πέρατα λέγοι, σύν-
τομος ἔσται ἡ πρὸς αὐτὸν ἀπόκρισις. εἰ γὰρ τὸ
μῆκος σῶμα ἐστίν, δεήσει τοῦτο εἰς τὰς τρεῖς
αὐτοῦ μερίζεσθαι διαστάσεις, ὧν ἑκάστη σῶμα
οὖσα πάλιν αὐτὴ διαιρεθήσεται εἰς διαστάσεις
ἄλλας τρεῖς, αἳ ἔσονται σώματα, καὶ ἐκεῖναι εἰς
ἄλλας ὁμοίως, καὶ τοῦτο μέχρις ἀπείρου, ὡς
ἀπειρομέγεθες γίνεσθαι τὸ σῶμα εἰς ἄπειρα μερι-
ζόμενον· ὅπερ ἄτοπον. οὐδὲ σώματα ἄρα εἰσὶν
αἱ προειρημέναι διαστάσεις. εἰ δὲ μήτε σώματά
εἰσι μήτε γραμμαὶ ἢ ἐπιφάνειαι, οὐδὲ εἶναι νομι-
σθήσονται.

45 Ἀκατάληπτος δέ ἐστι καὶ ἡ ἀντιτυπία. αὕτη
γὰρ εἴπερ καταλαμβάνεται, ἁφῇ καταλαμβάνοιτο
ἄν. ἐὰν οὖν δείξωμεν ὅτι ἀκατάληπτός ἐστιν ἡ
ἁφή, σαφὲς ἔσται ὅτι οὐχ οἷόν τέ ἐστι καταλαμβάνεσθαι τὴν ἀντιτυπίαν. ὅτι δὲ ἀκατάληπτός
ἐστιν ἡ ἁφή, διὰ τούτων ἐπιλογιζόμεθα. τὰ
ἁπτόμενα ἀλλήλων ἤτοι μέρεσιν ἀλλήλων ἅπτεται
ἢ ὅλα ὅλων. ὅλα μὲν οὖν ὅλων οὐδαμῶς· ἑνω-
θήσεται γὰρ οὕτω καὶ οὐχ ἅψεται ἀλλήλων. ἀλλ'
οὐδὲ μέρεσι μερῶν· τὰ γὰρ μέρη αὐτῶν ὡς μὲν
πρὸς τὰ ὅλα μέρη ἐστίν, ὡς δὲ πρὸς τὰ μέρη
46 ἑαυτῶν ὅλα. ταῦτα οὖν τὰ ὅλα, ἅ ἐστιν ἑτέρων
μέρη, ὅλα μὲν ὅλων οὐχ ἅψεται διὰ τὰ προειρη-

lies next to it breadth-wise with some of its parts and by others is united with the surface of which it is a limit, it will not be without breadth, and, consequently, it will not be a line. But if there exists in Body neither line nor surface, neither length nor breadth nor depth will exist in Body.

And should anyone assert that the Limits are 44 bodies, he can be answered very shortly. For if length is a body, it must needs be divided into its three dimensions, and each of these, in turn, being a body will be divided into three other dimensions, which will be bodies, and these likewise into others, and so on *ad infinitum*, so that the Body comes to be of infinite size, being divided into an infinity of parts: this result is absurd, and therefore the dimensions aforesaid are not bodies. But if they are neither bodies nor lines nor surfaces, they will be held to have no existence.

Solidity [a] also is inapprehensible. For if it is 45 apprehended, it must be apprehended by touch. If, then, we shall prove that touch is inapprehensible, it will be clear that it is impossible for solidity to be apprehended. That touch is inapprehensible we argue as follows. Things which touch one another either touch with their parts or as wholes touching wholes. Now they certainly will not touch as wholes; for then they will be unified instead of being in contact with one another. Nor yet through parts touching parts; for their parts, though in relation to the wholes they are parts, are wholes in relation to their parts. So these wholes, which are parts of 46 other things, will not touch as wholes touching wholes,

---

[a] Or " resistance," § 39 ; for this quality, as treated by Epicurus, *cf. Adv. Phys.* ii. 222.

SEXTUS EMPIRICUS

μένα, ἀλλ' οὐδὲ μέρεσι μερῶν· καὶ γὰρ τὰ τούτων
μέρη ὡς πρὸς τὰ ἑαυτῶν μέρη ὅλα ὄντα οὔτε ὅλα
ὅλων ἅψεται οὔτε μέρεσι μερῶν. εἰ δὲ μήτε κατὰ
ὁλότητα μήτε κατὰ μέρη γινομένην ἀφὴν καταλαμβάνομεν, ἀκατάληπτος ἔσται ἡ ἀφή. διὰ δὲ
τοῦτο καὶ ἡ ἀντιτυπία. ὅθεν καὶ τὸ σῶμα· εἰ γὰρ
οὐδέν ἐστι τοῦτο παρὰ τὰς τρεῖς διαστάσεις καὶ
τὴν ἀντιτυπίαν, ἐδείξαμεν δὲ ἀκατάληπτον τούτων
ἕκαστον, καὶ τὸ σῶμα ἔσται ἀκατάληπτον.

Οὕτω μὲν οὖν, ὅσον ἐπὶ τῇ ἐννοίᾳ τοῦ σώματος,
47 ἀκατάληπτόν ἐστιν εἰ ἔστι τι σῶμα· λεκτέον δὲ καὶ
τοῦτο εἰς τὸ προκείμενον. τῶν ὄντων τὰ μέν φασιν
εἶναι αἰσθητὰ τὰ δὲ νοητά, καὶ τὰ μὲν τῇ διανοίᾳ
καταλαμβάνεσθαι τὰ δὲ ταῖς αἰσθήσεσιν, καὶ τὰς
μὲν αἰσθήσεις ἁπλοπαθεῖς εἶναι, τὴν δὲ διάνοιαν
ἀπὸ τῆς τῶν αἰσθητῶν καταλήψεως ἐπὶ τὴν κατάληψιν τῶν νοητῶν ἰέναι. εἰ οὖν ἔστι τι σῶμα, ἤτοι
αἰσθητόν ἐστιν ἢ νοητόν. καὶ αἰσθητὸν μὲν οὐκ
ἔστιν· κατὰ γὰρ συναθροισμὸν μήκους καὶ βάθους
καὶ πλάτους καὶ ἀντιτυπίας καὶ χρώματος καὶ
ἄλλων τινῶν καταλαμβάνεσθαι δοκεῖ, σὺν οἷς θεω-
ρεῖται· αἱ δὲ αἰσθήσεις ἁπλοπαθεῖς εἶναι λέγονται
48 παρ' αὐτοῖς. εἰ δὲ νοητὸν εἶναι λέγεται τὸ σῶμα,
δεῖ τι πάντως ὑπάρχειν ἐν τῇ φύσει τῶν πραγμάτων αἰσθητόν, ἀφ' οὗ ἡ τῶν σωμάτων νοητῶν
ὄντων ἔσται νόησις. οὐδὲν δὲ ἔστι παρὰ τὸ σῶμα
καὶ τὸ ἀσώματον, ὧν τὸ μὲν ἀσώματον αὐτόθεν
νοητόν ἐστι, τὸ δὲ σῶμα οὐκ αἰσθητόν, ὡς ὑπ-

ᵃ Cf. § 38.
ᵇ This means that each sense is specialized, so that it is
capable of receiving only one kind of impression (e.g. the
sight is affected by colour, but not by sound or solidity);
cf. § 108.

fot the reasons aforesaid, nor yet through parts touching parts ; for their parts, too, being wholes relatively to their own parts, will not be in contact either as wholes with wholes or as parts with parts. But if we apprehend the occurrence of touch neither by way of wholeness nor by way of parts, touch will be inapprehensible. And, consequently, solidity also ; and, therefore, Body ; for if this is nothing more than the three dimensions *plus* Solidity, and we have proved that each of these is inapprehensible, Body also will be inapprehensible.

Thus, then, if we are to judge by the conception [a] of Body, it is inapprehensible whether any body exists ; and about this problem there is this also to be said. 47 Of existing things some, they say, are sensible, others intelligible, and the latter are apprehended by the reason, the former by the senses, and the senses are " simply-passive," [b] while the reason proceeds from the apprehension of sensibles to the apprehension of intelligibles. If then any body exists, it is either sensible or intelligible. Now it is not sensible ; for it is supposed to be apprehended as a conglomeration of length and depth and breadth and solidity and colour and various other things, along with which it is experienced ; whereas, according to their statements, the senses are " simply-passive." And if Body is said 48 to be intelligible, there must certainly be pre-existent in the nature of things some sensible object from which to derive the notion of bodies, they being intelligible. But nothing exists save Body and the Incorporeal, and of these the Incorporeal is essentially intelligible,[c] and Body, as we have shown, is not

[c] *i.e.* in the view of the Stoics, but not of the Sceptics, for the inapprehensibility of the " Incorporeal " is proved in § 50 *ad fin.*

ἐμνήσαμεν. μὴ ὄντος οὖν ἐν τῇ φύσει τῶν πραγμάτων αἰσθητοῦ τινὸς ἀφ' οὗ ἡ νόησις ἔσται τοῦ
σώματος, οὐδὲ νοητὸν ἔσται τὸ σῶμα. εἰ δὲ μήτε
αἰσθητόν ἐστι μήτε νοητόν, παρὰ δὲ ταῦτα οὐδὲν
ἔστι, λεκτέον ὅσον ἐπὶ τῷ λόγῳ μηδὲ εἶναι τὸ
49 σῶμα. διὰ ταῦτα οὖν ἡμεῖς ἀντιτιθέντες τοὺς
κατὰ τοῦ σώματος λόγους τῷ φαίνεσθαι [δοκεῖν]¹
ὑπάρχον τὸ σῶμα, συνάγομεν τὴν περὶ τοῦ σώματος ἐποχήν.

Τῇ δὲ τοῦ σώματος ἀκαταληψίᾳ συνεισάγεται
καὶ τὸ ἀκατάληπτον εἶναι τὸ ἀσώματον. αἱ γὰρ
στερήσεις τῶν ἕξεων νοοῦνται στερήσεις, οἷον
ὁράσεως τυφλότης καὶ ἀκοῆς κωφότης καὶ ἐπὶ τῶν
ἄλλων παραπλησίως. διόπερ ἵνα στέρησιν καταλάβωμεν, δεῖ τὴν ἕξιν ἡμᾶς προκατειληφέναι ἧς
λέγεται στέρησις εἶναι ἡ στέρησις· ἀνεννόητος γάρ
τις ὢν τῆς ὁράσεως οὐκ ἂν δύναιτο λέγειν ὅτι
ὅρασιν ὅδε οὐκ ἔχει, ὅπερ ἐστὶ τὸ τυφλὸν εἶναι.
50 εἰ οὖν στέρησις σώματός ἐστι τὸ ἀσώματον, τῶν
δὲ ἕξεων μὴ καταλαμβανομένων ἀδύνατον τὰς
στερήσεις αὐτῶν καταλαμβάνεσθαι, καὶ δέδεικται
ὅτι τὸ σῶμα ἀκατάληπτόν ἐστιν, ἀκατάληπτον
ἔσται καὶ τὸ ἀσώματον. καὶ γὰρ ἤτοι αἰσθητόν
ἐστιν ἢ νοητόν. εἴτε δὲ αἰσθητόν ἐστιν, ἀκατάληπτόν ἐστι διὰ τὴν διαφορὰν τῶν ζῴων καὶ τῶν
ἀνθρώπων καὶ τῶν αἰσθήσεων καὶ τῶν περιστάσεων
καὶ παρὰ τὰς ἐπιμιξίας καὶ τὰ λοιπὰ τῶν προειρημένων ἡμῖν ἐν τοῖς περὶ τῶν δέκα τρόπων· εἴτε
νοητόν, μὴ διδομένης αὐτόθεν τῆς τῶν αἰσθητῶν
καταλήψεως, ἀφ' ἧς ὁρμώμενοι τοῖς νοητοῖς ἐπιβάλλειν δοκοῦμεν, οὐδὲ ἡ τῶν νοητῶν αὐτόθεν

¹ [δοκεῖν] om. T.

sensible. Since, then, no sensible object exists in the nature of things from which we can derive the notion of Body, Body will not be intelligible either. And if it is neither sensible nor intelligible, and besides these nothing else exists, we must declare that, so far as this argument goes, Body has no existence. Accordingly 49 we, by thus opposing the arguments against Body to the apparent existence of Body, infer suspension of judgement concerning Body.

The inapprehensibility of Body involves also that of the Incorporeal. For privations are conceived as privations of states or faculties, as, for example, blindness of sight, deafness of hearing, and similarly with the rest. Hence, in order to apprehend a privation, we must first have apprehended the state of which the privation is said to be a privation ; for if one had no conception of sight one would not be able to assert that this man does not possess sight, which is the meaning of being blind. If then Incorporeality is 50 the privation of Body, and when states are not apprehended it is impossible for the privations of them to be apprehended, and it has been proved that Body is inapprehensible, Incorporeality also will be inapprehensible. Moreover, it is either sensible or intelligible. And if it is sensible, it is inapprehensible because of the variance amongst animals and men, the senses and the circumstances, and owing to the admixtures and all the other things we have previously described in our exposition of the Ten Tropes.[a] If, again, it is intelligible, since the apprehension of sensibles, which is supposed to form the starting-point from which we attain to the intelligibles,[b] is not immediately given, neither will the apprehension of

[a] *Cf.* i. 36 ff.   [b] *Cf.* ii. 10.

SEXTUS EMPIRICUS

κατάληψις δοθήσεται, διόπερ οὐδὲ ἡ τοῦ ἀσωμάτου.

51 Ὅ τε φάσκων καταλαμβάνειν τὸ ἀσώματον ἤτοι
αἰσθήσει τοῦτο παραστήσει καταλαμβάνειν ἢ διὰ
λόγου. καὶ αἰσθήσει μὲν οὐδαμῶς, ἐπειδὴ αἱ μὲν
αἰσθήσεις κατὰ ἐπέρεισιν καὶ νύξιν ἀντιλαμβάνεσθαι
δοκοῦσι τῶν αἰσθητῶν, οἷον ἡ ὅρασις, ἐάν τε κατὰ
ἔντασιν¹ γίνηται κώνου, ἐάν τε κατὰ εἰδώλων ἀπο-
κρίσεις τε καὶ ἐπικρίσεις, ἐάν τε ⟨κατ᾽⟩² ἀκτίνων
ἢ χρωμάτων ἀποχύσεις, καὶ ἡ ἀκοὴ δέ, ἥν τε ὁ
πεπληγμένος ἀὴρ ἥν τε τὰ μόρια τῆς φωνῆς
φέρηται περὶ τὰ ὦτα καὶ πλήττῃ τὸ ἀκουστικὸν
πνεῦμα ὥστε τὴν ἀντίληψιν τῆς φωνῆς ἀπεργά-
ζεσθαι. ἀλλὰ καὶ αἱ ὀδμαὶ τῇ ῥινὶ καὶ οἱ χυμοὶ
αὖ τῇ γλώττῃ προσπίπτουσιν, καὶ τὰ τὴν ἁφὴν
52 κινοῦντα ὁμοίως τῇ ἁφῇ. τὰ δὲ ἀσώματα ἐπέρεισιν τοιαύτην ὑπομένειν οὐχ οἷά τέ ἐστιν, ὥστε
οὐκ ἂν δύναιτο τῇ αἰσθήσει καταλαμβάνεσθαι.

Ἀλλ᾽ οὐδὲ διὰ λόγου. εἰ μὲν γὰρ λεκτόν ἐστιν
ὁ λόγος καὶ ἀσώματος, ὡς οἱ στωικοί φασιν, ὁ
λέγων διὰ λόγου καταλαμβάνεσθαι τὰ ἀσώματα
τὸ ζητούμενον συναρπάζει. ζητούντων γὰρ ἡμῶν
εἰ δύναται ἀσώματόν τι καταλαμβάνεσθαι, αὐτὸς
ἀσώματόν τι λαβὼν ἁπλῶς διὰ τούτου τὴν κατάληψιν τῶν ἀσωμάτων ποιεῖσθαι θέλει. καίτοι
αὐτὸς ὁ λόγος, εἴπερ ἀσώματός ἐστι, τῆς τῶν
53 ζητουμένων ἐστὶ μοίρας. πῶς οὖν ἀποδείξει τις

¹ ἔντασιν Kayser: ἔνστασιν mss., Bekk.
² ⟨κατ᾽⟩ add. T, cj. Bekk.

ᵃ The first of these theories of vision is that of Chrysippus
(a cone of light connecting eye with object), the second that
of Democritus and Epicurus, the third that of Empedocles,
Pythagoreans, Plato (*Tim.* 45 в) and Aristotle.

360

the intelligibles be given immediately, nor, consequently, that of Incorporeality.

Also, he who asserts that he apprehends the In- 51
corporeal will maintain that he apprehends it either
by sense or by means of reason. Certainly not by
sense, since it is supposed that the senses perceive
the sensibles by way of " impression " and " indenta-
tion,"—take sight, for instance, whether it occur by
reason of the tension of a cone, or of the emissions and
immissions of images, or by effusions of rays or
colours [a]; and hearing too, whether it be the smitten
air [b] or the parts of the sound that are carried round
the ears and smite the acoustic breath so as to effect
the perception of sound. Smells also impinge on the
nose and flavours on the tongue, and likewise objects
of touch on the sense of touch. But incorporeals are 52
incapable of submitting to impression of this kind, so
that they could not be apprehended by sense.

Nor yet by means of reason. For if the reason
is " verbally expressible " [c] and incorporeal, as the
Stoics assert, he who says that incorporeals are
apprehended by means of reason is begging the
question. For when our question is—" Can an
incorporeal object be apprehended ? " he assumes an
incorporeal object and then, by means of it alone,
claims to effect the apprehension of incorporeals. Yet
reason itself, if it is incorporeal, belongs to the class
of things which are in question. How, then, is one to 53

[b] Cf. Plato, *Tim.* 67 B; Diog. Laert. vii. 158; " acoustic
breath " is Stoic for the air within the ear, *cf.* ii. 70.
[c] For the Stoic theory of " expression " (λεκτόν) *cf.* ii.
81, 104. *Logos* (" reason " or " word ") is from the same stem
as *Lekton* (" what can be put into words " or " meaning "),
which—as contrasted with " uttered words "—was termed by
the Stoics " incorporeal."

ὅτι πρότερον τοῦτο τὸ ἀσώματον καταλαμβάνεται,
φημὶ δὲ τὸν λόγον· εἰ μὲν γὰρ δι' ἄλλου ἀσωμάτου,
κἀκείνου ζητήσομεν τὴν ἀπόδειξιν τῆς καταλήψεως, καὶ τοῦτο μέχρις ἀπείρου· εἰ δὲ διὰ σώματος,
ζητεῖται καὶ περὶ τῆς καταλήψεως τῶν σωμάτων·
διὰ τίνος οὖν δείξομεν ὅτι καταλαμβάνεται τὸ
σῶμα τὸ εἰς ἀπόδειξιν τῆς καταλήψεως τοῦ ἀσωμάτου λόγου λαμβανόμενον; εἰ μὲν διὰ σώματος,
εἰς ἄπειρον ἐκβαλλόμεθα, εἰ δὲ δι' ἀσωμάτου, εἰς
τὸν διάλληλον τρόπον ἐκπίπτομεν. μένοντος οὖν
οὕτως ἀκαταλήπτου τοῦ λόγου, εἴπερ ἀσώματός
ἐστιν, οὐκ ἂν δύναιτό τις λέγειν δι' αὐτοῦ καταλαμβάνεσθαι τὸ ἀσώματον.

54 Εἰ δὲ σῶμά ἐστιν ὁ λόγος, ἐπεὶ καὶ περὶ τῶν
σωμάτων διαπεφώνηται πότερον καταλαμβάνεται
ἢ οὔ, διὰ τὴν λεγομένην συνεχῆ ῥύσιν αὐτῶν, ὡς
μηδὲ τὴν τόδε[1] δεῖξιν ἐπιδέχεσθαι, μηδὲ εἶναι νο-
μίζεσθαι (παρὸ καὶ ὁ Πλάτων γινόμενα μὲν ὄντα
δὲ οὐδέποτε καλεῖ τὰ σώματα), ἀπορῶ πῶς ἐπικριθήσεται ἡ περὶ τοῦ σώματος διαφωνία, μήτε
σώματι μήτε ἀσωμάτῳ ταύτην ὁρῶν ἐπικρίνεσθαι
δυναμένην διὰ τὰς μικρῷ πρόσθεν εἰρημένας
ἀτοπίας. οὐκοῦν οὐδὲ λόγῳ δυνατόν ἐστι κατα-
55 λαμβάνειν τὰ ἀσώματα. εἰ δὲ μήτε αἰσθήσει
ὑποπίπτει μήτε διὰ λόγου καταλαμβάνεται, οὐδ'
ἂν ὅλως καταλαμβάνοιτο.

Εἰ τοίνυν μήτε περὶ τῆς ὑπάρξεως τοῦ σώματος
μήτε περὶ τῶν ἀσωμάτων οἷόν τέ ἐστι διαβεβαιώσασθαι, καὶ περὶ τῶν στοιχείων ἐστὶν ἐφεκτέον,

---

[1] τόδε Apelt: τότε mss., Bekk.

[a] The Heracleitean doctrine, cf. i. 217 ff.; §§ 82, 115 infra.

362

prove that this particular incorporeal (I mean reason) is previously apprehended ? For if it is by means of another incorporeal, we shall ask for the proof of its apprehension also, and so on *ad infinitum* ; whereas, if it is by means of a body, the apprehension of bodies is also in question ; by what means, then, are we to prove that the body which is assumed in order to prove the apprehension of the incorporeal reason is itself apprehended ? If by means of a body, we are plunged into infinite regress ; while if we do so by means of an incorporeal, we are wrecked on circular reasoning. Reason, then, since it is incorporeal, remaining thus inapprehensible, no one will be able to say that by means of it the incorporeal is apprehended.

But if reason is a body, inasmuch as about bodies 54 also there is much controversy as to whether or not they are apprehended, owing to what is called their " continual flux," [a] which gives rise to the view that they do not admit of the title " this " and are non-existent—just as Plato [b] speaks of bodies as " becoming but never being,"—I am perplexed as to how this controversy about Body is to be settled, as I see that it cannot be settled, because of the difficulties stated a moment ago, either by a body or by an incorporeal. Neither, then, is it possible to apprehend the incorporeals by reason. And if they are 55 neither objects of sense nor apprehended by means of reason, they will not be apprehended at all.

If, then, it is impossible to be positive either about the existence of Body or about the Incorporeals, we must also suspend judgement concerning the Elements, and possibly about the things

[b] *Cf.* ii. 28.

τάχα δὲ καὶ περὶ τῶν μετὰ τὰ στοιχεῖα, εἴγε
τούτων τὰ μὲν σώματα τὰ δὲ ἀσώματα, καὶ περὶ
ἀμφοτέρων ἠπόρηται. πλὴν ἀλλὰ τῶν τε δραστικῶν ἀρχῶν καὶ τῶν ὑλικῶν διὰ ταῦτα ἐφεκτῶν
οὐσῶν ἄπορός ἐστιν ὁ περὶ ἀρχῶν λόγος.

Η'.—ΠΕΡΙ ΚΡΑΣΕΩΣ

56   Ἵνα δὲ καὶ ταῦτα παραλίπῃ τις, πῶς ἄρα καὶ
γίνεσθαί φασι τὰ συγκρίματα ἐκ τῶν πρώτων
στοιχείων, μήτε θίξεως καὶ ἀφῆς ὑπαρχούσης
μήτε κράσεως ἢ μίξεως ὅλως; ὅτι μὲν γὰρ οὐδέν
ἐστιν ἡ ἀφή, καὶ μικρῷ πρόσθεν ὑπέμνησα, ὅτε
περὶ τῆς ὑποστάσεως τοῦ σώματος διελεγόμην·
ὅτι δὲ οὐδὲ ὁ τρόπος τῆς κράσεως ὅσον ἐπὶ τοῖς
λεγομένοις ὑπ' αὐτῶν δυνατός ἐστι, διὰ βραχέων
ἐπιστήσω. πολλὰ μὲν γὰρ λέγεται περὶ κράσεως,
καὶ σχεδὸν ἀνήνυτοι περὶ τοῦ προκειμένου σκέμ-
ματός εἰσι παρὰ τοῖς δογματικοῖς στάσεις· ὅθεν
εὐθέως ἅμα τῇ ἀνεπικρίτῳ διαφωνίᾳ καὶ τὸ ἀκατάληπτον τοῦ σκέμματος συνάγοιτ' ἄν. ἡμεῖς δὲ νῦν
τὴν πρὸς ἕκαστον αὐτῶν ἀντίρρησιν παραιτησάμενοι
διὰ τὴν πρόθεσιν τῆς συγγραφῆς, τάδε λέξειν ἐπὶ
τοῦ παρόντος ἀποχρώντως ὑπολαμβάνομεν.

57   Τὰ κιρνάμενα ἐξ οὐσίας καὶ ποιοτήτων συγκεῖ-
σθαι φασίν. ἤτοι οὖν τὰς μὲν οὐσίας αὐτῶν μί-

---

[a] For the four (or five) " elements " cf. §§ 30, 31 ; for " the
things behind " them (from the point of view of cognition),
i.e. primary bodies or stuff, cf. § 32.

[b] *i.e.* the primary bodies out of which, as "elements," the
(four) so-called " elements " (earth, air, fire, water) were
said by the Stoics to be compounded.

[c] For "touch" cf. i. 50, 96, iii. 45-46. " Mixture " (of
solids as well as fluids) is a wider term than " blending."

which lie behind the Elements [a] as well, seeing that of these some are bodies, others incorporeals, and both of these are matters of doubt. In fact, when both the active and the material Principles, for these reasons, call for suspense of judgement, the doctrine of Principles is open to doubt.

CHAPTER VIII.—CONCERNING MIXTURE

But, to pass over these problems, how do they 56 explain the production of the compounds from the primary elements,[b] when neither contact and touch nor mixture or blending [c] has any existence at all ? For that touch is nothing I showed a moment ago, when I was discussing the subsistence of Body ; and that the method of Mixture is equally impossible on their own showing, I shall briefly demonstrate. For there is much argument about Mixture, and the rival views held by the Dogmatists [d] on the problem propounded are well-nigh endless ; and hence we might straightway infer, along with the indeterminable controversy, the inapprehensibility of the problem. And we shall for the moment, owing to the design of our treatise, excuse ourselves from answering all their views in detail, deeming that the following remarks will amply suffice for the present.

They declare that mixed things are composed of 57 substance and qualities. If so, one must declare

---

[d] Especially Aristotle (*De gen. et corr.* i. 10) and the Stoics. The following argument is against the latter. As Aristotle says, " mixture " effects some change, but not a total change, in the things mixed, which must be such as are capable of mutually affecting one another, and capable also of being easily decomposed into their constituent particles : he defines " mixture " as " the union of mixables which have undergone alteration."

γνυσθαι φήσει τις τὰς δὲ ποιότητας μηδαμῶς, ἢ
τὰς μὲν ποιότητας ἀναμίγνυσθαι μηκέτι δὲ τὰς
οὐσίας, ἢ μηθέτερον ἀναμίγνυσθαι θατέρῳ, ἢ ἀμφότερα ἐνοῦσθαι ἀλλήλοις. ἀλλ' εἰ μὲν οὔτε αἱ
ποιότητες οὔτε αἱ οὐσίαι ἀναμίγνυνται ἀλλήλοις,
ἀνεπινόητος ἔσται ἡ κρᾶσις· πῶς γὰρ μία αἴσθησις
ἀπὸ τῶν κιρναμένων γίνεσθαι συμβήσεται, εἴγε
κατὰ μηδὲν τῶν προειρημένων μίγνυται ἀλλήλοις
58 τὰ κιρνάμενα; εἰ δὲ αἱ μὲν ποιότητες ἁπλῶς παρακεῖσθαι λεχθεῖεν ἀλλήλαις αἱ δὲ οὐσίαι μίγνυσθαι,
καὶ οὕτως ἄτοπον ἂν εἴη τὸ λεγόμενον· οὐ γὰρ
κεχωρισμένων τῶν ποιοτήτων τῶν ἐν ταῖς κρά-
σεσιν ἀντιλαμβανόμεθα, ἀλλ' ὡς μιᾶς ἀπὸ τῶν
κιρναμένων ἀποτελουμένης αἰσθανόμεθα. εἰ δὲ τὰς
μὲν ποιότητας μίγνυσθαι λέγοι τις τὰς δὲ οὐσίας
μηδαμῶς, ἀδύνατα λέξει· ἡ γὰρ τῶν ποιοτήτων
ὑπόστασις ἐν ταῖς οὐσίαις ἐστίν, διόπερ γελοῖον
ἂν εἴη λέγειν ὡς αἱ μὲν ποιότητες χωρισθεῖσαι
τῶν οὐσιῶν [καὶ]¹ ἰδίᾳ μίγνυνταί που ἀλλήλαις,
ἄποιοι δὲ αἱ οὐσίαι χωρὶς ὑπολείπονται.

59   Λείπεται λέγειν ὅτι καὶ αἱ ποιότητες τῶν κιρναμένων καὶ αἱ οὐσίαι χωροῦσι δι' ἀλλήλων καὶ μιγνύ-
μεναι τὴν κρᾶσιν ἀποτελοῦσιν. ὃ τῶν προειρημένων ἐστὶν ἀτοπώτερον· ἀδύνατος γάρ ἐστιν ἡ
τοιαύτη κρᾶσις. οἷον γοῦν ἐὰν δέκα κοτύλαις
ὕδατος κωνείου χυλοῦ κοτύλη μιχθῇ, παντὶ τῷ
ὕδατι συνανακίρνασθαι ἂν λέγοιτο τὸ κώνειον· εἰ
γοῦν καί τι βραχύτατον μέρος τοῦ μίγματος λάβοι

¹ [καὶ] om. T, Creuzer.

ᵃ Here " blend " is used merely as a synonym for " mix."
ᵇ Chrysippus held that " mixture " is not effected by
superficial " juxtaposition " but by the mutual " permeation "

either that their substances are blended[a] but not their qualities, or their qualities blended but not their substances any longer, or neither blended with the other, or both unified with each other. But if neither the qualities nor the substances are blended with one another, Mixture will be inconceivable ; for how will a single sensation result from the things mixed if the things mixed are blended with one another in none of the ways stated above ? And if it should be said 58 that the qualities are simply juxtaposed and the substances blended, even so the statement would be absurd ; for we do not perceive the qualities in the mixtures as separate objects but as a single sense-impression produced by the mixed things. And anyone who should assert that the qualities are blended, but the substances not, would be asserting the impossible ; for the reality of the qualities resides in the substances, so that it would be ridiculous to assert that the qualities by themselves, in separation from the substances, are somehow blended with one another, while the substances are left apart void of quality.

It only remains to say that both the qualities and 59 the substances of the mixed things permeate one another [b] and by their blending produce Mixture. But this is a more absurd view than any of the foregoing ; for such a mixture is impossible. Thus, for example, if a cup of hemlock juice were blended with ten cups of water, it will be said that the hemlock is mixed in with all the water ; for certainly if one were to take even the least portion of the mixture he would

or " interpenetration " of the constituents of the mixture : " qualities " as well as substances he regarded as corporeal and thus capable of being " penetrated."

τις, εὑρήσει πεπληρωμένον αὐτὸ τῆς τοῦ κωνείου
60 δυνάμεως. εἰ δὲ ἐπιμίγνυται τὸ κώνειον παντὶ
μέρει τοῦ ὕδατος καὶ παρεκτείνεται αὐτῷ ὅλον
ὅλῳ κατά τε τὴν τῶν οὐσιῶν καὶ τῶν ποιοτήτων
αὐτῶν δι' ἀλλήλων δίοδον, ἵν' οὕτως ἡ κρᾶσις
γένηται, τὰ δὲ παρεκτεινόμενα ἀλλήλοις καθ' ἅπαν
μέρος τὸν ἴσον ἐπέχει τόπον, διὸ καὶ ἴσα ἀλλήλοις
ἐστίν, ἴση ἔσται ἡ κοτύλη τοῦ κωνείου ταῖς δέκα
κοτύλαις τοῦ ὕδατος, ὡς εἴκοσι κοτύλας ὀφείλειν
εἶναι τὸ μῖγμα ἢ δύο μόνας, ὅσον ἐπὶ τῇδε τῇ
ὑποθέσει τοῦ τρόπου τῆς κράσεως· καὶ κοτύλης
πάλιν ὕδατος ταῖς εἴκοσι κοτύλαις ὅσον ἐπὶ τῷ
λόγῳ τῆς ὑποθέσεως ἐπεμβληθείσης τεσσαράκοντα
κοτυλῶν ὀφείλει τὸ μέτρον εἶναι ἢ πάλιν δύο μόνων,
ἐπειδὴ καὶ τὴν κοτύλην εἴκοσι κοτύλας ἐνδέχεται
νοεῖν, ὅσαις παρεκτείνεται, καὶ τὰς εἴκοσι κοτύλας
61 μίαν, ᾗ συνεξισοῦνται. δυνατὸν δὲ οὕτω κατὰ μίαν
κοτύλην ἐπεμβάλλοντα καὶ ὁμοίως συλλογιζόμενον
συνάγειν ὅτι αἱ εἴκοσιν ὁρώμεναι τοῦ μίγματος
κοτύλαι δισμύριαί που καὶ πρὸς ὀφείλουσιν εἶναι
ὅσον ἐπὶ τῇ ὑποθέσει τοῦ τρόπου τῆς κράσεως, αἱ
δὲ αὐταὶ καὶ δύο μόναι· ὅπερ ἀπεμφάσεως ὑπερβολὴν οὐκ ἀπολέλοιπεν. οὐκοῦν ἄτοπός ἐστι καὶ
62 αὕτη ἡ ὑπόθεσις τῆς κράσεως. εἰ δὲ οὔτε τῶν
οὐσιῶν μόνων μιγνυμένων ἀλλήλαις οὔτε τῶν
ποιοτήτων μόνων οὔτε ἀμφοτέρων οὔτε οὐθετέρου
δύναται γίνεσθαι κρᾶσις, παρὰ δὲ ταῦτα οὐδὲν
οἷον τέ ἐστιν ἐπινοεῖν, ἀνεπινόητος ὁ τρόπος τῆς
τε κράσεως καὶ ὅλως τῆς μίξεως ἐστιν. διόπερ
εἰ μήτε κατὰ θίξιν παρατιθέμενα ἀλλήλοις τὰ
καλούμενα στοιχεῖα μήτε ἀνακιρνώμενα ἢ μιγνύ-
μενα ποιητικὰ τῶν συγκριμάτων εἶναι δύναται,

find it full of the potency of the hemlock. Yet if the 60
hemlock is blended in with every particle of the water
and is distributed as a whole over the whole volume
of the water and through the mutual interpenetration
of both their substances and their qualities, so that
Mixture may in this way result; and if the things so
distributed over each other in every particle occupy
an equal space, so that they are equal to each other,—
then the cup of hemlock will be equal to the ten cups
of water, so that the blend must consist of twenty
cups or of only two, according to the assumption now
made as to the mode of Mixture. And if, again, a
cup of water were poured into the twenty cups,
then—according to the theory assumed—the quantity
is bound to be forty cups or, again, only two, since it
is admissible to conceive either the one cup as all
the twenty over which it is distributed, or the twenty
cups as the one with which they are equalized. And 61
by thus pouring in a cup at a time and pursuing the
same argument it is possible to infer that the twenty
cups seen in the blend must be twenty thousand and
more, according to the theory of Mixture assumed,
and at the same time only two—a conclusion which
reaches the very height of incongruity. Wherefore
this theory of Mixture also is absurd.

But if Mixture cannot come about by the mutual 62
blending either of the substances alone or of the
qualities alone or of both or of neither, and it is
impossible to conceive any other ways than these,
then the process of Mixture and of blending in
general is inconceivable. Hence, if the so-called
Elements are unable to form the compounds either
by way of contact through juxtaposition or by

SEXTUS EMPIRICUS

ἀνεπινόητός ἐστιν ἡ κατὰ τοὺς δογματικοὺς φυσιο-
λογία καὶ ὅσον ἐπὶ τούτῳ τῷ λόγῳ.

Θ.—ΠΕΡΙ ΚΙΝΗΣΕΩΣ

63 Πρὸς δὲ τοῖς προειρημένοις ἦν ἐπιστῆσαι τῷ
περὶ τῶν κινήσεων λόγῳ, ᾧ καὶ[1] ἀδύνατος ἂν
εἶναι νομισθείη ἡ κατὰ τοὺς δογματικοὺς φυσιο-
λογία. πάντως γὰρ κατά τινα κίνησιν τῶν τε
στοιχείων καὶ τῆς δραστικῆς ἀρχῆς ὀφείλει γίνεσθαι τὰ συγκρίματα. ἐὰν οὖν ὑπομνήσωμεν ὅτι
μηδὲν εἶδος κινήσεως ὁμολογεῖται, σαφὲς ἔσται ὅτι
καὶ διδομένων καθ᾽ ὑπόθεσιν τῶν προειρημένων
ἁπάντων μάτην ὁ καλούμενος φυσικὸς λόγος τοῖς
δογματικοῖς διεξώδευται.

Ι΄.—ΠΕΡΙ ΤΗΣ ΜΕΤΑΒΑΤΙΚΗΣ ΚΙΝΗΣΕΩΣ

64 Φασὶ τοίνυν οἱ δοκοῦντες ἐντελέστερον περὶ
κινήσεως διειληφέναι ἓξ εἴδη ταύτης ὑπάρχειν,
τοπικὴν μετάβασιν, φυσικὴν μεταβολήν, αὔξησιν,
μείωσιν, γένεσιν, φθοράν. ἡμεῖς οὖν ἑκάστῳ τῶν
προειρημένων εἰδῶν τῆς κινήσεως κατ᾽ ἰδίαν ἐπι-
στήσομεν, ἀπὸ τῆς τοπικῆς μεταβάσεως ἀρξάμενοι. ἔστιν οὖν αὕτη κατὰ τοὺς δογματικοὺς καθ᾽
ἣν τόπον ἐκ τόπου περιέρχεται τὸ κινούμενον ἤτοι
καθ᾽ ὁλότητα ἢ κατὰ μέρος, ὅλον μὲν ὡς ἐπὶ τῶν
περιπατούντων, κατὰ μέρος δὲ ὡς ἐπὶ τῆς περὶ
κέντρῳ κινουμένης σφαίρας· ὅλης γὰρ αὐτῆς
μενούσης ἐν τῷ αὐτῷ τόπῳ τὰ μέρη τοὺς τόπους
ἀμείβει.

[1] ᾧ καὶ ego : καὶ ὡς mss., Bekk. : καὶ om. Steph.

mixture or blending, then, so far as this argument goes, the physical theory of the Dogmatists is inconceivable.

CHAPTER IX.—CONCERNING MOTION

In addition to the foregoing we might have dwelt 63 on the argument about the kinds of motion, since this also might be held to render the physical theory of the Dogmatists impossible. For the formation of the compounds must certainly be due to some motion both of the elements and of the efficient Principle. If, then, we shall show that no one kind of motion is generally agreed upon, it will be clear that, even if all the assumptions mentioned above be granted, the Dogmatists have elaborated their so-called " Physical Doctrine " in vain.

CHAPTER X.—CONCERNING TRANSIENT MOTION

Now those who are reputed to have given the most 64 complete classification of Motion assert that six kinds of it exist—local transition, physical change, increase, decrease, becoming, perishing.[a] We, then, shall deal with each of the aforesaid kinds of motion separately beginning with local transition. According, then, to the Dogmatists, this is the motion by which the moving object passes on from place to place, either wholly or partially—wholly as in the case of men walking, partially as when a globe is moving round a central axis, for while as a whole it remains in the same place, its parts change their places.

[a] Cf. Adv. Phys. ii. 37 ff.; Aristot. Phys. vii. 2, Categ. 15 a 13; Plato, Laws, x. 894.

65 Τρεῖς δέ, οἶμαι, γεγόνασιν αἱ ἀνωτάτω περὶ κινήσεως στάσεις. ὁ μὲν γὰρ βίος[1] καί τινες τῶν φιλοσόφων εἶναι κίνησιν ὑπολαμβάνουσιν, μὴ εἶναι δὲ Παρμενίδης τε καὶ Μέλισσος καὶ ἄλλοι τινές. μὴ μᾶλλον δὲ εἶναι ἢ μὴ κίνησιν ἔφασαν οἱ σκεπτικοί· ὅσον μὲν γὰρ ἐπὶ τοῖς φαινομένοις δοκεῖν εἶναι κίνησιν, ὅσον δὲ ἐπὶ τῷ φιλοσόφῳ λόγῳ μὴ ὑπάρχειν. ἡμεῖς οὖν ἐκθέμενοι τὴν ἀντίρρησιν τῶν τε εἶναι κίνησιν ὑπολαμβανόντων καὶ τῶν μηδὲν εἶναι κίνησιν ἀποφαινομένων, ἐὰν τὴν διαφωνίαν εὑρίσκωμεν ἰσοσθενῆ, μὴ μᾶλλον εἶναι ἢ μὴ εἶναι κίνησιν λέγειν ἀναγκασθησόμεθα ὅσον ἐπὶ τοῖς
66 λεγομένοις. ἀρξόμεθα δὲ ἀπὸ τῶν ὑπάρχειν αὐτὴν λεγόντων.

Οὗτοι δὴ τῇ ἐναργείᾳ μάλιστα ἐπερείδονται· εἰ γὰρ μὴ ἔστι, φασί, κίνησις, πῶς μὲν ἀπὸ ἀνατολῶν ἐπὶ δυσμὰς ὁ ἥλιος φέρεται, πῶς δὲ τὰς τοῦ ἔτους ὥρας ποιεῖ, παρὰ τοὺς πρὸς ἡμᾶς συνεγγισμοὺς αὐτοῦ καὶ τὰς ἀφ' ἡμῶν ἀποστάσεις γιγνομένας; ἢ πῶς νῆες ἀπὸ λιμένων ἀναχθεῖσαι καταίρουσιν ἐπὶ λιμένας ἄλλους πάμπολυ τῶν προτέρων ἀφεστῶτας; τίνα δὲ τρόπον ὁ τὴν κίνησιν ἀναιρῶν πρόεισι τῆς οἰκίας καὶ αὖθις ἀναστρέφει; ταῦτα δὴ τελέως ἀναντίρρητα εἶναι. διὸ καὶ τῶν κυνικῶν τις ἐρωτηθεὶς κατὰ τῆς κινήσεως λόγον οὐδὲν ἀπεκρίνατο, ἀνέστη δὲ καὶ ἐβάδισεν, ἔργῳ καὶ διὰ τῆς ἐναργείας παριστὰς ὅτι ὑπαρκτή ἐστιν ἡ κίνησις.

[1] βίος T: βίας mss., Bekk.

---

[a] Lit. "by life," cf. i. 165, ii. 244.
[b] Such as Zeno and Diodorus Cronos, cf. ii. 242.

The main views held about motion are, I imagine, 65 three. It is assumed by ordinary people [a] and by some philosophers that motion exists, but by Parmenides, Melissus and certain others [b] that it does not exist ; while the Sceptics have declared that it is " no more " existent than non-existent ; for so far as the evidence of phenomena goes it seems that motion exists, whereas to judge by the philosophic argument it would seem not to exist. So when we have exposed the contradiction which lies between those who believe in the existence of motion and those who maintain that motion is naught, if we shall find the counter-arguments of equal weight,[c] we shall be compelled to declare that, so far as these arguments go, motion is " no more " existent than non-existent. We shall begin with those who affirm its real 66 existence.

These base their view mainly on " evidence." [d] If, say they, motion does not exist, how does the sun move from east to west, and how does it produce the seasons of the year, which are brought about by its approximations to us and its recessions from us ? Or how do ships put out from harbours and cast anchor in other harbours very far distant from the first ? And in what fashion does the denier of motion proceed from his house and return to it again ? These facts are perfectly incontestable. Consequently, when one of the Cynics [e] had an argument against motion put to him, he made no reply but stood up and began to walk, thus demonstrating by his action and by " evidence " that motion is capable of real existence.

[a] *Cf.* i. 26 for " equipollence " as leading to Sceptic " suspension."

[d] *i.e.* what is plainly obvious, *cf.* § 266.

[e] *Cf.* ii. 244.

Οὗτοι μὲν οὖν οὕτω δυσωπεῖν ἐπιχειροῦσι τοὺς
67 τῆς ἐναντίας αὐτοῖς στάσεως ὄντας· οἱ δὲ τὴν
ὕπαρξιν τῆς κινήσεως ἀναιροῦντες λόγοις ἐπιχειροῦσι τοιούτοις. εἰ κινεῖταί τι, ἤτοι ὑφ' ἑαυτοῦ
κινεῖται ἢ ὑφ' ἑτέρου. ἀλλ' εἰ μὲν ὑφ' ἑτέρου, [τὸ
γὰρ λεγόμενον ὑφ' ἑαυτοῦ κινεῖσθαι] ἤτοι ἀναιτίως
κινηθήσεται ἢ κατά τινα αἰτίαν. ἀναιτίως μὲν
οὐδέν φασι γίνεσθαι· εἰ δὲ κατά τινα αἰτίαν κινεῖται, ἡ αἰτία, καθ' ἣν κινεῖται, κινητικὴ αὐτοῦ
γενήσεται, ὅθεν εἰς ἄπειρον ἐκπίπτει κατὰ τὴν
68 μικρῷ πρόσθεν εἰρημένην ἐπιβολήν. ἄλλως τε καὶ
εἰ τὸ κινοῦν ἐνεργεῖ, τὸ δὲ ἐνεργοῦν κινεῖται,
κἀκεῖνο δεήσεται κινοῦντος ἑτέρου, καὶ τὸ δεύτερον
τρίτου, καὶ μέχρις ἀπείρου, ὡς ἄναρχον γίνεσθαι
τὴν κίνησιν· ὅπερ ἄτοπον. οὐκ ἄρα πᾶν τὸ κινούμενον ὑφ' ἑτέρου κινεῖται. ἀλλ' οὐδὲ ὑφ' ἑαυτοῦ.
ἐπεὶ γὰρ πᾶν τὸ κινοῦν ἤτοι προωθοῦν κινεῖ ἢ
ἐπισπώμενον ἢ ἀνωθοῦν ἢ ἐνθλῖβον, δεήσει τὸ
ἑαυτὸ κινοῦν κατά τινα τῶν προειρημένων τρόπων
69 ἑαυτὸ κινεῖν. ἀλλ' εἰ μὲν προωστικῶς ἑαυτὸ κινεῖ,
ἔσται ἐξόπισθεν ἑαυτοῦ, εἰ δὲ ἐπισπαστικῶς, ἔμπροσθεν, εἰ δὲ ἀνωστικῶς, ὑποκάτω, εἰ δὲ ἐν-
θλιπτικῶς, ἐπάνω. ἀδύνατον δὲ αὐτό τι ἑαυτοῦ
ἐπάνω εἶναι ἢ ἔμπροσθεν ἢ ὑποκάτω ἢ ὀπίσω·
ἀδύνατον ἄρα ὑφ' ἑαυτοῦ τι κινεῖσθαι. εἰ δὲ μήτε
ὑφ' ἑαυτοῦ τι κινεῖται μήτε ὑφ' ἑτέρου, οὐδὲ
κινεῖταί τι.
70   Εἰ δέ τις ἐπὶ τὴν ὁρμὴν καὶ τὴν προαίρεσιν κατα-
φεύγοι, ὑπομνηστέον αὐτὸν τῆς περὶ τοῦ ἐφ' ἡμῖν
διαφωνίας, καὶ ὅτι ἀνεπίκριτος αὕτη καθέστηκεν,

ᵃ An Aristotelian phrase : freedom of choice was denied
by fatalists, such as Democritus and the Stoics.

So these men attempt in this way to put to shame those who hold the contrary opinion ; but those who 67 deny the existence of motion allege such arguments as these : If a thing is moved, it is moved either by itself or by another thing. But if it is moved by another, it will be moved either causelessly or owing to some cause. Nothing, they assert, is moved causelessly ; but if it is moved owing to some cause, the cause owing to which it moves will be what makes it move, and thus we are involved in an infinite regress, according to the criticism stated a little while ago. Moreover, if the movent thing 68 is active, and what is active is moved, that movent thing will need another movent thing, and the second a third, and so on *ad infinitum*, so that the motion comes to have no beginning ; which is absurd. Therefore the thing that moves is not always moved by another. Nor yet by itself. Since every movent causes motion either by pushing forward or by drawing after or by pushing up or by thrusting down, what is self-movent must move itself in one of the aforesaid ways. But if it moves itself propulsively, it will be 69 behind itself ; and if by pulling after, it will be in front of itself ; and if by pushing up, it will be below itself ; and if by thrusting down, it will be above itself. But it is impossible for anything to be above or before or beneath or behind its own self ; therefore it is impossible for anything to be moved by itself. But if nothing is moved either by itself or by another, then nothing is moved at all.

And if anyone should seek refuge in the notions 70 of " impulse " and " purpose " we must remind him of the controversy about " what is in our power," [a] and

κριτήριον ἡμῶν τῆς ἀληθείας ἄχρι νῦν οὐχ εὑρηκότων.

71 Ἔτι κἀκεῖνο λεκτέον. εἰ κινεῖταί τι, ἤτοι ἐν ᾧ ἔστι τόπῳ κινεῖται ἢ ἐν ᾧ οὐκ ἔστιν. οὔτε δὲ ἐν ᾧ ἔστιν· μένει γὰρ ἐν αὐτῷ, εἴπερ ἐν αὐτῷ ἔστιν· οὔτε ἐν ᾧ μὴ ἔστιν· ὅπου γάρ τι μὴ ἔστιν, ἐκεῖ οὐδὲ δρᾶσαί τι οὐδὲ παθεῖν δύναται. οὐκ ἄρα κινεῖταί τι. οὗτος δὲ ὁ λόγος ἔστι μὲν Διοδώρου τοῦ Κρόνου, πολλῶν δὲ ἀντιρρήσεων τετύχηκεν, ὧν τὰς πληκτικωτέρας διὰ τὸν τρόπον τῆς συγγραφῆς ἐκθησόμεθα μετὰ τῆς φαινομένης ἡμῖν ἐπικρίσεως.

72 Φασὶν οὖν τινὲς ὅτι δύναταί τι ἐν ᾧ ἔστι τόπῳ κινεῖσθαι· τὰς γοῦν περὶ τοῖς κέντροις περιδινουμένας σφαίρας ἐν τῷ αὐτῷ μενούσας τόπῳ κινεῖσθαι. πρὸς οὓς μεταφέρειν χρὴ τὸν λόγον ἐφ' ἕκαστον τῶν μερῶν τῆς σφαίρας, καὶ ὑπομιμνήσκοντας ὅτι ὅσον ἐπὶ τῷ λόγῳ μηδὲ κατὰ μέρη κινεῖται, συνάγειν ὅτι μηδὲ ἐν ᾧ ἔστι τόπῳ κινεῖταί

73 τι. τὸ δὲ αὐτὸ ποιήσομεν καὶ πρὸς τοὺς λέγοντας ὅτι τὸ κινούμενον δυοῖν ἔχεται τόπων, τοῦ τε ἐν ᾧ ἔστι καὶ τοῦ εἰς ὃν φέρεται. πευσόμεθα γὰρ αὐτῶν πότε φέρεται τὸ κινούμενον ἀπὸ τοῦ ἐν ᾧ ἔστι τόπου εἰς τὸν ἕτερον, ἆρα ὅτε ἐν τῷ πρώτῳ τόπῳ ἔστιν ἢ ὅτε ἐν τῷ δευτέρῳ. ἀλλ' ὅτε μὲν ἐν τῷ πρώτῳ τόπῳ ἔστιν, οὐ μετέρχεται εἰς τὸν δεύτερον· ἔτι γὰρ ἐν τῷ πρώτῳ ἔστιν· ὅτε δὲ οὐκ

74 ἔστιν ἐν τούτῳ, οὐ μετέρχεται ἀπ' αὐτοῦ. πρὸς τῷ καὶ συναρπάζεσθαι τὸ ζητούμενον· ἐν ᾧ γὰρ μὴ ἔστιν, οὐδὲ ἐνεργεῖν ἐν αὐτῷ δύναται· οὐ γὰρ

---

[a] Cf. ii. 18 ff.   [b] Cf. ii. 245.

how it is still unsettled, since hitherto we have failed to find a criterion of truth.[a]

Further, there is this also to be said. If a thing 71 moves, it moves either in the place where it is or in that where it is not. But it does not move in the place where it is, for if it is in it, it remains in it; nor yet does it move in the place where it is not; for where a thing is not, there it can neither effect nor suffer anything. Therefore nothing moves. This argument is, in fact, that of Diodorus Cronos,[b] but it has been the subject of many attacks, of which we shall describe, owing to the character of our treatise, only the more formidable, together with a judgement of their value, as it seems to us.

Some, then, assert that a thing can move in 72 the place where it is; at any rate the globes which revolve round their axes move while remaining in the same place.[c] Against these men we should transfer the argument which applies to each of the parts of the globe, and, reminding them that, to judge by this argument, it does not move even in respect of its parts, draw the conclusion that nothing moves in the place where it is. And we shall take the same course 73 in replying to those who declare that the moving thing occupies two places, that wherein it is and that whereto it shifts. For we shall ask them *when* the moving object shifts from the place wherein it is to the other place—whether while it is in the first place or while it is in the second. But when it is in the first place it does not pass over into the second, for it is still in the first; and when it is not in this, it is not passing from it. And besides, the question is being 74 begged; for where it is not, there it cannot be active.

[a] *Cf. Adv. Phys.* ii. 93, 103.

δήπου φέρεσθαι εἴς τινα τόπον συγχωρήσει τις ἐκεῖνο ἁπλῶς ὃ μὴ δίδωσι κινεῖσθαι.

75 Τινὲς μέντοι κἀκεῖνο φασίν· τόπος λέγεται διχῶς, ὁ μὲν ἐν πλάτει, οἷον ὡς ἐμοῦ ἡ οἰκία, ὁ δὲ πρὸς ἀκρίβειαν, ὡς λόγου χάριν ὁ περιτετυπωκώς μου τὴν ἐπιφάνειαν τοῦ σώματος ἀήρ. λέγεται οὖν ἐν τόπῳ κινεῖσθαι τὸ κινούμενον οὐκ ἐν τῷ πρὸς ἀκρίβειαν ἀλλ' ἐν τῷ κατὰ πλάτος. πρὸς οὓς ἔνεστιν, ὑποδιαιροῦντας τὸν ἐν πλάτει τόπον, λέγειν ὅτι τούτου ἐν ᾧ μὲν ἔστι κυρίως τὸ κινεῖσθαι λεγόμενον σῶμα, ὡς ἐν τῷ πρὸς ἀκρίβειαν αὐτοῦ τόπῳ, ἐν ᾧ δὲ οὐκ ἔστιν, ὡς ἐν τοῖς λοιποῖς μέρεσι τοῦ κατὰ πλάτος τόπου· εἶτα συνάγοντας ὅτι μήτε ἐν ᾧ ἔστι τόπῳ κινεῖσθαί τι δύναται μήτε ἐν ᾧ μὴ ἔστιν, ἐπιλογίζεσθαι ὅτι μηδὲ ἐν τῷ κατὰ πλάτος καταχρηστικῶς λεγομένῳ τόπῳ κινεῖσθαί τι δύναται· συστατικὰ γάρ ἐστιν αὐτοῦ τό τε ἐν ᾧ ἔστι πρὸς ἀκρίβειαν καὶ ἐν ᾧ πρὸς ἀκρίβειαν οὐκ ἔστιν, ὧν ἐν οὐθετέρῳ κινεῖσθαί τι δύνασθαι δέδεικται.

76 Ἐρωτητέον δὲ κἀκεῖνον τὸν λόγον. εἰ κινεῖταί τι, ἤτοι κατὰ τὸ πρότερον πρότερον κινεῖται ἢ κατὰ ἄθρουν μεριστὸν διάστημα· οὔτε δὲ κατὰ τὸ πρότερον πρότερον δύναταί τι κινεῖσθαι, οὔτε κατὰ τὸ ἄθρουν μεριστὸν διάστημα, ὡς δείξομεν· οὐδὲ κινεῖταί τι ἄρα.

ᵃ Cf. §§ 119, 131. "Place" in the "exact" or narrow sense means the precise portion of space occupied by an object, as distinguished from "place" in the "broad" or "extended" sense in which it includes surrounding portions of space. The latter sense of "place" was adopted in order to make "motion in place" feasible; but Sextus argues that it fails to do so.

ᵇ The following sections, 76-80, criticize two kinds of motion, (1) *successive* motion, by which the moving body occupies the first part of the intervening space first with its

For surely no one will allow that any object to which he does not grant motion at all can shift to any place.

Some, however, make this statement: Place is 75 used in two senses, the broad sense, as for example " my house," and the exact sense,ᵃ as for instance " the air which enfolds the surface of my body." So the moving object is said to move in place, " place " being used not in the exact sense but in the broad sense. To these we can reply by dividing up " place " in the broad sense, and saying that in one part of it the body said to be moved properly exists, this being its own " place " in the exact sense, and in the other part it does not exist, this being the remaining portions of " place " in the extended sense ; next we shall argue that an object can move neither in the place where it is nor in that where it is not, and so conclude that nothing can move even in what is perversely termed " place " in the broad sense ; for this is composed of the place wherein it is in the exact sense and the place wherein it is not, and it has been proved that a thing cannot move in either of these.

We should also propound the following argument.ᵇ 76 If a thing moves it moves either by way of orderly, or gradual, progression or by occupying the divisible interval all at once ; but in neither of these ways can a thing move, as we shall prove ; so that it does not move at all.

own first part, next with its second part, and so on till all its parts have passed through all the parts of the " interval." (Here it is assumed that both the moving body and the spatial distance, or " interval," are divisible ; but, argues Sextus, whether they are infinitely divisible or divisible only into a limited number of indivisible parts, in either case motion is found to be impossible.) (2) *Momentaneous* motion (§§ 78-79), by which the moving body passes into the whole of the interval in a single moment of time.

Ὅτι μὲν οὖν κατὰ τὸ πρότερον πρότερον οὐκ ἐνδέχεταί τι κινεῖσθαι, αὐτόθεν δῆλον. εἰ μὲν γὰρ εἰς ἄπειρον τέμνονται τὰ σώματα καὶ οἱ τόποι καὶ οἱ χρόνοι οἷς κινεῖσθαι λέγεται τὰ σώματα, οὐ γενήσεται κίνησις, ἀδυνάτου ὄντος τοῦ πρῶτόν τι ἐν ἀπείροις εὑρεθῆναι, ἀφ' οὗ πρώτου κινήσεται τὸ 77 κινεῖσθαι λεγόμενον. εἰ δὲ εἰς ἀμερὲς καταλήγει τὰ προειρημένα, καὶ ἕκαστον τῶν κινουμένων ὁμοίως τὸ πρῶτον ἀμερὲς τοῦ τόπου τῷ πρώτῳ ἑαυτοῦ ἀμερεῖ μετέρχεται χρόνῳ, πάντα τὰ κινούμενα ἔστιν ἰσοταχῆ, οἷον ὁ ταχύτατος ἵππος καὶ ἡ χελώνη· ὅπερ τοῦ προτέρου ἐστὶν ἀτοπώτερον. οὐκ ἄρα κατὰ τὸ πρότερον πρότερον γίνεται ἡ κίνησις.

Ἀλλ' οὐδὲ κατὰ τὸ ἄθρουν μεριστὸν διάστημα. 78 εἰ γὰρ ἀπὸ τῶν φαινομένων, ὡς φασί, μαρτυρεῖσθαι τὰ ἄδηλα χρή, ἐπεί, ἵνα τις ἀνύσῃ σταδιαῖον διάστημα, δεῖ πρότερον αὐτὸν ἀνύσαι τὸ πρῶτον τοῦ σταδίου μέρος καὶ τὸ δεύτερον δεύτερον καὶ τὰ ἄλλα ὁμοίως, οὕτω καὶ πᾶν τὸ κινούμενον κατὰ τὸ πρότερον πρότερον κινεῖσθαι προσήκει, ἐπεί τοί γε εἰ ἀθρόως διιέναι τὸ κινούμενον λέγοιτο πάντα τὰ μέρη τοῦ τόπου ἐν ᾧ κινεῖσθαι λέγεται, ἐν πᾶσιν ἅμα ἔσται τοῖς μέρεσιν αὐτοῦ, καὶ εἰ τὸ μὲν ψυχρὸν εἴη μέρος τὸ δὲ θερμὸν τοῦ δι' οὗ ποιεῖται τὴν κίνησιν, ἢ τὸ μέν, εἰ τύχοι, μέλαν τὸ δὲ λευκὸν ὥστε καὶ χρῴζειν τὰ ἐντυγχάνοντα δύνασθαι, τὸ κινούμενον ἔσται θερμόν τε ἅμα καὶ 79 ψυχρὸν καὶ μέλαν καὶ λευκόν· ὅπερ ἄτοπον. εἶτα καὶ πόσον ἀθρόως διέξεισι τόπον τὸ κινούμενον

Now that a thing can not move in orderly progression is plain on the face of it. For if bodies, and also the places and the times in which the bodies are said to move, are divided to infinity, motion will not occur, it being impossible to discover amongst the infinite any first thing wherefrom the object said to move will derive its initial movement. And if the aforesaid 77 objects are reducible to atomic parts, and each of the moving things passes equally in an atomic period of time with its own first atom into the first atomic point of space, then all moving things are of equal velocity —the speediest horse, for instance, and the tortoise [a]; which is a result even more absurd than the former. Therefore motion does not take place by way of orderly progression.

Nor yet by way of immediate occupation of the divisible interval. For if one ought, as they declare, 78 to take the apparent as evidence for the non-apparent, since, in order to complete the distance of a stade a man must first complete the first portion of the stade, and secondly the second portion, and so on with the rest, so likewise everything that moves ought to move by way of orderly progression ; for surely if we should assert that the moving thing passes all at once through all the portions of the place wherein it is said to move, it will be in all the portions thereof at once, and if one portion of the place through which it has its motion should be cold, another hot, or, mayhap, one black, another white, so as to be able also to colour things in contact,—then the moving thing will be at once hot and cold and black and white, which is absurd. Next let them tell us how much space the 79

[a] *Cf.* the Eleatic puzzle of " Achilles " (and the tortoise); *cf.* Aristot. *Phys.* vi. 9.

εἰπάτωσαν. εἰ μὲν γὰρ ἀόριστον τοῦτον εἶναι
φήσουσιν, προσδέξονταί τι κινεῖσθαι διὰ πάσης
τῆς γῆς ἀθρόως· εἰ δὲ τοῦτο φεύγουσιν, ὁρισάτωσαν
ἡμῖν τὸ μέγεθος τοῦ τόπου. τὸ μὲν γὰρ πρὸς
ἀκρίβειαν ἐπιχειρεῖν ὁρίζειν τὸν τόπον οὗ πλέον
διάστημα οὐδὲ κατὰ τὸ ἀκαριαῖον δυνήσεται διελθεῖν τὸ κινούμενον ἀθρόως, πρὸς τῷ ἀποκληρωτικὸν καὶ προπετὲς ἢ καὶ γελοῖον ἴσως εἶναι, εἰς
τὴν ἀρχῆθεν ἀπορίαν ἐμπίπτει· πάντα γὰρ ἔσται
ἰσοταχῆ, εἴγε ἕκαστον αὐτῶν ὁμοίως κατὰ περι-
ωρισμένους τόπους τὰς μεταβάσεις τῶν κινήσεων
80 ποιεῖται. εἰ δὲ φήσουσιν ὅτι μικρὸν μέν, οὐ πρὸς
ἀκρίβειαν δὲ περιωρισμένον τόπον ἀθρόως κινεῖται
τὸ κινούμενον, ἐνέσται ἡμῖν κατὰ τὴν σωριτικὴν
ἀπορίαν ἀεὶ τῷ ὑποτεθέντι μεγέθει ἀκαριαῖον προσ-
τιθέναι μέγεθος τόπου. εἰ μὲν γὰρ στήσονταί που
τοιαύτην ποιουμένων ἡμῶν συνερώτησιν, πάλιν
εἰς τὸν ἀκριβῆ περιορισμὸν καὶ τὴν τερατείαν ἐκείνην ἐμπεσοῦνται· εἰ δὲ προσήσονται τὴν παραύξησιν,
ἀναγκάσομεν αὐτοὺς σωγχωρεῖν ἀθρόως τι δύνασθαι κινηθῆναι διὰ τοῦ μεγέθους τῆς γῆς ἁπάσης.
ὥστε οὐδὲ κατὰ ἄθρουν μεριστὸν διάστημα κινεῖται
81 τὰ κινεῖσθαι λεγόμενα.   εἰ δὲ μήτε κατὰ ἄθρουν
μεριστὸν τόπον μήτε κατὰ τὸ πρότερον πρότερον
κινεῖταί τι, οὐδὲ κινεῖταί τι.

Ταῦτα μὲν οὖν καὶ ἔτι πλείω τούτων φασὶν οἱ
τὴν μεταβατικὴν κίνησιν ἀναιροῦντες. ἡμεῖς δὲ

---

^a Cf. § 77. This is further explained in *Adv. Phys.* i. 154:
" If all is indivisible (time, bodies, and space), all moving
bodies will be of equal velocity (*e.g.* the sun and the tortoise),
since an indivisible interval is completed by all alike in an
indivisible moment of time." In this § 79 the difficulties as

moving thing passes through all at once. For if they shall assert that it is limitless, they will be granting that a thing moves through the whole of the earth all at once ; while if they shirk this conclusion, let them define for us the extent of the space. But, on the one hand, the attempt to define precisely the space or interval beyond which the thing moving all at once will be unable to advance so much as a hair's-breadth is probably not merely presumptuous and rash or even ridiculous, but plunges us again into the original difficulty [a] ; for all things will be of equal velocity, if each of them alike has its transitional movements over definite intervals of space. And if, on the other 80 hand, they shall assert that the moving thing moves all at once through a space that is small but not precisely determined, it will be open to us to adopt the *sorites* argument [b] and keep constantly adding a hair's-breadth of space to the breadth assumed. And if, then, they shall make a halt anywhere while we are pursuing this argument, they will be reverting to the monstrous theory of precise definition as before ; while if they shall assent to the process of addition, we shall force them to grant that a thing can move all at once through the whole of the earth. Consequently, objects said to be in motion do not move by occupying a divisible interval all at once. But if 81 a thing moves neither thus instantaneously nor by way of gradual progression, it does not move at all.

These, and yet more than these, are the arguments used by those who reject transient motion. But we,

regards the *quantity* of space passed through by the moving body on the *momentaneous* theory are exposed : it must be conceived either as (1) unlimited or (2) precisely limited, or (3) small, but not precisely limited ; but all these views lead to absurdities.　　　　　　　　　　　[b] *Cf.* ii. 253.

μήτε τοὺς λόγους τούτους μήτε τὸ φαινόμενον,
ᾧ κατακολουθοῦντες εἰσάγουσι τὴν ὑπόστασιν τῆς
κινήσεως, δυνάμενοι διατρέπειν, ὅσον ἐπὶ τῇ ἀντι-
θέσει τῶν τε φαινομένων καὶ τῶν λόγων, ἐπέχομεν
περὶ τοῦ πότερον ἔστι κίνησις ἢ οὐκ ἔστιν.

ΙΑ΄.—ΠΕΡΙ ΑΥΞΗΣΕΩΣ ΚΑΙ ΜΕΙΩΣΕΩΣ

82 Τῷ δὲ αὐτῷ χρώμενοι λογισμῷ καὶ περὶ αὐξή-
σεώς τε καὶ περὶ μειώσεως ἐπέχομεν· ἡ γὰρ ἐνάργεια δοκεῖ τὴν ὑπόστασιν αὐτῶν εἰσάγειν, ἣν
οἱ λόγοι διατρέπειν δοκοῦσιν. ἢ θέασαι γοῦν· τὸ
αὐξόμενον ὂν καὶ ὑφεστὼς εἰς μέγεθος ἐπιδιδόναι
προσήκει, ὡς εἴγε ἑτέρῳ προσθέσεως γενομένης
ἕτερον ηὐξηκέναι τις λέγοι, ψεύσεται. ἐπεὶ τοίνυν ἡ οὐσία οὐδέποτε ἔστηκεν ἀλλ᾽ ἀεὶ ῥεῖ τε
καὶ ἑτέρα ἀνθ᾽ ἑτέρας ἐπεισκρίνεται, τὸ ηὐξηκέναι
λεγόμενον οὐκ ἔχει τὴν προτέραν οὐσίαν καὶ μετὰ
ταύτης ἄλλην τὴν προστεθεῖσαν ἀλλ᾽ ὅλην ἑτέραν.
83 ὥσπερ οὖν εἰ, λόγου χάριν, ξύλου τριπήχεος ὄντος
δεκάπηχυ ἕτερον ἀγαγών τις ηὐξηκέναι τὸ τρίπηχυ
λέγοι, ψεύσεται διὰ τὸ ὅλον ἕτερον εἶναι τοῦτο
ἐκείνου, οὕτω καὶ ἐπὶ παντὸς τοῦ αὔξεσθαι λεγομένου, τῆς προτέρας ὕλης ἀπορρεούσης καὶ ἑτέρας
ἐπεισιούσης, εἰ προστίθεται τὸ προστίθεσθαι λεγόμενον, οὐκ ἂν αὔξησίν τις εἴποι τὸ τοιοῦτον εἶναι,
ἀλλ᾽ ἐξ ὅλου ἑτεροίωσιν.
84 Ὁ δὲ αὐτὸς καὶ περὶ τῆς μειώσεως λόγος· τὸ
γὰρ μὴ ὑφεστὼς ὅλως πῶς ἂν μεμειῶσθαι λέγοιτο;

---

^a Cf. § 66.
^b i.e. material substance, which Heracleitus and Plato said
was " in flux," cf. i. 217 ff., ii. 28.

384

being unable to refute either these arguments or the apparent facts on which the view of the reality of motion is based, suspend our judgement—in view of the contradiction between appearances and arguments—regarding the question as to the existence or non-existence of motion.

CHAPTER XI.—CONCERNING INCREASE AND DECREASE

Employing the same reasoning we suspend judge- 82 ment also concerning both increase and decrease. For the outward evidence [a] seems to support their reality, which the arguments seem to refute. For just consider : That which increases must grow in size as a stable substance, so that it will be false for anyone to say that one thing increases when an addition is made to another. Since then substance [b] is never stable but always in flux, one part supplanting another, the thing said to have increased does not retain its former substance together with the added substance but has its substance all different. Just 83 as if, for example, when there is a beam three cubits long a man should bring another of ten cubits and declare that the beam of three cubits had increased, he would be lying because the one is wholly different from the other ; so too in the case of every object which is said to increase, as the former matter flows away and fresh matter enters in its place, if what is said to be added is added, one should not call such a condition increase but complete alteration.

The same argument applies also to decrease.[c] For 84 how could that which has no stable existence be said

[c] *Cf. Adv. Phys.* i. 277 ff.

πρὸς δὲ τούτοις, εἰ ἡ μὲν μείωσις γίνεται κατὰ
ἀφαίρεσιν ἡ δὲ αὔξησις κατὰ πρόσθεσιν, οὐδὲν δέ
ἐστιν οὔτε ἀφαίρεσις οὔτε πρόσθεσις, οὐκοῦν οὐδὲ
ἡ μείωσις οὐδὲ ἡ αὔξησις ἔστι τι.

IB΄.—ΠΕΡΙ ΑΦΑΙΡΕΣΕΩΣ ΚΑΙ ΠΡΟΣΘΕΣΕΩΣ

85 Ὅτι δὲ οὐδέν ἐστιν ἀφαίρεσις, ἐντεῦθεν ἐπιλογίζονται. εἰ ἀφαιρεῖταί τι ἀπό τινος, ἤτοι τὸ ἴσον
ἀπὸ τοῦ ἴσου ἀφαιρεῖται ἢ τὸ μεῖζον ἀπὸ τοῦ
ἐλάσσονος ἢ τὸ ἔλασσον ἀπὸ τοῦ μείζονος. κατὰ
οὐδένα δὲ τῶν τρόπων τούτων ἀφαίρεσις γίνεται,
ὡς παραστήσομεν· ἀδύνατος ἄρα ἐστὶν ἡ ἀφαίρεσις.

Ὅτι δὲ κατ᾽ οὐδένα τῶν προειρημένων τρόπων
ἡ ἀφαίρεσις γίνεται, δῆλον ἐντεῦθεν. τὸ ἀφαιρούμενον ἀπό τινος ἐμπεριέχεσθαι χρὴ πρὸ τῆς
86 ἀφαιρέσεως τῷ ἀφ᾽ οὗ ἀφαιρεῖται. οὔτε δὲ τὸ
ἴσον ἐν τῷ ἴσῳ περιέχεται, οἷον τὰ ἓξ ἐν τοῖς ἕξ·
μεῖζον γὰρ εἶναι δεῖ τὸ περιέχον τοῦ περιεχομένου
καὶ τὸ ἀφ᾽ οὗ ἀφαιρεῖταί τι τοῦ ἀφαιρουμένου, ἵνα
μετὰ τὴν ἀφαίρεσιν ὑπολείπηταί τι· τούτῳ[1] γὰρ
διαφέρειν δοκεῖ τῆς παντελοῦς ἄρσεως ἡ ἀφαίρεσις·
οὔτε τὸ μεῖζον ἐν τῷ μικροτέρῳ, οἷον τὰ ἓξ ἐν τοῖς
87 πέντε· ἀπεμφαίνει γάρ. διὰ δὲ τοῦτο οὐδὲ τὸ
ἔλασσον ἐν τῷ μείζονι. εἰ γὰρ ἐν τοῖς ἓξ περιέχεται τὰ πέντε ὡς ἐν πλείοσιν ἐλάσσονα, καὶ ἐν
τοῖς πέντε περισχεθήσεται τὰ τέσσαρα καὶ ἐν τοῖς
τέτταρσι τὰ τρία καὶ ἐν τοῖς τρισὶ τὰ δύο καὶ ἐν
τούτοις τὸ ἕν. ἕξει οὖν τὰ ἓξ πέντε τέσσαρα τρία
δύο ἕν, ὧν συντεθέντων γίνεται ὁ πεντεκαίδεκα
ἀριθμός, ὃς ἐν τῷ ἓξ περιέχεσθαι συνάγεται διδο-

_____
[1] τούτῳ Mutsch.: τοῦτο mss., Bekk.

to have decreased ? Besides, if decrease takes place by way of subtraction, and increase by addition, and neither subtraction nor addition is anything, then neither decrease nor increase is anything.

CHAPTER XII.—CONCERNING SUBTRACTION AND ADDITION

That subtraction[a] is nothing they argue thus : If 85 anything is subtracted from anything, either equal is subtracted from equal, or greater from less, or less from greater. But in none of these ways does subtraction take place, as we shall show ; therefore subtraction is impossible.

That subtraction takes place in none of these ways is plain from what follows : What is subtracted from anything ought, before its subtraction, to be included in that from which it is subtracted. But 86 equal is not included in the equal—six, for instance, in six ; for what includes must be greater than what is included, and that from which the subtraction is made than what is subtracted, in order that there may be some remainder after the subtraction ; for it is this which is held to distinguish subtraction from complete removal. Nor is the greater included in the less—six, for instance, in five ; for that is irrational. And for this reason, neither is the less 87 included in the greater. For if five is included in six, as less in greater, four will be included in five, three in four, two in three, and one in two. Therefore six will contain five, four, three, two, and one, which when put together form the number fifteen, and this we conclude is included in six, if it be granted

• *Cf. Adv. Phys.* i. 297 ff.

μένου τοῦ τὸ ἔλασσον ἐν τῷ μείζονι περιέχεσθαι. ὁμοίως δὲ καὶ ἐν τῷ πεντεκαίδεκα τῷ ἐν τῷ ἓξ ἐμπεριεχομένῳ ὁ τριακονταικαιπέντε ἀριθμὸς περιέχεται καὶ κατὰ ὑπόβασιν ἄπειροι. ἄτοπον δὲ τὸ λέγειν ἀπείρους ἀριθμοὺς ἐμπεριέχεσθαι τῷ ἓξ ἀριθμῷ· ἄτοπον ἄρα καὶ τὸ λέγειν ὅτι ἐν τῷ μεί 88 ζονι περιέχεται τὸ ἔλασσον. εἰ οὖν χρὴ τὸ ἀφαιρούμενον ἀπό τινος περιέχεσθαι ἐν ἐκείνῳ ἀφ᾽ οὗ ἀφαιρεῖσθαι μέλλει, οὔτε δὲ τὸ ἴσον ἐν τῷ ἴσῳ περιέχεται οὔτε τὸ μεῖζον ἐν τῷ μικροτέρῳ οὔτε τὸ μικρότερον ἐν τῷ μείζονι, οὐδὲ ἀφαιρεῖταί τι ἀπό τινος.

Καὶ μὴν εἰ ἀφαιρεῖταί τι ἀπό τινος, ἢ ὅλον ἀπὸ ὅλου ἀφαιρεῖται ἢ μέρος ἀπὸ μέρους ἢ ὅλον ἀπὸ 89 μέρους ἢ μέρος ἀπὸ ὅλου. ὅλον μὲν οὖν ἀφαιρεῖσθαι λέγειν ἤτοι ἀπὸ ὅλου ἢ ἀπὸ μέρους ἀπεμφαίνει προδήλως, λείπεται δὲ λέγειν τὸ μέρος ἀφαιρεῖσθαι ἤτοι ἀπὸ ὅλου ἢ ἀπὸ μέρους· ὅπερ ἐστὶν ἄτοπον. οἷον γοῦν, ἵνα ἐπὶ ἀριθμῶν στήσωμεν τὸν λόγον τοῦ σαφοῦς ἕνεκα, ἔστω δεκάς, καὶ ἀπὸ ταύτης ἀφαιρεῖσθαι λεγέσθω μονάς. αὕτη οὖν ἡ μονὰς οὔτε ἀπὸ ὅλης τῆς δεκάδος ἀφαιρεῖσθαι δύναται οὔτε ἀπὸ τοῦ λειπομένου μέρους τῆς δεκάδος, τουτέστι τῆς ἐννεάδος, ὡς παραστήσω· οὐκοῦν οὐδὲ ἀφαιρεῖται.

90 Εἰ γὰρ ἡ μονὰς ἀπὸ ὅλης ἀφαιρεῖται τῆς δεκάδος, ἐπεὶ ἡ δεκὰς οὔτε ἕτερόν τί ἐστι παρὰ τὰς δέκα μονάδας οὔτε τις τῶν μονάδων ἀλλ᾽ ἡ συνέλευσις

---

[a] The addition of the numbers 1 . . . 5 gives 15; of 1 . . . 4, 10; of 1 . . . 3, 6; of 1 and 2, 3; so we get the total 35 = 15 + 10 + 6 + 3 + 1; cf. Adv. Phys. i. 304 ff. But perhaps we should read 105 for 35 (ἑκατόν for τριάκοντα), as 1 . . . 14 = 105.

that the less is included in the greater. So likewise in the fifteen which is included in the six there is included the number thirty-five,[a] and so on, step by step, to infinity. But it is absurd to say that infinite numbers are included in the number six ; and so it is also absurd to say that less is included in greater. If, then, what is subtracted from a thing must be 88 included in that from which it is to be subtracted, and neither equal is included in equal, nor greater in less, nor less in greater, then nothing is subtracted from anything.

Again, if anything is subtracted from anything, it is either a whole subtracted from a whole, or a part from a part, or a whole from a part, or a part from a whole. But to say that a whole is subtracted 89 from either a whole or a part is plainly nonsense. It remains, then, to say that a part is subtracted either from a whole or from a part ; which is absurd. Thus for example—basing our argument on numbers for the sake of clearness—let us take ten and suppose that from it one is subtracted. This one, then, cannot be subtracted either from the whole ten or from the remaining part of the ten, as I shall show ; therefore it is not subtracted at all.[b]

For if the one is subtracted from the whole ten, 90 since the ten is neither something other than the ten ones nor one of the ones, but the aggregate of

[b] In what follows it is argued (§§ 90, 91) that 1 cannot be subtracted from a "whole 10," 10 being ten ones, so that the subtracted 1 must be subtracted from each of those *ones*, including itself, and thus $10 - 1 = 0$. Further, as the number 1 (the "monad") is indivisible, it does not admit of subtraction : and the 1 to be subtracted must fall into 10 parts, and thus be itself a 10, if it is subtracted 10 separate times from the units of the 10.

πασῶν τῶν μονάδων, ἀπὸ ἑκάστης μονάδος ἀφαιρεῖσθαι ὀφείλει ἡ μονάς, ἵνα ἀπὸ ὅλης ἀφαιρῆται
τῆς δεκάδος. μάλιστα μὲν οὖν ἀπὸ μονάδος οὐδὲν
δύναται ἀφαιρεῖσθαι· ἀδιαίρετοι γάρ εἰσιν αἱ
μονάδες, καὶ διὰ τοῦτο οὐκ ἀφαιρεθήσεται ἡ
91 μονὰς ἀπὸ τῆς δεκάδος οὕτως. εἰ δὲ καὶ δοίη τις
ἀπὸ ἑκάστης τῶν μονάδων ἀφαιρεῖσθαι τὴν μονάδα,
δέκα ἕξει μέρη ἡ μονάς, δέκα δὲ ἔχουσα μέρη
δεκὰς[1] ἔσται. ἀλλὰ καὶ ἐπεὶ δέκα ἕτερα μέρη ἀπο-
λέλειπται, ἀφ' ὧν ἀφήρηται τὰ τῆς μονάδος λεγομένης δέκα μέρη, ἔσται τὰ δέκα εἴκοσι. ἄτοπον
δὲ λέγειν τὸ ἓν δέκα εἶναι καὶ τὰ δέκα εἴκοσι καὶ
τὸ ἀδιαίρετον κατὰ αὐτοὺς διαιρεῖσθαι. ἄτοπον
ἄρα τὸ λέγειν ἀπὸ ὅλης τῆς δεκάδος ἀφαιρεῖσθαι
τὴν μονάδα.
92 Ἀλλ' οὐδὲ ἀπὸ τῆς ὑπολειπομένης ἐννεάδος
ἀφαιρεῖται ἡ μονάς· τὸ μὲν γὰρ ἀφ' οὗ τι ἀφαιρεῖται οὐ μένει ὁλόκληρον, ἡ δὲ ἐννεὰς μετὰ τὴν
ἀφαίρεσιν ἐκείνης τῆς μονάδος ὁλόκληρος μένει.
καὶ ἄλλως, ἐπεὶ ἡ ἐννεὰς οὐδέν ἐστι παρὰ τὰς
ἐννέα μονάδας, εἰ μὲν ἀπὸ ὅλης αὐτῆς λέγοιτο
ἀφαιρεῖσθαι ἡ μονάς, ἐννεάδος ἀφαίρεσις ἔσται,
εἰ δὲ ἀπὸ μέρους τῶν ἐννέα, εἰ μὲν ἀπὸ τῶν
ὀκτώ, τὰ αὐτὰ ἄτοπα ἀκολουθήσει, εἰ δὲ ἀπὸ
τῆς ἐσχάτης μονάδος, διαιρετὴν εἶναι φήσουσι
93 τὴν μονάδα, ὅπερ ἄτοπον. οὐκοῦν οὐδὲ ἀπὸ τῆς
ἐννεάδος ἀφαιρεῖται ἡ μονάς. εἰ δὲ μήτε ἀπὸ
ὅλης τῆς δεκάδος ἀφαιρεῖται μήτε ἀπὸ μέρους

---

[1] δεκὰς T: μονὰς mss., Bekk.

---

a i.e. the Dogmatists, who assumed the indivisibility of
the " one."   In the next sections (92-93) it is shown that " a
390

the ones, the one ought to be subtracted from each of the ones in order to be subtracted from the whole ten. Now from a one, above all, nothing can be subtracted; for the ones are indivisible, and on this account the one will not be subtracted from the ten in this way. And even were we to grant that the 91 one is subtracted from each of the ones, the one will contain ten parts, and as containing ten parts it will be a ten. And further, since ten other parts remain, after the subtraction of the ten parts of the so-called one, the ten will be twenty. But it is absurd to say that the one is ten and the ten twenty, and to divide what, according to them,[a] is indivisible. Wherefore it is absurd to say that the one is subtracted from the whole ten.

Neither is the one subtracted from the remaining 92 nine; for that from which anything is subtracted does not remain entire, but the nine does remain entire after the subtraction of that one. Besides, since the nine is nothing more than the nine ones, if it should be said that the one is subtracted from the whole nine, the sum subtracted will be nine, or if from a part of it, then in case it be eight the same absurd results will follow, while if the subtraction is made from the last one, they will be affirming the divisibility of the one, which is absurd. So then, 93 neither from the nine is the one subtracted. But if it is neither subtracted from the whole ten nor from

part cannot be subtracted from a part," *i.e.*, in the case of the "Decad," you cannot subtract 1 from 9: for 10 − 1 still leaves an "entire" 9; and if 9 = 9 × 1, and 1 is subtracted from each of the 9 ones, the subtracted 1 will be 1 × 9; and the same applies to subtraction of 1 from other "parts" of the "Decad" (8, 7, 6, etc.), of which the last is 1, which, as indivisible, does not admit of subtraction.

αὐτῆς, οὐδὲ μέρος ἀπὸ ὅλου ἢ μέρους ἀφαιρεῖσθαι δύναται. εἰ οὖν μήτε ὅλον ἀπὸ ὅλου τι ἀφαιρεῖται μήτε μέρος ἀπὸ ὅλου μήτε ὅλον ἀπὸ μέρους μήτε μέρος ἀπὸ μέρους, οὐδὲ ἀφαιρεῖταί τι ἀπό τινος.

94 Ἀλλὰ καὶ ἡ πρόσθεσις τῶν ἀδυνάτων εἶναι παρ' αὐτοῖς ὑπείληπται. τὸ γὰρ προστιθέμενον, φασίν, ἤτοι ἑαυτῷ προστίθεται ἢ τῷ προϋποκειμένῳ ἢ τῷ ἐξ ἀμφοῖν συνεστῶτι· τούτων δὲ οὐδέν ἐστιν ὑγιές· οὐκοῦν οὐδὲ προστίθεταί τι τινί. οἷον γοῦν ἔστω τι τετρακοτυλιαῖον πλῆθος, καὶ προστιθέσθω κοτύλη. ζητῶ τίνι προστίθεται· ἑαυτῇ μὲν γὰρ οὐ δύναται, ἐπεὶ τὸ μὲν προστιθέμενον ἕτερόν ἐστι τοῦ ᾧ προστίθεται, οὐδὲν δὲ ἑαυτοῦ ἕτερόν ἐστιν.

95 ἀλλ' οὐδὲ τῷ ἐξ ἀμφοῖν, τοῦ τετρακοτυλιαίου καὶ τῆς κοτύλης· πῶς γὰρ ἂν προστεθείη τι τῷ μηδέπω ὄντι; καὶ ἄλλως, εἰ τῷ τετρακοτυλιαίῳ καὶ τῇ κοτύλῃ μίγνυται ἡ κοτύλη ἡ προστιθεμένη, ἑξακοτυλιαῖον ἔσται πλῆθος ἀπὸ τοῦ τετρακοτυλιαίου καὶ τῆς κοτύλης καὶ τῆς προστιθεμένης κοτύλης.

96 εἰ δὲ μόνῳ τῷ τετρακοτυλιαίῳ προστίθεται ἡ κοτύλη, ἐπεὶ τὸ παρεκτεινόμενόν τινι ἴσον ἐστὶν ἐκείνῳ ᾧ παρεκτείνεται, τῷ τετρακοτυλιαίῳ πλήθει ἡ κοτύλη παρεκτεινομένη διπλασιάσει τὸ τετρακοτυλιαῖον ὡς γίνεσθαι τὸ πᾶν πλῆθος ὀκτὼ κοτυλῶν· ὅπερ οὐ θεωρεῖται. εἰ οὖν μήτε ἑαυτῷ προστίθεται τὸ προστίθεσθαι λεγόμενον μήτε τῷ προϋποκειμένῳ μήτε τῷ ἐξ ἀμφοῖν τούτων, παρὰ δὲ ταῦτα οὐδὲν ἔστιν, οὐδὲ προστίθεται οὐδὲν οὐδενί.

a part of it, no part can be subtracted from either a whole or a part. If, then, nothing is subtracted either as whole from whole or as part from whole, nor as whole from part or as part from part, then nothing is subtracted from anything.

Moreover, addition is regarded by them [a] as one of 94 the impossibles. For, they say, that which is added is added either to itself or to what pre-exists or to the compound of both; but none of these alternatives is sound; therefore nothing is added to anything. Suppose, for instance, a measure of four cups,[b] and add to this a cup. To what, I ask, is it added? for it cannot be added to itself, since what is added must be other than that whereto it is added, but nothing is other than itself. Neither is it added to the com- 95 pound of the four cups and the one cup; for how could anything be added to what does not yet exist? Besides, if the added cup is blended with the four cups and the one cup, six cups will be the measure resulting from the four cups and the one cup and the added cup. And if the cup is added to the four 96 cups alone, since that which is extended over anything is equal to that over which it extends, the cup which extends over the measure of four cups will double the four cups so that the whole measure becomes eight cups—a result contrary to experience. If, then, what is said to be added is neither added to itself nor to what pre-exists nor to the compound of these, and besides these there are no other alternatives, then there is no addition of anything to anything.

[a] *i.e.* the Sceptics. [b] *Cf.* § 59.

Γʹ.—ΠΕΡΙ ΜΕΤΑΘΕΣΕΩΣ

97 Τῇ δὲ τῆς προσθέσεως καὶ τῆς ἀφαιρέσεως καὶ
τῆς τοπικῆς κινήσεως ὑποστάσει συμπεριγράφεται
καὶ ἡ μετάθεσις· αὕτη γὰρ ἀπὸ τινὸς μέν ἐστιν
ἀφαίρεσις τινὶ δὲ πρόσθεσις μεταβατικῶς.

ΙΔʹ.—ΠΕΡΙ ΟΛΟΥ ΚΑΙ ΜΕΡΟΥΣ

98 Καὶ τὸ ὅλον δὲ καὶ τὸ μέρος. κατὰ μὲν γὰρ
συνέλευσιν καὶ πρόσθεσιν τῶν μερῶν τὸ ὅλον
γίγνεσθαι δοκεῖ, κατ᾽ ἀφαίρεσιν δὲ τινὸς ἢ τινῶν
παύεσθαι τοῦ ὅλον εἶναι. καὶ ἄλλως δέ, εἰ ἔστι
τι ὅλον, ἤτοι ἕτερόν ἐστι παρὰ τὰ μέρη αὐτοῦ ἢ
99 αὐτὰ τὰ μέρη αὐτοῦ τὸ ὅλον ἐστίν. ἕτερον μὲν
οὖν τῶν μερῶν οὐδὲν φαίνεται τὸ ὅλον εἶναι· ἀ-
μέλει γοῦν ἀναιρουμένων τῶν μερῶν οὐδὲν ὑπο-
λείπεται, ἵνα ἕτερόν τι παρὰ ταῦτα λογισώμεθα τὸ
ὅλον. εἰ δὲ αὐτὰ τὰ μέρη τὸ ὅλον ἐστίν, ὄνομα
ἔσται μόνον τὸ ὅλον καὶ προσηγορία κενή, ὑπόστασιν δὲ ἰδίαν οὐχ ἕξει, καθάπερ οὐδὲ διάστασίς
ἐστί τι παρὰ τὰ διεστῶτα οὐδὲ δόκωσις παρὰ τὰ
δεδοκωμένα. οὐκ ἄρα ἔστι τι ὅλον.

100 Ἀλλ᾽ οὐδὲ μέρη. εἰ γὰρ ἔστι μέρη, ἤτοι τοῦ
ὅλου ταῦτά ἐστι μέρη ἢ ἀλλήλων ἢ ἑαυτοῦ ἕκαστον.
οὔτε δὲ τοῦ ὅλου, ἐπεὶ μηδὲ ἔστι τι παρὰ τὰ μέρη
(καὶ ἄλλως τὰ μέρη οὕτως ἔσται μέρη ἑαυτῶν,
ἐπεὶ ἕκαστον τῶν μερῶν συμπληρωτικὸν εἶναι
λέγεται τοῦ ὅλου), οὔτε ἀλλήλων, ἐπεὶ τὸ μέρος

ᵃ Lit. " is cancelled," cf. i. 13.
ᵇ Cf. ii. 215 ff., Adv. Phys. i. 330 ff.

Chapter XIII.—Concerning Transposition

Together with the existence of addition and sub- 97
traction and local motion transposition also is
abolished,[a] for this is subtraction from a thing and
addition to a thing by way of transition.

Chapter XIV.—Concerning Whole and Part

So too with both whole and part.[b] For the whole 98
is held to come about by the combination and addition
of the parts, and to cease from being a whole by the
subtraction of one or more parts. Besides, if a whole
exists, it is either other than its parts [c] or its parts
themselves form the whole. Now it is apparent that 99
the whole is nothing other than its parts ; for certainly
when the parts are removed there is nothing left, so
as to enable us to account the whole as something else
besides its parts. But if the parts themselves form
the whole, the whole will be merely a name and an
empty title,[d] and it will have no individual existence,
just as separation [e] also is nothing apart from the
things separated, or laying beams apart from the
beams laid. Therefore no whole exists.

Nor yet parts. For if parts exist, either they are 100
parts of the whole, or of one another, or each one of
itself. But they are not parts of the whole, since it
is nothing else than its parts (and besides, the parts
will on this assumption be parts of themselves, since
each of the parts is said to be complementary to the
whole) ; nor yet of one another, since the part is said

[c] The view of Epicurus ; the Stoics said that the whole is
neither the same as its parts nor different.
[d] Cf. ii. 214, 227.
[e] Cf. Adv. Phys. i. 344 f., ii. 27.

ἐμπεριέχεσθαι δοκεῖ ἐν ἐκείνῳ οὗ ἐστὶ μέρος, καὶ
ἄτοπόν ἐστι λέγειν τὴν χεῖρα, εἰ τύχοι, ἐν τῷ ποδὶ
101 περιέχεσθαι. ἀλλ᾽ οὐδὲ ἕκαστον ἑαυτοῦ μέρος
ἔσται· διὰ γὰρ τὴν περιοχὴν ἔσται τι ἑαυτοῦ μεῖζον
καὶ ἔλαττον. εἰ οὖν μήτε τοῦ ὅλου μήτε ἑαυτῶν
μήτε ἀλλήλων μέρη ἐστὶ τὰ λεγόμενα εἶναι μέρη,
οὐδενός ἐστι μέρη. εἰ δὲ μηδενός ἐστι μέρη, οὐδὲ
ἔστι μέρη· τὰ γὰρ πρός τι ἀλλήλοις συναναιρεῖται.
Ταῦτα μὲν οὖν ἁπλῶς[1] εἰρήσθω κατὰ παρέκ-
βασιν, ἐπειδὴ ἅπαξ ὅλου καὶ μέρους ἐπεμνήσθημεν.

ΙΕ΄.—ΠΕΡΙ ΦΥΣΙΚΗΣ ΜΕΤΑΒΟΛΗΣ

102 Ἀνυπόστατον δὲ εἶναι λέγουσί τινες καὶ τὴν
καλουμένην φυσικὴν μεταβολήν, λόγοις ἐπιχειροῦν-
τες τοιούτοις. εἰ μεταβάλλει τι, ἤτοι σῶμά ἐστι
τὸ μεταβάλλον ἢ ἀσώματον· ἑκάτερον δὲ τούτων
ἠπόρηται· ἄπορος ἄρα ἔσται καὶ ὁ περὶ τῆς μετα-
103 βολῆς λόγος. εἰ μεταβάλλει τι, κατά τινας ἐνεργείας αἰτίου καὶ πάσχον μεταβάλλει. ⟨ἀλλ᾽ οὐχ
ὡς πάσχον μεταβάλλει⟩·[2] διατρέπεται γὰρ ἡ τοῦ
αἰτίου ὑπόστασις, ᾧ τὸ πάσχον συμπεριτρέπεται
104 μὴ ἔχον ὑπὸ ὅτου πάθῃ. οὐδὲ μεταβάλλει τι ἄρα.
[ὃ] εἰ μεταβάλλει τι, ἤτοι τὸ ὂν μεταβάλλει ἢ τὸ
μὴ ὄν. τὸ μὲν οὖν μὴ ὂν ἀνυπόστατόν ἐστι καὶ
οὔτε πάσχειν τι οὔτε δρᾶν δύναται, ὥστε οὐδὲ

---

[1] ἁπλῶς ego : ἄλλως mss., Bekk.
[2] ⟨ἀλλ᾽ . . . μεταβάλλει⟩ addidi : ⟨ὃ ἀδύνατον⟩ add. Apelt.

---

[a] Cf. §§ 86 ff. supra. The notion of " part " involves that
of a " whole " which " includes " it, and of which it is
" part."
[b] " Part " and " whole " are " co-relative " notions, each
implying the other, and relative things are " apprehended

to be included [a] in that whereof it is part, and it is absurd to assert that, say, the hand is included in the foot. Neither will each be a part of itself; for, 101 because of the inclusion, it will be both greater and less than itself. If, then, the so-called parts are parts neither of the whole nor of themselves nor of one another, they are parts of nothing. But if they are parts of nothing, parts have no existence; for co-relatives are annulled together.[b]

Let thus much be said, then, of a general character, by way of digression, seeing that once already we have dealt with the subject of whole and part.

CHAPTER XV.—CONCERNING PHYSICAL CHANGE

Some, too, maintain that what is called " physical 102 change " is non-real, and the arguments they employ are such as these [c] : If a thing changes, what changes is either corporeal or incorporeal ; but each of these is matter of dispute ; therefore the theory of change will also be disputable. If a thing changes, it changes 103 through certain actions of a Cause [d] and by being acted upon. But it does not change by being acted upon, for the reality of Cause is refuted, and therewith is refuted also the object which is acted upon, as it has no agent to act upon it. Therefore nothing 104 changes at all. If a thing changes, either what is changes or what is not.[e] Now what is not is unreal and can neither act nor be acted upon at all, so that

together," the presence, or absence, of the one involving that of the other, cf. ii. 125, 175.

[c] With this section cf. §§ 38 ff., 49 and 64 where " physical change " is distinguished from " local transition " and other kinds of " motion."

[d] Cf. §§ 17 ff.   [e] With §§ 104-105 cf. 109 ff.

μεταβολὴν ἐπιδέχεται. εἰ δὲ τὸ ὂν μεταβάλλει,
ἤτοι καθὸ ὄν ἐστι μεταβάλλει ἢ καθὸ μὴ ὄν ἐστιν.
105 καθὸ μὲν οὖν μὴ ὄν ἐστιν, οὐ μεταβάλλει· οὐδὲ
γὰρ οὐκ ὄν ἐστιν· εἰ δὲ καθὸ ὄν ἐστι μεταβάλλει,
ἕτερον ἔσται τοῦ ὂν εἶναι, τουτέστιν οὐκ ὂν
ἔσται. ἄτοπον δὲ τὸ λέγειν τὸ ὂν οὐκ ὂν γίνε-
σθαι· οὐκ ἄρα οὐδὲ τὸ ὂν μεταβάλλει. εἰ δὲ μήτε
τὸ ὂν μεταβάλλει μήτε τὸ μὴ ὄν, παρὰ ταῦτα δὲ
οὐδὲν ἔστι, λείπεται λέγειν ὅτι οὐδὲν μεταβάλλει.
106 Ἔτι καὶ ταῦτά φασί τινες. τὸ μεταβάλλον ἔν
τινι χρόνῳ μεταβάλλειν ὀφείλει· οὔτε δὲ ἐν τῷ
παρῳχηκότι χρόνῳ μεταβάλλει τι οὔτε ἐν τῷ μέλλοντι, ἀλλ' οὐδ' ἐν τῷ ἐνεστῶτι, ὡς δείξομεν· οὐκ
ἄρα μεταβάλλει τι. ἐν μὲν οὖν τῷ παρεληλυθότι
ἢ μέλλοντι χρόνῳ οὐδὲν μεταβάλλει· τούτων γὰρ
οὐθέτερος ἐνέστηκεν, ἀδύνατον δέ ἐστι δρᾶν τι ἢ
πάσχειν ἐν τῷ μὴ ὄντι καὶ ἐνεστηκότι χρόνῳ.
107 ἀλλ' οὐδὲ ἐν τῷ ἐνεστῶτι. ὁ γὰρ ἐνεστὼς χρόνος
ἴσως μὲν καὶ ἀνύπαρκτός ἐστιν, ἵνα δὲ τοῦτο νῦν
ὑπερθώμεθα, ἀμερής ἐστιν· ἀδύνατον δέ ἐστιν ἐν
ἀμερεῖ χρόνῳ νομίζειν τὸν σίδηρον, εἰ τύχοι, ἀπὸ
τῆς σκληρότητος εἰς μαλακότητα μεταβάλλειν ἢ
τῶν ἄλλων μεταβολῶν ἑκάστην γίνεσθαι· παρα-
τάσεως γὰρ αὗται φαίνονται χρῄζειν. εἰ οὖν μήτε
ἐν τῷ παρεληλυθότι χρόνῳ μεταβάλλει τι μήτε ἐν
τῷ μέλλοντι μήτε ἐν τῷ ἐνεστῶτι, οὐδὲ[1] μεταβάλλειν τι ῥητέον.
108 Πρὸς τούτοις, εἰ ἔστι τις μεταβολή, ἤτοι
⟨αἰσθητή ἐστιν ἢ νοητή. καὶ αἰσθητὴ μὲν οὔκ
ἐστιν· αἱ μὲν γὰρ⟩[2] αἰσθήσεις ἁπλοπαθεῖς εἰσίν, ἢ

---

[1] οὐδὲ Pasquali: οὐ Bekk.
[2] ⟨αἰσθητὴ . . . γὰρ⟩ add. cj. Bekk.

it does not admit of change either. And if what is changes, it changes either in so far as it is in being or in so far as it is not in being. Now in so far as it is 105 not in being it does not change, for it is not even existent; while if it changes in so far as it is existent, it will be other than existent, which means that it will be non-existent. But it is absurd to say that the existent becomes non-existent; therefore the existent does not change either. And if neither the existent nor the non-existent changes, and besides these there is nothing else, it only remains to say that nothing changes.

Some also argue thus [a] : That which changes must 106 change in a certain time ; but nothing changes either in the past or in the future, nor yet in the present, as we shall prove ; nothing therefore changes. Nothing changes in the past or in the future, for neither of these times is present, and it is impossible to do or suffer anything in time that is not existent and present. Nor yet in time present. For the present 107 time is probably also unreal,[b] and—even if we set aside this point—it is indivisible ; and it is impossible to suppose that in an indivisible moment of time iron, say, changes from hard to soft, or any one of all the other changes takes place ; for they appear to require extension in time. If, then, nothing changes either in the past or in the future or in the present, we must declare that nothing changes at all.

Further, if change exists at all ⟨it is either sensible 108 or intelligible ; but it is not sensible, since the senses⟩ are specialized,[c] whereas change is thought to possess

[a] Cf. §§ 144 ff. ; Aristot. Phys. vi. 6.
[b] This is shown later, in §§ 144-145.
[c] Lit. " simply passive," i.e. each sense perceives only one class of objects, cf. § 47 supra.

δὲ μεταβολὴ συμμνημόνευσιν ἔχειν δοκεῖ τοῦ τε
ἐξ οὗ μεταβάλλει καὶ εἰς ὃ μεταβάλλειν λέγεται·
εἰ δὲ νοητή ἐστιν, ἐπεὶ περὶ τῆς ὑπάρξεως τῶν
νοητῶν ἀνεπίκριτος γέγονε παρὰ τοῖς παλαιοῖς
διαφωνία, καθάπερ ἤδη πολλάκις ὑπεμνήσαμεν,
οὐδὲν ἕξομεν λέγειν οὐδὲ περὶ τῆς ὑπάρξεως τῆς
μεταβολῆς.

Ιϛ′.—ΠΕΡΙ ΓΕΝΕΣΕΩΣ ΚΑΙ ΦΘΟΡΑΣ

109 Συμπεριτρέπεται μὲν οὖν καὶ ἡ γένεσις καὶ ἡ
φθορὰ τῇ προσθέσει καὶ τῇ ἀφαιρέσει καὶ τῇ
φυσικῇ μεταβολῇ· χωρὶς γὰρ τούτων οὔτε γένοιτο
ἄν τι οὔτε φθαρείη, οἷον γοῦν ἀπὸ τῆς δεκάδος
φθειρομένης, ὡς φασίν, ἐννεάδα γίνεσθαι συμβαίνει
κατὰ ἀφαίρεσιν μονάδος, καὶ τὴν δεκάδα ἀπὸ τῆς
ἐννεάδος φθειρομένης κατὰ πρόσθεσιν τῆς μονάδος,
καὶ τὸν ἰὸν ἀπὸ τοῦ χαλκοῦ φθειρομένου κατὰ
μεταβολήν. ὥστε ἀναιρουμένων τῶν προειρημένων
κινήσεων ἀναιρεῖσθαι καὶ τὴν γένεσιν καὶ τὴν
φθορὰν ἴσως ἀνάγκη.

110 Οὐδὲν δὲ ἧττόν τινες κἀκεῖνά φασίν. εἰ ἐγεν-
νήθη Σωκράτης, ἤτοι ὅτε οὐκ ἦν Σωκράτης ἐγένετο
Σωκράτης, ἢ ὅτε ἦν ἤδη Σωκράτης. ἀλλ᾽ εἰ μὲν
ὅτε ἦν ἤδη γεγενῆσθαι λέγοιτο, δὶς ἂν εἴη γεγενη-
μένος· εἰ δὲ ὅτε οὐκ ἦν, ἅμα καὶ ἦν Σωκράτης
καὶ οὐκ ἦν. ἦν μὲν τῷ γεγονέναι, οὐκ ἦν δὲ κατὰ
111 τὴν ὑπόθεσιν. καὶ εἰ ἀπέθανε Σωκράτης, ἤτοι ὅτε
ἔζη ἀπέθανεν ἢ ὅτε ἀπέθανεν. καὶ ὅτε μὲν ἔζη,
οὐκ ἀπέθανεν, ἐπεὶ ὁ αὐτὸς ἂν καὶ ἔζη καὶ ἐτε-

---

[a] A peculiar Stoic expression, cf. Adv. Phys. i. 353 ff., ii. 64.
[b] Cf. ii. 57 ff., i. 170.

" concurrent recollection " [a] both of that from which it changes and that into which it is said to change. And if it is intelligible, then, since (as we have frequently pointed out already [b]) there exists among the ancients an unsettled controversy as to the reality of intelligibles, we shall also be unable to make any assertion about the reality of change.

CHAPTER XVI.—CONCERNING BECOMING AND PERISHING

Both becoming and perishing are included in the 109 refutation of addition and subtraction and physical change ; for apart from these nothing would become or perish. Thus, for instance, it is as a result of the perishing of the ten, as they say, that the nine becomes by the subtraction of one, and the ten from the perishing of the nine by the addition of one ; and rust becomes from the perishing of bronze by means of change. Hence, if the aforesaid motions are abolished it is likely that becoming and perishing are also necessarily abolished.

Yet none the less some argue also as follows [c] : 110 If Socrates was born, Socrates became either when Socrates existed not or when Socrates already existed ; but if he shall be said to have become when he already existed, he will have become twice ; and if when he did not exist, Socrates was both existent and non-existent at the same time—existent through having become, non-existent by hypothesis. And if Socrates 111 died, he died either when he lived or when he died. Now he did not die when he lived, since he would

* Cf. Adv. Phys. i. 269, ii. 346 ff.

θνήκει· ἀλλ' οὐδὲ ὅτε ἀπέθανεν, ἐπεὶ δὶς ἂν εἴη
τεθνηκώς. οὐκ ἄρα ἀπέθανε Σωκράτης. τοῦτον
δὲ τὸν λόγον οἷόν τέ ἐστιν ἐφ' ἑκάστου τῶν γίνεσθαι
ἢ φθείρεσθαι λεγομένων ἱστάντα ἀναιρεῖν τὴν
γένεσιν καὶ τὴν φθοράν.

112 Ἔνιοι δὲ καὶ οὕτω συνερωτῶσιν. εἰ γίνεταί τι,
ἤτοι τὸ ὂν γίνεται ἢ τὸ μὴ ὄν. οὔτε δὲ τὸ μὴ ὂν
γίνεται· τῷ γὰρ μὴ ὄντι οὐδὲν συμβεβηκέναι
δύναται, ὥστε οὐδὲ τὸ γίνεσθαι. ἀλλ' οὐδὲ τὸ ὄν.
εἰ γὰρ γίνεται τὸ ὄν, ἤτοι καθὸ ὄν ἐστι γίνεται ἢ
καθὸ οὐκ ὄν ἐστιν. καθὸ μὲν οὖν οὐκ ὄν ἐστιν, οὐ
γίνεται. εἰ δὲ καθὸ ὄν ἐστι γίνεται, ἐπεὶ τὸ γινόμενον ἕτερον ἐξ ἑτέρου φασὶ γίνεσθαι, ἕτερον ἔσται
τοῦ ὄντος τὸ γινόμενον, ὅπερ ἐστὶν οὐκ ὄν. τὸ
113 ἄρα γινόμενον οὐκ ὂν ἔσται, ὅπερ ἀπεμφαίνει. εἰ
οὖν μήτε τὸ μὴ ὂν γίνεται μήτε τὸ ὄν, οὐδὲ
γίνεταί τι.

Κατὰ τὰ αὐτὰ δὲ οὐδὲ φθείρεται. εἰ γὰρ φθείρεταί τι, ἤτοι τὸ ὂν φθείρεται ἢ τὸ μὴ ὄν. τὸ μὲν
οὖν οὐκ ὂν οὐ φθείρεται· πάσχειν γάρ τι δεῖ τὸ
φθειρόμενον. ἀλλ' οὐδὲ τὸ ὄν. ἤτοι γὰρ μένον
ἐν τῷ ὂν εἶναι φθείρεται ἢ μὴ μένον. καὶ εἰ μὲν
μένον ἐν τῷ ὂν εἶναι, ἔσται τὸ αὐτὸ ἅμα καὶ ὂν
114 καὶ οὐκ ὄν· ἐπεὶ γὰρ οὐ φθείρεται καθὸ μὴ ὄν
ἐστιν ἀλλὰ καθὸ ὄν ἐστιν, καθὸ μὲν ἐφθάρθαι
λέγεται, ἕτερον ἔσται τοῦ ὄντος καὶ διὰ τοῦτο οὐκ
ὄν, καθὸ δὲ μένον ἐν τῷ εἶναι φθείρεσθαι λέγεται,

ᵃ Cf. Adv. Phys. ii. 326 ff. ; Aristot. Phys. i. 8.
ᵇ i.e. it is ("other" or) different after it has "become"
from what it was before it "became": "becoming" involves
a change of nature or character in the thing which undergoes the process.　　　ᶜ Cf. Adv. Phys. ii. 344 f.

have been at once both alive and dead ; nor yet when he died, since he would have been dead twice. Therefore Socrates did not die. And by applying this argument in turn to each of the things said to become or perish it is possible to abolish becoming and perishing.

Some also argue thus [a] : If a thing becomes, 112 either the existent becomes or the non-existent. But the non-existent does not become ; for to the non-existent nothing can occur ; neither, therefore, can becoming occur. Nor does the existent become. For if the existent becomes, it becomes either in so far as it is existent or in so far as it is non-existent. Now in so far as it is non-existent it does not become. But if it becomes in so far as it is existent, then, since they assert that what becomes becomes other from other,[b] what becomes will be other than the existent, and that is non-existent. Therefore what becomes will be non-existent, which is nonsense. If, then, 113 neither the non-existent becomes nor the existent, nothing becomes at all.

For the same reasons, neither does anything perish.[c] For if anything perishes, it is either the existent that perishes or the non-existent. Now the non-existent does not perish, for what perishes must be a subject of action. Nor yet does the existent perish. For it must perish either while continuing in existence or while not so continuing. And if it be while continuing in existence, it will be at one and the same time both existent and non-existent ; for since 114 it does not perish in so far as it is non-existent but in so far as it is existent, it will be other than the existent and therefore non-existent in so far as it is said to have perished, whereas in so far as it is said to

ὂν ἔσται. ἄτοπον δὲ τὸ λέγειν τὸ αὐτὸ εἶναι καὶ
ὂν καὶ οὐκ ὄν· οὐκ ἄρα μένον ἐν τῷ εἶναι φθείρεται
τὸ ὄν. εἰ δὲ οὐ μένον ἐν τῷ εἶναι τὸ ὂν φθείρεται,
ἀλλ' εἰς τὸ μὴ εἶναι περιίσταται πρῶτον, εἶθ'
οὕτως φθείρεται, οὐκέτι τὸ ὂν ἀλλὰ τὸ μὴ ὂν
φθείρεται· ὅπερ ἀδύνατον εἶναι ὑπεμνήσαμεν. εἰ
οὖν μήτε τὸ ὂν φθείρεται μήτε τὸ μὴ ὄν, παρὰ δὲ
ταῦτα οὐδὲν ἔστιν, οὐδὲ φθείρεταί τι.

Ταῦτα μὲν οὖν ὡς ἐν ὑποτυπώσει καὶ περὶ τῶν
κινήσεων ἀρκέσει λελέχθαι, οἷς ἕπεται τὸ ἀνύπαρκτον εἶναι καὶ ἀνεπινόητον τὴν κατὰ τοὺς
δογματικοὺς φυσιολογίαν.

ΙΖ'.—ΠΕΡΙ ΜΟΝΗΣ

115 Ἑπομένως δὲ καὶ περὶ τῆς ὡς πρὸς τὴν φύσιν
μονῆς ἠπόρησάν τινες, λέγοντες ὅτι τὸ κινούμενον
οὐ μένει, πᾶν δὲ σῶμα διαρκῶς κινεῖται κατὰ τὰς
τῶν δογματικῶν ὑπολήψεις, ῥευστὴν εἶναι λεγόντων τὴν οὐσίαν καὶ ἀεὶ διαφορήσεις τε καὶ προσθέσεις ποιουμένην, ὡς τὸν μὲν Πλάτωνα μηδὲ ὄντα
λέγειν τὰ σώματα ἀλλὰ γινόμενα μᾶλλον καλεῖν,
τὸν δὲ Ἡράκλειτον ὀξείᾳ ποταμοῦ ῥύσει τὴν
116 εὐκινησίαν τῆς ἡμετέρας ὕλης ἀπεικάζειν. οὐδὲν
ἄρα σῶμα μένει. τό γε μὴν λεγόμενον μένειν
συνέχεσθαι δοκεῖ ὑπὸ τῶν περὶ αὐτό, τὸ δὲ συν-
εχόμενον πάσχει· οὐδὲν δὲ ἔστι πάσχον, ἐπεὶ μηδὲ
αἴτιον, ὡς ὑπεμνήσαμεν· οὐδὲ μένει τι ἄρα.

---

[a] Cf. § 64.
[b] i.e. "rest" as the opposite of motion in general, not of
locomotion only (as in the Stoic use of the term); cf. Adv.
Phys. ii. 245 ff.   [c] Cf. §§ 51, 54 supra.
[d] i.e. "matter" (in the ordinary sense) of "our" physical

perish while continuing in existence it will be existent. But it is absurd to say that the same thing is both existent and non-existent; therefore the existent does not perish while continuing in existence. And if the existent does not perish while continuing in existence but passes first into non-existence and then in this way perishes, it is no longer the existent that perishes but the non-existent ; and this we have shown to be impossible. If, then, neither the existent perishes nor the non-existent, and besides these there is nothing else, nothing perishes at all.

This account of the motions [a] will suffice by way of outline, and therefrom it follows that the Physical Science of the Dogmatists is unreal and inconceivable.

Chapter XVII.—Concerning Rest

In like manner some have doubted about physical 115 rest,[b] saying that what is in motion is not at rest, but every body is constantly in motion according to the views of the Dogmatists who assert that Being is in flux [c] and always undergoing effluxes and additions— just as Plato does not even speak of bodies as " being" but rather calls them " becoming," and Heracleitus compares the mobility of our matter [d] to the swift current of a river. Therefore no body is at rest. What 116 is said to be at rest is, in fact, held to be embraced by the things which surround it, and what is embraced is acted upon ; but nothing acted upon exists, since no causal activity exists, as we have shown [e] ; therefore nothing is at rest.

universe, as distinct from any logical or metaphysical use of the term.

• *Cf.* §§ 13 ff., 103 *supra.*

Ἐρωτῶσι δέ τινες καὶ τοῦτον τὸν λόγον. τὸ
μένον πάσχει, τὸ δὲ πάσχον κινεῖται· τὸ ἄρα μένειν
117 λεγόμενον κινεῖται· εἰ δὲ κινεῖται, οὐ μένει. ἐκ
δὲ τούτων φανερόν ἐστιν ὅτι οὐδὲ τὸ ἀσώματον
ἐνδέχεται μένειν. εἰ γὰρ τὸ μένον πάσχει, τὸ δὲ
πάσχειν σωμάτων ἐστὶν ἴδιον, εἴπερ ἄρα, καὶ οὐχὶ
ἀσωμάτων, οὐδὲν [δὲ][1] ἀσώματον οὔτε πάσχειν
δύναται οὔτε μένειν· οὐδέν ἄρα μένει.
118 Τοσαῦτα μὲν καὶ περὶ μονῆς εἰρήσθω. ἐπεὶ δὲ
ἕκαστον τῶν προειρημένων οὐκ ἄνευ τόπου ἢ
χρόνου ἐπινοεῖται, μετιτέον ἐπὶ τὴν περὶ τούτων
σκέψιν· ἐὰν γὰρ ταῦτα δείξῃ τις ἀνυπόστατα,
ἀνυπόστατον ἔσται καὶ διὰ ταῦτα ἐκείνων ἕκαστον.
ἀρξώμεθα δὲ ἀπὸ τοῦ τόπου.

ΙΗ΄.—ΠΕΡΙ ΤΟΠΟΥ

119 Τόπος τοίνυν λέγεται διχῶς, κυρίως καὶ καταχρηστικῶς, καταχρηστικῶς μὲν [ὡς] ὁ ἐν πλάτει,
ὡς ἐμοῦ ἡ πόλις, κυρίως δὲ ὁ πρὸς ἀκρίβειαν
κατέχων, ὑφ᾽ οὗ περιεχόμεθα πρὸς ἀκρίβειαν.
ζητοῦμεν οὖν περὶ τοῦ [τόπου] πρὸς ἀκρίβειαν.
τοῦτον δὲ οἱ μὲν ἔθεσαν οἱ δὲ ἀνεῖλον, οἱ δὲ
120 ἐπέσχον περὶ αὐτοῦ. ὧν οἱ μὲν ὑπάρχειν αὐτὸν
φάσκοντες ἐπὶ τὴν ἐνάργειαν καταφεύγουσιν. τίς
γὰρ ἄν, φασί, λέξει μὴ εἶναι τόπον ὁρῶν τὰ μέρη
τοῦ τόπου, οἷον τὰ δεξιὰ τὰ ἀριστερά, τὰ ἄνω τὰ

[1] [δὲ] secl. Heintz.

---

[a] Cf. § 75 supra for this distinction between the " broad "
and narrow or " strict " senses of " place." In §§ 121-120 we
have the popular arguments for space based on (1) observed
facts as to " the parts of space," and the movement of bodies
406

Some, too, propound this argument: What is at rest is acted upon; but what is acted upon is in motion; therefore what is said to be at rest is in motion; but if it is in motion, it is not at rest. And [117] from this it is evident that neither does the incorporeal admit of being at rest. For if what is at rest is acted upon, and being acted upon is a property, if anything, of bodies and not of incorporeals, no incorporeal can either be acted upon or be at rest; therefore nothing is at rest.

So much for the subject of rest. And since no one [118] of the things we have mentioned is conceived apart from space or time, we must pass on to consider these; for if one should prove these to be unreal, then, because of them, each of the others also will be unreal. Let us begin with space.

CHAPTER XVIII.—CONCERNING SPACE

Space, or place, then, is used in two senses,[a] the [119] strict and the loose—loosely of place taken broadly (as " my city "), and strictly of exactly containing place whereby we are exactly enclosed. Our inquiry, then, is concerned with space of the strict kind. This some [b] have affirmed, others denied; and others have suspended judgement about it. And of these, those [120] who maintain its existence have recourse to the evidence of experience.[c] Who, they argue, could assert that space does not exist when he sees the parts of space, such as right and left, up and down, before

in space; and (2) traditional language, which assumes the existence of space; (3) if body exists, space must also exist.

    [b] *e.g.* the Stoics and Peripatetics, *cf.* §§ 124, 131.
    [c] *Cf.* Aristot. *Phys.* iv. 1.

κάτω, ἔμπροσθεν ὀπίσω, καὶ ἄλλοτε ἀλλαχοῦ
γιγνόμενος, βλέπων τε ὅτι ἔνθα ὁ ὑφηγητὴς ὁ
ἐμὸς διελέγετο, ἐνταῦθα ἐγὼ νῦν διαλέγομαι, τόπον
τε διάφορον καταλαμβάνων τῶν κούφων φύσει καὶ
121 τῶν φύσει βαρέων, ἔτι καὶ τῶν ἀρχαίων ἀκούων
λεγόντων '' ἤτοι μὲν γὰρ πρῶτα χάος ἐγένετο'' ;
εἶναι γάρ φασι χάος τὸν τόπον ἀπὸ τοῦ χωρητικὸν
αὐτὸν εἶναι τῶν ἐν αὐτῷ γινομένων. εἴγε μὴν ἔστι
τι σῶμα, φασίν, ἔσται καὶ ὁ τόπος· ἄνευ γὰρ
τούτου οὐκ ἂν εἴη τὸ σῶμα. καὶ εἰ ἔστι τὸ ὑφ'
οὗ καὶ τὸ ἐξ οὗ, ἔστι καὶ τὸ ἐν ᾧ, ὅπερ ἐστὶν ὁ
τόπος· τὸ δὲ πρῶτον ἐν ἑκατέρῳ· τὸ ἄρα δεύτερον
ἐν ἀμφοτέροις.

122 Οἱ δὲ ἀναιροῦντες τὸν τόπον οὔτε τὰ μέρη τοῦ
τόπου διδόασιν εἶναι· μηδὲν γὰρ εἶναι τὸν τόπον
παρὰ τὰ τούτου μέρη, καὶ τὸν συνάγειν πειρώμενον
ὅτι ἔστιν ὁ τόπος ἐκ τοῦ τὰ μέρη αὐτοῦ ὡς ὄντα
λαμβάνειν, τὸ ζητούμενον δι' ἑαυτοῦ κατασκευάζειν
βούλεσθαι. ὁμοίως δὲ ληρεῖν καὶ τοὺς ἔν τινι τόπῳ
γίνεσθαί τι ἢ γεγονέναι φάσκοντας, ὅλως μὴ διδομένου τοῦ τόπου. συναρπάζειν δὲ αὐτοὺς καὶ τὴν
τοῦ σώματος ὕπαρξιν μὴ διδομένην αὐτόθεν, καὶ
τὸ ἐξ οὗ καὶ τὸ ὑφ' οὗ δείκνυσθαι ἀνύπαρκτα
123 παραπλησίως τῷ τόπῳ. τὸν δὲ Ἡσίοδον μὴ ἀξιό-
χρεων εἶναι κριτὴν τῶν κατὰ φιλοσοφίαν. καὶ οὕτω

---

[a] Herodotus of Tarsus, cf. Introd. pp. xl f.
[b] Hesiod, Theog. 118.
[c] "Chaos" is here absurdly derived from χώρα, "room"
(the Stoics connected it with χεῖν, "to pour"). It means, in
fact, a "cavity" or abyss (from χάσκειν, "to yawn").
[d] "By which" is the "efficient," "from which" the
"material" cause: the Stoics regarded both these as
"bodies," and so involving the existence of space.

and behind ; and when he is now here, now there, and sees that where my teacher[a] was talking there I am talking now ; and when he observes that the place of things naturally light is different from that of things naturally heavy ; and when, also, he hears the 121 ancients declaring that " Verily first of all came Chaos into existence "[b]? For space, they say, is called Chaos from its capacity for containing[c] what becomes within it. Then, too, if any body exists, space also exists ; for without it body would not exist. And if "that-*by*-which" exists, and "that-*from*-which,"[d] there exists ; also " that-*in*-which," and this is space ; but the first is in each of the two, therefore the second is in both.[e]

But those who deny space do not admit the existence 122 of the parts of space ; for space, they say, is nothing else than its parts, and he who tries to deduce the existence of space from the assumption that its parts exist is seeking to establish the matter in question by means of itself. Equally silly is the language of those who assert that a thing becomes or has become in some place, when space in general is not admitted.[f] And they also presume the reality of body, which is not self-evident ; and, in much the same way as space, both that-*from*-which and that-*by*-which are proved to be unreal. Hesiod, too, is no competent 123 judge of philosophical problems. And while thus

[e] For the Stoic use of "first" and "second" in hypothetical syllogisms *cf.* ii. 104, 142. In the next sections (122-123) the arguments of the previous sections (120-121) are rebutted : (1) the "parts of space" are identical with space and in asserting their existence we are merely "begging the question"; (2) the reality of "body," or solid matter, as well as of the "efficient" and "material" causes, is likewise pure assumption. In §§ 124-130 the special views of the Stoics are expounded and refuted; in §§ 13 1ff. those of Aristotle and his School.   [f] *Cf.* §§ 38 ff. *supra.*

409

διακρουόμενοι τὰ εἰς κατασκευὴν φερόμενα τοῦ
εἶναι τόπον, ἤδη καὶ ποικιλώτερον κατασκευάζουσιν ὅτι ἀνύπαρκτός ἐστι, ταῖς ἐμβριθεστάταις
εἶναι δοκούσαις τῶν δογματικῶν στάσεσι περὶ τοῦ
τόπου προσχρώμενοι, τῇ τε τῶν στωικῶν καὶ τῇ
τῶν περιπατητικῶν, τὸν τρόπον τοῦτον.

124 Οἱ στωικοί φασι κενὸν μὲν εἶναι τὸ οἷόν τε ὑπὸ
ὄντος κατέχεσθαι μὴ κατεχόμενον δέ, ἢ διάστημα
ἔρημον σώματος, ἢ διάστημα ἀκαθεκτούμενον ὑπὸ
σώματος, τόπον δὲ διάστημα ὑπὸ ὄντος κατεχόμενον καὶ ἐξισαζόμενον τῷ κατέχοντι αὐτόν, νῦν
ὂν καλοῦντες τὸ σῶμα, χώραν δὲ διάστημα κατὰ
μέν τι κατεχόμενον ὑπὸ σώματος κατὰ δέ τι
ἀκαθεκτούμενον, ἐνίων χώραν εἰπόντων εἶναι τὸν
τόπον τοῦ μεγάλου σώματος, ὡς ἐν μεγέθει τὴν
διαφορὰν εἶναι τοῦ τε τόπου καὶ τῆς χώρας.

125 λέγεται οὖν ὅτι ἐπειδὴ διάστημα ὑπὸ σώματος
κατεχόμενόν φασιν εἶναι τὸν τόπον, πῶς καὶ λέγουσιν αὐτὸν εἶναι διάστημα; πότερον τὸ μῆκος τοῦ
σώματος ἢ τὸ πλάτος ἢ τὸ βάθος μόνον ἢ τὰς
τρεῖς διαστάσεις; εἰ μὲν γὰρ μίαν διάστασιν, οὐκ
ἐξισάζεται ὁ τόπος τῷ οὗ τόπος ἐστίν, πρὸς τῷ
καὶ μέρος τοῦ περιεχομένου τὸ περιέχον εἶναι, ὃ
126 παντάπασιν ἀπεμφαίνει. εἰ δὲ αἱ τρεῖς διαστάσεις,
ἐπεὶ οὔτε κενὸν ὑπόκειται ἐν τῷ λεγομένῳ τόπῳ
οὔτε ἄλλο σῶμα διάστασιν ἔχον, μόνον[1] δὲ τὸ ἐν

---

[1] μόνον Papp., Apelt: μένον mss., Bekk.

---

[a] The argument is: " Interval " cannot mean one " dimension " only (such as " length ") since (by definition) " Place "
must be " equated " to the " body " which is in it and must
therefore have all three dimensions; and further, the " in-

rebutting the arguments that tend to establish the existence of space, they also demonstrate its unreality more elaborately by making use of what are held to be the most weighty views of the Dogmatists about space, namely those of the Stoics and Peripatetics, in the following fashion.

The Stoics declare that Void is that which is capable 124 of being occupied by an existent but is not so occupied, or an interval empty of body, or an interval unoccupied by body ; and that Place is an interval occupied by an existent and equated to that which occupies it (" existent " being here the name they give to " body "); and that Room is an interval partly occupied by body and partly unoccupied—though some of them say that Room is the Place of the large body, so that the difference between Place and Room depends on size.   Their opponents then argue thus : 125 When the Stoics define Place as an " interval occupied by body," in what sense do they call it an " interval " ? Do they mean the length of the body or its width or its depth only, or all three dimensions ?   For if they mean one dimension, the place is not equated with the object of which it is the place, and besides, that which includes is part of what is included, which is pure nonsense.[a]   And if by " interval " is meant the 126 three dimensions, then, since in the so-called place there subsists neither a void nor another body which has dimensions, but only the body said to exist in

cluding " place of one " dimension " would be less than the body of three dimensions which it " includes."   Nor can it be all three dimensions, since the body which is " in " it is all these three dimensions and therefore identical with its " place "—the thing contained with the thing which contains it.   Thus " interval " and " place " are not explicable in terms of " dimensions."

τόπῳ λεγόμενον εἶναι σῶμα δ[1] συνέστηκεν ἐκ τῶν
διαστάσεων (ἔστι γὰρ τοῦτο μῆκος καὶ πλάτος καὶ
βάθος καὶ ἀντιτυπία, ᾗ δὴ συμβεβηκέναι λέγεται
ταῖς διαστάσεσι ταῖς προειρημέναις), αὐτὸ τὸ σῶμα
ἔσται ἑαυτοῦ τόπος, καὶ τὸ αὐτὸ περιέχον καὶ
περιεχόμενον, ὅπερ ἄτοπον. οὐκ ἄρα ἔστι τις
127 διάστασις τόπου ὑποκειμένου. διὰ δὲ τοῦτο οὐδὲ
ἔστι τι ὁ τόπος.

Ἐρωτᾶται δὲ καὶ οὗτος ὁ λόγος. ἐπεὶ διπλαῖ
αἱ διαστάσεις οὐ θεωροῦνται καθ' ἕκαστον τῶν ἐν
τόπῳ εἶναι λεγομένων, ἀλλ' ἓν μῆκος καὶ ἓν πλάτος
καὶ ἓν βάθος, πότερον μόνου τοῦ σώματός εἰσιν
αἱ διαστάσεις αὗται ἢ μόνου τοῦ τόπου ἢ ἀμφοτέρων; ἀλλ' εἰ μὲν μόνου τοῦ τόπου, οὐχ ἕξει τὸ
σῶμα ἴδιον μῆκος οὐδὲ πλάτος οὐδὲ βάθος οὐθέν,
128 ὥστε οὐδὲ σῶμα ἔσται τὸ σῶμα, ὅπερ ἄτοπον. εἰ
δὲ ἀμφοτέρων, ἐπεὶ τὸ κενὸν οὐδεμίαν ὑπόστασιν
ἔχει παρὰ τὰς διαστάσεις, εἰ αἱ διαστάσεις αἱ τοῦ
κενοῦ ὑπόκεινται ἐν τῷ σώματι συστατικαὶ οὖσαι
αὐτοῦ τοῦ σώματος, τὰ τοῦ κενοῦ συστατικὰ καὶ
τοῦ σώματος ἔσται συστατικά. περὶ μὲν γὰρ τῆς
ὑπάρξεως τῆς ἀντιτυπίας οὐκ ἔστι διαβεβαιώσασθαι, καθάπερ ἔμπροσθεν ὑπεμνήσαμεν[a]· μόνων δὲ
τῶν διαστάσεων φαινομένων κατὰ τὸ λεγόμενον
σῶμα, αἵπερ εἰσὶ τοῦ κενοῦ καὶ αἱ αὐταὶ τῷ κενῷ,
κενὸν ἔσται τὸ σῶμα. ὅπερ ἄτοπον. εἰ δὲ μόνου
τοῦ σώματός εἰσιν αἱ διαστάσεις, οὐδεμία ἔσται
διάστασις τόπου, διόπερ οὐδὲ ὁ τόπος. εἰ τοίνυν

---

[1] δ Papp. : οὐ mss., Bekk.

[a] Cf. § 39 supra.

place, and it is composed of the dimensions (for it is length and breadth and depth and solidity,[a] this last being said to be a property of the foregoing dimensions), the body itself will be its own place and at once both container and contained, which is absurd. Therefore no dimension of a subsisting place exists. 127 And, consequently, place is nothing.

This argument also is propounded.[b] Since the dimensions are not found to be twofold in the case of each of the objects said to exist in place, but there is one length, one breadth and one depth, do these dimensions belong to the body only, or to the place only, or to both ? If they belong only to the place, the body will have no length or breadth or depth of its own, so that the body will not even be body, which is absurd. If they belong to both, then, since the 128 Void has no reality apart from the dimensions, if the dimensions of the Void subsist in the body and serve to compose the body itself, the components of the Void will also be components of the body—for about the reality of solidity it is impossible to say anything positive, as we have shown above.[c] And since in the case of the so-called body only those dimensions appear which belong to the Void and are identical with the Void, the body will be Void, which is absurd. And if the dimensions belong to the body only, there will be no dimension of place, and therefore no place

---

[b] This argument raises the question—since "body" and "place" coincide (spatially), to which of the two do the "dimensions" belong, as we cannot assume two sets of dimensions in the same place? To ascribe them to the "body" annuls "place" and *vice versa*.

[c] *Cf.* §§ 45 f.; the "components" of "body" are the three "dimensions."

κατ' οὐδένα τῶν προειρημένων τρόπων εὑρίσκεται
τόπου διάστασις, οὐδὲ ἔστιν ὁ τόπος.

129 Πρὸς τούτοις λέγεται ὅτι ὅτε ἔπεισι τῷ κενῷ τὸ
σῶμα καὶ γίνεται τόπος, ἤτοι ὑπομένει τὸ κενὸν
ἢ ὑποχωρεῖ ἢ φθείρεται. ἀλλ' εἰ μὲν ὑπομένει,
τὸ αὐτὸ ἔσται καὶ πλῆρες καὶ κενόν, εἰ δὲ ὑποχωρεῖ
κινούμενον μεταβατικῶς ἢ φθείρεται μεταβάλλον,
σῶμα ἔσται τὸ κενόν· σώματος γὰρ ἴδιά ἐστι ταῦτα
τὰ πάθη. ἄτοπον δὲ τὸ αὐτὸ λέγειν κενὸν καὶ
πλῆρες, ἢ ὅτι σῶμά ἐστι τὸ κενόν. ἄτοπον ἄρα
τὸ λέγειν οἷόν τε εἶναι τὸ κενὸν ὑπὸ σώματος κατα-
130 σχεθῆναι καὶ γενέσθαι τόπον. διὰ δὲ ταῦτα καὶ
τὸ κενὸν ἀνυπόστατον εὑρίσκεται, εἴγε μὴ δυνατόν
ἐστιν αὐτὸ κατασχεθῆναι ὑπὸ σώματος καὶ γενέσθαι τόπον· ἐλέγετο γὰρ κενὸν εἶναι ὃ οἷόν τε
ὑπὸ σώματος κατασχεθῆναι. συμπεριτρέπεται δὲ
τούτοις καὶ ἡ χώρα· εἴτε γὰρ ὁ μέγας τόπος ἐστὶ
χώρα, συμπεριγράφεται τῷ τόπῳ, εἴτε ἡ κατὰ μέν
τι ὑπὸ σώματος κατεχομένη κατὰ δέ τι κενὴ διάστασις, ἀμφοτέροις συναναιρεῖται.

Ταῦτα μὲν οὖν καὶ ἔτι πλείω πρὸς τὴν στάσιν
131 τῶν στωικῶν περὶ τοῦ τόπου λέγεται· οἱ δὲ περι-
πατητικοί φασιν εἶναι τόπον τὸ πέρας τοῦ περιέχοντος, καθὸ περιέχει, ὡς ἐμοῦ τόπον εἶναι τὴν
ἐπιφάνειαν τοῦ ἀέρος τὴν περιτετυπωμένην τῷ
ἐμῷ σώματι. ἀλλ' εἴπερ τοῦτό ἐστιν ὁ τόπος, τὸ
αὐτὸ καὶ ἔσται καὶ οὐκ ἔσται. ὅτε γὰρ μέλλει
ἔν τινι τόπῳ γίνεσθαι τὸ σῶμα, καθὸ μὲν οὐδὲν
δύναται γενέσθαι ἐν τῷ μὴ ὑπάρχοντι, δεῖ προϋπάρχειν τὸν τόπον, ἵνα οὕτως ἐν αὐτῷ γένηται τὸ
σῶμα, καὶ διὰ τοῦτο ἔσται ὁ τόπος πρὶν ἐν αὐτῷ

———
[a] *Cf.* §§ 49 ff. ; and for the " affections," §§ 38, 52, 117.
414

either. If, then, no dimension of place is found in any of the ways described above, place does not exist.

Further, it is argued that when the body occupies 129 the Void and place comes about, the Void either remains or withdraws or perishes. But if it remains, the Plenum and the Void will be identical ; and if it withdraws by a movement of transition, or perishes by change, the Void will be a body [a] ; for these affections are peculiar to body. But it is absurd to say either that Void and Plenum are identical or that the Void is body. Therefore it is absurd to say that the Void can be occupied by body and become place. For these reasons also the Void is found to be unreal, 130 since it is impossible for it to be occupied by body and to become place ; for Void was defined [b] as " that which is capable of being occupied by body." And, in the refutation of these, Room also is involved ; for it is annulled along with place if " room is the large place," while if it is " that which is partly occupied by body and partly empty extension," its refutation is included in that of these two.

These arguments, and others besides, are directed against the views about place held by the Stoics. The Peripatetics [c] assert that place is " the limit of 131 what encloses in so far as it encloses," so that my place is the surface of the air that forms a mould round my body. But if this is place, the same thing will both be and not be. For when the body is about to become in a certain place, then, inasmuch as nothing can become in what is non-existent, the place must be pre-existent in order that the body may in this way become in it, and consequently the place will

[b] Cf. § 124.
[c] Cf. Adv. Phys. ii. 30 ff. ; Aristot. Phys. iv. 4, De cael. iv. 3.

γενέσθαι τὸ ἐν τόπῳ σῶμα. καθὸ δὲ περιτυπου-
μένης τῆς τοῦ περιέχοντος ἐπιφανείας τῷ περιεχομένῳ ἀποτελεῖται, οὐ δύναται ὑποστῆναι ὁ τόπος
πρὸ τοῦ ἐν αὐτῷ γενέσθαι τὸ σῶμα, καὶ διὰ τοῦτο
οὐκ ἔσται τότε. ἄτοπον δὲ τὸ αὐτὸ λέγειν καὶ
εἶναί τι καὶ μὴ εἶναι· οὐκ ἄρα ἔστι τόπος τὸ πέρας
τοῦ περιέχοντος, καθὸ περιέχει.

132 Πρὸς τούτοις, εἰ ἔστι τι ὁ τόπος, ἤτοι γεννητός
ἐστιν ἢ ἀγέννητος. ἀγέννητος μὲν οὖν οὐκ ἔστιν·
περιτυπούμενος γάρ, φασίν, τῷ ἐν αὐτῷ σώματι
ἀποτελεῖται. ἀλλ' οὐδὲ γεννητός· εἰ γὰρ ἔστι
γεννητός, ἤτοι ὅτε ἐν τόπῳ ἐστὶ τὸ σῶμα, τότε
γίνεται ὁ τόπος ἐν ᾧ ἤδη λέγεται εἶναι τὸ ἐν τόπῳ,
133 ἢ ὅτε οὐκ ἔστιν ἐν αὐτῷ. οὔτε δὲ ὅτε ἐν αὐτῷ
ἔστιν (ἔστι γὰρ ἤδη τοῦ ἐν αὐτῷ σώματος ὁ τόπος)
οὔτε ὅτε οὐκ ἔστιν ἐν αὐτῷ, εἴγε περιτυποῦται μέν,
ὡς φασίν, τῷ περιεχομένῳ τὸ περιέχον καὶ οὕτω
γίνεται τόπος, τῷ δὲ μὴ ἐν αὐτῷ ὄντι οὐδὲν δύναται περιτυπωθῆναι. εἰ δὲ μήτε ὅτε ἐν τόπῳ ἐστὶ
τὸ σῶμα, μήτε ὅτε οὐκ ἔστιν ἐν αὐτῷ, γίνεται ὁ
τόπος, παρὰ δὲ ταῦτα οὐδὲν ἔστιν ἐπινοεῖν, οὐδὲ
γεννητός ἐστιν ὁ τόπος. εἰ δὲ μήτε γεννητός ἐστι
μήτε ἀγέννητος, οὐδὲ ἔστιν.

134 Κοινότερον δὲ καὶ ταῦτα δύναται λέγεσθαι. εἰ
ἔστι τι ὁ τόπος, ἤτοι σῶμά ἐστιν ἢ ἀσώματον·
ἑκάτερον δὲ τούτων ἀπορεῖται, ὡς ὑπεμνήσαμεν·
καὶ ὁ τόπος ἄρα ἐστὶν ἄπορος. ὁ τόπος πρὸς τῷ
σώματι νοεῖται οὗ ἔστι τόπος· ἄπορος δέ ἐστιν ὁ
περὶ τῆς ὑπάρξεως τοῦ σώματος λόγος· καὶ ὁ περὶ
τοῦ τόπου ἄρα. ὁ τόπος ἑκάστου ἀΐδιος μὲν οὐκ

exist before the-body-in-the-place becomes therein. But inasmuch as it consists in the moulding of the surface of what encloses round the thing enclosed, place cannot be already subsisting before the body becomes within it, and therefore it will not be in existence then. But it is absurd to say that the same thing both is and is not ; therefore place is not " the limit of what encloses in so far as it encloses."

Furthermore, if place is anything, it is either created 132 or uncreate. Now it is not uncreate; for it is brought about, they say, by being moulded round the body within it. Nor yet is it created ; for if it is created, it is either when the body is in place that the place, in which the body in place is already said to be, comes into existence, or when the body is not in it. But it does not come into existence either when the 133 body is in it (for the place of the body within it exists already), or when it is not in it, since, as they assert, the container is moulded round the contained and in this way place becomes, and nothing can be moulded round that which is not within it. But if place does not become either when the body is in place or when it is not therein, and no other alternatives are conceivable, then place is not created at all. And if it is neither created nor uncreate, it has no existence.

These objections may also be stated more generally.[a] 134 If place is anything, it is either corporeal or incorporeal ; but each of these alternatives is, as we have shown, disputed ; therefore place is in dispute. Place is conceived in relation to the body whereof it is the place ; but the doctrine of the reality of body is disputed, therefore that of place is likewise disputable.

[a] The first objection is based on §§ 38-56, the second also on §§ 38 ff., the third on §§ 109 ff.

ἔστιν, γίνεσθαι δὲ λεγόμενος ἀνυπόστατος εὑρίσκεται γενέσεως μὴ ὑπαρχούσης.

135 Ἔνεστι δὲ καὶ ἄλλα πλείω λέγειν, ἀλλ' ἵνα μὴ
τὸν λόγον μηκύνωμεν, ἐκεῖνο ἐπακτέον ὅτι τοὺς
σκεπτικοὺς ἐντρέπουσι μὲν οἱ λόγοι, δυσωπεῖ δὲ
καὶ ἡ ἐνάργεια. διόπερ οὐθετέρῳ προστιθέμεθα
ὅσον ἐπὶ τοῖς λεγομένοις ὑπὸ τῶν δογματικῶν,
ἀλλ' ἐπέχομεν περὶ τοῦ τόπου.

ΙΘ'.—ΠΕΡΙ ΧΡΟΝΟΥ

136 Τὸ δὲ αὐτὸ πάσχομεν καὶ ἐν τῇ περὶ τοῦ χρόνου
ζητήσει· ὅσον μὲν γὰρ ἐπὶ τοῖς φαινομένοις δοκεῖ
τι εἶναι ὁ χρόνος, ὅσον δὲ ἐπὶ τοῖς περὶ αὐτοῦ
λεγομένοις ἀνυπόστατος φαίνεται. χρόνον γὰρ
εἶναί φασιν οἱ μὲν διάστημα τῆς τοῦ ὅλου κινήσεως
(ὅλον δὲ λέγω τὸν κόσμον), οἱ δὲ αὐτὴν τὴν κίνησιν
τοῦ κόσμου, Ἀριστοτέλης δέ, ἢ ὥς τινες Πλάτων,
ἀριθμὸν τοῦ ἐν κινήσει προτέρου καὶ ὑστέρου,
137 Στράτων δέ, ἢ ὥς τινες Ἀριστοτέλης, μέτρον
κινήσεως καὶ μονῆς, Ἐπίκουρος δέ, καθὼς Δη-
μήτριος ὁ Λάκων φησί, σύμπτωμα συμπτωμάτων,
παρεπόμενον ἡμέραις τε καὶ νυξὶ καὶ ὥραις καὶ
πάθεσι καὶ ἀπαθείαις καὶ κινήσεσι καὶ μοναῖς.

---

[a] *Cf.* §§ 66, 81. The Sceptics are here said to be "put
to shame," or "confusion" (*i.e.* caused to hesitate in their
judgement as to the nature of space) owing to the "equipollence" of the arguments against space and those for it
based on the obvious facts of experience.

[b] The Stoics, *cf.* Diog. Laert. vii. 141. This definition is
derived from the fact that Time is measured by the motions
of the planets and stars which compose the Universe.

[c] Aristot. *Phys.* iv. 10 mentions this (Platonic) definition,
cf. Plato, *Tim.* 47 D ff. Aristotle says that our notion of time
is derived from a sense of difference and of succession in our

The place of each thing is not eternal, but if we say that it becomes it is found to be unreal as becoming does not exist.

It is possible to adduce many other arguments. 135 But in order to avoid prolonging our exposition, we may conclude by saying that while the Sceptics are put to confusion by the arguments, they are also put to shame by the evidence [a] of experience. Consequently we attach ourselves to neither side, so far as concerns the doctrines of the Dogmatists, but suspend judgement regarding place.

CHAPTER XIX.—CONCERNING TIME

Our attitude is the same with respect to the inquiry 136 about time. For if we depend on appearances, time seems to be something, but if we depend on the arguments about it, it appears unreal. Some [b] define time as "the interval of the motion of the Whole" (meaning by "Whole" the Universe), others [c] as "the actual motion of the Universe"; Aristotle (or, as some say, Plato) as "the number of the prior and posterior in motion"; Strato (or, as some say, 137 Aristotle) as "the measure of motion and rest"; Epicurus (according to Demetrius the Laconian [d]) as "a concurrence of concurrences, concomitant with days and nights and seasons and affections and non-affections and motions and rests." And, in point of 138

thoughts and perceptions, which brings with it a distinction between "before" and "after"—between "past," "present," and "future." Thus "time" is a thing "numbered" or "measured" by the conscious mind, and Aristotle defines it as "a numeration of motion in respect of priority and posteriority" (*Phys.* iv. 11).

[d] An Epicurean, *cf. Adv. Log.* ii. 318.

138 κατ᾽ οὐσίαν τε οἱ μὲν σῶμα αὐτὸν ἔφασαν εἶναι,
ὡς οἱ περὶ τὸν Αἰνησίδημον, (μηδὲν γὰρ αὐτὸν
διαφέρειν τοῦ ὄντος καὶ τοῦ πρώτου σώματος), οἱ
δὲ ἀσώματον. ἤτοι οὖν πᾶσαι αἱ στάσεις αὐταί
εἰσιν ἀληθεῖς, ἢ πᾶσαι ψευδεῖς, ἢ τινὲς μὲν ἀληθεῖς
τινὲς δὲ ψευδεῖς· οὔτε δὲ πᾶσαι ἀληθεῖς ὑπάρχειν
δύνανται (μάχονται γὰρ αἱ πλεῖσται) οὔτε πᾶσαι
ψευδεῖς εἶναι δοθήσονται ὑπὸ τῶν δογματικῶν.
139 καὶ ἄλλως, εἰ δοθείη ψεῦδος μὲν εἶναι τὸ σῶμα
εἶναι τὸν χρόνον, ψεῦδος δὲ καὶ τὸ ὅτι ἀσώματός
ἐστιν, αὐτόθεν δοθήσεται ἡ τοῦ χρόνου ἀνυπαρξία·
παρὰ γὰρ ταῦτα οὐδὲν εἶναι δύναται ἕτερον. οὔτε
τινὲς μέν εἰσιν ἀληθεῖς τινὲς δὲ ψευδεῖς δυνατὸν
καταλαβεῖν διά τε τὴν ἰσοσθενῆ διαφωνίαν καὶ τὴν
ἀπορίαν τὴν κατὰ ⟨τὸ⟩[1] κριτήριόν τε καὶ τὴν
140 ἀπόδειξιν. ὥστε διὰ ταῦτα οὐδὲν ἕξομεν περὶ
χρόνου διαβεβαιώσασθαι.

Εἶτα, ἐπεὶ οὐκ ἄνευ κινήσεως ἢ καὶ μονῆς ὁ
χρόνος ὑφεστάναι δοκεῖ, τῆς κινήσεως ἀναιρου-
μένης, ὁμοίως δὲ καὶ τῆς μονῆς, ἀναιρεῖται ὁ
χρόνος. οὐδὲν δὲ ἧττον καὶ τάδε φασί τινες κατὰ
τοῦ χρόνου. εἰ ἔστι χρόνος, ἤτοι πεπέρασται ἢ
141 ἄπειρός ἐστιν. ἀλλ᾽ εἰ μὲν πεπέρασται, ἀπό
τινος χρόνου ἤρξατο καὶ εἴς τινα χρόνον λήξει·
διὰ δὲ τοῦτο ἦν ποτὲ χρόνος ὅτε οὐκ ἦν χρόνος,
πρὸ τοῦ ἄρξασθαι αὐτόν, καὶ ἔσται ποτὲ χρόνος
ὅτε οὐκ ἔσται χρόνος, μετὰ τὸ λῆξαι αὐτόν, ὅπερ
142 ἄτοπον. οὐ τοίνυν πεπέρασται ὁ χρόνος. εἰ δὲ
ἄπειρός ἐστιν, ἐπεὶ τὸ μέν τι αὐτοῦ λέγεται παρ-
ῳχηκὸς τὸ δὲ ἐνεστὼς τὸ δὲ μέλλον, ὁ μέλλων καὶ
ὁ παρῳχηκὼς ἤτοι εἰσὶν ἢ οὐκ εἰσίν. ἀλλ᾽ εἰ οὐκ

---

[1] ⟨τὸ⟩ add. Mutsch.

420

substance, some have affirmed that it is corporeal
—for instance, Aenesidemus, arguing that it differs
in nothing from Being and the prime body,—others,[a]
that it is incorporeal. Either, then, all these theories
are true, or all false, or some true and some false ;
but they cannot all be true (most of them being
in conflict), nor will it be granted by the Dogmatists that all are false. And besides, should it 139
be granted that the assertion of the corporeality
of time is false, and that of its incorporeality likewise false, then, *ipso facto*, the unreality of time will
be granted ; for it cannot be anything but one or
other of these. Nor yet can we apprehend which
theories are true, which false, owing to the equal
weight [b] of the rival opinions as well as the perplexity
regarding the criterion and proof.[c] Hence for these 140
reasons we shall be unable to affirm anything positively about time.

Further, since time does not seem to subsist without
motion or even rest, if motion is abolished, and
likewise rest, time is abolished. None the less the
following objections against time are made by some.
If time exists, it is either limited or unlimited. But 141
if it is limited, it began at a certain time and will end
at a certain time. Consequently, there was once a
time when time was not (before it began), and there
will once be a time when time will not be (after it has
ended) ; which is absurd.[d] So then time is not limited.
But if it is unlimited, since part of it is said to be 142
past, part present, and part future, the future and
past are either existent or non-existent. But if they

---

[a] *i.e.* the Stoics.   [b] *Cf.* i. 8.
[c] *Cf.* ii. cc. 3-7, 12, 13.
[d] *Cf.* Aristot. *Met.* xii. 6.

εἰσίν, μόνου τοῦ ἐνεστῶτος ὑπολειπομένου, ὅς
ἐστιν ἀκαριαῖος, πεπερασμένος ἔσται ὁ χρόνος καὶ
ἀκολουθήσουσιν αἱ ἀρχῆθεν ἀπορίαι. εἰ δὲ ὁ
παρῳχηκὼς ἔστι καὶ ὁ μέλλων ἔστιν, ἐνεστὼς
ἔσται ἑκάτερος αὐτῶν. ἄτοπον δὲ τὸ λέγειν ἐνεστῶτα τὸν παρῳχηκότα καὶ τὸν μέλλοντα χρόνον·
οὐκοῦν οὐδὲ ἄπειρός ἐστιν ὁ χρόνος. εἰ δὲ μήτε
ἄπειρος μήτε πεπερασμένος, οὐδὲ ἔστιν ὅλως χρόνος.

143 Πρὸς τούτοις, εἰ ἔστιν ὁ χρόνος, ἤτοι μεριστός
ἐστιν ἢ ἀμέριστος. ἀμέριστος μὲν οὖν οὐκ ἔστιν·
διαιρεῖται γὰρ εἴς τε τὸν ἐνεστῶτα καὶ εἰς τὸν
παρῳχηκότα καὶ εἰς τὸν μέλλοντα, ὡς αὐτοί φασιν.
ἀλλ᾽ οὐδὲ μεριστός. ἕκαστον γὰρ τῶν μεριστῶν
καταμετρεῖται ὑπό τινος ἑαυτοῦ μέρους, καθ᾽
ἕκαστον μέρος τοῦ μετρουμένου γινομένου τοῦ
μετροῦντος, ὡς ὅταν δακτύλῳ πῆχυν μετρῶμεν.
ὁ δὲ χρόνος οὐ δύναται καταμετρεῖσθαι ὑπό τινος
ἑαυτοῦ μέρους. εἰ γὰρ ὁ ἐνεστὼς λόγου χάριν
καταμετρεῖ τὸν παρῳχημένον, ἔσται κατὰ τὸν
παρῳχηκότα καὶ διὰ τοῦτο παρῳχηκώς, καὶ ἐπὶ
τοῦ μέλλοντος ὁμοίως μέλλων. καὶ ὁ μέλλων εἰ
καταμετροίη τοὺς ἄλλους, ἐνεστὼς ἔσται καὶ
παρῳχηκώς, καὶ ὁ παρῳχηκὼς παραπλησίως μέλλων ἔσται καὶ ἐνεστώς· ὅπερ ἀπεμφαίνει. οὐκοῦν
οὐδὲ μεριστός ἐστιν. εἰ δὲ μήτε ἀμέριστος μήτε
μεριστός, οὐδὲ ἔστιν.

144 Ὅ τε χρόνος λέγεται τριμερὴς εἶναι, καὶ τὸ μὲν
παρῳχηκὼς τὸ δὲ ἐνεστὼς τὸ δὲ μέλλων. ὧν ὁ
μὲν παρῳχηκὼς καὶ ὁ μέλλων οὐκ εἰσίν· εἰ γὰρ
εἰσὶ νῦν ὅ τε παρῳχηκὼς καὶ ὁ μέλλων χρόνος,
ἔσται ἐνεστὼς ἑκάτερος αὐτῶν. ἀλλ᾽ οὐδὲ ὁ ἐνεστώς. εἰ γὰρ ἔστιν ὁ ἐνεστὼς χρόνος, ἤτοι ἀ-

are non-existent, and there remains only the present, which is momentary, time will be limited and the original difficulties [a] will follow. And if the past exists and the future exists, each of these will be present. But it is absurd to call past and future time present; neither, then, is time unlimited. But if it is neither unlimited nor limited, time does not exist at all.

Further, if time exists it is either divisible or 143 indivisible. Now it is not indivisible; for it is divided, as they themselves declare, into present, past, and future. Yet it is not divisible either. For each divisible thing is measured by some part of itself, the measure coinciding with each part of the measured, as when we measure a cubit by a finger. But time cannot be measured by any part of itself. If, for instance, the present measures the past, it will coincide with the past and will therefore be past, and similarly it will be future in the case of the future. And if the future should measure the rest, it will be present and past, and so likewise the past will be future and present; which is nonsense. Neither, then, is time divisible. But if it is neither indivisible nor divisible, it does not exist.

Time, too, is said to be tripartite, partly past, partly 144 present, and partly future. Of these the past and the future are non-existent; for if past and future time exist now, each of them will be present. Neither is the present existent; for if present time exists

---

[a] *e.g.* that there was once a time when no time was.

μέριστός ἐστιν ἢ μεριστός. ἀμέριστος μὲν οὖν οὐκ
ἔστιν· ἐν γὰρ τῷ ἐνεστῶτι χρόνῳ λέγεται τὰ
μεταβάλλοντα μεταβάλλειν, οὐδὲν δὲ ἐν ἀμερεῖ
χρόνῳ μεταβάλλει, οἷον ὁ σίδηρος εἰς μαλακότητα
ἢ τῶν ἄλλων ἔκαστον. ὥστε οὐκ ἔστιν ἀμέριστος
145 ὁ ἐνεστὼς χρόνος. ἀλλ᾽ οὐδὲ μεριστός· εἰς ἐν-
εστῶτας μὲν γὰρ οὐκ ἂν μερισθείη, ἐπεὶ διὰ τὴν
ὀξεῖαν ῥύσιν τῶν ἐν κόσμῳ ἀνεπινοήτως[1] ὁ ἐνεστὼς
εἰς παρῳχηκότα μεταβάλλειν λέγεται· ἀλλ᾽ οὐδ᾽
εἰς παρῳχηκότα καὶ μέλλοντα· ἔσται γὰρ οὕτως
ἀνύπαρκτος, τὸ μέν τι μηκέτι ὂν ἔχων μέρος ἑαυτοῦ,
146 τὸ δὲ μηδέπω ὄν. ὅθεν οὐδὲ τέλος τοῦ παρῳχημένου καὶ ἀρχὴ τοῦ μέλλοντος εἶναι δύναται ὁ
ἐνεστώς, ἐπεὶ καὶ ἔσται καὶ οὐκ ἔσται. ἔσται μὲν
[οὖν] ὡς ἐνεστώς, οὐκ ἔσται δὲ ἐπεὶ μὴ ἔστιν αὐτοῦ
τὰ μέρη. οὐκοῦν οὐδὲ μεριστός ἐστιν. εἰ δὲ μήτε
ἀμέριστός ἐστιν ὁ ἐνεστὼς μήτε μεριστός, οὐδὲ
ἔστιν. μὴ ὄντος δὲ τοῦ ἐνεστῶτος μηδὲ τοῦ
παρῳχημένου μηδὲ τοῦ μέλλοντος, οὐδὲ ἔστι τι
χρόνος· τὸ γὰρ ἐξ ἀνυπάρκτων[2] συνεστὼς ἀνύπαρκτόν ἐστιν.
147 Λέγεται κατὰ τοῦ χρόνου κἀκεῖνος ὁ λόγος. εἰ
ἔστι χρόνος, ἤτοι γενητός ἐστι καὶ φθαρτὸς ἢ
ἀγένητος καὶ ἄφθαρτος. ἀγένητος μὲν οὖν καὶ
ἄφθαρτος οὐκ ἔστιν, εἴγε αὐτοῦ τὸ μὲν παρῳχηκέναι
λέγεται καὶ μηκέτι εἶναι τὸ δὲ μέλλειν καὶ μηδέπω
148 εἶναι. ἀλλ᾽ οὐδὲ γενητὸς καὶ φθαρτός. τὰ γὰρ
γινόμενα ἔκ τινος ὄντος γίγνεσθαι δεῖ καὶ τὰ

---

[1] ἀνεπινοήτως Kayser : ἀπερινοήτως mss., Bekk.
[2] ἀνυπάρκτων Kayser : ἀνυπάρκτου mss., Bekk.

---

[a] Cf. Aristot. Phys. vi. 6.

it is either indivisible or divisible. Now it is not
indivisible ; for what changes is said to change in
the present time, but nothing changes in indivisible
time [a]—iron, for instance, into softness, and so on.
Hence present time is not indivisible. Neither 145
is it divisible ; for it could not be divided into a
plurality of presents, since time present is said to
change into time past imperceptibly owing to the
rapid flux of the things in the Universe. Nor yet into
past and future ; for so it will be unreal, having one
part of itself no longer existent and the other part
not yet existent. Hence, too, the present cannot be 146
the end of the past and the beginning of the future,
since then it will both be and not be existent ; for it
will exist as present, but will not exist because its
parts are non-existent. Therefore it is not divisible
either. But if the present is neither indivisible nor
divisible, it does not exist. And when neither the
present nor the past nor the future exists, time too is
non-existent; for what is compounded of things unreal
is unreal.

This argument, too, is alleged against time : If 147
time exists it is either generable and perishable or
ingenerable and imperishable.[b] Now it is not ingenerable and imperishable, since part of it is said
to be past and no longer in existence, and part to be
future and not yet in existence. Neither is it generable and perishable. For things generated must be 148
generated from something existent, and things which

[b] Time " came into existence " (γέγονεν), said Plato (*Tim.*
38 B): " No," said Aristotle (*Met.* xii. 6). In §§ 147-148 I
render γενητός (" capable of coming into existence ") by
" generable," and γίνεται by " is generated "; but in § 149,
and elsewhere, I usually render γίνεται by " becomes,"
γινόμενα by " becoming," etc.

φθειρόμενα εἴς τι ὂν φθείρεσθαι κατὰ τὰς τῶν δογματικῶν αὐτῶν ὑποθέσεις. εἰ οὖν εἰς τὸν παρῳχημένον φθείρεται, εἰς οὐκ ὂν φθείρεται, καὶ εἰ ἐκ τοῦ μέλλοντος γίνεται, ἐξ οὐκ ὄντος γίνεται· οὐθέτερος γὰρ αὐτῶν ἔστιν. ἄτοπον δὲ τὸ λέγειν τι ἐξ οὐκ ὄντος γίνεσθαι ἢ εἰς τὸ μὴ ὂν φθείρεσθαι. οὐκ ἄρα γενητὸς καὶ φθαρτός ἐστιν ὁ χρόνος. εἰ δὲ μήτε ἀγένητος καὶ ἄφθαρτός ἐστι μήτε γενητὸς καὶ φθαρτός, οὐδὲ ὅλως ἔστιν.

149 Πρὸς τούτοις, ἐπεὶ πᾶν τὸ γινόμενον ἐν χρόνῳ γίγνεσθαι δοκεῖ, εἰ γίνεται ὁ χρόνος, ἐν χρόνῳ γίνεται. ἤτοι οὖν αὐτὸς ἐν ἑαυτῷ γίνεται ἢ ἕτερος ἐν ἑτέρῳ. ἀλλ' εἰ μὲν αὐτὸς ἐν ἑαυτῷ, τὸ αὐτὸ καὶ ἔσται καὶ οὐκ ἔσται. ἐπεὶ γὰρ τὸ ἐν ᾧ τι γίγνεται τοῦ ἐν αὐτῷ γιγνομένου ὀφείλει προϋπάρχειν, ὁ γιγνόμενος ἐν ἑαυτῷ χρόνος, ᾗ μὲν γίνεται, οὐδέπω
150 ἔστιν, ᾗ δὲ[1] ἐν ἑαυτῷ γίνεται, ἤδη ἔστιν. ὥστε οὐδὲ γίνεται ἐν ἑαυτῷ. ἀλλ' οὐδ' ἐν ἑτέρῳ ἕτερος. εἰ γὰρ ὁ ἐνεστὼς ἐν τῷ μέλλοντι γίγνεται, μέλλων ἔσται ὁ ἐνεστώς, καὶ εἰ ἐν τῷ παρῳχηκότι, παρ- ῳχηκώς. τὰ δὲ αὐτὰ λεκτέον καὶ περὶ τῶν ἄλλων χρόνων. ὥστε οὐδὲ ἕτερος χρόνος ἐν ἑτέρῳ γίνεται χρόνῳ. εἰ δὲ μήτε αὐτὸς ἐν ἑαυτῷ γίνεται μήτε ἕτερος ἐν ἑτέρῳ, οὐδὲ γενητός ἐστιν ὁ χρόνος. ἐδείκνυτο δὲ ὅτι οὐδὲ ἀγένητός ἐστιν. μήτε οὖν γενητὸς ὢν μήτε ἀγένητος οὐδ' ὅλως ἔστιν· ἕκαστον γὰρ τῶν ὄντων ἤτοι γενητὸν ἢ ἀγένητον εἶναι προσήκει.

_____
[1] ᾗ μὲν . . . ᾗ δὲ Heintz: εἰ μὲν . . . εἰ δὲ mss., Bekk.

perish must perish into something existent, according to the postulates of the Dogmatists themselves.[a] If, then, time perishes into the past, it perishes into a non-existent ; and if it is generated out of the future, it is generated out of a non-existent ; for neither of these is in existence. But it is absurd to say that anything is generated from a non-existent or perishes into the non-existent. Therefore time is not generable and perishable. But if it is neither ingenerable and imperishable nor generable and perishable, it does not exist at all.

Further, since everything which becomes seems to 149 become in time, time, if it becomes, becomes in time. Either, then, it becomes itself in itself or as one time in another. But if it becomes in itself, it will be at once both existent and non-existent. For since that within which a thing becomes must exist before the thing which becomes within it, the time which becomes in itself does not yet exist in so far as it becomes, but does already exist in so far as it becomes in itself.[b] Consequently it does not become in itself. Nor yet 150 in another. For if the present becomes in the future, the present will be future, and if in the past, it will be past. And the same may be said of all the other times ; so that one time does not become in another. But if time neither becomes in itself nor as one time in another it is not generable. And it has been shown that it is not ingenerable either. Being, then, neither generable nor ingenerable, it is wholly non-existent ; for each existing thing is bound to be either generable or ingenerable.

[a] *e.g.* Aristotle, Epicurus, Poseidonius ; *cf.* Lucr. i. 151.
[b] *Cf.* § 133 *supra*.

SEXTUS EMPIRICUS

Κ'.—ΠΕΡΙ ΑΡΙΘΜΟΤ

151 Ἐπεὶ δὲ ὁ χρόνος δοκεῖ μὴ ἄνευ ἀριθμοῦ θεωρεῖσθαι, οὐκ ἂν εἴη ἄτοπον καὶ περὶ ἀριθμοῦ βραχέα διεξελθεῖν. ὅσον μὲν γὰρ ἐπὶ τῇ συνηθείᾳ καὶ ἀδοξάστως ἀριθμεῖν τί φαμεν καὶ ἀριθμὸν εἶναί τι ἀκούομεν· ἡ δὲ τῶν δογματικῶν περιεργία καὶ
152 τὸν κατὰ τούτου κεκίνηκε λόγον. αὐτίκα γοῦν οἱ ἀπὸ τοῦ Πυθαγόρου καὶ στοιχεῖα τοῦ κόσμου τοὺς ἀριθμοὺς εἶναι λέγουσιν. φασὶ γοῦν ὅτι τὰ φαινόμενα ἔκ τινος συνέστηκεν, ἁπλᾶ δὲ εἶναι δεῖ τὰ στοιχεῖα· ἄδηλα ἄρα ἐστὶ τὰ στοιχεῖα. τῶν δὲ ἀδήλων τὰ μέν ἐστι σώματα, ὡς αἱ ἄτομοι[1] καὶ οἱ ὄγκοι, τὰ δὲ ἀσώματα, ὡς σχήματα καὶ ἰδέαι καὶ ἀριθμοί. ὧν τὰ μὲν σώματά ἐστι σύνθετα, συνεστῶτα ἔκ τε μήκους καὶ πλάτους καὶ βάθους καὶ ἀντιτυπίας ἢ καὶ βάρους. οὐ μόνον ἄρα
153 ἄδηλα ἀλλὰ καὶ ἀσώματά ἐστι τὰ στοιχεῖα. ἀλλὰ καὶ τῶν ἀσωμάτων ἕκαστον ἐπιθεωρούμενον ἔχει τὸν ἀριθμόν· ἢ γὰρ ἕν ἐστιν ἢ δύο ἢ πλείω. δι᾽ ὧν συνάγεται ὅτι τὰ στοιχεῖα τῶν ὄντων εἰσὶν οἱ ἄδηλοι καὶ ἀσώματοι καὶ πᾶσιν ἐπιθεωρούμενοι ἀριθμοί. καὶ οὐχ ἁπλῶς, ἀλλ᾽ ἥ τε μονὰς καὶ ἡ κατὰ ἐπισύνθεσιν τῆς μονάδος γινομένη ἀόριστος δυάς, ἧς κατὰ μετουσίαν αἱ κατὰ μέρος γίγνονται

[1] αἱ ἄτομοι Papp.: οἱ ἀτμοὶ mss., Bekk.

---

* With this chapter cf. Adv. Phys. ii. 248-309. In §§ 152-156 the Pythagorean doctrine of numbers as the primary constituents, or "elements," of the Universe is expounded; in
428

Chapter XX.—Concerning Number

Since time, it seems, is not found apart from 151
number, it will not be out of place to discuss number
briefly.[a] In the customary way we speak undogmatically [b] of numbering a thing and hear number
talked of as something which exists; but the extreme
methods of the Dogmatists have provoked the attack
upon number also. Thus, for example, the School of 152
Pythagoras declare that numbers are also elements
of the Universe. They assert, in fact, that phenomena are constructed from something, and that the
elements must be simple; therefore the elements
are non-evident. But of things non-evident, some are
corporeal, like atoms and masses, others incorporeal,
like figures [c] and forms and numbers. Of these
the corporeal are composite, being constructed from
length and breadth and depth and solidity, or even
weight. The elements, therefore, are not only non-
evident but also incorporeal. Moreover, each of the 153
incorporeals involves the perception of number, for
it is either one or two or more. Thus it is inferred
that the non-evident and incorporeal numbers which
are involved in all perception are the elements of
existing things. Yet not simply ⟨these numbers⟩,
but both the Monad also and the Indefinite Dyad
which is generated by the expansion of the Monad,
and by participation in which the particular dyads

§§ 156-157 the Pythagorean proof that numbers are distinct
from things numbered ("numerables") is set forth; in §§ 158 ff.
the Sceptical arguments against the Pythagorean doctrine of
the real existence of numbers (as distinct from "numerables")
are developed.
    [b] Cf. i. 15.
    [c] i.e. "the limits of bodies" of § 32 supra, cf. § 153.

154 δυάδες δυάδες. ἐκ τούτων γὰρ καὶ τοὺς ἄλλους
γίγνεσθαι ἀριθμούς, τοὺς ἐπιθεωρουμένους τοῖς
ἀριθμητοῖς, καὶ τὸν κόσμον κατασκευάζεσθαι
λέγουσιν. τὸ μὲν γὰρ σημεῖον τὸν τῆς μονάδος
ἐπέχειν λόγον, τὴν δὲ γραμμὴν τὸν τῆς δυάδος
(δύο γὰρ σημείων μεταξὺ θεωρεῖσθαι ταύτην), τὴν
δὲ ἐπιφάνειαν τὸν τῆς τριάδος (ῥύσιν γὰρ εἶναί
φασι τῆς γραμμῆς εἰς πλάτος ἐπ᾽ ἄλλο σημεῖον ἐκ
πλαγίου κείμενον), τὸ δὲ σῶμα τὸν τῆς τετράδος·
ἐπανάστασιν γὰρ γίγνεσθαι τῆς ἐπιφανείας ἐπί τι
155 σημεῖον ὑπερκείμενον. καὶ οὕτω τά τε σώματα
καὶ ὅλον τὸν κόσμον ἀνειδωλοποιοῦσιν, ὅντινα καὶ
διοικεῖσθαί φασι κατὰ ἁρμονικοὺς λόγους, τόν τε
διὰ τεσσάρων, ὅς ἐστιν ἐπίτριτος, ὡς ἔχει πρὸς τὰ
ἐξ τὰ ὀκτώ, καὶ τὸν διὰ πέντε, ὅς ἐστιν ἡμιόλιος,
ὡς ἔχει πρὸς τὰ ἐξ τὰ ἐννέα, καὶ τὸν διὰ πασῶν,
ὅς ἐστι διπλάσιος, ὡς ἔχει πρὸς τὰ ἐξ τὰ δώδεκα.
156 Ταῦτά τε οὖν ὀνειροπολοῦσιν, καὶ ὅτι ἕτερόν τι
ἐστὶν ὁ ἀριθμὸς παρὰ τὰ ἀριθμητὰ κατασκευάζουσι,
λέγοντες ὅτι εἰ τὸ ζῷον κατὰ τὸν ἑαυτοῦ λόγον
ἐστίν, εἰ τύχοι, ἕν, τὸ φυτόν, ἐπεὶ μή ἐστι ζῷον,
οὐκ ἔσται ἕν· ἔστι δὲ καὶ ⟨τὸ⟩[1] φυτὸν ἕν· οὐκ ἄρα
τὸ ζῷον, ⟨καθὸ ζῷον⟩,[2] ἕν ἐστιν, ἀλλὰ κατά τι
ἕτερον ἐπιθεωρούμενον ἔξωθεν αὐτῷ, οὗ μετέχει

---

[1] ⟨τὸ⟩ add. Rüstow.
[2] , ⟨καθὸ ζῷον⟩, addidi: καθὸ ζῷόν ἐστιν, ἕν cj. Bekk.: ⟨ὡς
ζῷον⟩, Mutsch.

---

[a] The existence of the "elemental" numbers is said to be
due to "participation" in either the principle of "Unity"
("the Monad") or the principle of Duality ("the indefinite
Dyad")—odd numbers in the first, even in the second. These
principles are the "genera" of which odd and even numbers
are "particulars."

become dyads.[a] For they say that it is from these 154 that the rest of the numbers are generated—those, that is, which are involved in the perception of numerables—and the Universe is arranged. For the point presents the relation, or character, of the Monad,[b] and the line that of the Dyad (it being regarded as lying between two points), and the surface that of the Triad (for they describe it as a flowing of the line breadth-wise up to another point placed transversely), and the ⟨solid⟩ body that of the Tetrad; for Body is formed by an ascension of the surface up to a point placed above. It is in this way 155 that they image forth both the bodies and the whole Universe, which also they declare to be arranged according to harmonic ratios[c]—namely, that of the " By-Fours," which is " epitrite," as is the ratio of 8 to 6; and that of the " By-Fives," which is one and a half times, as is the ratio of 9 to 6; and that of the " By-Alls," which is double, as is the ratio of 12 to 6.

These are the fictions they imagine; and they 156 also make out that number is something else apart from numerables, arguing that if " animal " according to its proper definition[d] is (say) one, the plant, since it is not an animal, will not be one; but the plant is one; therefore the animal is not one ⟨*qua* animal⟩ but in virtue of some other attribute perceived outside itself, whereof each animal partakes and because

[b] *i.e.* it is an indivisible unit, and begins the line as the One begins the number-series; *cf. Adv. Phys.* ii. 278.

[c] 'The terms here used are those of the Pythagorean musical ("octave") system, and denote the ratios 4:3, 3:2, 2:1. *Cf.* Plato, *Tim.* 36 A; *Adv. Arith.* 6-9, *Adv. Mus.* 46.

[d] Or " in its own essence," apart from relation to anything else.

ἕκαστον καὶ γίνεται δι' αὐτὸ ἕν. καὶ εἰ τὰ ἀριθμητά ἐστιν ὁ ἀριθμός, ἐπειδὴ ἄνθρωποί εἰσιν οἱ
ἀριθμητοὶ καὶ βόες, εἰ τύχοι, καὶ ἵπποι, ἄνθρωποι
καὶ βόες καὶ ἵπποι ἔσται ὁ ἀριθμός, καὶ λευκὸς
[ἀριθμὸς]¹ καὶ μέλας καὶ γενειήτης, εἰ τύχοιεν
157 τοιοῦτοι τυγχάνοντες οἱ μετρούμενοι. ταῦτα δέ
ἐστιν ἄτοπα· οὐκ ἄρα τὰ ἀριθμητά ἐστιν ὁ ἀριθμός,
ἀλλ' ἰδίαν ὑπόστασιν ἔχει παρὰ ταῦτα, καθ' ἣν
καὶ ἐπιθεωρεῖται τοῖς ἀριθμητοῖς καὶ ἔστι στοιχεῖον.

Οὕτως οὖν ἐκείνων συναγαγόντων ὅτι ἀριθμὸς
οὐκ ἔστι τὰ ἀριθμητά, παρεισῆλθεν ἡ κατὰ τοῦ
ἀριθμοῦ ἀπορία. λέγεται γὰρ ὅτι εἰ ἔστιν ἀριθμός,
ἤτοι αὐτὰ τὰ ἀριθμητά ἐστιν ὁ ἀριθμὸς ἢ ἕτερόν
τι παρὰ ταῦτα ἔξωθεν· οὔτε δὲ αὐτὰ τὰ ἀριθμητά
ἐστιν ὁ ἀριθμός, ὡς ἀπέδειξαν οἱ Πυθαγορικοί,
οὔτε ἕτερόν τι παρὰ ταῦτα, ὡς ὑπομνήσομεν·
οὐδὲν ἄρα ἐστὶν ὁ ἀριθμός.

158 Ὅτι δὲ οὐδὲν ἔξωθέν ἐστι παρὰ τὰ ἀριθμητὰ ὁ
ἀριθμός, παραστήσομεν ἐπὶ τῆς μονάδος τὸν λόγον
στήσαντες εὐσήμου διδασκαλίας ἕνεκεν. εἰ γὰρ
ἔστι τι καθ' ἑαυτὴν ἡ μονάς, ἧς μετέχον ἕκαστον
τῶν μετεχόντων αὐτῆς γίνεται ἕν, ἤτοι μία ἔσται
αὕτη ἡ μονὰς ἢ τοσαῦται ὅσα τὰ μετέχοντα αὐτῆς
ἐστίν. ἀλλ' εἰ μὲν μία ἐστίν, πότερον ὅλης αὐτῆς
μετέχει ἕκαστον τῶν μετέχειν αὐτῆς λεγομένων ἢ
μέρους αὐτῆς; εἰ μὲν γὰρ πᾶσαν ἔχει τὴν μονάδα,
εἰ τύχοι, ὁ εἷς ἄνθρωπος, οὐκέτι ἔσται μονὰς ἧς
μεθέξει ὁ εἷς ἵππος ἢ ὁ εἷς κύων ἢ τῶν ἄλλων
159 ἕκαστον ὃ λέγομεν εἶναι ἕν, ὥσπερ καὶ πολλῶν

¹ [ἀριθμὸς] om. M (? ἄνθρωπος).

of which it becomes one. And if number is the numerables, since the numerables are men (say) and oxen and horses, number will be men and oxen and horses—and number will be white and black and bearded, if the objects counted should happen to be such. But these things are absurd; therefore number 157 is not the numerables, but it has a reality of its own apart from them whereby it is involved in the perception of the numerables and is an element.

So when they had thus concluded that number is not the numerables, there arose in consequence the difficulty about number. For it is argued that if number exists, number is either the actual numerables or something else apart from them; but number is neither the actual numerables, as the Pythagoreans have proved, nor something else apart from them, as we shall show; number, therefore, is nothing.

That number is nothing apart from the numerables 158 we shall demonstrate by basing our argument on the Monad, for the sake of lucidity of exposition.[a] If the Monad, by partaking in which each of its participants becomes one, is in itself a real object, this Monad will be either one or as many as are its participants. But if it is one, does each of the things said to partake thereof partake of all of it or of a part of it? For if the one man (say) takes all the Monad, there will no longer exist a monad for the one horse to partake of, or the one dog or any one of all the other things which we declare to be one—just as, supposing there 159

[a] The argument here is that "participation" of things in the Monad involves either (1) the division of the Monad into an infinite number of parts (§§ 158-159), or (2) the multiplication of the Monad into an infinite number of whole Monads (§§ 160-162), both which results violate the conception of the Monad as unique principle of Unity.

ὑποτεθέντων γυμνῶν ἀνθρώπων, ἑνὸς δὲ ὄντος
ἱματίου καὶ τοῦτο ἑνὸς ἀμφιασαμένου, γυμνοὶ
μενοῦσιν[1] οἱ λοιποὶ καὶ χωρὶς ἱματίου. εἰ δὲ μέρους
αὐτῆς μετέχει ἕκαστον, πρῶτον μὲν ἕξει τι μέρος ἡ
μονάς, καὶ ἄπειρά γε ἕξει μέρη, εἰς ἃ διαιρεῖται·
ὅπερ ἄτοπον. εἶτα ὡς τὸ μέρος τῆς δεκάδος, οἷον
ἡ δυάς, οὐκ ἔστι δεκάς, οὕτως οὐδὲ τὸ μέρος τῆς
μονάδος ἔσται μονάς, διὰ δὲ τοῦτο οὐδὲ μεθέξει
τι τῆς μονάδος. ὥστε οὐκ ἔστι μία ἡ μονὰς ἧς
μετέχειν λέγεται τὰ κατὰ μέρος.

160 Εἰ δὲ ἰσάριθμοι τοῖς ἀριθμητοῖς, ἐφ’ ὧν λέγεται
τὸ ἕν, αἱ μονάδες εἰσὶν ὧν κατὰ μετοχὴν ἕκαστον
τῶν κατὰ μέρος λέγεται ἕν, ἄπειροι ἔσονται αἱ
μετεχόμεναι μονάδες. καὶ αὗται ἤτοι μετέχουσιν
ἐπαναβεβηκυίας μονάδος ἢ μονάδων ἰσαρίθμων
αὐταῖς, καὶ διὰ τοῦτό εἰσι μονάδες, ἢ οὐ μετέχουσιν ἀλλὰ χωρίς τινος μετοχῆς μονάδες εἰσίν.

161 εἰ μὲν οὖν[2] χωρὶς μετοχῆς μονάδες εἶναι δύνανται
αὗται, δυνήσεται καὶ τῶν αἰσθητῶν ἕκαστον
χωρὶς μονάδος μετοχῆς ἓν εἶναι, καὶ αὐτόθεν
περιτρέπεται ἡ καθ’ ἑαυτὴν θεωρεῖσθαι λεγομένη
μονάς. εἰ δὲ ἀπὸ μετοχῆς κἀκεῖναι μονάδες εἰσίν,
ἤτοι μιᾶς μετέχουσι πᾶσαι ἢ μία ἑκάστη ἰδίας.
καὶ εἰ μὲν πᾶσαι μιᾶς, ἤτοι κατὰ μέρος ἑκάστη ἢ
ὅλης λεχθήσεται μετέχειν, καὶ μένουσιν αἱ ἀρχῆθεν
162 ἀτοπίαι· εἰ δὲ ἑκάστη ἰδίας, καὶ ἐκείνων τῶν
μονάδων ἑκάστῃ μονάδα ἐπιθεωρεῖσθαι δεῖ, καὶ
ταῖς ἐπιθεωρουμέναις ἐκείναις ἄλλας, καὶ μέχρις
ἀπείρου. εἰ οὖν ἵνα καταλάβωμεν ὅτι εἰσί τινες

---

[1] μενοῦσιν Mutsch.: μένουσιν mss., Bekk.
[2] οὖν cj. Bekk.: γὰρ mss.

are a number of naked men, who possess only one garment amongst them, which one man had put on, all the rest will remain naked and without a garment. And if each thing partakes of a part of it, then, in the first place, the Monad will have a part. and parts, too, infinite in number into which it is divided ; which is absurd. And further, just as the part of the Decad, such as the Dyad, is not a Decad, so neither will the part of the Monad be a Monad, and for this reason nothing will partake of the Monad. Hence the Monad whereof the particular objects are said to partake is not one.

But if the monads, by participation in which each 160 of the particular objects is called one, are equal in number to the numerables to which the term " one " is applied, the monads partaken of will be infinite in number. And these either partake of a superior [a] monad or of monads equal in number to themselves, or else they do not so partake but are monads apart from any participation. Yet if these 161 can be monads without participation, each of the sensibles also will be able to be one without participation in a monad, and so at once the monad said to be perceived as real in itself is overthrown. Whereas, if those monads are monads by participation, either they all partake of one monad, or each partakes of a monad of its own. And if all partake of one, each will be said to partake either of a part or of the whole, and the original difficulties will still remain ; but if each 162 partakes of its own monad, we must posit a new monad for each of those monads, and others again for the former, and so on *ad infinitum*. If then, in order to apprehend that there are certain self-sub-

[a] *i.e.* " Unity " as a *summum genus*, *cf.* i. 38.

καθ' ἑαυτὰς μονάδες, ὧν κατὰ μετοχὴν ἕκαστον
τῶν ὄντων ἐστὶν ἕν, δεῖ κατειληφέναι ἀπειράκις
ἀπείρους νοητὰς μονάδας, ἀδύνατον δὲ καταλαβεῖν
ἀπειράκις ἀπείρους μονάδας νοητάς, ἀδύνατον ἄρα
ἐστὶν ἀποφήνασθαι ὅτι εἰσί τινες νοηταὶ μονάδες
καὶ ἕκαστον τῶν ὄντων ἐστὶν ἕν κατὰ μετοχὴν
ἰδίας μονάδος γινόμενον ἕν.

163   Ἄτοπον ἄρα τὸ λέγειν ὅτι τοσαῦταί εἰσιν αἱ
μονάδες ὅσα τὰ μετέχοντα αὐτῶν. εἰ δὲ μήτε μία
ἐστὶν ἡ καθ' ἑαυτὴν λεγομένη μονὰς μήτε τοσαῦται
ὅσα τὰ μετέχοντα αὐτῆς ἐστιν, οὐδὲ ἔστιν ὅλως
μονὰς καθ' ἑαυτήν. ὁμοίως δὲ οὐδὲ τῶν ἄλλων
ἀριθμῶν ἕκαστος καθ' ἑαυτὸν ἔσται· χρῆσθαι γὰρ
ἔνεστιν ἐπὶ πάντων τῶν ἀριθμῶν τῷ λόγῳ, παρα-
δειγματικῶς νῦν ἐπὶ τῆς μονάδος ἠρωτημένῳ.
ἀλλ' εἰ μήτε καθ' ἑαυτόν ἐστιν ὁ ἀριθμός, ὡς
ὑπεμνήσαμεν, μήτε αὐτὰ τὰ ἀριθμητὰ ὁ ἀριθμός
ἐστιν, ὡς οἱ ἀπὸ Πυθαγόρου παρέστησαν, παρὰ δὲ
ταῦτα οὐδὲν ἔστι, λεκτέον μηδὲ εἶναι ἀριθμόν.

164   Πῶς δὲ καὶ γίνεσθαί φασιν ἐκ τῆς μονάδος τὴν
δυάδα οἱ ἔξωθέν τι δοκοῦντες εἶναι τὸν ἀριθμὸν
παρὰ τὰ ἀριθμητά; ὅτε γὰρ συντίθεμεν μονάδα
ἑτέρᾳ μονάδι, ἤτοι προστίθεταί τι ταῖς μονάσιν
ἔξωθεν, ἢ ἀφαιρεῖταί τι ἀπ' αὐτῶν, ἢ οὔτε προστίθεταί τι οὔτε ἀφαιρεῖται. ἀλλ' εἰ μὲν οὔτε προστίθεταί τι οὔτε ἀφαιρεῖται, οὐκ ἔσται δυάς. οὔτε
γὰρ χωρὶς ἀλλήλων οὖσαι αἱ μονάδες εἶχον τὴν
δυάδα[1] ἐπιθεωρουμένην αὐταῖς κατὰ τὸν ἴδιον
αὐτῶν λόγον, οὔτε νῦν τι αὐταῖς ἔξωθεν προσ-
γέγονεν, ὥσπερ οὐδὲ ἀφῄρηται, κατὰ τὴν ὑπόθεσιν.

---

[1] δυάδα Kayser, Papp.: μονάδα mss., Bekk.

sistent monads by participation in which each existing thing is one, it is necessary to apprehend an infinite infinity of intelligible monads, and to apprehend an infinite infinity of intelligible monads is a thing impossible, then it is impossible to show that there are certain intelligible monads and that each existing thing is one through becoming one by participation in its own monad.

It is absurd, therefore, to say that the monads are 163 as numerous as the things which partake of them. But if the so-called self-subsistent monad is neither one nor as many as its participants, a self-subsistent monad does not exist at all. So likewise none of the other numbers will be self-subsistent; for one may apply to all the numbers the argument which has now been employed in the typical case of the monad. But if number is neither self-subsistent, as we have shown, nor consists in the actual numerables, as the Pythagoreans have demonstrated, and beyond these there is no other alternative, then we must declare that number does not exist.

In what way, too, is the Dyad said to be generated 164 from the Monad by those who believe that number is something else apart from the numerables? For when we combine a monad with another monad either something external is added to the monads, or something is subtracted from them, or nothing is either added or subtracted. But if nothing is either added or subtracted, there will not be a Dyad. For neither did the monads, when existing apart from each other, contain the Dyad as involved in the perception of them, according to their own definition, nor has any addition now been made to them from without, just as, by hypothesis, nothing has been subtracted.

SEXTUS EMPIRICUS

165 ὥστε οὐκ ἔσται δυὰς ἡ σύνθεσις τῆς μονάδος πρὸς τὴν μονάδα, μήτε ἀφαιρέσεως μήτε προσθέσεως ἔξωθέν τινος γινομένης. εἰ δὲ ἀφαίρεσις γίνεται, οὐ μόνον οὐκ ἔσται δυάς, ἀλλὰ καὶ μειωθήσονται αἱ μονάδες. εἰ δὲ προστίθεται αὐταῖς ἔξωθεν ἡ δυάς, ἵνα ἐκ τῶν μονάδων γένηται δυάς, τὰ δύο δοκοῦντα εἶναι τέσσαρα ἔσται· ὑπόκειται γὰρ μονὰς καὶ ἑτέρα μονάς, αἷς προστιθεμένης ἔξωθεν δυάδος

166 ἢ τέσσαρα ἀριθμὸς ἀποτελοῖτο ἄν. ὁ δὲ αὐτὸς λόγος καὶ ἐπὶ τῶν ἄλλων ἀριθμῶν τῶν κατὰ σύνθεσιν ἀποτελεῖσθαι λεγομένων.

Εἰ οὖν μήτε κατὰ ἀφαίρεσιν μήτε κατὰ πρόσθεσιν μήτε ἄνευ ἀφαιρέσεως καὶ προσθέσεως γίγνονται οἱ σύνθετοι λεγόμενοι εἶναι ἀριθμοὶ ἐκ τῶν ἐπαναβεβηκότων, ἀσύστατός ἐστιν ἡ γένεσις τοῦ κατ᾽ ἰδίαν καὶ παρὰ τὰ ἀριθμητὰ εἶναι λεγομένου ἀριθμοῦ. ὅτι δὲ οὐδὲ ἀγένητοι τυγχάνουσιν ὄντες οἱ κατὰ σύνθεσιν ἀριθμοί, δηλοῦσιν αὐτοὶ συντίθεσθαί τε αὐτοὺς καὶ γίγνεσθαι φάσκοντες ἐκ τῶν ἐπαναβεβηκότων, οἷον τῆς τε μονάδος καὶ

167 δυάδος τῆς ἀορίστου. οὐκοῦν οὐχ ὑφέστηκε κατ᾽ ἰδίαν ὁ ἀριθμός. εἰ δὲ μήτε κατ᾽ ἰδίαν ὁ ἀριθμὸς θεωρεῖται μήτε ἐν τοῖς ἀριθμητοῖς ἔχει τὴν ὑπόστασιν, οὐδέ ἔστι τι ὁ ἀριθμὸς ὅσον ἐπὶ ταῖς περιεργίαις ταῖς ὑπὸ τῶν δογματικῶν εἰσενηνεγμέναις.

Τοσαῦτα μὲν καὶ περὶ τοῦ φυσικοῦ καλουμένου τῆς φιλοσοφίας μέρους ἀρκοῦντα ὡς ἐν ὑποτυπώσει λελέχθω.

438

Hence the combination of the monad with the monad 165
will not be a dyad, as no addition or subtraction
from without takes place. But if subtraction does
take place, not only will there not be a dyad but the
monads will even be diminished. And if the dyad is
added to them from without, so that a dyad may be
generated from the monads, the things which appear
to be two will be four ; for there exists already a
monad and a second monad, and when an outside
dyad is added to these the result will be the number
four. And the same argument applies to all the 166
other numbers which are said to be formed as a
result of combination.

If, then, the numbers which are said to be compounded from the superior[a] numbers are formed
neither by subtraction nor by addition nor without
subtraction and addition, the formation of the number
which is said to be independent and apart from the
numerables is non-composite. But they themselves
make it clear that the numbers formed by combination
are not ungenerated by asserting that they are compounded and generated from the superior numbers
—from the monad, for example, and the Indefinite
Dyad.[b] So then number does not subsist of itself. 167
But if number neither is conceived as self-existent,
nor subsists in the numerables, then, to judge from
the subtleties introduced by the Dogmatists, number
is nothing.

Let this, then, suffice as an account in outline of
what is called the Physical section of philosophy.

[a] *Cf.* § 160 *supra.* [b] *Cf.* § 153 *supra.*

SEXTUS EMPIRICUS

ΚΑ΄.—ΠΕΡΙ ΤΟΥ ΗΘΙΚΟΥ ΜΕΡΟΥΣ ΤΗΣ ΦΙΛΟΣΟΦΙΑΣ

168 Λείπεται δὲ τὸ ἠθικόν, ὅπερ δοκεῖ περὶ τὴν
διάκρισιν τῶν τε καλῶν καὶ κακῶν καὶ ἀδιαφόρων
καταγίγνεσθαι. ἵνα οὖν κεφαλαιωδῶς καὶ περὶ
τούτου διαλάβωμεν, περὶ τῆς ὑπάρξεως τῶν τε
ἀγαθῶν καὶ κακῶν καὶ ἀδιαφόρων ζητήσομεν, τὴν
ἔννοιαν ἑκάστου προεκθέμενοι.

ΚΒ΄.—ΠΕΡΙ ΑΓΑΘΩΝ ΚΑΙ ΚΑΚΩΝ ΚΑΙ ΑΔΙΑΦΟΡΩΝ

169 Φασὶν οὖν οἱ στωικοὶ ἀγαθὸν εἶναι ὠφέλειαν ἢ
οὐχ ἕτερον ὠφελείας, ὠφέλειαν μὲν λέγοντες τὴν
ἀρετὴν καὶ τὴν σπουδαίαν πρᾶξιν, οὐχ ἕτερον δὲ
ὠφελείας τὸν σπουδαῖον ἄνθρωπον καὶ τὸν φίλον.
ἡ μὲν γὰρ ἀρετὴ πως ἔχον ἡγεμονικὸν καθεστηκυῖα
καὶ ἡ σπουδαία πρᾶξις ἐνέργειά τις οὖσα κατ᾽
ἀρετὴν ἄντικρύς ἐστιν ὠφέλεια, ὁ δὲ σπουδαῖος
170 ἄνθρωπος καὶ ὁ φίλος οὐχ ἕτερος ὠφελείας. μέρος
μὲν γὰρ τοῦ σπουδαίου ἐστὶν ὠφέλεια, τὸ ἡγεμονικὸν αὐτοῦ ὑπάρχουσα· τὰ δὲ ὅλα οὔτε τὰ αὐτὰ τοῖς
μέρεσιν εἶναι λέγουσιν, οὐ γάρ ἐστιν ὁ ἄνθρωπος
χείρ, οὔτε ἕτερα παρὰ τὰ μέρη, οὐκ ἄνευ γὰρ τῶν
μερῶν ὑφέστηκεν. διόπερ οὐχ ἕτερα τῶν μερῶν
τὰ ὅλα λέγουσιν. ὅθεν τὸν σπουδαῖον ὅλον ὄντα
ὡς πρὸς τὸ ἡγεμονικὸν ἑαυτοῦ, ὅπερ ἔφασαν ὠφέλειαν, οὐχ ἕτερον ὠφελείας εἶναι λέγουσιν.

---

[a] Lit. " fair " (honestum): the Stoics used καλόν as a
synonym for ἀγαθόν " good " (bonum), and in this section the
terms are used as synonymous.

[b] Or "regent part," i.e. the mind, cf. i. 128, ii. 81; Introd.
p. xxv. The doctrine that "the good man" is "not other"
than goodness (virtue or "utility") strikes one as curious.
The Stoics, we must remember, regarded attributes or
qualities as corporeal and parts of the "substance" (οὐσία)

CHAPTER XXI.—CONCERNING THE ETHICAL DIVISION OF PHILOSOPHY

There remains the Ethical division, which is sup- 168 posed to deal with the distinguishing of things good,[a] bad, and indifferent. In order, then, to treat of this branch also in a summary way, we shall inquire into the reality of things good, bad, and indifferent, explaining first the conception of each.

CHAPTER XXII.—CONCERNING THINGS GOOD, BAD, AND INDIFFERENT

The Stoics, then, assert that good is " utility or not 169 other than utility," meaning by " utility " virtue and right action, and by " not other than utility " the good man and the friend. For " virtue," as consisting in a certain state of the ruling principle,[b] and " right action," being an activity in accordance with virtue, are exactly " utility " ; while the good man and the friend are " not other than utility." For 170 utility is a part of the good man, being his ruling principle. But the wholes, they say, are not the same as the parts (for the man is not a hand), nor are they other than the parts (for without the parts they do not subsist). Wherefore they assert that the wholes are not other than the parts. Hence, since the good man stands in the relation of a whole to his ruling principle, which they have identified with utility, they declare that he is not other than utility.

to which they belong—here the mind (" regent part ") of " the good man." For the equation of " virtue " (or " goodness ") with " utility " (or " benefit ") as " the source (or agency) from which benefit results " see Diog. Laert. vii. 94. For Stoic Ethics cf. Introd. pp. xxvi ff.

171 Ἐντεῦθεν καὶ τριχῶς τὸ ἀγαθόν φασι λέγεσθαι. καθ᾽ ἕνα μὲν γὰρ τρόπον φασὶν εἶναι ἀγαθὸν τὸ ὑφ᾽ οὗ ἔστιν ὠφελεῖσθαι, ὃ δὴ ἀρχικώτατόν ἐστι καὶ ἀρετή, καθ᾽ ἕτερον δὲ καθ᾽ ὃ συμβαίνει ὠφελεῖσθαι, ὡς ἡ ἀρετὴ καὶ αἱ κατ᾽ ἀρετὴν πράξεις, κατὰ τρίτον δὲ τρόπον τὸ οἷόν τε ὠφελεῖν, τοῦτο δὲ καὶ ἀρετὴν εἶναι καὶ κατὰ ἀρετὴν πρᾶξιν καὶ τὸν σπουδαῖον καὶ τὸν φίλον θεούς τε καὶ σπουδαίους δαίμονας, ὡς τὸ μὲν δεύτερον σημαινόμενον τοῦ ἀγαθοῦ ἐμπεριληπτικὸν εἶναι τοῦ πρώτου σημαινομένου, τὸ δὲ τρίτον τοῦ δευτέρου καὶ τοῦ
172 πρώτου. τινὲς δέ φασιν ἀγαθὸν εἶναι τὸ δι᾽ ἑαυτὸ αἱρετόν, ἄλλοι δὲ τὸ συλλαμβανόμενον[1] πρὸς εὐδαιμονίαν ἢ τὸ συμπληρωτικόν· εὐδαιμονία δέ ἐστιν, ὡς οἱ στωικοί φασιν, εὔροια βίου.

Τοιαῦτα μέν τινα εἰς τὴν ἔννοιαν τοῦ ἀγαθοῦ
173 λέγεται. εἴτε δὲ τὸ ὠφελοῦν εἴτε τὸ δι᾽ ἑαυτὸ αἱρετὸν εἴτε τὸ συνεργοῦν πρὸς εὐδαιμονίαν ἀγαθόν τις εἶναι λέγοι, οὐχὶ τί ἐστι τὸ ἀγαθὸν παρίστησιν, ἀλλά τι τῶν συμβεβηκότων αὐτῷ λέγει. ὅπερ ἐστὶ μάταιον. ἤτοι γὰρ μόνῳ τῷ ἀγαθῷ συμβέβηκε τὰ προειρημένα ἢ καὶ ἑτέροις. ἀλλ᾽ εἰ μὲν καὶ ἑτέροις, οὐκ ἔστι χαρακτηριστικὰ τοῦ ἀγαθοῦ κοινοποιούμενα, εἰ δὲ μόνῳ τῷ ἀγαθῷ, οὐκ ἐνδέχεται ἡμᾶς
174 ἀπὸ τούτων νοεῖν τὸ ἀγαθόν· ὡς γὰρ ὁ ἀνεννόητος ἵππου οὔτε τὸ χρεμετίζειν τί ἐστιν οἶδεν, οὔτε διὰ τούτου δύναται εἰς ἔννοιαν ἐλθεῖν ἵππου, εἰ μὴ

---

[1] συλλαμβανόμενον cj. Bekk.: συλλαμβάνον mss.

---

[a] *i.e.* " primary, fundamental, good "—the source of other goods. Good in the first sense is the central good, which

Hence also they assert that good has three mean- 171
ings. In one of its meanings, good, they say, is that
by which utility may be gained, this being the most
principal good [a] and virtue; in another meaning, good
is that of which utility is an accidental result, like
virtue and virtuous actions; and thirdly, it is that
which is capable of being useful; and such is virtue
and virtuous action and the good man and the friend,
and gods and good daemons; so that the second signification of good is inclusive of the first signification,
and the third of both the second and the first. But 172
some define good as " what is to be chosen for its
own sake " [b]; and others as " that which contributes
to happiness or is supplementary thereto "; and
happiness, as the Stoics declare, is " the smooth
current of life."

These, or such as these, are their statements with
reference to the notion of the Good. But in describ- 173
ing as good what is useful or what is choiceworthy
for its own sake or what is contributory to happiness,
one is not exhibiting the essence of the good but
stating one of its properties. And this is senseless.
For the properties aforesaid belong either to the good
only or to other things as well. But if they belong to
other things as well, they are not, when thus extended,
characteristic marks of the good; while if they belong
only to the Good, it is not possible for us to derive
from them a notion of the good. For just as the man 174
who has no notion of " horse " has no knowledge of
what " neighing " is and cannot arrive thereby at a
notion of " horse," unless he should first meet with a

expands into the second and third senses as into concentric
circles—the third including the second, the second the first.
  [b] Cf. Aristot. Rhet. i. 6; the other definition is Stoic.

443

πρότερον ἵππῳ χρεμετίζοντι ἐντύχοι, οὕτως ὁ διὰ
τὸ μὴ εἰδέναι τὸ ἀγαθὸν ζητῶν τί ἐστιν ἀγαθόν,
οὐ δύναται γινώσκειν τὸ ἰδίως αὐτῷ καὶ μόνῳ
ὑπάρχον, ἵνα δι᾽ αὐτοῦ τὸ ἀγαθὸν αὐτὸ νοῆσαι
δυνηθῇ. πρότερον γὰρ δεῖ μαθεῖν τὴν αὐτοῦ τοῦ
ἀγαθοῦ φύσιν, εἶθ᾽ οὕτω συνεῖναι ὅτι ὠφελεῖ καὶ ὅτι
δι᾽ αὐτὸ αἱρετόν ἐστι καὶ ὅτι εὐδαιμονίας ποιητικόν.
175 ὅτι δὲ τὰ προειρημένα συμβεβηκότα οὐκ ἔστιν
ἱκανὰ μηνῦσαι τὴν ἐπίνοιαν καὶ τὴν φύσιν τοῦ
ἀγαθοῦ, δηλοῦσιν ἔργῳ οἱ δογματικοί. ὡς μὲν
γὰρ ὠφελεῖ τὸ ἀγαθὸν καὶ ὅτι αἱρετόν ἐστι, παρὸ
καὶ ἀγαθὸν εἴρηται τὸ οἱονεὶ ἀγαστόν, καὶ ὅτι
εὐδαιμονίας ἐστὶ ποιητικόν, πάντες ἴσως συγ-
χωροῦσιν· ἐρωτώμενοι δὲ τί ἐστιν ᾧ ταῦτα συμβέβηκεν, εἰς ἄσπειστον ἐμπίπτουσι πόλεμον, οἱ
μὲν ἀρετὴν λέγοντες, οἱ δὲ ἡδονήν, οἱ δὲ ἀλυπίαν,
οἱ δὲ ἄλλο τι. καίτοι εἰ ἐκ τῶν προειρημένων
ὅρων ἐδείκνυτο τί ἐστι τὸ ἀγαθὸν αὐτό, οὐκ ἂν
ἐστασίαζον ὡς ἀγνοουμένης τῆς τούτου φύσεως.
176 Οὕτω μὲν οὖν διαφέρονται περὶ τῆς ἐννοίας τοῦ
ἀγαθοῦ οἱ δοκιμώτατοι δοκοῦντες εἶναι τῶν δογ-
ματικῶν· ὁμοίως δὲ διηνέχθησαν καὶ περὶ τοῦ
κακοῦ, λέγοντες κακὸν εἶναι βλάβην ἢ οὐχ ἕτερον
βλάβης, οἱ δὲ τὸ δι᾽ ἑαυτὸ φευκτόν, οἱ δὲ τὸ
κακοδαιμονίας ποιητικόν. δι᾽ ὧν οὐχὶ τὴν οὐσίαν
τοῦ κακοῦ ἀλλά τινα τῶν συμβεβηκότων ἴσως
αὐτῷ φάσκοντες εἰς τὴν προειρημένην ἐμπίπτουσιν
ἀπορίαν.

―――――――――

[a] Deriving ἀγαθόν from ἀγαστόν, cf. Plato, Cratyl. 412 c,
422 A and § 184 infra.
[b] The Stoics said " virtue," Cyrenaics and Epicureans
" pleasure," some Peripatetics " painlessness " (cf. Aristot.
Rhet. i. 7).

neighing horse, so too one who is seeking the essence of the good, because he has no knowledge of the good, cannot perceive the attribute which is peculiar to it alone in order that he may be enabled thereby to gain a notion of the good itself. For he must first learn the nature of the good itself, and then pass on to apprehend that it is useful, and that it is choice-worthy for its own sake, and that it is productive of happiness. But that the aforesaid attributes are 175 not sufficient to indicate the concept and the real nature of the good is made plain by the practice of the Dogmatists. All, probably, agree that the good is useful and that it is choiceworthy (so that the good is said to be, as it were, "the delightful"[a]) and that it is productive of happiness ; but when asked what the thing is to which these properties belong, they plunge into a truceless war, some saying it is virtue, others pleasure, others painlessness,[b] and others some-thing else. And yet, if the essence of the good had been proved from the foregoing definitions, they would not have been at feud as though its nature were unknown.

Such, then, is the discord amongst those who are 176 reputed the most eminent of the Dogmatists regarding the notion of the Good ; and they have differed like-wise regarding Evil, some defining Evil as "damage or not other than damage,[c]" others as "what is to be shunned for its own sake," others as "what is pro-ductive of unhappiness." But since they express by these phrases not the essence of evil but some of its possible attributes they are involved in the logical *impasse* mentioned above.

[c] "Damage " or " harm " being the opposite of " utility " or " benefit "—the Stoic definition of " good."

177 Τὸ δὲ ἀδιάφορόν φασι λέγεσθαι μὲν τριχῶς, καθ᾽ ἕνα μὲν τρόπον πρὸς ὃ μήτε ὁρμὴ μήτε ἀφορμὴ γίνεται, οἷόν ἐστι τὸ ἀρτίους εἶναι τοὺς ἀστέρας ἢ τὰς ἐπὶ τῆς κεφαλῆς τρίχας, καθ᾽ ἕτερον δὲ πρὸς ὃ ὁρμὴ μὲν ἢ ἀφορμὴ γίνεται, οὐ μᾶλλον δὲ πρὸς τόδε ἢ τόδε, οἷον ἐπὶ δυοῖν τετραδράχμων ἀπαραλλάκτων, ὅταν δέῃ τὸ ἕτερον αὐτῶν αἱρεῖσθαι· ὁρμὴ μὲν γὰρ γίνεται πρὸς τὸ αἱρεῖσθαι τὸ ἕτερον αὐτῶν, οὐ μᾶλλον δὲ πρὸς τόδε ἢ τόδε. κατὰ τρίτον δὲ τρόπον φασὶν ἀδιάφορον εἶναι τὸ μήτε εὐδαιμονίαν μήτε πρὸς κακοδαιμονίαν συμβαλλόμενον, ὡς ὑγίειαν πλοῦτον· ᾧ γὰρ ἔστιν ὁτὲ μὲν εὖ ὁτὲ δὲ κακῶς χρήσασθαι, τοῦτο ἀδιάφορον εἶναι φασίν. περὶ οὗ μάλιστα ἐν τοῖς ἠθικοῖς

178 διαλαμβάνειν λέγουσιν. τίνα μέντοι καὶ περὶ ταύτης τῆς ἐννοίας δεῖ φρονεῖν, δῆλον καὶ ἐκ τῶν εἰρημένων ἡμῖν περί τε ἀγαθῶν καὶ κακῶν.

Οὕτω μὲν οὖν σαφές ἐστιν ὅτι οὐκ ἐπέστησαν ἡμᾶς τῇ ἐννοίᾳ τῶν προειρημένων ἑκάστου· οὐδὲν δὲ ἀπεικὸς πεπόνθασιν ἐν ἀνυποστάτοις τάχα πράγμασι σφαλλόμενοι. ὅτι γὰρ οὐδὲν τῇ φύσει ἐστὶν ἀγαθὸν ἢ κακὸν ἢ ἀδιάφορον, ἐντεῦθέν τινες ἐπιλογίζονται.

ΚΓ΄.—ΕΙ ΕΣΤΙ ΤΙ ΦΥΣΕΙ ΑΓΑΘΟΝ ΚΑΙ ΚΑΚΟΝ ΚΑΙ ΑΔΙΑΦΟΡΟΝ

179 Τὸ πῦρ φύσει ἀλεαῖνον πᾶσι φαίνεται ἀλεαντικόν, καὶ ἡ χιὼν φύσει ψύχουσα πᾶσι φαίνεται ψυκτική, καὶ πάντα τὰ φύσει κινοῦντα ὁμοίως πάντας κινεῖ τοὺς κατὰ φύσιν, ὥς φασιν, ἔχοντας. οὐδὲν δὲ

* Cf. i. 27.

The term " indifferent," they say, is used in three 177
senses—in one sense, of that which is an object of
neither inclination nor disinclination, as for instance
the fact that the stars or the hairs of the head are
even in number ; in another sense, of that which is an
object of inclination or disinclination, but not towards
this particular object any more than towards that, as
in the case of two indistinguishable tetradrachms,
when one has to choose one of them ; for there arises
an inclination to choose one of them, but not this
one more than that one; and a third sense of the term
" indifferent " is, they say, " that which contributes
neither to happiness nor to unhappiness," as health,
or wealth ; for what a man may use now well, now
ill, that, they say, is indifferent, and they claim to
discuss it specially in their Ethics. But what view we 178
ought to take regarding this conception is plain from
what we have already said about things good and evil.

Thus, then, it is plain that they have not guided
us to a clear conception of the several things above-
mentioned ; yet, in thus failing with regard to
matters that, perhaps, have no real existence, their
experience is by no means strange. For there
are some who argue on the following grounds
that nothing is by nature [a] either good or evil or
indifferent.

CHAPTER XXI.—IS ANYTHING BY NATURE GOOD,
BAD, OR INDIFFERENT ?

Fire which heats by nature appears to all as heat- 179
ing, and snow which chills by nature appears to all as
chilling, and all things which move by nature move
equally all those who are, as they say, in a natural

τῶν λεγομένων ἀγαθῶν πάντας κινεῖ ὡς ἀγαθόν,
ὡς ὑπομνήσομεν· οὐκ ἄρα ἔστι φύσει ἀγαθόν. ὅτι
δὲ οὐδὲν τῶν λεγομένων ἀγαθῶν πάντας ὁμοίως
180 κινεῖ, δῆλον, φασίν. ἵνα γὰρ τοὺς ἰδιώτας παρῶμεν,
ὧν οἱ μὲν εὐεξίαν σώματος ἀγαθὸν εἶναι νομίζουσιν,
οἱ δὲ τὸ λαγνεύειν, οἱ δὲ τὸ ἀδηφαγεῖν, οἱ δὲ οἰνο-
φλυγίαν, οἱ δὲ τὸ χρῆσθαι κύβοις, οἱ δὲ πλεονεξίαν,
οἱ δὲ καὶ χείρω τινὰ τούτων, αὐτῶν τῶν φιλοσόφων
τινὲς μὲν τρία γένη φασὶν εἶναι ἀγαθῶν, ὡς οἱ
περιπατητικοί· τούτων γὰρ τὰ μὲν εἶναι περὶ ψυχὴν
ὡς τὰς ἀρετάς, τὰ δὲ περὶ σῶμα ὡς ὑγίειαν καὶ
τὰ ἐοικότα, τὰ δὲ ἐκτὸς ὡς φίλους, πλοῦτον, τὰ
181 παραπλήσια. οἱ δὲ ἀπὸ τῆς στοᾶς τριγένειαν μὲν
καὶ αὐτοί φασιν εἶναι ἀγαθῶν· τούτων γὰρ τὰ μὲν
εἶναι περὶ ψυχὴν ὡς τὰς ἀρετάς, τὰ δὲ ἐκτὸς ὡς
τὸν σπουδαῖον καὶ φίλον, τὰ δὲ οὔτε περὶ ψυχὴν
οὔτε ἐκτός, οἷον τὸν σπουδαῖον ὡς πρὸς ἑαυτόν·
τὰ μέντοι περὶ σῶμα [ἢ ἐκτός],[1] ἃ φασιν οἱ ἐκ τοῦ
περιπάτου ἀγαθὰ εἶναι, οὔ φασιν ἀγαθά. ἔνιοι δὲ
τὴν ἡδονὴν ἠσπάσαντο ὡς ἀγαθόν, τινὲς δὲ κακὸν
αὐτὴν ἄντικρυς εἶναι φασίν, ὥστε καί τινα τῶν ἐκ
φιλοσοφίας ἀναφθέγξασθαι " μανείην μᾶλλον ἢ
ἡσθείην."
182 Εἰ τοίνυν τὰ μὲν φύσει κινοῦντα πάντας ὁμοίως
κινεῖ, ἐπὶ δὲ τοῖς λεγομένοις ἀγαθοῖς οὐ πάντες
ὁμοίως κινούμεθα, οὐδέν ἐστι φύσει ἀγαθόν. καὶ
γὰρ οὔτε πάσαις ταῖς προεκκειμέναις στάσεσι
πιστεύειν ἐνδέχεται διὰ τὴν μάχην οὔτε τινί. ὁ

----

[1] [ἢ ἐκτός] del. Apelt.

* Cf. Plato, Laws iii. 697 ; Aristot. Eth. Nic. i. 8.

condition. But none of the so-called " goods," as we shall show, moves all men as being good ; therefore no natural good exists. And that none of the so-called goods moves all men alike is, they assert, an evident fact. For, not to mention ordinary folk—of whom 180 some regard right bodily condition as good, others chambering, others gluttony, others drunkenness, others gambling, others greed, and others still worse things,—some of the philosophers themselves (such as the Peripatetics) say that there are three kinds of goods [a]; of these some concern the soul, like the virtues, others the body, like health and similar things, while others are external, such as friends, wealth and the like. The Stoics themselves, too, 181 assert that there is a trinity [b] of goods ; of these some have to do with the soul, like the virtues, others are external, like the good man and the friend, while others are neither of the soul nor external, as for instance the good man in relation to himself ; but they deny that the bodily states, which the Peripatetics declare to be goods, are goods. And some have accepted pleasure as a good, whereas some affirm that it is a downright evil, so that one professor of philosophy [c] actually exclaimed, " I would sooner be mad than merry."

If, then, things which move by nature move all 182 men alike, while we are not all moved alike by the so-called goods, there is nothing good by nature. In fact it is impossible to believe either all the views now set forth, because of their conflicting character, or any one of them. For he who asserts that one

[b] Apparently a unique sense of the rare word τριγένεια (from τριγενής, " thrice-born ").

[c] Antisthenes, the Cynic.

γὰρ λέγων ὅτι τῇδε μὲν πιστευτέον τῇ στάσει
τῇδε δὲ οὐδαμῶς, ἐναντιουμένους τοὺς παρὰ τῶν
ἀντιδοξούντων λόγους αὐτῷ ἔχων, μέρος γίνεται
⟨τῆς⟩[1] διαφωνίας, καὶ τοῦ κρινοῦντος αὐτὸς
δεήσεται διὰ τοῦτο μετὰ τῶν ἄλλων, ἀλλ' οὐχ
ἑτέρους κρινεῖ. μήτε οὖν κριτηρίου ὄντος ὁμο-
λογουμένου μήτε ἀποδείξεως, διὰ τὴν ἀνεπίκριτον
καὶ περὶ τούτων διαφωνίαν εἰς τὴν ἐποχὴν κατ-
αντήσει, καὶ διὰ τοῦτο οὐχ ἕξει διαβεβαιοῦσθαι
τί ἐστι τὸ φύσει ἀγαθόν.

183 Ἔτι κἀκεῖνο λέγουσί τινες ὅτι ἀγαθόν ἐστιν ἤτοι
τὸ αἱρεῖσθαι αὐτὸ ἢ ἐκεῖνο ὃ αἱρούμεθα. τὸ μὲν
οὖν αἱρεῖσθαι οὐκ ἔστιν ἀγαθὸν κατὰ τὸν ἴδιον
λόγον· οὐ γὰρ ἂν ἐσπεύδομεν τυχεῖν ἐκείνου ὃ
αἱρούμεθα, ἵνα μὴ ἐκπέσωμεν τοῦ ἔτι αὐτὸ αἱρεῖσθαι, οἷον εἰ ἀγαθὸν ἦν τὸ ἀντιποιεῖσθαι ποτοῦ, οὐκ
ἂν ἐσπεύδομεν ποτοῦ τυχεῖν· ἀπολαύσαντες γὰρ
τούτου τῆς ἀντιποιήσεως αὐτοῦ ἀπαλλαττόμεθα.
καὶ ἐπὶ τοῦ πεινῆν ὁμοίως καὶ ἐπὶ τοῦ ἐρᾶν καὶ
τῶν ἄλλων. οὐκ ἄρα τὸ αἱρεῖσθαι δι' αὑτὸ αἱρετόν
ἐστιν, εἰ μή γε καὶ ὀχληρόν· καὶ γὰρ ὁ πεινῶν
σπεύδει μετασχεῖν τροφῆς, ὅπως ἀπαλλαγῇ τῆς
ἐκ τοῦ πεινῆν ὀχλήσεως, καὶ ὁ ἐρῶν ὁμοίως καὶ
ὁ διψῶν.

184 Ἀλλ' οὐδὲ τὸ αἱρετόν ἐστι τὸ ἀγαθόν. τοῦτο
γὰρ ἤτοι ἔξωθέν ἐστιν ἡμῶν ἢ περὶ ἡμᾶς. ἀλλ' εἰ
μὲν ἔξωθεν ἡμῶν, ἤτοι ποιεῖ περὶ ἡμᾶς ἀστείαν
κίνησιν καὶ ἀποδεκτὸν κατάστημα καὶ ἀγαστὸν
πάθος, ἢ οὐδαμῶς ἡμᾶς διατίθησιν. καὶ εἰ μὲν
οὐκ ἔστιν ἡμῖν ἀγαστόν, οὔτε ἀγαθὸν ἔσται οὔτε

_____

[1] ⟨τῆς⟩ add. cj. Bekk.

[a] Cf. ii. 18 ff., 134 ff.

must believe this view, but not that, becomes a party to the controversy, since he has opposed to him the arguments of those who take the rival view, and therefore he himself, along with the rest, will need an adjudicator instead of pronouncing judgement on others. And as there does not exist any agreed criterion or proof [a] owing to the unsettled controversy about these matters, he will be reduced to suspending judgement, and consequently he will be unable to affirm positively what the good by nature is.

Further, it is asserted by some that Good is either 183 the Choice [b] itself or that which we choose. Now Choice is not good according to its proper meaning ; else we would not have been hurrying to obtain that which we choose, for fear of losing the power of continuing to choose it ; for example, if the seeking to get drink were good, we would not have hurried to obtain drink ; for when we have enjoyed it we are quit of seeking to get it. So, too, with hunger and love and the rest. Choice, then, is not choiceworthy in itself, even if it is not actually disagreeable ; for in fact the hungry man hurries to partake of food in order to get quit of the discomfort due to his hunger ; and so likewise the man in love and the thirsty man.

But neither is the good the choiceworthy. For this 184 is either external to us or in connexion with us. But if it is external to us either it produces in us a soothing motion and a welcome condition and a delightful feeling, or it does not affect us at all. And if it is not a delight to us it will not be good,[c] nor will it attract

[b] Literally, "the (act of) choosing" or "trying to get for oneself." "Choice" (as the context shows) involves "desire" and the striving for satisfaction.

[c] For the connexion of "good" (ἀγαθόν) with "delightful" (ἀγαστόν) cf. § 175.

SEXTUS EMPIRICUS

ἐπάξεται ἡμᾶς πρὸς τὸ αἱρεῖσθαι αὐτὸ οὔτε ὅλως
αἱρετὸν ἔσται. εἰ δὲ [ἐγ]γίνεταί τι περὶ ἡμᾶς ἀπὸ
τοῦ ἐκτὸς προσηνὲς κατάστημα καὶ ἀσμενιστὸν
πάθος, οὐχὶ δι᾽ ἑαυτὸ αἱρετὸν ἔσται τὸ ἐκτός, ἀλλὰ
διὰ τὴν περὶ ἡμᾶς ἐπ᾽ αὐτῷ γινομένην διάθεσιν·
185 ὥστε οὐ δύναται τὸ δι᾽ αὐτὸ αἱρετὸν ἐκτὸς εἶναι.
ἀλλ᾽ οὐδὲ περὶ ἡμᾶς. ἤτοι γὰρ περὶ σῶμα εἶναι
λέγεται μόνον ἢ περὶ ψυχὴν μόνην ἢ περὶ ἀμφότερα.
ἀλλ᾽ εἰ μὲν περὶ σῶμα μόνον, ἐκφεύξεται τὴν
γνῶσιν ἡμῶν· ψυχῆς γὰρ αἱ γνώσεις εἶναι λέγονται,
τὸ δὲ σῶμα ἄλογον εἶναί φασιν ὅσον ἐφ᾽ ἑαυτῷ.
εἰ δὲ καὶ μέχρι τῆς ψυχῆς διατείνειν λέγοιτο, τῇ
τῆς ψυχῆς ἀντιλήψει καὶ τῷ ταύτης ἀγαστῷ πάθει
δοκοίη ἂν αἱρετὸν εἶναι· τὸ γὰρ κρινόμενον ὡς
αἱρετὸν τῇ διανοίᾳ κρίνεται κατὰ αὐτοὺς καὶ οὐκ
ἀλόγῳ σώματι.
186 Λείπεται λέγειν ὅτι περὶ ψυχὴν μόνην τὸ ἀγαθόν
ἐστιν. καὶ τοῦτο δὲ ἐξ ὧν οἱ δογματικοὶ λέγουσιν
ἀδύνατόν ἐστιν. ἡ γὰρ ψυχὴ τάχα μὲν καὶ ἀνύπαρκτός ἐστιν· εἰ δὲ καὶ ὑπάρχει, ὅσον ἐφ᾽ οἷς
λέγουσιν οὐ καταλαμβάνεται, καθὼς ἐπελογισάμην
ἐν τῷ περὶ κριτηρίου λόγῳ. πῶς δ᾽ ἂν θαρροίη
τις ἐν ἐκείνῳ τι γίνεσθαι λέγειν ὃ μὴ καταλαμβάνει;
187 ἵνα δὲ καὶ ταῦτα παραλίπωμεν, πῶς ἄρα καὶ
λέγουσιν ἐν τῇ ψυχῇ τὸ ἀγαθὸν γίνεσθαι· εἰ γοῦν
ὁ Ἐπίκουρος ἐν ἡδονῇ τίθεται τὸ τέλος καὶ φησὶ
τὴν ψυχήν, ἐπεὶ καὶ πάντα, ἐξ ἀτόμων συνεστάναι,
πῶς ἐν ἀτόμων σωρῷ δυνατὸν ἡδονὴν γίγνεσθαι
καὶ συγκατάθεσιν ἢ κρίσιν τοῦ τόδε μὲν αἱρετὸν
εἶναι καὶ ἀγαθὸν τόδε δὲ φευκτὸν καὶ κακόν,
ἀμήχανον εἰπεῖν.

ᵃ Cf. ii. 31 ff., which also deals with " the Criterion."

452

us to the choosing of it, nor will it be choiceworthy at all. And if there arises within us, from the external object, a congenial condition and an agreeable feeling, it is not for its own sake that the external object will be choiceworthy but for the sake of the internal condition which follows upon it ; so that what is choice- 185 worthy in itself cannot be external. Nor can it be personal to us. For it is said to belong either to the body alone or to the soul alone or to both. But if it belongs to the body alone, it will elude our perception; for our perceptions are said to be properties of the soul, and they assert that the body, viewed by itself, is irrational. And if it should be said to extend to the soul also, it would seem to be choiceworthy owing to its affecting the soul and to the agreeable feeling therein ; for, according to them, what is judged to be choiceworthy is judged by the intellect and not by the irrational body.

There remains the alternative that the good is in 186 the soul only. But this, too, is impossible if we go by the statements of the Dogmatists. For the soul is, perhaps, actually non-existent [a] ; and even if it exists, judging by what they say it is not apprehended, as I have argued in my chapter "On the Criterion." How then could one venture to affirm that something takes place in a thing which he does not apprehend ? But, to pass over these objections, in what manner 187 does the good, according to them, come about in the soul ? For certainly, if Epicurus makes the End consist in pleasure and asserts that the soul, like all else, is composed of atoms, it is impossible to explain how in a heap of atoms there can come about pleasure and assent or judgement that this object is choiceworthy and good, that object to be avoided and evil.

ΚΔ΄.—ΤΙ ΕΣΤΙΝ Η ΛΕΓΟΜΕΝΗ ΤΕΧΝΗ ΠΕΡΙ ΒΙΟΝ

188 Πάλιν οἱ στωικοὶ περὶ ψυχὴν ἀγαθά φασιν εἶναι
τέχνας τινάς, τὰς ἀρετάς· τέχνην δὲ εἶναί φασι
σύστημα ἐκ καταλήψεων συγγεγυμνασμένων, τὰς
δὲ καταλήψεις γίγνεσθαι περὶ τὸ ἡγεμονικόν. πῶς
οὖν ἐν τῷ ἡγεμονικῷ, πνεύματι κατ᾽ αὐτοὺς ὑπάρχοντι, ἐναπόθεσις γίνεται καταλήψεων καὶ ἀ-
θροισμὸς τοσούτων ὡς γενέσθαι τέχνην, οὐχ οἷόν τε
ἐννοῆσαι, τῆς ἐπιγινομένης τυπώσεως ἀεὶ τὴν πρὸ
αὐτῆς ἀπαλειφούσης, ἐπεὶ χυτόν τέ ἐστι τὸ πνεῦμα
καὶ ἐξ ὅλου κινεῖσθαι λέγεται καθ᾽ ἑκάστην τύπω-
189 σιν. τὸ γὰρ τὴν Πλάτωνος ἀνειδωλοποίησιν λέγειν
ἐπιδεκτικὴν εἶναι δύνασθαι τοῦ ἀγαθοῦ, φημὶ δὲ
τὴν κρᾶσιν τῆς ἀμερίστου καὶ μεριστῆς οὐσίας καὶ
τῆς θατέρου φύσεως καὶ ταὐτοῦ, ἢ τοὺς ἀριθμούς,
τέλεον ληρῶδές ἐστιν. ὅθεν οὐδὲ περὶ ψυχὴν εἶναι
190 δύναται τὸ ἀγαθόν. εἰ δὲ μήτε τὸ αἱρεῖσθαι αὐτὸ
ἀγαθόν ἐστι, μήτε ἐκτὸς ὑπόκειται τὸ δι᾽ αὐτὸ
αἱρετόν, μήτε περὶ σῶμά ἐστι μήτε περὶ ψυχήν,
ὡς ἐπελογισάμην, οὐδ᾽ ὅλως ἔστι τι φύσει ἀγαθόν.

Διὰ δὲ τὰ προειρημένα οὐδὲ κακόν τι ἔστι φύσει·
τὰ γὰρ ἑτέροις δοκοῦντα εἶναι κακά, ταῦτα ἕτεροι
διώκουσιν ὡς ἀγαθά, οἷον ἀσέλγειαν ἀδικίαν φιλ-
αργυρίαν ἀκρασίαν, τὰ ἐοικότα. ὅθεν εἰ τὰ μὲν

ᵃ It is a mistake (of the mss.) to make a new chapter here,
as §§ 188 ff. carry on the argument of 185 ff. about the connexion of " good " with the soul. The " Art of Living " is
first dealt with in § 239.

ᵇ Cf. Cic. Acad. iv. 7. 22 "ars . . . ex multis animi per-
ceptionibus constat." The virtues, said the Stoics, are " arts "
because they are forms of knowledge and consist in the use
or " exercise " of a large number of perceptions or " apprehensions " related to one another in a systematic way. These

CHAPTER XXIV.—WHAT IS THE SO-CALLED ART
OF LIVING ? [a]

Again, the Stoics declare that goods of the soul 188
are certain arts, namely the virtues. And an art,
they say, is " a system composed of co-exercised
apprehensions," [b] and the perceptions arise in
the ruling principle. But how there takes place
in the ruling principle, which according to them
is breath,[c] a deposit of perceptions, and such
an aggregation of them as to produce art, it is
impossible to conceive, when each succeeding impression obliterates the previous one, seeing that
breath is fluid and it is said to move as a whole at
each impression. For it is perfect nonsense to say 189
that Plato's imaginary construction of the soul—I
mean the mixture of the indivisible and the divisible
essence and of the nature of the Other and of the
Same,[d] or the Numbers—is capable of being receptive
of the Good. Hence the good cannot belong to the
soul either. But if the good is not choice itself, and 190
what is choiceworthy in itself neither exists externally
nor belongs to either body or soul—as I have argued,
—then there does not exist at all any natural good.

For the foregoing reasons also there exists no
natural evil. For things which seem to some to be
evil are pursued as goods by others—for instance,
incontinence, injustice, avarice, intemperance, and the
like. Hence, if it is the nature of things naturally

"apprehensions" are "deposited" in the mind which is
conceived as an elastic fluid *pneuma* of which the whole
moves when any part of it is moved. *Cf.* §§ 241, 251 *infra.*

[c] *Cf.* i. 128, ii. 70.

[d] *Cf.* Plato, *Tim.* 35 ff. But " the Numbers " may refer to
the Pythagorean theory.

φύσει πάντας ὁμοίως πέφυκε κινεῖν, τὰ δὲ λεγόμενα
εἶναι κακὰ οὐ πάντας ὁμοίως κινεῖ, οὐδέν ἐστι
φύσει κακόν.

191 Ὁμοίως δὲ οὐδ' ἀδιάφορόν ἐστί τι φύσει διὰ τὴν
περὶ τῶν ἀδιαφόρων διαφωνίαν. οἷον γοῦν οἱ μὲν
στωικοὶ τῶν ἀδιαφόρων φασὶ τὰ μὲν προηγμένα
εἶναι τὰ δὲ ἀποπροηγμένα τὰ δὲ οὔτε προηγμένα
οὔτε ἀποπροηγμένα, προηγμένα μὲν τὰ ἱκανὴν
ἀξίαν ἔχοντα ὡς ὑγίειαν πλοῦτον, ἀποπροηγμένα
δὲ τὰ μὴ ἱκανὴν ἔχοντα ἀξίαν ὡς πενίαν νόσον,
μήτε δὲ προηγμένα μήτε ἀποπροηγμένα ὡς τὸ
192 ἐκτεῖναι ἢ συγκάμψαι τὸν δάκτυλον. τινὲς δὲ
οὐδὲν τῶν ἀδιαφόρων φύσει προηγμένον ἢ ἀποπροηγμένον εἶναι λέγουσιν· ἕκαστον γὰρ τῶν
ἀδιαφόρων παρὰ τὰς διαφόρους περιστάσεις ὁτὲ
μὲν προηγμένον φαίνεσθαι ὁτὲ δὲ ἀποπροηγμένον.
εἰ γοῦν, φασίν, οἱ μὲν πλούσιοι ἐπιβουλεύοιντο
ὑπὸ τυράννου οἱ δὲ πένητες εἰρηνεύοιντο, πᾶς
ἂν ἕλοιτο εἶναι πένης μᾶλλον ἢ πλούσιος, ὡς
193 ἀποπροηγμένον γίνεσθαι τὸν πλοῦτον. ὥστε ἐπεὶ
ἕκαστον τῶν λεγομένων ἀδιαφόρων οἱ μὲν ἀγαθὸν
εἶναί φασιν οἱ δὲ κακόν, ἅπαντες δ' ἂν ὁμοίως
ἀδιάφορον αὐτὸ ἐνόμιζον εἶναι εἴγε ἀδιάφορον ἦν
φύσει, οὐδέν ἐστι φύσει ἀδιάφορον.

Οὕτως καὶ εἴ τις φύσει αἱρετὴν εἶναι λέγοι τὴν
ἀνδρίαν διὰ τὸ τοὺς λέοντας φυσικῶς τολμᾶν καὶ[1]
ἀνδρίζεσθαι δοκεῖν, καὶ ταύρους, εἰ τύχοι, καὶ
ἀνθρώπους τινὰς καὶ ἀλεκτρυόνας, λέγομεν ὅτι
ὅσον ἐπὶ τούτῳ καὶ ἡ δειλία τῶν φύσει αἱρετῶν
ἐστίν, ἐπεὶ ἔλαφοι καὶ λαγωοὶ καὶ ἄλλα πλείονα

---

[1] τολμᾶν καὶ T: τολμᾶν ἐπὶ τὸ MSS.: ὁρμᾶν ἐπὶ τὸ edd., Bekk.

existent to move all men alike, whereas the things said to be evil do not move all alike, nothing is naturally evil.

Similarly there is nothing naturally indifferent, 191 because of the divergence of opinion about things indifferent. The Stoics, for example, assert that of the indifferents some are preferred, some rejected, and others neither preferred nor rejected,[a]—the preferred being such as have sufficient value, like health and wealth ; the rejected such as have not sufficient value, like poverty and sickness ; while extending the finger or bending it in are cases of the neither preferred nor rejected. Some, however, maintain 192 that none of the indifferents is by nature preferred or rejected ; for, owing to the differences in the circumstances, each of the indifferents appears at one time preferred, at another rejected. For certainly, they argue, if the rich were being threatened with attack by a tyrant while the poor were being left in peace, everyone would prefer to be poor rather than rich, so that wealth would be a thing rejected. Consequently, 193 since of each of the so-called indifferents some say that it is good, others bad, whereas all alike would have counted it indifferent had it been naturally indifferent, there is nothing that is naturally indifferent.

So also, should anyone declare that courage is naturally choiceworthy because lions seem to be naturally bold and courageous, bulls too, it may be, and some men and cocks, we reply that, as for that, cowardice also is one of the things naturally choiceworthy, since deer and hares and many other animals

---

[a] *Cf.* Introd. p. xxvii, Cic. *De fin.* iii. 15 f., iv. 9, 16.

SEXTUS EMPIRICUS

ζῷα φυσικῶς ἐπ' αὐτὴν ὁρμᾷ. καὶ οἱ πλεῖστοι
δὲ τῶν ἀνθρώπων δειλοὶ θεωροῦνται· σπανίως
μὲν γάρ τις ὑπὲρ πατρίδος ἑαυτὸν ἐπέδωκεν εἰς
θάνατον [βλακευσάμενος]¹ ἢ ἄλλως θερμόν τι
τυφωθεὶς ἔδοξέ τις διαπράττεσθαι, ὁ δὲ πλεῖστος
ὅμιλος τῶν ἀνθρώπων πάντα τὰ τοιαῦτα ἐκκλίνει.

194 Ὅθεν καὶ οἱ Ἐπικούρειοι δεικνύναι νομίζουσι
φύσει αἱρετὴν εἶναι τὴν ἡδονήν· τὰ γὰρ ζῷά φασιν
ἅμα τῷ γενέσθαι, ἀδιάστροφα ὄντα, ὁρμᾶν μὲν
195 ἐπὶ τὴν ἡδονὴν ἐκκλίνειν δὲ ἀλγηδόνας. καὶ πρὸς
τούτους δέ ἐστι λέγειν ὅτι τὸ ποιητικὸν κακοῦ
οὐκ ἂν εἴη φύσει ἀγαθόν. ἡ δέ γε ἡδονὴ κακῶν
ἐστὶ ποιητική· πάσῃ γὰρ ἡδονῇ παραπέπηγεν
ἀλγηδών, ἥ ἐστι κατ' αὐτοὺς φύσει κακόν. οἷον
γοῦν ἥδεται ὁ μέθυσος ἐμφορούμενος οἴνου καὶ ὁ
γαστρίμαργος τροφῆς, καὶ ὁ λάγνος ἀφροδισίοις
ἀμέτροις χρώμενος· ἀλλὰ ταῦτα καὶ πενίας καὶ
νόσων ἐστὶ ποιητικά, ἅπερ ἀλγεινά ἐστι καὶ κακά,
ὡς φασίν. οὐκ ἄρα φύσει ἀγαθόν ἐστιν ἡ ἡδονή.
196 παραπλησίως δὲ καὶ τὸ ποιητικὸν ἀγαθῶν οὐκ
ἔστι φύσει κακόν, ἡδονὰς δὲ ἀποτελοῦσιν ἀλγηδόνες·
καὶ γὰρ ἐπιστήμας ἀναλαμβάνομεν πονοῦντες, καὶ
πλούτου καὶ ἐρωμένης οὕτως ἐγκρατὴς γίνεταί τις,
καὶ ὑγίειαν περιποιοῦσιν αἱ ἀλγηδόνες. οὐκ ἄρα
ὁ πόνος φύσει κακόν. καὶ γὰρ εἰ φύσει ἀγαθὸν
μὲν ἦν ἡ ἡδονὴ φαῦλον δὲ ὁ πόνος, πάντες ἂν
ὁμοίως διέκειντο περὶ αὐτῶν, ὡς ἐλέγομεν· ὁρῶμεν
δὲ πολλοὺς τῶν φιλοσόφων τὸν μὲν πόνον καὶ τὴν
καρτερίαν αἱρουμένους, τῆς ἡδονῆς δὲ καταφρο-
νοῦντας.

¹ [βλακευσάμενος] delevi, post ἀνθρώπων transp. Apelt: ⟨οὐ⟩
βλακ. cj. R. Philippson.
458

are naturally impelled thereto. The majority of men, too, show themselves to be cowardly ; for it is rare for a man to give himself up to death for the sake of his country,[a] or to seem inspired to do any other daring deed, the great majority of mankind being averse to all such actions.

Hence, also, the Epicureans suppose themselves to 194 have proved that pleasure is naturally choiceworthy ; for the animals, they say, as soon as they are born, when still unperverted, seek after pleasure and avoid pains. But to these we may reply that what is pro- 195 ductive of evil cannot be naturally good ; but pleasure is productive of evils ; for to every pleasure there is linked a pain, and pain, according to them, is a natural evil. Thus, for example, the drunkard feels pleasure when filling himself with wine, and the glutton with food, and the lecher in immoderate sexual intercourse, yet these things are productive of both poverty and sickness, which, as they say, are painful and evil. Pleasure, therefore, is not a natural good. Similarly, 196 too, what is productive of good is not naturally evil, and pains bring about pleasures ; it is, in fact, by toil that we acquire knowledge, and it is thus also that a man becomes possessed both of wealth and of his lady-love, and pains preserve health. Toil, then, is not naturally evil. Indeed if pleasure were naturally good, and toil bad, all men, as we said, would have been similarly disposed towards them, whereas we see many of the philosophers choosing toil and hardship and despising pleasure.

[a] The word bracketed in the Greek text (βλακευσάμενος) means "being lazy, or spiritless," and is obviously out of place here, though it would fit well enough in the next clause (as Apelt suggests).

197 Ὁμοίως δ' ἂν περιτρέποιντο καὶ οἱ τὸν ἐνάρετον
βίον φύσει ἀγαθὸν εἶναι λέγοντες ἐκ τοῦ τινὰς τῶν
σοφῶν τὸν μεθ' ἡδονῆς αἱρεῖσθαι βίον, ὡς ἐκ τῆς
παρ' αὐτοῖς ἐκείνοις διαφωνίας τὸ φύσει τι τοῖον
ἢ τοῖον εἶναι διατρέπεσθαι.

198 Οὐκ ἄτοπον δ' ἂν ἴσως εἴη πρὸς τούτοις καὶ
εἰδικώτερον ἐπιστῆσαι διὰ βραχέων ταῖς ὑπολήψεσι
ταῖς περὶ αἰσχρῶν καὶ οὐκ αἰσχρῶν ἀθέσμων τε
καὶ οὐ τοιούτων καὶ νόμων καὶ ἐθῶν καὶ τῆς εἰς
θεοὺς εὐσεβείας καὶ τῆς περὶ τοὺς κατοιχομένους
ὁσιότητος καὶ τῶν ἐοικότων· καὶ γὰρ οὕτω περὶ
τῶν πρακτέων ἢ μὴ πολλὴν εὑρήσομεν ἀνωμαλίαν.

199 Οἷον γοῦν παρ' ἡμῖν μὲν αἰσχρόν, μᾶλλον δὲ καὶ
παράνομον νενόμισται τὸ τῆς ἀρρενομιξίας, παρὰ
Γερμανοῖς δέ, ὡς φασίν, οὐκ αἰσχρὸν ἀλλ' ὡς ἕν
τι τῶν συνήθων. λέγεται δὲ καὶ παρὰ Θηβαίοις
τὸ παλαιὸν οὐκ αἰσχρὸν τοῦτο εἶναι δόξαι, καὶ τὸν
Μηριόνην τὸν Κρῆτα οὕτω κεκλῆσθαί φασι δι'
ἔμφασιν τοῦ Κρητῶν ἔθους, καὶ τὴν Ἀχιλλέως
πρὸς Πάτροκλον διάπυρον φιλίαν εἰς τοῦτο ἀν-
200 άγουσι τινές. καὶ τί θαυμαστόν, ὅπου γε καὶ οἱ
ἀπὸ τῆς κυνικῆς φιλοσοφίας καὶ οἱ περὶ τὸν Κιτιέα
Ζήνωνα καὶ Κλεάνθην καὶ Χρύσιππον ἀδιάφορον
τοῦτο εἶναι φασίν; καὶ τὸ δημοσίᾳ γυναικὶ μίγ-

---

[a] e.g. the Cyrenaics.
[b] Cf. the examples in i. 145 ff. "Amongst us" here, and throughout this chapter (as in i. 145 ff.), means "amongst the Greeks" and refers in special to the laws or customs of Athens.
[c] Prob. not " Germans," but a Persian tribe, cf. i. 152.
[d] i.e. Μηριόνης is derived from μηρός (" thigh "): cf. § 245 infra.   [e] Cf. Plato, Symp. 180 A.
[f] Cf. §§ 205, 245 ; and i. 148, 153, 160 for what follows. The repellent features of Stoic ethical theory mentioned in

And so, too, those who assert that the virtuous life 197 is naturally good might be refuted by the fact that some of the sages choose the life which includes pleasure,[a] so that the claim that a thing is by nature of this sort or that is contradicted by the divergence of opinion amongst the Dogmatists themselves.

And perhaps it may not be amiss, in addition to 198 what has been said, to dwell more in detail, though briefly, on the notions concerning things shameful and not shameful, unholy and not so, laws and customs, piety towards the gods, reverence for the departed, and the like. For thus we shall discover a great variety of belief concerning what ought or ought not to be done.

For example,[b] amongst us sodomy is regarded as 199 shameful or rather illegal, but by the Germani,[c] they say, it is not looked on as shameful but as a customary thing. It is said, too, that in Thebes long ago this practice was not held to be shameful, and they say that Meriones the Cretan was so called by way of indicating the Cretans' custom,[d] and some refer to this the burning love of Achilles for Patroclus.[e] And 200 what wonder, when both the adherents of the Cynic philosophy and the followers of Zeno of Citium, Cleanthes and Chrysippus, declare that this practice is indifferent?[f] Having intercourse with a woman,

this chapter are passed over in most expositions of Stoicism, though confirmed by Plutarch (*De Stoic. repugn.*). We may ascribe them to the " Back to Nature" movement, which the early Stoics shared with the Cynics. The dictum " Live according to Nature" might be taken to mean " Disregard conventional morals," "Cease to repress your natural instincts." But, as Sextus says in § 249, they did not (like some of the Cynics) carry out in practice these shocking theories.

νυσθαι, καίτοι παρ' ἡμῖν αἰσχρὸν εἶναι δοκοῦν,
παρά τισι τῶν Ἰνδῶν οὐκ αἰσχρὸν εἶναι νομίζεται·
μίγνυνται γοῦν ἀδιαφόρως δημοσίᾳ, καθάπερ καὶ
201 περὶ τοῦ φιλοσόφου Κράτητος ἀκηκόαμεν. ἀλλὰ
καὶ τὸ τὰς γυναῖκας ἑταιρεῖν παρ' ἡμῖν μὲν αἰσχρόν ἐστι καὶ ἐπονείδιστον, παρὰ δὲ πολλοῖς τῶν
Αἰγυπτίων εὐκλεές· φασὶ γοῦν ὅτι αἱ πλείστοις
συνιοῦσαι καὶ κόσμον ἔχουσι περισφύριον, σύνθημα
τοῦ παρ' αὐταῖς σεμνολογήματος. παρ' ἐνίοις
δὲ αὐτῶν αἱ κόραι πρὸ τῶν γάμων τὴν προῖκα ἐξ
ἑταιρήσεως συνάγουσαι γαμοῦνται. καὶ τοὺς στωικοὺς δὲ ὁρῶμεν οὐκ ἄτοπον εἶναι λέγοντας τὸ
ἑταίρᾳ συνοικεῖν ἢ τὸ ἐξ ἑταίρας ἐργασίας διαζῆν.
202   Ἀλλὰ καὶ τὸ ἐστίχθαι παρ' ἡμῖν μὲν αἰσχρὸν
καὶ ἄτιμον εἶναι δοκεῖ, πολλοὶ δὲ Αἰγυπτίων καὶ
203 Σαρματῶν στίζουσι τὰ γεννώμενα. τό τε ἐλλόβια
ἔχειν τοὺς ἄρρενας παρ' ἡμῖν μὲν αἰσχρόν ἐστι,
παρ' ἐνίοις δὲ τῶν βαρβάρων, ὥσπερ καὶ Σύροις,
εὐγενείας ἐστὶ σύνθημα. τινὲς δὲ ἐπιτείνοντες τὸ
σύνθημα τῆς εὐγενείας, καὶ τὰς ῥῖνας τῶν παίδων
τιτρώσκοντες κρίκους ἀπ' αὐτῶν ἀργυρέους ἢ
χρυσοῦς ἀπαρτῶσιν, ὃ παρ' ἡμῖν οὐκ ἂν ποιήσειέ
204 τις, ὥσπερ οὐδὲ ἀνθοβαφῆ καὶ ποδήρη τις ἄρρην
ἐνταῦθα ἂν ἀμφιέσαιτο ἐσθῆτα, καίτοι παρὰ
Πέρσαις εὐπρεπεστάτου τοῦ παρ' ἡμῖν αἰσχροῦ
τούτου δοκοῦντος εἶναι. καὶ παρὰ Διονυσίῳ δὲ
τῷ τῆς Σικελίας τυράννῳ τοιαύτης ἐσθῆτος Πλάτωνι καὶ Ἀριστίππῳ τοῖς φιλοσόφοις προσενεχ-
θείσης ὁ μὲν Πλάτων ἀπεπέμψατο, εἰπὼν

too, in public, although deemed by us to be shameful, is not thought to be shameful by some of the Indians ; at any rate they couple publicly with indifference, like the philosopher Crates, as the story goes. Moreover, 201 prostitution is with us a shameful and disgraceful thing, but with many of the Egyptians it is highly esteemed ; at least, they say that those women who have the greatest number of lovers wear an ornamental ankle-ring as a token of their proud position.[a] And with some of them the girls marry after collecting a dowry before marriage by means of prostitution. We see the Stoics also declaring that it is not amiss to keep company with a prostitute or to live on the profits of prostitution.

Moreover, with us tattooing is held to be shameful 202 and degrading, but many of the Egyptians and Sarmatians tattoo their offspring. Also, it is a 203 shameful thing with us for men to wear earrings, but amongst some of the barbarians, like the Syrians, it is a token of nobility. And some, by way of marking their nobility still further, pierce the nostrils also of their children and suspend from them rings of silver or gold—a thing which nobody with us would do, just 204 as no man here would dress himself in a flowered robe reaching to the feet, although this dress, which with us is thought shameful, is held to be highly respectable by the Persians. And when, at the Court of Dionysius the tyrant of Sicily, a dress of this description was offered to the philosophers Plato and Aristippus,[b] Plato sent it away with the words—

[a] *Cf.* Hdt. iv. 176.
[b] *Cf.* Diog. Laert. ii. 78, and i. 155 *supra.* The verses are from Eurip. *Bacchae* 836 and 317.

οὐκ ἂν δυναίμην θῆλυν ἐνδῦναι στολήν
ἄρρην πεφυκώς,

ὁ δὲ Ἀρίστιππος προσήκατο, φήσας
καὶ γὰρ ἐν βακχεύμασιν
οὖσ' ἥ γε σώφρων οὐ διαφθαρήσεται.

οὕτω καὶ τῶν σοφῶν ᾧ μὲν οὐκ αἰσχρὸν ᾧ δὲ
205 αἰσχρὸν ἐδόκει τοῦτο εἶναι. ἄθεσμόν τέ ἐστι παρ'
ἡμῖν μητέρα ἢ ἀδελφὴν ἰδίαν γαμεῖν· Πέρσαι δέ,
καὶ μάλιστα αὐτῶν οἱ σοφίαν ἀσκεῖν δοκοῦντες,
οἱ Μάγοι, γαμοῦσι τὰς μητέρας, καὶ Αἰγύπτιοι
τὰς ἀδελφὰς ἄγονται πρὸς γάμον, καὶ ὡς ὁ
ποιητής φησιν,

Ζεὺς Ἥρην προσέειπε κασιγνήτην ἄλοχόν τε.

ἀλλὰ καὶ ὁ Κιτιεὺς Ζήνων φησὶ μὴ ἄτοπον εἶναι
τὸ μόριον τῆς μητρὸς τῷ ἑαυτοῦ μορίῳ τρῖψαι,
καθάπερ οὐδὲ ἄλλο τι μέρος τοῦ σώματος αὐτῆς
τῇ χειρὶ τρῖψαι φαῦλον ἂν εἴποι τις εἶναι. καὶ ὁ
Χρύσιππος δὲ ἐν τῇ πολιτείᾳ δογματίζει τόν τε
πατέρα ἐκ τῆς θυγατρὸς παιδοποιεῖσθαι καὶ τὴν
μητέρα ἐκ τοῦ παιδὸς καὶ τὸν ἀδελφὸν ἐκ τῆς
ἀδελφῆς. Πλάτων δὲ καὶ καθολικώτερον κοινὰς
206 εἶναι τὰς γυναῖκας δεῖν ἀπεφήνατο. τό τε αἰ-
σχρουργεῖν ἐπάρατον ὂν παρ' ἡμῖν ὁ Ζήνων οὐκ
ἀποδοκιμάζει· καὶ ἄλλους δὲ ὡς ἀγαθῷ τινι τούτῳ
χρῆσθαι τῷ κακῷ πυνθανόμεθα.
207 Ἀλλὰ καὶ τὸ ἀνθρωπείων γεύεσθαι σαρκῶν παρ'
ἡμῖν μὲν ἄθεσμον, παρ' ὅλοις δὲ βαρβάροις ἔθνεσιν
ἀδιάφορόν ἐστιν. καὶ τί δεῖ τοὺς βαρβάρους λέγειν,

---

[a] Cf. i. 152.   [b] Homer, Il. xviii. 356.
[c] Cf. § 246, i. 160.

A man am I, and never could I don
A woman's garb ;

but Aristippus accepted it, saying—

For e'en midst revel-routs
She that is chaste will keep her purity.

Thus, even in the case of these sages, while the one of them deemed this practice shameful, the other did not. And with us it is sinful to marry one's mother 205 or one's own sister ; but the Persians, and especially those of them who are reputed to practise wisdom— namely, the Magi,—marry their mothers ; and the Egyptians [a] take their sisters in marriage, even as the poet says [b]—

Thus spake Zeus unto Hera, his wedded wife and his sister.

Moreover, Zeno of Citium says that it is not amiss for a man to rub his mother's private part with his own private part, just as no one would say it was bad for him to rub any other part of her body with his hand. Chrysippus,[c] too, in his book *The State* approves of a father getting children by his daughter, a mother by her son, and a brother by his sister. And Plato,[d] in more general terms, has declared that wives ought to be held in common. Masturbation, too, which we 206 count loathsome, is not disapproved by Zeno ; and we are informed that others, too, practise this evil as though it were a good thing.

Moreover, the eating of human flesh is sinful with 207 us, but indifferent amongst whole tribes of barbarians.[e] Yet why should one speak of " barbarians "

[d] *Cf. Rep.* v. 457.   [e] *Cf.* § 225 *infra.*

465

ὅπου καὶ ὁ Τυδεὺς τὸν ἐγκέφαλον τοῦ πολεμίου
λέγεται φαγεῖν, καὶ οἱ ἀπὸ τῆς στοᾶς οὐκ ἄτοπον
εἶναί φασι τὸ σάρκας τινὰ ἐσθίειν ἄλλων τε ἀν-
208 θρώπων καὶ ἑαυτοῦ· τό τε ἀνθρωπείῳ μιαίνειν
αἵματι βωμὸν θεοῦ παρ' ἡμῖν μὲν τοῖς πολλοῖς
ἄθεσμον, Λάκωνες δὲ ἐπὶ τοῦ βωμοῦ τῆς Ὀρ-
θωσίας Ἀρτέμιδος μαστίζονται πικρῶς ὑπὲρ τοῦ
πολλὴν αἵματος ἐπὶ τοῦ βωμοῦ τῆς θεοῦ γενέσθαι
ῥύσιν. ἀλλὰ καὶ τῷ Κρόνῳ θύουσιν ἄνθρωπόν
τινες, καθάπερ καὶ Σκύθαι τῇ Ἀρτέμιδι τοὺς
ξένους· ἡμεῖς δὲ χραίνεσθαι τὰ ἱερὰ δοκοῦμεν ἀν-
209 θρώπου φόνῳ. τούς γε μὴν μοιχοὺς κολάζει παρ'
ἡμῖν νόμος, παρὰ δέ τισιν ἀδιάφορόν ἐστι ταῖς
τῶν ἑτέρων γυναιξὶ μίγνυσθαι· καὶ φιλοσόφων δέ
τινές φασιν ἀδιάφορον εἶναι τὸ ἀλλοτρίᾳ γυναικὶ
μίγνυσθαι.

210   Τοὺς πατέρας τε ὑπὸ τῶν παίδων ἐπιμελείας
ἀξιοῦσθαι κελεύει παρ' ἡμῖν νόμος· οἱ Σκύθαι δὲ
ὑπὲρ τὰ ἑξήκοντα ἔτη γενομένους αὐτοὺς ἀποσφάτ-
τουσιν. καὶ τί θαυμαστόν, εἴγε ὁ μὲν Κρόνος τῇ
ἅρπῃ τὰ αἰδοῖα ἐξέτεμε τοῦ πατρός, ὁ δὲ Ζεὺς
τὸν Κρόνον κατεταρτάρωσεν, ἡ δὲ Ἀθηνᾶ μετὰ
Ἥρας καὶ Ποσειδῶνος τὸν πατέρα δεσμεύειν ἐπ-
211 εχείρησεν; ἀλλὰ καὶ τοὺς ἑαυτοῦ παῖδας ὁ Κρόνος
ἀναιρεῖν ἔκρινεν, καὶ ὁ Σόλων Ἀθηναίοις τὸν περὶ
τῶν ἀκρίτων νόμον ἔθετο, καθ' ὃν φονεύειν ἑκάστῳ
τὸν ἑαυτοῦ παῖδα ἐπέτρεψεν. παρ' ἡμῖν δὲ τὸ
τοὺς παῖδας φονεύειν ἀπαγορεύουσιν οἱ νόμοι. οἵ
τε Ῥωμαίων νομοθέται τοὺς παῖδας ὑποχειρίους

ᵃ Tydeus, father of Diomede; his "enemy" was Melan-
ippus (Il. xiv. 114 ff.).

when even Tydeus [a] is said to have devoured the brains of his enemy, and the Stoic School declare that it is not wrong for a man to eat either other men's flesh or his own ? And with most of us it is 208 sinful to defile an altar of a god with human blood, but the Laconians lash themselves fiercely over the altar of Artemis Orthosia [b] in order that a great stream of blood may flow over the altar of the goddess. Moreover, some sacrifice a human victim to Cronos, just as the Scythians [c] sacrifice strangers to Artemis ; whereas we deem that holy places are defiled by the slaying of a man. Adulterers are, of 209 course, punished by law with us, but amongst some peoples [d] intercourse with other men's wives is a thing indifferent ; and some philosophers, [e] too, declare that intercourse with the wife of another is indifferent.

With us, also, the law enjoins that the fathers 210 should receive due care from their children ; but the Scythians cut their throats when they get to be over sixty years old. And what wonder, seeing that Cronos cut off his father's genitals with a sickle, and Zeus plunged Cronos down to Tartarus, and Athena with the help of Hera and Poseidon attempted to bind her father with fetters ? [f] Moreover, Cronos 211 decided to destroy his own children, and Solon gave the Athenians the law " concerning things immune," by which he allowed each man to slay his own child ; but with us the laws forbid the slaying of children. The Roman lawgivers also ordain that the children

[b] Boys were scourged at the altar of Artemis Orthia in Laconia.
[c] Cf. i. 149.
[d] Cf. Hdt. iv. 180 ; Aristot. Pol. ii. 3.
[e] e.g. Diogenes the Cynic, cf. Diog. Laert. vi. 72.
[f] Cf. Hom. Il. xiv. 204, i. 399.

SEXTUS EMPIRICUS

καὶ δούλους τῶν πατέρων κελεύουσιν εἶναι, καὶ
τῆς οὐσίας τῶν παίδων μὴ κυριεύειν τοὺς παῖδας
ἀλλὰ τοὺς πατέρας, ἕως ἂν ἐλευθερίας οἱ παῖδες
τύχωσι κατὰ τοὺς ἀργυρωνήτους· παρ' ἑτέροις δὲ
212 ὡς τυραννικὸν τοῦτο ἐκβέβληται. νόμος τέ ἐστι
τοὺς ἀνδροφόνους κολάζεσθαι· οἱ μονομάχαι δὲ
φονεύοντες πολλάκις καὶ τιμῆς τυγχάνουσιν. ἀλλὰ
καὶ τὸ τύπτειν ἐλευθέρους οἱ νόμοι κωλύουσιν· οἱ
ἀθληταὶ δὲ τύπτοντες ἐλευθέρους ἄνδρας, πολλάκις καὶ ἀναιροῦντες, τιμῶν καὶ στεφάνων ἀξιοῦν-
213 ται. νόμος τε παρ' ἡμῖν κελεύει μιᾷ συνοικεῖν
ἕκαστον, Θρᾳκῶν δὲ καὶ Γαιτούλων (Λιβύων δὲ
214 ἔθνος τοῦτο) πολλαῖς ἕκαστος συνοικεῖ. τό τε
ληστεύειν παρ' ἡμῖν μὲν παράνομον καὶ ἄδικόν
ἐστι, παρὰ δὲ πολλοῖς τῶν βαρβάρων οὐκ ἄτοπον.
φασὶ δὲ ὅτι καὶ εὐκλεὲς τοῦτο οἱ Κίλικες ἐνόμιζον
εἶναι, ὡς καὶ τοὺς ἐν λῃστείᾳ τελευτήσαντας τιμῆς
ἀξίους εἶναι δοκεῖν. καὶ ὁ Νέστωρ δὲ παρὰ τῷ
ποιητῇ, μετὰ τὸ φιλοφρονήσασθαι τοὺς περὶ τὸν
Τηλέμαχον, φησὶ πρὸς αὐτοὺς

ἦ μαψιδίως ἀλάλησθε
οἷά τε λῃστῆρες;

καίτοι εἰ ἄτοπον ἦν τὸ ληστεύειν, οὐκ ἂν ⟨ἦν⟩[1]
οὕτως αὐτοὺς φιλοφρονησάμενος διὰ τὸ ὑποπτεύειν
μὴ ἄρα τοιοῦτοί τινες εἶεν.
215 Ἀλλὰ καὶ κλέπτειν [μὲν] παρ' ἡμῖν μὲν ἄδικον
καὶ παράνομόν ἐστιν· οἱ δὲ καὶ κλεπτίστατον εἶναι
θεὸν λέγοντες τὸν Ἑρμῆν οὐκ ἄδικον τοῦτο νομί-
ζεσθαι ποιοῦσιν· πῶς γὰρ ἂν θεὸς εἴη κακός;
φασὶ δέ τινες ὅτι καὶ οἱ Λάκωνες τοὺς κλέπτας

[1] ⟨ἦν⟩ addidi: ⟨ὠνείδισε⟩ post φιλοφρ. cj. Mutsch.

468

are subjects and slaves of their fathers, and that power over the children's property belongs to the fathers and not the children, until the children have obtained their freedom like bought slaves ; but this custom is rejected by others as being despotic. It is the law, too, 212 that homicides should be punished ; but gladiators when they kill often receive actual commendation. Moreover, the laws prevent the striking of free men ; yet when athletes strike free men, and often even kill them, they are deemed worthy of rewards and crowns. With us, too, the law bids each man to 213 have one wife, but amongst the Thracians and Gaetulians (a Libyan tribe) [a] each man has many wives. Piracy, too, is with us illegal and criminal, 214 but with many of the barbarians it is not disapproved. Indeed they say that the Cilicians used to regard it as a noble pursuit, so that they held those who died in the course of piracy to be worthy of honour. So too Nestor—in the poet's account [b]—after welcoming Telemachus and his comrades, addresses them thus—

> Say, are you roaming
> Aimlessly, like sea-rovers ?

Yet, if piracy had been an improper thing, he would not have welcomed them in this friendly way, because of his suspicion that they might be people of that kind.

Moreover, thieving is with us illegal and criminal ; 215 yet those who declare that Hermes is a most thievish god cause this practice to be accounted not criminal— for how could a god be bad ? And some say that the Laconians also punished those who thieved, not be-

[a] Cf. Sallust, Bell. Iug. 21, 82.
[b] Homer, Od. iii. 73. For early Greek piracy cf. Thucyd. i. 5.

ἐκόλαζον οὐ διὰ τὸ κεκλοφέναι ἀλλὰ διὰ τὸ πεφω-
216 ρᾶσθαι. ἀλλὰ καὶ ὁ δειλὸς καὶ ὁ ῥίψασπις ἀνὴρ
κολάζεται παρὰ πολλοῖς νόμῳ· διὸ καὶ ἡ τὴν ἀσπίδα τῷ παιδὶ ἐπὶ πόλεμον ἐξιόντι διδοῦσα Λάκαινα
" σὺ " ἔφη, " τέκνον, ἢ ταύταν ἢ ἐπὶ ταύταν."
Ἀρχίλοχος δέ, ὥσπερ σεμνυνόμενος ἡμῖν ἐπὶ τῷ
τὴν ἀσπίδα ῥίψας φυγεῖν, ἐν τοῖς ποιήμασι περὶ
ἑαυτοῦ φησὶν

ἀσπίδι μὲν Σαΐων τις ἀγάλλεται, ἣν παρὰ θάμνῳ
ἔντος ἀμώμητον κάλλιπον οὐκ ἐθέλων,
αὐτὸς δ᾿ ἐξέφυγον θανάτου τέλος.

217 αἱ δὲ Ἀμαζόνες καὶ ἐχώλευον τὰ ἄρρενα τῶν παρ᾿
αὐταῖς γεννωμένων ὑπὲρ τοῦ μηδὲν ἀνδρεῖον αὐτὰ
ποιῆσαι δύνασθαι, περὶ πόλεμον δὲ ἔσχον αὐταί,
τοῦ ἐναντίου παρ᾿ ἡμῖν καλῶς ἔχειν νενομισμένου.
καὶ ἡ μήτηρ δὲ τῶν θεῶν προσίεται τοὺς θηλυδρίας,
οὐκ ἂν οὕτω κρίνασα ἡ θεός, εἴγε φύσει φαῦλον
218 ἦν τὸ μὴ ἀνδρεῖον εἶναι. οὕτω καὶ τὰ περὶ τῶν
δικαίων καὶ ἀδίκων καὶ τοῦ κατὰ τὴν ἀνδρίαν
καλοῦ πολλὴν ἀνωμαλίαν ἔχει.

Καὶ τὰ περὶ εὐσεβείας δὲ καὶ θεῶν πεπλήρωται
πολλῆς διαφωνίας. θεοὺς γὰρ οἱ μὲν πολλοί φασιν
εἶναι τινὲς δὲ οὐκ εἶναι, ὥσπερ οἱ περὶ Διαγόραν
τὸν Μήλιον καὶ Θεόδωρον καὶ Κριτίαν τὸν Ἀθη-
ναῖον. καὶ τῶν εἶναι θεοὺς ἀποφηναμένων οἱ μὲν
τοὺς πατρίους νομίζουσι θεούς, οἱ δὲ τοὺς ἐν ταῖς

---

[a] A. of Paros, famous for his iambic poems, *circa* 680 b.c.
Alcaeus, a later poet, also flung away his shield in battle;
and Hor. *Od.* ii. 7 is based on one or other of these incidents.
[b] *Cf.* Hdt. iv. 114.
[c] Cybele, whose priests were eunuchs, *cf.* Catullus 63.

cause they had thieved, but because they had been found out. Moreover, the coward and the man 216 who throws away his shield are in many places punished by law; and this is why the Laconian mother, when giving a shield to her son as he set out for the war, said, "Either with this, my child, or upon it." Yet Archilochus,[a] as though vaunting to us of his flight after flinging away his shield, speaks thus of himself in his poems—

> Over my shield some Saïan warrior gloats,—
> The shield I left, though loth, beside the bush—
> A flawless piece of armour; I myself
> Fled and escaped from death which endeth all.

And the Amazons[b] used to maim the males amongst 217 their offspring so as to make them incapable of any manly action, while they themselves attended to warfare; though with us the opposite practice is regarded as right. The Mother of the gods,[c] also, approves of effeminates, and the goddess would not have decided thus if unmanliness were naturally a bad thing. So it is that, in regard to justice and 218 injustice and the excellence of manliness, there is a great variety of opinion.

Around all matters of religion and theology also, there rages violent controversy.[d] For while the majority declare that gods exist, some deny their existence, like Diagoras of Melos, and Theodorus, and Critias the Athenian.[e] And of those who maintain the existence of gods, some believe in the ancestral gods, others in such as are constructed

---

[d] Cf. for this subject Adv. Phys. i. 13 ff., 50 ff.

[e] Diagoras, atomist and poet, circa 420 B.C.; Theodorus, a Cyrenaic, circa 310 B.C.; Critias, orator and poet, one of the "Thirty Tyrants" (404 B.C.) of Athens.

δογματικαῖς αἱρέσεσιν ἀναπλασσομένους, ὡς ᾿Αρι-
στοτέλης μὲν ἀσώματον εἶπεν εἶναι τὸν θεὸν καὶ
πέρας τοῦ οὐρανοῦ, στωικοὶ δὲ πνεῦμα διῆκον καὶ
διὰ τῶν εἰδεχθῶν, ᾿Επίκουρος δὲ ἀνθρωπόμορφον,
219 Ξενοφάνης δὲ σφαῖραν ἀπαθῆ. καὶ οἱ μὲν προνοεῖν τῶν καθ᾿ ἡμᾶς, οἱ δὲ μὴ προνοεῖν· τὸ γὰρ
μακάριον καὶ ἄφθαρτον ὁ ᾿Επίκουρός φησι μήτε
αὐτὸ πράγματα ἔχειν μήτε ἑτέροις παρέχειν. ὅθεν
καὶ τῶν κατὰ τὸν βίον οἱ μὲν ἕνα φασὶν εἶναι θεόν,
οἱ δὲ πολλοὺς καὶ διαφόρους ταῖς μορφαῖς, ὡς
καὶ εἰς τὰς τῶν Αἰγυπτίων ὑπολήψεις ἐκπίπτειν,
κυνοπροσώπους καὶ ἱερακομόρφους καὶ βόας καὶ
κροκοδείλους καὶ τί γὰρ οὐχὶ νομιζόντων τοὺς
θεούς.
220 Ὅθεν καὶ τὰ περὶ θυσιῶν καὶ τῆς περὶ τοὺς
θεοὺς θρησκείας ὅλως πολλὴν ἀνωμαλίαν ἔχει· ἃ
γὰρ ἔν τισιν ἱεροῖς ὅσια, ταῦτα ἐν ἑτέροις ἀνόσια.
καίτοι εἰ φύσει τὸ ὅσιον καὶ τὸ ἀνόσιον ἦν, οὐκ ἂν
τοῦτο ἐνομίσθη. οἷον γοῦν Σαράπιδι χοῖρον οὐκ
ἂν θύσειέ τις, ῾Ηρακλεῖ δὲ καὶ ᾿Ασκληπιῷ θύουσιν.
πρόβατον ῎Ισιδι θύειν ἄθεσμον, τῇ μητρὶ μέντοι
λεγομένῃ τῶν θεῶν καὶ θεοῖς ἄλλοις καλλιερεῖται.
221 τῷ Κρόνῳ ⟨οἱ Καρχηδόνιοι⟩[1] θύουσιν ἄνθρωπον,
ὃ τοῖς πλείστοις ἀσεβὲς εἶναι νομίζεται. αἴλουρον
ἐν ᾿Αλεξανδρείᾳ τῷ ῞Ωρῳ θύουσι, καὶ Θέτιδι
σίλφην· ὃ παρ᾿ ἡμῖν οὐκ ἂν ποιήσειέ τις. ἵππον

---

[1] ⟨οἱ Καρχηδόνιοι⟩ addidi: ⟨τινὲς δὲ⟩ ante τῷ cj. Mutsch.

[a] This definition of God is not in our Aristotle, but cf. De
caelo, i. 9, 278 b 14: "We are wont to give the name of
'Heaven' especially to the outermost and highest (part of
the Universe), in which all the Divinity, we say, is situated."

in the Dogmatic systems—as Aristotle asserted
that God is incorporeal and " the limit of heaven,"[a]
the Stoics that he is a breath which permeates even
through things foul, Epicurus that he is anthropomorphic,[b] Xenophanes that he is an impassive sphere.
Some, too, hold that he cares for human affairs, others 219
that he does not so care ; for Epicurus declares that
"what is blessed and incorruptible neither feels trouble
itself nor causes it to others." Hence ordinary people
differ also, some saying that there is one god, others
that there are many gods and of various shapes ;
in fact, they even come to share the notions of the
Egyptians [c] who believe in gods that are dog-faced, or
hawk-shaped, or cows or crocodiles or anything else.

Hence, too, sacrificial usages, and the ritual of wor- 220
ship in general, exhibit great diversity. For things
which are in some cults accounted holy are in others
accounted unholy. But this would not have been so
if the holy and the unholy existed by nature. Thus,
for example, no one would sacrifice a pig to Sarapis,
but they sacrifice it to Heracles and Asclepius. To
sacrifice a sheep to Isis is forbidden, but it is offered
up in honour of the so-called Mother of the gods
and of other deities. To Cronos [d] a human victim is 221
sacrificed ⟨at Carthage⟩, although this is regarded by
most as an impious act. In Alexandria they offer a
cat to Horus and a beetle to Thetis—a thing which
no one here would do. To Poseidon they sacrifice a

It is this outermost circumference—the abode of Fire, the
finest and most divine of elements—which is here termed
" the limit " ($\pi\acute{\epsilon}\rho\alpha\varsigma$).

[b] *Cf.* Diog. Laert. vii. 138 f. (Stoics), x. 139 (Epicureans).
For Xenophanes *cf.* i. 225.

[c] *Cf.* Hdt. ii. 41, Juvenal xv. 2 ff.

[d] *Cf.* § 208 *supra.*

τῷ Ποσειδῶνι καλλιεροῦσιν· Ἀπόλλωνι δέ, ἐξαιρέτως τῷ Διδυμαίῳ, τὸ ζῷον ἀπεχθές. αἶγας Ἀρτέμιδι θύειν εὐσεβές, ἀλλ' οὐκ Ἀσκληπιῷ.

222 καὶ ἄλλα δὲ τούτοις ὅμοια παμπληθῆ λέγειν ἔχων ἐῶ, τῆς συντομίας [παρα]στοχαζόμενος. εἰ μέντοι τι ἦν ὅσιον φύσει θῦμα καὶ ἀνόσιον, παρὰ πᾶσιν ἂν ὁμοίως ἐνομίζετο.

Παραπλήσια δὲ τούτοις ἔστιν εὑρεῖν καὶ τὰ ἐν τῇ κατὰ τὴν δίαιταν τῶν ἀνθρώπων θρησκείᾳ περὶ

223 τοὺς θεούς. Ἰουδαῖος μὲν γὰρ ἢ ἱερεὺς Αἰγύπτιος θᾶττον ἂν ἀποθάνοι ἢ χοίρειον φάγοι, Λίβυς δὲ προβατείου γεύσασθαι κρέως τῶν ἀθεσμοτάτων εἶναι δοκεῖ, Σύρων δέ τινες περιστερᾶς, ἄλλοι δὲ ἱερείων. ἰχθῦς τε ἐν τισὶ μὲν ἱεροῖς θέμις ἐσθίειν, ἐν ἄλλοις δὲ ἀσεβές. Αἰγυπτίων δὲ τῶν σοφῶν εἶναι νενομισμένων οἱ μὲν κεφαλὴν ζῴου φαγεῖν ἀνίερον εἶναι νομίζουσιν, οἱ δὲ ὠμοπλάτην, οἱ δὲ

224 πόδα, οἱ δὲ ἄλλο τι. κρόμμυον δὲ οὐκ ἄν τις προσενέγκαιτο τῶν καθιερουμένων τῷ κατὰ Πηλούσιον Κασίῳ Διί, ὥσπερ οὐδὲ ἱερεὺς τῆς κατὰ Λιβύην Ἀφροδίτης σκορόδου γεύσαιτο ἄν. ἀπέχονται δὲ ἐν οἷς μὲν ἱεροῖς μίνθης, ἐν οἷς δὲ ἡδυόσμου, ἐν οἷς δὲ σελίνου. ἔνιοι δὲ θᾶττον ἂν τὰς κεφαλὰς φαγεῖν φασι τῶν πατέρων ἢ κυάμους.

225 ἀλλὰ παρ' ἑτέροις ταῦτα ἀδιάφορα. κυνείων τε γεύσασθαι δοκοῦμεν ἡμεῖς ἀνίερον εἶναι, Θρακῶν δὲ ἔνιοι κυνοφαγεῖν ἱστοροῦνται. ἴσως δὲ καὶ παρ' Ἕλλησι τοῦτο ἦν σύνηθες· διόπερ καὶ Διοκλῆς ἀπὸ τῶν κατὰ τοὺς Ἀσκληπιάδας ὁρμώμενος τισὶ τῶν

ᵃ i.e. of Didymus, near Miletus.
ᵇ Cf. Hdt. ii. 47.   ᶜ Cf. Hdt. ii. 39.
ᵈ Cf. Juv. xv. 9.   ᵉ East of the Nile Delta.

horse; but to Apollo (especially the Didymaean [a] Apollo) that animal is an abomination. It is an act of piety to offer goats to Artemis, but not to Asclepius. And I might add a host of similar instances, but I 222 forbear since my aim is to be brief. Yet surely, if a sacrifice had been holy by nature or unholy, it would have been deemed so by all men alike.

Examples similar to these may also be found in the religious observances with regard to human diet. For a Jew or an Egyptian priest [b] would sooner die 223 than eat swine's flesh; by a Libyan it is regarded as a most impious thing to taste the meat of a sheep, by some of the Syrians to eat a dove, and by others to eat sacrificial victims. And in certain cults it is lawful, but in others impious, to eat fish. And amongst the Egyptians some of those who are reputed to be sages believe it is sinful to eat an animal's head,[c] others the shoulder, others the foot, others some other part. And no one would bring an onion [d] 224 as an offering to Zeus Casius of Pelusium,[e] just as no priest of the Libyan Aphrodite would taste garlic. And in some cults they abstain from mint, in others from catmint, in others from parsley. And some declare that they would sooner eat their fathers' heads than beans.[f] Yet, amongst others, these things 225 are indifferent. Eating dog's flesh, too, is thought by us to be sinful, but some of the Thracians are reported to be dog-eaters. Possibly this practice was customary also amongst the Greeks; and on this account Diocles, too, starting from the practices of the Asclepiadae,[g] prescribes that hounds' flesh should

[f] *Cf.* Emped. *Frag.* 141; probably a Pythagorean (or Orphic) " taboo "; *cf.* Hdt. ii. 37.
[g] The earliest Greek medical guild; Diocles was a famous physician of the fourth century B.C.

SEXTUS EMPIRICUS

πασχόντων σκυλάκεια δίδοσθαι κελεύει κρέα. τινὲς δὲ καὶ ἀνθρώπων σάρκας, ὡς ἔφην, ἀδιαφόρως ἐσθίουσιν, ὅπερ ἀνίερον παρ' ἡμῖν εἶναι νενόμισται. 226 καίτοι εἴγε ἦν φύσει τὰ τῆς θρησκείας καὶ τῶν ἀθέσμων, παρὰ πᾶσιν ἂν ὁμοίως ἐνομίζετο.

Παραπλήσια δὲ ἔστι λέγειν καὶ περὶ τῆς εἰς τοὺς κατοιχομένους ὁσιότητος. οἱ μὲν γὰρ ὁλοκλήρως περιστείλαντες τοὺς ἀποθανόντας γῇ καλύπτουσιν, ἀσεβὲς εἶναι νομίζοντες ἡλίῳ δεικνύειν αὐτούς· Αἰγύπτιοι δὲ τὰ ἔντερα ἐξελόντες ταριχεύουσιν αὐτοὺς καὶ σὺν ἑαυτοῖς ὑπὲρ γῆς ἔχουσιν. 227 Αἰθιόπων δὲ οἱ ἰχθυοφάγοι εἰς τὰς λίμνας ἐμβάλλουσιν αὐτούς, ὑπὸ τῶν ἰχθύων βρωθησομένους· Ὑρκανοὶ δὲ κυσὶν αὐτοὺς ἐκτίθενται βοράν, Ἰνδῶν δὲ ἔνιοι γυψίν. Τρωγλοδύτας δέ φασιν ἐπί τινα γεώλοφον ἄγειν τὸν ἀποθανόντα, εἶτα δεσμεύσαντας αὐτοῦ τὴν κεφαλὴν πρὸς τοὺς πόδας λίθοις βάλλειν μετὰ γέλωτος, εἶθ' ὅταν χώσωσιν αὐτὸν τοῖς βαλ- 228 λομένοις ἀπαλλάσσεσθαι. τινὲς δὲ βάρβαροι τοὺς μὲν ὑπὲρ ἑξήκοντα ἔτη γεγονότας θύσαντες ἐσθίουσιν, τοὺς δὲ ἐν νεότητι ἀποθανόντας γῇ κρύπτουσιν. ἔνιοι δὲ καίουσι τοὺς τετελευτηκότας· ὧν οἱ μὲν ἀναλαβόντες αὐτῶν τὰ ὀστέα κηδεύουσιν, οἱ δὲ ἀφροντίστως καταλείπουσιν ἐρριμμένα. Πέρσας δέ φασιν ἀνασκολοπίζειν τοὺς ἀποθανόντας καὶ νίτρῳ ταριχεύειν, εἶθ' οὕτω τελαμῶσι συνειλεῖν. ἄλλοι δὲ ὅσον πένθος ἐπὶ τοῖς τελευτήσασιν ὑπομένουσιν ὁρῶμεν.

---

[a] § 207 *supra*.

be given to certain patients. And some, as I have said,[a] even eat human flesh indifferently, a thing which with us is accounted sinful. Yet, if the rules 226 of ritual and of unlawful foods had existed by nature, they would have been observed by all men alike.

A similar account may be given of reverence towards the departed.[b] Some wrap the dead up completely and then cover them with earth, thinking that it is impious to expose them to the sun; but the Egyptians take out their entrails and embalm them and keep them above ground with themselves. The fish-eating tribes of the Ethiopians cast them 227 into the lakes, there to be devoured by the fish; the Hyrcanians[c] expose them as a prey to dogs, and some of the Indians to vultures. And they say that some of the Troglodytes[d] take the corpse to a hill, and then after tying its head to its feet cast stones upon it amidst laughter, and when they have made a heap of stones over it they leave it there. And some 228 of the barbarians[e] slay and eat those who are over sixty years old, but bury in the earth those who die young. Some burn the dead; and of these some recover and preserve their bones,[f] while others show no care but leave them scattered about. And they say that the Persians[g] impale their dead and embalm them with nitre, after which they wrap them round in bandages. How much grief others endure for the dead we see ourselves.

[b] For this subject cf. Diog. Laert. ix. 84; Cic. Tusc. i. 45; Sir T. Browne, Hydriotaphia, chap. i.

[c] South of the Caspian Sea.

[d] i.e. "cave-dwellers" of west coast of the Red Sea.

[e] Cf. § 210 supra.

[f] Cf. Tibull. iii. 2. 17 for the practice of ossilegium.

[g] Cf. Hdt. i. 140.

229 Καὶ τὸν θάνατον δὲ αὐτὸν οἱ μὲν δεινὸν καὶ
φευκτὸν εἶναι νομίζουσιν, οἱ δὲ οὐ τοιοῦτον. ὁ
γοῦν Εὐριπίδης φησὶν

τίς δ' οἶδεν εἰ τὸ ζῆν μέν ἐστι κατθανεῖν,
τὸ κατθανεῖν δὲ ζῆν κάτω νομίζεται;

καὶ ὁ Ἐπίκουρος δέ φησιν " ὁ θάνατος οὐδὲν πρὸς
ἡμᾶς· τὸ γὰρ διαλυθὲν ἀναισθητεῖ, τὸ δὲ ἀναισθη-
τοῦν οὐδὲν πρὸς ἡμᾶς." φασὶ δὲ καὶ ὡς εἴπερ
συνεστήκαμεν ἐκ ψυχῆς καὶ σώματος, ὁ δὲ θάνατος
διάλυσίς ἐστι ψυχῆς καὶ σώματος, ὅτε μὲν ἡμεῖς
ἐσμέν, οὐκ ἔστιν ὁ θάνατος (οὐ γὰρ διαλυόμεθα),
ὅτε δὲ ὁ θάνατος ἔστιν, οὐκ ἐσμὲν ἡμεῖς· τῷ γὰρ
μηκέτι τὴν σύστασιν εἶναι τῆς ψυχῆς καὶ τοῦ
230 σώματος οὐδὲ ἡμεῖς ἐσμέν. ὁ δὲ Ἡράκλειτός
φησιν ὅτι καὶ τὸ ζῆν καὶ τὸ ἀποθανεῖν καὶ ἐν τῷ
ζῆν ἡμᾶς ἐστὶ καὶ ἐν τῷ τεθνάναι· ὅτε μὲν γὰρ
ἡμεῖς ζῶμεν, τὰς ψυχὰς ἡμῶν τεθνάναι καὶ ἐν
ἡμῖν τεθάφθαι, ὅτε δὲ ἡμεῖς ἀποθνήσκομεν, τὰς
ψυχὰς ἀναβιοῦν καὶ ζῆν. ἔνιοι δὲ καὶ βέλτιον
εἶναι τὸ ἀποθανεῖν τοῦ ζῆν ἡμᾶς ὑπολαμβάνουσιν.
ὁ γοῦν Εὐριπίδης φησὶν

ἐχρῆν γὰρ ἡμᾶς σύλλογον ποιουμένους
τὸν φύντα θρηνεῖν, εἰς ὅσ' ἔρχεται κακά,
τὸν δ' αὖ θανόντα καὶ κακῶν πεπαυμένον
χαίροντας εὐφημοῦντας ἐκπέμπειν δόμων.

231 ἀπὸ δὲ τῆς αὐτῆς ὑπολήψεως καὶ ταῦτα εἴρηται·

_____

ᵃ Eurip. *Frag.* 638 (Nauck).
ᵇ Epic. p. 61. 6 ; 71. 6 (Usener); *cf.* Lucret. iii. 830.

Some, too, believe death itself to be dreadful and 229
horrible, others do not. Thus Euripides says [a]:

> Who knows if life be but the state of death,
> And death be counted life in realms below?

And Epicurus [b] declares: " Death is nothing to us;
for what is dissolved is senseless, and what is senseless
is nothing to us." They also declare that, inasmuch as
we are compounded of soul and body, and death is a
dissolution of soul and body, when we exist death
does not exist (for we are not being dissolved), and
when death exists we do not exist, for through the
cessation of the compound of soul and body we too
cease to exist. And Heracleitus [c] states that both life 230
and death exist both in our state of life and in our
state of death ; for when we live our souls are dead
and buried within us, and when we die our souls
revive and live. And some even suppose that dying
is better for us than living. Thus Euripides says [d]:

> Rather should we assemble to bewail
> The babe new-born, such ills has he to face ;
> Whereas the dead, who has surcease from woe,
> With joy and gladness we should bear from home.

These lines, too, spring from the same sentiment [e]: 231

---

[c] *Cf.* Heracl. *Frag.* 67, 78 (B 88 Diels). Part of the
" Upward and Downward Way " of H. (see Introd. p. viii)
is the cycle of generation by which every creature is simultaneously both living and dying. The soul, which consists
of " fire," is continually passing into the other elements,
and the other elements into it. But the second clause (" for
when we live " etc.) looks rather like a contamination of
Heracleitus's doctrine with the $\sigma\hat{\omega}\mu\alpha$—$\sigma\hat{\eta}\mu\alpha$ (" body a tomb ")
theory of Pythagoreanism.

[d] *Frag.* 449 ; *cf.* Cic. *Tusc.* i. 48, Lucr. v. 222 ff.

[e] Theognis 425 ff. ; *cf.* Soph. *Oed. Col.* 1227.

ἀρχὴν μὲν μὴ φῦναι ἐπιχθονίοισιν ἄριστον,
μηδ' ἐσιδεῖν αὐγὰς ὀξέος ἠελίου,
φύντα δ' ὅπως ὤκιστα πύλας Ἀΐδαο περῆσαι
καὶ κεῖσθαι πολλὴν γαῖαν ἐφεσσάμενον.

καὶ τὰ περὶ Κλέοβιν δὲ καὶ Βίτωνα ἴσμεν, ἅ φησιν
ὁ Ἡρόδοτος ἐν τῷ περὶ τῆς Ἀργείας ἱερείας λόγῳ.
232 ἱστοροῦνται δὲ καὶ Θρᾳκῶν ἔνιοι περικαθεσθέντες
τὸν γεννηθέντα θρηνεῖν. οὐδὲ ὁ θάνατος οὖν τῶν
φύσει δεινῶν εἶναι νομίζοιτο ἄν, ὥσπερ οὐδὲ τὸ ζῆν
τῶν φύσει καλῶν. οὐδὲ τῶν προειρημένων τί ἐστι
φύσει τοῖον ἢ τοῖον, νομιστὰ δὲ πάντα καὶ πρός τι.
233 Τὸν αὐτὸν δὲ τρόπον τῆς ἐπιχειρήσεως μεταφέρειν ἔστι καὶ ἐφ' ἕκαστον τῶν ἄλλων, ἃ μὴ
ἐξεθέμεθα νῦν διὰ τὴν συντομίαν τοῦ λόγου. εἰ
δὲ καὶ περί τινων μὴ ἔχομεν εἰπεῖν αὐτόθεν ἀνωμαλίαν, λεκτέον ὅτι ἔν τισιν ἔθνεσιν ἀγνοουμένοις
ἡμῖν ἐνδέχεται καὶ περὶ αὐτῶν εἶναι διαφωνίαν.
234 ὡς οὖν εἰ μὴ ἐγιγνώσκομεν, εἰ τύχοι, τὸ περὶ τοῦ
τὰς ἀδελφὰς γαμεῖν τῶν Αἰγυπτίων ἔθος, οὐκ ἂν
ὀρθῶς διεβεβαιούμεθα ὁμολογούμενον παρὰ πᾶσιν
εἶναι τὸ μὴ δεῖν ἀδελφὰς γαμεῖν, οὕτως οὐδὲ περὶ
τῶν πραγμάτων ἐκείνων ἐν οἷς οὐχ ὑποπίπτουσιν
ἡμῖν ἀνωμαλίαι διαβεβαιοῦσθαι προσήκει μὴ εἶναι
διαφωνίαν ἐν αὐτοῖς, ἐνδεχομένου, καθάπερ ἔφην,
τοῦ παρά τισιν ἔθνεσι τῶν ἡμῖν μὴ γινωσκομένων
τὴν περὶ αὐτῶν εἶναι διαφωνίαν.

---

[a] Cf. Hdt. i. 31 ; Cic. Tusc. i. 47. Their mother Cydippe
(the " Argive priestess " of Hera) prayed the goddess to grant
her sons, C. and B., the best of boons for mortals : the same
night both died in their sleep.

> Not to have been begotten at all were the best thing for mortals,
> Nor to have lookèd upon fiery rays of the sun :
> Or, if begotten, to hasten amain to the portals of Hades,
> And to lie unmoved robèd in masses of earth.

We know, too, the facts about Cleobis and Biton which Herodotus [a] relates in his story of the Argive priestess. It is reported, also, that some of the 232 Thracians sit round the new-born babe and chant dirges.[b] So, then, death should not be considered a thing naturally dreadful, just as life should not be considered a thing naturally good. Thus none of the things mentioned above is naturally of this character or of that, but all are matters of convention and relative.

The same method of treatment may be applied also 233 to each of the other customs, which we have not now described owing to the summary character of our exposition. And even if, in regard to some of them, we are unable to declare their discrepancy offhand, we ought to observe that disagreement concerning them may possibly exist amongst certain nations that are unknown to us.[c] For just as, if we had been 234 ignorant, say, of the custom amongst the Egyptians of marrying sisters,[d] we should have asserted wrongly that it was universally agreed that men ought not to marry sisters,—even so, in regard to those practices wherein we notice no discrepancy, it is not proper for us to affirm that there is no disagreement about them, since, as I said, disagreement about them may possibly exist amongst some of the nations which are unknown to us.

* *Cf.* Hdt. v. 4.   c *Cf.* ii. 40.
          d *Cf.* § 205 *supra.*

SEXTUS EMPIRICUS

235 Ὁ τοίνυν σκεπτικὸς τὴν τοσαύτην ἀνωμαλίαν
τῶν πραγμάτων ὁρῶν ἐπέχει μὲν περὶ τοῦ φύσει
τι ἀγαθὸν ἢ κακὸν ἢ ὅλως πρακτέον ἢ μὴ πρακτέον
εἶναι, κἂν τούτῳ τῆς δογματικῆς ἀφιστάμενος προ-
πετείας, ἕπεται δὲ ἀδοξάστως τῇ βιωτικῇ τηρήσει,
καὶ διὰ τοῦτο ἐν μὲν τοῖς δοξαστοῖς ἀπαθὴς μένει,
236 ἐν δὲ τοῖς κατηναγκασμένοις μετριοπαθεῖ· ὡς μὲν
γὰρ ἄνθρωπος αἰσθητικῶς[1] πάσχει, μὴ προσδοξά-
ζων δὲ ὅτι τοῦτο ὃ πάσχει κακόν ἐστι φύσει; με-
τριοπαθεῖ. τὸ γὰρ προσδοξάζειν τι τοιοῦτο χεῖρόν
ἐστι καὶ αὐτοῦ τοῦ πάσχειν, ὡς ἐνίοτε τοὺς μὲν
τεμνομένους ἢ ἄλλο τι τοιοῦτο πάσχοντας φέρειν,
τοὺς δὲ παρεστῶτας διὰ τὴν περὶ τοῦ γινομένου
237 δόξαν ὡς φαύλου λειποψυχεῖν. ὁ μέντοι γε ὑπο-
θέμενος τὸ φύσει τι ἀγαθὸν ἢ κακὸν ἢ ὅλως πρακτέον ἢ μὴ πρακτέον εἶναι ταράσσεται ποικίλως.
καὶ γὰρ παρόντων αὐτῷ τούτων ἃ νομίζει φύσει
κακὰ εἶναι ποινηλατεῖσθαι δοκεῖ, καὶ τῶν φαινομένων ἀγαθῶν αὐτῷ γινόμενος ἐγκρατὴς ὑπό τε
τοῦ τύφου καὶ τοῦ περὶ τὴν ἀποβολὴν αὐτῶν φόβου,
καὶ εὐλαβούμενος μὴ πάλιν ἐν τοῖς φύσει κακοῖς
νομιζομένοις παρ' αὐτῷ γένηται, ταραχαῖς οὐχὶ
238 ταῖς τυχούσαις περιπίπτει· τοὺς γὰρ ἀναπόβλητα
εἶναι τὰ ἀγαθὰ λέγοντας ἐφέξομεν ἐκ τῆς ἀπορίας τῆς κατὰ τὴν διαφωνίαν. ὅθεν ἐπιλογιζόμεθα
ὅτι εἰ τὸ κακοῦ ποιητικὸν κακόν ἐστι καὶ φευκτόν,
ἡ δὲ πεποίθησις τοῦ τάδε μὲν εἶναι φύσει ἀγαθὰ

---

[1] αἰσθητικῶς Heintz : αἰσθητικὸς mss., Bekk.

ᵃ *Cf.* i. 13, 25 ff.

Accordingly, the Sceptic, seeing so great a diversity 235
of usages, suspends judgement as to the natural
existence of anything good or bad or (in general) fit
or unfit to be done, therein abstaining from the rashness of dogmatism[a]; and he follows undogmatically
the ordinary rules of life, and because of this he
remains impassive in respect of matters of opinion,
while in conditions that are necessitated his emotions
are moderate; for though, as a human being, he 236
suffers emotion through his senses, yet because he
does not also opine that what he suffers is evil by
nature, the emotion he suffers is moderate. For the
added opinion that a thing is of such a kind is worse
than the actual suffering itself, just as sometimes the
patients themselves bear a surgical operation, while
the bystanders swoon away because of their opinion
that it is a horrible experience. But, in fact, he who 237
assumes that there exists by nature something good
or bad or, generally, fit or unfit to be done, is disquieted in various ways. For when he experiences
what he regards as natural evils he deems himself to
be pursued by Furies, and when he becomes possessed
of what seems to him good things he falls into no
ordinary state of disquiet both through arrogance and
through fear of losing them, and through trying to
guard against finding himself again amongst what he
regards as natural evils; for those who assert that goods 238
are incapable of being lost[b] we shall put to silence
by means of the doubts raised by their dissension.
Hence we conclude that if what is productive of evil
is evil and to be shunned, and the persuasion that
these things are good, those evil, by nature produces

[b] So said the Cynics, and some Stoics; other Stoics gave
up the doctrine; *cf.* Diog. Laert. vi. 105, vii. 127.

SEXTUS EMPIRICUS

τάδε δὲ κακὰ ταραχὰς ποιεῖ, κακόν ἐστι καὶ
φευκτὸν τὸ ὑποτίθεσθαι καὶ πεποιθέναι φαῦλόν τι
ἢ ἀγαθὸν ὡς πρὸς τὴν φύσιν εἶναι.

Ταῦτα μὲν οὖν ἐπὶ τοῦ παρόντος ἀρκεῖ λελέχθαι
περὶ ἀγαθῶν καὶ κακῶν καὶ ἀδιαφόρων.

ΚΕ΄.—ΕΙ ΕΣΤΙ ΤΕΧΝΗ ΠΕΡΙ ΒΙΟΝ

239 Δῆλον δὲ ἐκ τῶν προειρημένων ὅτι οὐδὲ τέχνη
τις ἂν εἴη περὶ τὸν βίον. εἰ γὰρ ἔστι τοιαύτη
τέχνη, περὶ τὴν θεωρίαν τῶν τε ἀγαθῶν καὶ τῶν
κακῶν καὶ τῶν ἀδιαφόρων ἔχει· διὸ τούτων ἀνυπάρκτων ὄντων ἀνύπαρκτός ἐστι καὶ ἡ περὶ τὸν
βίον τέχνη. καὶ ἄλλως, ἐπεὶ μὴ ὁμοφώνως μίαν
ἀπολείπουσι πάντες οἱ δογματικοὶ τέχνην περὶ τὸν
βίον, ἀλλ' ἄλλοι ἄλλην ὑποτίθενται, ὑποπίπτουσι
τῇ διαφωνίᾳ καὶ τῷ ἀπὸ τῆς διαφωνίας λόγῳ, ὃν
ἠρώτησα ἐν τοῖς περὶ τἀγαθοῦ λελεγμένοις ἡμῖν.
240 εἰ μέντοι καὶ μίαν εἶναι πάντες λέγοιεν καθ' ὑπόθεσιν τὴν περὶ τὸν βίον τέχνην, οἷον τὴν ἀοίδιμον
φρόνησιν, ἥτις ὀνειροπολεῖται μὲν παρὰ στωικοῖς,
μᾶλλον δὲ πληκτικωτέρα τῶν ἄλλων εἶναι δοκεῖ,
καὶ οὕτως οὐδὲν ἧττον ἀτοπίαι παρακολουθήσουσιν.
ἐπεὶ γὰρ φρόνησίς ἐστιν ἀρετή, τὴν δὲ ἀρετὴν
μόνος εἶχεν ὁ σοφός, οἱ στωικοὶ μὴ ὄντες σοφοὶ
241 οὐχ ἕξουσι τὴν περὶ τὸν βίον τέχνην. ὅλως τε,
ἐπεὶ μὴ δύναται κατ' αὐτοὺς ὑποστῆναι τέχνη, οὐδὲ
περὶ τὸν βίον ἔσται τέχνη τις ὅσον ἐφ' οἷς λέγουσιν.

Οἷον γοῦν τέχνην εἶναί φασι σύστημα ἐκ κατα-

---

[a] Cf. Adv. Eth. 167 ff. ; Cic. De fin. i. 13, v. 6 ff.
[b] Cf. §§ 180, 238 supra.
[c] For the sage as " indiscoverable " cf. Adv. Phys. i. 133,
Introd. p. xxix. " Prudence " (φρόνησις), or " practical
484

disquiet, then the assumption and persuasion that anything is, in its real nature, either bad or good is evil and to be shunned.

For the present, then, this account of things good, evil, and indifferent is sufficient.

CHAPTER XXIII.—DOES THERE EXIST AN ART OF LIVING?

It is plain from what has been said above that there 239 can be no art of living.[a] For if such an art exists, it has to do with the consideration of things good, evil, and indifferent, so that these being non-existent the art of living also is non-existent. Further, since the Dogmatists do not all with one accord lay down one single art of living, but some propound one art, some another, they are guilty of discrepancy and open to the argument from discrepancy which I stated in our discussion of the Good.[b] Yet, even if they were 240 all to agree in assuming that the art of living is one —such as, for example, the celebrated " prudence " whereof the Stoics dream, and which seems to be more convincing than all the rest,—even so equally absurd results will follow. For since " prudence " is a virtue, and the Sage alone was in possession of virtue, the Stoics, not being sages,[c] will not be in possession of the art of living. And in general, since, according 241 to them, no art[d] can have real existence, an art of living cannot exist, so far as their statements go.

Thus, for example, they declare that art is " a com-

wisdom," is distinguished from " wisdom " (σοφία). Note that in this argument " the art of living " is identified with " prudence."

[d] *Cf.* §§ 188 ff. ; ii. 53 ff.

SEXTUS EMPIRICUS

λήψεων, κατάληψιν δὲ καταληπτικῇ φαντασίᾳ
συγκατάθεσιν. ἀνεύρετος δέ ἐστιν ἡ καταληπτικὴ
φαντασία· οὔτε γὰρ πᾶσα φαντασία καταληπτική
ἐστιν, οὔτε ποία τίς ἐστιν ἀπὸ τῶν φαντασιῶν ἡ
καταληπτικὴ φαντασία ἐπιγνωσθῆναι δύναται, ἐπεὶ
μήτε πάσῃ φαντασίᾳ δυνάμεθα κρίνειν ἁπλῶς τίς
μέν ἐστι καταληπτικὴ τίς δὲ οὐ τοιαύτη, χρῄζοντές
τε καταληπτικῆς φαντασίας εἰς τὴν ἐπίγνωσιν τοῦ
ποία τίς ἐστιν ἡ καταληπτικὴ φαντασία εἰς ἄπειρον
ἐκβαλλόμεθα, εἰς ἐπίγνωσιν τῆς λαμβανομένης ὡς
καταληπτικῆς φαντασίας καταληπτικὴν φαντασίαν
242 ἄλλην αἰτούμενοι. ταῦτά τοι καὶ οἱ στωικοὶ ἐν τῇ
τῆς καταληπτικῆς φαντασίας ἐννοίας ἀποδόσει οὐχ
ὑγιῶς φέρονται· καταληπτικὴν μὲν γὰρ φαντασίαν
λέγοντες τὴν ἀπὸ ὑπάρχοντος γινομένην, ὑπάρχον
δὲ εἶναι λέγοντες ὃ οἷόν τε κινεῖν καταληπτικὴν
φαντασίαν, εἰς τὸν διάλληλον ἐμπίπτουσι τῆς
ἀπορίας τρόπον. εἰ τοίνυν, ἵνα μὲν περὶ τὸν βίον
ᾖ τις τέχνη, δεῖ πρότερον εἶναι τέχνην, ἵνα δὲ
ὑποστῇ τέχνη, κατάληψιν προϋφεστάναι, ἵνα δὲ
ὑποστῇ κατάληψις, καταληπτικῇ φαντασίᾳ συγκατάθεσιν κατειλῆφθαι, ἀνεύρετος δέ ἐστιν ἡ καταληπτικὴ φαντασία, ἀνεύρετός ἐστιν ἡ περὶ τὸν βίον
τέχνη.

243 Ἔτι κἀκεῖνο λέγεται. πᾶσα τέχνη ἐκ τῶν ἰδίως
ὑπ᾽ αὐτῆς ἀποδιδομένων ἔργων καταλαμβάνεσθαι
δοκεῖ, οὐδὲν δέ ἐστιν ἴδιον ἔργον τῆς περὶ τὸν βίον
τέχνης· ὃ γὰρ ἂν ἔργον εἶναι ταύτης λέγῃ τις, τοῦτο
κοινὸν εὑρίσκεται καὶ τῶν ἰδιωτῶν, οἷον τὸ τιμᾶν
γονεῖς, τὸ παραθήκας ἀποδιδόναι, τἆλλα πάντα.
οὐκ ἄρα ἔστι τις περὶ τὸν βίον τέχνη. οὔτε γὰρ

ᵃ Cf. ii. 4, 53 ff., Introd. p. xxv.

posite of apprehensions," and apprehension is "assent to an apprehensive impression." [a] But the apprehensive impression is indiscoverable ; for every impression is not apprehensive, nor is it possible to decide which one of the impressions is the apprehensive impression, since we cannot simply decide by means of every impression which one is apprehensive and which not, while if we require an apprehensive impression in order to determine which is the apprehensive impression we are wrecked on the *ad infinitum* fallacy, since we are asking for another apprehensive impression so as to determine the impression taken to be apprehensive. And herein, too, the procedure of the Stoics, 242 in presenting the notion of the apprehensive impression, is logically unsound ; for in stating, on the one hand, that an apprehensive impression is that which is derived from a real object,[b] and, on the other hand, that a real object is that which is capable of giving rise to an apprehensive impression, they fall into the fallacy of circular reasoning. If, then, in order that an art of living may exist, there must first exist art, and in order that art may subsist apprehension must pre-exist, and in order that apprehension may subsist assent to an apprehensive impression must be apprehended, but the apprehensive impression is indiscoverable,—then the art of living is indiscoverable.

Another argument is this. Every art appears to 243 be apprehended by means of its own special products, but there is no special product of the art of living ; for anything you might mention as its product—such as honouring parents, paying back deposits, and all the rest—is found to be common to ordinary folk as well. Therefore no art of living exists. For we

[b] *Cf. Adv. Log.* ii. **88.**

ἐκ τοῦ ἀπὸ φρονίμης διαθέσεως φαίνεσθαι λεγό-
μενόν τι ὑπὸ τοῦ φρονίμου ἢ ποιούμενον, ὡς φασί
τινες, ἐπιγνωσόμεθα ὅτι τῆς φρονήσεως ἔργον
244 ἐστίν. αὐτὴ γὰρ ἡ φρονίμη διάθεσις ἀκατάληπτός
ἐστι, μήτε ἐξ αὑτῆς ἁπλῶς καὶ αὐτόθεν φαινομένη
μήτε ἐκ τῶν ἔργων αὑτῆς· κοινὰ γάρ ἐστι ταῦτα
καὶ τῶν ἰδιωτῶν. τό τε λέγειν ὅτι τῷ διομαλισμῷ
τῶν πράξεων καταλαμβάνομεν τὸν ἔχοντα τὴν περὶ
τὸν βίον τέχνην, ὑπερφθεγγομένων ἐστὶ τὴν ἀνθρώπων φύσιν καὶ εὐχομένων μᾶλλον ἢ τἀληθῆ
λεγόντων·

τοῖος γὰρ νόος ἐστὶν ἐπιχθονίων ἀνθρώπων
οἷον ἐπ᾽ ἦμαρ ἄγῃσι πατὴρ ἀνδρῶν τε θεῶν τε.

245   Λείπεται λέγειν ὅτι ἐξ ἐκείνων τῶν ἔργων καταλαμβάνεται ἡ περὶ τὸν βίον τέχνη ἅπερ ἀναγρά-
φουσιν ἐν ταῖς βίβλοις· ὧν πολλῶν καὶ παραπλησίων
ἀλλήλοις ὄντων ὀλίγα ἐκθήσομαι παραδείγματος
χάριν. οἷον γοῦν ὁ αἱρεσιάρχης αὐτῶν Ζήνων ἐν
ταῖς διατριβαῖς φησὶ περὶ παίδων ἀγωγῆς ἄλλα τε
ὅμοια καὶ τάδε " διαμηρίζειν μηδὲν μᾶλλον μηδὲ
ἧσσον παιδικὰ ἢ μὴ παιδικά, μηδὲ θήλεα ἢ ἄρρενα·
οὐ γὰρ [ἐστι] παιδικοῖς ἄλλα ἢ μὴ παιδικοῖς, οὐδὲ
θηλείαις ἢ ἄρρεσιν, ἀλλὰ ταὐτὰ πρέπει τε καὶ πρέ-
246 ποντα ἐστίν." περὶ δὲ τῆς εἰς τοὺς γονεῖς ὁσιότητος ὁ αὐτὸς ἀνήρ φησιν εἰς τὰ περὶ τὴν Ἰοκάστην
καὶ τὸν Οἰδίποδα ὅτι οὐκ ἦν δεινὸν τρίβειν τὴν
μητέρα. " καὶ εἰ μὲν ἀσθενοῦσαν ἑτέρόν τι μέρος
τοῦ σώματος τρίψας ταῖς χερσὶν ὠφέλει, οὐδὲν
αἰσχρόν· εἰ δὲ ἕτερα μέρη τρίψας εὔφραινεν, ὀδυνω-

shall not ascertain (as some assert) from the apparent derivation of some speech or operation of the prudent man from a state of prudence that it is a product of prudence. For the state of prudence itself is inappre- **244** hensible, not being directly apparent either of itself or from its products, these being common to ordinary folk as well. And to say that we apprehend the possessor of the art of living by the unvarying quality of his actions [a] is the assertion of those who over-estimate human nature and are visionaries rather than truth-tellers :

> As is the day which upon them is brought by the sire immortal,
> So are the minds of mortal men.[b]

There remains the assertion that the art of living **245** is apprehended by means of those effects which they describe in their books ; and these being numerous and much alike, I will extract a few of them by way of examples. Thus, for instance, Zeno, the Master of their sect, in his treatises, amongst many other statements regarding the rearing of children, says this : " Have carnal knowledge no less and no more of a favourite than of a non-favourite child, nor of a female than of a male ; favourite or non-favourite, males or females, no different conduct, but the same, befits and is befitting to all alike." And as concerns piety **246** towards parents, the same man states,[c] in reference to the story of Jocasta and Oedipus, that there was nothing dreadful in his rubbing his mother : " If she had been ailing in one part of her body and he had done her good by rubbing it with his hands, it had not been shameful ; was it, then, shameful for

---

[a] *i.e.* always consistently good, impeccable.
[b] Homer, *Od.* xviii. 136-137. [c] *Cf.* § 205.

μένην παύσας, καὶ παῖδας ἐκ τῆς μητρὸς γενναίους
ἐποίησεν, αἰσχρόν;’’ τούτοις δὲ ὁμογνωμονεῖ καὶ
ὁ Χρύσιππος· ἐν γοῦν τῇ πολιτείᾳ φησὶ ‘‘δοκεῖ δέ
μοι ταῦτα οὕτω διεξάγειν καθάπερ καὶ νῦν οὐ
κακῶς παρὰ πολλοῖς εἴθισται, ὥστε καὶ τὴν μητέρα ἐκ τοῦ υἱοῦ τεκνοποιεῖσθαι καὶ τὸν πατέρα
ἐκ τῆς θυγατρὸς καὶ τὸν ὁμομήτριον ἐκ τῆς ὁμο-
247 μητρίας.’’ καὶ ἀνθρωποφαγεῖν ἐν τοῖς αὐτοῖς συν-
τάγμασιν ἡμῖν ἐπεισάγει· φησὶ γοῦν ‘‘ καὶ ἐὰν τῶν
ζώντων ἀποκοπῇ τι μέρος πρὸς τροφὴν χρήσιμον,
μήτε κατορύττειν αὐτὸ μήτε ἄλλως ῥίπτειν, ἀνα-
λίσκειν δὲ αὐτό, ὅπως ἐκ τῶν ἡμετέρων ἕτερον
248 μέρος γένηται.’’ ἐν δὲ τοῖς περὶ τοῦ καθήκοντος
περὶ τῆς τῶν γονέων ταφῆς ῥητῶς φησὶν ‘‘ ἀπο-
γενομένων δὲ τῶν γονέων ταφαῖς χρηστέον ταῖς
ἁπλουστάταις, ὡς ἂν τοῦ σώματος, καθάπερ
ὀνύχων ἢ ὀδόντων ἢ τριχῶν, οὐδὲν ὄντος πρὸς
ἡμᾶς, καὶ οὐδὲν ἐπιστροφῆς ἢ πολυωρίας προσ-
δεομένων ἡμῶν τοιαύτης τινός. διὸ καὶ χρησίμων
μὲν ὄντων τῶν κρεῶν τροφῇ χρήσονται αὐτοῖς,
καθάπερ καὶ τῶν ἰδίων μερῶν, οἷον ποδὸς ἀπο-
κοπέντος, ἐπέβαλλε χρῆσθαι αὐτῷ καὶ τοῖς παρα-
πλησίοις· ἀχρείων δὲ ὄντων ἢ κατορύξαντες ἐά-
σουσιν, ἢ κατακαύσαντες τὴν τέφραν ἀφήσουσιν, ἢ
μακρότερον ῥίψαντες οὐδεμίαν αὐτῶν ἐπιστροφὴν
ποιήσονται καθάπερ ὄνυχος ἢ τριχῶν.’’
249 Τοιαῦτα μὲν πλεῖστα ὅσα λέγουσιν οἱ φιλόσοφοι·
ἅπερ οὐκ ἂν τολμήσειαν διαπράττεσθαι, εἴγε μὴ
παρὰ Κύκλωψιν ἢ Λαιστρυγόσι πολιτεύοιντο. εἰ
δὲ τούτων μὲν ἀνενέργητοι παντάπασίν εἰσιν, ἃ
δὲ πράττουσι, κοινὰ καὶ τῶν ἰδιωτῶν ἐστίν, οὐδὲν

---

him to stop her grief and give her joy by rubbing other parts, and to beget noble children by his mother?" And with this opinion Chrysippus also agrees. At least he says in his *State*: " I approve of carrying out those practices—which, quite rightly, are customary even nowadays amongst many peoples —according to which a mother has children by her son,[a] the father by his daughter, the brother by his full sister." And he proceeds, in the same 247 treatises, to introduce amongst us cannibalism,[b] saying : " And if from a living body a part be cut off that is good for food, we should not bury it nor otherwise get rid of it, but consume it, so that from our parts a new part may arise." And in his book 248 *On Duty* he says expressly, regarding the burial of parents : " When our parents decease we should use the simplest forms of burial, as though the body—like the nails or teeth or hair—were nothing to us, and we need bestow no care or attention on a thing like it. Hence, also, men should make use of the flesh, when it is good, for food, just as also when one of their own parts, such as the foot, is cut off, it would be proper that it and the like parts should be so used ; but when the flesh is not good, they should either bury it and leave it, or burn it up and let the ashes lie, or cast it far away and pay no more regard to it than to nails or hair."

Of such a kind are most of the philosophers' 249 theories ; but they would not dare to put them into practice unless they lived under the laws of the Cyclopes or Laestrygones.[c] But if they are totally incapable of acting thus, and their actual conduct is common to ordinary folk as well, there is no action

[c] For C. and L., as savages of ancient Sicily, *cf.* Hom. *Od.* i. 69, x. 81 ; Thuc. vi. 21.

ἴδιον ἔργον ἐστὶ τῶν ἔχειν ὑποπτευομένων τὴν
περὶ τὸν βίον τέχνην. εἰ οὖν αἱ μὲν τέχναι πάντως
ὀφείλουσιν ἐκ τῶν ἰδίων ἔργων καταλαμβάνεσθαι,
οὐδὲν δὲ ἴδιον ἔργον ὁρᾶται τῆς περὶ τὸν βίον
λεγομένης τέχνης, οὐ καταλαμβάνεται αὕτη. διόπερ
οὐδὲ διαβεβαιοῦσθαι περὶ αὐτῆς δύναταί τις ὅτι
ἔστιν ὑπαρκτή.

Κϛ΄.—ΕΙ ΓΙΝΕΤΑΙ ΕΝ ΑΝΘΡΩΠΟΙΣ Η ΠΕΡΙ ΤΟΝ
ΒΙΟΝ ΤΕΧΝΗ

250 Καὶ μὴν εἰ γίνεται ἐν ἀνθρώποις ἡ περὶ τὸν βίον
τέχνη, ἤτοι φύσει ἐγγίνεται αὐτοῖς ἢ διὰ μαθήσεως
καὶ διδασκαλίας. ἀλλ᾿ εἰ μὲν φύσει, ἤτοι καθὸ
εἰσὶν ἄνθρωποι ἐγγίνοιτο ἂν αὐτοῖς ἡ περὶ τὸν βίον
τέχνη, ἢ καθὸ οὐκ εἰσὶν ἄνθρωποι. καθὸ μὲν οὖν
οὐκ εἰσὶν ἄνθρωποι, οὐδαμῶς· οὐδὲ γὰρ οὐκ εἰσὶν
ἄνθρωποι. εἰ δὲ καθὸ εἰσὶν ἄνθρωποι, πᾶσιν
ἀνθρώποις ὑπῆρξεν ἂν ἡ φρόνησις, ὡς πάντας εἶναι
φρονίμους τε καὶ ἐναρέτους καὶ σοφούς. φαύλους
251 δὲ τοὺς πλείστους λέγουσιν. οὐκοῦν οὐδὲ καθὸ
εἰσὶν ἄνθρωποι ὑπάρξειεν ἂν αὐτοῖς ἡ περὶ τὸν βίον
τέχνη. οὐδὲ φύσει ἄρα. καὶ ἄλλως, ἐπειδὴ τὴν
τέχνην σύστημα ἐκ καταλήψεων εἶναι βούλονται
συγγεγυμνασμένων, διὰ πείρας τέ τινος καὶ μαθήσεως ἐμφαίνουσι μᾶλλον ἀναλαμβάνεσθαι τάς τε
ἄλλας τέχνας καὶ ταύτην περὶ ἧς ὁ λόγος.

ΚΖ΄.—ΕΙ ΔΙΔΑΚΤΗ ΕΣΤΙΝ Η ΠΕΡΙ ΤΟΝ ΒΙΟΝ ΤΕΧΝΗ

252 Ἀλλ᾿ οὐδὲ διδασκαλίᾳ καὶ μαθήσει ἀναλαμβά-
νεται. ἵνα γὰρ ὑπόστασιν ἔχῃ ταῦτα, δεῖ τρία

peculiar to those who are suspected of possessing the art of living. So then, if the arts must certainly be apprehended by means of their peculiar effects, and no effect is observed that is peculiar to the so-called art of living, this art is not apprehended. Consequently, no one can positively affirm regarding it that it is really existent.

CHAPTER XXVI.—DOES THE ART OF LIVING
ARISE IN MANKIND ?

Moreover, if the art of living comes into existence 250 in men, it so comes either by nature or through learning and teaching. But if it is by nature, then the art of living will arise in them either in so far as they are men, or in so far as they are not men. Certainly not in so far as they are not men ; for it is not a fact that they are not men. But if it is in so far as they are men, then prudence [a] would have belonged to all men, so that all would have been prudent and virtuous and wise. But they describe most men as bad. Neither, then, in so far as they are men will the art of 251 living belong to them. Therefore it does not accrue by nature. And again, since they insist that art is "a system of co-exercised apprehensions," [b] they make it evident that the art under discussion, as well as all other arts, is acquired rather by some sort of effort and learning.

CHAPTER XXVII.—IS THE ART OF LIVING
CAPABLE OF BEING TAUGHT ?

But neither is it acquired by teaching and learning. 252 For in order that these should subsist, three things

[a] For " prudence," or practical " wisdom," *cf.* § 240.
[b] *Cf.* §§ 188, 241, 261.

προωμολογῆσθαι, τὸ διδασκόμενον πρᾶγμα, τὸν διδάσκοντα καὶ τὸν μανθάνοντα, τὸν τρόπον τῆς μαθήσεως. οὐδὲν δὲ τούτων ὑφέστηκεν· οὐδὲ ἡ διδασκαλία ἄρα.

ΚΗ΄.—ΕΙ ΕΣΤΙ ΤΙ ΔΙΔΑΣΚΟΜΕΝΟΝ

253 Οἷον γοῦν τὸ διδασκόμενον ἤτοι ἀληθές ἐστιν ἢ ψεῦδος· καὶ εἰ μὲν ψεῦδος, οὐκ ἂν διδάσκοιτο· ἀνύπαρκτον γάρ φασιν εἶναι τὸ ψεῦδος, ἀνυπάρκτων δὲ οὐκ ἂν εἴη διδασκαλία. ἀλλ' οὐδ' εἰ ἀληθὲς εἶναι λέγοιτο· ὅτι γὰρ ἀνύπαρκτόν ἐστι τὸ ἀληθές, ὑπεμνήσαμεν ἐν τοῖς περὶ κριτηρίου. εἰ οὖν μήτε τὸ ψεῦδος μήτε τὸ ἀληθὲς διδάσκεται, παρὰ δὲ ταῦτα διδακτὸν οὐδέν ἐστιν (οὐ γὰρ δὴ τούτων ἀδιδάκτων ὄντων τοὺς ἀπόρους μόνους διδάσκειν 254 ἐρεῖ τις), οὐδὲν διδάσκεται. τό τε διδασκόμενον πρᾶγμα ἤτοι φαινόμενόν ἐστιν ἢ ἄδηλον. ἀλλ' εἰ μὲν φαινόμενόν ἐστιν, οὐκ ἔσται διδασκαλίας δεόμενον· τὰ γὰρ φαινόμενα πᾶσιν ὁμοίως φαίνεται. εἰ δὲ ἄδηλον, ἐπεὶ τὰ ἄδηλα διὰ τὴν ἀνεπίκριτον περὶ αὐτῶν διαφωνίαν ἀκατάληπτά ἐστιν, ὡς πολλάκις ὑπεμνήσαμεν, οὐκ ἔσται διδακτόν· ὃ γὰρ μὴ καταλαμβάνει τις, πῶς ἂν τοῦτο διδάσκειν ἢ μανθάνειν δύναιτο; εἰ δὲ μήτε τὸ φαινόμενον μήτε τὸ ἄδηλον διδάσκεται, οὐδὲν διδάσκεται.

255 Ἔτι τὸ διδασκόμενον ἤτοι σῶμά ἐστιν ἢ ἀ-σώματον, ἑκάτερον δὲ αὐτῶν ἤτοι φαινόμενον ἢ

---

[a] *Cf.* ii. 85 ff.

[b] "Dubious lessons": if the text is right, we must supply λόγους (sayings, "lessons") with τοὺς ἀπόρους. It was laid

must first be agreed upon—the matter which is being taught, the teacher and the learner, and the method of learning. But none of these subsists; neither, then, does teaching.

CHAPTER XXVIII.—DOES A MATTER OF INSTRUCTION EXIST?

Thus, for instance, the matter of instruction is 253 either true or false; if false it would not be taught; for they assert that falsehood is non-existent, and of non-existents there could be no teaching. Nor yet if it were said to be true; for we have shown in our chapter "On the Criterion"[a] that truth is non-existent. If, then, neither the false nor the true is being taught, and besides these there is nothing capable of being taught (for no one, to be sure, will say that, though these are unteachable, he teaches only dubious lessons[b]), then nothing is taught. And the matter taught is either apparent or non- 254 evident. But if it is apparent, it will not require teaching; for things apparent appear to all alike. And if it is non-evident, then, since things non-evident are, as we have often shown, inapprehensible owing to the undecided controversy about them, it will be incapable of being taught; for how could anyone teach or learn what he does not apprehend? But if neither the apparent is taught nor the non-evident, nothing is taught.

Again, what is taught is either corporeal or in- 255 corporeal, and each of these being either apparent or

down (cf. Adv. Math. i. 29) that "the dubious (ἄπορον) cannot be taught": it is intermediate between truth and falsehood

ἀδηλούμενον οὐ δύναται διδάσκεσθαι κατὰ τὸν μικρῷ πρόσθεν ἡμῖν εἰρημένον λόγον. οὐκ ἄρα διδάσκεταί τι.

256 Πρὸς τούτοις ἤτοι τὸ ὂν διδάσκεται ἢ τὸ μὴ ὄν. τὸ μὲν οὖν μὴ ὂν οὐ διδάσκεται· εἰ γὰρ διδάσκεται τὸ μὴ ὄν, ἐπεὶ τῶν ἀληθῶν δοκοῦσιν εἶναι αἱ διδασκαλίαι, ἀληθὲς ἔσται τὸ μὴ ὄν. ἀληθὲς δὲ ὂν καὶ ὑπάρξει· ἀληθὲς γὰρ εἶναί φασιν ὃ ὑπάρχει καὶ ἀντίκειταί τινι. ἄτοπον δέ ἐστι λέγειν ὑπάρχειν τὸ μὴ ὄν· οὐκ ἄρα διδάσκεται τὸ μὴ ὄν. 257 ἀλλ' οὐδὲ τὸ ὄν. εἰ γὰρ διδάσκεται τὸ ὄν, ἤτοι καθὸ ὄν ἐστι διδάσκεται ἢ κατ' ἄλλο τι. ἀλλ' εἰ μὲν καθὸ ὄν ἐστι διδακτόν, τῶν ὄντων ἔσται, διὰ δὲ τοῦτο οὐδὲ διδακτόν· τὰς γὰρ διδασκαλίας ἐκ τινῶν ὁμολογουμένων καὶ ἀδιδάκτων γίνεσθαι προσήκει. οὐκ ἄρα τὸ ὂν καθὸ ὄν ἐστι διδακτόν ἐστιν. 258 καὶ μὴν οὐδὲ κατ' ἄλλο τι. τὸ γὰρ ὂν οὐκ ἔχει ἄλλο τι συμβεβηκὸς αὐτῷ ὃ μὴ ὄν ἐστιν, ὥστε εἰ τὸ ὂν καθὸ ὄν ἐστιν οὐ διδάσκεται, οὐδὲ κατ' ἄλλο τι διδαχθήσεται· ἐκεῖνο γὰρ ὅ τι ποτέ ἐστι συμβεβηκὸς αὐτῷ, ὄν ἐστιν. καὶ ἄλλως, εἴτε φαινόμενον εἴη τὸ ὂν ὃ λέξουσι διδάσκεσθαι, εἴτε ἄδηλον, ταῖς εἰρημέναις ἀπορίαις ὑποπῖπτον ἀδίδακτον ἔσται. εἰ δὲ μήτε τὸ ὂν διδάσκεται μήτε τὸ μὴ ὄν, οὐδέν ἐστι τὸ διδασκόμενον.

---

[a] For the Stoic doctrine of "the true" and "truth" cf. ii. 80 ff. What "the true" is "opposed to" is presumably "the false."

[b] Cf. Aristot. Anal. Post. i. 1.

non-evident is incapable of being taught, according to the argument we have just now stated. Nothing, therefore, is taught.

Further, either the existent is taught or the non- 256 existent. Now the non-existent is not taught; for if the non-existent is taught the non-existent will be true, since teaching is held to be of things true. And if it is true, it will also subsist; for they declare that " a true thing is what subsists and is opposed to something." [a] But it is absurd to say that the non-existent subsists; therefore the non-existent is not taught. Yet neither is the existent. For if the 257 existent is taught, it is taught either in so far as it is existent or in so far as it is something else. But if it is to be taught in so far as it is existent, it will be one of the existing things, and therefore a thing incapable of being taught; for teaching ought to proceed from certain acknowledged facts which require no teaching.[b] Therefore the existent, in so far as it is existent, is not capable of being taught. Nor, in fact, 258 in so far as it is something else. For the existent has not anything else which is non-existent attached to it, so that if the existent in so far as it is existent is not taught, neither will it be taught in so far as it is something else; for whatsoever thing is attached to it is existent. And further, whether the existent thing which, they will say, is taught be apparent or non-evident, as it is subject to the absurdities we have stated, it will be incapable of being taught. But if neither the existent nor the non-existent is taught, there is nothing that is taught.

KΘ΄.—ΕΙ ΕΣΤΙΝ Ο ΔΙΔΑΣΚΩΝ ΚΑΙ Ο ΜΑΝΘΑΝΩΝ

259 Συμπεριτρέπεται μὲν οὖν τούτῳ ὅ τε διδάσκων
καὶ ὁ μανθάνων, οὐδὲν δὲ ἧττον καὶ κατὰ ἰδίαν
ἀποροῦνται. ἤτοι γὰρ ὁ τεχνίτης τὸν τεχνίτην
διδάσκει ἢ ὁ ἄτεχνος τὸν ἄτεχνον ἢ ὁ ἄτεχνος τὸν
τεχνίτην ἢ ὁ τεχνίτης τὸν ἄτεχνον. ὁ μὲν οὖν
τεχνίτης τὸν τεχνίτην οὐ διδάσκει· οὐθέτερος γὰρ
αὐτῶν, καθό ἐστι τεχνίτης, δεῖται μαθήσεως. ἀλλ᾿
οὐδὲ ὁ ἄτεχνος τὸν ἄτεχνον, ὥσπερ οὐδὲ τυφλὸν
ὁδηγεῖν δύναται τυφλός. οὐδὲ ἄτεχνος τὸν τεχνί-
260 την· γελοῖον γάρ. λείπεται λέγειν ὅτι ὁ τεχνίτης
τὸν ἄτεχνον· ὃ καὶ αὐτὸ τῶν ἀδυνάτων ἐστίν.
ὅλως γὰρ ὑποστῆναι τεχνίτην ἀδύνατον εἶναι
λέγεται, ἐπεὶ μήτε αὐτοφυῶς τις καὶ ἅμα τῷ
γενέσθαι τεχνίτης ὑφιστάμενος βλέπεται μήτε ἐξ
ἀτέχνου γίνεταί τις τεχνίτης. ἤτοι γὰρ ἓν θεώρημα
καὶ μία κατάληψις δύναται ποιῆσαι τὸν ἄτεχνον
261 τεχνίτην ἢ οὐδαμῶς. ἀλλ᾿ εἰ μὲν κατάληψις μία
τὸν ἄτεχνον τεχνίτην ἀπεργάζεται, πρῶτον μὲν
ἐνέσται λέγειν ὅτι οὐκ ἔστι σύστημα ἐκ καταλήψεων ἡ τέχνη· ὁ γὰρ μηδὲν ὅλως εἰδώς, εἰ ἓν
θεώρημα διδαχθείη τέχνης, τεχνίτης ἂν οὕτω
λέγοιτο εἶναι. εἶτα καὶ ἐὰν λέγῃ τις ὡς ὁ τινὰ
θεωρήματα τέχνης ἀνειληφὼς καὶ προσδεόμενος
ἑνὸς ἔτι καὶ διὰ τοῦτο ὢν ἄτεχνος, ἂν τὸ ἓν ἐκεῖνο
προσλάβῃ, τεχνίτης ἐξ ἀτέχνου ἀποτελεῖται ἐκ

---

[a] For this saying cf. Matt. xv. 14 ; Hor. Epist. i. 17.

[b] The argument here is that the non-expert cannot become
an expert either (1) by a *single* lesson, §§ 261-262, or (2) by
a course of lessons, which must follow each other *singly*,
§ 263. " Apprehension " here means the grasp of a truth
or principle of the art or craft which is being imparted, the

CHAPTER XXIX.—DO THE TEACHER AND THE
LEARNER EXIST ?

Now with the refutation of this is involved that of 259
both the teacher and the learner ; though they are
just as much open to doubt on their own account.
For either the expert artist teaches the expert, or
the non-expert the non-expert, or the non-expert the
expert, or the expert the non-expert. Now the expert
does not teach the expert ; for neither of them, *qua*
expert, needs teaching. Nor does the non-expert
teach the non-expert, any more than the blind can
lead the blind.[a] Nor the non-expert the expert, for
it would be ridiculous. The only thing left is to say 260
that the expert teaches the non-expert ; and this,
too, is a thing impossible. For it is declared to be
wholly impossible that an expert artist should exist,
since neither do we see anyone existing spontaneously
and from birth as an expert, nor does anyone turn
into an expert from being a non-expert. For either
one lesson and one apprehension can make an expert
of the non-expert or they cannot do so at all.[b]
But if one apprehension makes the non-expert an 261
expert, it will be open to us to declare, firstly, that
art is not a system of apprehensions [c] ; for the man
who knows nothing at all would be termed an expert
if only he were taught a single lesson of art. And,
secondly, should anyone assert that, as soon as a man
who has acquired some principles of art and still
needs one more, and because of this is non-expert,
acquires also that one principle, he at once becomes
an expert instead of a non-expert by means of one

"art" itself being defined as a "system" of such pieces
of knowledge.   [c] *Cf.* § 251 *supra.*

262 καταλήψεως μιᾶς, ἀποκληρωτικὸν λέξει. ἐπὶ γὰρ
τῶν κατὰ μέρος οὐκ ἂν δύναιτο δεῖξαί τινα ἄτεχνον
μὲν ἔτι, τεχνίτην δὲ ἐσόμενον ἐὰν ἕν τι θεώρημα
προσλάβῃ· οὐ γὰρ δήπου τὴν ἐξαρίθμησιν τῶν
θεωρημάτων ἑκάστης τέχνης ἐπίσταταί τις, ὥστε
ἀπαριθμησάμενος τὰ ἐγνωσμένα θεωρήματα, πόσα
λείπεται πρὸς τὸν πλήρη τῶν θεωρημάτων τῆς
τέχνης ἀριθμὸν εἰπεῖν ἔχειν. οὐκοῦν ἑνὸς θεωρή-
263 ματος γνῶσις οὐ ποιεῖ τὸν ἄτεχνον τεχνίτην. εἰ
δὲ τοῦτό ἐστιν ἀληθές, ἐπεὶ μὴ πάντα ἀθρόως τὰ
θεωρήματα τῶν τεχνῶν ἀναλαμβάνει τις, ἀλλ᾽
εἴπερ ἄρα, καθ᾽ ἓν ἕκαστον, ἵνα τις καὶ τοῦτο καθ᾽
ὑπόθεσιν διδῷ, ὁ κατὰ ἓν θεώρημα τῆς τέχνης
ἀναλαμβάνειν λεγόμενος οὐκ ἂν τεχνίτης γένοιτο·
ὑπεμιμνήσκομεν γὰρ ὅτι οὐ δύναται θεωρήματος
ἑνὸς γνῶσις τὸν ἄτεχνον ποιῆσαι τεχνίτην. οὐδὲ
ἐξ ἀτέχνου τοίνυν γίνεταί τις τεχνίτης. ὥστε καὶ
διὰ ταῦτα φαίνεται ἀνυπόστατος εἶναι ὁ τεχνίτης.
διὰ δὲ τοῦτο καὶ ὁ διδάσκων.

264 Ἀλλ᾽ οὐδὲ ὁ μανθάνειν λεγόμενος, ἄτεχνος ὤν,
δύναται τὰ τῆς τέχνης θεωρήματα, ἧς ἐστιν ἄτεχνος, μανθάνειν τε καὶ καταλαμβάνειν. ὡς γὰρ ὁ
ἐκ γενετῆς πηρός, εἰς ὅσον ἐστὶ πηρός, οὐκ ἂν
λάβοι χρωμάτων ἀντίληψιν, οὐδὲ ὁ ἐκ γενετῆς
κωφὸς ὁμοίως φωνῆς, οὕτως οὐδὲ ὁ ἄτεχνος κατα-
λάβοι ἂν τὰ τῆς τέχνης θεωρήματα ἧς ἐστιν ἄτεχνος. καὶ γὰρ ἂν οὕτως ὁ αὐτὸς εἴη τεχνίτης τε
καὶ ἄτεχνος τῶν αὐτῶν, ἄτεχνος μὲν ἐπεὶ οὕτως
ὑπόκειται, τεχνίτης δὲ ἐπεὶ κατάληψιν ἔχει τῶν

ᵃ Cf. § 79 supra.
ᵇ These comparisons are ascribed to Anacharsis, the

apprehension, he will be making a random assertion.[a] 262
For in the case of individual men we could not point
to one who, being still a non-expert, will become an
expert by acquiring one additional principle ; for no
one, to be sure, has such a command of the numeration of the principles of each art as to be able to say,
by numbering off the known principles, how many
are still needed to make up the full number of the
principles of the art. So then the learning of one
principle does not make the non-expert an expert.
But if this is true, seeing that no one acquires all the 263
principles of the arts at once, but each one singly,
if at all—this point also being granted by way of
assumption—the man who is said to acquire the principles of the art one by one will not be termed an
expert ; for we recall the conclusion that the learning
of one principle cannot make an expert of the non-
expert. No one, then, becomes an expert from
being a non-expert. Hence, on these grounds too,
the expert artist appears to be non-existent. And
therefore the teacher also.

Neither can the so-called learner, if he is non- 264
expert, learn and apprehend the principles of the art
wherein he is non-expert. For just as the man who
is blind from birth, in so far as he is blind, will not
acquire perception of colours, nor, similarly, he who
is deaf from birth, of sound,[b] so too the non-expert
will not apprehend the principles of the art wherein
he is non-expert. For should he do so the same man
would be both expert and non-expert in the same
things—non-expert since he is such by hypothesis,
and expert since he has apprehension of the prin-

Scythian sage of Solon's time (*circa* 590 B.C.); *cf. Adv. Log.*
i. 55.

SEXTUS EMPIRICUS

τῆς τέχνης θεωρημάτων. ὥστε οὐδὲ ὁ τεχνίτης
265 τὸν ἄτεχνον διδάσκει. εἰ δὲ μήτε ὁ τεχνίτης τὸν
τεχνίτην διδάσκει μήτε ὁ ἄτεχνος τὸν ἄτεχνον μήτε
ὁ ἄτεχνος τὸν τεχνίτην μήτε ὁ τεχνίτης τὸν
ἄτεχνον, παρὰ δὲ ταῦτα οὐδὲν ἔστιν, οὔτε ὁ
διδάσκων ἔστιν οὔτε ὁ διδασκόμενος.

Λ'.—ΕΙ ΕΣΤΙ ΤΙΣ ΜΑΘΗΣΕΩΣ ΤΡΟΠΟΣ

Μὴ ὄντος δὲ μήτε τοῦ μανθάνοντος μήτε τοῦ
διδάσκοντος καὶ ὁ τρόπος τῆς διδασκαλίας παρ-
266 έλκει· οὐδὲν δὲ ἧττον καὶ διὰ τούτων ἀπορεῖται.
ὁ γὰρ τρόπος τῆς διδασκαλίας ἤτοι ἐναργείᾳ
γίνεται ἢ λόγῳ· οὔτε δὲ ἐναργείᾳ γίνεται οὔτε
λόγῳ, καθάπερ παραστήσομεν· οὐδὲ ὁ τρόπος ἄρα
τῆς μαθήσεώς ἐστιν εὔπορος.

Ἐναργείᾳ μὲν οὖν οὐ γίνεται διδασκαλία, ἐπεὶ
τῶν δεικνυμένων ἐστὶν ἡ ἐνάργεια. τὸ δὲ δεικνύμενον πᾶσίν ἐστι φαινόμενον· τὸ δὲ φαινόμενον, ᾗ
φαίνεται, πᾶσίν ἐστι ληπτόν· τὸ δὲ κοινῶς πᾶσι
ληπτὸν ἀδίδακτον· οὐκ ἄρα τι ἐναργείᾳ διδακτόν
ἐστιν.

267 Καὶ μὴν οὐδὲ λόγῳ διδάσκεταί τι. οὗτος γὰρ
ἤτοι σημαίνει τι ἢ οὐδὲν σημαίνει. ἀλλὰ μηδὲν
μὲν σημαίνων οὐδὲ ἔσται τινὸς διδασκαλικός. εἰ
δὲ σημαίνει τι, ἤτοι φύσει σημαίνει τι ἢ θέσει.
καὶ φύσει μὲν οὐ σημαίνει διὰ τὸ μὴ πάντας πάντων ἀκούοντας συνιέναι, οἷον Ἕλληνας βαρβάρων

---

[a] Cf. i. 138, 178.   [b] Cf. ii. 214.

ciples of the art. Hence, neither does the expert teach the non-expert. But if neither the expert 265 teaches the expert, nor the non-expert the non-expert, nor the non-expert the expert, nor the expert the non-expert, and these are all the alternatives possible, then neither the teacher exists nor the taught.

CHAPTER XXX.—DOES THERE EXIST ANY METHOD OF LEARNING ?

And if neither the learner nor the teacher exists, the method of teaching also is abolished. And it is no 266 less disputed on the following grounds. The method of teaching comes to exist either by ocular evidence or by speech *a*; but it does not come to exist either by ocular evidence or by speech, as we shall show ; therefore the method of learning also is not easy to discover.

Now teaching does not come by ocular evidence, since ocular evidence consists in things exhibited. But what is exhibited is apparent to all ; and the apparent, *qua* apparent, is perceptible by all ; and what is perceptible by all in common is incapable of being taught ; therefore nothing is capable of being taught by ocular evidence.

Nor, in fact, is anything taught by speech. For 267 speech either signifies something or signifies nothing. But if it signifies nothing, neither will it be capable of teaching anything. And if it signifies something, it does so either by nature or by convention. But it is not significant by nature *b* because all men do not understand all when they hear them, as is the case with Greeks hearing barbarians

268 καὶ βαρβάρους Ἑλλήνων. θέσει δὲ εἰ σημαίνει, δῆλον ὡς οἱ μὲν προκατειληφότες καθ' ὧν αἱ λέξεις εἰσὶ τεταγμέναι ἀντιλήψονται τούτων, οὐκ ἐξ αὐτῶν διδασκόμενοι ἅπερ ἠγνόουν, ἀλλὰ ἀναμιμνησκόμενοι καὶ ἀνανεούμενοι ταῦτα ἅπερ ᾔδεσαν, οἱ δὲ χρῄζοντες τῆς τῶν ἀγνοουμένων μαθήσεως, καὶ μὴ εἰδότες καθ' ὧν εἰσὶν αἱ λέξεις τεταγ-
269 μέναι, οὐδενὸς ἀντίληψιν ἕξουσιν. διόπερ οὐδὲ ὁ τρόπος τῆς μαθήσεως ὑποστῆναι δύναιτο ἄν. καὶ γὰρ ὁ διδάσκων κατάληψιν τῶν θεωρημάτων τῆς διδασκομένης τέχνης ἐμποιεῖν ὀφείλει τῷ μανθάνοντι, ἵνα οὕτως ἐκεῖνος τὸ σύστημα τούτων καταλαβὼν τεχνίτης γένηται. οὐδὲν δέ ἐστι κατάληψις, ὡς ἐν τοῖς ἔμπροσθεν ὑπεμνήσαμεν· οὐκοῦν οὐδὲ ὁ τρόπος τῆς διδασκαλίας ὑφεστάναι δύναται. εἰ δὲ μήτε τὸ διδασκόμενον ἔστι μήτε ὁ διδάσκων καὶ ὁ μανθάνων μήτε ὁ τρόπος τῆς μαθήσεως, οὔτε μάθησις ἔστιν οὔτε διδασκαλία.

270 Ταῦτα μὲν οὖν κοινότερον ἐπικεχείρηται περὶ μαθήσεως καὶ διδασκαλίας· ἔνεστι δὲ ἀπορεῖν οὕτω καὶ ἐπὶ τῆς λεγομένης περὶ τὸν βίον εἶναι τέχνης. οἷον γοῦν τὸ μὲν διδασκόμενον πρᾶγμα, τουτέστι τὴν φρόνησιν, ἀνυπόστατον ἐδείξαμεν ἐν τοῖς ἔμπροσθεν· ἀνυπόστατος δέ ἐστι καὶ ὁ διδάσκων καὶ ὁ μανθάνων. ἤτοι γὰρ ὁ φρόνιμος τὸν φρόνιμον διδάξει τὴν περὶ τὸν βίον τέχνην ἢ ὁ ἄφρων τὸν ἄφρονα ἢ ὁ ἄφρων τὸν φρόνιμον ἢ ὁ φρόνιμος τὸν ἄφρονα· οὐδεὶς δὲ τούτων οὐδένα διδάσκει· οὐκ ἄρα διδάσκεται ἡ περὶ τὸν βίον εἶναι λεγομένη
271 τέχνη. καὶ περὶ μὲν τῶν ἄλλων ἴσως περιττὸν καὶ λέγειν· εἰ δὲ ὁ φρόνιμος τὸν ἄφρονα διδάσκει

• Cf. § 214.   ᵇ Cf. §§ 240 ff.

talk or barbarians hearing Greeks. And if it 268
is significant by convention, evidently those who
have grasped beforehand the objects to which the
several words are assigned will perceive those objects,
not through being taught by the words things of
which they were ignorant, but by recollecting and
recovering things which they knew ; whereas those
who require to learn what they do not know, and
who are ignorant of the objects to which the words
are assigned, will have no perception of anything.
Consequently, the method of learning also will be 269
incapable of subsisting. For, in fact, the teacher
ought to impart to the learner an apprehension of
the principles of the art he is teaching, so that the
latter by apprehending them as a system may thus
become an expert artist. But, as we have shown
above,[a] apprehension is nothing ; therefore also the
method of teaching cannot subsist. But if neither
the matter taught exists, nor the teacher and the
learner, nor the method of learning, then neither
learning exists nor teaching.

Such, then, are the objections put forward regard- 270
ing learning and teaching in general. And the same
difficulties may also be alleged in the case of the
so-called art of living. Thus, for instance, we have
shown above[b] that the matter taught, namely prudence, is non-existent ; and both the teacher and the
learner are non-existent. For either the prudent
man will teach the prudent the art of living, or the
imprudent the imprudent, or the imprudent the
prudent, or the prudent the imprudent ; but none
of these teaches any other ; therefore the so-called
art of living is not taught. Probably it is superfluous 271
even to refer to the other cases ; but if the prudent

τὴν φρόνησιν, ἡ δὲ φρόνησις ἐπιστήμη ἐστὶν ἀγαθῶν καὶ κακῶν καὶ οὐθετέρων, ὁ ἄφρων μὴ ἔχων
τὴν φρόνησιν ἄγνοιαν ἔχει τῶν ἀγαθῶν καὶ κακῶν
καὶ οὐθετέρων, ἄγνοιαν δὲ τούτων ἔχων πάντως
διδάσκοντος αὐτὸν τοῦ φρονίμου τὰ ἀγαθὰ καὶ
κακὰ καὶ οὐθέτερα ἀκούσεται μόνον τῶν λεγομένων, οὐ γνώσεται δὲ ταῦτα. εἰ γὰρ ἀντιλαμ-
βάνοιτο αὐτῶν ἐν ἀφροσύνῃ καθεστώς, ἔσται καὶ
ἡ ἀφροσύνη τῶν τε ἀγαθῶν καὶ κακῶν καὶ οὐθ-
272 ετέρων θεωρητική. οὐχὶ δέ γε τούτων κατὰ αὐτοὺς
ἡ ἀφροσύνη θεωρητικὴ καθέστηκεν, ἐπεὶ ὁ ἄφρων
ἔσται φρόνιμος. ὁ ἄρα ἄφρων οὐκ ἀντιλαμβάνεται τῶν ὑπὸ τοῦ φρονίμου λεγομένων ἢ πραττο-
μένων κατὰ τὸν τῆς φρονήσεως[1] λόγον. μὴ ἀντι-
λαμβανόμενος δὲ οὐκ ἂν διδάσκοιτο ὑπ᾽ αὐτοῦ,
ἄλλως τε καὶ ἐπεὶ μήτε ἐναργείᾳ μήτε διὰ λόγου
δύναται διδάσκεσθαι, καθὰ προειρήκαμεν. πλὴν
ἀλλ᾽ εἰ μήτε διὰ μαθήσεως καὶ διδασκαλίας ἐγ-
γίνεταί τινι ἡ περὶ τὸν βίον λεγομένη τέχνη μήτε
φύσει, ἀνεύρετός ἐστιν ἡ παρὰ τοῖς φιλοσόφοις
θρυλουμένη τέχνη περὶ τὸν βίον.
273 Εἰ μέντοι καὶ δοίη τις ἐκ πολλοῦ τοῦ περιόντος
ἐγγίνεσθαί τινι τὴν ὀνειροπολουμένην τέχνην περὶ
τὸν βίον, βλαβερὰ καὶ ταραχῆς αἰτία φανήσεται
μᾶλλον τοῖς ἔχουσιν αὐτὴν ἢ ὠφέλιμος.

ΛΑ΄.—ΕΙ ΩΦΕΛΕΙ Η ΠΕΡΙ ΤΟΝ ΒΙΟΝ ΤΕΧΝΗ ΤΟΝ
ΕΧΟΝΤΑ ΑΥΤΗΝ

Αὐτίκα γοῦν, ἵνα παραδείγματος ἕνεκεν ὀλίγα
ἀπὸ πολλῶν εἴπωμεν, ὠφελεῖν ἂν δοκοίη τὸν σοφὸν

---

[1] τῆς φρονήσεως Mutsch.: τῆς μαθήσεως Bekk.: τήσσεως
mss.: τῆς ζητήσεως T.

man teaches prudence to the imprudent, and prudence is " knowledge [a] of things good and evil and neither," the imprudent man, as he does not possess prudence, possesses ignorance of the things that are good and evil and neither ; and since he possesses nothing but ignorance thereof, when the prudent man teaches him what things are good and evil and neither, he will merely hear what is said and will not get to know the things. For if he should grasp them while in a state of imprudence, then imprudence too will be capable of perceiving what things are good and evil and neither. But, according to them, imprudence is certainly not capable of perceiving these things, since, if it were, the imprudent man will be prudent. Therefore, according to the definition of prudence, the imprudent man does not grasp what is said or done by the prudent. And, as he fails to grasp, he will not be taught by him, especially since, as we have said above, he cannot be taught either by ocular evidence or by means of speech. But, in fine, if the so-called art of living is not imparted to anyone either by means of learning and teaching or by nature, then the art of living, so harped on by the philosophers, is indiscoverable.

Yet even were one to grant, as an act of bounty, 273 that this visionary art of living is imparted to someone, it will show itself to be hurtful to its possessors, and a cause of perturbation, rather than beneficial.

CHAPTER XXXI.—DOES THE ART OF LIVING BENEFIT ITS POSSESSOR ?

Thus, for instance—to take a few arguments out of many by way of example—the art of living might

[a] *Cf.* § 168.

ἡ περὶ τὸν βίον τέχνη ἐγκράτειαν αὐτῷ παρεχο-
μένη ἐν ταῖς πρὸς τὸ καλὸν ὁρμαῖς καὶ ἐν ταῖς
274 ἀπὸ τοῦ κακοῦ ἀφορμαῖς. ὁ οὖν λεγόμενος κατ᾽
αὐτοὺς ἐγκρατὴς σοφὸς ἤτοι κατὰ τοῦτο λέγεται
ἐγκρατὴς καθόσον ἐν οὐδεμιᾷ γίνεται ὁρμῇ τῇ
πρὸς τὸ κακὸν καὶ ἀφορμῇ τῇ ἀπὸ τοῦ ἀγαθοῦ,
ἢ καθόσον εἶχε μὲν φαύλας ὁρμὰς καὶ ἀφορμάς,
275 περιεκράτει δὲ αὐτῶν τῷ λόγῳ. ἀλλὰ κατὰ μὲν
τὸ μὴ γίνεσθαι ἐν φαύλαις κρίσεσιν οὐκ ἂν εἴη
ἐγκρατής· οὐ γὰρ κρατήσει οὗ οὐκ ἔχει. καὶ ὡς
οὐκ ἂν εἴποι τις τὸν εὐνοῦχον ἐγκρατῆ πρὸς ἀφρο-
δίσια καὶ τὸν κακοστομαχοῦντα πρὸς ἐδεσμάτων
ἀπόλαυσιν (οὐδ᾽ ὅλως γὰρ ἐπιζήτησις αὐτοῖς γίνεται τῶν τοιούτων, ἵνα καὶ ἐγκρατῶς κατεξαναστῶσι
τῆς ἐπιζητήσεως) τῷ αὐτῷ τρόπῳ οὐδὲ τὸν σοφὸν
ἐγκρατῆ ῥητέον διὰ τὸ μὴ φύεσθαι ἐν αὐτῷ πάθος
276 οὗ ἔσται ἐγκρατής. εἰ δὲ κατὰ τοῦτο ἀξιώσουσιν
αὐτὸν ὑπάρχειν ἐγκρατῆ καθόσον γίνεται μὲν ἐν
φαύλαις κρίσεσιν περιγίνεται δὲ αὐτῶν τῷ λόγῳ,
πρῶτον μὲν δώσουσιν ὅτι οὐδὲν ὠφέλησεν αὐτὸν ἡ
φρόνησις, ἀκμὴν ἐν ταραχαῖς ὄντα καὶ βοηθείας
δεόμενον, εἶτα καὶ κακοδαιμονέστερος τῶν φαύλων
λεγομένων εὑρίσκεται. εἰ μὲν γὰρ ὁρμᾷ ἐπί τι,
πάντως ταράσσεται, εἰ δὲ περικρατεῖ τῷ λόγῳ,
συνέχει ἐν ἑαυτῷ τὸ κακόν, καὶ διὰ τοῦτο μᾶλλον
ταράσσεται τοῦ φαύλου ἐκείνου μηκέτι τοῦτο

---

[a] For the Stoic definition of this virtue *cf. Adv. Phys.* i. 153.
It denotes "self-mastery" by which the rational self (or
"Logos") overcomes the irrational appetites and passions.

[b] *Cf.* § 177 for the Stoic use of "inclination" and "aversion" as ethical terms. The Stoic ideal being complete

be thought to benefit the wise man by furnishing him with temperance [a] in his impulses towards good and repulsions from evil. He, then, who is termed by **274** them a temperate sage is called temperate either in virtue of his never feeling the impulse towards good or repulsion from evil,[b] or in virtue of his possessing slight impulses in either direction and overcoming them by reason. But in respect of his freedom from **275** bad resolutions he will not be self-controlled; for he will not control what he does not possess. And just as one would not call a eunuch temperate in sex-indulgence, or a man with a poor stomach temperate in respect of the pleasures of the table (for they feel no attraction at all towards such things, so that they might rise superior to the attraction through temperance),—in the same way we ought not to term the sage temperate, because he possesses no natural feeling over which he may exercise control. And **276** if they shall claim that he is temperate in virtue of his forming bad resolutions but overcoming them by reason, then, firstly, they will be admitting that prudence was of no benefit to him just when he was in a state of perturbation and needed assistance, and, secondly, he is found to be even more unfortunate than those they term bad.[c] For if he feels an impulse towards anything, he is certainly perturbed; while if he overcomes it by reason, he retains the evil, and because of this he is more perturbed than the bad man who no longer experiences this feeling;

absence of passion and emotion ("apathy"), the less "temperance" a man exercised the better he was. "The Sage," being a purely rational self, needs no "self-mastery." *Cf.* Introd. p. xxviii.

[c] The "not-wise" of the Stoics, *cf.* § 251.

SEXTUS EMPIRICUS

277 πάσχοντος· εἰ μὲν γὰρ ὁρμᾷ, ταράσσεται, εἰ δὲ
τυγχάνει τῶν ἐπιθυμιῶν, παύεται τῆς ταραχῆς.
Οὐ τοίνυν ἐγκρατὴς γίνεται ὅσον ἐπὶ τῇ φρο-
νήσει ὁ σοφός· ἢ εἴπερ γίνεται, πάντων ἀνθρώπων
ἐστὶ κακοδαιμονέστατος, ὥστε οὐκ ὠφέλειαν ἀλλὰ
ταραχὴν αὐτῷ μεγίστην ἡ περὶ τὸν βίον παρέσχε
τέχνη. ὅτι δὲ ὁ νομίζων ἔχειν τὴν περὶ τὸν βίον
τέχνην καὶ δι' αὐτῆς ἐπεγνωκέναι τίνα τέ ἐστιν
ἀγαθὰ ὡς πρὸς τὴν φύσιν καὶ τίνα φαῦλα, ταράσσεται σφόδρα καὶ τῶν ἀγαθῶν αὐτῷ παρόντων
καὶ τῶν κακῶν, ἐν τοῖς ἔμπροσθεν ὑπεμνήσαμεν.
278 λεκτέον οὖν ὅτι εἰ μήτε ἡ τῶν ἀγαθῶν τε καὶ
κακῶν καὶ ἀδιαφόρων ὑπόστασις ὁμολογεῖται, ἥ
τε περὶ τὸν βίον τέχνη τάχα μὲν καὶ ἀνυπόστατός
ἐστιν, εἰ δὲ καὶ ὑφεστάναι δοθείη καθ' ὑπόθεσιν,
οὐδεμίαν ὠφέλειαν τοῖς ἔχουσιν αὐτὴν παρέχει,
τοὐναντίον δὲ ταραχὰς αὐτοῖς ἐμποιεῖ μεγίστας,
μάτην ὠφρυῶσθαι δοκοῖεν ἂν οἱ δογματικοὶ κἂν τῷ
λεγομένῳ ἠθικῷ μέρει τῆς καλουμένης φιλοσοφίας.
279 Τοσαῦτα καὶ περὶ τοῦ ἠθικοῦ τόπου συμμέτρως
ὡς ἐν ὑποτυπώσει διεξελθόντες, ἐνταῦθα περιγράφομεν καὶ τὸ τρίτον σύνταγμα καὶ τὸ πᾶν τῶν
Πυρρωνείων ὑποτυπώσεων σπούδασμα, ἐκεῖνο ἐπει-
πόντες.

ΛΒ'.—ΔΙΑ ΤΙ Ο ΣΚΕΠΤΙΚΟΣ ΕΝΙΟΤΕ ΑΜΥΔΡΟΥΣ
ΤΑΙΣ ΠΙΘΑΝΟΤΗΣΙΝ ΕΡΩΤΑΝ ΕΠΙΤΗΔΕΥΕΙ ΛΟΓΟΥΣ

280 Ὁ σκεπτικὸς διὰ τὸ φιλάνθρωπος εἶναι τὴν τῶν
δογματικῶν οἴησίν τε καὶ προπέτειαν κατὰ δύναμιν
ἰᾶσθαι λόγῳ βούλεται. καθάπερ οὖν οἱ τῶν σω-

---
[a] Cf. §§ 236 f. supra, i. 27.
[b] Cf. i. 20, 177 ; ii. 256, 258.

510

for the latter, though he is perturbed if he is feeling **277** an impulse, yet ceases from his perturbation if he gains his desires.

So, then, the sage does not become temperate in virtue of his prudence ; or if he does become so, he is of all men the most miserable, so that the art of living has brought him no benefit but the uttermost perturbation. And we have shown above *a* that the man who believes that he possesses the art of living, and that by means of it he discerns what things are naturally good and what bad, is extremely perturbed both when good things are his and when evil things. We must, then, declare that, if there is no agree- **278** ment as to the existence of things good and bad and indifferent, and the art of living is possibly non-existent, or—if its existence is provisionally admitted —brings no benefit to its possessors but, on the contrary, causes them extreme perturbations, then the Dogmatists would seem to be vainly puffed up in respect of the so-called Ethical division of what they term " philosophy."

Having now treated of the subject of Ethics also **279** at sufficient length for an account in outline, we con-clude at this point our third book, and with it the complete treatise on " Pyrrhonean Outlines," adding only this final section :

CHAPTER XXXII. — WHY THE SCEPTIC SOMETIMES PURPOSELY PROPOUNDS ARGUMENTS WHICH ARE LACKING IN POWER OF PERSUASION

The Sceptic, being a lover of his kind, desires to **280** cure by speech, as best he can, the self-conceit and rashness *b* of the Dogmatists. So, just as the

ματικῶν παθῶν ἰατροὶ διάφορα κατὰ μέγεθος
ἔχουσι βοηθήματα, καὶ τοῖς μὲν σφοδρῶς πεπονθόσι
τὰ σφοδρὰ τούτων προσάγουσι τοῖς δὲ κούφως τὰ
κουφότερα, καὶ ὁ σκεπτικὸς οὕτως διαφόρους
281 ἐρωτᾷ [καὶ] κατὰ ἰσχὺν λόγους, καὶ τοῖς μὲν ἐμ-
βριθέσι καὶ εὐτόνως ἀνασκευάζειν δυναμένοις τὸ
τῆς οἰήσεως τῶν δογματικῶν πάθος ἐπὶ τῶν
σφόδρα τῇ προπετείᾳ κεκακωμένων χρῆται, τοῖς
δὲ κουφοτέροις ἐπὶ τῶν ἐπιπόλαιον καὶ εὐίατον
ἐχόντων τὸ τῆς οἰήσεως πάθος καὶ ὑπὸ κουφοτέρων
πιθανοτήτων ἀνασκευάζεσθαι δυναμένων. διόπερ
ὁτὲ μὲν ἐμβριθεῖς ταῖς πιθανότησιν ὁτὲ δὲ καὶ
ἀμαυροτέρους φαινομένους οὐκ ὀκνεῖ λόγους συνερωτᾶν ὁ ἀπὸ τῆς σκέψεως ὁρμώμενος, ἐπίτηδες,
ὡς ἀρκοῦντας αὐτῷ πολλάκις πρὸς τὸ ἀνύειν τὸ
προκείμενον.

physicians who cure bodily ailments have remedies which differ in strength, and apply the severe ones to those whose ailments are severe and the milder to those mildly affected,—so too the Sceptic propounds arguments which differ in strength, and employs those **281** which are weighty and capable by their stringency of disposing of the Dogmatists' ailment, self-conceit, in cases where the mischief is due to a severe attack of rashness, while he employs the milder arguments in the case of those whose ailment of conceit is superficial and easy to cure, and whom it is possible to restore to health by milder methods of persuasion. Hence the adherent of Sceptic principles does not scruple to propound at one time arguments that are weighty in their persuasiveness, and at another time such as appear less impressive,—and he does so on purpose, as the latter are frequently sufficient to enable him to effect his object.